P9-AOI-461

LEFTISM
REVISITED

LEFTISM REVISITED

From de Sade and Marx to Hitler and Pol Pot

Erik von Kuehnelt-Leddihn

Preface by

William F. Buckley, Jr.

REGNERY GATEWAY
Washington, D.C.

LIBRARY
COLBY-SAWYER COLLEGE
NEW LONDON, NH 03257

JC
571
.K793
1990
C.1

#21975557

Text © 1990 by Erik von Kuehnelt-Leddihn
Introduction © 1990 by William F. Buckley, Jr.

Library of Congress Cataloging-in-Publication Data

Kuehnelt-Leddihn, Erik von, 1909-
Leftism Revisited : from de Sade and Marx to Hitler and Pol Pot / Erik von
Kuehnelt-Leddihn.
p.   cm.
Includes bibliographical references and index.
ISBN 0-89526-537-0
1. Liberalism—History.   2. Democracy—History.   3. Conservatism—
History.   4. Political science—History.   I. Title.
JC571.K793   1990
320.5'09—dc20   90-8821
                                                                      CIP

Published in the United States by
Regnery Gateway
1130 17th Street, NW
Washington, DC 20036

Distributed to the trade by
National Book Network
4720-A Boston Way
Lanham, MD 20706

1990 printing
Printed on acid free paper
Manufactured in the United States of America

LIBRARY
COLBY-SAWYER COLLEGE
NEW LONDON, NH

Acknowledgements

I wish to thank both the Historical Research Foundation and the Earhart Foundation for grants that made possible the culmination of this book.

And I wish especially to thank Patricia B. Bozell, the Executive Secretary of the Foundation, who labored over my work for over six months, editing it, correcting my English when it lapsed, calling to my attention material whether missing or redundant. I am infinitely obliged to her for her creative and sophisticated contribution.

E v. K-L
Lans, Tyrol, Austria
August 30, 1990

Contents

PART III **Liberalism**

PART IV **The Left and U.S. Foreign Policy**

Preface

by William F. Buckley, Jr.

Many years ago at dinner with Max Eastman he asked me if I had read *Liberty or Equality?* by Erik von Kuehnelt-Leddihn. As a matter of fact, I had just then read it (this was in 1953 shortly after the book had been published by Caldwell). "Amazing!" Eastman, the learned essayist, critic, and philosopher, remarked. "Reading it is like going to college and graduate school all over again."

I agreed. Moreover, my affinity for the mind of K-L would prove extensive. He is the only writer whose column appeared in *National Review* when the magazine was founded and continues to appear in it today, thirty-five years later. The mind of K-L is more fully stacked than that of anyone I have ever known, but not merely in the $64,000 Question sense, in which wandering scholars can be found who can answer questions about the dates of the Second Peloponnesian War. If such a question were directed to K-L, he would tell you why the years of that war were important, and the impact they had on the thinking of Aquinas after he had discovered Aristotle. There was never (that I know of) a mind better fixed on the reticulations that, if diligently pursued, will take you from Mother Teresa to Sister Boom Boom.

Now the reader should know a little about the extraordinary author of this extraordinary book. This is important because after a half-dozen pages the temptation may occur to you to conclude that you are in the hands of an exhibitionist. It is important to know that this isn't the case: an exhibitionist seeks merely to display the knowledge he has achieved. K-L seeks with agonizing effort to put that knowledge to the service of a set of ideas he has hammered out from his conversance with the history of the world, and the history of the human mind. He now and again takes obvious delight in the historical or linguistic *bon mot*, but only because he is convinced that you and I will share in that delight: he is never just showing off. Two or three novels back I wrote about Berlin during the time that the Wall went up, and my story began in the awful days when Hitler was preparing to go to war. K-L liked the novel immensely, and sent along a pleasant single-spaced four-page letter wherein he engagingly pointed out seventy or eighty errors, traceable to historical solecisms, proper names improperly attributed to characters from that particular region of Germany, misleading street addresses. . . I was both appalled (at the size of the accumulation), and amused (by the arcana brought together). I wrote to ask his permission to publish his letter in my little corner of *National Review* (it is called "Notes & Asides") where I publish correspondence that especially appeals, for one reason or another. He wrote back instantly and said under no circumstances was I to do any such thing, the letter had been only for my own amusement. A year later I had mislaid the critical letter and wished to show it to someone as a rogue example of K-L's voluminous knowledge: would he be so good as to send me a copy of it? He hadn't a copy.

Kuehnelt-Leddihn tells us, in this learned and opinionated book, what he feels about major political and philosophical problems. All his cards are on the table: K-L does not know the meaning of casuistry, one of the few arts he does not practise. He tells us without delay that he is a Christian, indeed a Catholic thinker. He rejects with a kind of wholesome scorn much that is held holy even by his fellow conservatives in America. He is determined to use the word "ideology" (loathed by most of us) to describe that collection of ideas and insights he seeks to serve. He dismisses with derision the use of "liberalism" to describe what approximately 100 percent of thinking Americans know of as "liberalism." He is absolutely certain that the election of Andrew Jackson marked the turning point in American history in the wrong direction. He uses a few words ("identitarian," for example) which his patient and talented editor Patricia Bozell literally begged him to retire, in place of substitutes better recognized: and he declined, athwart his chivalrous disposition to oblige. He believes (rather persuasively) that the French Revolution was the central cause of the malformation of modern ideological thought; and that the Reformation was the crowning historical event in a kind of philosophical stratification that had the opposite effect of what was intended.

And, supremely, he believes that democracy is the enemy of good government, believing resolutely that the minority should rule the majority rather than the other way around, on the grounds that the minority are far less prone to exploit the complementary body, or to stoop to the use of ingratiation, ostensibly to serve the public, in fact, to damage the public. His recital of the performance of democracies in this century is not reassuring, and he disposes of the question, Were the majority of Germans in favor of Hitler? with a very simple answer: Yes. You see, they were without an offsetting ideology. "Ideology."

The great events of 1989, during which communism ceased to be a creed (remaining only a threat) do not disturb his analysis. Communism as an economic system was always surrealistic, and although defective diplomacy is substantially responsible for the high watermark of Soviet imperialism, the whole idea of it was *contra naturam*, and one always looked on it as the human desecration it was, and prayed that it would dissipate without death throes accompanied by nuclear exchanges. There is no substantial insight in this bountiful book that is wounded, let alone anachronized, by the happy developments that came just after its completion.

There is ever so much here to cause the reader to wonder out loud. A lot to cause the reader to look up and say, Well, I'm not so sure. . . Some thought and analysis—inevitably—that will cause this reader or that to jump up and down with frustration/indignation/fury. But not enough, I warrant, to cause any (respectable) reader to take the volume and toss it into the fireplace. Because, I suspect, any intellectually sentient man would feel that to do so would be the equivalent of tossing into the sea a huge collection of valuable stones, irregularly set, perhaps; eccentrically cut, yes: but giving out shafts of brilliant light.

Introduction

I

*We are now so stultified in
our thinking and so priggish in our
expressions that it becomes
unavoidably offensive to tell the truth.*

—Johann Georg Hamann

Sixteen years have elapsed since *Leftism: From de Sade and Marx to Hitler and Marcuse* was published in the United States. Since then much has changed. We no longer speak about Marcuse, who has gone to his reward as have two of his most outstanding companions at the highly destructive Frankfurt School. When one of them, Theodor W. Adorno, gave his last university lecture in 1969, his male students hooted him while the females, stripped to the waist, stormed the dais and fell on him with kisses. To his students, he was an old, useless fogey. He suffered a nervous breakdown and explained in tears to reporters that his former disciples did not understand him. A few weeks later he was dead. Max Horkheimer, the other companion, turned to religion (the liberalization of which he considered nonsense) and passed away in a highly spiritualized version of the faith of his childhood. The revolt of 1968 is nearly forgotten.

In the ensuing years in the United States the beliefs of a small elite burgeoned into a solid conservative movement. More and more Americans came to the conclusion that Right is right and Left is wrong.

A variety of reasons accounts for this evolution. As this volume points out, the United States is rooted in the political philosophy of the Founding Fathers of whom the majority were politically right of center. They despised democracy and followed the nauseating drama of the French Revolution with utter disgust. Rightist ideas continued among eminent American thinkers even after 1828 (which Henry Adams considered a watershed in the history of the United States). Herman Melville, for example, spoke about the "Dark Ages of Democracy"; other like-minded notables included James F. Cooper, Orestes A. Brownson, William Graham Sumner, Paul Elmer Moore, Irving Babbitt, Albert Jay Nock, Ralph Adams Cram, and H. L. Mencken, not to mention the Southern Agrarians and, even later, writers like Richard M. Weaver and Bernard Iddings Bell—the list goes on and on. But after the war, the concept of democracy wove a spell on the intelligentsia in the United States.

I was one of the first authors to attack frontally the imported French ideology of democracy. In *The Menace of the Herd* (Milwaukee, 1943), I demonstrated that not only socialism and communism, but national socialism as well were intrinsically tied to democracy in varying degrees—that they all belonged to the Left. In a more scholarly way I made the same point in *Liberty or Equality?* (London and Caldwell, 1952).

The year 1953 saw the publication of Russell Kirk's *The Conservative Mind*, and in 1955 *National Review* was founded by William F. Buckley Jr. The existing associations, institutes, and periodicals fostering the free market economy and anticollective philosophy blended with the budding conservative movement. Of course, this blending process had and continues to have its difficulties. Today, for example, the conservative label is used by near-anarchists who want to abolish the armed forces and slaughter the unborn as well as by genuine traditionalists.

The early postwar conservative movement had a distinctly intellectual and elitist character, while the pseudo-intellectual leftist establishment wallowed in sentimentality and took pains to hide its contempt for the man in the street. The conservative movement—partly liberal in the classic sense, partly traditional and nostalgic—had also at that time a rather distinctly Catholic leadership; Catholic converts were not rare. Only a minority of the leading minds were agnostic or belonged to the Reformation or Jewish religions.

Conservatism became a broad, popular movement—and thus politically important—only with the revival of the orthodox Reformation faiths. (I avoid the term "Protestant" because it is a Catholic term of abuse coined in

1529 and has nearly no official standing in the Old World.)[1] While in Europe the three faiths—Lutheran, Calvinist and Anglican—were almost hopelessly perverted and watered down by the First Enlightenment,[2] in the United States "religious liberalism" hit the mainline churches hard, but not the masses of the people. A number of denominations, despite the ridicule heaped upon them, continued to adhere to the essentials of Christianity. The Fundamentalists survived infinitely better in America than in Europe. These Christians were for generations the backbone of the country. From them evolved the so-called Silent Majority which in time gained real momentum. In the 1980s it may not have given the conservative movement many intellectual generals—although names like Rushdoony, Schlossberg, Opitz, and Neuhaus come to mind—but it did offer junior officers, troops, good organizers, and popular leaders. The ecumenical spirit that pervaded the United States no less than Europe made this political interfaith collaboration possible.

Nor should one overlook another development: the sizable shift of American Jews from their solid support of the Democratic to the Republican party. A small number, of course, have been right-wingers ever since the forties. During World War II, moreover, a whole group consistently warned against the American-Soviet honeymoon. Today a considerable number of Jewish intellectuals are on the Right.

The present conservative wave in the United States has of course no guarantee of permanence. Liberal democracy (i.e., majority rule combined with certain freedoms) not only embodies the contradictory elements of equality and liberty but is a frame into which free elections can put all sorts of pictures. The present U.S. Congress, moreover, is far from impressive, and today's voter a very fickle creature. Loyalty is a virtue and an ideal that belongs to the feudal age; it is intimately connected with the monarchy and religion—with the vertical order. By contrast, every election campaign is a constitutional attempt to shake the loyalty of supporters of other parties, to encourage some sort of treason. The result can be veritable orgies of infidelity.

In this respect we must also remember that the modern voter is very much an economic animal prone to connect his financial well-being with his government. If he is doing well economically, he tends to keep his government in power; if not, he seeks a change. It matters very little whether the government is responsible for either the good or the bad economic situation, or whether the verdict of the majority is right or wrong. Economic favors may be distributed as a result of irresponsible preelection promises, but only at the expense of burdensome debts and/or horrifying inflation.

The democratic process being what it is, we cannot be certain that the present conservative trend will continue. Leftists, after all, are most adroit in demagoguery; the half-educated that dominate the mass media have an easy time with the uneducated.

Many American conservatives nevertheless put their faith in the "good sense" of the average man (Rousseau's "common man," if you like), hoping that he will vote the "right" way. American conservatives only too firmly believe that if properly informed, nicely educated, and instructed by the right people in the right way, the dear people will vote for the right party. This reminds one of Europe's Christian Democrats who, questioned about the true meaning of Christian Democracy, express the pious hope that the masses will some day faithfully vote for the Christian Democratic parties.[3]

The questions remain whether today in large nations (we omit the direct democracy of small Swiss cantons) the man in the street is capable of understanding the content and nature of the occasionally momentous problems facing his country and whether in a great emergency he would not thoroughly lose his head. The case of Germany's two economic collapses (1923 and 1931) with millions of unemployed followed by the electoral victories of the brown and red enemies of parliamentary government should be as much in our minds as the support given by the peasant masses to the red armies during Russia's civil war of 1918-1920. *Sins will get punished beyond the grave, but follies right here on Earth.* The German sheep were led by their National Socialist butchers to the battlefields on three continents and were roasted alive by the Allies in their cities. The Russian peasants, hellbent on grabbing the remaining good-sized estates, were collectivized or, if they resisted, murdered—quickly or slowly—by the millions. History is pitiless.

We all have to face the grim, indisputable fact that the abyss between the *Scita*—the political, economic, technological, scientific, military, geographical, psychological knowledge of the masses *and* of their representatives—and the *Scienda*—the knowledge in these matters that is necessary to reach logical-rational-moral conclusions—is incessantly and cruelly widening. In a sense we are all becoming more and more ignorant. And he who no longer acts with the support of knowledge or experience can only rely on intuition (as Wilson, F. D. Roosevelt, Beneš, and Hitler admittedly did) or on mere feelings. In a constantly shrinking globe such a thoroughly antique form of government is hopelessly obsolete.

There is nothing more fatal than sentimental amateurism. The switches were wrongly set in 1789 with the French Revolution. The three fundamentally leftist revolutions, those that spawned France's democracy, Russia's international socialism, and Germany's national socialism, formed and fashioned the history of the last two hundred years and established the "Centuries of the G"—guillotines, gaols, gallows, gas chambers, and gulags.

To see the issues of our times clearly it is abolutely necessary for those on both sides of the Atlantic and even of the Pacific to distinguish between what is "left" and what is "right" and to learn which basic constructive principles best guide us in safeguarding our personalized, freedom-oriented ideals.

In this updated edition of my book I have stressed the importance of establishing a true understanding between the "conservative-rightists" in the English-speaking world and those on the Continent. We must try to establish a common language, mindful also of the words of Confucius, "When words lose their meaning, people lose their liberty," and of God's complaint that the people in Niniveh were too ignorant to distinguish between "right" and "left" (Jonah, 4.11).

The American people, I am convinced, have great qualities. I have always put the average American above the average European. But the political and educational system of the United States has tremendous, perhaps fatal, weaknesses. (America's two Achilles heels, foreign and military affairs, will be dealt with later on.)

This volume is a Continental book, not at all in the tradition of Hooker, Hume, Locke, Paine, or J. S. Mill. What I write and, even more, what I propose might shock many an American ear, but I have composed these lines precisely in order to give a wholesome jolt to my readers. Americans (or Britishers) are basically conservative. Being evolutionary rather than revolutionary they like familiar things and ideas in bigger and better editions, but they are easily horrified or disgusted by the essentially new, the different or unexpected. To me, on the other hand, nothing is sacred but the sacred. *Nihil mihi sacrum nisi sacrum.* Complacency is out. I am admittedly a radical, a man who tries to get to the root of the matter. Charles de Gaulle told us that one can never take a holiday from history. At present, less than ever, although so many are tempted to retire from the fray. The lure is great!

II

*In dictatorships one has to
howl with the wolves. . .
and in democracies one has
to bleat with the sheep.*

—HERMANN FUNKE

The purpose of this book is to describe the character of leftism and to show to what extent and in what way the vast majority of the leftist ideologies now dominating or threatening most of the modern world are *competitors* rather than *enemies*. The distinction is important. Shoe factory A is a *competitor* of shoe factory B, but a movement promoting the abolition of footwear is the *enemy* of both.

In the political field today, the distinction between competition and enmity is, unfortunately, less obvious; it is largely obscured by a confusion in semantics which, bad enough in Europe, is even worse in the United States. It has adversely influenced the foreign policy of the United States, a policy that has been and is being determined not only by what—really or seemingly—is in the best interests of the country but also by ideological prejudices. Very often these ideological convictions, by coloring the outlook of those Americans responsible for the course of foreign affairs (presidents, congressmen, professors, the media elite), have actually run counter to America's—and mankind's—best interests.

Ideologies—i.e., coherent political-social philosophies, with or without a religious background—did not spring full-blown in the United States in this century, a time that has seen the country engaged in two European crusades under two Democratic administrations. Nor am I of the opinion, so dear to certain "conservatives," that leftism is equitable to ideology. I believe rather that from its very birth in the late eighteenth century the United States was deep in the throes of warring political philosophies which contained both positive and negative aspects. The ideological impact of these ideas was, moreover, keenly felt in Europe where, sad to admit, their inner content was often misunderstood and perverted. The American

War of Independence (*not* "Revolution") had an undeniable influence on the French Revolution, and the latter, in its turn, had a terrible impact on the United States.

It was nevertheless not until the twentieth century—in our lifetime—that the United States decisively intervened in world affairs and that Europe suddenly found itself on the receiving end of American foreign policy. Decisions made in Washington (with or without consultation with refugees) affected Central Europe—which I consider my home—deeply and often adversely. During the long years that I spent in and out of the United States, I came to understand the reasons for and the psychological roots of the Great Euramerican Misunderstanding. As one might expect, there were several aspects to the problem: (1) a lack of self-knowledge on the part of the United States (paralleled in Europe by the blind acceptance of American myths); (2) misinformation in America about Europe (paralleled by European ignorance of America); and (3) the totally inadequate realization of where we all stand historically, what the big, dynamic ideologies truly represent, and how they are related to one other.

These three points are somewhat interconnected, since both America (or, better still, the English-speaking world) and Europe (or, more concretely, the Continent) cannot be properly understood without an excursion into the field of ideology. Even the folklore of a place is deeply affected by "philosophies." A sentence such as, "One man is as good as any other man if not a little bit better," is an automatic reminder of a certain type of American thought. It smacks of Sandburgian folkloric romanticism. At another level and in another place, the words *suum cuique* (to everybody his due) are still inscribed at Innsbruck University's law school. Yet it is equally true that Ulpian's great legal principle makes sense to a number of Americans while egalitarian notions are rampant in Europe. The Atlantic Ocean, no less than the Channel, is shrinking and slowly but surely our confusions are fusing. Unfortunately, our respective semantics are still far apart, which makes matters worse.

A positive and constructive understanding between the United States and Free Europe is no less necessary than the knowledge of which political and economic order is good, right, and fruitful. This book, therefore, tries to serve a double purpose: to reduce, if not eliminate, the Great Intercontinental Misunderstanding, and to institute a Quest for Truth, which entails an exposé of the multifaced, multiheaded enemy—Leftism.

In all fairness I owe it to the reader to explain my starting point, the premises from which I work. I am a Christian: I am emphatically not a democrat but a devotee of personal liberty. I thoroughly subscribe to the words of Alexis de Tocqueville, "Despotism appears to me particularly to be dreaded in democratic ages. I think that I would have loved liberty at all times, but in the present age I am ready to worship it." I am a liberal of the far Right, a term that will be explained in due course.

There are, of course, selfish European reasons for my writing this book, which is replete with views often not properly represented or understood in the United States. For example, the unwarranted identification of democracy with liberty is precisely what has caused a great many of the recurrent tragedies of American foreign policy (as well as a number of internal woes). One need only recall all the wars, all the propaganda, all the pressure campaigns for the cause of democracy, how every hailed victory of democracy has ended in terrible defeat for *personal liberty,* the one cause really dear to American hearts.

This is by no means a new story. Even Burke, in the beginning, welcomed the French Revolution, and eminent Americans praised it. But it all ended in a forest of guillotines. Mr. Woodrow Wilson enthusiastically welcomed Alexander Kerenski's government which would make Russia "fit for a league of honor."But how long did it last? The Weimar Republic, the near-republican Italian monarchy, the Spanish Republic, the decolonized free nations from Haiti to Tanzania, North Vietnam to Indonesia, Nicaragua to Buenos Aires—all have been grievous disappointments to "progressive" Americans, terminating as they have in dictatorships, civil wars, crowded jails, confiscated newspapers, gallows and firing squads, tyrannies and sequestrations, nationalizations and social engineering.

Yet beyond these obvious failures, beyond the brutal overt elimination of liberty and decency, the democratic evolution leading to nonviolent slavery is traceable to a turn of mind and outlook basically the same as the one that brings about the more obvious forms of tyranny. One should not be surprised, because the roots of the evil are historically-genetically the same all over the Western world.

The fatal year is 1789, and the symbol of iniquity is the Jacobin Cap. Its heresy is the denial of personality and of personal liberty. Its concrete realizations are mass democracy, all forms of national collectivism and statism, Marxism, which produces socialism and communism, fascism and national socialism—in short, leftism in all its modern guises and manifestations. It is to this that in America the old familiar term "liberalism," perversely enough, is being applied. The issue is between man created in the image of God and the termite in a human guise. It is in defense of man and in opposition to the false teachings that lower man to the status of an insect that this book has been written, and rewritten.

PART I

The Leftist Mind

To flatter the vices of the people
is even more cowardly and more dirty
than to flatter the vices of the great.

—CHARLES PÉGUY,
Mémoires et dossiers

CHAPTER 1

Identity and Diversity

The Lord our God
delights in variety.[4]

—HERMAN BORCHARDT

Viewed from a certain angle, we are all subject to two basic drives: *identity* and *diversity*. Neither in the lives of persons nor in the histories of nations are these drives always the same in intensity and balance.

How do they manifest themselves? All of us experience a mood during which we feel the desire to be in the company of people of our own age, our own class, sex, conviction, religion, or taste. Quite possibly, we share this drive towards conformity with the animal world, for a strong feeling of identity is like a herd instinct, a strong common feeling of community that regards another group with hostility. In race riots and ethnic demonstrations, this collective sentiment can display great force. The conformist herd instinct was, for example, the driving motor behind the nationalistic gymnastic organizations of the Germans and the Slavs,[5] so potent in the first half of this century. Watching five or ten thousand identically dressed men or women carrying out identical movements, one gets an overpowering impression of homogeneity, synchronization, symmetry, uniformity.

Identity and its drives tend to efface self, tend towards a "nostrism" ("usness") in which the ego becomes submerged. Of course, "nostrism" (a term created by the Austrian National Socialist Walther Pembaur) can be and usually is a clever multiplication of egoisms. Whoever praises a collective unit in which he participates (a nation, a race, a class, a party) also praises himself. And therefore all drives towards conformity not only take a stand for sameness and oppose otherness, but are also self-seeking. Homosexuality has an aspect of sameness to it along with the refusal to establish the sometimes difficult bridge—intellectual, spiritual, and psychological—to the other sex. In this respect, homosexuality is a form of narcissism, of immaturity, and implies the limitations of the "simpleton."[6]

Luckily, man in his maturity and in the fullness of his qualifications has not only drives towards identity but also towards diversity, not only a *herd instinct* but also a *romantic sentiment*. More often than not we yearn to meet people of the other sex, another age group, mentality, class, even of another faith and political conviction. All varieties of curiosity for the new—the eagerness to travel, to eat other food, to hear different music, to get in touch with varied cultures and civilizations—derive from the tendency to diversify. A dog has no wish to travel, nor does he much object to eating the same food. The stage of the ant or the termite can remain unaltered throughout the centuries. But man's desire for change results in history as we know it. There is something in us that cannot stand repetition. This hunger for the new can be quite fatal, of course, if it is not blended with an element of permanence—and prudence. In other words, we share with the beast the instinct to seek identity with another; we become fully human only through our drive and enthusiasm for diversity.

The danger notwithstanding, all higher theist religions rest squarely on this longing, this love for otherness. Though I would not subscribe to Karl Barth's formula of *Gott als der ganz andere* (God as the totally different One), no theist would deny God's otherness. We are created in His image, though we are not a facsimile of God. This is one reason why the Incarnation moves man so profoundly, why the first Ecumenical Council raged with bitterness over its exact nature, why it gave rise to tragic heresies and schisms.

Viewing these two drives, identity and diversity (both have psychological foundations, but only the latter has an intellectual character), we must conclude that modern times are more favorable to the herd instinct than to diversity. This may not be immediately evident, because in some ways the opposite seems to be the case: the craving for travel can now more easily be satisfied, and in the arts a greater variety of tastes and schools exists. But in other, more important realms, identity has been fostered in every way, partly by passions (mostly of the animal order), and partly by modern technology and the procedures that form modern civilization. Although it is fashionable to speak of present-day pluralism, in fact all modern trends point to the specter of a terrifying, bigger, and more pitiless conformity.

In this connection, identity is a cousin of equality. Everything that is identical is automatically equal. Two fifty-cent coins of the same issue are not only identical, they are also equal. Two quarters are equal to a fifty-cent coin, but they are not identical to it. Identity *is* equality: it is equality at first sight, an equality that takes no lengthy reasoning or painstaking investigation to discover. Therefore, all political or social forms that are inspired by the idea of equality will almost inevitably point to the concept of identity and foster the herd instinct, with subsequent suspicion, if not hatred, for those who dare to be different or who claim superiority.

There is a dull, animalistic leaning towards social conformity (identity) as well as a programmatic, fanatical drive in that direction. Nietzsche[7] was aware of it, as was Jacob Burckhardt.[8] Its driving motor is fear, formed by an inferiority complex and engendering hatred, with envy as its blood brother. This fear stems from feeling inferior to another person (or to a situation); hatred is possible *only* through feeling helpless before a more powerful person. A feeble and cowardly slave can fear and hate his master; the master, in contrast, will not hate but rather feel contempt for his slave. Haters throughout history have committed horrible acts of cruelty (the inferior's revenge),[9] whereas contempt—always coupled with a feeling of superiority—has rarely produced cruelty.

The demand for equality and identity arises precisely in order to avoid that fear, that feeling of inferiority. Nobody is better, nobody is superior, nobody feels challenged, everybody is "safe." Furthermore, if identity, if sameness has been achieved, then the other person's actions and reactions can be forecast. With no (disagreeable) surprises, a warm herd feeling of brotherhood emerges. These sentiments—this rejection of quality (which ineluctably differs from person to person)—explain much concerning the spirit of the mass movements of the last two hundred years. Simone Weil has told us that the "I" comes from the flesh, but the "we" comes from the Devil.

Identity's other factor is envy. Envy has several complex psychological roots. There is, first of all, the curious feeling that whatever one person possesses has in some way been taken away from another: "I am poor because he is rich." This inner, often unspoken sentiment rests on the assumption that all good things in this world are finite. In the case of money, or even more so of landed property, this might have some substance. (Hence the enormous envy of peasants for one another's real estate.) This contention, however, is often unconsciously extended to values that are not finite. Isabel is beautiful; Eloise is ugly. Yet Isabel's beauty is not the result of Eloise's plainness, nor Bob's brightness of Tim's stupidity. Envy sometimes subconsciously uses a statistical argument: "Not all of us sisters can be pretty, nor all of us brothers bright. Fate has discriminated against me!"

The second aspect of envy lies in the superiority of another person in a different respect. A burning envy can be created by the mere suspicion that the other person *feels* superior on account of looks, brains, brawn, money, or whatever. The only way to compensate is to find inferior qualities in the object of envy: "He is rich, but he is evil," "He is successful, but his family life is miserable." The envied person's shortcomings serve as a consolation: sometimes they serve as an excuse for attack, especially if the shortcomings are moral.

In the last two hundred years the exploitation of envy—its mobilization among the masses—coupled with the denigration of individuals, but more frequently of classes, races, nations, or religious communities, has been the key to political success. [10] The history of the Western world since the end of the eighteenth century cannot be written without this fact constantly in mind. All leftist "isms" harp on this theme; i.e., on the privilege of groups, which are the objects of envy and, at the same time, deemed inferior in an intellectual or moral respect. They have no right to their exalted position, runs the cant. They ought to adjust, become identical with "the people," renounce their privileges, *conform*. If they speak another language, they should eschew it in favor of the common tongue. If they are wealthy, their riches should be taxed away or confiscated. If they adhere to an unpopular ideology, they should renounce it. [11] Everything special, everything esoteric, everything not easily understood by the many becomes suspect and evil (as, for instance, the increasingly "undemocratic" modern art and poetry). [12] One type of unpopular minority, which cannot conform and therefore is always in danger of being exiled, suppressed, or slaughtered, is the racial minority.

Because—as always—hypocrisy is the compliment which vice pays to virtue, the ugly incitement of envy will never be publicly invoked. The nonconforming person or group sinning against the sacred principle of sameness will instead be treated as a traitor, and if he is not a traitor the envious majority will push him in that direction. (As late as 1934 some German Jews tried to form a Nazi group of their own; they naively considered anti-Semitism a "passing phase." But can one imagine a German Jew in 1943 *not* praying for an Allied victory? They were pushed in that direction.)

Thus, to be different means being treated as or being turned into a traitor. Even if the formula, nonconformist-traitor, is not openly spoken, it frequently lurks at the back of modern man's mind, whether or not he overtly embraces totalitarianism. How many people who sincerely reject all totalitarian creeds today would subscribe to the famous dictum of St. Stephen, King of Hungary, who wrote in his will to his heir presumptive, St. Emmeric: "A kingdom of only one language and one custom is a fragile and stupid thing"?[13] Unity and uniformity have been blended in our minds.

The modern allure of sameness has been enhanced not only by a technology that produces identical objects (one type of car owned "commonly" by half-a-million people), but also by the subconscious realization that sameness is related to cheapness and that it makes for greater intelligibility, especially for simpler minds. Identical laws, identical measurements, identical language, identical currency, identical education, identical intellectual levels, identical political power ("one-man-one-vote"), identical or near-identical clothes (the blue Maoist denim)—all this seems highly desirable. It simplifies matters. It is cheaper. It saves thinking. To certain minds it even seems "more just."

But these identical tendencies run into two obstacles: nature and man (who is part nature). Of the two nature can more easily be pressed into identical patterns by human endeavor, as witness certain types of gardening or hills that are leveled. But to fit man into an identical mold is a more difficult task, although not hopeless to the dolt who cheerfully declares, "All men are equal," and "All people are more alike than unlike." It evokes Procrustes, the legendary Greek robber and sadist, who flung his victims onto a bed: Those who were too short were stretched and hammered down until they fit, those who were too long were cut to size. Procrustes is the forerunner of modern tyranny.

But inevitably the leveler comes up against the mystery of personality. Human beings are different. They are of different ages, different sexes; they vary in physical strength, intellect, education, ambition. They have different characters, different dispositions, and different kinds of memory; they react differently to the same treatment (all of which antagonizes the leveler). Whereas the shoemaker takes diversity for granted, it is a headache for the shoe manufacturer. Natural to the governess and no mystery to the parent, it can become an insoluble problem to the teacher of a large class. In effect, large groups tend to give up at least part of the personality. Massman has the tendency to think, act, and react in synchromesh with the crowd (a phenomenon that might have a scientific explanation).

Precisely, then, because human identity is difficult to achieve, a poor substitute often has to be brought in. This substitute is equality—and it is equally unworkable.

CHAPTER 2

Equality and Liberty

Legislators and revolutionaries
who promise equality and liberty
at the same time are either
psychopaths or mountebanks.

—GOETHE [14]

Various clichés regarding equality must be dealt with at the start. One popular cliché states that all men are equal, not physically or intellectually, but "in the eyes of God." This, of course, is by no means the case. None of the Christian faiths teaches that we are all equally loved by God; on the contrary, we have it from Scripture that Christ loved some of his disciples more than others. Nor does any Christian religion maintain that grace is given in equal amounts to all men. Catholic doctrine, more optimistic than Lutheranism or Calvinism, teaches that everyone is given sufficient grace to be able to save himself. The Reformers, who were determinists, did not grant even that minimum. The Marquis de Sade and St. Jean Vianney or Pastor von Bodelschwingh were obviously not "equal in the eyes of God." Otherwise, Christianity would make no sense; the sinner would equal the saint; bad would be the same as good.

It is interesting, however, to observe the inroads that secular democratic thinking has made among theologians. Although freedom is mentioned several times in Scripture, equality does not figure at all. Yet far too many

9

religious thinkers try to bridge the gap between religion, i.e., their Christian faith, and current political notions. Hence they talk about *adverbial* equality, unaware that they are playing tricks. They begin by saying that all men have souls *equally*, that they are *equally* called upon to save their souls, that they are *equally* created in the image of God, and so forth. But two persons who equally have noses or banking accounts do not have equal noses or equal banking accounts.

While our physical and intellectual differences—our inferiorities and superiorities—can be fairly obvious, our spiritual status is much more difficult to determine. Since we do not know who among us is nearer to God, we should treat each other as equals. This, however, is merely procedural. We are similar to the postman who delivers two sealed letters indiscriminately, one carrying a worthless ad and the other tidings of great joy, unaware of what is inside. The comparison is admittedly far from perfect, because all human beings, having the same Father, are therefore brothers—even if on different spiritual levels with different functions in human society. (Socially, one person can be more important than another; but since everybody is unique, *everybody is indispensable*. To state the contrary is democratic nihilism.)

Another cliché speaks of equality before the law. At times, this equality is an administrative expedient to save money and the strain of lengthy investigations. In other words, equality before the law can be "practical." But certain questions obtrude: is it desirable, is it just, should it be adhered to?

A child of four who has committed manslaughter should obviously be treated differently from an adolescent of seventeen, or an adult of thirty. The egalitarian will accept this but will hasten to add that all men or women at age thirty should be punished alike. Yet most courts take circumstances into consideration. St. Thomas insisted that stealing in a real emergency—a desperate beggar stealing a loaf of bread to feed his family—is no sin. And in Austria, the law in such circumstances would invoke *unwiderstehlicher Zwang* (irresistible urge) and the "criminal" would get a suspended sentence or go free. Yet again, when the Germans were freezing in the winter of 1945–46 Cardinal Frings of Cologne told the faithful that, given the circumstances, to steal coal was no sin, no crime in the eyes of God. (Hence the phrase *Kohle fringsen*, to "fringsize coal.")

In other cases, the difference between the sexes will put obstacles in the path of equality before the law. Women, for instance, can decide to conceive and thereby get pregnancy leave with pay, but a man cannot. When the topless bikini appeared in 1964 a German paper humorously protested against police interference because they had violated the highly democratic and egalitarian basic law of the country which forbade all discrimination between the sexes—why should women be compelled to cover the upper part of their bodies and not men? But has not God discriminated physically between the sexes? Equality before the law might be highly unjust: witness the outcry, *Summum ius, summa iniuria* ("The strictest law can be the greatest injustice"). Indeed, justice is better served by Ulpian's previously stated principle—*Suum cuique*, to everybody his due.

A third cliché which is invoked by a great many people is equality of opportunity. In the narrow sense of the term it can never be achieved, and should never be attempted. For in employing labor we must discriminate between the skilled and the inexperienced, the industrious and the lazy, the dull and the smart, and so on. Unfortunately, the trend in many labor unions is to protest against such just discrimination and to insist on indiscriminate wage rates and employment security. It would be far wiser to demand the abolition of *unjust* discrimination, arbitrary discrimination without solid factual foundation. Some trade unions have an ugly record of racial discrimination, as in the Republic of South Africa where the common man tends to be a racist whereas big business is color-blind. [15]

Just discrimination, or preference based on merit, is conspicuously absent in a sanctified process that has great influence in our society— political elections. Whether it is a genuinely democratic election in the West or a plebiscitary comedy in the East, the one-man-one-vote principle is a commonplace today. The voter's knowledge, experience, merit, sex, wealth, his military record, his standing in the community—nothing counts except the vegetable principle of age: he must be eighteen, twenty-one, twenty-four years old. The twenty-one-year-old semiliterate prostitute and the sixty-five-year-old professor of political science who has lost an arm in the war, has a large family, carries a considerable tax burden, and has studied the political problems on the ballot, are politically equal as citizens. Compared with a nineteen-year-old student of, say, government, our friendly prostitute actually rates higher as a voter. It is not surprising, therefore, that in the emerging nations—and some others—literacy is not required in order to vote. This egalitarianism of the voters has psychologically fathered (as we shall see later on) other egalitarian notions and has been severely criticized by Pope Pius XII. [16] And not only by him. [17]

But back to equality of opportunity: In a concrete sense, not even a totalitarian tyranny can bring it about because no country can decree that a child, upon entering the world, have equal parents. They might be equal to other parents as far as wealth is concerned, but will they have equal pedagogical qualifications? Will they bestow equal heredity? Will they give their child the same nutrition as other parents? The same education?

The cry for an identical and equal education has been raised again and again in democracies, totalitarian and otherwise; in accordance, variety in schools is deemed "undemocratic." To achieve their ends, egalitarians have been forced to advocate not only intensive schooling, but boarding schools so as to counter the fact that parents are very different (every marriage offers another "constellation"). Children, they argue, should be taken out of their homes and educated collectively twenty-four hours a day. (In the Soviet Union a plan—supported by the "liberal" Khrushchev, butcher of the Ukraine and Hungary—dictated that 90 percent of all children over the age six be put in boarding schools by 1980. How this idea would have affected the low birth rate is another question.)[18] Yet even these measures will never result in complete equality of opportunity unless attributes such as capacity and skills are disregarded. If this should happen, a general decline at all levels would set in.

There is also the problem of racial and/or intellectual inequality. God endowed the various nations and races with different qualities and handicaps. The Japanese have relatively poor eyesight, the Bambutis (African dwarfs) have short legs, the Watussis very long ones, the Eskimos rarely suffer from heart disease, Mediterranean people have a nervous system that reacts faster than that of Northern people. And, since the brain is part of the body, IQs differ all over the globe. For a religious person concerned mainly with eternity, all this is of no importance; to a pagan, it presents a vital problem. To deny these differences is unscientific and demonstrates an ideologically conditioned infantilism.

But, as Friedrich August von Hayek has pointed out, a certain equality of treatment is necessary in a free society.[19] Only by treating people equally can one discover who is superior to whom. A group must undergo the same test in order to classify its members; horses in a race must all start from the same line. By treating people equally (back to the adverb), we do not of course make them equal, because in a free and open society the better qualified will get ahead faster ("Honor to whom honor is due").

There can be no doubt that from the point of view of the common good, the commonweal, the open society is best, because talents have a better chance of developing in it than in societies divided by castes or estates.[20] But it would be a great mistake to think that the absence of fixed social handicaps increases personal happiness. The gifted bourgeois who failed in prerevolutionary French society had the consolation of blaming an iniquitous system for his inability to rise to the top. The failure in a free society must either blame himself (which leads to the melancholia of those plagued by inferiority complexes) or lash out at imaginary conspiracies of ill-wishers or wicked enemies. Thus, psychologically his position has become far more difficult. A mobile society may contribute to many achievements but, because of the nature of things, to even more disappointments. Psychological disturbances—nervous breakdowns, even suicides—may possibly increase in a socially mobile society (as well as with the loss of religious conviction). This, however, does not cancel the intrinsic superiority of an open over a closed society.

Egalitarianism, as already intimated, cannot make much progress without the use of force: perfect equality is only possible in total slavery. Since nature (and naturalness, implying freedom from artificial constraints) is not biased against even gross inequalities, force must be used to establish equality. Imagine an average class of students in a boarding school, with the normal variety of talents, interests, and inclinations for hard work. One fine day the dictatorial principal demands that all students score B in a given subject. The C, D, or E students would be forced to work harder, so much so that some would collapse. At the other end, the A students would have to be restrained—given drugs or locked up with copies of *Playboy* or *The New Masses*, or simply hit over the head. In sum, force would have to be used, much as Procrustes used it. Yet the use of force limits and in most cases destroys freedom.

A "free" landscape has hills and valleys. To make the landscape "egalitarian" would entail blowing off the tops of the hills and filling the valleys with the rubble. To become even, a hedge must be clipped regularly. To equalize wealth (as in so many progressive countries on either side of the former Iron Curtain) the government must ordain equal wages and salaries or tax away the surplus—to the extent that those earning above average would refuse additional work. Since the hard workers are usually gifted people with stamina and ideas, their refusal would effectively paralyze the commonweal.

In other words, a real antagonism, an incompatibility, a mutual exclusiveness exists between liberty and enforced equality. The situation is curious given that in the popular mind these two concepts are closely linked. Is this due to the fact that the French Revolution chose as its slogan "Liberty, Equality, Fraternity"—or is there another reason?

None comes to mind except for the psychological nexus mentioned earlier. If A is superior to B—more powerful, more handsome, more intelligent, more influential, more wealthy—then B will feel inferior, ill at ease, probably afraid of A. And, as we have seen, inequalities engender fear—and envy, though it is rarely mentioned. Fear and envy are twin brothers, or perhaps triplets with hate added for good company.

However one looks at it, equality and freedom are mutually hostile. Since equality is the dynamic element in democracy, and liberty lies at the base of true liberalism, the two political concepts are equally exclusive.

A word is needed here about equality in the United States. As is well known, that which people praise highly, they usually lack. The hungry speak about food, the poor about money, the fat about slenderness, the sick about health, and so forth. This is equally true of nations. One hears of the loyalty of the Germans, the golden heart of the Viennese, the collectivist tendencies of the Russians, the frivolity of the French, the individualism of the Reformers, the obedience of Catholics—all are so many myths.

So too is the wish for equality in the United States. Americans are only "programmatically" egalitarian, and this results in a schizoid attitude towards life. Told to admire democracy, an imported French ideology, they think (being very serious people) that they have to "live up to it." But by nature they are anything but egalitarian; on the contrary, they are intensely interested in quality and in individual performance, as is evident in their professional life which is (by European standards) brutally elitist. If you do not perform well, you fail, and to be a failure is the nightmare of every American; he is not at all eager to be equal, he wants to be successful, he wants to *excel*. A constant testing and comparing is going on in the United States.

"One man is as good as another" is said glibly, but not for a moment believed—and rightly so. Could anybody in his right mind imagine that a society could be simultaneously competitive and egalitarian? The three most important fields in American life are business, sports, and politics, and in all of them numbers and measurements, which express quantities and qualities, figure prominently. The egalitarian hysteria currently sweeping the United States, which invades life with countless and sometimes ridiculous laws and regulations, has been brought on by the impact of French democracy, a highly illiberal and completely un-American import. William Dean Howells in his *Impressions and Experiences* (1896) spoke the simple truth: "Inequality is as dear to the American heart as liberty itself."

CHAPTER 3

Democracy and Liberalism

*Had every Athenian been a
Socrates, every Athenian assembly
would have been a mob.*

—*Federalist*, No. 55

Democracy is a political form, a system of government. It has no social content, although the word is frequently misused in that sense. It is wrong to say, "Mr. Green is very democratic; on his trips he has lunch with his chauffeur." Mr. Green is, rather, a friend of simple people, and so should appropriately be described as *demophile*, not *democratic*.

"Democracy" is a Greek word combining *demos* (the people) and *krátos* (power in a strong, almost brutal sense). The milder form would be *arché*, which implies leadership rather than rule. Hence "monarchy" is the fatherly rule of one man in the interest of the common good, whereas "monocracy" is a one-man tyranny. Aristotle and the early and late Scholastics divided the forms of government according to the table below.

GOOD FORMS	BAD FORMS
Monarchy, the rule of one man in the interest of the common good.	*Tyranny*, the rule of one man for his own benefit.

GOOD FORMS	BAD FORMS
Aristocracy, the rule of a group in the interest of the common good.	*Oligarchy*, the rule of a group for its own benefit.
Republic or Polity, the rule of the better part of the people in the interest of the common good.	*Democracy*, the rule of the worse part of the people for their own benefit.

"Aristocracy," originally a form of government, came to mean the highest social layer. Similarly, the term "republic" came to mean every (external) form of government that was nonmonarchical and "public." *Rzeczpospolita* was a term used for the Polish state prior to 1795 and after 1918, while American and British scholars speak about the Polish Commonwealth when referring to the elective kingdom after 1572. Yet the term republic covers a multitude of forms of government—from the Polish Kingdom prior to 1795, to the highly aristocratic Republic of Venice (the *Christianissima Res Publica*), the Soviet Republic (USSR), the present (presidential) French Republic, and the (presidentless) Republic of San Marino with its five *capitani reggenti*. The United States is *de facto* a republic, although not so designated in the Constitution; only the states of the Union are required to have "a republican form of government" (Article IV.4).

Given these historical semantics, the question today is how to define a democracy (once a pejorative label)? To the question, "Who should rule?" Democracy would answer, "The majority of politically equal citizens, either in person or through representatives" (direct or indirect democracy). This formulation raises a number of subsidiary interpretations.

One school insists that only direct democracy is real democracy, that elected delegates constitute an oligarchy with a time limit. This interpretation of democracy, the "oligarchic school," comes principally from Vilfredo Pareto, Gaetano Mosca, and Roberto Michels (an Italianized former German Socialist). All three might conceivably be called fascist sympathizers, but it was probably the intellectual and realistic climate of Italy, so hostile to all forms of illusion, that influenced their critical thinking.[21]

Another school maintains that the election of representatives, bound in conscience to voice the views of their electors, is a *democratic* performance, while representatives who are guided by their own lights, their own knowledge, their own conscience, are the executors of a *republican* spirit.[22] Many ancient commentators believe that a republic, no less than a democracy, is ruled by a majority. But in the case of a republic the majority is not only the *pars maior*, but the *pars sanior*, whereas in a democracy, the majority can be the worst part of the nation. In every nation, the lower half of the social pyramid (if the expression is permitted) is by far the bigger half, which means that the people of quality can always be outvoted. Not inevitably, of course. The natural *aristoi* can be included in the party that wins the election. They are out of luck, however, if a demagogue (in ancient Greece, a "leader of the people" in a democratic state) successfully mobilizes the masses against them.

The definition of "full citizen," as when one speaks of "politically equal citizens," is *always* arbitrary. In pre-1971 Switzerland and Haiti, for instance, women were excluded from the suffrage. Yet it is hard to argue that Switzerland was therefore not a democracy. The main Swiss counterargument, one that is typical of this militarized nation, was to the effect that since women did not serve in the armed forces, they did not have equal duties and, thus, should not have equal rights.[23]

Even more arbitrary are the age limits that supposedly define the "mature voter." One man or woman can achieve an early maturity, another does so at the voting age, a third later in life, a fourth never. There is maturity without knowledge, and knowledge without wisdom—but these analytical probings could lead us far astray. For those who insist that human beings are not only *animalia socialia*, but also *zoa politika*, arbitrarily set voting ages are a serious and insoluble matter; for, given this reasoning, some people are being deprived of their "God-given right" (inherent in their God-given nature). In many a country, as a result of the Swiss argument concerning rights and duties, the voting age was lowered to the age of military service. The same argument, applied in reverse, led to conscription and the *levée en masse* in the First French Republic.

Our marginal remarks notwithstanding, it remains that democracy rests on two pillars: *majority rule and political equality*. And this although certain constitutions make it possible (with or without gerrymandering) for a minority of citizens to elect a majority of deputies or representatives. Proportional representation (P.R.) eliminates this possibility. But although the many disadvantages of proportional representation are frequently pointed out and the idea pilloried,[24] P.R. is undoubtedly more "democratic" than the majority system as it exists in the United States and Britain—although not necessarily better.

Freedom, however, has nothing to do with democracy as such—nor has a republic. The repression of 49 percent of the people by 51 percent, or of 1 percent by 99 percent, is most regrettable, but it is not undemocratic. Bear in mind that only democracy has made the concept of majority/minority an absolute political reality;[25] naturally the whole people can never act as ruler, but a majority can (usually) through its representatives. If this majority, however, is lenient towards those it has defeated in the prior election, it will have been motivated not by democratic principles but by tolerance. And if this tolerance is ideologically systemized, it is *liberalism* in the geniune sense, not in the totally perverted American sense. (See chapter 8.)

Thus, in the democratic order, the phrase "rule of the people" is misleading. The majority rules over the minority, or in George Orwell's famous phrase in *Animal Farm*, "All animals are equal, but some are more equal than others." The notion that one part lords it over another is displeasing to the "democratist," i.e., the supporter of democrat*ism*, which is democracy raised to the status of an ideology. He will argue that those who have been beaten in an election have, by their cooperation in the process, helped the majority in furthering their plans, just as the man who chooses a losing lottery ticket contributes to the jackpot won by somebody else. This, however, will certainly not be the case where only part of the population believes in democracy as an article of faith. (In the German elections in July and November 1932, only a very small part of the electorate genuinely believed in democratic processes.)

Yet even if the entire electorate were convinced of the dogmas of "democratism," the "yes" of the disappointed voter would be qualified and sometimes most unhappy. In an existential sense democracy is not self-government at all, and self-government (unless we stand for unanimity in a democratic procedure) is an illusion. Herman Melville expressed this view when he said, "Better to be secure under one king, than exposed to violence from twenty millions of monarchs, though oneself be one of them."[26]

Actually, the voter never knows precisely what effect his vote will have— whether it will make him a winner or a loser. He might, the morning after the election, ascertain whether he is among the winners or the losers. But in many a country he will have to wait, as, for example, if none of the parties has an absolute majority, in which case a government will be formed only after lengthy negotiations concerning which the voter has no influence whatsoever. He can only watch joyfully or angrily how his vote is utilized. Existentially, he is faced with a preestablished situation: he has to choose between candidates he rarely had a hand in picking (certainly never picked singlehandedly); thus he is usually left to choose the least objectionable among various undesirables. In large nations, moreover, the voter is a microscopic unit. If the electorate of the United States were equal to a thick black line as high as the Empire State Building in New York City, graphically a single vote would be about 3mu, which is three times the thousandth part of a millimeter (and a millimeter is the twenty-eighth part of an inch). The formula "self-government" under these circumstances makes hardly any sense.

Yet self-government is understandably a dream. Since government (the state) would not exist without Original Sin,[27] "democratism" is looked upon as a paradisaical movement, promising an Eden-like utopia more often than not depicted as a return to a lost Golden Age. (In the secular view, this Golden Age was not lost owing to the rebellious sin of our ancestors but as a result of a wicked conspiracy of evil minorities.) The notion of self-government implies that we will not be ruled by somebody else: we will do it ourselves and thereby we will be free. Rule, force, and subservience will come to an end. Nudism, this type of thinking holds, will solve the sexual problem by disposing of clothes. But, in fact, people get used to nudity while the sexual problems continue (as in the case of Japan).

There is just no return to Paradise by the back door or by political legerdemain. The hardship of being ruled by somebody else remains; it can be alleviated only if we love those who rule us. Servitude can only be dissolved in love.[28] But how can there be love for the rulers when we hire and fire them like obnoxious menials? Have not the words "politics" and "politicians" assumed pejorative meanings in democracies? Do they not express contempt, suspicion, sarcasm, and irony? Sir Henry Campbell-Bannerman, the Liberal British Prime Minister, declared that "self-government is better than good government." If this were true, medical self-help would be preferable to professional treatment. The Austrian Peter Wolf, on the other hand, said that the first right of a nation is to be *well* governed. Personal freedom, which can be brutally curtailed by majority rule, belongs essentially to good government.

To speak of tolerance as the essence of liberalism, which might or might not exist alongside democracy, implies a readiness to "carry" (*tolerare*), to "put up with" the presence, the propagation of views and ideas that we reject or oppose. Marshaling our charity, we would suppress our indignation and give our fellowmen the opportunity for open dissent despite our disagreement. Tolerance is a real virtue because it entails self-control and an ascetic attitude.

There are nevertheless certain limits to tolerance. All behaviors, all political ideologies cannot be tolerated at all times. The United States severely restricted the immigration of anarchists. Anarchists believed in the Propaganda of Deeds, which meant assassination and open revolution. Nor could all faiths be tolerated. Some religions encourage murder, such as the East Indian Thugs who assassinated travelers for the greater glory of Kali. And what about the People's Temple, the American sect that climaxed in Guyana with nearly one thousand murders and suicides?[29] (Whether religious polygamy should be outlawed is a moot question. When I was born about half a million of my fellow citizens were Muslims. Here in the United States, Mormon fundamentalism is certainly an authentic American religion; besides, almost all American states permit polygamy on the installment plan.)[30] On the political front, West Germany outlawed the Communist party for years, yet it is legal in Austria. Ironically, the brown-clad murderers, supporters of the gas chamber, cannot have a political party, but the red executioners, who shoot through the nape of the neck, can. In these matters, arbitrariness once again prevails.

Those who have no principles, no grounded convictions, no dogmas, cannot be tolerant—they can only be *indifferent*, which is quite another matter. An agnostic is expected to be indifferent, not tolerant, because he has no good reason to oppose another opinion. To him truth is either nonexistent or humanly unattainable. A strict agnostic makes no value judgments, and thus for him there is no "good" or "bad," while "right" and "wrong" have only practical, circumstantial meanings. To a person like Oliver Wendell Holmes, Jr., man is no better than a baboon or a grain of sand. According to Holmes, "Man at present is a predatory animal. I think that the sacredness of human life is a purely municipal idea of no validity outside the jurisdiction."[31] An agnostic, a philosophic relativist, can only say to his adversary, "I *think* that I am right in *my own way*, and although you differ from me, you may be right in your own way. So let's compromise." All of which recalls the delightful conversation between Franklin D. Roosevelt and Stalin at the Teheran Conference when Stalin wanted to execute 50,000 "junkers and militarists," and Roosevelt counterproposed 49,000 and then, in compromise, 49,500. The conversation was facetious, but, in a way, not so facetious. It disgusted even such an immoralist as Winston Churchill.[32]

Yet, whether out of tolerance or indifference, the readiness to yield and to compromise is the quintessence of parliamentary life in a democracy. (No stump orator, of course, will promise to be a superb compromiser once he is elected—rather the opposite.) Compromise does not belong per se to democracy, but it is the *conditio sine qua non* of democracy. It can equally be assumed that when the majority of people inspired by liberal principles in the Western world talk about democracy, they usually refer to *liberal* democracy. This brings about such errors as calling the confiscation of a newspaper "undemocratic." If the majority of the people approve of it, such an act is highly democratic, but assuredly not liberal. Democracy is the concept of the totally politicized nation; it is a populism, like ethnicism (nationalism) or racism, and therefore leftist—and consequently totalitarian.

When then is liberalism correctly understood? Liberalism is not an exclusively political term. It can be applied to a prison reform, to an economic order, to a theology. Within the political framework, the question is not (as in a democracy), "*Who* should rule?" but "*How* should rule be exercised?" The reply is, "Regardless of who rules—a monarch, an elite, a majority, or a benevolent dictator—governments should be exercised in such a way that each citizen enjoys the greatest possible amount of personal liberty." The limit of liberty is obviously the common good. But, admittedly, the common good (material as well as immaterial) is not easily defined, for it rests on value judgments. Its definition is therefore always somewhat arbitrary. Speed limits curtail freedom in the interest of the common good, yet there is arbitrariness in setting the limits. Is there a watertight case for forty, forty-five, or fifty miles an hour? Certainly not.

It is obvious that liberty is only relative, that the true liberal wants to push it to its feasible limits, and that it cannot be identical at all times, in all places, under all circumstances, for the same persons. (One might permit an eighteen year-old to drive a car but not a thirteen year-old, and so forth.) Only God—not man—is perfectly free. But freedom does pertain to man (Wust's *animal insecurum*)[33] because man is created in the image of God. Liberty, for the same reason, belongs neither to the animal world nor to the sphere of inanimate matter.

Freedom thus is the only postulate of liberalism—of genuine liberalism. If, therefore, democracy is liberal, the life, the whims, the interests of the minority will be just as respected as those of the majority. Yet surely not only a democracy, but a monarchy (absolute or otherwise) or an aristocratic (elitist) regime can be liberal. In fact, the affinity between democracy and liberalism is not at all greater than that between, say, monarchy and liberalism or a mixed government and liberalism. (People under the Austrian monarchy, which was not only symbolic but an effective mixed government, were not less free than those in Canada, to name only one example.)[34]

Viewed in the light of the terminology favored by leading political scientists,[35] it seems that monarchs such as Louis XIV, Joseph II, or George III were genuine liberals—*by modern standards*. None of them could have issued a decree drafting male subjects into his army, nor a decree regulating the diet of his citizens, nor one demanding a general confession of all economic activities from the head of each household. Not until the democratic age were conscription, Prohibition, and income tax declarations made into law by the people's representatives, who have far greater power than absolute monarchs ever dreamed of. (In Western and Central Europe, "absolute" monarchs—thanks to the *corps intermédiaires*—were never for that matter really absolute: the local *parlements* in France and the regional *Landtage* and *Stände* in the Germanies never failed to convene.) Modern parliaments can be more peremptory than the old monarchies because they operate under the auspices of the magic democratic formula: "We are the people, and the people—that's us."

Monarchs, in a way, skated on thin ice. They desperately tried to bequeath their countries to their heirs, for if they failed, they sometimes had their heads chopped off. They could not conveniently retire to a quiet law office like deputies or presidents who fail to get reelected. *There are totalitarian and monolithic tendencies inherent in democracy* that are not present even in a so-called absolute monarchy, much less so in a mixed government which, without exaggeration, can be called *the* great Western political tradition. (insert)

Inescapably, then, democracy and totalitarianism are not mutually exclusive terms. Professor J. L. Talmon has rightly entitled one of his books (on the French Revolution) *The Origins of Totalitarian Democracy*.[36] Nor is it an accident that the isms that have menaced liberty from the eighteenth century to our days were called democratic. Their proponents all claimed that the majority, nay, the vast majority of the people supported their particular "wave of the future." At times this claim had a solid statistical foundation. Genuine liberalism, on the other hand, rarely became a real mass movement—and conservatism never. The marriage between democracy and liberalism (again, in the etymological sense of the term) came late in history and bore the seeds of divorce. De Tocqueville saw only too clearly that while democracy could founder into chaos, the greater danger was in its gradual evolution into oppressive totalitarianism, a type of tyranny the world would never have seen before and for which it would have been partly conditioned by modern administrative methods and technological inventions.[37]

CHAPTER 4

Right and Left

The heart of the wise man
beats on his right side,
the heart of the
fool on his left.

—ECCLESIASTES, 10, 2

Much of the semantic rubble in the vocabulary used in the Western world (though sometimes not in the United States) has been cleared up in the foregoing pages. We deal now with a necessary definition that has no universal acceptance—the definition of the terms "right" and "left."

If a workable definition existed, or if the two words could be entirely dispensed with, there would be no problem. On the other hand, they can be very useful, for as handy labels they can often truly simplify matters.

"Right" and "left" have been used in Western civilization from time immemorial with certain meanings; right has a positive and left a negative connotation. In all European languages (including Hungarian and the Slavic idioms) right is related to "right" (ius), rightly, rightful—in German *gerecht* (just), in Russian *pravo* (law), *pravda* (truth). Left, on the other hand, is *gauche* in French, which also means "awkward," "clumsy" (Bulgar: *levitsharstvo*). The Italian *sinistro* can mean "left," "unfortunate," or "calamitous." The English "sinister" can mean "left" or "threatening." The Hungarian word for "right" is *jobb*, which also means "better," while "left" (*bal*) is used in composite nouns in a negative sense: *balsors* is "misfortune." The same distinction prevails in Sanskrit (*dakśina*, *vamah*) and in Japanese (*hidarimae*, which means "in front of the left" or "adversity").[38]

In biblical languages, the just on the Day of Judgment will be on the right,[39] with the damned on the left. Christ sits *ad dexteram Patris* (at the right hand of the Father), as the Nicene Creed asserts. In Britain, it is customary to allocate seats to the supporters of the government on the right side and to the opposition on the left side in Parliament. And when a vote is taken in the House of Commons the "ayes" pass into the right lobby behind the Speaker's chair while the "noes" go to the left lobby. (They are counted by four members who then inform the Speaker of the outcome.) Thus in the Mother of Parliaments, right and left imply affirmation and negation respectively.

On the Continent, where most parliaments, beginning with France, gathered in a horseshoe shape (rather than facing each other), the most conservative parties were seated to the right, usually flanked by the liberals, then came the parties of the center (which frequently held key positions in the formation of government coalitions), followed by the "radicals," and finally the Socialists, Independent Socialists, and Communists.

In Germany after World War I, the National Socialists, most unfortunately, were seated on the far right because to simple-minded people nationalists were rightists, if not conservatives—a grotesque idea when one remembers the antinationalism (anti-ethnicism) of Metternich, the monarchical families, and Europe's ultraconservatives. Ethnicism, (nationalism), indeed, was a by-product of the French Revolution (as was militarism). Nationalism (as the term is understood in Europe, though not in America), is after all "identitarian," a form of conformity, whereas patriotism is not. In Central Europe nationalism has a purely ethnic connotation and implies an exaggerated enthusiasm for culture, language, folklore, ways of life. Patriotism, on the other hand, emphasizes the country. A patriot will be happy if numerous nationalities live in his Fatherland, whose outstanding characteristic ought to be variety, not uniformity. The nationalist is hostile to all those who do not conform ethnically. Thus nationalism, as understood on the Continent, is the blood brother of racism.[40]

The mislocation of the National Socialists in the *Reichstag* compounded a confusion in semantics and logical thinking that had started some time earlier. The Communists, the Socialists, and the Anarchists were identified with the Left, the Fascists and the National Socialists with the Right. At the same time, it was evident that there were a number of similarities between the National Socialists on the one side and the Communists on the other. This gave rise to the famous and idiotic formula: "We are opposed to all extremism, be it from the Left or from the Right. Besides, the Reds and the Browns are practically the same: extremes always meet."

The thinking is incredibly sloppy: extremes never meet. Extreme cold and extreme heat, extreme distance and extreme nearness, extreme strength and extreme weakness, extreme speed and extreme slowness never meet. They do not become identical or even alike. If the pontificator on extremes were to be asked what he understands by the Right and the Left, he would be unable to analyze the terms coherently. Lamely, he would imply that the reactionaries—the Fascists, for instance—were extreme. Asked whether Mussolini's *Repùbblica Sociale Italiana* was a reactionary or a leftist establishment, he would mumble anew about those paradoxical extremes, adding with certainty that the Left is collectivist and progressive, and the Communists "extreme progressivists." Should he persist in this nonsense, it would be well to inform him that certain primitive African societies with a tribal collectivism are not in fact "extremely progressive." At this point, the conversation would undoubtedly expire.

The first failure with this loose reasoning lies in the belief that "extremes meet," the second in the lack of a clear definition of the Left and the Right. In other words, both logic and semantic clarity are missing. Logic lies beyond our ministrations, but clear definitions can be provided.

Right, then, is what is truly right for man, above all his freedom. Because man has a personality, because he is a riddle, a piece of a puzzle that never completely fits into any preestablished social or political picture, he needs room, space. He needs a certain *Lebensraum* in which he can develop, expand, in which he has a tiny personal kingdom. *L'enfer, c'est les autres.* "Hell, that's the others," is voiced by Sartre, a pagan existentialist, near the end of his play *Huis Clos*. The Great Menace is all around us. In a state-insured, government-prescribed, and—to make matters worse—socially endorsed collectivism, our liberty, our "Western" personality, our spiritual growth, our true happiness is at stake.

All the great dynamic isms of the last two hundred years have been mass movements attacking—even as they mouthed the word "freedom"—the liberty, the independence of the person. This was done programmatically in the name of all sorts of high- and even low-sounding ideals: nationality, race, better living standards, social justice, security, ideological conviction, restoration of ancient rights, a happier world for all. But in reality the driving motor of these movements was always the mad ambition of intellectuals—oratorically or, at least, literarily gifted—and the successful mobilization of the masses filled with envy and a thirst for revenge.

The Right has to be identified with *personal freedom*, not with some utopian vision whose realization, were such a thing possible, demands tremendous collective efforts. It stands for free, organically grown forms of life. And this in turn implies a respect for tradition. The Right is truly progressive, unlike leftist utopianism with its lack of real advance, its almost inevitable demand—as in the *Internationale*—to "make a clean sweep" of the past, *du passé faisons table rase*, or *dyelayem gladkuyu dosku iz proshlago*. If we return to point zero, we have to start from scratch.[41] Bernard of Chartres said that generations were "like dwarfs seated on the shoulders of giants, thereby capable of seeing more things than their forebears and at a greater distance."[42] Almost all utopias, though "futuristic" in temperament, have preached a return to an assumed Golden Age, glowing with the false colors of a romantic dream. The true rightist is not a man who wants to go back to this or that institution for the sake of return; he wants first to find out what is eternally true, eternally valid, and then either to restore or to reinstall it, regardless of whether it seems obsolete, whether it is ancient, contemporary, brand new, or ultramodern. Old truths can be rediscovered, entirely new ones found. The Man of the Right does not have a time-bound mind but a sovereign mind. If a Christian, he is, in the words of the Apostle Peter, the steward of a *Basileion Hieráteuma*, a Royal Priesthood.[43]

The Right stands for liberty, a free, unprejudiced form of thinking; a readiness to preserve traditional values (provided they are true values); a balanced view of the nature of man, seeing in him neither beast nor angel, insisting on the uniqueness of human beings which cannot be transformed into or treated as mere numbers or ciphers. The Left is the advocate of the opposite principles; it is the enemy of diversity and the fanatical promoter of identity. Uniformity is stressed in all leftist utopias, paradises in which everybody is the same, envy is dead, and the enemy is either dead, lives outside the gates, or is utterly humiliated. Leftism loathes differences, deviations, stratifications. The only hierarchy it can accept is functional. The word "one" is its symbol: one language, one race, one class, one ideology, one ritual, one type of school, one law for everybody, one flag, one coat of arms, one centralized world state. Leftism is horizontal and collectivist, rightism is vertical and personalist. The word "person" comes from the Etruscan *phersú*, mask. The mask represents the nontransferable role of an actor. The person is unique and irreplaceable. Left and right tendencies can be observed not only in the political domain but in many other areas of human interest and endeavor. Concerning the structure of the state, leftists believe in strong centralization. Rightists, on the other hand, are federalists—in the European sense—state-righters. Since they believe in local rights and privileges, they stand for the principle of subsidiarity. Decisions, in other words, should be made and carried out at the lowest possible level—by the person, the family, the village, the borough, the city, the county, the federated state, and only finally at the top, by the government in the nation's capital. The breakup of the glorious old French provinces with their local *parlements* and their replacement with small *départements*, named after some geographic feature and totally dependent upon the government in Paris, was a typically leftist reform.

Concerning education, the leftist is always a statist. He has all sorts of grievances and animosities against personal initiative and private enterprise. The notion of the state doing everything, until finally it replaces all private existence, is the Great Leftist Dream. Thus the leftist tends to have city or state schools—or a ministry of education—control all aspects of education. As an example there is the famous story of the French Minister of Education who pulls out his watch and, glancing at its face, says to his visitor, "At this moment in 5,431 public elementary schools, they are writing an essay on the joys of winter." Church schools, parochial schools, private schools, personal tutors, none is in keeping with leftist sentiments. The reasons are manifold. Not only is delight in statism involved, but also the idea of uniformity and equality—the notion that social differences in education should be eliminated and all pupils be given a chance to acquire the same knowledge, the same type of information, in the same fashion, and to the same degree. This should enable them to think in identical or at least in similar ways. Quite naturally, it is especially true in countries where "democratism"—democracy as an ism—is promoted, where pains are taken to ignore differences in IQs and in personal effort, where marks tend to be eliminated and promotion to the next grade becomes automatic.

Leftism does not like religion for a variety of reasons. Its ideologies, its omnipotent, all-permeating states demand undivided allegiance. And religion, of course, demands allegiance to God and at times to a church. Leftism deals with religion in two widely divergent ways. One is through the separation of church and state, which eliminates religion from the marketplace and tries to atrophy it by not permitting it to exist anywhere

outside sacred precincts. The other is through the transformation of the
Church into a fully state-controlled establishment, asphyxiating rather
than starving it to death. The National Socialists and the Soviets used the
former method, Czechoslovakia the latter.

But the antireligious bias of leftism rests not only on anticlericalism,
antiecclesiasticism, and antagonism to the existence of another body, another organization within the boundaries of the state; it gets its impetus not
only from jealousy but above all from the rejection of a supranatural, a
spiritual order. *Leftism is basically materialistic.*

The Provider State, Hilaire Belloc's *Servile State*, is obviously a creation of
the leftist mentality. It should not be called the Welfare State for, after all,
every state exists for the welfare of its citizens. Alexis de Tocqueville in
Democracy in America anticipated with great accuracy the possibility, nay,
the probability that the democratic state would evolve in a totalitarian
way towards the Provider State. In this state, two leftist wishes find
fulfillment—the extension of government, and the dependence of the
person upon the state, which controls his destiny from the cradle to the
grave. Every aspect of the citizen—his birth and his death, his marriage
and his income, his illness and his education, his military training and his
transportation, his real estate and his travels—everything is known by the
state.

In the practical order of things, of course, there are exceptions to the
rule, because leftism is a disease, an ideology, that does not necessarily
spread in a coherent, systematic way. Here and there an isolated manifestation can even appear in the opposite camp. Spain under Franco's rule, for
example, had a partly leftist character, such as strong centralizing tendencies, restrictions on languages other than Castilian, monopoly of the state
syndicates, censorship.

Concerning the first two failings—leftist tendencies *are* failings—it is
good to remember the effects of Spain's immediate historic past. Catalonian, Basque, and Galician nationalism took on a radically leftist
character—since nationalism, in the European sense, *is* leftism—when
they opposed "Castilian" centralization. Hence, in Madrid, almost all
movements promoting local rights and privileges, whether political or
ethnic, were suspect as leftist, enemies of the regime and inimical to the
unity of Spain. (Spain is *"Una*, Grande, Libre"!) Oddly enough—but
understandable to anybody with a real knowledge of Spanish history—the
far Right in Spain, represented by the Carlists and not, as popularly
assumed, by the Falangists, is federalist ("localist," anticentralist) in the
European sense. The Carlists are also opposed to the centralizing tendencies

of Madrid. When in 1964 the central government tried to cancel the privileges (the *fueros*) of Navarre, the Carlists threatened to issue a call to rebellion, causing the government quickly to back down, declaring it all a mistake.

All conservative movements in Europe are federalist and opposed to centralization. Thus, ironically, we encounter in Catalonia a desire for autonomy and the cultivation of the Catalan language among supporters of the extreme Right as well as of the Left. The notorious Catalonian Anarchists have always supported autonomy, but formal anarchism has been a curious *mixtum compositum*. Whereas anarchism's ultimate goals are leftist, socialistic in essence, its temper is rightist. Much of present-day communism in Italy and Spain is merely popularly misunderstood anarchism. On the other hand, it is significant that in 1937 open war broke out in Barcelona between the Communists and the Anarchists. It was, moreover, the Anarchists who resisted the Communists in Russia longer than any other group, until in 1924 they were literally exterminated in all Soviet jails and camps. Hope of "taming" them had been abandoned.

Or let us take the Metternich regime in Central Europe. Basically it had a rightist character, but although born in conscious opposition to the French Revolution, it had—as so often tragically happens—learned too much from the enemy. True, it never became totalitarian, but it assumed authoritarian features and aspects that were nothing other than leftist, such as the elaborate police system based on espionage, informers, censorship, and controls in every direction. Still, when Sir William Wilde, Oscar's father, studied in Austria in 1840, he found the country superior to England in many respects, especially education.

Something similar is true of Maurrasism, which was also a curious blend of rightist and leftist notions, characterized by deep inner contradictions. Charles Maurras was, simultaneously, a monarchist and a nationalist. Yet monarchy is basically a supranational institution. Usually the monarch's wife, his mother, and the spouses of his children are foreigners. With two exceptions—Serbia and Montenegro—[44] all the sovereign ruling houses of Europe in the year 1910 were foreign in origin. By contrast, nationalism is "populist," and the typical republican constitution requires that the president be a native of the country. Maurras undoubtedly had brilliant insights, and many a European has borrowed from him. But it was by no means accidental that he collaborated when the German National Socialists occupied his country. Nor was he a Christian during the better part of his life, although he returned to the Faith some time before his death.[45]

To identify, in a rough way, the Right with freedom, personalism, and variety, and the Left with slavery, collectivism, and uniformity, is to make sense of semantics. It negates once and for all the moronic statement that communism and national socialism are alike because "extremes always meet." In the same camp with socialism and fascism can be found that particularly vague leftism which in the United States is known perversely enough as liberalism (taken up in detail in chapter 14). European liberalism is quite distinct in nature. In Italy, significantly, the Italian Liberal party (the PLI) is seated to the right of the *Democristiani*, next to the monarchists.

Right and left will be used in these pages as outlined here; the proper distinction in semantics is vital in discussing the political scene of our age. (For a list of leftist characteristics, see the Appendix.) Words are important. Confucius told us that if words lose their meaning, people lose their liberty. [46]

PART II

Leftism in History

*In certain historical periods
one has to make the full circle
of follies in order to
return to reason.*

—BENJAMIN CONSTANT DE REBECQUE

CHAPTER 5

The Historic Origins of Leftism

*He who wants to get to the
source must swim against
the current.*

—STANISLAW LEC

In the Western world the roots of leftism reach way back into the dim past. Leftist tendencies, according to the terminology outlined above, existed in ancient Greece. Hellenic (Athenian) democracy not only insisted on the rule of the many, it had a strong egalitarian slant. Naturally, the notion of equality only applied to full citizens, which excluded women, slaves, and foreigners (*metoikoi*), so that the electorate in Greek democracies was always a minority.

Greek democracies, while frequently oppressive, did contain certain liberal aspects: no respect was given to men in elevated positions and there was no strong, concretized ruling class or anything resembling a "presidency" to weaken the people's authority. Elements of equality and social liberty appear in Plato's and Aristotle's descriptions of democracy: envy was writ large and excellence suspect. Fear of a monarchical restoration was ever-present and inspired a dread of all concentration of power. If anybody excelled in merit and prestige, he was menaced by exile through ostracism. Social liberties were nevertheless evident but political liberties were few,

33

LIBRARY
COLBY-SAWYER COLLEGE
NEW LONDON, NH 03257

although it is well to recall that the concept of the person as we know it did not exist in antiquity. It appeared in the Western world—and only in the Western world—with the advent of Christianity. When Aristotle called man a *zoon politikon* he meant a creature all but absorbed by the city or the state.

The hostility of Plato to democracy (more apparent in the *Politeia* than in the *Nomoi*) was similar to Aristotle's; in the end, Aristotle fled the democratic rule of Athens and went to Chalcis on Euboea to avoid the fate of Socrates. Plato's antidemocratic bias was not only the automatic reaction of the intellectual against a form of government that put no premium on reason or knowledge; it was also the result of the depth of his feelings over his master's death. The average American or European, though aware that Socrates was put to death on account of his "impiety" in introducing strange gods and for "corrupting" the young, is rarely aware of the full story. The last charge, far from having anything to do with sex, was subdivided (according to Xenophon) into several accusations: (1) that he taught his disciples to treat the institutions of the state with contempt; (2) that he taught the young to disobey their parents; (3) that he had associated with Critias and Alcibiades; and (4) that he constantly quoted Homer and Hesiod against morality and democracy (especially *Iliad, II,* 198-206). Not only the democratic government, but the "dear people" were opposed to Socrates, and he can, without exaggeration, be called a victim of democracy, of the *vox populi*.[47]

Salvador de Madariaga has said that Western civilization rests on two deaths—the death of Socrates and the death of Christ. And indeed the Crucifixion was also a democratic event. When our Lord was brought before Pilate, He told him that He had come as a witness to the Truth, and the governor, a true agnostic, asked Him, "What is Truth?" And without waiting for an answer, he passed Him by and consulted "the people." The *vox populi* condemned our Lord to death as it had Socrates more than three centuries earlier. But if we despair of truth, if we believe that truth either does not exist or cannot humanly be attained, we are left with two alternatives: we have either to leave things to chance, or we must be content with preferences—personal preferences or "preferences statistically arrived at," which often means accepting the "verdict of the majority." The latter, although a handy way to settle differences of opinion, neither tells us the truth nor offers us *rational* solutions to burning problems.

Greek democracy was buried under the power drive of Sparta and then Macedonia, a conquest which was, incidentally, applauded by both Pho-

kion and Isocrates.[48] Rome, in its turn, sprang up, but was never a real democracy, not even in the broad sense of the term used by antiquity. The Roman Marius can nevertheless be said to have represented the Roman Left, while his wife's nephew, Julius Caesar, became a leftist dictator, thereby fulfilling the *anakyklosis* as defined by Polybius[49] and foreseen by Plato: the evolution of monarchy into aristocracy, aristocracy into democracy, democracy into tyranny, and tyranny again into monarchy. But it is a moot question whether Roman Caesarism was ever genuinely monarchical or only, as Metternich argued,[50] a form of "Bonapartism," i.e., military dictatorship. By the end of the third century, even the simplest Romans presumably realized that the Republic had gone the way of all flesh and that Rome had developed a fundamentally different constitution (a fact which Tacitus had strongly suspected).[51]

During the Middle Ages "democracy" had a bad reputation among intellectuals, who alone knew its meaning. It existed in small private societies, such as in the high valleys of the Alps and the Pyrenees, in Iceland and Norway, and in Slavic villages in the form of the *vyetche*.

The larger and more developed political societies in medieval times were for the most part ruled by mixed governments, with a monarch at the top who owed his status either to birth or to election by a small elite. The *Regimen Mixtum* normally had a Diet (or even two "Houses") composed of representatives of the three or four estates. (Originally only the nobility and clergy were represented. Later a new element was added, the Third Estate, i.e., the burghers, and in many cases yet another, the peasantry, or Fourth Estate, as in Sweden and the Tyrol.)

The mixed governments were balanced. The king was not all-powerful—*rex sub lege*[52] was the standard formula. The king had no right to levy taxes, as witness the penury of monarchs, which was a permanent feature of medieval and postmedieval society. The king's power was curtailed by powerful vassals—the Church, the Diet in which the Estates were represented, and the free municipalities which had great privileges. Absolutism and totalitarianism were unknown in the Middle Ages.[53] The Middle Ages were obviously not "progressive."

All during that period the word "democracy" appeared only in learned treatises, but insidious religious sects with leftist social and political programs were nevertheless active in large parts of Europe. The Albigenses (Bogumilians, *Catharoi*) were not themselves egalitarian, but a strong leftist character was evident in the earlier Waldensians (founded by Peter Waldo). They scorned not only the "rich, sinful Church," but all luxury, ostentation, power, the high and the mighty. These dualistic sects with their Manichaean roots made their way from the Near East into the Balkans and from there to northern Italy, southern France, Belgium, Bohemia, and England. They had apocalyptic visions of the wickedness of wealth, the punishment of the arrogant, the destruction of the two great organizations, Church and state. These visions were not uniform; their accents changed and compromises with reality were frequent. But a red thread was distinct throughout. As far as their ideas went, the sects had a definite influence on the origins of the Reformation.[54]

What distinguished these sectarians from the Reformers was the cult of poverty, as found among the Poor of Lyons, an early Waldensian group. The Waldensians from Lombardy (as distinct from those of France) insisted that their faithful live on the fruits of manual labor. Specializing in weaving, they lived and worked together, were hostile to military service, rejected oaths, and hated sumptuous churches. They seemed also to have an anti-intellectual bent. From Lombardy they spread as far as Bohemia.

In northern France, the Turlupins, a Christian sect, preached a human equality that suggests some connection with the ideas of the monk Joachim de Floris, such as his pantheistic chiliasm. They may also have been behind the big peasant rising, the *Jacquerie*.

In England, the revolt of the farmers led by John Ball and Wat Tyler also had a certain religious motivation. (John Ball was a priest, and his revolutionary sermons were frequently on the theme, "When Adam delved and Eve span, who was then the gentleman?")[55] These revolts were connected with the teachings of Wycliffe, whose new doctrines had far-reaching political effects.

Wycliffe began by denouncing papal supremacy, thus earning the sympathy of the king. He then proceeded to question transubstantiation and the prerogatives of the clergy, for which he received the support of the nobility. Finally, he advanced democratic theories and denounced wealth altogether, thereby giving impetus to the agrarian revolt. A partially analogous development took place when Luther (who knew the writings of Wycliffe) declared the Pope to be the Antichrist and received the protection of the princes against the Emperor; he subsequently won the applause of the nobility when he denounced the clergy and the monastic institutions. But Luther never went further in these matters.

When the enormous wave of criticism of the existing order reached the peasantry and resulted in violent rebellion, and the lower middle classes in various regions embraced Anabaptism (Münster, for example) or engaged in iconoclastic orgies, Luther applied the brakes and denounced the extremism. At one time Wycliffe also half-heartedly protested against Ball and Tyler (who insisted they were his followers), but he died before the full development of Lollardy (a sect composed largely of Wycliffe's followers). Wycliffe's Poor Preachers were definitely an effort to "democratize" religion, a populist outburst along semiecclesiastical lines. The Poor Preachers were past masters at exploiting the envy of the masses.

Wycliffe, despite his prominence, did not stand at the beginning of a new development. He was, rather, a student of the prime mover, Marsilius of Padua, as was Luther much later on. Marsilius, in support of Emperor Ludwig I, tried to undermine the political claims of the papacy, attacked its hierarchical status, and ended up developing a democratic theory of government.[56] He declared that original political power resided in the people collectively, or at least in their better (*valentior*) part. Another source of Wycliffe's inspiration came from extreme factions of the Franciscan Order with their emphasis on poverty. Significantly, the mendicant order at first strongly supported Wycliffe.[57] The curious relationship between a misconceived notion of the monastic idea and the leftist currents in every age will be taken up in another chapter. The phenomenon evokes the outcry of St. Thomas, "*Corruptio optimi pessima*" ("When the best is corrupted, it becomes the worst").

Lollardy, which survived Wycliffe right up to the beginning of the sixteenth century,[58] was not only the religious attitude of the poor people, it had great support from the landed gentry as well. The wealth of the Church was heavily criticized as inconsistent with the teachings of Christ. Nor was the attack confined to the Church. The legend, prevalent at the time, was that Christ, the indigent son of a poor carpenter, and His Apostles were a band of paupers anxious to avoid contamination by the rich.[59]

A second type of envy was intellectual rather than material. Theology was looked at askance as something complicated, not easily comprehended by the uneducated, the private property of the intellectually *beati possidentes*. Soon after its founding, a bitter struggle developed in the Franciscan Order between intellectual and nonintellectual factions. The former emerged victorious, thanks to which we have such outstanding representatives of Christian theology as St. Bonaventure, Alexander Hales, Occam, and Duns Scotus.

And, finally, the third kind of envy had a spiritual cause. The clergy reserved the Chalice of Holy Communion for itself. This was largely due to the fear of infection from the plague.

Thus the demand for equality—the rebellion against differences and privileges—was mounting. It is no coincidence that the cry first went up in England, one of the most class-conscious countries in Western civilization, due to the invasion of conquerors that created different social layers. It was repeated in the seventeenth century when egalitarian sects rose and, for the first time in Christian European history, a king was formally put to death.

But the first truly concrete, systematic, egalitarian revolution in Europe was Taboritism, the radical form of Hussitism. Hus was not only Wycliffe's translator and commentator, he was his most faithful imitator. All the new currents were hostile to hierarchies and differentiation; they stood for brotherhood and assailed fatherhood. In the political sphere, this meant questioning the monarchy as well as mixed governments with a monarchic head (evidence once more that new religious doctrines affect political ideas). Inevitably, this development shook the position of the father in the family, not surprising since the patriarchal[60] order forms a coherent unity.[61]

Psychological affinities are not necessarily logical. It is possible, for instance, to be a Lutheran monarchist, or a Unitarian tyrannical *paterfamilias*. Some Catholic republicans believe (erroneously) that every papal encyclical is infallible, and some agnostic monarchists reject the papacy, as they reject the heavenly Father. Yet these affinities should never be overlooked. The early New Englanders who were convinced that George III had secretly become a Catholic were factually in error[62] as far as that British monarch was concerned, but in regard to the institution, their suspicion was not grotesque. Kierkegaard (to quote just one example) thought that all genuine royalists leaned towards the Catholic faith.[63]

But back to the sectarian upheavals. Hus, like Wycliffe, was not really a champion of the "common people." Like Wycliffe he had the support largely of the lower nobility and, like Wycliffe, he was a nationalist. Wycliffe was an "England Firster" while Hus became the spokesman for the Czech people against the German element in Bohemia-Moravia. And there, in the land of the Crown of St. Wenceslas, for the first time European history witnessed outbreaks of national hatred, clashes at the university between national student organizations—the type of collective fury that was to bring ruin to Europe in the nineteenth and twentieth centuries. The stage for leftist mass movements was set. A fairly strong underground movement was already at work in Bohemia, a movement made up of late Waldensians and Beghards (Pickarts), the male counterpart of the Béguine Order, but disorganized and riddled with heretical ideas.[64]

The martyr-death of Hus, who was burned at the stake in Constance, led to a fiery outbreak of popular wrath in the Czech parts of Bohemia. The responsibility for Hus's ignoble death was partly that of the counter-pope, John XXIII.[65] The Emperor, however, was even more responsible, having given Hus the safe conduct that was not honored by the Council.

The death of Hus resulted in the establishment of two groups: the Utraquists, a more moderate group content with administering communion under both species, bread and wine, and the Taborites, a radical group that found its center in the newly established city of Tábor. (*Tábor* means "camp" in Czech, as it does in Latin.) The Taborites, extreme fanatics, were organized militarily. Their first leader was Jan Žižka, scion of a newly noble family of German origin. Their ideology was chiliastic, nationalistic, puritanical, democratic, and socialistic—*a real and concrete prefiguration of the isms of our times* in dynamic synthesis. The mass movements of our days are related to Taboritism perhaps more by filiation than by analogy.

Taboritism, however, was more deeply influenced by the Waldensians and the Beghards than by pure Hussite theology. In its earlier phase the socialistic and puritanical ideas were pronounced, and the ultraextremists—the nudist Adamites—were severely persecuted by Žižka. Still, the Taborites believed in the coming of a millennium in the form of a Third Kingdom (taken from the prophecies of Daniel). A radically socialist program regarding property was adopted at first, but after the death of Žižka, under the leadership of Prokop Holý (also, apparently, of German origin), the egalitarian spirit weakened. Hussite armies invaded the surrounding German areas and a crusade was preached against the Taborites. When the army of the crusaders was routed near Domažlice (Taus), the old leading classes finally woke up to the danger. Allied with the Utraquists, who had kept the original moderate Hussite spirit, the Taborites were in due course defeated in the battle of Lipan and Prokop was killed.

Proudhon has stated that it is surprising how theology is always found to be the basis of politics.[66] The emphasis in these pages on theological ("religious") ideas, movements, and arguments is thus not due merely to the profoundly religious character of the Middle Ages. Looking back through the centuries at the tragedy of Socrates, it is clear that the tragedy was largely conditioned by an intermingling of political, philosophical, and religious sentiments and concepts, an interconnection that persisted throughout the first 1,700 years of Christian history. But for the ensuing two hundred years, the prevailing isms have been unable to coexist peacefully with theistic religions. On the contrary, they have fought them with all the means at their disposal. And vice versa.

Precisely because modern totalitarian ideologies—from simple leftism

to national socialism, international socialism, and communism—have a
pseudomonastic as well as a "heretical" aspect, they are unacceptable to the
great religions of the West: Christianity, Judaism, and, up to a point,
Islam. These isms derive their strength, as will be discussed later on, from
the secularized version of a few Christian tenets. They are therefore
Religionsersatz (substitutes for religion), and the parties representing them
are secular "churches" with hierarchies, rituals amounting to a real liturgy,
secular ministries of propaganda,[67] and a system of worldwide missions,
among other things.

Comparisons between the Vatican and the Kremlin are usually made in a
spirit of hostility, but they are not without substance if we bear in mind
that the various isms, as fundamental heresies, are indeed evil caricatures of
fragments of Christian doctrine, of Christian institutions. Our isms could
not, in the first instance, have grown on non-Christian soil, although they
could have been transferred to areas where Christianity was not indigenous.

The influence of Hus, Wycliffe, and Marsilius on Luther and the beginnings of the Reformation is not pertinent to this book.[68] But it is important to remember that the Reformation, contrary to an obsolete concept
that survives in English-speaking countries,[69] was by no means the "beginning of liberalism" (genuine or fake), nor anything like the fulfillment of
the Renaissance, but a late medieval and "monastic" reaction[70] against
Humanism and the spirit of the Renaissance. To Luther, the Renaissance
(no less than Humanism) was a foul compromise between Christianity and
paganism. According to Luther, Plato, Socrates, and Aristotle were all
broiling in the eternal fires of Hell.[71]

The picture of Luther as taught to American Catholics and Protestants is
unfortunately totally false. He was in reality a true "wrestler with Christ"[72]
and not a neurotic. He was not a neurotic who wanted to marry a nun; nor
was he a libertarian subjectivist who wanted to promote "private interpretation" of the Bible; nor did he yearn for "personal freedom." He was an
unequivocal rigorist who wanted to go *back* to what he considered the
original purity of the Church. That he was shocked when in Rome by the
depravity of the hierarchy is nonsense. The moral situation in Germany at
the time was not a whit better. Moreover, in scholastic theology the moral
virtues were not highly rated.[73] (Luther was a typical medievalist in this
respect also.) Far from advocating anything like classic liberalism, Luther
taught the omnipotence of the state and opposed all forms of rationalism,
Christian or otherwise, as well as the "worship of man"—*Soli Deo Gloria*
was Calvin's battle cry, but it could as easily have been Luther's. He was

convinced that man could not contribute anything substantial to his own salvation: only the blood of the Lamb could wash away sins; good works were of no avail. Hence also Luther's dislike for the Epistle of St. James.

All of which means that the Reformation was (in the literal sense of the term) conservative in character and communitarian in spirit; Luther and Calvin were by no means pioneers of liberal democratic relativism. It is highly significant that in Catholic European countries, not a single party calls itself "conservative." The Catholic faith is not conservative. It is, rather, like a tree, rooted to the same spot but changing in shape, shedding old leaves and branches, adding new ones.

Because the Reformation was a reaction *against* Humanism and the Renaissance, the Middle Ages continued in a certain sense in the Reformed world; the Gothic style, for instance, was seen in churches and colleges. In the Catholic world, the Renaissance style evolved slowly into the Baroque and later into the Rococo styles. And while the world of the Reformation espoused discipline, commercialism, industry, and hard work—a sort of secular monasticism—the Catholic world retained its monastic and medieval ideas in monasteries and convents[74] while its secular life proceeded on its artistic, intellectual, and anarchical course.

The "wild sects," meantime, continued to exist almost solely in the *Mundus Reformatus*. The sixteenth century saw a furious outbreak of sectarian chiliasm in various parts of Germany, in the southwest along the Rhine and, above all, in Münster and Thuringia. Thomas Münzer, a German Anabaptist, after visiting the Hussite circles in Prague in 1521, started a series of popular uprisings in the name of religion. He attacked the Reformers for their half-hearted work—for not having gone far enough in religion and for failing to change the state and society. Through preaching and writing, he attempted to establish a communist theocracy (completely opposed by Luther). After contacting the Swiss Anabaptists, Münzer (together with the former monk Pfeifer) seized the Thuringian town of Mühlhausen where he deposed the local government and plundered both convents and the houses of the rich. In 1525 he joined the Peasant Revolt, but his warfare against the "godless princes and priests" ended in failure. Beaten in battle, he and Pfeifer were taken prisoner and beheaded.

Jan van Leyden, also called Jan Bokelszoon, born in Holland, became master of Münster after the Anabaptists had taken the town and Jan Matthys, his predecessor and a fanatical preacher, had been killed in battle. He established a communist "Kingdom of Zion" based on a weird mixture of socialist and Old Testament notions—everyone received goods "according to his needs,"[75] the sexual corruption of his court knew no limits, and the entire population was terrorized. The city was finally taken back by Bishop Count Bernhard von Galen, and Jan van Leyden was put to death.

The Anabaptists set up the most famous model of their political order in Münster, but their settlements in southern Moravia in the late 1520s and early 1530s were more concretely communist. In the religious area, their principles were set down in the Nikolsburg Articles, which featured their opposition to organized government and to all forms of learning, especially theology. (The Scriptures, admittedly not easy for the common man to understand, were only necessary for the wicked and the heathen; the children of God did not need them. Christ, of course, was not the Son of God but merely a prophet.)[76]

The social arrangement in that part of the Holy Roman Empire was more interesting than the religious faith. Carl A. Cornelius gives a short but vivid description:

> The Zürich Doctrines were obeyed in their most uncompromising and radical form. Government offices, oaths and the use of arms were strictly outlawed. Nobody owned property. The stranger who asked for Baptism had to surrender all his earthly goods to the community, and in the case of excommunication or banishment nothing was returned to him. Family life, which cannot be imagined without property, was replaced with a different order. Marriages, without consultation of the partners, were decreed and blessed by the Servants of the Word. Children soon after their birth were handed over to wet nurses and later placed in the common schoolhouse. Dressed and fed in an identical way, adults lived according to their occupation in large households under the supervision of a Servant of the Necessity. All of life moved, day in and day out, within the narrowest limits. Any manifestation of personal independence or freedom led to banishment, which meant to bottomless misery.[77]

As in the case of the Low German Anabaptists (finally centered in Münster), the expectation of an imminent Day of Judgment, dooming the wicked and exalting the faithful, was very strong. In our time, though in a more secular sense, the far Left also believes either in a millennium or, in anticipation, an earthly Day of Judgment crowned by the triumph of the chosen race, whether of the Aryans (over the Jews), or the proletarians (over the idle rich), or merely the "progressive forces of mankind" (over the dark forces of reaction), to use the Nazi expression from the Night of the Long Knives.

The collapse of Anabaptism in northeastern Germany under the joint blows of Catholics and Lutherans seems to have stopped the first great leftist wave for roughly two hundred years. This wave was essentially medieval in character, much like the pseudomonasticism mentioned above. Even the Waldensians were able to impress on their contemporaries that they were friars *manqués*.[78] The medieval spirit continued only in the north of Europe (owing to the "medieval" and "Gothic" character of the Reformation). The different spirits of the Catholic and Reformed outlook are, I believe, best symbolized in Botticelli's *Birth of Venus* and Grant Wood's *American Gothic*. Botticelli was a pious man, and his Venus was "baptized"; her face expresses the loving goodness of Christianity.

England, however, witnessed another explosion of religious leftism in the midseventeenth century. With the downfall of the first Stuart monarchy and the execution of Charles I (a truly world-shaking event), there was a new outbreak of populism from the lower classes, which endangered even Cromwell's regime when the Levellers under John Lilburne threatened army discipline. Lilburne saw clearly that Cromwell's and Ireton's leadership was leading to oligarchic rule—Cromwell rejected egalitarianism outright—and thus he came out strongly for the prerogative of Parliament. Lilburne himself defended private property and protested the "Leveller" label, but the most radical Levellers, the Diggers, espoused far more leftist ideas.

England in the seventeenth century thus proved a breeding ground for heresies. And certain religious-political notions born there at the time found their way to the United States. Unfortunately, it is not easy to put them into proper focus—neither to underestimate nor to exaggerate their impact on the Thirteen Colonies and, more especially, on the young American republic.

Still, it would be a great mistake to think that there was any specifically leftist or "progressivist" element in New England Puritanism. Even the anti-Episcopalian (and anti-Catholic and antimonarchical) attitude of the Pilgrim Fathers and their more immediate descendants lacked egalitarian overtones.[79]

There is no egalitarianism inherent in Calvinist theology; on the contrary, predestination brutally separates mankind into the damned and the saved, and in the best Old Testament tradition the saved from the beginning partake of divine favor. A dim reflection of their eternal bliss descends upon them on this earth. (Hence, the efforts of individuals to prove by deeds and facts that they were saved resulted in the tremendous economic upsurge of the Calvinist countries, according to the thesis of Max Weber and Müller-Armack.)[80] Paul Kecskeméti said correctly that "the basic idea upon which the Puritan political system was founded was that church members alone could have political rights. This ensured that the Puritan commonwealth could be nothing but an oligarchy. As wealth was one of the criteria (though by no means the only one) on the basis of which it was determined whether one belonged to the 'elect,' the commonwealth was necessarily controlled by the wealthy."[81]

CHAPTER 6

Nascent America

As was said long afterward,
the founders of the Republic in general,
whether Federalist or Republican, feared
democracy more than they feared original sin.

—CHARLES A. AND MARY BEARD
America in Mid-Passage, Vol. 3

The Pilgrim Fathers and the Puritans were neither democrats nor liberals. John Winthrop declared that democracy was "the meanest and worst of all forms of government." John Cotton was equally blunt: "Democracy, I do not conceyve that God did ever ordeyne as a fitt government either for the church or commonwealth. If the people be governors, who shall be governed? As for the monarchy and aristocracy, they are both of them clearly approved and directed in Scripture."

The government of New Amsterdam (New York), the Dutch establishment in the New World, was in no way democratic. Pennsylvania's constitution (William Penn's *Concessions*) was democratic only in that freemen and proprietors could vote; it could better be characterized as liberal. In Maryland, at least one "democratic" practice had an ambivalent history: religious tolerance, shaken in 1692, came to an end in 1715 when Catholics were disenfranchised. South of the Potomac, democracy held no appeal. By the end of the eighteenth century, only one state had an egalitarian franchise—Vermont, not admitted until 1791 into the Union.

And yet it is undoubtedly the American War of Independence (which is not to be confused with a revolution) that provided the main psychological, but not ideological, momentum for the French Revolution. Other intellectual and political currents of course contributed to it. There was the "example" of England, tirelessly cited by Voltaire, who owed much to this northern neighbor of France. Then there was Switzerland, which fit so well the romantic temper of the times: the beautiful, rustic, well-regulated, republican, progressive community next door. There were also the Encyclopedists, Rousseau (from Geneva) and, last but not least, the Marquis de Sade, the grandfather of modern democracy.

But Voltaire's picture of England and the sentimental portrait of Switzerland had little to do with the reality of those countries. The Swiss federation did not become a democracy until passage of its constitution in 1878, and it is arguable that certain Swiss cantons remained oligarchic-aristocratic units until the dawn of this century. But it was the image of the United States, far from French shores, that most allured the revolutionists. Its very remoteness ensured mistaken perceptions: a foreign country, a foreign culture and, above all, a foreign political movement is fraught with potential misinterpretations.

In other words, the filiation between the American War of Independence and the French Revolution existed in a psychological sense, *but there was a tremendous and catastrophic misunderstanding as far as ideas and content were concerned*—the first in a row of never-ending mutual transatlantic misinterpretations and misjudgments.

The United States owes its political structure and its Constitution to the Thirteen Colonies who fought to escape the domination of "London," of its two institutions: Parliament and the Crown. At the time, there was no practical way to achieve genuine representation in the Mother of Parliaments. England's ruler (who was intermittently insane) had little sympathy for the just grievances of his subjects beyond the seas. In fact, Britishers as a whole, with the exception of certain radical Whigs and a few Irish (Burke among them), neither understood nor particularly cared for the colonists. In their quarrel with them, the British failed in public relations and in presenting their financial claims, which provoked the critical cry, "No taxation without representation!" The demands by both sides were probably just: the British wished to recover part of the expenses for the war that led to the annexation of Canada, and the colonists insisted on full citizenship. Almost inevitably, the conflicting desires led to severance and the establishment of a republican form of government. Concerning the inevitability of the latter—the form of government chosen—history tells a different tale.

If one part of a country, with no leading family, secedes from another which is ruled by a monarchy, the simplest solution would seem to be to establish a republican form of government.[82] But the history of the last 150 years teaches otherwise. During the nineteenth and early twentieth centuries, republican-democratic forms of government were generally considered so intrinsically inferior—the murder of Socrates and the chaotic end of the Roman Republic affected educated Europeans, as did the French Revolution and the sanguinary anarchy of Latin America—that secessions ended in monarchical instaurations. When the Belgians broke away from the Dutch in 1830, they called in a Lutheran prince of the Saxe-Coburg family (although the secession was largely motivated by denominational animosities). The new King Leopold I played an important part in European politics. (This shows, incidentally, the character of a Christian monarchy—international, interracial, "diversitarian"—unlike a republic which by its very nature is a national institution).[83] When the Norwegians terminated their "personal union" with Sweden in 1905, they called in the Danish Prince Charles who, as Haakon VII, ruled the country until 1957. Yet again: The Balkan countries, throwing off the Turkish yoke in the nineteenth century in two cases established local dynasties (the Petrović-Njegoš in Montenegro and the Karagjorgjević in Serbia), while the Greeks, Bulgars, and Rumanians sent for foreign princes. (The Rumanians began with a native, but ended up importing the Catholic Hohenzollerns.) In 1910, Serbia and Montenegro had the only *native* sovereign dynasties in Europe.[84]

In other words, the establishment of an American republic (in fact, if not in name) was not inevitable. As late as 1787 Nathan Gorham, president of the Congress under the old constitution, and Baron von Steuben "conspired" to persuade Prince Henry of Prussia, brother of Frederick II (the "Great") to come to the United States to assume the office of "hereditary stadhouder." It seems that the Dutch republic (officially transformed into a kingdom in 1815) served as a pattern. The *stadhouders* belonging to the House of Oranje-Nassau served in a hereditary capacity and held the title of "prince," a true *regimen mixtum*. Prince Henry, however, declined. He probably feared that the American adventure would be abortive.[85]

When about forty years later General San Martín met Simón Bolívar in Guayaquil, he beseeched *El Libertador* to let him find a prince to become the ruler of Spanish America, but Bolívar flatly refused. San Martín went into exile with a broken heart. The Latin American tragedy that began then has yet to end. [86]

In effect, monarchical solutions to the governance of lands that have seceded have not been rare. They were the logical alternative to what the *New York Gazette and Weekly Mercury* wrote on April 23, 1770: "God forbid that we should ever be so miserable as to sink into a Republic." [87]

The idea of a monarchy was not total anathema to the colonists. One of the Founding Fathers, Alexander Hamilton, perhaps the most gifted of them all, regretted that the United States could not become a monarchy. [88] (Hamilton was himself considered a monarchist, [89] by Van Buren for one, a reasonable assumption given Hamilton's speeches at the Federal Convention in 1787 and 1788 in New York City.) Francis Lieber very rightly pointed out that Jefferson's Declaration of Independence was not really an antimonarchical document. [90] The sentence, "A prince whose character is thus marked by every act which may define a tyrant, is unfit to be the ruler of a free people," merely condemned George III; at the same time, it voiced great respect for the royal office. The average American today would consider the term "ruler of a free people" a paradox. But such formulations are good examples of Jefferson's contradictory character. He stands near the mainstream of American leftist thought (well deserving Hamilton's strictures). [91] But then again, he also was the man who, in a letter to Mann Page, spoke about the "swinish multitudes." [92] And another Founding Father, the far right Gouverneur Morris, for his part wrote to Nathanael Green in 1781, "I will go farther, I have no hope that our Union can subsist except in the form of an absolute monarchy." [93]

But these rightist traits were only part of a mixed bag of beliefs and traditions in the Thirteen Colonies; antimonarchical and even leftist sentiments also existed. Generally speaking, their religious and political traditions stemmed from the British trait of independence. The civil war in Britain and the Jacobite-Hanoverian antagonism also left their imprint on North America, as did the political crystallization of British parliamentary life with its two factions: the Tories and the Whigs. The term Whig had originally a Scottish and Presbyterian connotation with republican undertones and an implicit toleration of the Dissenters; they were related to the Roundheads. Tory was an Irish word and initially denoted loyalty to the Stuarts and "popish" tendencies; they were related to the Cavaliers. Both terms were originally nicknames and underwent a certain evolution.

By the middle of the eighteenth century, it was evident that the Tories were the party of royal privileges, of the small nobility with aulic leanings, of the clergy of the Established Church, while the Whigs stood for the big, independent-minded, rich, landed nobility. Thus the Whigs, and not the Tories, represented the true aristocratic spirit. The French Revolution has somewhat obscured this reality by creating a curious alliance between Crown and nobility, opponents throughout most of European history. A genuine aristocracy never advocates an absolute or excessively strong monarchy unless the monarch, as the "first among equals," is merely the executor of the will of the nobility. *"Und der König absolut, wenn er unsren Willen tut!"* ("The king may be absolute so long as he does our will!").

Aristocrats can often be quite republican in spirit. In a monarchy the nobility must take second place to the king. Moreover, monarchs, by their power to make a noble, are able to foster social mobility and thus impinge on aristocratic exclusiveness. Republics, on the other hand, have often been exclusively aristocratic in character. This was especially true in ancient Venice and Genoa, as well as in a number of Swiss city-cantons. The aristocratic republics (sometimes dominated by a patriciate without titles but even more exclusive than many a titled aristocracy) were often highly static and conservative states. Old Geneva was a far more hidebound city than, say, Munich, Berlin, or even St. Petersburg.

Towards the end of the eighteenth century, Britain was split between the New Whigs and the Old Whigs, an evolution that did not take place in North America. In the Western Hemisphere, it was the Whigs who were critical of the Crown and, therefore, of ties with Britain. The Tories were the Loyalists, as in seventeenth- and early eighteenth-century Ireland. The Whigs were frequently inspired by republican notions; they felt they were "just as good as the king." It was they who were responsible for the War of Independence against Britain, against the Tories—against the Tories abroad and at home.

We owe thanks to the pen of Kenneth Roberts, a first-rate amateur historian as well as a good novelist, for his *Oliver Wiswell*, which presents a "live" picture of one aspect of the War of Independence—the civil war between Whigs and Tories. Naturally, the struggle had its analogies and repercussions in England where Whigs, quite unpatriotically, could not suppress their elation at the victory of their "coreligionists" in America.

Since the Whig, then, was the true aristocrat,[94] the American War of Independence found a friendly, if not enthusiastic, echo among Europe's noblemen. They flocked to North America as volunteers, primarily the French who had not forgotten the years of the *Fronde* and were imbued with liberal ideas. Indeed, Jackson Square, which faces the White House in the capital of the United States, has at its center the equestrian statue of Andrew ("Old Hickory") Jackson, the first U.S. president to call himself a Democrat. But at the corners of the square, four statues honor European noblemen who fought, not for American democracy, but for American freedom—Tadeusz Kościuszko, von Steuben, the Comte de Rochambeau, and the Marquis de Lafayette. (The Polish nobleman Kazimierz Pulaski, has a monument in Savannah, Georgia, and Jean de Kalb or "Baron de Kalb," whose nobility is rather spurious, has been honored in various parts of America. But the most valiant and characteristic of them all, Charles-Armand Tuffin, Marquis de la Roüerie, has not been commemorated in any way.)[95]

Thus the foundations of the American republic are aristocratic and Whiggish with an antimonarchic slant. The antimonarchical tradition in the United States has long roots, which have probably deepened over the years. It has certainly affected U.S. foreign policy in a most fatal way—fatal to those on the receiving end, fatal to American self-interest. Antimonarchism, which will be taken up later on, has cost untold billions of dollars and, far worse, thousands upon thousands of American lives, victims of a piece of American folklore propagated by leftist prejudices.

Whiggery was nevertheless not the only source of republican sentiment in the Thirteen Colonies prior to 1776. The disposition was nourished by religions such as the Congregationalist and Presbyterian, and perhaps also by the Dutch Reformed, Quaker, and Unitarian—although not by the Church of England. The whole tradition of the Independents (connected with the Cromwellian Commonwealth) was not only violently anti-Catholic (and moderately anti-Anglican) but antihierarchical and therefore also antimonarchical.

John C. Miller, in his *Origins of the American Revolution*, speaks of the effect of this anti-Catholic-antimonarchical animosity which was particularly strong in New England in the years preceding the War of Independence.[96] Even more interesting material can be culled from Ray Allen Billington's *The Protestant Crusade 1800–1860*. Billington quotes Daniel Barber's *History of My Own Time* on the anti-Catholic sentiment: "This feeling remained so strong through the early part of the Revolution that the President of Princeton University [John Witherspoon] believed the common hatred of Popery, caused by the Quebec Act, the only thing that cemented the divergent religious groups in the colonies together sufficiently to allow them to make war, an opinion which was shared by British observers."[97] The Quebec Act, granting religious freedom to the French

Canadians, by a curious twist of reasoning was considered a major menace to freedom. It inspired a ditty sung during the Revolution:

> If Gallic Papists have the right
> To worship their own way,
> Then farewell to the liberties
> Of poor Americay.

The suspicion arose that George III (who had so stoutly resisted the emancipation of Catholics) had secretly become a Catholic: kings, after all, must admire popes, and popes will support kings. John Trumbull in his satirical poem *McFingal* accused the King in these terms:

> Struck bargains with the Romish churches
> Infallibility to purchase.
> Set wide for popery the door,
> Made friends with Babel's scarlet whore.

As already mentioned, these accusations, though unfounded, were not psychologically baseless since the Catholic political tradition leans to mixed governments with a monarchical head. And even today, despite that the majority of "Protestant" nations are at least symbolically ruled by monarchs, the Catholic-monarchic equation continues to survive in the United States. It is alluded to by professional anti-Catholics and resented by the sort of American Catholic who, eager to be accepted as a 200 percent American,[98] makes a play of his democratic-republican credentials.[99] These desperate efforts earn little intellectual respect. Those who engage in "political theology" almost always try to prove too much.[100]

Although antimonarchical dispositions, and, occasionally, what might even be termed egalitarian feelings, existed in the Thirteen Colonies, the character of the young American polity was actually deeply Whiggish, that is, aristocratic. One ought not to forget that the term "democratic" appears neither in the Declaration of Independence nor in the Constitution. Nor does the word "republic"; the Constitution merely insists that the member states of the Union have a "republican" form of government. The Constitution, if analyzed *in its original form*, is a serious attempt to establish a mixed government with democratic, aristocratic, and monarchical elements, a government of checks and balances. Had the three elements derived their power from different sources, the attempt might have been successful, but the Constitution provided for a republican polity rather than for a *regimen mixtum*.

Ever since its inception, the American republic has been exposed through the Constitution to democratizing influences—the dependence of the electors upon the voters, the direct election of senators, even the two-term amendment, the impending direct election of the President, and so on. The older republican (and more strongly democratic) constitutions of other countries do not provide for a president—nor for a head of state, nor a head of government. In Switzerland, the equivalent of a president is merely the chairman of the council of cabinet ministers, elected by both Houses of Parliament; and he is elected for one year only. His portrait is not found in public buildings but rather that of the commanding colonel. (Only in times of mobilization does Switzerland have a general.)[101] Switzerland is a military democracy.

The Founding Fathers, educated men of the period, rejected democracy outright and even more intensely when totalitarian repression came to dominate the French Revolution. (Modern Americans forget too easily that the forces of the French Revolution, and later of the Napoleonic regime, murdered or exiled the three godfathers of the American republic—the kings of France and Spain and the *Stadhouder* of the Netherlands.)[102] George Washington, the master of Mount Vernon, was anything but a democrat.[103] And John Adams, the second President of the United States, had nothing but contempt for this form of government. Only remotely related to Samuel Adams of Boston, who had been a bit of a rabble-rouser if not an early leftist, John Adams was a real patrician with a strong aristo-cratic outlook. "Noble blood," he wrote in his *Discourses on Davila* which created an enormous outcry in the budding American Left, "whether the nobility be hereditary or elective, and indeed, *more in republican governments than in monarchies, least of all in despotisms*, is held in estimation for the same reason"[104] (italics mine). In fact, he considered democratic leanings with egalitarian undertones a sign of immaturity. Jefferson tells about a conver-sation between Dr. Ewen and John Adams during which the doctor in-formed the President that he had a younger son who was a "democrat" and an older one who was an "aristocrat." "Well," said the President, "a boy of fifteen who is not a democrat is good for nothing, and he is no better who is a democrat at twenty."[105]

Yet when John Adams came to judge democracy as such, his criticism was far more stringent. In a letter to John Taylor, Adams insisted that democracy would inevitably evolve into oligarchy and oligarchy into despo-tism,[106] a notion he shared with Plato and Aristotle. He flatly equated democracy with ignorance and maintained that "the moment you give knowledge to a democrat, you make him an aristocrat."[107] In *A Defence of the Constitution of the Government of the United States* he wrote, "Democracy, simple democracy, never had a patron among men of letters. The people have almost always expected to be served gratis, and to be paid for the honor of serving them, and their applause and adoration are bestowed too often on artifice and tricks, on hypocrisy and superstition, on flattery, bribes and largesses."

In the same work he wrote that "we may appeal to every page of history. . . for proofs irrefragable that the people, when they have been unchecked, have been as unjust, tyrannical, brutal, barbarous and cruel as any king or senate possessed by an uncontrollable power. The majority has eternally and without any one exception usurped over the rights of the minority." And he added in another passage, "All projects of government formed upon a supposition of continual vigilance, sagacity, virtue, and firmness of the people, when possessed of the exercise of supreme power, are cheats and delusions." This tallies with his remark, "The proposition that the people are the best keepers of their own liberties is not true. They are the worst conceivable, they are no keepers at all: they can neither judge, act, think, or will, as a political body. Individuals have conquered themselves: nations and large bodies never." Adams fired his heaviest artillery at democracy in the same work when he advanced twelve points, of which we quote only a few:

1. No democracy ever did or ever can exist. . . .
4. That no love of equality, at least since Adam's fall, ever existed.
5. That no love of frugality ever existed as a passion, but always as a virtue.
6. That therefore the democracy of Montesquieu . . . [is] all mere fragments of the brain, a delusive imagination.
7. That his passion of love for democracy would be in the members of the majority only a love of the majority. . . .
11. That in reality, the word democracy signifies nothing more nor less than a nation or people without any government at all. . . .[108]

And in a letter to Jefferson, Adams stated that "Democracy will envy all, contend with all, endeavor to pull down all, and when by chance it happens to get the upper hand for a short time, it will be revengeful, bloody and cruel."[109] John Adams saw clearly that private property was basically endangered by democracy which would almost always be in the hands of the lower and far more numerous part of the pyramid. In his letter to John

Taylor he said, "If you give more than a share in the sovereignty to the democrats, that is, if you give them the command or the preponderance in the sovereignty, that is, the legislature, they will vote all property out of the hands of you aristocrats, and if they let you escape with your lives, it will be more humanity, consideration and generosity than any trimphant democracy ever displayed since the creation."[110]

Madison, fourth President of the United States, had the same fears concerning democracy. This is evident in his letter to Jared Sparks where he says that laws must be "capable of protecting the rights of property against the spirit of democracy."[111] Madison, of course, distinguished between pure democracy and the spirit of democracy. To him, pure democracy was direct democracy, as can be gleaned from his definitions in the *Federalist*, No. 10 and No. 14. Yet E. M. Burns is right when he says that "instead of defending the absolute sovereignty of the majority, Madison detested it so strongly that he sought in almost every conceivable way to prevent its exercise."[112] Nor, of course, was Madison an egalitarian (not surprising given Montpelier, his palatial manor in Virginia). In a letter to Edmund Randolph he admitted that "there are subjects to which the capacity of the bulk of mankind are unequal and on which they must and will be governed by those with whom they happen to have acquaintance and confidence."[113] This is a far cry from the views of Andrew Jackson who said in his first annual message that "the duties of all public offices are . . . so plain and simple that men of intelligence may readily qualify themselves for their performance."[114]

Until the end of the nineteenth century an American Republican (capital "R") would never have termed his country a "democracy" but rather a "representative republic."[115] Madison, however, seems to have been more influenced by Jefferson than by Hamilton in his political views. But given the way Madison referred to Hamilton's monarchical views, and his reservations concerning the republic during the Philadelphia Convention, Madison seems to have been sympathetic to monarchism.[116]

Americans frequently compare "Jeffersonian democracy" with "Jacksonian democracy." But the question surely remains: was Jefferson, the third President of the United States, a convinced democrat? Dr. Mortimer Adler is more right than wrong when he says that "the dawn of American democracy really begins with Jackson."[117] And a careful perusal of the Washington and Ford editions of Jefferson's *Works* elicits only one positive allusion to the terms "democrat" and "democracy."[118] Even more: in a letter written to Lafayette, Jefferson insisted that the 1791 constitution would work out in France, provided it was kept within the framework of a constitutional monarchy.[119] Still, Jefferson had an exaggerated notion of the qualities of the American people (only somewhat modified in his declining years) when he wrote that "if all the sovereigns of Europe were to set themselves to work to emancipate the minds of their subjects from their present ignorance and prejudice . . . a thousand years would not place them on that high ground on which our people are now setting out."[120]

But in order to understand Jefferson more fully—by no means an easy task—it must be remembered that he was an agrarian romantic who believed in the high virtues and qualities of a free yeomanry. His was not the language of one of his relatives, John Randolph of Roanoke, who told the Virginia Constitutional Convention, "I am an aristocrat: I love liberty, I hate equality."[121]

"Those who labor in the earth," Jefferson wrote, "are the chosen people of God if ever he had a chosen people."[122] To Madison he wrote, "I think that our government will remain virtuous for many centuries, as long as they are chiefly agricultural, and this will be as long as there are vacant lands in any part of America. When they get piled upon one another as in the large cities of Europe, they will become corrupt as in Europe."[123] Since Jefferson figures in the folklore of the American Left—the Communists in New York City ran a Jefferson School in the 1930s and 1940s—it is interesting to read what the slave-owning master of Monticello thought about the urban working class. "The mobs of the great cities add just so much to the support of pure government, as sores do to the strength of the human body," he wrote to John Jay in 1785.[124] And then he confessed, "I consider the class of artificers as the panders of vice, and the instruments by which the liberties of the country are generally perverted."[125] In a letter to John Adams, speaking about the United States and using the same "reactionary" language, he insisted that "everyone by his property, or by his satisfactory situation is interested in the support of law and order. And such men may safely and advantageously reserve to themselves wholesome control over their public affairs, and a degree of freedom, which in the hands of the *canaille* of the cities of Europe, would be instantly perverted to the demolition and destruction of everything public."[126]

What then did he hope for? Who really should govern? In the same letter Jefferson proves himself a true timocrat: "The natural aristocracy I consider as the most precious gift of nature, for the instruction, the trusts and governments of society. And indeed, it would have been inconsistent in creation to have formed men for the social state, and not to have provided virtue and wisdom enough to manage the concerns of society. May we not even say that that form of government is the best, which provides most effectually for a pure selection of these natural *aristoi* into the offices of government?"[127]

All too many benighted minds regard the preamble of Jefferson's Declaration of Independence, with the phrase that all men are created equal, as a revolutionary, egalitarian program. But the statement, part of a broad statement of independence, was intended to make clear that Americans were equal, not inferior, to Britishers. Read out of context, the relevant sentence, in a document composed and signed by a good number of slaveholders, would amount to a gigantic piece of hypocrisy. There was practically no lessening in the commonly accepted inequalities after July 4, 1776, but rather an increase for the hapless Loyalists. [128]

Thus, quite clearly, the Founding Fathers of the United States were not professed democrats, and the United States was not established as a "democracy." Albert Jay Nock wrote, "One sometimes wonders how our Revolutionary forefathers would take it if they could hear some flatulent political thimblerigger charge them with having founded 'the great and glorious democracy of the West.' "[129] Senator Arthur H. Vandenberg once remarked that "the government of the United States is a representative republic and not a pure democracy. The difference is as profound today as it was when the foundations of the Constitution were set in the ages. . . . We are a representative republic. We are not a pure democracy. . . . Yet we are constantly trying to graft the latter on the former, and every effort we make in this direction, with but few exceptions, is a blow aimed at the heart of the Constitution."[130]

So much for the character and mind of nascent America.

CHAPTER 7

The French Revolution

*The French Revolution was an
insurrection of mules and horses against
men, conducted by apes with
the throats of parrots.*

—HIPPOLYTE-ADOLPHE TAINE

It is time to search out the roots of a heinous iniquity, the French Revolution, historically the mother of most of the ideological evils besetting civilization, not only of the West but of the entire world.

Among the myriad factors responsible for the French Revolution are the misinterpretations and distortions of events surrounding America's War of Independence. In the first phase of the great misunderstanding, the French rather than the Americans (and English) were the more culpable. They propagated false ideas in France by misinterpreting what they saw and experienced in America. England, although physically not part of Europe, comes into this equation because ideologically its impact on the Continent was very similar to that of the United States.

As for the Americans, in the early days, their reactions to Europe were varied and in the main had political implications. Philip Rahv's *Discovery of Europe*[131] speaks of the enthusiasm of Americans for the Continent, giving the lie to Adet, a French agent of the *Directoire* living in the United States, who maintained that all Americans were "born enemies of all the people of

Europe."[132] Rahv does in fact depict John Adams as too unbending and Jefferson as too provincial.[133]

Concerning Jefferson's role in French events, Hamilton was convinced that as American minister in Paris before the French Revolution, Jefferson had played a rather negative part. Hamilton wrote that "in France he [Jefferson] saw government only on the side of its abuses. He drank freely of the French philosophy, in religion, in science, in politics. He came from France in the moment of fermentation, which he had a share in exciting, and in the passions and feelings of which he shared both from temperament and situation."[134]

A successor of Jefferson, Gouverneur Morris, was of a different breed. He spent several years in Paris and Western Europe before being appointed United States Minister to France. In his diary he relates, "At dinner I sit next to M. de Lafayette who tells me I injure the cause, for that my sentiments are continually quoted against the good party. I seize this opportunity to tell him that I am opposed to the democracy from regard to liberty."[135] Yet Morris was a voice crying in the wilderness. As an American aristocrat he moved in the highest French circles and was sickened by the leftist sentiments he encountered everywhere, not only among the nobility but among the clergy. His eulogies of aristocracy did not please the republican countesses and princesses.[136] The Bishop of Arras, who thought to make Morris happy by praising the American Constitution which he had helped draft, found that he pleased him not at all. Morris, in fact, was forever haunted by the specter of dictatorship in America.[137]

But of all the nobility, Lafayette probably irritated Morris the most. Talking to him, Morris "pointed out for the hundredth time that each country needed to have its own form of government, that an American Constitution could not do for France and that, above all, France needed stability. He gave the reasons for his advice clearly and forcibly, but poor Lafayette flinched from it, and could not be persuaded to make any effectual step."[138] This was the same Gouverneur Morris who at a banquet he gave in New England in 1815 exclaimed, "The long agony is over. The Bourbons are restored. France reposes in the arms of the legitimate prince. We may now express our attachments to her consistently with the respect we owe to ourselves. . . . Thank God, we can, at length, avow the sentiments of gratitude to that august family under whose sway the fleets and armies of France and Spain were arrayed in defence of American liberty. . . . The Bourbons are restored. Rejoice France! Spain! You are governed by your legitimate kings! Europe! Rejoice!"[139] Imagine the outcry among the early Americans when the full text of this address was aired!

That a "technical" affiliation exists between 1776 and 1789 can hardly be denied. And this "factual" connection is precisely what effectively produced various misunderstandings. To begin with, 1789 did not *necessarily* lead to 1792 and to totalitarianism throughout Europe and, later, the globe. Georges Bernanos has emphasized the difference between the initial stage of the French Revolution, which had the all but unanimous support of the French nobility[140] (and a large sector of the clergy), and the terror regime of the lower middle class which was followed by a proletarian-agrarian movement under Gracchus Babeuf. Yet a godless, human "Titanism" did exist from the very beginning, and it snowballed during the five years of the Revolution.

In other words, the aristocratic character of the American Revolution and of the *initial* stage of the French Revolution was very similar. But in the latter, the activity of bloodthirsty mobs grew dynamically stronger until the fall of the Robespierre regime.[141] The nobility, as de Tocqueville pointed out, nursing old grievances against royal absolutism, forced the issue by insisting that the King convoke the Estates General; the *noblesse de la robe* spearheaded the movement. The historian A. Mathiez has coined the phrase *révolte nobiliaire*,[142] a development that shows the dangers of tampering radically with a political structure in a period of transition, an era when reforms have already been initiated.

Other factors were at work besides the Whiggish tendency of the aristocracy to oppose the monarch.[143] One was the ancient hatred of the Jansenists for the Crown, which was expressed in various ways.[144] Bishop Henri Grégoire, a member of that faction, headed the Constitutionalist priests, who were in schism with Rome. The bishop played an eminent part during the revolution; he voted against the monarchy ("kings are in the political order what monsters are in the natural order") and was one of the first in the National Convention to demand a trial of the King.

Other religious opposition to the King came from the Huguenots, who were equally unrelenting. Edmund Burke who, as an Anglican, belonged to a faith in some ways as remote from Rome as theirs, had to acknowledge "that they have behaved shockingly since the very beginning of the rebellion, and have been uniformly concerned in its worst and most atrocious acts. Their clergy are just the same atheists as those Constitutional Catholics, but still more wicked and daring. Three of their number have met from their republican associates the rewards of their crimes."[145] The attitude of the rebels can be understood given the past intolerance of French kings to various Reformed religions, such as Calvinism. Yet in 1787 Brienne, bishop of Toulouse, proposed that the Calvinists be emancipated and a year later it was done. Nevertheless, André Siegfried, himself a Calvinist, confessed that a French Calvinist even then had "naturally, almost necessarily to be a partisan of the French Revolution, which means, in other words, that he is congenitally an enemy of the *ancien régime* and of anything that might be styled 'reactionary.' "[146]

The president of the Constitutional Assembly, Jean Paul Rabaut Saint-Etienne, was the son of a distinguished Reformed minister; belonging to the more moderate Girondins, he met with a tragic fate. But, such individual cases notwithstanding, in the popular mind the Huguenots became so identified with support of the French Revolution (and not without cause) that after the restoration anti-Huguenot riots took place, notably the so-called *massacres de Nîmes* (a reaction against the *bagarres de Nîmes*).[147]

Among the foreign influences (mostly misinterpreted) were the popular images of Switzerland and England. Voltaire was truly bewitched by England, and it was he who spearheaded Anglomania in France.[148] Metternich, who was haunted by the thought that copying England had been the undoing of France, if not of the entire Continent, was equally certain that England in its turn would come to be ruined by imitating French patterns, by submitting to the *école française*.[149] In a secret memorandum to Alexander I, written around December 1820, Metternich said, "It is difficult to overlook the influence which England for a long time has exercised on France. England, however, is in such a unique situation that we can maintain without exaggeration that none of the forms congenial to that State, none of its habits or institutions can be adopted by any of the states of the Continent, and when these are actually taken for models, the result is nothing but troubles and dangers without any accompanying advantages."[150] Alfred Müller-Armack also discerned this decisive English influence on the ideology of the French Revolution.[151] And Charles Seignobos insisted that a sketchy forerunner of the *Déclaration des Droits de l'Homme et du Citoyen* was shown to the rebelling citizens of Bordeaux by Colonel Sexby, an Englishman. This outline was the preamble of a constitutional draft proposed in 1648 by the British army to Parliament.[152]

The English and Swiss influences, needless to say, were effective, thanks to their emphasis on personal liberty and to the economic well-being of their respective upper classes. (The general prosperity of Switzerland stems from a much later period. Emigration and foreign military service characterized the Swiss experience until the early part of the nineteenth century.[153] The patricians, however, always lived in great comfort.)

Because the United States was at such a great distance, its example was less concrete than that of the English and Swiss and was ringed by a highly romantic halo. It was transmitted first to the French volunteers who arrived prior to the break between Paris and London, then to the regular army men who fought side by side with the Americans. There was also a Rousseauistic aura surrounding the new country—virgin forests, noble savages, freemen, simple lives, log cabins, and town halls in Grecian style. And the Americans in Paris—Thomas Jefferson, Benjamin Franklin, Silas Deane—excited the French imagination beyond belief. But although these Americans naively played a part in fathering the French Revolution, they were not nearly so instrumental as the French volunteers and regular officers who fought in the New World and returned imbued with half-digested notions ill understood.

Evidence of the misunderstanding of the returning French soldiery is well documented in a number of works. Of these, some stand out, such as the writings of Lafayette,[154] Count Louis Philippe de Ségur,[155] Madame de Staël,[156] Madame Campan,[157] Lamartine,[158] Chateaubriand,[159] and many others. Later Alexis de Tocqueville,[160] Lord Acton,[161] Taine,[162] Philippe Sagnac,[163] Georg Jellinek,[164] and Felix Somary,[165] while discussing the American roots of the French Revolution, insisted that the ideas prevailing in America at the time of the War of Independence had been grossly misinterpreted by the French. Transplanted to French soil, they assumed a new meaning and degenerated rapidly.

Concerning the influence of Americans in Paris, Hamilton was certain that Jefferson had not been innocent in the events that transpired in France after 1789. John Adams, for his part, was tortured by the thought that the United States, and he himself, were to blame in large share for the horrors that followed the storming of the Bastille. The former President of the United States wrote to Dr. Benjamin Rush in a letter dated August 28, 1811: "Have I not been employed in mischief all my days? Did not the American Revolution produce all the calamities and desolation to the human race and the whole globe ever since? I meant well, however. My conscience was clear as a crystal glass, without scruple or doubt. I was borne by an irresistible sense of duty. God prospered our labors, and, awful, dreadful, and deplorable as the consequences have been, I cannot but hope that the ultimate good of the world, of the human race, and of our beloved country, is intended and will be accomplished by it."[166]

But the ultimate good had not as yet been achieved, and Adams himself knew that the dictator who sprang to power after the French Revolution was its offspring. "Napoleon and all his generals were but creatures of democracy," he wrote to John Taylor of Caroline, Virginia. [167]

Yet other men were infinitely more responsible than John Adams in pushing the ideas of the French Revolution, men like the Anglo-American Thomas Paine who much later became the hero of the National Socialist playwright Hanns Johst. [168] Other Nazis, for instance a certain Dr. Friedrich Schönemann, praised Jefferson and damned Hamilton, seeing in the former a precursor of the view of historic evolution leading to the victory of the Common Man—and of German national socialism. [169] Earlier European authors dealing with the United States have extolled George Washington and Alexander Hamilton but critized Jefferson and, later, the young American Democratic party for fostering the "party of the revolution" [170] in Europe. Then—as now, to be sure—only a few Europeans recognized the United States for what it really was and, in a certain temperamental way, still is: an aristocratic state. [171]

Charles-Armand Tuffin, Marquis de la Roüerie, a Frenchman who participated in the War of Independence, clearly perceived the difference between that noble struggle and the French Revolution. Of far more distinction than the vain and morbidly ambitious Lafayette, [172] the little-known marquis should be an inspiration to young Americans and Frenchmen as well as to lovers of liberty and defenders of human values everywhere. He came to America before Lafayette, left after Lafayette, and fought bravely *for* freedom and *against* democracy. No monument, no street, no stamp, no memorial whatsoever can be found to commemorate him in the United States.

Among the other noblemen (Lafayette and Maximilien de Robespierre were two of them) [173] who contributed to the French Revolution, is a man known as the "grandfather of modern democracy," the Comte de Sade, sometimes called "the Divine Marquis." He is better known for his sexual aberrations—"sadism" is named after him. But his real importance lies in the domain of politics, in his one historic intervention and, later, in the dissemination of his political ideas.

Research on de Sade began, slowly, during this century. The first serious efforts were made by Dr. Eugen Dühren (a pseudonym for Iwan Bloch) who, however, was interested only in de Sade's sexual pathology. After World War I, Maurice Heine, originally a Socialist, became interested in de Sade. In the schism that split the French Socialist party, Heine joined the radical group and became editor of *L'Humanité,* the Communist daily. In common with many people in Latin countries, he confused communism with anarchical libertinism. Fired from the paper on Moscow's orders and later ousted from the party, he concentrated on de Sade[174] and came to admire him as a totally free, unfettered, and diabolical spirit.

The events of World War II increased public interest in de Sade. He emerged from a number of essays as "a fellow like you and me," as can be seen in M. Pierre Klossowski's book called, significantly, *Sade, notre prochain.* (A private edition of de Sade's collected works has been published, and a serious, if perhaps not definitive, biography by Gilbert Lely.)[175] By and large, the crimes of the Divine Marquis have been exaggerated. His deeds were neither so numerous nor so ferocious as reputed, since he spent most of his time in jails and hospitals for the criminally insane. But he was not *mentally* ill. As a fanatical and confirmed atheist, he more or less acted in accordance with his views. He was undoubtedly in need of the aid of skilled theologians and philosophers and, perhaps, psychiatrists, although he was neither schizophrenic nor paranoic, being fully responsible for his actions.

What has *not* been done so far is a systematic investigation of de Sade's political and philosophical thought, some of which can be found in a few pamphlets and minor essays. The larger part, unfortunately, is dispersed among his pornographic works. One would have to wade through an ocean of smut (shocking at first, merely tiring in the long run) in order to get a coherent whole. For the brave man who dares undertake the Herculean task, a system of thought lies waiting to be examined. There was method and logic to the man. His books were widely read but rarely quoted, being far from respectable even then, the end of the eighteenth century. This hampered efforts to prove *unequivocally* how influential they were at the time of their publication—and after. But their effect is evident in the oblique reflections in the sayings, writing, and actions of others.

De Sade's ideology-philosophy was probably the outcome of his inclinations and aberrations—and not the other way around. Perhaps we all have sadistic drives, but in normal people they are kept within limits. But de Sade not only broke all restraints, he came to justify his yielding to his base urges until he finally became their slave. They dominated his imagination, his daydreams, his writings, his whole intellect.

Donatien Aldonse François Comte de Sade was born on June 2, 1740, in Paris, a scion of an ancient Provençal family. He served in the army and in 1763 married Mademoiselle de Montreuil whose wealthy family belonged to the *noblesse de la robe.* A few months after the wedding, he tortured a prostitute sadistically and was jailed for fifteen days as a consequence. A similar though graver case occurred in 1768 when he cruelly flogged a girl and was again committed to prison. Released, he engaged in an orgy in a brothel in Marseille which resulted in a more severe sentence in 1772. Imprisoned in Miolans, he succeeded in escaping but was again arrested in Paris in 1777 and brought back to the south of France where, thanks to another escape, he enjoyed thirty-nine days of liberty. Arrested yet again, he spent five-and-a-half years at the Vincennes fortress followed by another five-and-a-half years in the Bastille, a jail reserved for the nobility. This last long stretch in prison was not due to a jail sentence but to a *lettre de cachet* from the King, issued upon the request of de Sade's mother-in-law, the présidente de Montreuil.

De Sade was transferred to the Bastille from Vincennes fortress, whose prison area had been demolished. But during the reform year of 1788, the government wanted to raze this state prison as well and sell the ground for real estate development. History only precipitated events.

During his imprisonment de Sade wrote assiduously, expressing his libertine, atheistic, and leftist views. Aware of the unrest in Paris, he began to harangue the people from his window, using a funnel to magnify his voice, charging that the prisoners were tortured and assassinated in the dark dungeons of the Bastille. M. de Launay, governor of the prison, wrote a letter dated July 2, 1789, to M. de Villedeuil, minister of state, insisting that under the circumstances his prisoner should be transferred to the hospital for the criminally insane in Charenton.[176] After repeating his performance on July 3, the prisoner was transferred the following day. The documentation concerning de Sade's noisy appeals is fairly complete,[177] and when he was later arrested at the height of the Terror, he boasted of his contribution to the fall of the Bastille. He spoke of the "ardor with which I called the people on the third of July to destroy the Bastille where the despots had me imprisoned: thus I possess the most glittering civic record of which a republican can pride himself."[178]

Was de Sade really the main culprit in this sordid affair? Quite possibly, because the government's plan to destroy the Bastille was well known, and besides, political prisoners were rarely, if ever, locked up behind its walls.

The governor of the Bastille, M. de Launay, an enlightened liberal, had a tiny garrison of Swiss guards and some invalid veterans at his disposal when the mob finally gathered around the building on July 14. He offered only token resistance. The delegates of the Town Hall and two appointees of the mob were received and invited to join the governor at his meal. In the meantime, the drawbridge of the outer court was let down and guns were directed at the inner court. The soldiers, sensing that they had a weak commander, surrendered.

After atrocious torture, the governor, imploring the monsters to finish him off, was finally given the *coup de grace*. A young cook "who knew how to handle meat" cut off his head with a small kitchen knife, and it was carried around in triumph into the late evening hours. Three officers were also murdered fiendishly, two of the invalids who had once fought heroically for France were hanged by the howling mob, and, their blood lust unassuaged, the hands of a Swiss guard were chopped off.

The surprise came when the "victors" found only seven prisoners. Four were forgers who quickly decamped, two were insane (they were there for observation), and one was a dissolute young man of noble descent who considered himself the real hero of the day for having harangued the people with revolutionary phrases. All in all, a nauseating and disgraceful performance, one inspired by and reflecting in every way the Divine Marquis. The anniversary of this ghoulish leftist orgy was chosen as the ideal date for a national holiday, first celebrated by the Third Republic in 1880. The two-hundredth anniversary celebration of the glorious event, in 1989, carefully avoided all grisly details of "the happening," emphasizing the Declaration of Human Rights, and did not even mention the storming of the Bastille.

Donatien de Sade only remained in Charenton until April 2, 1790, when he was released, thanks to a decree of the National Assembly which declared all *lettres de cachet* of the King null and void. It was Good Friday. His wife sued for and obtained a separation from the monstrous man. De Sade felt "betrayed." Yet he soon engaged in local politics and became a leader of the Place Vendome *Section des Piques*, an auxiliary police unit in Paris. After the September massacres in 1792, he was appointed its secretary. He was evidently torn between a certain snobbery—after all, the de Sades belonged to the highest nobility—and his materialistic-atheistic convictions which drew him to the Left. His noble origin, however, proved to be no obstacle, in his case or in that of others, to a "career" in republican circles. Yet at the height of the Terror, although his section had been directed by Robespierre, de Sade was in danger of being guillotined. The 9th Thermidor, the day of Robespierre's fall, saved his life.

However interesting his life, de Sade's writings are of even greater interest. In 1791 he published his first great pornographic novel *Justine, ou les malheurs de la vertu*. In it, philosophical remarks and debates are wedged in between scenes of sexual debauchery. His *Addresse d'un citoyen de Paris au roi des Français*, issued that same year, is purely political but it does not as yet show the extreme leftist materialistic views of his later writings, such as *Aline et Valcour, ou le Roman Philosophique*, a "novel" in four volumes that was reprinted three times between 1793 and 1795. Totaling more than 1,700 pages, it had an enormous impact on the French Revolution which was, in so many ways, a sanguinary sex orgy. Hence its great popular appeal.

Even worse, from a moral-aesthetic and ideological point of view, were *La philosophie dans le boudoir* (1795) and *La Nouvelle Justine, suivi de l'histoire de Juliette ou les prospérités du vice* (1797). De Sade, especially during his jail terms and his sojourn in Charenton, must have had a prodigious capacity for work and a truly limitless imagination, because the above list by no means exhausts his *opera omnia*. Some of his manuscripts were destroyed by his son or by the police, others were published posthumously—such as the important *Dialogue entre un prêtre et un moribond* which contains the quintessence of de Sade's materialistic outlook—while the more scandalous *Les 120 Jours de Sodome ou l'École du libertinage* is pure pornography.

Lely's biography of de Sade[179] lists, in all, thirty-one published and twenty-three unpublished books and pamphlets, and thirty-five lost manuscripts. Among these were seven smaller (published) political pamphlets (between four and eight pages), seven of which were issued by the *Section des Piques* (Vendome) during the time "Citizen Sade" was politically active. Among the unpublished manuscripts are a large number of plays. One of these, *Le Comte Oxtiern ou les Effets du Libertinage*, was performed in the Théâtre Molière (October 1791).

De Sade's outlook—materialistic-atheistic-totalitarian—has a curiously contradictory anarchical bent. He believed that human beings were not superior to animals. The whole animal and plant kingdom (he drew the line at minerals) contained no hierarchic superiorities or inferiorities.[180] All were "equal." His determinism was complete. "Pedantic louts, hangmen, scribblers, legislators, tonsured scum, what are you going to do once we prevail? What will happen to your laws, your morality, your religion, your powers, your paradise, your gods, your hell, when it is proved that such and such a flow of humor, a certain type of fibre, a specific degree of acidity in the blood or in the animal spirit will make a man the object of your punishment or your reward?"[181] The idea, he believed, that murder, destruction, and annihilation could be "bad" contradicted the workings of nature: there could be no creation without preliminary destruction[182]—an idea also expressed in Oliver Wendell Holmes's writings.

The nihilism of de Sade went so far that he contemplated with a certain satisfaction the possibility that mankind could annihilate itself. "This total self-destruction would merely return to nature the opportunity of creation which we have taken from her by propagating ourselves."[183]

Needless to say, children should belong to the state, a constant demand of leftists who have an innate hatred for the family as an "individualistic" cell that tries to separate itself from the state and society.[184] De Sade's hatred of the family also took more extreme forms. He insisted that any society based on fraternity should make incest mandatory between brothers and sisters. (Interestingly enough, this theme recurs in the writings of Thomas Mann, a leftist of great literary talent.)[185] Promiscuity in whatever form would naturally end the concept of fatherhood, which rests on a man's ability to identify children as his own through faith and conviction. But motherhood would survive; and there would be a fatherland, a *patria*, and this would be sufficient.[186] Just as creation-propagation loses its value, so too does murder lose its horror.[187]

The French Revolution truly lived up to de Sade's visions. In a sense, the Divine Marquis is the patron saint of all leftist movements. But bear in mind that only leftists produce "movements"; rightists, at best, only "organize" in a relatively hierarchic fashion. Spengler has said correctly that the concept of the "party" is itself leftist.[188] Thus if movements and parties are not conducive to a genuinely rightist outlook, it follows that the principles of the Right within the parliamentary-democratic framework could only prevail in the wake of a catastrophic default or collapse of leftism. Generally speaking, the Right cannot win by virtue of its goodness, its truth, or its values, because it cannot enthrall the masses. It may attract extraordinary and superior people but it will only occasionally win over the average man.

Neither de Sade nor the confused French veterans of the American rebellion could be blamed entirely for the French Revolution. Nor even Voltaire, who was instrumental in undermining and eroding the principles of religion and order on which the *ancien régime* rested. His part was similar to that of the post-World War I German leftists—the pseudoliberal intellectuals and artists, the spiritual Kerenskis of the decaying Weimar Republic.[189]

Voltaire was certainly not an ardent republican, nor was he a democrat. His ideal was a constitutional monarchy headed by a *roi sage*, Plato's philosopher-king.[190] Voltaire believed that a republic represented a social order that would lead to tyranny.[191] "Independent of my love for freedom," he wrote, "I still would prefer to live under a lion's paw than under the teeth of a thousand rats who are my fellow citizens."[192] In a letter to d'Alembert he said flatly that the *canaille* were not made for reason. And in another letter he insisted that "we never intended to enlighten shoemakers and servants, that is up to the apostles."[193] Speaking of democracy, in the *Dictionnaire de Philosophie*, Voltaire deemed that a democracy "would only be feasible in a very small country which must also have a very fortunate geographic location. And in spite of its smallness it will commit many mistakes because it will consist of human beings, which means that discord will rule in it as in a monastery."[194] Yet he forgot his geographic reservations when he sang his oft-repeated praises of the British constitution. Once, when he embarked anew on his panegyric, the Prince de Ligne interrupted him, saying, "Add to it the protection of Britain by the ocean, without which she would not last a year."[195]

Rousseau was also convinced that the democratic republic was fit only for small states; larger ones needed a monarchical government.[196] But it was not this thought that gave Rousseau his importance as a political theorist but rather his concept of the social contract, a theory that opened an era of totalitarianism in whose midst we live today. The French Revolution was obviously deeply indebted to Rousseau. After his death in 1778, his memory was honored at every possible (or impossible) opportunity. At the Feast of Reason in Notre Dame the busts of Voltaire, Rousseau, and Franklin were objects of veneration.[197] In 1794 Rousseau's remains were solemnly buried in the Pantheon where they remained for twenty years.

A vain person, a shabby immoralist burdened with an unbalanced mind (especially during the last years of his life when he verged on insanity), Rousseau helped to father the French Revolution and subsequent developments. He also made an impact on the American scene—from a folkloric as well as from an intellectual point of view. (This can be seen in George D. Herron's enthusiasm for Rousseau and Calvin.)[198] Jacques Maritain was convinced that Rousseau influenced the rise of democracy and "democratism" in the United States, although less so than in France.[199] Walter Lippmann, on the other hand, stated unequivocally that "Jacobinism became the creed of American democracy"[200] and that Rousseau's ideas (as well as those of two other Swiss, Fröbel and Pestalozzi)[201] influenced American education. But then again, Alfred Müller-Armack insisted that it was neither Rousseau nor Montesquieu, but *seventeenth-century* England[202] that originally provided the French Revolution with its ideological foundations.

Rousseau, of course, hailed from Geneva, and his original faith was Calvinism. There are various analogies, as well as dialectic contradictions, between his thought and Calvin's. A certain emotional trait pervades the thinking of both, a fact clearly brought out by A. J. M. Cornelissen, a Dutch author.[203] Rousseau referred to his *sentiment interieur* and avowed that he "never thought out anything," that he felt everything, while Calvin spoke of the "inner gifts of the spirit, the *autópiston*, which one should never subject to demonstration or reason"[204] —all in all, a language quite distinct from that of the Scholastics.

Yet along with the analogies there were the dialectic contradictions. The antinomian reaction of Rousseau to Calvin and Calvinism was, moreover, stronger than his willingness to copy the Reformers.[205] Temperamentally, too, these two men were poles apart: Maître Jehan, the man from Noyon, was, after all, a cold spirit and a methodical thinker; Jean-Jacques, the native Genevan, was a confused emotionalist.

Still, both men[206] were absolutists, and Jellinek quite correctly saw Hobbes as a forerunner of Rousseau. "It was obviously the concept of the sovereign king in his own glory which engendered the demand for a free, sovereign people. The omnipotent king became the ancestor of the omnipotent people and Thomas Hobbes found a master in the pupil that surpassed him—in J. J. Rousseau."[207] But Jellinek also recognized the emotionalist in Rousseau, the man who has to experience everything before formulating a theory.[208] And in Rousseau there is possibly even a deist—more than in the theocentric Calvin—with pantheistic inclinations, a sort of mystic (in the general sense of the term).[209]

Both Calvin and Rousseau were nevertheless not only "absolutists" but totalitarian in their thinking, by no means the same thing. Benjamin Constant, a genuine liberal, rightly denounced Rousseau's theory of the social contract as "the most terrible aid to all types of despotism."[210] In a way, Rousseau's concept of the people is reminiscent of the totality of the Greek city-state. It is also the precursor of modern nationalism. Irving Babbitt understood that nationalism and internationalism (as opposed to genuine patriotism or a feeling of universality) are different in degree, not in essence, and rightly accused Rousseau of having given a new impetus to both collectivist drives. At the same time he admitted that Rousseau "in his final phase [was] an emotional nationalist, and that is because he saw that the patriotic virtue is a more potent intoxicant than the love of humanity."[211]

This emotional nationalism—if exploited by an able imperialistic leader who spurns all ethical discipline and lusts for knowledge, for feeling, but even more for power—gives rise to the "most sinister of all types, the efficient megalomaniac. When, finally, science becomes the tool of power-lust, it is used, in Burke's phrase, to 'improve the mystery of murder.' "[212] Indeed, these were prophetic words published in 1919 by Babbitt, one of the most brilliant American conservative minds.

In this connection, it would be wrong to think only of the obvious mass assassins—Hitler and Stalin—or the butchers of Hamburg, Dresden, Hiroshima, and Nagasaki. "The leadership of the Occident is no longer here," Babbitt wrote scathingly. "The leaders have succumbed in greater or lesser degree to naturalism (the Church, so far as it has become human-itarian, has itself succumbed to naturalism), and so have been tampering with the moral law. That the brutal imperialist who brooks no obstacle to his lust for domination has been tampering with this law goes without saying, but the humanitarian, all adrip with brotherhood and profoundly convinced of the loveliness of his own soul, has been tampering with it also, *and in a more dangerous way*, for the very reason that it is less obvious" (italics mine).[213]

To what extent Rousseau not only laid the foundations of the French Revolution but also of the modern totalitarian state can be gleaned even better from Werner Kägi's fascinating essay, "The Constitutional State and Democracy."

"Rousseau," Kägi writes, "might be a representative of the idea of local rights, but within the state he had denied all manifestations of pluralism as a menace to democracy. This monistic—unitary-centralistic—thinking has determined the very character of the French Revolution's ideology. The *république une et indivisible* became the great postulate of constitutional evolution, and 'simplification' was equated with 'progress.' Thus the uni-tary centralistic state became the prevailing form of state structure,"[214] and we are finally faced with a "democratic Leviathan."[215] No wonder, for the "massively absolutistic democratism of the twentieth century is not domi-nated by the notion of representation, but by identity, because the represen-tatives do not have a well-grounded position of constitutional power, but have merely the unstable status of 'agents' as defined by Rousseau."[216] These seminal ideas did not reach maturity until our age.[217]

Rousseau made the choice between uniformity, equality, and free-dom—although he cagily used the latter term. "Whoever refuses to pay obedience to the general will," he wrote, "shall be liable to be compelled to it by the force of the whole body. And this is in effect nothing more than that he may be compelled to be free."[218] This formulation is not surprising given that Rousseau, entirely in keeping with much of demo-cratic thought, insisted on the *a priori* consent of every citizen to all laws, including those against which he voted and to which he objected.[219] Naturally, he wrote, "the most generally expressed will, the will of the majority [*la volonté la plus générale*] is the most just because the voice of the people is the voice of God."[220] (This emphasis on majority rule was not alien to Jefferson.)[221]

Rousseau started with the individualism of eighteenth-century romanticism, antiroyalism, and the concept of the noble savage ("people born free are now in chains");[222] he then made a programmatic switch from the rule of one to the rule of all, thus paving the way for totalitarianism. In his ideology, the glorified individual reappeared as a cipher, and the foundations of socialism were thereby laid. The old individualistic man, of course, who had grown up in the *ancien régime* was hardly ideal material for this new society of obedient nonentities ready to be submerged in the mass: Man had to be created anew. "He who dares to legislate to a people," Rousseau wrote, "has to be capable, so to say, of changing human nature . . . he must transform human nature in order to strengthen it."[223]

A statement like this shows an absolute contempt for personality, for the character of individuals as well as of entire nations—a mixture of ignorance and arrogance that is typical of the entire modern Left bent upon putting mankind into a straitjacket. A Girondist like Condorcet manifested the same outlook when he wrote, "One law is good for all nations just as a theorem in geometry is good for all minds."[224]

In Rousseau, there was not only the sloppy, contradictory thinker, but also the sentimentalist with exhibitionist tendencies and, above all, there was the visionary, the prophet.[225] Jean-Jacques died eleven years before the outbreak of the French Revolution, but the great revolutionary leaders thought and acted in his spirit. His totalitarian attitude was echoed in a speech by Saint-Just on October 10, 1793. "You have to punish not only the traitors," he shouted, "but even those who are indifferent. You have to punish whosoever behaves in the Republic in a passive spirit and does nothing for her, because ever since the French people have manifested their will, everything outside of the sovereign is an enemy."[226] This is the same man who declared on February 26, 1794: "You wanted a republic. . . what constitutes a republic is the total destruction of everything that places itself in its way."[227] And Maximilien de Robespierre, with a contradictory Rousseauistic concept of "collective liberty," stated on February 7, 1794, "The government of the Revolution is the despotism of liberty against tyranny."[228] The same phraseology reappeared under the National Socialists in Germany who were ideologically nurtured by Fichte, the great defender of the French Revolution.

The French Revolution which, like the Russian Revolution of 1917, broke out in a period of reforms is still with us in every way. Not only are its ideas ever-present, but there is much in its historical evolution worth learning—by North Americans no less than by Europeans. Its initial period began with the undermining of traditional values and ideas, coupled with the demand for moderate reforms. With Voltaire, a whole series of scoffers, facile critics, and agnostics in the literal sense of the term made their appearance. They subverted religion, convictions, traditions, and the loyalties on which state and society rest.

The process of decomposition and putrefaction always starts at the top—in the royal palace, the presidential mansion, among the intellectuals, the aristocracy, the wealthy, the clergy—and then gradually enmeshes the lower social layers. In the process, *the powerful develop a sense of guilt coupled with a readiness to abdicate*, to yield to expropriation, to submit to the loss of privileges—*to commit suicide politically and economically*. The ideological propaganda emanating from their own ranks prepares them more than sufficiently for this masochistic act.

The French Revolution is a case in point. Louis XVI was not a representative of either "reaction" or "conservatism" but an avid reader of the *Encyclo-pédie* and (not so improbably) he was perhaps even a Freemason. The members of the nobility who took an active part in the intellectual or political undermining of the *ancien régime* and participated in the ensuing revolution were numerous; without their support the French Revolution would have been well-nigh unimaginable. Among the revolution's forerunners were nobles Holbach, Grimm, and Madame d'Epernay, followed by Mirabeau, Noailles, Malesherbes, Victor Claude de Broglie,[229] Clootz, Condorcet, Robespierre, Custine, Saint-Just, Clermont-Tonnerre, de Séchelles, Boissy d'Anglas, Barras, Collot d'Herbois, Corday d'Armont, Rouget de Lisle, de Sade, Lafayette, Lanjuinais, the brothers Lameth, Barère de Vieuzac, and the Duc d'Orléans. The first president of the Jacobin Society in 1790 was the Duc d'Auguillon. Even Napoleon, the man who in moderation spread the revolution across the map of Europe, came from a noble family. Such an inventory evidences the fact that, statistically speaking, the natural death of states and nations as well as of classes and estates is not murder but suicide. This act of suicide, however, is usually preceded by a period of delusion and folly. *Quem deus vult perdidi prius dementat.*

The pioneers of the revolution were also frequently members of the clergy. The "philosophizing abbés" could be found everywhere, men such as Siéyès, Raynal, (Bishop) Grégoire, Mably, St. Pierre, and Barthélmy.

Voltaire owed his deism to the Abbé de Châteauneuf, and Rousseau, not without reason, put the summary of his sentimental-deistic philosophy into the mouth of his *Vicaire Savoyard*. The Enlightenment and the revolution had little to fear from the more intellectual clergy. Voltaire and Diderot were both educated by the Jesuits. And since the totalitarian movements of the last hundred years, so reminiscent of the French Revolution, are in part or even predominantly Christian heresies, men and women with a distinctly Christian background are attracted to them. Neither seminary training nor the clerical state serves as a prophylactic against such deviations. Who could imagine the French Revolution without the participation of clerics and ex-clerics, or Russian Bolshevism without Stalin and Mikoyan, both former seminarians? Or earlier leftist currents without such men as Arnaldo di Brescia, Joachim de Floris, John Ball, John Wycliffe, and Campanella?

The second lesson to be learned from the French Revolution concerns the danger inherent in reforms that are not carried out by a firm hand.[230] Human beings on the whole do not respond to generosity with gratitude, and frequently the loosening of reins becomes a signal for general unrest and mutiny.[231] The Reformation instilled in radical illiterate groups the feeling that there were no fixed laws, no eternal rules, no set standards, no permanent authority—and all of this even though the Reformation was by no means a liberal revolution but a rigoristic movement, a spiritual revolt against the rationalism of Rome; it was, in other words, the very reverse of the Enlightenment —which was, in turn, the bastard grandchild of the Renaissance.

Still, because radical changes took place in the Reformation, the inner balance of the masses was completely upset. Anarchical peasant risings occurred and mad, weird sects made their ubiquitous appearance. Luther, in forceful response, invoked the secular arm, and since secular authority had not been shaken by this purely religious evolution, order was restored. In the French Revolution, however, secular authority was undermined and attacked after religious loyalties had been gravely weakened. Only outside military intervention could have helped the old order. But the energies let loose by the revolutionary volcano were too strong; for twenty years Continental Europe was at the mercy of the French Revolution and its Bonapartist aftermath, which found the United States a virtual ally of Napoleon in the War of 1812.

Kerenski types usually appear on the scene at a time of reform. They take over and pretend to be the originators of all improvements. They continue the reforming-liberalizing policy of their "reactionary" forerunners, but then, quite soon, they lose their hold and cede power to a combination of wild demagogues and frantic mobs. The Lafayettes, Lameths, Mirabeaus, in precisely this fashion, failed to stem the mounting tide of radicalism. As in a Greek tragedy, events ran their inevitable course. The anarchical tyranny of the many evolved into the despotism of a single man. Civilian chaos became military order. *Skytalismos*, the rule of the club, yielded to the rule of the sword. Tyranny "settled down" into monarchy, as foreseen by Plato, Aristotle, and Polybius.

But today, the "royalization" of tyranny is unfortunately no longer possible. Totalitarian tyrannies no longer evolve because Big Brother cannot become a Father. Thus we get endless intrigues, palace revolts, and assassinations. Only total military defeat can break the evil chain.

(During the years 1789–1815, France was a classic example of the evolution of political revolution, but just as a disease does not always follow the pattern of a medical textbook, just so the classic does not always prevail. In history, nothing can be prophesied with certainty, only with likelihood, with lesser or greater possibilities. Nothing is inevitable. Yet only a fool would disregard the lessons of history; individuals sometimes learn, but nations, as Hegel remarked, *never*. Personal memory and personal learning exist. But collective memory is problematic, and the masses never study. The real historian, beyond finding facts, is neither a determinist nor a pure pragmatist. Still, Friedrich Schlegel was right when he called the historian a backward-looking prophet.)[232]

The horrors of the French Revolution were the direct and logical outcome of the philosophy of the First Enlightenment. The atrocities surprised only the British and the American observers (as did the nightmarish deeds of Communists and Nazis a century-and-a-half later) because, owing to the relativistic and weakened post-Protestant mind of the English-speaking world, extremism and absolutism in thought and deed became "unimaginable." By the end of the eighteenth century the American and British intellectuals were beginning to veer from deism to agnosticism. On the Continent, the recession of Catholic (and Eastern) religiousness did not give way to agnosticism but to atheism and antitheism. Absolutism in thinking was not replaced with polite doubt, but with other radical attitudes, with secular faiths of a sentimental or pseudorational character. Anatole France, who was certainly not a convinced Christian nor a hidebound secular dogmatist, once remarked that "only extremes are bearable."[233]

This was the same Anatole France who in his novel, *Les Dieux ont soif*, described the blood orgies of the French Revolution, a revolution that pleased and inspired the budding American Left more than 190 years ago. Although the delirious horrors committed by the National Socialists and the international Communists in our century were quantitatively even worse, the French Revolution, marking the rebirth of democracy after it had foundered in antiquity, laid down a pattern of inhumanity that set a lasting example.

In fact, the revolutionaries in France (more even than the Bolsheviks) engaged in tortures and massacres with a truly popular *élan*, quite different from their Nazi imitators who perpetrated their crimes in a bureaucratic and almost always clandestine way. The tortures to which the officers of the Bastille were submitted were carried out by the "dear people" in full daylight. The fiendish dissection of the Princesse de Lamballe, the frenetic work of these sadists and sex maniacs, can be ascribed to "ignoble savages," to our deified friend, the Common Man. (The reader is spared the details, which can be got elsewhere.)[234] The ghoulish procession in which the private parts of this unfortunate woman were carried on a pike through the streets was a fitting symbolic overture to the democratic tragedy that was to become the nightmare of Europe. The princess, of course, was not alone. On August 10, 1792, a young defender of the Tuileries, employed in the kitchen, was rolled in butter and fried alive. All these niceties were hushed up in the 1989 celebrations.

Metternich's reaction to the French Revolution led him to remark, "When I saw what people did in the name of fraternity, I resolved, if I had a brother, to call him cousin."[235] And, indeed, the history of the revolution is a nauseating mixture of idealistic verbiage, of treachery and intrigue, of sentimental incantations and senseless butcheries, of envy and outbursts of sadism. The *colonnes infernales* of the revolutionary army under General Turreau[236] massacred the population of entire villages in the Vendée and eastern Brittany. Women and girls of all ages were raped (as during the Soviet occupation of Eastern Europe), from three- and four-year-olds to tottering matrons. The republican regional governor, Président Cholet, wrote to Turreau that his soldiers committed horrors of which not even cannibals would be capable.[237] Some of the worst cruelties were committed when Le Mans fell into the hands of the Republicans, who promptly murdered all the wounded counterrevolutionaries in the military hospitals. Almost everyone who had not fled was butchered. The women and girls, after being undressed, raped, and slain, were placed alongside naked male corpses in obscene postures—scenes which General Turreau perhaps failed to notice in his official *promenades* (as he called them). These slaughters were also designed to reduce the *grande armée de bouches inutiles*.[238] The *Noyades* in the Loire had homosexual overtones and were indescribable, despicable.[239]

These nightmares were repeated in Arras, where the guillotine was placed in front of the theater from whose balcony the revolutionary leader Lebon and his dear wife could watch the spectacle. After an arduous day with a big crop, the executioners amused themselves by imitating the *batteries nationales* of Le Mans; they denuded the decapitated corpses of both sexes, mixing the macabre with the lascivious. On a different occasion, the hangman fastened a *ci-devant* marquis on the board of the guillotine and proceeded for ten minutes to read aloud from the local newspaper. Finally he exhorted the wretched marquis to inform his friends and relatives in the beyond about the victories of the French armies.[240]

During the September Massacres, which took place in the Paris jails (1792), the butcher-volunteers received six francs each and as much wine as they could drink. But it was not only the *aristos* who suffered; the children in reformatories and the prostitutes (temporarily arrested) in the Bicêtre and La Salpêtrière jails were not spared. Indeed, indescribable scenes of bestiality took place among the prostitutes. Big butcheries among prostitutes were also organized by the Left during the Spanish Civil War in Barcelona and by SS units in Eastern Poland—for "hygienic" reasons. For the genuine materialist there is no fundamental, only a gradual, "evolutionary" difference, between a man and a pest, a noxious insect.

The revolutionary fervor spared nobody. When Lavoisier, the great mathematician, physicist, and chemist, was accused of counterrevolutionary activities and condemned to death, his lawyer cried out that he was a great scientist. It was unavailing, for to a convinced democrat one man is as good as another. Coffinhal, the president of the Law Court, replied quite truthfully, *"La République n'a pas besoin de savants."*[241] In spite of the cult of reason, true intellectuality soon became suspect. Envy of titles and honors rapidly evolved into envy of knowledge, and it was only a question of time before the strongest form of this vice appeared, envy of material possessions—which had played such a potent part in the radical democratic movements in seventeenth-century England.

The *Enragés*, the left wing of the *Montagne*, with men such as Roux, Varlet, and Leclerc, increasingly protested against the inequality of wealth. The equality of civil rights, they insisted, was senseless without financial equality. Hébert spoke in the same way, and Saint-Just declared war on the rich. It was Joseph Lebon, the butcher of Arras, who started the methodical warfare against the "rich" in the north: 392 were guillotined in Arras, 149 in Cambrai. In a famous speech before the National Convention Jacques Roux demanded equal incomes for all. "Identitarianism" wanted to go all the way, and only the fall of Robespierre and later the defeat of Gracchus Babeuf, the first modern communist leader (1797), prevented a further development in this direction. In the course of the French Revolution, however, the inner connection between "democratism" and socialism became clearly visible once again.

It would be wrong to believe, as "sensible" but badly informed people like to do, that the French Revolution, like many others, was a "swinging of the pendulum in the other direction" or a "just reaction to earlier abuses." In American high schools and colleges, such an interpretation of history is quite popular. And it is often conveyed, with the best intentions, to provide students with a story that "makes sense" and simultaneously to suggest that reason and justice, though not always effective, are forces to be reckoned with in the gradual evolution of mankind. The alternative seems to be an endless enumeration of names, places, and dates—the inventory of a madhouse or a vale of tears, leaving the Beyond as the only consolation.

The average teacher is afraid to tell young people who look for security on this earth that Luther was right in calling the world *des Teufels Wirtshaus*, the "Devil's Inn." The deeper meaning of history is theological, and he who flees theology can only try to solve the riddles of history by offering banalities of a moralizing nature, such as the optimistic old liberalism and Marxism (only remotely related) have tried to do. But this world *is* a vale of tears, and man, from a purely terrestrial viewpoint, a tragic creature. The trouble is that America and Europe, after a long process of de-Christianization, are no longer capable of assimilating a philosophy of the tragic or a theology of the Cross.[242]

Attempts to explain history also indulge in myriad rationalizations, the pendulum theory, the conviction that "where there's smoke there's fire." This latter theory ignores the fact that there can be an enormous fire with little smoke and a tiny fire, maybe only a glow, enveloping a whole area in dark fumes. These phenomena rise up again and again in this study. The egregious reaction to "provocation" in the French Revolution later emerged between the Jews and the National Socialists, the Armenians and the Young Turks, the white Russians and the Bolsheviks. (It could also be seen in the horrors perpetrated by the savage monsters of Holden Roberto's Liberation Front against the Portuguese in Angola, the atrocities of Gbenye and Mulele against the Belgians in the Congo, and the barbarities of the Mau-

Mau against the British in Kenya.) The fact must be faced: man is not "good"—only the extraordinary man is good, only the heroic saint or the saintly hero. The noble savage belongs to the world of fairy tales. The Bible is very explicit on this subject. Genesis 8, 21 says: "The tendency of man's heart, from his youth on, is set toward evil."

From a social viewpoint, the French Revolution took place in a period of general well-being and growing prosperity. External trade had quadrupled since the death of Louis XIV: the value of exchanged goods exceeded a billion francs in 1788, a record met only once since (in 1848).[243] Moreover, the richest, not the poorest, regions of France were the most revolutionary, those where the mirage of limitless wealth had driven cupidity to new heights.[244] The same phenomenon could be observed in Spain during the Civil War (1936–39) and in Italy after the last war, where communism was (and is) strongest in areas where equitable social conditions existed. Another example can be found in the strong communist or agrarian-socialist movement in pre-World War II Bulgaria, a country with no upper crust and only a small middle class, a nation where the factor of envy should hardly have come into play.

In France the relationship between the old nobility and the peasantry ranged from fair to good. (The largely fake nobility of the newly rich[245] did not have the demophile-patriarchal qualities of the ancient *noblesse de l'épée*.) Serfdom survived only in a few remote corners of the eastern reaches and in the Bourbonnais. Louis XVI himself had eliminated the last vestiges of serfdom in his domain. About half the land in France was owned by the peasantry, and the peasants, although proprieters, as a rule also rented land from those who had large estates. In addition there were numerous home industries. But given the French rural mentality, there were nevertheless endless minor frictions over rents, borders and title deeds.[246] There was, of course, no slavery.

Edmund Burke, who traveled in France fairly widely before the revolution, gave a good picture of the character of the classes and their mutual relationships.[247] He noted that the nobility showed "something more nearly approaching familiarity [with the lower classes] than is generally practiced with us."[248] And he added that the aristocracy had no "manner of power in the cities" and very little in the country. Still, he berated them for their foolish Anglomania which (politically at least) was to contribute to their downfall. They were also morally lax and hesitant to take in the new moneyed class. "All this violent outcry against the nobility I take to be a mere work of art," he wrote. As for the Catholic hierarchy of France, Burke remarked that they were "liberal and open, with the hearts of gentlemen and men of humour, neither insolent nor servile. They seemed to me a rather superior class."

But the question remains, would the French Revolution have taken place without an ideological preparation in which large sectors of the nobility and a significant number of the clergy had an appreciable share? Even when the mask was off and the face of the beast clearly recognizable, some silly priests and sillier friars of the "constitutional" type, as well as formally unfrocked clerics, enthusiastically supported the revolution. It was, in fact, Claude Royer, a pastor from Chalon-sur-Saône and a member of the Paris Jacobin Club in the rue Saint-Honoré, who made the first great appeal for a regime of sheer terror. "Let us stop talking," he shouted, "yet let our silence be terrible. It should be the signal for combat, putting fear into the hearts of the conspirators and acting as a call to men hesitating to support liberty. . . . Yes, my friends, let us be terrible but save liberty!" Royer repeated this speech before the Convention and demanded that the *Leveé en Masse* and the jailing of all suspects be decreed. Danton and Robespierre seconded the proposition. Mass arrests were voted immediately, and Royer had a pamphlet printed carrying the headline, "Let us make terror the order of the day!"[249] In another instance, one of the shrillest propagandists for the execution of the royal couple was the ex-Capuchin monk Chabot who supported Moras in his bloodcurdling attacks.[250] The perversion of basic Christian sentiments comes easiy to priests who have neglected their spiritual life and who, secularizing theology, become real masters of the mob—as witness what is happening in Latin America, and even farther north.[251]

Royalist authors later intimated that the "Jacobin Fathers" of the rue Saint-Honoré (who were Dominicans) had been imbued with an antiroyalist spirit since the time of the *Ligue*, but this is an exaggeration. Still, they eagerly invited the Jacobins into their monastery and undoubtedly had leftist leanings—unlike the monks of the same order who were domiciled in the rue Saint-Jacques.[252]

The tragedy of the intellectual leftist nobleman is best personified by Chrétien de Lamoignon de Malesherbes, a liberal of somewhat sectarian cast and a pillar of the Enlightenment. In 1750, at the age of twenty-nine, he became president of the *Cour des Aides* of the Paris *parlement* while his father was made chancellor (but left all the work to his son). Malesherbes used his position to promote the Enlightenment and, trying desperately to appear "tolerant," "progressive," and "broadminded," he gave every imaginable aid to those who undermined the old order and persecuted opponents of the Enlightenment. This was easily done as his office handled the censorship of all printed matter published in France. (The Holy Illiberal Inquisition was working effectively even in those days.) Then as now, the pink intellectual, fearing to be out of step with the times, cut a contemptible figure.

Baron Grimm did not exaggerate when he commented that "without the assistance of Malesherbes the *Encyclopédie* would probably never have been published."[253] Pierre Gaxotte called him *"le type achevé du libéral qui a toujours peur de passer pour un réactionnaire."* Elie Fréron, an enemy of Voltaire, along with d'Alembert and Marmontel, published a relatively conservative journal, *L'Année Littéraire*, which was repeatedly confiscated. In 1758 he was almost jailed for having published a discussion of a book opposed to the *Encyclopédie*. Although he was constantly attacked by the men of the Enlightenment, he was actively prevented by Malesherbes from defending himself. Malesherbes also forbade the publication of a work by Father Julien Louis Geoffroy because it was critical of Diderot. And when Father Thomolas of Lyons dared reply to the article "Collège"[254] in the *Encyclopédie*, he was warned not to be impudent. In other instances, Father Charles Palissot de Montenoy, an Oratorian, was persecuted by Malesherbes, as was also the gifted and short-lived Nicholas Laurent Gilbert. "The philosophers shouted that they were being tyrannized," Gaxotte remarked, "yet they were the ones who exercised a tyrannical rule over the literary world."

Malesherbes, one can safely assume, finally saw the light, but by then it was too late. He returned from Switzerland, where he had been given asylum, to defend the King before his judges, and it was his bitter task to tell the monarch that he had been sentenced to death. He then retired to the country but was arrested in December 1793, together with his daughter, son-in-law, and grandchildren. They were all condemned to death and, with the great delicacy that always distinguishes convinced leftists, the executioner had all the family beheaded in the presence of the old man (the grandfather of Alexis de Tocqueville) before his turn came (April 23, 1794). Certainly he expiated all his sins. The road leading to the hell of leftist radicalism is not only broad, it is also fast and steep. Under such circumstances the brakes rarely work.

The significance of the French Revolution lies not only in the revival of democracy and in the adoption of political patterns prevailing in antiquity and among primitives, but in the new impetus it gave to state worship and ethnic nationalism. The all-powerful *polis*-state again made its appearance. In other words, the "identitarian" drives culminated in a frantic demand both for equality (which went so far that only Robespierre's fall prevented the destruction of all steeples and towers)[255] and for ethnic sameness. The chapter dealing with the German National Socialists will show how much they owe, directly and indirectly, to the French Revolution and to what extent "well-meaning," "moderate," "enlightened," and "progressive" leftists contributed to the rise of the brown scourge.

Another aspect of the French Revolution has to do with the radical clubs of the era, a subject dealt with in *The Jacobins*, an excellent book by Professor Crane Brinton. The volume was published in New York in 1930, three years before Hitler came to power. It reads exactly as if the author were trying methodically to prove that the National Socialists knowingly imitated the plans and actions of the Jacobins—who were by no means internationalists.

"When the war went wrong," Brinton wrote, referring to the first defeats inflicted by the Prussian-Austrian alliance, "and the peoples refused to rise, Frenchmen were almost obliged to consider themselves the only virtuous people. The [Jacobin] society of Gueret waited nobly until January 1794, and then removed the American and English flags from the tree of liberty. The tricolor flew alone."[256]

Yet Professor Brinton argued rightly that, even without a foreign war, the *patriote* would have evolved from a lover of mankind into a nationalist because equality could not remain an abstraction: it had to find concrete expression. All other qualities were accidental, but Frenchness now became the touchstone of equality.[257] All Frenchmen should have a common language. And soon the Jacobin clubs began a minor crusade against all other languages—Provençal, Breton, German, Flemish, Basque. The Jacobin Club of Strasbourg even suggested that all Alsatians who refused to learn French be deported and in their stead *sans-culottes* imported.[258] To make France linguistically uniform, some people proposed the swift guillotining of ethnic units, like the stubborn Alsatians. Auschwitz was beckoning. French was *la langue républicaine*[259] and the French people the historically predestined bearers of truth, of a messianic message. This gives a hint of the extent to which the French Revolution was not only a forerunner but an ideological stepping-stone to the slow growth of ideas that found their concrete expression in our time in national socialism.

Some might object that, as far as fanaticism, extremism, and savagery are concerned, the National Socialists far outdid their precursors. In a purely quantitative way this is surely the case. Yet *la terreur* was far more programmatic during the French Revolution than the sytem inaugurated by Hitler. It is difficult for outsiders to believe how effectively the truth about systematic murder was kept from the Germans; they certainly knew about the concentration camps and even about the killing of the insane, but not about the extermination camps.[260] In Germany *Schrecklichkeit*—terribleness—was used to paralyze resistance through fear, but it was used quite sparingly. To speak the truth about Auschwitz, Tręblinka, Majdanek, and the other horror chambers was to risk one's life. Those Jews still at liberty did not know what was in store for them. Here and there rumors leaked out, but they were vague, and people's minds understandably shied away from accepting the tales of horror. We were all still too conditioned by the centuries of Christianity.[261]

The French Revolution was, however, quite different. In spite of Rousseauistic fancies, the depravity of which the average man is capable soon became evident. People literally danced around the guillotines. Various military and civil commanders openly and officially boasted about their bestial deeds, which in all their sick horror were perpetrated above all against the "internal enemy." Thus General Westermann in his message to the Committee of Public Welfare, after the defeat of the *Chouans* near Savenay, could declare:

> The Vendée, republican fellow citizens, no longer exists. She is dead under our sabres, together with her women and children. I have just buried her in the swamps and forests of Savenay. Following the orders you gave me, I have trampled the children to death with our horses, I have massacred the women, and they are no longer going to give birth to any more brigands. I am not guilty of taking a single prisoner, I have exterminated them all. . . . The roads are covered with corpses. There are so many of them at several places they form pyramids. The firing squads work incessantly at Savenay since every moment brigands arrive who pretend that they will surrender as prisoners . . . but we are not taking any. One would be forced to feed them with the bread of liberty, but compassion is not a revolutionary virtue.[262]

The unspeakable Westermann, an Alsatian, belonged to the faction around Danton. He was to be arrested and guillotined on April 5, 1794. But his spirit lived on. An official report to Paris from Avranches said, "The Hospital was also filled with wounded and they too were subjected to the national vengeance. They have been finished off." Doctor Gainou wrote his friend Robespierre from Fougères that "the soldiers have killed all the wounded and the sick in the hospital. Several wives of brigands were there in a state of illness. They were raped and their throats cut." Marceau-Desgraviers, a real soldier who participated in the war against the Vendée, was tormented for the rest of his life—he was killed in action in 1796—by nightmares of the horrors perpetrated by this renascent democracy. At Le Mans he rescued a royalist girl and barely escaped the guillotine in consequence. Meanwhile, the commissioner of Angers wrote triumphantly to the mayor of Paris, "Our Holy Mother Guillotine is working full time. . . ." It was in Angers that the Republicans issued an order to have the heads of the "brigands" (the *Chouans*) scalped, dissected, and exposed on small pikes on the ramparts of the city. Since the doctors picked for this appetizing job were too slow, and since the Republicans needed quick demonstrations of democratic fervor, they proceeded to guillotine what civilian prisoners they had, among them the eighty-two-year-old Abbess of Fontevault. She was blind but, as the chronicler tells us, *"pleine de vertus et de charité."*[263]

It is worth reading the reports by the minions of the victorious revolution as well as the accounts of other eyewitnesses. There are descriptions of the Le Mans massacre, where Bourbotte and Prieux watched not only the raping of naked women and girls whose throats were subsequently slit, but the raping of corpses—real orgies of necrophilia. Beauvais, writing about the event after the retreat from Fougères, relates that "all the wounded in the hospital were massacred in the most fiendish way . . . all their members without exception were cut off bit by bit. The women were treated in exactly the same way until, finally, cartridges were inserted in their private parts in order to terminate their lives and their sufferings with an explosion." Tortures of this sort were also perpetrated by the admirable Loyalists in the Spanish Civil War, but instead of hospitals, they selected churches for their expressions of sexual democracy.

Some of the worst horrors occurred in the Vendée, where, as the chronicler writes, "young girls were hung stark naked from trees after they had been raped, their hands tied behind their backs. The lucky ones were rescued . . . by charitable passers-by from this shameful torture. Pregnant women," he continues, "were crushed to death by wine presses. A poor woman, also pregnant, was cut open alive in the Chapelet Wood near Maillou. A certain Jean Lainé from Croix de Beauchêne, consigned to his bed by illness, was burned alive. Madame Sauson from Pé Bardon met with the same fate after she had been gravely wounded. Blood-covered limbs and babies were carried in truimph on bayonets!

"A young girl from La Chappelle, after having been raped by soldiers, was hung feet first on an oak tree. Each leg stretched as far as possible, was tied to a separate branch. In this position they cut her body in two down to her head."

And here another witness of the glorious "Birth of Democracy." Beauvais relates how Amey, a leader of the *colonnes infernales,* fired houses and set bakers' ovens ablaze; when they were well heated, he put women and children in them. "Then we protested, but he claimed that this was the way the Republic wanted to bake its bread. The soldiers of Turreau were delighted by this procedure, and since there were not a sufficient number of wives of 'brigands' [i.e., royalists], even the wives of patriots [i.e., republicans] were baked alive.'[264] There were, in fact, numerous reports of republicans massacred in the Vendée, for the Jacobins wished to exterminate the entire population of this "reactionary" province.

Mass murder had become the order of the day in France. If in Germany the National Socialists succeeded in slaughtering millions, thanks to the development of technology, the French revolutionaries, given their limited means, certainly tried very hard. The chemical engineer Fourcroy, at the command of Robespierre, Collot d'Herbois, Barère, and Fouché, invented a poison gas, but it was not very effective. Carrier then proposed to poison the rivers and the lakes with arsenic. What Renan was later to call the "zoological wars" had already begun.[265]

The spirit of the *Marseillaise* was Nazi and racist: "To arms, citizens, form your battalions, let us march, march, so that impure blood will drench our furrows." A clever inversion of the blood-soil complex, *Blut und Boden,* seems to be contained in these lines.

The fall of Robespierre on July 27, 1794, came as a blessing for most Frenchmen, but the political scientists, psychologists and historians may feel a kind of regret for having thus been deprived of the full realization of early leftism in its democratic, identitarian form. The ethnic-linguistic problem of Alsace was never solved (by mass deportations or worse) and two plans never carried out: to put all Frenchmen and Frenchwomen into uniform[266] and to level all church towers for being "arrogant" and "undemocratic." The church of Besse-en-Chandesse was the first victim of this barbarism, and later the church of Ars (where St. Jean Vianney was to become the famous *curé*) suffered the same fate. In all of France churches and cathedrals still show the wounds inflicted by leftist savagery, although the desecrated and emptied tombs of saints, kings, and queens have been carefully restored. Not surprisingly, the National Socialists were also past masters at violating cemeteries (Jewish in their case), as were the red Spaniards.

CHAPTER 8

From Democracy to Romantic Socialism

*The butcher is held
in great esteem in Harmony.*

—FRANÇOIS FOURIER

The concept of socialism and communism is a great deal older than St. Thomas More's *Utopia*, generally considered to be the first "Communist Manifesto." *Utopia* is a half serious, half humorous, profound, yet satirical effort to visualize a state and a society based purely on the four natural virtues—prudence, fortitude, temperance, and justice. Faith, hope, and charity, the three theological virtues, naturally do not figure in this imaginary non-Christian sector of the world. But Platonic notions play a certain part in More's highly rational polity, which proclaims a sweeping equality among its citizens (women, it seems, must also serve in the army). There is no private property, but scholars enjoy privileges, and monasteries are allowed to exist.

Utopia also has its ironic aspect. It tries to portray a perfect pagan society and indirectly points out that Christian nations, although favored by God, often fall below pagan levels. Freedom, though not totally lacking, is rather limited in Utopia, and state controls are ubiquitous and severe.

But this leveling concept did not spring full-grown with More. The

85

basic idea of the communist order—lack of private property, equality, a nonhereditary government, common work, common social life—can be found not only in Western civilization but also in the most diverse parts of the world. It is concretely expressed in monasticism. But this way of life presupposes a *vocation*, the *sacrifice* of innate rights and a *voluntary* act of surrender. Although monastic life also normally provides for certain non-spiritual advantages, such as regular and regulated work, free medical care, and material security, it is basically a *sacrificial* form of existence (even if outsiders, at the sight of the thick walls of some monastery, sigh enviously, "It's easy for them!"—without joining, of course).

The purpose of a monastery is spiritual. Nobody is going to measure the success of a monastic order by its economic record (which, more often than not, is modest, to say the least). Yet historically, certain purely external monastic features have been unconsciously and roughly imitated by modern institutions, such as prisons, barracks and, above all, in some ways, *factories*, all of which practice a separation of the sexes.

The monastic spirit in the West seems to have made its first appearance in the Essene communities in the Holy Land. The earliest Christian monks were—as their name indicates—*monachoi*, men living singly, anchorites, hermits. Somewhat later the *monachoi* began to live together in groups as *coenobites*. At a still later period, St. Benedict established an order with formal vows of obedience, chastity, and poverty, the three "councils of perfection." The Middle Ages were the great period of monasticism. For centuries the monasteries and convents were the fortresses not only of religious life, but of learning, of the arts, and of the higher crafts. Many of the intellectual treasures of antiquity were saved by the monks who copied and recopied ancient texts.

With the decline of the Middle Ages, in the fifteenth century, the monasteries too began to decline and the orders founded after the Reformation lacked the monastic character. Jesuits, Redemptorists, and Salesians are not monks; they are not cloistered. The Oratorians (founded by St. Philip Neri) are not even an order but simply a congregation of priests. And with the twentieth century there appeared mixed lay and clerical institutions, such as the *Opus Dei* with its own prelature in Rome.

The Reformation was started by a monk, an Augustinian hermit, and, as previously mentioned, it was essentially a reaction against the spirit of the Renaissance and humanism. While Martin Luther was in Rome, he became convinced that the popes had sold out to paganism. Luther was aghast when he learned that the medieval concept of the universe, the circle with

God at its center, had been exchanged for an elliptical concept with two focal points, God *and* man. Luther decried human worship (the saints elevated to the honor of the altar) and protested against the enthusiasm for the cultural and intellectual treasures of antiquity. These were, after all, pagan in origin and everything pagan was damned for all eternity.[267] The entire theological and philosophical intellectualism and "rationalism," which began before St. Thomas and finally fused with the new learning, was odious to him. Reason did not lead to God;[268] man could be saved *by faith alone.*

This fideism was one of the many aspects of Luther's teaching that alienated the leading humanists—Erasmus, Pirckheimer, Adelmann, and even the very anticlerical Reuchlin—and resulted in real enmity toward the new teaching by the universities.[269] Luther, of course, never taught the doctrine of "private interpretation";[270] he was not a precursor of liberalism.[271] He was basically a rigorist and a disciplinarian[272]—a conservative by inclination. The term "freedom" as used by him had no personal meaning.[273] He was a predestinarian as much as Calvin, but thanks to Melanchthon's intervention his notion of the enslaved will[274] was not inserted in the *Confessio Augustana.* Melanchthon thought, quite rightly, that such a teaching would prove an important obstacle to eventual reunion of Lutheranism and the Catholic Church. Calvin's reforms had a far stricter character than Luther's.[275] Geneva under Calvin and later under Besa and Farel actually became the first totalitarian state in Europe.[276] (Calvin's *Soli Deo Gloria!* hardly made up for any "polycentrism.")

The Reformation did not sweep through the European Continent as a torrent of freedom.[277] True, in certain areas the changes were adopted with great popular enthusiasm. The Reformation was riding the wave of greater religious awareness, of an increased religious *Innerlichkeit* (inner-directedness) and popular piety. But in other areas, as in Scandinavia, the changes were dictated by the secular authorities. It was generally felt that greater asceticism and greater strictness were needed: Luther's monastic severity descended on Central Europe like a second coming of the Irish monks.[278] Sebastian Franck, an ex-Dominican, speaking from experience, declared: "Now we think we have escaped the monastery, but actually we have to be monks all our life."[279] (The Catholic world, meanwhile, continued in the spirit of the Renaissance, the Baroque, and the Rococo; it remained individualistic, anarchical, and revolutionary, torn between holy and unholy passions.)

The areas converted by the Reformation settled down to law and order and a strong community spirit. The community, the congregation, the group dominated religious life to a large extent. The monarchical-patriarchal idea was badly shaken in the Calvinist world and republican ideas were soon on the march. Strong egalitarian and communistic notions were felt in England during the time of the Commonwealth (Levelers, Diggers) and, later on, in the northern American colonies. Puritanism was, after all, a half-religious, half-secular kind of monasticism.

The monasteries, as mentioned, prefigured the big communities that are bounded by real or symbolic walls—boarding schools, barracks, hospitals, jails, factories—communities consisting usually (or predominantly) of a single sex. Other monastic traits found in such institutions are the habit (uniform), mental and physical discipline, order, conformity, regulated work, community spirit, common meals, equality in hierarchy, cells (as in jails) or dormitories (as in barracks), self-control, subordination, mental concentration, simplicity, sobriety, an ascetic way of life—altogether an autonomous but collective existence, to the average Catholic a holy life of great sacrifice. There is no place in the monastery for sloth and individualism. (The opposite of this would be the bohemian family of a wild but prosperous artist in which everybody dressed, acted, created, loafed, came, and went according to whim and inclination.)

The monastery, of course, has a positive value since it rests on voluntary sacrifice unlike the more or less coercive character of the barracks, jails, boarding schools, hospitals, and factories. (This is equally true of the "hybrids" such as the military hospital and the reformatory.)

The issue has been oversimplified, however, because the monastery is not all pure sacrifice. Although weakly developed, most of us have a monastic instinct, most of us sometimes envy the monks and nuns their "secure" life. The curious dilemma in this complexity of feelings is illustrated by the well-known questions: "Who is secure in all his basic needs? Who has work, spiritual care, medical care, housing, food, occasional entertainment, free clothing, free burial, free everything?" The answer might be, "monks and nuns," but the standard reply is, "prisoners." And inevitably this conjures up citizens of the Provider State who have material protection from "the cradle to the grave." But here again, to sacrifice an eye for a dear friend is one thing; to be blinded by an executioner is quite another.

Yet the monastic yearning *is* in us, and therefore some of us readily respond to the appeal of a false monasticism. The security element most certainly motivates this allure. But the person with the *genuine* monastic vocation seeks security merely to rid himself of material distractions in his heroic struggle to live a life of complete spiritual devotion. (In bygone ages there have naturally been men and women attracted to the monastic life by purely material considerations. In our overeroticized and highly materialistic age, such a "temptation" hardly exists.)

The situation is quite different in the "world," where millions crave security and dread responsibility. Interestingly enough, the two historic epochs most inclined to a sort of secular monasticism were the Reformation and the French Revolution, two periods in which genuine monasteries and convents were confiscated and dissolved by the thousands. (In Russia the same thing happened after 1917.) The smaller the number of religious monasteries, the more perverted the secular monasticism. The most extreme form of secular monasticism is communism, and the communist movement's strength in a given area often can be measured by the number of empty or ruined monasteries. This is also true of countries outside Western Europe and North America, such as China, Southeast Asia, and Mexico.

The eccentric or ex-monk is often an ardent advocate of secular monasticism in one form or another. Joachim de Floris and Tomaso Campanella were typical of this type of mind and outlook. Joachim (1145–1202), a radical Cistercian, preceded Campanella (1568–1639), a rather odd Dominican. Both were of noble birth and both came from Calabria.

The ideas of Joachim profoundly affected the "spiritual" wing of the Franciscans and created grave theological and monastic disturbances. His views, considered quite orthodox during his lifetime, had an apocalyptic and eschatological character. Like François Fourier and other visionary socialists, he arbitrarily divided history into "ages," past and future. In Joachim's case they were: the Age of the Father, characterized by obedience; the Age of the Son (the "present time"), guided by reading; and the Age of the Spirit, devoted to prayer and song. The last and final age was to be entirely monastic in character: Humanity would consist entirely of monks and nuns in preparation for the Day of Judgment. Joachim's "gnostic" ideas were widely spread; they were to influence Wycliffe and Roger Bacon and bear on the Reformation.

Joachim de Floris (like Jansenius, Bishop of Ypres, who unknowingly started the Jansenist heresy) had little trouble during his lifetime. Joachim's foundation, the Abbey of San Giovanni in Fiore on Monte Nero, even enjoyed the favors of Frederick II, *stupor mundi*, after its founder's death. Tomaso Campanella, on the other hand, had grave political difficulties and spent many years in jail for opposing Spanish rule in Naples. He wrote several philosophical treatises but owed his fame to his *"Civitas Solis,"* the "Sun State," published in 1602. This interesting and intellectually contradictory man was also one of the first "one-worlders," and F. Meinecke, the great German historian, has called his concept "one of the greatest psychological riddles in the new history of ideas." *"Civitas Solis,"* published as part of Campanella's *Realis Philosophiae Partes Quattuor*—like Thomas More's *Utopia*—may be a mere intellectual exercise.

In this essay Campanella envisaged an idealist state with no Christian characteristics nor any political-social aura reminiscent of Catholic concepts. (This dichotomy was typical of all Campanella's intellectual efforts: his philosophy did not tally with his theology, nor his theology with his political theory, nor his basic political views with his practical notions.) His "Sun State" had a monarchical head, an intellectual-elitist leadership, no private property, and no lasting marriages. Sterile women automatically became public harlots, and pregnant women could have sexual intercourse with everyone. Yet women who used makeup, put on high heels, or wore long skirts to conceal their feet were condemned to death as "liars." Incest, except between mothers and sons, was encouraged. (Could this have been a forerunner of de Sade?)

Campanella was liberated from his Spanish jail in Naples by Pope Urban VIII through a ruse. He fled to Rome and later settled in Paris where he enjoyed the favors of Cardinal Richelieu who saw in him an *esprit fort*, an emancipated spirit. (This controversial friar, with the vivid sexual imagination, preceded Morelly by only a century.) He was a political agent, a theoretical libertine, a socialist thinker, a defender of absolute monarchy and papalism, and an enemy of Machiavelli's teachings. Indeed, there was nobody like him. He died, oddly enough, in the Dominican monastery of the rue Jacob in Paris, which spawned the smaller monastery in the rue St. Honoré. The Dominicans in Paris were nicknamed *Les Jacobins* after the first monastery, but the name stuck to the radically leftist club established in the smaller house across the Seine. So even today, in a purely historical sense, Jacobin means Dominican.[280]

It was obvious that religious monasticism had to shed its Christian roots if it was to evolve, however perversely, into secular socialism. This was not always the case, as witness the monastic bent in the younger William Morris, who later developed socialist tendencies.

But Morelly was a man quite divorced from traditional values. Little is known of Morelly, even his first name and his beginnings in Vitry-le-François are matters of conjecture. He authored several dull epics but also a very important utopian socialist treatise, the *Code de la Nature*, published in

1755 in Amsterdam. At first Diderot was thought to be its author, but this theory was exploded in the 1820s. It has been reprinted at various times, most recently by a communist publishing house in Paris, and its influence on later socialist thinking cannot be underestimated. Alexis de Tocqueville dealt with it very seriously in his *L'Ancien Régime et La Révolution*. And V. P. Volgin, a Soviet "politologist" who wrote the preface for the Paris edition in 1953, called Morelly "the purest interpreter of socialism."

The fourth part of the book, "Model of Legislation in Conformity with Nature," is the most important segment. Law No. I.2 stipulates that "every citizen will be fed, housed, and employed at public expense." No goods are to be exchanged, bartered, bought, or sold. Every transaction in this ideal order has to go through the hands of the state. "All non-perishable products shall be stored in public warehouses in order to be distributed" (II.6). There are jails for those with short sentences, but penitentiaries will hold those serving long terms (IV.2). The dangerous maniacs and enemies of humanity who attempt to abolish the sacred laws and introduce property will be jailed for life in the midst of cemeteries. They will die a "civil death" and be separated from the rest of mankind in perpetuity by thick walls and iron grills (XII.2). The size of all cities and the quality of all houses will be about the same (IV.2-3). Everybody between the ages of ten and thirty will wear a uniform, one for work and one for holidays. Vanity will be repressed by the "chiefs." Education for all children will be uniform and anybody teaching metaphysics or trying to define the Divinity in human terms will be severely censured (X.9). Freedom to teach is allowed only in the natural sciences—not in the humanities (XI.5). Private property is strictly outlawed; severe marriage laws attend obligatory marriage; and equally strict sanctions are applied against adultery (XII.3). Children will be taken from their parents at the age of five, but occasional contacts through the schools will be permitted (X.4). The laws, needless to say, can never be changed. The political structure of this socialist utopia is in essence a hierarchic system of councils, a system of *Soviets*.[281]

Gracchus Babeuf knew the nightmarish works of Morelly, and so in all probability did Comte Henri de Saint-Simon, the first nineteenth-century socialist in Europe and another French leftist aristocrat.

Henri de Saint-Simon belonged to a junior branch of the Ducs de Saint-Simon. Born in 1760, he owed a great deal of his education and intellectual inspiration to d'Alembert, while he himself profoundly influenced Auguste Comte, the founder of positivism.[282] An enthusiastic young man, Saint-Simon and a host of aristocratic friends volunteered to fight for the young American republic. Endowed with a great deal of imagination, he subsequently offered the viceroy of New Spain (Mexico) a plan for a canal between the two oceans. Back in France his great interest in economics earned him a tidy little sum. Although he did not participate in the revolution, he was temporarily imprisoned during the Terror as a *ci-devant*. He then contracted an unfortunate marriage, got a divorce, was completely ruined, and took a menial position at $200 a year which he gave up when a former valet, who had become well-to-do in the turbulent times, offered him food and shelter.

Saint-Simon's earlier works dealt with scientific, political, and social problems and brought neither fame nor fortune, for his ideas were not taken seriously. But after the fall of Napoleon and the restoration of the Bourbon monarchy, Saint-Simon became more aggressive. His writings dealt extensively with the growing class of workers, a new social element and the product of the Industrial Revolution. This working class developed mainly on the outskirts of the bigger cities and was neglected both intellectually and spiritually. (It cannot, incidentally, be said that the Church "lost" the working class—it had never properly "found" it.) This new class consisted partly of urban workers, but was mostly made up of the uprooted sons and daughters of the peasantry, young people unwilling to work for years as apprentices and journeymen in order to acquire skills, and unwilling to put up with the discipline meted out by those families to which young craftsmen were made subject. They wanted to leave their dull villages and earn money immediately.

Thus, not only in France, but everywhere in Western Europe (as in England at an earlier period) there rose a propertyless, ill-paid class, the industrial proletariat. Whether wages could have been substantially higher at that stage of technological development is not easily ascertained. A good deal of historical, sociological, and economic research would have to be undertaken, but it is highly probable that the factory hands working on the new, rather primitive, yet quite expensive machines could not have achieved materially better living standards. (If better paid, who could have bought their more expensive products?) At this stage of industrial development, figures indicate that the manufacturers lived rather spartan lives and that reinvestments were enormous.[283] But whatever the reason for their misery, the fact remains that an entire race of melancholic, desperate, destitute paupers was growing up as "wild animals," a potential menace to society.[284]

Saint-Simon's compassion for these victims of an economic-social transformation may have been influenced by a variety of factors: his own

financial misery, the indifference of his relatives, his intellectual condition-
ing by the Encyclopedists, and the kindness of his former valet, which
strenghtened his conviction that the lower classes were morally superior to
the upper ones.[285] In a book published in 1820, he insisted that the death
of ten thousand workers would be a much greater loss to France than that of
ten thousand noblemen and members of the royal family. In 1821–22 he
published *l'Industriel*, a work dedicated to industrialists, in which he
proclaimed that he wrote for the managers and against the courtiers, for the
bees and against the hornets.

In vain, and quite naively, he appealed to Louis XVIII for support. A few
idealistic young men admired him, but public reaction to his work was
weak, and he despaired of the success of his ideas. The valet who had
supported him died and he was forced to live almost entirely on alms. In a
fit of depression, he tried to commit suicide (1823) but only managed to
hurt one of his eyes. He lived two more years, just long enough to see the
publication of his *Nouveau Christianisme*. In this last work he proposed the
creation of a social-sentimental religion with a global hierarchic organization based on brotherly love.

This book was the most influential among the "Saint-Simonists," above
all for a man called Barthélémy Prosper Enfantin. Based on Saint-Simon's
ideas, Enfantin, together with Armand Bazard, founded an organization
which published *Le Producteur* and later controlled *Le Globe*. At this point,
the rather odd ideas of Saint-Simon developed in the direction of real
madness. The crazy radicalism that characterized the French Revolution—
beginning with Rousseau's nature worship and ending with a utopianism
totally alien to nature—now demonstrated its full dynamism. Whoever
wanted to establish utopia had to change, to reform, to rebuild—to smash
existing forms.

Barthélémy Enfantin did not intend to decree total equality of wealth.
His goal was the destruction of the family. To this end he wanted to do away
with inheritance; that is, allow only the state to inherit. The Steering
Committee of the Neo-Saint-Simonists that met in Paris and published
l'Organisateur did not divulge the entire program of the New Theocracy,
which was to be administrated by a brand new type of priest. But it did
reveal that the priests would run an agency to control production. On
religious matters, the new "theology" advocated by Enfantin accused
Christianity of having retarded humanity by its dualism of flesh and spirit
and preached instead the "Emancipation of the Flesh."

The revolution of 1830 gave new impetus to these weird teachings, and

Enfantin's *Economic Politique* created a minor sensation among the more literate representatives of the working class. *Le Globe* was now published under the title *Journal de la doctrine de Saint-Simon*, and since the organization was represented in most of the leading cities of France, Enfantin had himself declared "Le Père," "The Father," head of the Saint-Simonist Church of Tomorrow. He began openly to preach total promiscuity (his version of the "Emancipation of the Flesh"), but Bazard disagreed and a schism resulted. In the summer of 1832 Enfantin established some sort of monastery at Menilmontant with forty-odd members who donned weird-looking habits and worked collectively in the fields of the estate. But the police intervened, and Enfantin was brought to court and the "family" dissolved. The provincial centers were also liquidated. Thus the first phase of ideological-practical French socialism came to an end.

Another forerunner of romantic socialism (aside from Morelly and Babeuf) was J. P. Brissott de Warville, later the leader of the Girondists and one of the many genuine links between democracy and socialism. As far back as 1780 he opined that owning property was the equivalent of theft; people should have an income sufficient to cover normal living expenses, and no more.[286]

The Abbé de Mably, whose real name was Gabriel de Bonnot and who was the brother of the philosopher Etienne Bonnot de Condillac, was yet another precursor of socialism and communism. The Abbé was invited in 1771 to visit Poland with Rousseau to draft a new constitution for the Polish Commonwealth. He was born in 1709 in Grenoble and died in 1785 leaving a number of works that enthusiastically championed the cause of democracy and socialism.

Gabriel Bonnot de Mably was a priest for the sake of convenience (as was his more famous younger brother). But as Spengler has pointed out, there have been a profusion of priests in leftist movements (Spengler called them *Priesterpöbel*). Just as monasticism "suggests" socialism, so too, to the more naive mind, does Christianity itself. Socialism and communism (the fulfillment of socialism) take their *initial* inspiration from basic Christian tenets. Universal brotherhood, altruism, mutual aid, social justice, all-pervading charity, humility-in-equality—all these notions have Christian roots, a Christian background. But *corruptio optimi pessima*! Due to a common source and ensuing confusions, "left Catholicism" and "left Protestantism" have sprung up, fanatical isms whose errors, deviations, and transgressions must be understood in the light of this Christian root. It is not surprising that Beatrice Webb (Lady Passfield), one of the great Fabian apologists for the USSR, was an enthusiastic admirer of monasteries.

The temptation to inject Christian precepts into the practical order so naively that they become self-defeating is especially great in a society where Christian trends have a sentimental and historic basis. Socialism and communism, though able to invade areas with no Christian tradition, could have sprouted only from civilizations with a strong Christian background. Not only the ethical content of Christianity, but its imagery and doctrine foster socialism. In the socialist utopia, a day of judgment will come when the humble will be exalted and the rich and mighty brutally dispossessed. [287] The utopians paint a picture of paradise lost—and regained: of a new age of innocence, of peace and brotherly love, with envy, crime, and hatred banished forever. [288]

Of course, this "Edenism" can be found in democracy, which, like nudism, is a conscious-subconscious effort to recreate paradise. Democracy uses the magic formula, "We are not ruled, we rule ourselves," to relativize the state—the painful result of Original Sin[289] —just as nudism tries to solve the sexual problem by shedding clothes.

Christian imagery is important in the socialist-communist vision, with its accent on saving the world through the proletariat. But so too is the glaring misinterpretation of Christ and early Christianity. Unfortunately, the Christian churches are not entirely innocent in this respect. In Christian folklore, the Saviour appears as the Son of the humble carpenter, the poor Boy from a lowly family, born in the stable and venerated by the Magi as He lies among domestic animals. He is the simple Man who talked to uneducated fishermen and associated primarily with the indigent. Early Christianity, furthermore, is presented as a movement of the outcasts of the Roman Empire, of slaves, paupers, and illiterates, a proletarian movement which—according to communist doctrine—was taken over by the high and mighty who proceeded to exploit and lull the masses into subservience by offering them salvation in the hereafter. Which led easily to Marx's formula: "Religion is the opium of the people."

The most obvious mistake concerns the beloved picture of the Magi in front of the manger. Scripture tells us clearly (Math. 2:11) that they entered a house, probably the house of Joseph and Mary. As for the "Son of the carpenter," *tekton* in Greek means carpenter but also house-builder, architect, contractor. Joseph, moreover, was not an "ordinary Jew," but as a descendant of David he was of royal blood and, therefore, in the eyes of his compatriots, a potential heir to the Throne of Judea. The angel characteristically addressed him as "son of David." (Christ too was addressed as "Son of David" [for instance, in Math. 20:31; Mark 10:48; Luke 18:38] and had to flee to avoid being proclaimed king [John 6:15]. He made his position clear: "My kingdom is not of this world." Yet when Pilate asked Him whether He was a king, Christ answered in the affirmative.) As for the Virgin Mary, she was the niece or grandniece of Zacharias and Elizabeth, both Aaronites and therefore of the priestly caste; thus she also belonged to the highest Jewish social layer, and, like her spouse, was of Davidic descent. (Gabriel reaffirmed this royal descent in his words to the Virgin.) Although Joseph and Mary were *probably* not rich, they still rated very high socially. Joseph must also have been a landowner in Bethlehem, the Davidic village, which explains why he had to be there for the census.[290]

Our Lord certainly did not concentrate on the proletariat or on the illiterate in His teaching years. Peter seems to have been head man of a group of fishermen. John, the most beloved disciple, obviously was an intellectual of the first order (as was Paul later on), and the other Evangelists certainly belonged to the educated classes. Nor did Our Lord shun the company of the rich.[291]

The notion that Christianity was a religion of outcasts in the Roman Empire, as maintained by Friedrich Engels, is totally erroneous. One need only peruse the Roman Missal and note the social background of the early martyrs to see that Christians could be found in all layers of society—among the families of the emperor and senators, among patricians, intellectuals, and actors. Nor can anyone maintain that the early Fathers of the Church were mostly simpleminded illiterates. Ignatius of Antioch, Tatian, Justin, Origen, Tertullian, Cyprian, Clement of Rome, Lactantius, Minucius Felix, Clement of Alexandria, Polycarp of Smyrna, Irenaeus, and Novatian were first-rate spiritual men—certainly not "social reformers." The picture of a religion of slaves undermining an aristocratic-heroic commonwealth is totally unhistorical.[292] One has only to read Adolf von Harnacks' *Militia Christi* to realize how well entrenched Christianity was in the Roman army. But a certain breed of "conservatives" with a pagan-heroic outlook—such as Winston S. Churchill, and Maurras, to some extent—is always prone to see Christianity as a weak, unmanly, and self-pitying faith. The antics of certain Christian leftists only confirm this view.

Yet it has a powerful effect as a myth. There are good Christians who believe that a rich man is bound to be bad; a rich man, rather, ought not become enslaved by his wealth, he ought to be "poor in spirit," *ptochos to pneumati*. Rarely pondered is the possibility that a wealthy man might in fact not serve Mammon, while a man of fewer material goods might struggle desperately to achieve them, and thereby neglect his spiritual life. Nobody will deny that the rich man who gives away his possessions liberally in a spirit of charity is acting virtuously. But is poverty *in itself* sanctifying? Is laziness with resulting poverty more admirable than the industry and thrift that produce material well-being? Hardly.

Yet in today's Christian world, with many Catholics and Evangelical Christians suffused in romanticism, there is not only a wholesome readiness to live a life of poverty, but also a tendency to worship the poor—the agrarian pauper and above all the "proleterian." Curiously enough the socialist sentiment in Christendom is nourished by this weird romantic enthusiasm—an oddity, because socialism and communism *hate* poverty. Socialism indeed is opposed to it. It copies from monasticism the idea of collective work, of a regulated life, of obedience and sobriety, of "mutualism" and equality. It *hopes*, however, to eliminate poverty, to achieve general material well-being.

The grim fact remains that some Christians will always cast longing glances at the socialist camp, sincerely regretting that Marxism is by its very nature atheistic.[293] They dream of a "Christian communism," of the possiblity of transforming dialectic materialism by "baptizing" the concept of a collective society. Communism operates on the notion of the "dictatorship of the proletariat" (i.e., of the party); and so-called "democratic socialism"[294] wants to achieve the same end by peaceful, democratic means. If 51 (or 99) percent vote for socialism, the rest (49 or only 1 percent) have to go along. The genuine democrat has no difficulty with this, for, according to Locke's thesis, "Right is what the majority wills—what the majority wills is right."[295]

The tendency in our ecumenical age is to open up dialogues not only with and among the various Christian faiths, but with every imaginable body of thought, to show a readiness to learn from everybody, and to compromise wherever and whenever compromise is possible—or impossible. (So far nobody has offered to start a fruitful dialogue with the National Socialists and other advocates of genocide—so far!)

The strong trend in our age to use Christian tenets, knowingly or unknowingly, to justify a reconciliation with leftism, can be found, unsurprisingly, in bygone centuries. The above pages have mentioned Saint-Simon and his *Nouveau Christianisme*, and his secretary of many years, August Comte, the founder of positivism, who dreamed of a completely secular Catholic Church. But there was a distinctly non-Christian competitor of Saint-Simon in the ancestral gallery of early socialist thought, yet another Frenchman, François Charles Marie Fourier.

Born in 1772, son of a small manufacturer, Fourier survived Saint-Simon by twelve years. He surprised the public with his first work in 1808, his *Théorie des quatres mouvements*. His vision was rather different from Saint-

Simon's. The blueprint he proposed for a socialist society was based on his monomaniacal notion of *harmony*, which he saw as a crucial human drive. Numbers and geometric notions played a decisive part in his utopia where the arbitrary was curiously mingled with the prophetic, and odd rationalizations alternated with dreams of utter unreality—tendencies and propensities that increased in him as he grew older.

Fourier wanted to divide humanity into groups of 1,600 people, the *phalanges* which were to live in monastery-like buildings called *phalanstères* (reminiscent of Morelly's jointly housed "tribes"). Economically each of these units was to be self-sufficient; each was to have its fields and workshops. As in the case of Saint-Simon's utopian reveries, Fourier's visionary elements combined with pure rationalism to form weird blueprints. Since madness is very often a combination of cold reason and fantasy severed from all reality, Fourier evinced madness in a pure form. Surprisingly, or perhaps not so surprisingly, the response to his ideas was considerable.[296] Although all efforts to realize his dreams failed—repeated attempts were made on both sides of the Atlantic—followers of Fourier existed in all countries, in Russia no less than in the United States.

Fourier's writings betray a truly sick mind, far more removed from sanity than Saint-Simon's. Fourier's utopianism worked both ways: "constructively" in planning for the future, retrospectively in explaining and expounding a totally unreal past. His descriptions of the earth's past were entirely imaginary. He assumed that the earth had another satellite named Phoebe which in the dim past had fallen on our globe. The ensuing destruction and confusion helped bring 150 new species of snakes and forty-three new races of bedbugs into existence. His views of life on the planets were equally interesting. He insisted that the inhabitants of planets, the *solariens*, who lived on or around the sun, had a physical organ not found in the *terriens*, the inhabitants of the earth. This member had the following properties: protection in falling, power in defense, splendor in ornamentation, with gigantic strength, a remarkable dexterity, and the cooperation and support of all bodily movements. From his description it sounded like a sort of trunk or tail, and his enemies used his own words to lampoon the *solariens* in delightful cartoons.

As for our history, he divided it in the following way:

A. Periods Anterior to History
   1. Bastards, no human beings
   2. Primitive, called Paradise
   3. Savagery or inertia

B. Divided Industry: repulsive
1. Patriarchalism with small industry
2. Barbarism with middle-size industry
3. Civilization with big industry
C. United Industry: attractive
1. Guaranteeism: half-association
2. Sociantism: simple association
3. Harmonism: full association

The final goal was "harmony"—the earth divided into a number of completely peaceful empires with monarchical rather than republican constitutions,[297] without total equality and with a slight difference in income (according to a key granting percentages for capital investment, work, and "talent"). These sixty-odd empires had small "armies" working together in large economic and technological projects. Sexual life was finally freed from all shackles; free unions were formed and abandoned every day.

The true social unit was the "*phalanstère*," in which the most intensive social life took place. People slept from 10:00 P.M. to 3:00 A.M. At three they washed and dressed to make the assembly by four. There the chronicle of the night was read to satisfy everyone's curiousity as to who shared what bed with whom. Half an hour later the "délite," the first meal, was eaten, followed by the "industrial parade." A shooting and hunting party was organized for 5:00 A.M. At seven fishing began. Breakfast was from eight to nine, at which time the newspapers were distributed and read; at ten there was divine service. Then came a break, during which the people watched the pheasants, until eleven, which was library time. Dinner was at 1:00 P.M., after which people repaired to the hothouses, to the exotic plants, and to the fish ponds until six when they enjoyed a champagne party, followed by a visit to the merino sheep. At eight the "phalansterians" marched to the stock exchange. Supper was at nine, followed by music and dancing until bedtime at ten.

This daily timetable tells the story—the unrealism of a man who believed that five hours of sleep was a good average and that a two-hour workday—as fun!—could be wedged in here and there. Religion was not eliminated: Fourier believed that God had endowed man with passions, but not with reason, which was a purely human and ungodly inclination. And in spite of his socialism, he was not an egalitarian. He would not even have objected to titles in his *phalanstères* so long as they did not handicap brotherliness and human harmony. These rested on the free interplay of the

passions which should not be resisted, merely "harnessed." (The influence
of Saint-Simon is not certain, but Rousseau's is obvious.)

Unlike the later "scientific" socialists, Fourier was a real epicurean. He
not only envisioned sexual libertinism (as found in Campanella and Saint-
Simon) but had a marked penchant for the joys of the palate and stomach—
joys which somehow would not impair the health of the *harmoniens*
scheduled to live at least 150 years. Fourier planned to have semiculinary,
semimedical specialists, the *gastrosophes*, to supervise the alimentation.
"The *gastrosophes* thus become unofficial doctors for each individual, protectors of his health by means of pleasure. It should be their ambition to see to
it that each *phalanstère* become well known for its appetite and the enormity
of its food consumption."[298] Altogether a rather French vision.

Of course there would be a uniform type of school with an identical basic
education for everybody, while not overeducating those children who
preferred to develop their bodies. (Instincts and passions were of course
better guides than idle ratiocination.) On the other hand, the penchant of
children to band together would be fostered assiduously. Fourier proposed
the establishment of delightful organizations such as the *petites bandes*,
consisting of two-thirds little girls and one-third boys, and the *petites
hordes*, with an inverse ratio of the sexes. The predominantly masculine
petites hordes would be dressed in Tartar costumes, all of different colors so
that from a distance they would look like a "well-mixed field of tulips."

For the *petites bandes* our great visionary reserved the task of controlling
the language. People with bad accents and bad grammar would be persecuted by this largely female horde. If anybody fell below the standard set
for the universal language, he would receive from the chancellery of the
petites bandes a list of his errors and be exhorted not to repeat them.

Smaller children would be trained as scavengers (because of their natural
inclination to play with dirt), thus keeping the *phalanstère* in perfect order.
Adolescents, according to their sexual activity, would be divided into *vestels*
and *vestales*, leading a continent life, while *damoiseaux* and *damoiselles* were
those who opted for more tantalizing sexual behavior.

All of this—life in the *phalanstère*—was only a part of Fourier's grandiose view of the future. The enormous work-armies of the age of harmony
would engage in huge enterprises. They would pierce the Isthmus of Suez
and of Panama, they would transform the Sahara into fertile land, they
would perfume the Arctic Ocean. (All in a two-hour workday!) Most
interesting were the plans to create (through careful cross-breeding) animals such as the "antilion," a superb, docile, "elastic" quadruped, which

would transport its rider in almost no time from one corner of France to the other. Starting in the morning from Calais, one might lunch in Paris and dine in Marseilles. The animal would be about three times the size of our own miserable lions and would cover eight yards with every step. "It would be a pleasure to live in this world if one could enjoy such wonderful service,"[299] observed Fourier wistfully.

Indeed it would, since even the hardest work would be sheer delight. Take farming, for instance. "We would see all these active groups well distributed over a beautiful valley, well housed in colored tents, working in separate groups, moving about with flags and instruments, and singing hymns in chorus. Then we would behold the whole canton spotted with castles and rural palaces with columns and turrets instead of huts covered with straw. Would we not believe that this is an enchanted landscape, a country of fairies, an olympic dwelling place?"[300]

The pleasure of these visions overpowered Fourier. "He who has seen the interior galleries of a *phalanstère* will consider the most beautiful palace to be merely a place of exile, a manor for idiots who after three thousand years of experimenting with architecture have still not learned to house themselves in a healthy and comfortable way."[301]

These visions—most of them quite detailed—fill hundreds of pages. Why, then, are the musings of an unbalanced man of any interest except to a psychologist or a psychiatrist? The fact is, they are of considerable importance. Fourierism is a crucial stage not only in the gradually unfolding history of socialism and communism, but also in the development of leftist thought in the United States. The chasm beween the early utopian socialists and the scientific socialists of a later period is not so great as the latter would like us to believe. The psychological foundations are practically the same; only the intellectual "superstructure" is different.

Friedrich Engels in his *Anti-Dühring* praised Fourier very highly, especially for his attitude toward women and for the skill with which he "managed" dialectics. In this, Engels likened him to Hegel, Fourier's contemporary.

In the revolutionary movements of 1848–49, Victor Considérant, Fourier's leading disciple, played a key part as an aide to the great demagogue Ledru-Rollin. Considérant was a former student of the *École Polytechnique* and became editor of *La Phalange* after Fourier's death. He managed to persuade a rich Englishman to finance a *phalanstère* in Condé-sur-Vègre in central France. It collapsed and with it *La Phalange*. But the paper was replaced with another, *La dèmocratie pacifique*. During these years Considérant published a number of books, the majority of them almost as fantastic and as remote from reality as those of his mentor. He was elected to the National Assembly in 1848 and again in 1849. Since he sided with what was then called *La Montagne*, he had to flee to Belgium.[302] From there he went to Texas where he founded another *phalanstère*, called *La Réunion*, near San Antonio.[303] This project also failed. In 1869 Considérant was permitted to return to France where he died in 1893 at the age of eighty-five.

It was not from its Texas roots that Fourierism came to affect American intellectuals, but rather via George Ripley and Brook Farm, which began as an experiment of the New England Transcendentalists. Its original purpose was to combine manual labor and intellectual life into an ideal example of collective living. The Transcendentalists, moreover, had a certain antirational bent and leaned toward "intuitivism." All in all, the influence of monastic ideals (in spite of their Unitarian background) was very obvious, the secular-sentimental imitation of the monastery quite apparent. It was probably not accidental that the founder of the Paulists, Father Isaac Hecker, was connected with Brook Farm in his pre-Catholic days: a rare example of an evolution back to the original (and healthy) source of a concept. (Evolution in the opposite direction is far more frequent.)[304]

In 1845, under the influence of Fourierism, George Ripley transformed Brook Farm into a *phalanstère*, but a year later the unfinished main building burned down, and by the end of 1847 the whole experiment had come to an end. Still, Brook Farm had many friends and supporters, inmates and sympathizers: Ralph Waldo Emerson (who favored it from a distance), Francis J. Barlow, Charles A. Dana, James Russell Lowell, William H. Channing, Elizabeth Palmer Peabody, Margaret Fuller, and Horace Greeley's *New York Tribune*, a most respectable daily and the forerunner of the *New York Herald Tribune*. After Greeley and Ripley, Arthur Brisbane[305] was the most active in promulgating Fourier's ideas. He organized the North American Phalanx in New Jersey which soon failed. (A Wisconsin Phalanx met the same fate.)

Meanwhile, Fourierism, as evidenced by Dostoyevski's *The Possessed*, also had a marked influence on the Russian Left, the precursors of bolshevism. Even Alexander I in his earlier, leftist period (prior to 1812) was a reader of Fourier. Byelinski too was profoundly impressed by Fourier,[306] and, not unexpectedly, Alexander Herzen who, however, saw in him and in Saint-Simon merely the forerunners of the real socialist ideology of tomorrow.[307]

Fourier also made a deep impression on Nikolay Gavrilovitch Chernyshevski, son of a priest whose novel *What to do?*[308] stands at the very beginning of the intellectual and emotional trends that led almost directly to bolshevism in Russia. There is only one cleverly masked reference to Victor Considerant's *La destinée sociale* in this highly programmatic novel, but Fourierism is evident throughout. (The attitude toward female emancipation, the theory that delight in work is rendered disagreeable only through "circumstances" are typical of Fourier). Yet another avid reader of Fourier was Peter Lavrov, a nobleman and revolutionary who lived mostly in exile in France.

Thus, clear for all to see, raving madness was at the cradle of the revolutionary movement that led to Red October and the terrible ensuing events; its weird, dark specter is with us yet.[309]

CHAPTER 9

From Romantic to Scientific and International Socialism

> *Capitalism is the uneven distribution*
> *of wealth, and socialism the even*
> *distribution of poverty.*
>
> —WINSTON S. CHURCHILL

Fourierism in France was eclipsed by the rise of a man with a clearer and deeper socialist mind than Fourier's, a man who, unfortunately for us, was overshadowed in turn by Karl Marx. His name was Pierre Joseph Proudhon, and like Fourier, he was a native of Besançon. Whereas Fourier's father was a shopkeeper of certain means, Proudhon's father came from a "proletarian" milieu. Pierre Joseph nevertheless succeeded in getting a good education in a *collège*[310] where he was taught Latin and Greek, later supplemented with Hebrew. He soon lost his Faith and became influenced by socialistic ideas, but in time he revolted against the mad speculations and prophecies of Fourier and his disciple Considérant whom he attacked in pamphlets.

Proudhon became the first truly methodical and scientific socialist thinker, yet unlike his bitter opponent, Karl Marx, he always kept—even in his "atheism"—a certain human and metaphysical outlook.[311] He was, in a way, an atheist tormented by doubts, and toward the end of his life he fought bitterly against the fanaticism of antireligious haters. His socialism was distributist rather than collectivist; the key word to his economic thinking is "mutualism." He was strongly opposed to economic liberalism because he feared bigness—the concentration of wealth, mammoth enterprises—yet he was equally an enemy of the omnipotent centralized state, which is at the root of most leftist thinking.

Proudhon's numerous books are full of notions and ideas that any true lover of liberty or any true conservative could underwrite, concepts that are part and parcel of the "arsenal" of rightist thought. He belonged to that not so rare category of theorists who, given the right contacts, the right friends, and the right ambiance could have overcome the magnetism of the Left.

In his *Confessions of a Revolutionary* Proudhon says that it "is surprising to observe how constantly we find all our political questions complicated by theology."[312] And, in fact, he never entirely divorced himself from his theological outlook. He always remained a healthy antistatist and a convinced antidemocrat. Indeed, one of the leading contemporary Catholic theologicans, Henri de Lubac, S.J., wrote a profound study on *Proudhon et le christianisme.*[313] Constantin Frantz, the great German conservative, could not hide his admiration for Proudhon. He only regretted having to cite a "French radical" since Germany, the classic country of thinkers, had become intellectually sterile.[314] Proudhon was himself convinced that France was the nation of "golden mediocrity."[315]

The few passages cited below give at least a vague idea of that part of Proudhon's mind that was bound to conflict with his later socialist outlook—dictatorial, centralizing, and "democratic."

The February Revolution replaced the system of voting by "classes":[316] democratic Puritanism still was not satisfied. Some wanted the vote given to children and women. Others protested against the exclusion of financial defaulters, released jailbirds, and prisoners. One wonders that they did not demand the inclusion of horses and donkeys.[317]

Democracy is the idea of the state without limits.[318]

Money, money, always money—this is the crux (*le nerf*) of democracy.[319]

Democracy is more expensive than monarchy; it is incompatible with liberty.[320]

Democracy is nothing but tyranny of the majorities, the most execrable tyranny of all because it rests neither on the authority of a religion, nor on the nobility of race, nor on the prerogatives of talent or property. Its foundation is numbers and its mask is the name of the people.[321]

Democracy is an aristocracy of mediocrities.[322]

Authority, which in monarchy is the principle of the governing activity, is in democracy the aim of the government.[323]

The people, thanks to their inferiority and their misery, will always form the army of liberty and progress—but due to their ignorance and the primitiveness of their instinct, as a result of the urgency of their needs and the impatience of their desires, they incline toward simple forms of authority. What they are looking for are by no means legal guarantees of which they have no concrete notions nor any realization of their power . . . they have faith in a leader whose intentions are known to them. . . . To such a leader they accord authority without limits and irresistible power. . . . The people do not believe in principles which alone could save them: they lack the "religion of ideas."[324]

Democracy is, in fact, essentially militaristic.[325]

Every state is by its very nature "annexationist."[326]

Left to themselves or led by a tribune, the masses will never accomplish anything. They have their faces turned to the past. No tradition is formed among them . . . about politics they understand nothing but intrigues, about the government only waste and sheer force; of justice only the accusations; of liberty only the erection of idols which are destroyed the next day. The rise of democracy starts an era of backwardness that will lead nation and state to their death.[327]

Accept in a manly way the situation in which you are and convince yourself once and for all that the happiest of men is the one who knows best how to be poor.[328]

My views on the family are not unlike those of the ancient Roman law. The father of the family is to me a sovereign . . . I consider all our dreams about the emancipation of women to be destructive and stupid.[329]

When we say "the People" we always unavoidably mean the least progressive part of society, the most ignorant, the most cowardly, the most ungrateful.[330]

If democracy is reason, then it ought to represent above all *demopedy*, "education of the people."[331]

The twentieth century is going to open up a period of federation, or humanity will enter a purgatory of a thousand years.[332]

In view of the above, it was inevitable that this man of the people, largely self-educated but possessed of a certain earthly wisdom, would clash with a man whose mind was strangely divorced from reality, who was a fervent hater, an illusionist, but at the same time a skilled demagogue— Karl Marx. These two men, even though they shared a claim to the label "socialist," were temperamentally poles apart. Proudhon, in spite of his anticlericalism (which abated toward the end of his life) was deeply imbued with Christian moral principles.[333] He led an exemplary pure and studious life and made every sacrifice for his ideas,[334] always guided by deep and lasting affections.

In 1846, Proudhon published a book, *Système des contradictions économiques ou Philosophie de la misère*, which precipitated the clash with Marx. The bourgeois from Trier furiously assailed Proudhon in a savage writ, *La Misère de la philosophie*. Proudhon and Marx both dreamed of a "withering away of the state." Marx sought to fulfill his ideas by revolutionary means, by the use of brute force, by the "dictatorship of the proletariat." Proudhon, on the other hand, was an "evolutionist": the right order of things should be *discovered*, not arbitrarily blueprinted. Socialism should come gradually, in stages, without upheavals, by persuasion: it should encompass the globe through voluntary consent of the people and finally unite mankind, not under one centralized superstate, but in a federal system—by federations deeply rooted in local customs, institutions, and traditions. De Lubac points to Proudhon's sentimental attachment to the part of France in which he was born and reared—the Franche Comté, which had been under Spanish rule for a long time and where an attachment to *personal liberty* was particularly strong.

When the savage and perhaps not unexpected attack from Marx came, Proudhon did not reply. This sensitive and noble man probably considered it beneath his dignity to react to that boorish piece of writing. Although Proudhon could rise to great heights of enthusiasm, although he was the man who had coined the term "scientific socialism," he had none of the bitter unbending dogmatism of Karl Marx. Had Proudhon retained leadership of the socialist movement, he would have stamped it with a more anarchical, "personalistic" character, a greater plasticity and humaneness. The Western world would have coped with it more easily. Instead, Karl Marx prevailed with the rigid, secular monasticism that was to plunge civilization into abysmal misery. Daniel Halévy wrote quite rightly that "there was a place for a great dialogue between the two men: Marx, the protagonist of the revolution of the proletarian masses, and Proudhon, the champion of the personalist revolution. The dialogue foundered and Marx is to blame for it, because the tone he gave to it right in the beginning rendered the expected discussions impossible."[335]

Who was this Karl Marx, source of so much evil for the past three generations? He was born in 1818 into the famiy of a Jewish lawyer in the old bishopric of Trier, a subject of King Frederick William III, the Congress of Vienna having allotted the Rhenish bishoprics to Prussia. When he was six years old his father embraced the Lutheran faith of the new Prussian master rather than the Catholic religion of the area, whether for religious or social reasons is unclear. The entire family gradually followed suit. But, interestingly, as soon as little Karl was able to read, he studied, together with his father, the works of Voltaire—not precisely an atheist but certainly a scoffer of orthodox Christianity. After finishing his *Gymnasium* (the classical high school and college), he studied law and philosophy at the Universities of Bonn and Berlin. He wrote a dissertation on Epicurus, whose philosophy has a decidedly materialistic flavor, for the University of Jena where he received his Ph.D.

In Berlin young Marx became strongly influenced by Hegel and his school. It is interesting to analyze the emotional as well as the intellectual development of the young Marx. His relations with his mother were bad; he truly hated her. But he somewhat admired her relative Lionel Philips, whose family founded the worldwide industrial empire in Eindhoven (NORELCO in the United States is part of it). Karl's relations with his father, on the other hand, were intimate; he always carried a picture of his father, which, at his death, Engels placed in his coffin. His father, nevertheless, fully understood his son's weaknesses, such as his expenditures of large sums of money (for purposes as yet not determined). When he wrote to his father that he was a "torn" (*zerrissene*) person, his father replied, "To be quite candid, my dear Karl, I do not like this modern word which serves as a cloak for weaklings who are at odds with the world because they cannot own, without effort and toil, beautifully furnished palaces, vast fortunes, and elegant carriages. This 'tornness' [*Zerrissenheit*] to me is disgusting, and I expect it least of all from you. What reasons can you have for it?" [336] The reasons were the precocious young man's mad ambitions combined with the sometimes unwholesome influence of German romanticism. Professor Ernst Kux reminds that Marx, who by no means had a "scientific mind" in his younger years, belonged to the *mainstream of German romanticism*. He always "felt" first and then looked for "scientific proof of his emotions." [337]

Young Marx, who has considerable appeal for the New Left, knew Bettina von Arnim and Arnold Ruge and was a close friend of Heinrich Heine. But the latter soon found him intolerable. He called Marx a *docteur en révolution* and a "godless self-god."[338] Yet young Marx was basically an artist, or at least a would-be artist, who wrote mediocre poetry and planned to publish a theatrical review. The nonfulfillment of his dreams made him a revolutionary. And here there emerges a strong analogy with Hitler: the frustrated artist who wants to destroy the world which does not appreciate him. Understandable, surely, for art is creation, and a man not permitted to create is thoroughly thwarted. For Marx, artistic activity was the very essence of human activity.[339] His great dream was a communist society where the "rich and profound all-around person is not restricted to an exclusive domain of action, but can develop himself in every branch, where society regulates general production and makes it possible for him to do this today and that tomorrow, to hunt in the morning, to fish at noon, to do some stock-farming in the evening, to engage in criticisms after meals, just as he feels inclined—without ever becoming a hunter, a fisherman, a shepherd, or a critic."[340] Marx's thinking can here be clearly traced to the ideas of Fourier, to his utopianism and his dreams of an earthly paradise.

At the same time, Marx became increasingly Promethean in his visions. He replaced God with man, and the notion of the *Übermensch*, the superman, began to appear in his writings.[341] Needless to say, all this is a far cry from Leninism, far more akin to the New Left. Yet the purely artistic vein, his interest in art (like Hitler's), never entirely disappeared. Marx always remained an aesthete,[342] yet his thinking and writing showed no preoccupation with ethics. He felt that a person could not be held responsible for historical processes that came about automatically as a result of scientific laws. (Such reflections were typical of a later period of his life.)[343] "The Communists preach no morality,"[344] he insisted. All morality leads to ideology, and ideology leads, not to tragedy, but to comedy. Any philosopher, he maintained, who preached a system of ethics would be childish enough to believe that a different conscience could change the order of things.[345] (Yet how could this be if the historic process is preordained and immutable?)

Originally Marx thought to enter upon an academic career and applied for an extraordinary professorship at the University of Bonn. His friends, however, dissuaded him, and in 1842 (at the age of twenty-four) he became editor-in-chief of the *Rheinische Zeitung* in Cologne. A year later the daily was suppressed by government order and Marx, undaunted by this failure, married Jenny von Westphalen. (Ladies of noble blood play a major role in almost all socialist movements. There is probably a deep psychological reason for this phenomenon.)[346] Marx, initially at least, undoubtedly loved his wife and his daughters dearly, but he was basically not only a critic and a scoffer, but also a hater, as witness his treatment of Proudhon. Arnold Ruge, with whom he collaborated (before falling out with him in Paris) wrote to Fröbel that "gnashing his teeth and with a grin Marx would slaughter all those who got in the way of this new Babeuf. He always *thinks* about this feast which he cannot *celebrate*."[347]

Yet the key to Karl Marx's personality is his poetry which, to a very large extent, consists of volcanic eruptions of hatred strewn with expressions of abounding megalomia. One of his poems ends with the bitter line, "we apes of a cold god." The statuette of an ape, brooding over a skull, sits on one of Darwin's books in Lenin's reconstructed study. (It is a gift of Armand Hammer.)

The best description of Marx in his thirtieth year came from Carl Schurz, the German-born American senator who met him in Cologne at a public session of democratic leagues and wrote in his *Lebenserinnerungen*: "The stocky, heavily built man with his broad forehead, with pitch-black hair and full beard, attracted general attention. . . . What Marx said was indeed substantial, logical and clear. But never did I meet a man of such offensive arrogance in his demeanor. No opinion deviating in principle from his own would he give the slightest consideration. Anybody who contradicted him was treated with hardly veiled contempt. Every argument which he happened to dislike was answered either with biting mockery about the pitiful display of ignorance or with defamatory suspicions as to the motives of the interpellator. I still well remember the sneering tone with which he spat out the word *bourgeois*. And as *bourgeois*, that is to say, as an example of a profound intellectual and moral depravity, he denounced anybody who dared to contradict his views."[348]

Marx, who as an educated German was fully conversant with French, transferred his residence late in 1843 to Paris, where he expected greater liberty under Louis-Philippe than in the Rhineland dominated by Prussians. With Arnold Ruge he started to publish the *German-French Yearbooks*, but after the the first issue the editors quarrelled and the periodical folded. While in France Marx broke with orthodox Hegelianism, retaining only Hegel's concept of the dialectic process of history. Here too he met with Proudhon, received his first communications from Engels, and wrote his first bitterly hostile essay on the Jews. Marx nurtured a real hatred for the Jews, in whom he saw the very embodiment of bourgeois capitalism.[349] But his prejudice had a racist as well as a sociological character.

Perhaps his anti-Semitism could partly be traced to Bruno Bauer, a

Lutheran theologian, one of the originators of biblical criticism, and a friend of Marx's younger years. Bauer's views showed a marked anti-Jewish bias. A Hegelian in his philosophical outlook, Bauer incurred Marx's hatred after the latter broke with Hegel's philosophy. As a result, together with Engels, Marx wrote one of his most venomous pamphlets: *The Holy Family Against Bruno Bauer and Company*. Engels was one of the few people with whom Marx was able to maintain a lasting friendship. (Unfriendly remarks about Engels in his correspondence were eliminated by his daughters. He had three, two of whom committed suicide.) This wealthy manufacturer from the Ruhr valley also had sufficient funds to support the penurious cofounder of international socialism and communism. Lenin's "useful idiots" thus existed long before Lenin.

The materialism of Ludwig Feuerbach made the deepest and most lasting impression on both Marx and Engels, and it hastened their break with German idealism. Feuerbach's criticism of religion in general and of Christianity in particular, combined with a violent materialism ("*Der Mensch ist, was er isst*"—"Man is what he eats") laid the foundation for Marx's unwavering rejection and hatred of all religions. Feuerbach's notion that culture and education can and should supplant religion bears a rather German and romantic tinge, but his idea that the readiness to "believe" must be replaced with the readiness to "will" points to the direction in which Marx and Engels were also moving. Morality, Feuerbach insisted, would never be sustained by religion, but only by an *improvement in living conditions*—in other words, by "social betterment."

This concept became typically Marxist, and it is currently shared by the American moderate Left, if not by American folklore. After all, the great consolation of so many in this vale of tears is the childlike belief in the automatic character of progress. Herein too the fulfillment of Dostoyevski's prophecy (through the mouth of his "Grand Inquisitor" in *The Brothers Karamazov*) that the time will come when science and the sages will proclaim no more criminals and and no more sinners—only hungry people will continue to exist. In popular terms this means "poverty. . . . Poverty breeds socialism: If people have not enough to eat, they will develop a 'communism of the stomach.' " But this was just another fallacy. And while Marx learned from Feuerbach only through books and articles, he established direct contact in Paris with disciples of Saint-Simon as well as with the count's former secretary, Auguste Comte, the father of positivism. Comte's effort to explain social laws by the laws of nature (which are not the "natural law") also left a permanent imprint on Marx's thinking.

In 1845 the Prussian government asked the French to expel Marx as a dangerous agitator, and the French complied. Thus he went to Brussels where in 1847 he published his pamphlet attacking Proudhon. In 1848, together with Engels, he issued the *Communist Manifesto*. A month later he was asked by the Belgian authorities to leave Brussels, whereupon he returned with Engels to a Paris seething with revolution during which Louis-Philippe was overthrown. From Paris the pair went to the Rhineland, to Cologne, where the revolutionary fervor reached a high pitch. There Marx published a daily paper, *Die Neue Rheinische Zeitung* with the subtitle *Demokratisches Organ*. In November the paper advised its readers not to pay taxes and, moreover, incited them to engage in armed resistance against the Prussian government, which had dissolved the National Assembly. Thereupon the newspaper was confiscated and Marx was arrested and tried, but subsequently acquitted by a middle-class jury. To avoid another arrest he returned to France. But the government there had become less radical in temper and he was given the choice either to settle somewhere outside Paris or to leave France altogether. Since Marx had to be near big libraries—he was a real bookworm—he went to a country that already had its own socialist movement—Britain. He found an abode in London and stayed there, working ceaselessly in the reading room of the British Museum until his dying day. His financial support came mainly from Engels, whose Calvinist-pietist family had "paid him out," and from the *New York Tribune*. Without the dollars and marks of capitalism, there probably would have been no socialist or communist movements.

But to return to the *Manifesto of the Communist Party*. While in Brussels, where he had written the *Manifesto,* Marx had joined the "League of the Just," which later became the *Bund der Kommunisten* ("League of Communists")—the official name, incidentally, of the former Communist party of Yugoslavia, *Savez komunista*. The *Manifesto*, a short pamphlet of about twelve thousand words, gives a vivid if unmethodical insight into the basic notions of Marxism. It was written jointly with Engels in a forceful, pungent style, yet its (German) vocabulary is such that it could scarcely be understood by the average worker and only by a minority of the working class. My edition, published in 1921[350] when education had substantially improved, contains a glossary of twelve closely printed pages. It gives further evidence that socialism (no less than communism) was emphatically a movement of intellectuals with complex psychological motives, intellectuals capable of mobilizing the masses through their writings, their oratorical gifts, or both. International socialism and communism were *not* born from among the "toiling masses." Nor were they conceptualized and organized by men with effusive affection for the downtrodden but rather—with few exceptions—by venomous haters. Neither love nor pity nor compassion plays a role in Marx's heart and mind.

The *Communist Manifesto*, first published in London, starts with the famous words: "A specter haunts Europe—the specter of communism."[351] After a preamble it sets out to explain all of the past as the history of class struggle. But the authors are also convinced that in prehistoric society there had been no classes and property had been held in common. In other words, they adopt the Rousseauistic notion of a paradisiacal past, a Golden Age, a secular version of the biblical story.

The *Manifesto* goes on to praise the "bourgeoisie" (a term, by the way, without any real equivalent in other European languages) for having over-thrown feudalism and its culture, but berates it for having created an iron rule of its own. A violent critique of bourgeois civilization follows, a passage that highlights the dominant characteristic of Marx: self-hatred. Marx, the typical product of bourgeois culture, is antibourgeois; Marx, of Jewish origin, is anti-Jewish; Marx, a permanent resident of capitalist Britain, is anticapitalist; Marx, married to an aristocrat, is antiaristocratic. In the third part of his *Manifesto* Marx's bile spills over onto "aristocratic socialism"—the proworker attitude of aristocratic opponents of the bour-geois outlook. The self-hater typically wants no allies, no help from anybody.

Marx nevertheless praises the bourgeoisie for having effected the domi-nation of the city over the countryside, for having caused mass migrations of countrymen to the cities, "tearing them away from the idiocy of rural life." Here is the voice of the rootless intellectual.

Marx also extolls the bourgeoisie for its antifeudal, antiaristocratic trend, the trend to centralize by promoting "one nation, one government, one law, one national class interest, one customs area." After raving over these achievements, he proceeds to try to prove that technology is opposed to the current methods of production. The bourgeoisie, Marx asserts, is in the midst of a terrible crisis. Wars, pervasive starvation, and economic chaos are menacing bourgeois society from every side. Production is too high; the only solution is to conquer new markets and brutally exploit the old. The bourgeoisie has to create new crises to survive. But to no avail, for the bourgeois themselves created the working class, the proletariat that will eliminate them as they themselves did away with the old ruling aristocracy.

What then follows is somewhat surprising—although less so in the light of German romanticism. It is a furious and not entirely unjust critique of modern industry, of the entire machine age, of the servitude it imposes on the worker. The worker, Marx says, is enslaved by the machine and by the overseers who serve the exploiting bourgeoisie. And the other evil is that the worker receives only a fraction of the wages due him.

But there is one consolation. The big bourgeois have pressed everybody down to the level of the proletariat. Bigness is seemingly victorious all along the line. Some of the petty bourgeois have joined the ranks of the proletariat willy-nilly. And within the proletariat itself a new civilization already exists: the relationship of the proletarian to wife and child, to state and nation, is already radically different from the former pattern. He has no fatherland, no bourgeois morality, no religion. And whereas in the past only minorities fought for their interests, the proletarian movement today is an "independent movement of the vast majority in the interest of a vast majority." Since, in addition, the proletariat is the lowest layer of society, its basis, it cannot rise without blowing up the rest of society.

While in the past, the authors continue, small social segments could rise socially, the worker was unable to do so. He grew poorer and poorer under the iron heel of the bourgeoisie. But the bourgeoisie has spawned its own gravediggers. Its downfall and the victory of the proletariat are unavoidable.

The ensuing critique of "bourgeois" property, education, morality, and sentiment is filled with weasel words, little insincerities, and flippancies. In an oblique attack, these values or assets are declared unattainable by the vast majority of the people. Nine-tenths of the population, Marx and Engels claim, have no property at all. And while arguing that the Communists will not abolish the right to own individual objects, they simultaneously maintain that private property will cease to exist in the communist order. "Bourgeois marriage," moreover, is bankrupt.

"The first step in the Revolution of the Workers is the transformation of the proletariat into the ruling class which is to enforce democracy."[352] Unlike what actually ensued later on in Russia, the transformation would occur step-by-step. "The proletariat is going to use its political domination to deprive the bourgeois gradually of their capital, to place all the instruments of production into the hands of the state, which means to centralize it in the hands of the proletariat organized into a ruling class, and to increase mass productive energies as fast as possible.

"This, of course, can only be achieved by despotic interventions against property rights . . . measures that might seem economically insufficient and untenable, but which in the course of development achieve a wider scope and are unavoidable as the means for the transformation of the entire sytem of production."

Apparently, then, the economic aspects are subordinate to the messianic vision.[353] "The measures," the authors add, "will be different in the various countries, but for the nations that have progressed furthest, the following could be enacted:

"1. Expropriation of real estate, the rent being used for the expenses of the government.

"2. Highly progressive taxation.

"3. Abolition of the right to inherit.

"4. Confiscation of all property of emigrants and rebels.

"5. Centralization of all credit in the hands of the state through the agency of a national bank with state capital and an exclusive monopoly.

"6. Centralization of all means of transport under state control.

"7. Increase of national factories and the means of production. Improvements of lands based on a common plan.

"8. Universal conscription of labor. Organization of industrial armies, especially for agricultural purposes.

"9. Unification of industrial and agrarian production. Efforts to eliminate gradually the differences between town and country.

"10. Public and free education for all children. Abolition of factory work for children in its present form. Amalgamation of education with material production."

A large section follows bitterly criticizing and ridiculing all the other socialist and leftist trends and parties. The *Manifesto* ends with the declaration that Communists are ready everywhere to support the despised bourgeois in their struggle against the remnants of feudalism and monarchism. "The Communists foster the cooperation and mutual understanding of democratic parties of all countries. The Communists disdain to keep their views and plans secret. They openly declare that their aims can only be achieved through a violent overturn of the present social order. Let the ruling classes tremble before the Communist Revolution. The proletarians have nothing to lose but their chains. They have a world to win. *Proletarians of all countries, unite!*"

This document is interesting because it reveals the mentality of its authors, their quasireligious vistas, their petty insincerities, their romantic outlook, their dogmatism and the inconsistencies of their views. (For instance, even granting the deadening character of modern industrial work, which "alienates" the laborer from his toil, how would the situation in this respect differ in a "progressive" communist world state?)[354] But the most intriguing aspect of the *Manifesto* lies in its vision of a secular "Day of Judgment" and in the relation of the "Preparatory Program" just cited to the existing trends in the free world today. In other words, this program can be used as a measuring rod to see to what extent we have all become Marxists and, especially, to what extent the befuddled scions of good old liberalism in the United States and Britain have succumbed to Marxist notions. Anybody condemned to listen to the loose talk in drawing rooms or political meetings where socialism is certainly not considered officially accepted, is astonished to observe how much headway the "false but clear ideas" of Marxism have made, how pervasively accepted they are. ("Vietnam? But that's only Wall Street wanting to profit from the rice paddies!")

The "Preparatory Program" has made unmistakable headway.

Point One was carried out by a number of highly "bourgeois" states, such as Czechoslovakia, Estonia, Latvia, and Rumania, between the two wars, and by Italy after World War II. (Hungary, Spain, and Poland enforced minor agrarian reforms.) In the free world, agricultural lands were also somewhat redistributed, but to benefit the farming class and not the state. (The most radical agrarian reforms before World War I were carried out by Imperial Russia—in the nineteenth century in conjunction with the liberation of the serfs, and again fifty years later under Stolypin.) Agrarian reforms nevertheless constitute a far-reaching intervention, of doubtful legitimacy, into the domain of private property.[355]

Point Two has become the rule in the vast majority of Western nations. From the government's point of view it brings in amazingly little revenue.[356] The "soaking of the rich" formula serves primarily to satisfy the envy of the masses.[357] Yet sometimes there is another reason for progressive taxation—the state's instinctive fear of the rich and therefore *independent* person.

Point Three is practiced in the West in another form. In certain countries death duties have reached a level that renders them confiscatory. As a result fortunes are frequently amassed in a manner that allows easy and invisible transfer of funds at home or abroad. The millionaire who dies in a hotel room with three suits in his closet, having gradually given everything away, is a symbol of our times. (Here again the "wicked reactionary fascist aristocratic landowner" who refuses to cede his property pays the full penalty.)

Point Four is only of academic interest in the free world, but it is fervently practiced elsewhere.

Point Five menaces all of free Europe. Although an "exclusive monopoly" does not yet generally exist, there is a strong tendency to nationalize banks. Thus all the big banks of France and Austria are fully nationalized and, as a result, the smaller banks literally have to compete with the state.

Point Six, the centralization and nationalization of transport, is a hard fact all over Western Europe. The same is true of the means of communication. Only in the United States do some private railroads still exist and compete against one another[358] and against an efficient network of bus companies and airlines. The American telephone system, although "redistributed," is still privately owned and one of the best in the world.

Point Seven is far advanced in free Europe and elsewhere in the world— India, Africa, and Latin America. In 1945–46, in the shadow of the red hysteria that affected even "Christian Democratic" parties from the Channel to Vienna, nationalizations were enacted right and left—partly to please the Socialists, partly as a manifestation of "Christian social consciousness."

Point Eight, the introduction of a compulsory labor service, has been adopted not so much by the free world as by national socialist and similar regimes. But "labor armies" on a voluntary basis were also seen in the United States during the New Deal.

Point Nine has to be understood in the light of the Marxist notion of the "idiocy of rural life." The farmer was and remains the stumbling block to socialist experiments everywhere. Since he raises his own food and tends to live in his own house, he is less "controllable" than, say, the urban dweller. The urbanization of our civilization is, moreover, a worldwide phenomenon that needs no aid or planning. Whether it is a blessing is quite another question. In Russia the dream of an *Agrogorod*, an "Agrarian City," can be found time and again in leading communist circles, even today.

Point Ten, the demand of all leftist parties, has been largely fulfilled. Its underlying motive is the hope that intellectual-social leveling and the standardization of knowledge at a tender age will foster equality and uniformity.[359]

The *Manifesto* by no means provides the full Marxist theory. The point is made, however: the list of steps that must be put into effect immediately following the proletarian victory clearly reflects the mind of the allegedly "non-Marxist" Left which, partly knowingly but largely unknowingly, has imbibed a good dose of Marxist thought.

Marx's subsequent work was largely based on the *Manifesto*. He merely intellectualized and rationalized his emotions. Positivism and a concomitant atheism were the foundations of his thinking. Auguste Comte and Feuerbach were his initial guiding stars. Added to them was the Hegelian dialectic,[360] and, as further stimuli, French socialism (Proudhon), English socialism (Robert Owen), certain tenets of Ricardo, and the personally experienced misery of the British working class, whose horrors should not be underestimated.[361] Since Britain, moreover, was the industrial leader of the world, Marx was convinced that all the other Continental nations would have to go through the same stages of debasement—a prophesy which, like almost all his others, proved untrue. The distance of a bookworm from reality can be considerable.

Marx's books, letters, and essays give a more complete and full view of his ideas. Only the first volume of *Das Kapital* was published during his lifetime. The other two (in certain editions, three) volumes were compiled and edited by Engels and Kautsky from material left by Marx after his death. But a more concrete view of the future utopia does not emerge clearly from these pages. The critical side in Marx was stronger than his prophetic gifts. And his hatred was stronger than the creative urge which needs love as a driving motor. Of all his theories concerning the iniquities, dangers, and pitfalls of capitalism, only *one* can still be taken seriously. That is the theory of concentration and monopolization, which the classic old liberals consider as inane as the rest of Marxist doctrine. (They have a point if they bring worldwide free trade into their calculations.) Neoliberalism, on the other hand, which is profoundly interested in continued competition as the lifeblood of a free economy, is strictly antitrust and anticartel. (This, however, does not mean that every neoliberal would subscribe to every bit of American antitrust legislation which, at times, is animated not by a sincere devotion to the cause of economic liberty but by anticapitalist prejudices.)[362] Yet, as history shows, the trend toward concentration is a problem that free enterprise in a free society can cope with. Concentration and bigness, on the other hand, is the life principle of socialism, which *is* state capitalism.

None of Marx's prophecies relating to the evolution of "capitalism" (an unhappy term) came true. Marx lived too early: he wrote about a free economy like a young man, who only knows his own age group, writes about life. What that youngster has to say about older people—sheer guesswork—is bound to be erroneous. Later in life Marx became convinced of the importance of technology, and it figured strongly in his calculations.

But at the time it was much too new and evolving much too rapidly to serve as a fixed cipher in economic equations. (Just as today the final impact of computers and automation cannot be accurately assessed.) But there seems to be some indication that Marx was so deeply immersed emotionally in his theories that he overlooked (consciously-subconsciously) a number of new phenomena which must have come to his attention between the publication of the *Communist Manifesto* and his death in 1883.

Added to the conflict between his fanaticism and his burning intellectuality was a quasireligious vision patterned after biblical concepts. It conceived the past as starting with an innocent, paradisiacal prehistory, followed by the evil rise of classes, family, religions, government, and iniquitous exploiting systems of production. This continued until he (a real prophet) and his friends appeared to preach the new Gospel of Salvation contained in the new Holy Scriptures. The millennium of the Dictatorship of the Proletariat was not far off, and it would lead to the original Paradise Lost in a better, more progressive and modern version. But Marx was too clever and too cautious to paint his picture of a redeemed humanity with the ridiculous precision of the utopian Socialists. He wanted to be a "scientific Socialist," a logician, rationalist, scholar, researcher—even though his daydreams led him completely astray.

Marx's monumental hatreds seriously conflicted with his biblical pretensions. It is difficult to say whom he loathed more, the "deviationists" in his own camp—men such as Proudhon, Bakunin, Lassalle—or the faceless, impersonal enemy, the *Grande Bourgeoisie Capitaliste* whom he attacked more objectively, in a far more general way, than his fellow leftists. In all this he was aided by a very facile pen, a brilliant style that made use of purple passages to enliven even such a basically dry work as *Das Kapital*.

But the real Marx came to life in his letters, especially when he vented his hatred on former friends, collaborators, or sympathizers. Marx actually vied with Engels in heaping anti-Jewish invectives upon the head of Lassalle, insults of a descriptive physical nature reminiscent of the smutty Nazi weekly *Der Stürmer*, edited by Julius Streicher. Marx saw in Lassalle a "niggerlike Jew," and Engels' invectives were no more moderate.[363] In a way these attitudes are not surprising because socialism and the Jewish outlook, the Jewish mind, the Jewish character do not easily mix.[364] Belonging to a religious minority within Christendom (with which they remain mysteriously connected), the Jews are apt to have the critical bent of small religious bodies everywhere. These minorities question much of the intellectual-spiritual foundations upon which the majority live, and they are often emphatic in their criticisms. Thus they easily become unpopular, because the Philistine hates the critic. Let such minorities rise financially and opposition to them will increase—envy will be added to discomfort and suspicion. The situation is by no means unique, as witness the Calvinists in France, the Copts in Egypt, the Parsees in India, the Indians in Africa, the Viets in Cambodia, or the Chinese in Indonesia.

Jews might initially be attracted by the *critical* aspect of socialist theory and some have even played important parts in nascent socialist movements—the names of Trotsky, Kamenev, Zinovyev, Kún, Bernstein, Eisner, Blum, Bauer come to mind—but they are constitutionally averse to its conformism, its anti-individualism, its moralizing cant and intellectual controls.[365] This may be less evident to an American or an East European, and for the same reason: the most indigent part of the Continent's Jewry lived in Eastern Europe, and it was largely they who emigrated to the United States in the last three decades before World War I. For sociological reasons, they were the most likely to embrace leftist ideas.[366] This was by no means the case with the old established American Jewry.

But there were also men like Theodor Herzl, founder of Zionism. Originally, he felt that the solution to the "Jewish Problem" lay in the conversion of all Hebrews, but then he witnessed the waning of religion, the rise of Darwinism, and the subsequent biologism, which turned against his people. And thus the idea of Israel was born. Herzl, however, was in the stream of all great Western thinkers, a man of the Right. In his programmatic book *Der Judenstaat*, he proposed that Israel be ruled by an aristocratic constitution: a monarchy was untenable, for David's line had been extinguished, and democracy was out of the question.

Yet even in Eastern Europe a break between the socialist and communist forces and the Jews had to come. (For a while this was obscured by the fact that the Nazis literally drove these Jews into the arms of organized leftism.) A latent, sometimes even an open, anti-Jewish sentiment existed in the ranks of Europe's socialist parties[367]—and it was prominent in Red Russia as well.[368] By the time World War II broke out, Stalin had killed many more Jews than Hitler.[369] Needless to say, Jewish *haute finance* was never really procommunist. If Jewish bankers did business with the Soviet Union, gentile manufacturers and financiers are even more guilty in this respect.[370]

Antonio Machado, the great Spanish poet who died in exile, predicted the inevitable turn to anti-Judaism that Marxism would take.[371] Marx himself started it, of course: "What is the secular basis of Judaism?" he asked. "Practical needs, egoism. What is the secular cult of the Jew? Huckstery. What is his secular God? Money."[372] No wonder Goebbels declared eighty years later that National Socialism was "anti-Semitic" because it was socialistic.[373]

Marxism does not harmonize with the Jewish mind, which is individualistic and commercially oriented; nor has it in any way a "proletarian" character. Marx ended his revolting pamphlet against the Jews, in his *Die Frühschriften*, with the remark that the true emancipation of the Jews consisted in "the emancipation of *society from Jewry*" (his emphasis). This is precisely what the National Socialists attempted with the *Endlösung*.

Marx's attitude toward the proletariat had similar traits. When he talked about workers he used untranslatable German terms of abuse—*Knoten* or *Straubinger*. Throughout his life he never once set foot in a factory—never, of course, worked in one. The worker's mentality was alien to him.

Marxism is absolutely bourgeois and therefore appeals strongly to the left-of-center, middle-class mind with its commercial background. Waldemar Gurian was very much to the point when he wrote, "Marxism, and therefore Russian Bolshevism, does but voice the secret and unavowed philosophy of bourgeois society when it regards society and economics as absolute. It is faithful, likewise, to its morality when it seeks to order this absolute, the economic society, in such a way that justice, equality, and freedom, the original war cries of the bourgeois advance, might apply to all. The rise of the bourgeoisie and the evolution of bourgeois society have made economics the lot of all."[374] It was the late Ben Hecht who admonished his readers not to believe in the picture of the Communist as a man with a bomb in one hand and a dagger in the other. To Hecht, bolshevism was a movement that evolved logically from nice middle-class democracy. "Democracy," he wrote, "was the most atrocious insult leveled at the intelligence of the race by its inferiors. Bolshevism goes one better, however." He thought that in time it would be fostered in the United States by "our lowest types"—politicians, thinkers, and writers.[375]

Yet the partial victories of Marxism—which, *as a doctrine*, found a resonance only among the partly educated, the "lowest types"—were due to a religious crisis which was moral, philosophical, and theological. As E. F. W. Tomlinson explained, "Because men cannot do without a philosophy . . . if they reject the good one they must do with the dregs of all the rest. Dialectical materialism is an agglomeration of all the dregs of the wayward metaphysics of the nineteenth century."[376] And, as previously noted, there is also in Marxism a curious eschatological vision, which is consciously-subconsciously copied from Christianity, an ecstatic waiting for the Second Coming of the Pan-Proletarian Christ, oddly counterbalanced by the antinomy of a purely mechanical predetermined notion of history with loud if not hysterical appeals to sanguinary revolutions and sacrifices. Jointly, this dogmatism and orthodoxy manage to infuse watered-down Marxists, Western-style "Social Democrats," and Labourites, with a bad conscience when they are confronted by Communists. This bad conscience is the reason why so many Social Democrats or Socialists in the satellite world let themselves be forced or coaxed into unitary Socialist parties (*de facto* completely Moscow-controlled), of which the Socialist Unitary party (*Sozialistische Einheitspartei Deutschlands*, SED) of the so-called German Democratic Republic (DDR) was the most typical. This also explains why Western Socialist parties, when hearing the "call of the wild," suddenly get weak in the knees.

In England Marx had contacts with the English Socialists who were, in a way, the forerunners of the Labour party. The founder of British socialism was Robert Owen, the son of a shopkeeper. At the age of twenty, this gifted man was the director of a textile factory and soon succeeded in becoming independent. In New Lanark, Scotland, he established a model factory, a social rather than a socialistic experiment.[377] Yet Owen did not stop at the realization of social ideas. Soon he began to show an interest in socialistic dreams. In 1824 he went to the United States where he bought the lands, property, and livestock of Georg Rapp, leader of a German communist sect, who had established a settlement in New Harmony, Indiana, not far from Evansville. In due course the "Rappites" left for Pennsylvania, but, in 1826, New Harmony was revived with a fresh crop of immigrants under Owen's guidance. Some of them were men of intelligence, education, and high moral qualities; others were eccentrics and "marginal characters" who disturbed the entire community. Thus the experiment failed totally within two years.

Owen returned to England in 1829. The man of mere reforms had become a radical Socialist. Because of his attacks on "organized religion" and on the basic tenets of Christianity he lost much of the general respect and public support he had received in earlier years. Although he was a cofounder of the first trade union in 1833, Owen's real interest lay in the more old-fashioned guilds and cooperatives. With advancing years his crotchety and cranky ideas multiplied. In fact, he founded a new ethical system (rather than a religion), which his supporters spread all over England in "Halls of Science." The essence of this teaching was that man was *essentially a product of his environment*, an idea that profoundly influenced Marx and that has become an almost essential part of the folklore of Western "education." For Marx it was the system of production that formed man and created the superstructure of all thinking: Marx attacked free will no less than Owen, who was convinced that through environment anyone's character could be formed, made to order. His strong belief in education found a powerful echo in Northern Europe and North America. Yet despite his determinism, his attitude towards ethics was far more positive than that of Marx. Before his death, Owen turned to spiritualism.

Marx founded his International Workers' Association in 1864, six years after Owen's death. The history of this First International was marked by the bitter struggle between the real Socialists and the Anarchists under Bakunin's leadership.[378] Marx's strong dislike for Russia and Russians[379] was partly due to his hatred of Bakunin, the Russian anarchist nobleman who converted Prince Kropotkin to his ideas.[380] Marx had Bakunin expelled from the party in 1872, and the seat of the First International was transferred to New York where the organization died a lingering death. The antagonism between the professorial, petty stickler, Marx, and the dashing ex-officer of the Imperial Russian army, Bakunin, had been ruinous.

Nor did Marx get along with another dashing person, Ferdinand Lassalle. Son of a Jewish merchant in Breslau and the first organizer of German workers, Lassalle was an immensely colorful character. Again and again accused of this or that political misdemeanor, he was frequently acquitted. Courageous, witty, a lover of the fair sex, a playwright, he was liked neither by Marx nor by Engels. Long connected with Countess Sophie Hatzfeld, whose lawyer he was, Lassalle was finally killed in a duel with a Rumanian near Geneva over the hand and heart of Helene von Dönniges, the daughter of a Bavarian diplomat.

Lassalle's lifestyle, his friendships with aristocratic ladies, thoroughly irritated the envious Marx who was a less successful snob, though he managed to take part a few times in an English fox hunt and sported a monocle.

Lassalle was not intellectually unique, but he had an excellent mind and published several essays on a variety of political and social questions as well as a volume on Heraclitus, from a Hegelian viewpoint. He dreamed of the emancipation of the German worker through state aid and made a passionate appeal to William I to transform the Kingdom of Prussia into a "social monarchy." Bismarck, who knew him well and respected him, said in his eulogy to him in the Diet that Lassalle had been a thorough royalist, though not quite sure whether Prussia should be ruled by the Hohenzollerns or the Lassalles. A gourmet, impeccably dressed, a brilliant conversationalist, this high-living man who was the idol of the German working class inevitably provoked the intense hatred of Marx. Had he lived longer—he was only thirty-nine years old when he died—he would in all likelihood have given an entirely different hue to the development of socialism in the heart of Europe, and thus in the world. Marx must have breathed more freely when in 1864 his competitor died.

Three years later the first volume of *Das Kapital* was published. In it, as some critics have pointed out, no difference emerged between "capitalists" (financiers), managers-entrepreneurs, and employees. (Our modern industries are "triangular"!)

The weaknesses of Marxist thought are manifold. The "mature" Marx was less interested in philosophical quests. His general disillusionment due to political disappointments (above all the failure of the Paris *Commune*) and constant financial worries increased his bitterness.[381] His character alienated all his friends, except for Engels. He sought forgetfulness in the arms of his housekeeper, Helene Demuth (which means "humility"), who bore him a son whom Engels loyally claimed to have begotten. (The true story leaked out much later.)[382]

Perhaps bitterness also acted as a brake on Marx's mind and work, which made very slow progress. His solitude and isolation caused him to make grave errors precisely concerning human character, errors that subsequently affected the entire Marxist landscape, primarily in countries where Marxism became the state religion. Marx seemed to have been unaware of Pascal's dictum that man is neither beast nor angel, and he who wants to turn man into an angel will inevitably degrade him to the level of a beast— a thought similar to our thesis of the enforced monastic life. Indeed, the coercive "paradise" becomes a Hell.

Another short-circuit in his line of thought was caused by his rejection of ideology while simultaneously he himself created one.[383] He would of course have denied that what he preached was an ideology. Ideologies, after all, rest only on ideas, and, he would add, what he advocated was an outline of scientific facts and laws which were active in this world. All he was doing was to proclaim the shape of things to come, against which resistance was vain, just as an exact meteorological forecast could not be forestalled. But if this really *were* the case, why the movements, the parties, the intrigues, the secret police, the concentration camps, the armies, the wars, the propaganda, the broadcasts? Only to speed up a "natural evolution"? In that case, shouldn't a little patience be called for?

Questions such as these have remained unanswered for some time. Yet Marx had and still has a fairly universal appeal. He appeals to the "left" in us, he personifies a temptation which we have to overcome. Jean Paul in his *Quintus Fixlein* says that in every century the Almighty sends an evil genius to tempt us. In the nineteenth century that genius was Karl Marx.

Marx died in 1883. German socialism, which means the German Social Democratic party, went through a very difficult period. It became more and more evident that many of the ideas and theories of Marx were not true to fact, true to life. Revisionism loomed around the corner. In 1889 the Second International was established, and in 1895 Engels died. By this time only fanatics still insisted that the "forces of reaction" were hell-bent on humiliating, exploiting, and destroying the working class, which, in fact, had friends and defenders in every camp and layer of society. One of the major reasons for the break between William II and Bismarck was their different attitudes toward organized labor and social legislation. The young emperor was prolabor. Bismarck had to remind him that the owners and directors of factories were also his subjects and expected loyalty from him as he expected loyalty from them.[384]

It was not until 1890 that the Fabians (in this respect strongly animated by Beatrice Webb) tried to hitch their wagon to the rising star of trade unions. Fabians were among the founders of the Independent Labour party in 1893 and the British Labour party in 1900, but they tried to propagandize the ranks of other parties as well. They were particularly successful with the left wing of the Liberal party which gradually veered under Lloyd George's leadership toward espousing social ideas and legislation. (During this time, there arose a young ambitious Tory apostate with very radical ideas who delighted Lloyd George and enchanted Beatrice Webb. His name was Winston S. Churchill.)[385] Indeed, many of the great social reforms before World War I were enacted by the Liberals but they were promoted and sponsored by the Fabians—the program adopted by the Labour party in 1918 was drawn up by Sidney Webb. In the years to come the Fabians were not only extremely active in the field of social legislation but also in foreign politics where they later strongly supported the League of Nations and methodically promoted leftist causes all over the globe.

The influence of the Fabians on the American scene was and remains considerable. They maintained intimate connections with a number of American universities and with the Foreign Policy Association, which they often provided with speakers who lectured all over the United States. Typical of them was Professor Harold Laski, famous for his correspondence with Oliver Wendell Holmes, Jr., for his clever formulations, and for his sometimes unbridled imagination.[386] The Fabians played an eminent role in the moral disarmament of the English-speaking countries vis-à-vis the Soviet Union. They loved disarmament—an affection that influenced labor policies during the 1930s and led, in combination with Tory provincialism, to the dangerous unpreparedness that prevailed when the Nazi menace appeared on the horizon. One really could not disarm, ridicule "Colonel Blimp," sneer at "militarism," and make a stand against the brown bullies. And it was dangerous to rely on the Red Army alone.

Fabians, on the other hand, supplied socialism in Eastern Europe with ample intellectual ammunition. One of the Fabians, J. A. Hobson, together with G. D. H. Cole, an initiator of "Guild Socialism," authored *Imperialism*, published in 1902.[387] This book inspired Lenin to write his pamphlet *Imperialism as the Last Stage of Capitalism* which came out in 1915. In this work the Russian Social Democrat living in his Swiss exile claimed that capitalism, as a last means of expansion, had to engage in aggressive wars not only to conquer new markets, but also to divert the masses from the class struggle—an argument that has helped fuel leftist disarmament and pacifist movements in the West and which was as untrue then as it is manifestly untrue today: a characteristic that places it firmly in the tradition of historical Marxism, which has been proved wrong on almost every account, but which has still been able to exact such a frightful cost in human suffering.

Looking back at Marx's message, and in view of the recent events of 1989—the bankruptcy of Marxism in Eastern Europe—one is tempted to believe that Marxism has come to its end. This would be dangerously premature; a *fausse idée claire*, a clear but false idea, does not die so quickly. Many people, especially in the Third World, still believe that "capitalism" is like a prison cell in which three little thieves are brutalized by a muscular mass murderer who waxes stronger as they weaken, deprived by him of their just rations. This is blatant nonsense. It has no connection to collective bargaining in the Free World.

Today, the incomes of the working class in the industrial nations have reached middle-class levels, thanks to managers, technologists, and scientists. . . not because of the efforts of the "social-minded" elite. Economics is an extremely involved science and thus thoroughly incomprehensible to the average man.

CHAPTER 10

From Socialism to Communism

*Once in our lives we wanted to make
the people happy and this is something
for which we will never forgive ourselves.*

—AN OLD RUSSIAN LEFTIST TO
NADEJDA MANDELSTAM

It was not in the industrial West, as Marx had predicted, but in Eastern Europe that socialism reaped its first concrete, tangible victories. When Marx and Engels wrote the *Communist Manifesto* they arranged for a Danish—but not a Russian—edition. Yet the socialist victory in Russia is one of the most important events in modern history and well worth special study. For present purposes, however, only three aspects, or problems, concerning the Russian Revolution will be probed.

Problem One concerns whether there is something inherently "communist" or collectivist in the Russian soul.

Problem Two concerns whether the Russian Revolution was in any way a "natural reaction" to the "horrors of czarism," a swinging of the pendulum to the other side, rather than a continuation of the old regime in a new form.

Problem Three examines the strength of the "Majority Wing of Russian Social Democracy" (Bolshevism) at the time of the revolution.

As to the first question, there is, emphatically, nothing inherently collectivist or conformist about the Russian mind and outlook; on the contrary, Russians are extremely individualistic with an anarchical bent of mind. Those who defend the theory of the "inborn trend toward collectivism" usually cite the institutions of the *mir* (land communities) and of the *artel'* (common workshops), as well as the principle of *sobornost'* (commonality) in the theology of the Eastern Church. As for the *mir*, it was such an abysmal failure that Stolypin had to liquidate it in the early twentieth century. *Sobornost'*, for its part, has its (admittedly not too close) analogy in the Catholic concept of the Mystical Body. Of course, the Catholic world no less than that of the Eastern Church has always been the cradle of anarchist parties. It is the Protestant world of the Reformation churches that demands strict order, discipline, frugality, conformity, cooperation, and consensus through massive persuasion and compromise. (In Europe *black* has always been the symbolic color for Catholics *and* anarchists!) Russia, on the other hand, has stood for extremes at all times; conformity is only possible where the accepted norm is the "happy medium," which is remote from all absolutes, the *juste milieu* which Alexander Herzen despised so heartily.

Edward Crankshaw was perhaps the first author in the English-speaking world to suggest that the Russians' anarchical mentality was a key to their character and thus to their political behavior. "The Russian," he wrote, "is a man who regards compromises not as a sign of strength, but as a sign of the dilution of the personality, or self-betrayal, who is, moreover, susceptible in the extreme to outside influence of every kind, who is, in a word, completely experimental and mentally *free*, in a way that, in the West, only artists are experimental and free (and by no means all of those)." He went on to explain how such a profoundly anarchical people, in despair of finding an inner cohesion, were willing to accept "control from above" as a necessary evil. He added, finally, "All this, I suggest, is the rigidity of a naturally fluid people who have to forge hoops of iron around themselves or disintegrate utterly. And it all comes from a natural individualism which makes our vaunted, rugged individualism look like an abandonment of personality." [388]

Russia, Spain, Italy, and France had, by no means accidentally, the largest anarchist parties at the turn of the century. In Russia it was the Anarchists (SR, or "Social Revolutionaries") who committed practically all the acts of violence. The Communists were too shrewd, too clever to engage in mere terrorism. They preferred conspiracy, organization, and mass risings.

The anarchical bent of the Southern and Eastern Europeans (and of the Catholic or Orthodox nations living in other parts of the world) also makes for a proliferation of political parties which, together with an uncompromising extremism, renders parliamentary life difficult if not impossible. Hence the almost inevitable failure of the "democratic experiment" in those areas.

Point Two is concerned with the swinging of the pendulum. In order to address the "pendulum" argument convincingly, it is necessary to take a fresh look at prerevolutionary Russia. To begin with, the Bolsheviks did not replace an absolute or even a constitutional monarchy, but a democratic republic—the republic of Alexander Kerenski, a moderate social revolutionary; if, moreover, the pendulum theory were to be applied to Germany, then the Weimar Republic must have been unmitigated hell—which was not the case either. History does not make "sense" in a mathematical or mechanical way, no more than does great drama.

After 1905, Imperial Russia was in many ways very different from what it had been in, say, 1890. A bearded man with a newspaper under his arm walking along a street in St. Petersburg in 1912 might easily be a deputy of the bolshevik wing of the Russian Social Democratic party—in other words, a Bolshevik sitting in the Duma. What paper is he carrying? *Pravda*. Where did he buy it? There, at the street corner. (I personally read that 1912 paper, and I can attest that no American editor would have lambasted his government as violently as did the editors of *Pravda* back then.)

Before 1905, of course, people were less free. Nevertheless, in 1878, Vyera Zassulitch, who tried to assassinate the police prefect Tryepov, was acquitted by a jury; Trotski described the benignity of Russian jails and the respect with which political "criminals" were treated by their wardens; and although Lenin suffered *ssylka*, exile in Siberia, simple exile merely meant that one was forced to live in or near a certain village on a meager pension while still able to read, write, hunt, and fish. Life in Siberia around 1900 was no worse than life in North Dakota or Saskatchewan at that time. (A friend of mine has even seen the copy of the letter Lenin's wife wrote from Shushenskoye to the governor in Irkutsk protesting against the insufficient staff allotted her.)

The agrarian situation in Russia is also beset by wrong conceptions. At the time of the outbreak of the revolution in 1917, the peasantry owned nearly 80 percent of the arable land,[389] whereas in Britain more than half the fertile soil belonged to large estates (yet Britain had no violent agrarian movement and Russia had). Illiteracy was down to about 56 percent, and the schools were multiplying by leaps and bounds. Also important, from a sociological viewpoint, the lower classes were much better represented in the Russian high school-colleges than in Western Europe. The majority of university students, moreover, had scholarships.[390]

The misconceptions, moreover, about the Russian class structure that prevail in the Western world are so manifold and so deeply rooted that they seem ineradicable. The three brilliant volumes by Anatole Leroy-Beaulieu on late nineteenth-century Russia, *L'Empire des tsars et les Russes*, give a glimpse of a totally mixed society based neither on birth nor on money. Needless to say, the same impression is conveyed by the great Russian novelists of that period.[391] Actually, before Red October Russia was Europe's "Eastern America," a country where social mobility was greater than elsewhere, where titles had none of the nimbus they had in the West, where fortunes could be made overnight by intelligent and thrifty people regardless of their social background. Skilled European workers and specialists in many fields emigrated to Russia rather than to the United States. And, even before 1905, knowing *how* to speak and to write gave total liberty.

A true understanding of prerevolutionary Russia presupposes not only a mastery of Russian (an exceedingly difficult language with an enormous vocabulary), but also years of research. The major problems surround proper distinctions and understanding—of the various, rapidly succeeding periods, of the vastness of the country and, above all, of the innumerable prevailing and erroneous clichés. Serfdom? It did exist until 1861, but it was no more and no less characteristic of Russia than slavery was of the United States. It was, moreover, incomparably milder than slavery and did not exist at all in the majority of the empire.[392] Some serfs were rich— with fortunes amounting to from 30 to 60 million dollars (present purchasing power)—and they paid only a microscopic head tax. Some were doctors, lawyers, or engineers who lived in the cities but held onto their tax-exempt status.[393] Under Catherine II, workers in the iron and steel industry toiled twelve hours a day for one week, twelve hours a night for the second, and were free for the third (which adds up to an eight-hour workday).[394]

Industry, which made enormous strides after the 1880s, was quite substantial in Russia, a fact attested to by the Soviet economist E. Tarle in his *Collected Works* (Moscow 1958, vol.IV, p. 443–468). It caused apprehension in Germany and Austria-Hungary where references to the "Russian steamroller" signified something other than military strength. The West invested considerable capital in Russia and supplied engineers and scientists in large numbers. After 1900 Russia's industrial progress and its GNP increase were more spectacular than those of the United States.[395]

Naturally, the lot of the worker was as difficult in Imperial Russia as it was *everywhere else in a nascent industrial society*. This was as true of England in the first third of the nineteenth century as it is of contemporary socialist India. That is not to say that the Imperial government ever intentionally favored the manufacturers, nor, for that matter, the large landowners. (The emancipation of the serfs was the work of the "autocracy" against the wishes of the landowning class.) Manya Gordon (in her book *Workers Before and After Lenin*) could say without exaggeration that "records have proved conclusively that Russia was a pioneer in labor legislation."[396] The *Okhrana*, the secret police, actually took steps to help the workers organize trade unions to defend against exploitation. Moreover, a quarter of a century after Red October the living standards of the workers were lower than in 1914, as Manya Gordon's book convincingly attests. And, in his memoirs, Ilya Ehrenburg writes that in the early 1950s there were fewer domestic animals in the USSR than in 1916.[397] The situation has not changed much since.[398]

No doubt certain aspects of the Imperial regime did not improve much even after 1905. There was discrimination against Catholics (but not against Lutherans) in the higher ranks of the administration—as there was in Scandinavia. (The Jesuits were outlawed in Switzerland until twenty years ago.) Jews could not reside in the northern and eastern provinces unless they held university degrees or were "merchants first class." (These restrictions were lifted for those who became Christians: that is, the discrimination was religious, not ethnic or racial.) Only a certain percentage of university students could be of the Jewish faith, but a *numerus clausus* of this sort was not unknown in American universities, especially in medical schools that prided themselves on their "liberalism."

Old Russia was also a pioneer in higher female education (in Finland, then part of the Russian Empire, women were enfranchised by Nicholas II in 1906). And it was the literary leader of Europe before World War I: its universities were as good as any in the Western world with some of the best textbooks on the Continent. Its *intelligentsiya* (a Russian word) was perhaps confused, but in richness and diversity of ideas it was unexcelled.[399]

To the question whether Russian bolshevism is merely "czarism [whatever that means] painted red," or the swing of the pendulum, the answer is:

neither. Imagine a very popular, intelligent, conscientious, good-looking and responsible young man, obviously destined for a highly successful life. One day, having had a few drinks too many, he runs his car into a tree and ends up a paraplegic. Accidents happen not only in the lives of persons, but also in the lives of nations. But high school teachers, eager to discover logic and sense in history, do not like to admit as much. Yet bolshevism is due precisely to such an accident, admittedly aided by two Russians, Minister of War Sukhomlinov and Chief of the General Staff Yanushkyevitch, who in 1914 transformed the Austro-Serb armed conflict into a world war and thus dug the grave for their country.[400]

This brings us to Problem Three: How did it happen that communism could overpower that great nation? Obviously, the turmoil following the lost war—not the industrial proletariat—provided the setting for the revolution. There were practically no workers among the leaders of the Russian Social Democratic Party. When, back in 1903 at the London congress of the then-illegal party, the majority voted for a radical program while the minority held out for more moderate demands, a real schism took place. The *bol'sheviki* (majoritarians) opposed the *men'sheviki* (minoritarians), though both still called themselves Social Democrats. Only the Boksheviks favored the communist label, which they used officially for the first time one year after Red October. By 1921 the schism had become worldwide and permanent; the old Social Democrats remained loyal to the Second International while the Communists established the Third International.

The Bolsheviks, no less than the Mensheviks, were led by men who either belonged to the lower nobility (*dvoryane*),[401] or had a middle-class intellectual background (both Jews and gentiles), or were ex-seminarians. When Joseph de Maistre prophesied that the coming Russian revolution would be led by a "Pugatshov with a university background,"[402] he was not far wrong. The description fits Lenin[403] only too well; but it could also be applied to most of the other leaders who combined in various degrees the three great revolutionary gifts: intellectuality, a talent for organization, and oratorical magnetism.

Yet all the talkers and doers among the radical Social Democrats rolled into one could never have won without the aid of the rebellious soldiers and sailors, mostly peasants and sons of peasants. At that time the working class of Russia was only a very small percentage of the population (we have no exact statistics). And the middle classes were relatively small, unorganized, and lacked all cohesion. Thus the soldiers and sailors, having fought a rough foreign enemy under oppressive discipline, looked foward to an easy victory—and to getting rid of their officers. Strongly represented in the "Councils (*Sovyety*) of Workers, Peasants and Soldiers," they helped the intellectual rabble-rousers win the day.

The Kerenski government fought the rebellious soldiers in the final stage of the rebellion with a female regiment that was decimated, defeated, and taken prisoner by the half-drunken red heroes. The scenes that followed would have delighted the Divine Marquis, as would the bestial slaughter of the Imperial family in Yekaterinburg.[404] Kerenski wanted to ship the family to Britain, but Lloyd George refused. To the "liberal" British prime minister, eager to achieve victory at all costs, Nicholas II, who desperately wanted peace, was a traitor. The British public would not stand for it, Lloyd George declared.[405] In World War I, the "moderate Left" was, manifestly, the force most opposed to peace, most prone to the worst excesses of nationalism. In England the main culprit was the leftist David Lloyd George, in America the Democratic Party of Woodrow Wilson, in France the old *Communard* Clemenceau, and in Russia the "progressive republican" regime of Alexander Kerenski.[406] Those who were eager for peace were the crowned heads, the Pope—and representatives of the working class, who tried to gather in Stockholm but were thwarted by the Allies.

In Russia, the fall of the monarchy in March 1917 destroyed the center and object of all loyalty. It was impossible to stabilize the country on a *juste milieu*—a middle-of-the-road position. Opposition to the Communists came only from the Right and the Anarchists. A series of civil wars (1918-20) was fought on a military rather than on a revolutionary basis, from which the Communists emerged victorious—not only because they held the center of the Russian railroad network but because they had the support of the peasantry which was thoroughly intoxicated by dreams of further land gains.

The first big agrarian partition had taken place after the emancipation of the serfs, when land was allotted in the form of the *mir* to entire communities. When the *mir* failed completely, Stolypin,[407] minister of the interior and later prime minister, decided to carve up the *mir* lands and give them permanently to individual holders, thus effectively ending the periodic famines. His plans for additional partitions of latifundia would have resulted in large landowners holding no more than 11 percent of the arable land by 1930. (They had only slightly more than 22 percent in 1916.)[408] While thrifty peasants now got ahead, the lazy ones sold their plots to the more ambitious, the so-called *kulaks* ("fists"). And since ambition is not considered a great virtue in Russia,[409] the *kulaks* became generally disliked.

The Communists promised to divide *all* estates not owned by the peasants, which resulted, generally, in bonding the peasantry to the Communists—although less so in the Ukraine and the Cossack (the Don and Kuban) areas. The "Whites" fought a losing battle because the soldiers (practically all of them peasants and peasant's sons) defected to the Red Army which promised them land. After the collapse of the White armies (some of whose battalions consisted of officers and noncoms only), there were new famines, for the peasants had failed to till the land they had, and the red authorities started to confiscate food. This resulted in a further lessening of production—money, after all, was worthless—and collectivization was enforced. First the *kulaks* were denounced, attacked, frequently deported, their goods expropriated. Next the lesser peasants were enslaved. The Russian countryside, far more so than the cities, went through incredible agonies; untold millions died. It was, in a sense, poetic justice. To this day the agrarian sector of the USSR is the poorhouse—and the unhappiest part—of the nation.[410]

Clearly, each part of Russia has its share of guilt in the revolution. So too, of course, have other "Christian" nations, not least those Germans, such as General Ludendorff, who transported Lenin back into Russia in 1917. (Which proves that it is criminal to commit immoralities for national benefit. Right causes *are* universal causes—such is the Christian tradition in government. The thinly disguised contempt with which the Bolsheviks treated the Germans during the peace negotiations in Brest-Litovsk was well deserved.)

Among the Russians, the working class was perhaps the least guilty, the avaricious peasants were eminently guilty, and the brilliant, scintillating, amiable *intelligentsiya* were the guiltiest of all. For generations they had undermined the fabric of Holy Mother Russia, either by siding with the Social Revolutionaries, the *Narodnaya Volya*, the Social Democrats, or by being "open-minded,"[411] by deriding the national heritage, by spreading polite doubt, by stupidly imitating Western patterns, ideas, and institutions that would never do for Russia. Dostoyevski in *The Possessed* (*Byessy*) showed vividly how liberal relativism and skepticism spawned the monstrosities that surfaced in the last decades before the revolution.[412] And Dostoyevski knew; in his youth he had been a leftist himself and, as a member of the Petrashevski conspiracy, had been condemned to death and had lived in a Siberian prison, in "The House of the Dead."[413]

In one of the most brilliant books on the Communist Revolution, *Tsarstvo Antikhrista*,[414] Dmitri Myerezhkovski wrote: "Not on account of their own strength are the Bolsheviks powerful but only thanks to your weakness. They know what they want, but you do not know what you want. They all want the same thing: among you everybody wants something else." He also quotes Rozanov: "The deeper reason for all that has happened is found in the fact that vanishing Christianity has created enormous cavities in the civilized world and now everything is tumbling into them."[415]

But in Russia (and later on in Germany), these cavities were not only of a religious but of a political nature. For there is always a more-or-less obvious, more-or-less subtle, more-or-less invisible connection beween the two. In the case of Russia it was the small, evil glow of communism that lit up the entire dark void until, at last, in our days the residue of Christianity along with the natural protest of man against an inhuman ideology combined to generate a spirit of resistance.

The picture painted by dogmatic socialism[416] in action is strikingly similar to that of the French Revolution. And no wonder, since the leadership had a very similar sociological structure: bitter and confused members of the nobility,[417] murderously idealistic intellectual bourgeois, and alienated wicked priests, friars, and seminarians. There was almost the same mob violence, high-flown speeches, declamatory writings, destruction of ancient buildings, desecration of tombs and cemeteries, furious attacks against religion, one-track political thinking, and turmoil in the countryside accompanied by arson and robbery. Gracchus Babeuf was, after all, worshiped and exalted by the *Bolsheviki* as their forerunner. And instead of the virtuous *citoyen*, the virtuous proletarian, the new ideal, was now arrayed against the "rotten old order."

This was an image to gladden the hearts of "progressives" the world over. But what they overlooked was the price of introducing to the world what was really a retrogressive system: the thousands of people, male and female soldiers, killed in the revolution;[418] the 2 million slain in the ensuing two years of civil war; the 6 million dead in the famines of 1920-1922; the 8 million dead under similar circumstances; the hundreds of thousands executed by the Tshe-Ka (Cheka),[419] the GPU, the NKVD, the MVD, the KGB; the millions dead in Stalin's concentration camps, including Estonians, Latvians, Lithuanians, Tartars, Jews, and Volga-Germans, all deported under inhuman conditions. In addition there were the intimately related misdeeds of Soviet armed and financed "ventures." Various foreign "local" enterprises of the Left also resulted in millions of deaths: the

Violencia in Columbia, the revolutionary guerrilla warfare in El Salvador, Guatemala, and Nicaragua, organized terrorism in Rhodesia, South Africa, Namibia, Angola, Mozambique, Argentina, Peru, Chile, and Bolivia. The civil wars in Malaysia and the Philippines, the horrors of Ethiopia and, last but by no means least, the military ventures in Vietnam, Laos, Cambodia, and Afghanistan—all were and are accompanied by slaughter and mass extermination.

But even these gigantic massacres are dwarfed by the record of Red China. In a shorter period, Mao Tse-tung murdered millions more than Lenin, Stalin, and his successors combined. To these staggering numbers must be added those killed in "foreign wars" fought over ideological issues.

Indeed, the calamities caused by Soviet communism were not confined to Russia—just as Chinese communism did not remain a "local" affair. The question has to be asked, whether without the Communist challenge the rise of fascism in Italy and of national socialism in Germany could be imagined. And, of course, World War II would never have taken place had not Stalin given the "green light" to Hitler by promising a simultaneous attack against Poland.[420] One of the consequences (with Western acquiescence, to be sure) was the tyranny imposed on Eastern Europe.

In character and basic doctrine these reactions—fascism, national socialism—greatly resembled "communistic socialism" (which is genuine socialism), differing only in financial techniques. While the Western totalitarians accepted statism and the total subordination of the individual to the whole, while they clearly represented another form of materialism, they nevertheless revolted against the danger of the Russian edition of communism, against the new imperialism emanating from Moscow.[421] They were not the "enemies" of communism but its "competitors," which is a very different matter; there can be greater bitterness in rivalry than in opposition. And, indeed, the tensions and hatred amounted to a cutthroat competition, a term that suitably illustrates this tragic and terrifying issue, expressed geographically in one of the worst wars history has ever seen, the "Third War of Austrian Succession," commonly called World War II. In this struggle the economic Left overpowered the biological Left; the "moderate Left" shared in none of the spoils and was, in spite of every effort and merit, nothing more than another loser.

CHAPTER 11

From Marxism to Fascist Statism

Youth, youth!
Springtime of beauty
In Fascism lies the salvation
Of our freedom.

—ORIGINAL FASCIST HYMN

The first systematic leftist and nationalistic opposition to Moscow-centered communism came from Italy. It was *fascism*; and it had clearly socialistic origins. The *fasces* ("bundles") were Roman symbols of authority; they reappeared as republican symbols during the French Republic and, later, on the American dime. In the early 1890s *fasci* ("leagues") of workers, so-called *fasci dei lavoratori*, created grave disturbances, primarily in Sicily but also in parts of Tuscany.

The founder of this century's fascism was Benito Mussolini, the elder of two sons of an Italian socialist blacksmith; he was called Benito (and not, in the Italian way, Benedetto) after Benito Juárez, the Mexican Indian who, supported by the United States, defeated and then executed Emperor Maximilian Ferdinand Joseph, brother of Franz Joseph. The younger Mussolini was baptized Arnaldo after the medieval revolutionary Arnaldo di Brescia.

Young Benito grew up a fanatical socialist like his father and started out to become a teacher, like his mother. Later he went to Switzerland to take literature courses at the Universities of Lausanne and Geneva while earning his livelihood as a mason. He had difficulties with the police, was temporarily jailed, and later went to Trent, then in Austria, where he worked as a journalist for two Italian-language newspapers with nationalistic and socialistic tendencies. (The future *duce del fascismo* also used his stay to study German quite thoroughly.) But he became convinced that the local population, though ethnically Italian in its vast majority, preferred Austrian to Italian rule. Mussolini also came to consider the Austrian administration superior to that of his own country.[422]

But he was finally expelled by the Austrian authorities who were suspicious of his nationalist and irredentist propaganda. In 1913 he published a book in Rome. The book was called *Giovanni Hus, il veridicò* (John Hus, the Truthful). Badly written, it showed a marked anti-Catholic bias (as did his one and only novel *The Cardinal's Mistress*), but it was far more political than religious. (In earlier years, Mussolini had been attracted by unorthodox Socialists, such as Sorel, and by Anarchists, such as Prince Kropotkin.)[423]

What interested Mussolini more than anything else was the popular movement that had sprung up after the burning of Hus at the stake in 1415—one of the great blunders the history of the Catholic Church abounds in. The more moderate followers of Hus, the Utraquists, soon made their peace with the Church and were given concessions in their rite, but the Taborites, the radical wing, embraced extreme religious, social, and political positions.[424] In the Taborite movement, nationalism ("ethnicity"), democracy, and various socialistic trends were united in a new synthesis for the first time in Europe. Inevitably, this violently *collectivist and "identitarian"* current encountered strong opposition from the Catholic Church, which is supranational and has always upheld the principle of idoneity—fitness, suitability, aptitude—against all egalitarian manias.[425]

The Taborites waged violent racial-ideological wars not only in the Lands of the Crown of St. Wenceslas (Bohemia, Moravia, Silesia), but also in the surrounding areas (Austria, Saxony, Upper Hungary). They were feared for their utter inhumanity: for their tendency to kill all men, women, and children in the cities they conquered; and for their limitless hatred of all things German. In Komotau, for instance, all males were slaughtered—except for thirty who had to bury the rest.[426] The Hussite women were completely "emancipated" and treated women more viciously than the men. In one case they undressed their victims and burned them in groups, reserving special cruelties for those who were pregnant.[427] When the

Taborites stormed Prachatitz (Prachatice) in 1420 they spared the lives of Utraquists but burned all the other men alive.[428]

Their hostility to everything Catholic and German was matched only by their loathing of the nobility—and this although, as in the later leftist revolution, members of the nobility frequently acted as leaders for the bestialized masses. Žižka of Trocnov was one example. But sadistic tortures are the expression of hatreds, and hatreds always originate from some sense of inferiority or from some sort of weakness. Almost always, inferior majorities try to *exterminate* superior minorities. Privileged minorities might have a strong *libido dominandi*, but the drive toward physical extermination has roots in the inferiority complex of the suspicious and envious masses, who in a deeper sense always are and feel helpless; hence their cruelty.

The importance of the events that centered in fifteenth-century Bohemia cannot be exaggerated, which is why we return to the subject. They constitute a phase in the development of the entire Western world that produced currents of a decisive and irrevocable nature. True, John Hus is unthinkable without the intellectual fatherhood of John Wycliffe, an early nationalist (not in the British-American sense of the term).[429] And Hus himself was a theologian rather than a political theorist. (The connections between Hus and Luther have been discussed elsewhere.)[430] Still, Hus's ideas were alive in German-speaking regions adjoining Bohemia until Luther's days.

What then, precisely, was the political character of the Taborite, the radical Hussite, movement? The importance here is not so much the *reality* of the movement's character as the historical evolution of its *image*. (Something similar can be said of the American War of Independence which in American folklore has become the "American Revolution" and as such frequently affects the thinking of the average American.) For however exaggerated the picture of Taboritism, it had a great effect, primarily on the Czechs, but in time also on their German neighbors (the so-called "Sudeten Germans"). They were prepared to ignore the anti-German character of Taboritism while cherishing its anti-Catholic and, at times, anti-Austrian bias. Above all, the historic picture of the Taborite "identitarian" revolution made a strong impact on a group of Czech Socialists who despaired of achieving international socialism. Hence in 1896 they formed the Czech National Socialist party, and this induced Mussolini to study the "doubly collectivist" Taborite-Hussite movement.

Professor Josef Pekař was probably right in his hotly contested thesis that the Taborites were neither quite so democratic nor quite so socialistic as earlier maintained, and that the presentation of other scholars (Masaryk, Palacký, Krofta, Hajn, Czerwenka) was at least in part erroneous.[431] Until the middle of the nineteenth century the Taborite movement had been rejected on moral grounds by the vast majority of Czechs and Germans as an outbreak of primeval savagery. But Palacký's mythological presentation changed all this. With the simultaneous rise of nationalism, democracy, and socialism, the Czechs came to cherish the idea that they were the forerunners of modernity, and Taboritism was reinterpreted, which went hand in hand with the reevaluation of Hus among the Germans.

The end of the nineteenth century saw the organization of the Evangelical "Away from Rome" movement (*Los-von-Rom-Bewegung*),[432] especially strong among the Germans from Bohemia and Moravia, and the memory of Hus, hitherto a despised Czech nationalist hero, suddenly became sacred. An entire German nationalist literature sprang up in praise of Hus (whose name, with a "double s," happily sounded quite German). Interestingly, Czech nationalists (then as now) viewed the Catholic Church as the German-Austrian church of the Habsburgs; thus when Thomas G. Masaryk joined the Bohemian Brethren (*bratři*), his break with Rome had simultaneously a religious and a national significance. (Needless to say, German nationalists and Nazis looked upon the "Church of Rome" as "Latin-Slav" and "alien"—*artfremd*. Similarly, Masaryk excoriated the allegedly pro-Slav Jews for being pro-German Habsburg protégés.)

Race-conscious nationalism, a form of neurosis, almost always ignores logic and knowledge: in the East European civil wars between 1918 and 1920 Jews were slaughtered for a variety of contradictory reasons, as capitalists, as communists, as friends of the Ukrainians, as Polonophiles, as pro-German—however circumstances dictated. (During World War I, the Jews in Eastern Europe did in fact sympathize with the Central Powers who gave them civil equality, as in the 1918 Treaty of Bucharest.)

What other momentous effects the "national socialist" aspects of Taboritism had on Central Europe will be discussed in due course. The importance here is to study the effect on Mussolini. As an Italian Socialist with a national outlook, Mussolini did not hesitate to favor intervention at the outbreak of World War I; he berated the Catholic Church, the House of Savoy, and conservative circles for not immediately bringing Italy into the war on the side of the Allies. True, he received monetary aid from France for his newly founded dissident socialist newspaper, *Il Popolo d'Italia*, but in his heart he really stood for intervention on the side of the Western Powers;

and this although Italy, along with Germany and Austria-Hungary, formed the Triple Alliance, and its national interests would have been better served had it remained in it.[433] But Mussolini had *ideological* reasons for his switch from pacifism to belligerence, for his espousal of the "wrong" side. When Italy joined England and France, he immediately volunteered and was wounded near the front by an exploding mortar.[434] By that time he had given up his purely Marxist views and, according to his own disavowal, became increasingly interested in Proudhon, Sorel, and the French Syndicalist movement.[435] Péguy, Nietzsche, and Lagardelle also made a deep impression on him.[436]

Mussolini returned from the war a non-Socialist. In his efforts to stem the tide of chaos and anarchy, this still staunch republican and leftist, in March 1919, founded the *fasci di combattimento*, whose real fighting force were the *squadristi*. They wanted to save Italy from the total anarchy toward which the country was undoubtedly headed. The formal founding of the National Fascist party, however, did not take place until late in 1921, the March on Rome a year later, on October 1922 (Mussolini went most of the way by train). By that time the *Fascisti* already had wide support, not only from ex-Socialists, but also from the middle and upper classes.

Who was to blame for this development? Primarily the Communists and Socialists who had plunged the country into indescribable confusion leading to near collapse. One strike followed the other. Communist bands occupied factories, paralyzed communications, established local soviets, and defied central authority. The constitutional monarchy, adhering far too loyally to the constitutional laws, could obviously no longer cope with the situation. Although it was the duty of the Crown to establish, with the help of the army, a temporary royal dictatorship, Victor Emmanuel III probably considered it more "democratic" for an existing party to shoulder the responsibility and thus he refused to proclaim the state of emergency craved by the weak Facta government, which thereupon resigned.

Mussolini, appointed prime minister, had a hard time restraining the more radical (and more emphatically leftist) Fascists. Full dictatorship did not develop until 1925-26. The transition period lasted several years and the diarchy (King and *Duce*) until 1943, when the monarchy saved the country by having Mussolini arrested. (Such a finale was not possible in Germany where Hitler fought to the bitter end and left the country divided and in ruins.) Mussolini, "rescued" by Otto Skorzeny, was taken to Hitler's headquarters where he proclaimed (in all likelihood upon Hitler's advice) the Italian Social Republic which collapsed in 1945.[437] A year later the

republic was revived, without the title "Social" but with decisive communist support.

Today, it is possible to review Italian fascism with some dispassion and in
the proper context—as an ideology *and* as an historic phenomenon within
the Italian setting. As Hannah Arendt has pointed out, compared to Nazi
Germany or the Soviet Union, Italy under fascism was hardly totalitarian;
fascist Italy was far more humane than the two tyrannies to the north.[438]
The temperament of nations is a highly important factor in the character of
any government.

There was another aspect to fascism—a drive for national discipline—
that was less apparent in Russian communism and not at all present in
German national socialism. The countries of Southern Europe, having
played such an eminent part in history until enlightenment, liberalism,
and technology speeded the evolution of the north, were fatally eclipsed and
"left behind." Italy was no exception. While Britain, the Netherlands,
Germany, and Scandinavia were forging ahead, acquiring military and
naval fame, and rapidly increasing their living standards, the Mediterranean nations, engaged in *dolce vita* and in *dolce far niente*, enjoyed blue skies,
soft melodies, and delightful conversations—and great poverty. The influx
of tourists from the affluent north, moreover, created an inferiority complex
which in turn fostered the desire to compete successfully with these
progressive and powerful nations. The remedy seemed to be hard work,
discipline, punctuality, cleanliness, anticorruption measures, control of
morality, military prowess, artificial industrialization, obligatory sports,
and propaganda for "national greatness."

Fascism tried to promote all these efforts and drives. Foreign tourists
were gratified to see beggars disappear from the streets and have trains
running on time. George Bernard Shaw, the great Fabian, had nothing but
praise for Mussolini and thereby elicited cries of protest from Socialists. He
was called a traitor, but he persisted: Fascists were "progressive." (André
Siegfried remarked quite rightly that Americans are far more attracted to
Germany and Switzerland, where order and discipline rule supreme, than
to France, which is anarchical.) Somewhat similar to the fascist attitude,
many a Russian nationalist was delighted by the industrialization of the
USSR. Russian refugees gloated: "We are going to show the decadent
West." The Soviets desired above all to outdo the United States.[439]

But apart from the competitive urge conditioned by an inferiority
complex, there was a purely ideological aspect to fascism, a solid piece of
socialist heritage, and also of *Religionsersatz*, synthetic religion, which

made coexistence between fascism and the Catholic Church extremely difficult.[440] Fascism had as well a Maurassian side (with Machiavellian, pragmatic overtones) insofar as it assented to the Catholic faith as a "national religion."[441] In this and in other respects fascism differed strongly from Spanish falangism and the Rumanian Iron Guard ideology, which was spiritual as well as savage.[442]

The pertinent passages about Italian fascism in the interesting diaries of Victor Serge, a dissident Russian Communist, help explain the deep and lasting connection between national and international leftist ideologies— socialism-communism and fascism. Serge writes about Nicola Bombacci, a Socialist who returned to Italy and "collaborated." When Serge met him in exile in Berlin (1923-24), Bombacci told him that Mussolini owed much to communist ideas. "Why," Serge asked, "didn't you get rid of Mussolini at the time of the destruction of the cooperatives?" "Because our most militant and energetic men had gone over to him," was the answer. Serge confessed that he then realized how much he was tortured by the attraction fascism exercised over the extreme Left. Just as the "reddest" areas in Germany changed from red to brown and back to red, so it occurred in Italy. The Romagna, very red today, was very fascist in the 1920s and 1930s.

Equally interesting are the confessions made to Serge by Henri Guilbeaux, another founder of the Komintern. Guilbeaux considered Mussolini Lenin's real heir. Serge concluded that fascism attracted many revolutionaries not only because of its "plebeian force and violence," but also because of its constructive program to build schools, drain swamps, promote industrialization, and found an empire. There was, moreover, a vision—a New Order—which, the leftists believed, would come about when the groundwork done by the Fascists was crowned with socialism. "It is impossible to review the fascist phenomenon without discovering the importance of its interrelations with revolutionary socialism," Serge confessed.[443]

Massimo Rocca's well-documented *How Fascism Became a Dictatorship* has even more material about the leftist ties of fascism. Rocca insists that in his last days Mussolini thought of surrendering to the Socialist party, expecting to be spared by his old comrades. (Twice he had saved the life of Pietro Nenni.) Toward the end of 1922 (the very beginning of fascist rule) Mussolini was still trying in the Chamber to win over the extreme Left through fiery appeals.[444] "For Mussolini," Rocca writes, "fascism was nothing but an interlude beween his exit from the Socialist party and his future triumphal readmission, a hope nourished for twenty years."[445] Back in 1919 Mussolini had praised the communist seizure of the factories in Dalmine and in 1921 he had offered to cooperate with the Socialist party (PSI) in an antimonarchical and anticapitalist revolution. Mussolini's "conversion" to the monarchy came a few weeks before the *Marcia su Roma*, but the last friend whom he truly trusted was a Socialist, Carlo Silvestri.

During his rule of the "Social Republic" (with the capital in Salò) Mussolini's loathing for the "bourgeoisie" and the "capitalists" again came out into the open. His hatred and contempt for the aristocracy had been strong at all times, as Vittorio, his son, confirmed. This explains in part his hostile attitude toward his daughter Edda's marriage.[446] In this respect he felt very much like Hitler, to whose spell he succumbed tragically toward the end of his life. Hitler had been influenced by the Taborite image in a more devious way. In *practice* Hitler certainly subscribed to Mussolini's *"Tutto nello Stato, niente al fuori dello Stato, nulla contro lo Stato"* ("Everything within the State, nothing outside the State, nothing against the State").[447] Theoretically, both could have adhered to another monistic formula in respect to their intended rule: "government of the people, by the people, and for the people."

"Hitler and Mussolini," Jules Romains wrote in *Les hommes de bonne volonté*, "are despots belonging to the age of democracy. They fully profit from the doubtful service which democracy has rendered to man in our society by initiating him into politics, by getting him used to that intoxicant, by making him believe that the domain of catastrophes is his concern, that history calls for him, consults him, needs him every moment. Dictatorship of the nazi type is a late cancer which has blossomed on the soil of the French Revolution."[448]

CHAPTER 12

National Socialism and Socialist Racism

*We call our movement National Socialism,
and with the victory of the movement
Socialism has conquered the
People and the State.*

—WALTER HAID

At heart Mussolini was always a Socialist. Hitler, on the other hand, never formally belonged to the Socialist party, although he had drunk from almost the same ideological sources. His *Weltanschauung* had also been largely fathered by the national socialist Taborites.

This leads back to the revived interest in the Taborites in Bohemia during the second half of the nineteenth century. At that time, Bohemia had a Social Democratic Czech party that cooperated fully with the Austrian Social Democrats. Both belonged to the Second International. But the nationalistic fervor of that period strongly affected the Czech party and led to a split in 1896. A faction under the leadership of Klofáč, Stříbrný, and Franke seceded and formed the *Národně Socialistická Strana Česká* (the Czech National Socialist party), thus introducing for the first time in European history a party sporting the National Socialist label.

The popular ideas of the Taborite movement were immediately adopted as guides by the new party.[449] Practically any Czech handbook or encyclopedia[450] will show that the main characteristic of this important new party

145

was its emphasis on the Hussite-Taborite tradition, which, in fact, became the "official myth" of Czechoslovakia after the country was formed in 1918. After 1919 the NSSČ took Dr. Edvard Beneš as its leader and changed its name to the Czechoslovak National Socialist party. Karel Hoch in his essay *The Political Parties of Czechoslovakia* lists the predominant features of the NSSČ as follows: "Collectivizing by means of development, surmounting of class struggle by national discipline, moral rebirth and democracy as the conditions of socialism, a powerful popular army, etc."[451]

A study of its programs reveals other important points: anticlericalism, an intimate synthesis between nationalism and socialism, trust in the working class, the peasantry, and the lower middle class, opposition to the nobility—all reminiscent of German national socialism except for the lack of an anti-Jewish sentiment. But contrary to a widespread notion, anti-Jewish feelings had been quite strong among the Czechs, leading to outbreaks of popular violence against the Jews in Prague and elsewhere. Ironically, anti-German riots led to demonstrations against Jewish shop-keepers, who spoke German, during which, on December 1, 1897, three persons were killed. Moreover, Thomas G. Masaryk criticized the Habsburgs for their support of the Jews, a stand that was seconded by Wickham Steed, the great British apostle of the Czech cause.[452]

Czech national socialism was also strongly identitarian, far more so than Italian fascism, which put the accent on the state rather than on the people. As a political party the NSSČ disappeared under German occupation only to reemerge in 1945, when, still headed by Beneš, it eagerly collaborated with the Communists.

It is not accidental that the big *Masaryk Encyclopedia* (*Masarykův Ottův Naučný*), under the heading "National Socialism," features both the Czech and the German National Socialist parties. The foundations for the latter were laid among the Germans of Bohemia in 1897 when a small periodical, *Der Hammer*, was moved from Vienna to Eger (in northwest Bohemia). Its editor was Franko Stein, a member of an organization called the German National Workers' League. Backed by his paper, Stein was able to organize a German National Workers' Congress in Eger in 1898, where a twenty-five point program was adopted, a program rather similar to the Linz program of Georg von Schönerer, Austria's most prominent nationalist leader. (The Linz program had been partly drawn up by Victor Adler, who later left the nationalist camp and became Austria's leading Social Democrat.) But these nationalist workers (soon headed by a bookbinder called Ferdinand Burschofsky) distrusted Schönerer; they considered him too "bourgeois" to rally or lead class-conscious workers. They wanted socialism; they wanted a nationalism with distinctly leftist features.

They were not unsuccessful. In April 1902 a meeting of the Organization of Nationalistic Labor took place in Saaz, and in December of the same year a mass demonstration was held in Reichenberg. The group, renamed the German Political Labor League for Austria, boasted 26,000 members, and Schönerer's national-liberal attitude was flatly rejected. On November 15, 1903, a further step was taken in Aussig: A *political party* was formed called the German Worker's Party in Austria (DAP). Its program was formulated a year later in Trautenau, where the following declaration was made: "We are a liberty-loving nationalistic party that fights energetically against reactionary tendencies as well as feudal, clerical, or capitalistic privileges and all alien influences."[453]

There were other demands, such as separation of church and state, adherence to democratic principles in army appointments, nationalization of mines and railroads—the usual postulates of "progressive" leftist parties in Europe. In the next year (1904), however, a move was made to change the name of the rising new party. Hans Knirsch, who hailed from Moravia, proposed calling it the German Social Workers' party or the National Socialist German Workers' party. After a long debate the move was rejected by the Bohemian delegates for an obvious reason: they were afraid of being charged with copying the Czech National Socialists. And yet their programs were almost identical and similar to that of the Social Democrats, members of the Second International. Karel Engliš, professor at the Masaryk University in Brünn (Brno), speaking about the program of the successors of the German Workers' Party, said that "German Socialism does not differ from Marxism in its critique of capitalism nor in its concept of the class struggle."[454]

At a local election in Reichenberg in 1905, the German Workers' Party was able to marshal 14,000 votes. In 1906 it sent three deputies to the *Reichsrat*, the Parliament in Vienna, thus appearing for the first time at the center of Austrian life. An "All-Austrian" congress of the German Workers' Party took place in Prague in 1909, and again the Moravian effort to change its name was defeated. But now new men were coming up. There was an engineer, Rudolf Jung, who had been transferred from Vienna to Bohemia by the state railway for having overtly engaged in nationalistic propaganda, and a lawyer, Dr. Walter Riehl—"bourgeois" elements, to be sure, but these are found in all socialist parties.

In the beginning, World War I had a paralyzing effect on all political activities, but in 1916 *Die Freien Stimmen*, the paper of the DAP, started to agitate anew for the adoption of the term "National Socialist." In April 1918 a motion to rename the party was again defeated by a vote of 29-14 in Aussig, but a month later the change was effected at a large congress in Vienna. Thus the German National Socialist Workers' Party (DNSAP, not yet NSDAP) was born months before the end of the war, while Hitler was still a *Gefreiter*, a private first class, on the Western Front.

The program formulated in Vienna had a totally leftist character. It said: "The German National Socialist Workers' Party is not a worker's party in the narrow sense of the term: It represents the interests of all honestly creative labor. It is a liberty-loving and strictly nationalist party and therefore fights against all reactionary trends, against ecclesiastical, aristocratic, and capitalist privileges and every alien influence, but above all against the overpowering influence of the Jewish-commercial mentality in all domains of public life. . . .

". . . it demands the amalgamation of all regions of Europe inhabited by Germans into a democratic, social-minded German Reich. . . .

". . . it demands plebiscites for all key laws in the Reich, the states and provinces. . . .

". . . it demands the elimination of the rule of Jewish banks over business life and the creation of national people's banks with a democratic administration. . . ."[455]

This program simply oozed the spirit of leveling leftism: it was democratic, it was anti-Habsburg (it demanded the destruction of the Danube monarchy in favor of the Pan-German program); it was against all unpopular minorities, an attitude that is the magnetism of all leftist ideologies. The Jews of Austria had been slowly evolving (as they had further west) into a new upper crust.[456] A Jewish proletariat, such as existed in Poland, Russia, or the Ukraine, no longer existed in Austria—Jews had even been ennobled—and envy was easily mobilized against them. In short, war was declared against all non-national, cosmopolitan elements like the Jews, the bankers, the clergy, the aristocracy, and royalty.

Six months later the Austro-Hungarian monarchy was no more. But Germany survived. Lloyd George, Wilson, and Clemenceau actually helped to realize the noble program of the DNSAP by eliminating the biggest stumbling block in the path of Pan-Germanism—the Habsburg monarchy. True, the birth of Czechoslovakia did not quite fit the plans of the National Socialists. But Hans Knirsch was able to congratulate Masaryk and Tusar, the Czech leaders, for having helped to destroy the old monarchy,[457] while he wept for the unfulfilled "old nostalgic dream of all German democrats"—the Pan-German state.[458] Still, in the first elections held in Czechoslovakia, the DNSAP received 42,000 votes. But it also suffered some losses; men who lacked legal grounds for Czechoslovak citizenship were expelled—Rudolf Jung went to Munich, Dr. Walter Riehl to Vienna. The party now had three branches: one in the newly founded Czechoslovakia, a smaller one in what remained of Austria (headed by Dr. Riehl), and a tiny one in Poland whose members were German-speaking. It was Rudolf Jung who contacted a small nationalist group in Munich (the German Workers' Party) and instilled in it the spirit of early National Socialism. Referring to this, Josef Pfitzner, a Sudenten German Nazi author, wrote with pride that "the synthesis of the two great dynamic powers of the century, of the socialist and national idea, had been perfected in the German borderlands which thus were far ahead of their motherland."[459]

What, in the meantime, had happened inside Germany? Konrad Heiden, Hitler's earliest biographer, mentions the creation early in 1918 of a Free Committee for a German Workers' Peace. Anton Drexler organized a branch of the league on March 7, 1918, in Munich.[460] And in January 1919 this local group was renamed the German Workers' Party with Drexler the proud holder of membership card number 1. The seventh member was a certain Adolf Hitler; but he did not like the name of the budding organization and proposed calling it the Social Revolutionary party. Rudolf Jung, who joined these men bringing with him much material and literature from the DNSAP,[461] persuaded them to adopt the slightly reshuffled name of the National Socialist German Workers' Party (NSDAP). Hitler contributed several ideas on foreign policy to the party program, while a teacher and organizer of the Democratic Party from Franconia by the name of Julius Streicher provided some additional, anti-Jewish motifs.[462]

Who was this amazing person, Adolf Hitler? As with every human being, the development of this tragic and unattractive figure must be studied in the context of his environment, personal experiences, and the ideas to which he was exposed. To understand him fully it is necessary to comprehend the Austrian and especially the Viennese atmosphere.

There are suspicions that Adolf Hitler's father was partly of Jewish origin, which helps explain the son's twin hatred of his father and the Jews. His father's mother, a Fräulein Schicklgruber, after bearing Hitler's father,[463] married a man called Hiedler or Hitler, which automatically legitimized the child. Hitler's father married twice and was a custom official in the city of Braunau on the Austro-German (Austro-Bavarian) border.

Braunau and the house where Hitler was born are well worth visiting.[464] The city's main square is completely open to the Inn River separating Braunau from (Bavarian) Simbach. The town, a country seat, seems to be cut in half as with a knife. Hitler's father spent much of his time on the bridge, stopping the passersby to inspect their suitcases, bundles, and sacks, thus symbolizing to his son the separation of Austria from Germany. There were, of course, several reasons why Hitler, who had qualms about his father' origin, did not get along with him. As for his heritage, given the importance attached by the Nazis to "racial purity," much about Hitler's ancestry remained "ambiguous," although a number of people seemed, nevertheless, to be rather well informed.[465]

Since his despised father, wearing a uniform with the imperial insignia, personified to young Hitler the Habsburg monarchy, he soon developed a real loathing for the country of his birth. His teachers in the secondary school were mostly Pan-Germans and thus anticlericalists; he himself never evidenced a religious bent. Rather, as an adolescent and a young man he seemed to be possessed by endless animosities. Before concentrating on the Jews his morbid hatred was turned against the higher social classes: military officers and the aristocracy.[466] He entered a high school-college of the scientific type[467] but, intellectually unable to make the grade, he took to painting and became interested in architecture. He wanted to study at the Art Academy (*Akademie der bildenden Künste*) of Vienna but was not admitted because he had neither a B.A. nor a B.S., nor did he show the extraordinary talent that would have served in lieu of a degree. The examining professor advised him to study architecture, but this too proved impossible because he lacked a degree which the Polytechnic required.

His hatred for the Imperial regime was so strong that he did everything within his power to avoid military service in Austria. (Those without a degree had to spend three years in the service, while those with one served one year and almost automatically received a commission.) Thus the young Hitler emigrated to Bavaria and at the outbreak of World War I joined the Bavarian army.[468] After the war, when Hitler, already the recognized leader of the national socialist movement, wanted to extend his oratory to Austria, the Austrian federal chancellor, Monsignor Seipel, warned him that he would have him arrested and tried for desertion. This further nourished Hitler's hatred of the Catholic Church.

Hitler, though never a paperhanger, allegedly sold hand-colored post-cards in coffee houses, a far more humiliating livelihood than any honest craft. (Theoretically, it is quite possible that he hawked his art to Lenin, Stalin, Trotski, or de Gasperi, all of whom frequented the Café Central in Vienna's Herengasse.) Easily hurt, quickly offended, tortured by inferiority complexes, he was also highly superstitious. Because he was born in Braunau, he became fixated with the color brown. The Nazi storm troopers wore brown shirts; the headquarters of the National Socialists in Munich was called the Brown House: Hitler became a German by acquiring the citizenship of Braunschweig (Brunswick) where the local Nazi government gave him an administrative post;[469] and, finally, he married his mistress—Eva Braun.[470]

Hitler also had a florid imagination. He read fiction and may have read *Der Diktator* by Paul Albrecht (Berlin-Schlachtensee: Siegfried, 1923), a utopian novel about a hoped-for German dictator. This dreadful literary product, however, has so far never been alluded to as a source of inspiration for Hitler.

Hitler's social inferiority weighed heavily on him. Carl Burckhardt, grandnephew of the famous Jacob Burckhardt and the last League of Nations commissioner in Danzig, explained to what extent this factor contributed to the outbreak of World War II. In *Meine Danziger Mission 1937–1939* Burckhardt reports his conversation with Hitler in August 1939 about the prospects of war and peace. Hitler shouted, "I have read idiotic reports in the French press to the effect that I have lost my nerve, whereas the Poles have kept theirs." (Hitler was so furious that for a few moments he was unable to continue.)

Burckhardt: "You do these journalists too much honor if you take their views so seriously. A Chancellor of the Reich ought not to get upset about such trifles. . . ."

Hitler: "This I cannot do. As a proletarian and due to my origin, my rise, and my character, I am incapable of seeing things in this light. This the statesmen have to understand if they want to avoid a catastrophe."[471]

Here is exemplified a man with a genuinely leftist turn of mind, an identitarian, a *leader*, not a ruler, a personifier of the masses.[472] Big Brother, but not father, a loveless man who wanted Germany in monotones—local traditions eliminated, regional self-government destroyed, flags of the *Länder* outlawed, differences between the Christian faiths eradicated, churches desiccated and forcibly amalgamated. He dreamed of making the Germans themselves more uniform, even physically, by planned breeding[473] and the extermination, sterilization, or deportation of those who deviated from the norm. The tribes (*Stämme*) should cease to exist. All this notwithstanding, Hitler's lack of education and preparation for the enormous power he held, the astonishing mediocrity of his tastes (especially in art) and of his views on almost all subjects, endeared him to the masses (who usually adore the successful amateur). Here was a "regular guy," a "fellow like you and me," an "ordinary, decent chap!"

His *Table Talks* noted down by a physician, Dr. Henry Picker, are a most frightening human document because they show the banality and the diabolism—the final logical consequences—in the thinking of the man in the street.[474] And, as so often happens with basically mediocre neurotics, certain romantic notions had taken a firm hold on Hitler. Before his emigration to Bavaria he had read the curious pamphlets of a defrocked Cistercian monk from Heiligenkreuz Abbey, Georg Lanz, who called himself Lanz von Liebenfels.[475] This somewhat mentally disturbed man had published a periodical propagating Nordic racism. These ideas, combined with his increasing hatred of the Jews and his violent rejection of the multinational Austrian Empire, impressed Hitler deeply. A close community can only be establised among near-identical people, and all this tied in well with the haunting vision of a perverted, secularized monastery.

Connections between the newly emerging NSDAP and the DNSAP of Czechoslovakia, Austria, and Poland were quickly established. In 1920 and 1922, so-called Interstate Meetings of Deputies of the three (or four) Nazi parties were held in Salzburg (Austria).[476] In the 1920 meeting a violent clash occurred between Hitler and two Austrian representatives, Dr. Riehl and Karl Schulz, during which Hitler, in the best proletarian fashion, declared that he would "prefer to be hanged in a bolshevik Germany than be happy in a gallicized *Reich*."[477] At the same meeting the Vienna program of 1918 was repeated almost verbatim, evidence of how strongly even German national socialism was determined by the Bohemian pattern. The new declarations were signed collectively by the National Socialist parties of the German people. Even at the 1922 meeting the German Nazi group seems to have been the smallest—if we discount the tiny German-Polish splinter.

In November 1923 Hitler tried a *Putsch* in Munich, which ended fatally. The revolutionary demonstrators were met by the *Reichswehr* under General von Lossow and the police and mowed down by bullets. Hitler and General Ludendorff[478] got away with their lives by throwing themselves on the ground. The conservative prime minister of Bavaria, August von Kahr, also helped to quell the rebellion, and for this "betrayal of the national revolution" Kahr paid with his life in the *Reichsmordwoche* (the mass executions on and after June 30, 1934) and German conservatives as a whole earned Hitler's undying hatred. After the Munich *Putsch* Hitler was apprehended and jailed in Landsberg fortress, where he found a splendid opportunity to write *Mein Kampf*.[479]

Released from jail, he was accepted by all three National Socialist parties as their undisputed leader, though Schulz established a dissident group in Austria. In Czechoslovakia, the National Socialist parties were dissolved in October 1933 and replaced by the *Sudetendeutsche Partei*, which was firmly national socialist in character and led by Konrad Henlein, a gymnastic teacher. The most militant element in the Czech national movement had always been the *Sokol*, a calisthenics association founded by Miroslav Tyrš, a fervent admirer of Jahn and Darwin. The majority of the German and Austrian calisthenic leagues, the *Turnvereine*, were nationalistic and suffused with an identitarian fervor that gloried in identically dressed men and women making identical movements in mass performances!

Although in 1923 Hitler failed to wrest Germany by force, theWeimar Republic's democratic constitution offered ideal conditions for a peaceful and legal takeover—through the electoral process. Any party could achieve supreme power either by winning a majority and thus running the government or, as a strategically placed minority in the Parliament, by making a mockery of democratic principles. Of course, the Weimar Constitution was thoroughly democratic in its intentions: it prescribed proportional representation, providing one deputy for every sixty thousand voters. The number of deputies was thus flexible; it depended upon the size of the electorate.

A study of the development of the different parties in the four elections preceding Hitler's advent to power is most interesting. Much can be learned from the voters' geographic-regional distribution as well as from changes in the support the parties received. Maps (which I have published elsewhere) show distinctly that religion was a decisive factor in the territorial growth of national socialism.[480] In Germany at that time, the denominations lived in specific circumscribed areas—the result of the historic principle *cuius regio eius religio* (roughly, "the ruler determines the faith of his subjects")—and even today, after the tragic migrations following the collapse of the Third Reich, the old pattern survives with surprisingly few differences.

There is no doubt that the Nazi victories were gained with the aid primarily of the Evangelicals or, to be more precise, the "progressive post-Protestants"; a mere glance at the areas shown in the statistical maps is proof enough. On the other hand, one of the maps shows that there were *no* denominational implications in the Communist voting.[481] This is not too surprising: Luther was a firm political authoritarian who believed that *utter* severity in government was essential in view of the totally corrupt nature of man; and, moreover, he became one of the world's most rabid Jew-haters and racists after vainly striving for the conversion of the Jews to his faith.[482] The idea of a concentration camp for Jews was his;[483] in fact, at the Nuremberg trial Julius Streicher invoked Luther, insisting that, if the Reformer were still alive, he would be sitting among the defendants.[484] Streicher (and not only Streicher) had carefully studied Luther's anti-Jewish pamphlets. It shows the ignorance and confusion in which we live that America's late leading black antiracist carried the Reformer's name.

These facts must unfortunately be mentioned because they are essential to an understanding of the German tragedy which has aspects of a global calamity.[485] Hitler, to be sure, never showed any specific enthusiasm for Luther and he despised the Evangelicals even more than the Catholics—he had, for all practical purposes, left the Catholic Church.[486] As for national socialism, Hitler declared that it was not a "cultic religion" but a "popular movement based on the exact sciences."[487]

Perhaps even more interesting than the denominational aspects of the spread of national socialism were its ideological conquests. The three or four elections that preceded the brown tidal wave paint a curious picture. The various parties can be separated into three categories: the parties of national socialism; the parties with fixed ideologies (Communists, Social Democrats, Catholic Centrists, German Nationalists, People's Conservatives, and Bavarian People's); and the parties belonging to the liberal-democratic dispensation (German People's, Democratic, Economic). The German People's Party was a successor of the National Liberals of Bismarck's day and was led by Dr. Gustav Stresemann until his death. The Democratic party had been renamed the State Party. The Bavarian People's party was monarchist and conservative. The following tabulations include the March 1933 elections, though their genuineness is most questionable. The 1933 elections were held under Nazi control and, in specific cases, the results were falsified.

To begin with, only 481 deputies had been elected in 1928 as against 647 in 1933, an increase explained by the participation at the polls of those

who had previously not voted—the withdrawn, the indifferent, the skeptical. By 1933, their imagination had obviously been caught by the National
Socialists, who owed much of their victory to these new constituents. (This
cannot, of course, be proved "scientifically"; *theoretically* it is possible that
the new voters cast their ballots for the Socialists, Centrists, or Nationalists, while former voters became Nazis, but those cognizant of the German
scene would scoff at such an idea.)

Election Date	Deputies		
	National Socialists	*Non-Nazi Ideologists*	*Demo- Liberal*
May 20, 1928	12	363	116
September 14, 1930	107	351	119
July 31, 1932	230	358	20
November 6, 1932	196	364	24
March 5, 1933	288	346	13

Yet just as important as the mobilization of the nonvoters was the switch
of the "Demo-Liberals," the uncommitted Left, the progressivists, and the
middle-roaders to the National Socialist Party. The Democratic Party,
which in 1919 had 80 deputies, was reduced to 2 in November 1932; the
Economic Party of the Middle Class went down from 23 in 1928 to zero.
The German People's Party (the former National Liberals) decreased from
45 in 1928 to a mere 2 in March 1933, but the Catholic Centrists increased
during the same period from 61 to 73, the Bavarian royalists rose from 17
to 19, and even the questionably conservative German Nationalists gained
6 seats in the years 1930-33, from 44 to 53 seats. This shows quite clearly
who resisted, who tried to stem the Nazi tide: certainly not the forces of
agnosticism, polite doubt, left-of-centrism, progressivism, and enlightenment.

How many of these people were executed by the National Socialists?
None (other than those executed for purely racial reasons). How many
Evengelical Christians gave their lives for their faith (rather than for their
political views)? Only Pastor Bonhoeffer comes to mind. On the other
hand, hundreds of Catholics, lay and religious, died for their faith in
Germany and Austria (not to mention Poland). Among them were Dr. Paul
Metzger, a priest who headed the Ecumenical Movement and was therefore
doubly suspect. And who really fought the Red armies in Russia's civil war
(1918–20)? Democrats? Liberals? By no means. Only monarchists and

anarchists—the religiously and ideologically motived. But back to the German elections.

The Social Democrats decreased, but only slightly. From May 1928 to November 1932 their seats in the *Reichstag* numbered 153, 143, 133, and 121. To whom did they lose?

A hint can be found in the totals of their fellow Marxists, the Communists: 44, 77, 89, and 100. This shows that by July 1932 the two big totalitarian parties, the National Socialist and the Communist, held 319 seats out of 608—an absolute majority, indicating that *more than half of all Germans emphatically rejected parliamentary democracy* and that another large sector regarded it with the greatest skepticism. This means in turn that the democratic republic uncompromisingly demanded by Wilson was the basis of future slavery in Germany, the door through which tyranny entered. Plato's and Aristotle's dictum that tyranny springs from democracy was well confirmed.

The German democratic parliamentarian system had reached a complete impasse by 1932. Chancellor Brüning knew that there was only one way to preserve the basic liberties—to restore the monarchy through a referendum. But the president, Paul von Hindenburg, rejected the solution because he considered a plebiscite on the monarchy incompatible with the principle of legitimacy, and also because he had given his oath of allegiance to the Republic (in which basically he did not believe).[488] A cabinet, moreover, enjoying the confidence of the majority could not be formed. Finally, Franz von Papen, a dissenter from the Centrist party and one of the stupidest men ever to emerge in German political life,[489] tried to rule without Parliament, depending only on the old War Emergency laws. But he was supplanted by General Kurt von Schleicher, an intellectual military man who tried desperately to find a formula resembling that of Primo de Rivera's regime in Spain—a dictatorship combining the army and trade unions.[490]

But the conservative forces, already deeply imbued with democratic notions, did not believe that, in the long run, a government could subsist without popular support; in consequence, they suffered a genuine failure of nerve. Thus, on January 30, 1933, a government was formed which included the National Socialists; these, unfortunately, had a relative plurality in the *Reichstag*. Hindenburg, too old and too tired to resist, and ill-advised by his nephew, also gave in—to what was, in actuality, the victory not of the liberal but of *the democratic principle*.

It had been Papen's idea to form a coalition government in which a non-

Nazi would be appointed to counterbalance every Nazi in an important ministerial post. Hitler would be chancellor of the *Reich*, Papen vice-chancellor, and so on along the line. Papen and his friends expected—as did the outside world—that Hitler would never be able to master either the gigantic economic difficulties or those pertaining to foreign policy. But Hitler surprised the savants. Internally, he solved the unemployment problem by producing armaments and instituting public works, and, in foreign matters, the West was so frightened of him that it made every concession formerly denied to Dr. Brüning.

Earlier, an offer by Papen for a coalition government had been rejected by Hitler in a haughty letter whose salient passages highlight the leftist character of the Nazi movement. In his analysis of Papen's predicament Hitler puts the following words into his mouth:

"In this emergency only one thing could help. We wanted to invite them, i.e., the National Socialists, into our cabinet which enjoys not only the support of all Jews, but also of many aristocrats, conservatives, and members of the *Stahlhelm*. We were certain that they would accept our invitation without suspecting guile, freely and gladly. Then we would slowly have started to draw their poison fangs. Once they had shared our company, they could hardly withdraw. Caught together, hanged together!"

The "open letter," printed by the thousands and distributed widely, closed in the best leftist "common man" tradition:

"As to the rest, Herr von Papen, stay in the world in which you are, I will go on fighting in mine. I am happy to know that my world is the community of millions of German workers of the forehead and the fist, and of German peasants who, although mostly of humble origin and living in dire poverty, want to be the most faithful sons of our people—for they fight not only with their lips, but also with a suffering borne thousandfold and with innumerable sacrifices for a new and better German *Reich*."[491]

In January 1933 Papen gave in on disadvantageous terms, and subsequently was duly cheated and outsmarted. The tragedy ran its full course, with an outcome only too well known. Golo Mann, son of Thomas Mann and perhaps Germany's most outstanding historian, summed up the events concisely: "There was no trickery about Hitler's ascent to power, because he was virtually the strongest of them all and the organizer of the most violent popular movement. Once such a movement exists, victory is in the offing according to the rules of democracy and the laws of history. The individual events of the last act do not alter these facts."[492] What happened in Germany merely confirmed Harold Laski's theory that government by parliament is viable only if there is (1) a two-party system, and (2) a common framework of reference, a common philosophy uniting the parties. Germany, with a free society and a variety of radically individual outlooks, satisfied neither premise. (Nor do most other Continental countries.)[493] A strong monarchy can afford the luxury of multiplicity and variety, a republic hardly. (This fact, well known to Washington and Hamilton, his ghostwriter, was mentioned in the *Farewell Address*.)

In the meantime, misinterpretations as to the real character of national socialism continued almost unchallenged. In truth, national socialism—in the judgment of historians and political scientists as well as of its own leaders and ideologues—had a distinctly leftist pattern, clearly traceable to the French Revolution.

Hermann Rauschning, from Danzig, was the first man to analyze from a conservative viewpoint Hitler's words spoken to him in private. In his highly revealing *Gespräche mit Hitler* he tells of Hitler's utter contempt for Italian fascism,[494] his special hatred for the Habsburgs, and his complete nihilism,[495] so reminiscent of the legal positivism in the United States. Naturally, Hitler knew all too well that the Nazi Revolution was "the exact counterpart of the French Revolution"; and he thought of himself not only as "the conqueror but also the executor of Marxism—of that part that is essential and justified, stripped of its Jewish-Talmudic dogma."[496] He was particularly proud of the extent to which he had learned from the political methods of the Social Democrats. He averred on record that "worker-calisthenic associations, cells from the factory workers, mass demonstrations, propaganda pamphlets written especially for the multitudes, all these new means of political struggle used by us are Marxist in origin."[497] Little wonder, since socialism brought the principle of totalitarian organization to Germany, an event duly noted by the late Wilhelm Röpke.[498] "National socialism is socialism in evolution," Hitler insisted, "a socialism in everlasting change."[499] And, he went on to admit, "There is more that unites us with than divides us from bolshevism. . . above all the genuine revolutionary mentality. I was always aware of this and I have given the order that former Communists should be admitted to the party immediately."[500]

Needless to say, for military, but above all, for ideological reasons, Hitler greatly regretted having given aid to Franco, whom he sincerely detested. Too late he discovered, when he met them in France, his deep affinity for red Spaniards, whom he ironically planned to use as allies at some future date. [501] Hitler's instincts were true, however, for the socialism within national socialism was genuine. A rich literature exists on the subject, such as Walter Haid's *Sozialismus als Träger des Dritten Reichs*.[502] And there are countless corroborative declarations by national socialist leaders; Hermann Neubacher, for example, the new mayor of Vienna after the *Anschluss*, emphasized to local social democratic leaders the rigid socialist character of the brown ideology.[503]

Speaking of the coming war, Hitler said, "I am not afraid of destruction. We will have to part with much that seems to us dear and irreplaceable. Cities are going to be transformed into ruins, noble edifices will disappear forever. This time our sacred soil will not be spared, but I am not afraid. We will set our teeth and fight to the bitter end. From these ruins Germany will rise bigger and more beautiful than any country in the world."[504] The master of mobs repeated this idea ecstatically in the last weeks of his rule. Demolition delights all leftists, fills them with diabolic glee. Mr. Herbert Read (quite some time before he was knighted, to be sure) praised destruction in a book appropriately called *To Hell with Culture* (No. 4. of the series, "The Democratic Order") in which he spoke about the necessity of destroying all "nondemocratic, aristocratic or capitalist" cultures. "To hell with such culture!" Read wrote, "To the rubbish-heap and furnace with it all! Let us celebrate the democratic revolution with the biggest holocaust in the history of the world. When Hitler has finished bombing our cities, let the demolition squads complete the good work. Then let us go out into the wide open spaces and build anew."[505] This was written in 1941 when the barbarians dominated *everywhere*. Still, Sir Herbert had the courage to write in 1943, "Communism is an extreme form of democracy, and it is totalitarian: but equally the totalitarian state in the form of fascism is an extreme form of democracy. All forms of socialism, whether state socialism of the Russian kind, or national socialism of the German kind, or democratic socialism of the British kind, are professedly democratic, that is to say, they all obtain popular assent by the manipulation of mass psychology." He then went on to explain why the Third Reich was much more thoroughly democratic than either Britain or the United States.[506]

Official utterances abound claiming that nazism stood firmly on the Left, that it represented an ideology that was democratic and republican, socialistic and anti-aristocratic. With a fanaticism equal to that of a British Labourite Hitler attacked the English public schools, Eton and Harrow.[507] He called himself an "arch-democrat,"[508] national socialism the "most genuine democracy,"[509] and the nazi constitution "truly democratic."[510]

And in *Mein Kampf* he wrote about the "Germanic democracy of the free election of a leader."[511]

Goebbels, for his part, called national socialism an "authoritarian democracy" or a "Germanic democracy," the "noblest form of European democracy."[512] He maintained that although National Socialists did not talk much about democracy, they were nevertheless the executors of the "general will." [513] Rudolf Hess termed national socialism "the most modern democracy in the world," one which rested on the "confidence of the majority."[514] And Michael Oakeshott of the London School of Economics said, very much to the point, in confirming Goebbels' stand, "An authoritarian regime, no doubt, can 'liquidate' the liberal supporters which, for one reason or another, helped to bring it into being, but no modern authoritarian doctrine can liquidate its debt to the doctrine of democracy. . . . It is impossible to understand either communism, fascism or national socialism without first understanding the doctrine of representative democracy. . . . It is the parent of these ungracious children."[515]

No wonder, then, that Goebbels averred that he "paid homage to the French Revolution for all the possibilities of life and development that it brought to the people. In this sense, if you like, I am a democrat."[516] Although, to be sure, there was a more radical wing among the national socialists led by Röhm and the brothers Strasser—a group that had suffered as much in the *Reichsmordwoche* as the conservative opposition—men like Goebbels were even more vocal than they in expressing their hatred of the traditional forces of Germany. Dr. Goebbels asked in 1932: "From where would we take the moral right to fight for the proletarian struggle between the classes, if the bourgeois class-state were not first destroyed and replaced by a new socialist structure of the German community?"[517] And when Mussolini was arrested by the King of Italy, Goebbels' indignation knew no limits. He declared on October 31, 1943, in the Sports Palace in Berlin, that something of this sort would never happen in the Third Reich because, "first of all, the Reich is headed by the *Führer* and not by a traitor like Badoglio. And secondly, because we have kings only in fairy tales and musical comedies. Germany is a republican *Führer*-state." Hitler, in fact, always loathed the King of Italy, and after his last official visit to Rome before the war, he said openly, "Now I would most certainly become an antimonarchist, if I had not always been one."[518]

The leftist character of national socialism was also apparent in its attitude toward Christianity. For a variety of reasons, national socialism was bound to take an anti-Christian stance. Not only did it reject the

Jewish background of Christianity and the Old Testament, but Christian ethics—compassion, charity, mercy—militated against the Nazi creed no less than against Marxism.

National socialism was, moreover, a materialism deeply pledged to Darwinian and Spencerian ideas. Anti-Judaism had practically died out in the early nineteenth century, due largely to the influence of the Enlightenment,[519] which brought about a rapid integration of the "Israelites" into Christian society. Theodor Herzl, the founder of Zionism, initially wanted to have all Jews converted to Christianity, but he changed his mind when biological materialism raised its ugly head. Instead of the nearly extinct anti-Judaism, something called anti-Semitism made its appearance; it inspired not only Zionism but National Socialism as well.[520]

Darwinism preached biological determinism. A conflict ensued (not truly realized) between belief in the automatic survival of the fittest and the urge to intervene in legislation which would sterilize, castrate, exile—exterminate—all "undesirables." The bellicosity of the Nazis blinded them to the fact that war takes the lives of the best, not the cowards. *Ares ouk agathôn pheidetai allá kakôn* ("Mars does not spare the good but the bad").[521] Aside from its anti-Semitism, one of the most criminal aspects of brown racism was the way its party minions handled the Russian and Ukrainian people. The German troops were initially greeted as liberators—Russia could have been had on a platter. But then the party moved in and the Russians were treated as slaves, the Ukrainians were never allowed self-government;[522] as a result, the disappointed and disgusted masses started to resist. Evil prejudices and a false doctrine destroyed a unique opportunity.

Yet the National Socialists were at first slow in showing their cards, which explains why, at the beginning of their rule, many well-meaning, naive people willingly collaborated with them. The plans forcibly to amalgamate the churches emerged slowly, for instance, but they foundered when it became evident that a sizable majority of upright Lutherans and Calvinists were resisting "nazification." Nor did "mercy killings" of the incurably insane get under way until the beginning of the war, and it immediately aroused protests from the Catholic bishops.

But as time went on and the population became occupied more and more with the war, the food problem, the losses at the front, and the shattering air attacks, the National Socialists became bolder. A circular letter, violently anti-Christian, like the one issued by Martin Bormann, the deputy leader, early in 1942, would have been unthinkable a few years earlier—

and this despite a rather frank forerunner, Alfred Rosenberg's *Mythus des Zwanzigsten Jahrhunderts*.[523] Bormann's massive attack was entirely in keeping with scientism and materialism and could have emanated from a Soviet propagandist (or from certain American professors). Plans were made to crush Christianity totally; they would be carried out after the victory which, fortunately, never eventuated—the crushing was left to the Nazi's Communist rivals who went to work in the eastern two-thirds of Europe.

The fundamentally leftist and "identitarian" character of national socialism can certainly not be questioned. The Marxists tried to prove that nazism was "financed by the rich" in order to browbeat organized labor, an interesting theory which implies that political persuasions (elections) are merely a matter of cash: the greater the propaganda—posters, newspaper ads, and so on—the more certain the victory at the polls. But this theory would be a most powerful argument against parliamentary democracy, because in the light of it, the man in the street is either a venal little swine or a spineless parrot. A computer, in fact, might well determine the amount of money needed to "affect" a vote. But, as Gustav Stolper has demonstrated,[524] the National Socialists were quite capable of financing themselves with the millions they received from their membership dues. The contributions of industrialists and bankers (some of them "non-Aryan") were tainted in the same manner as the sums shamefacedly paid to gangsters by shopkeepers who prefer playing safe to trusting in the police.

The economic order under the National Socialists was thoroughly socialistic. And this although German manufacturers and other entrepreneurs continued in their positions. (The same anomaly occurred in Mao's China where the "patriotic capitalists" retained jobs for which they had both the experience and the qualifications.) German entrepreneurs became mere stewards in a planned economy; they worked for a totalitarian state that admitted neither genuine private property nor individual decisions. In explanation, Ludwig von Mises pointed out that, in the end, the entrepreneurs preferred being reduced to the status of shop managers by the National Socialists to being "liquidated" by the Communists in the Russian manner. Conditions being what they then were in Germany, no third way was open to them.[525]

Not by accident was the Nazi flag the *red* banner. In early 1933 many Nazi flags were only adapted communist and socialist flags—the center cut out and replaced by a white cloth or covered by a sewn-on "mirror" (when it rained, the red shone through). The socialist ties extended to the Nazi concentration camps, where the Communists, who were very well organized, were able to murder their rightist opponents under the very noses of the aloof jailers.[526] Nazi-Soviet cooperation was in fact planned at an early date, as witness the well-documented Reventlow-Radek negotiations. This joint red-brown hatred was directed mainly against Poland, the *bête noire* of leftists all over the world.[527] In this respect Stalin, Hitler, Lloyd George, and the American Left formed an unholy alliance.

Who were the real "Nazis?" Professor Theodor Abel found that among the leading National Socialists (i.e., those known to the broad public, the historians, etc.), 7 percent belonged to the upper class, 7 percent were peasants, 35 percent workers, and 51 percent those who could be described as middle class. In the party the largest single occupational group was made up of elementary school teachers, well known in Europe for their authoritarian leanings and an intellectual curiosity sadly combined with scholarly vacuity. (European elementary schools as a rule last only four or five years, and in the past the teachers almost never had the equivalent of a college education.) But what about the army? Since army officers (and even soldiers) were *not* permitted to belong to the National Socialist party, the brown fanatics with military ambitions were almost all in the *Waffen-SS*; it paralled the *Wehrmacht*, the regular army, where there were very few high-ranking officers with Nazi leanings (men such as Keitel—"la Keitel"—and Jodl were exceptions).

The situation changed radically following the final attempted assassination of Hitler (there had been several). After July 1944, members of the NSDAP and *Gottgläubige* (non-Christian theists) could be members of the officers' corps; and the German Greeting (*Heil Hitler!*) was made obligatory. Thus, not until that late date was the army finally nazified. Before these events even the draftees had to return their party membership cards and show a deposit slip as proof. Membership could be resumed only after military service. Until July 1944, moreover, the higher officers' corps, including the general staff, consisted of about half noblemen and half commoners, and most of the latter were "anti-Nazi." (Names such as Beck, Halder, Rommel, Speidel immediately come to mind.) Yet after the Jews, those most hated by the Nazi leaders were the royalty and the nobility. And, indeed, it was primarily the nobility within the armed forces that, as a group, struck in July 1944. The retribution was terrible. Hitler *filmed* the hanging of the conspirators—including their naked corpses suspended on butchers' hooks. Here again is evidence of the sadistic drives of a genuine, Sade-inspired leftism.

Still, the horrors perpetrated by the Nazis during the war in occupied areas and inside their own country were perfectly "logical." Leftists around the world have tried to portray these horrors as typical of "reactionaries," "right extremists," "counterrevolutionaries," if not of "conservatives." Another school has tried to nail these chilling crimes to the German character. But nobody in Europe has attempted to pin the delirious crimes perpetrated by the French revolutionaries on the dark and seamy side of the French character. And few people have ascribed the atrocities of the Spanish Civil War to the Spanish soul, or the frightfulness of the Russian Revolution to an inherent trait in Eternal Russia.

The shock of the Nazi atrocities was stunning because they followed two hundred years of Rouseauistic propaganda about the goodness of human nature. And, besides, Germans were literate, clean, sober, technologically progressive, hard working, and so forth. (The Bible has, in fact, more concrete and pertinent information about human nature than do statistics dealing with secondary education, the number of bathtubs, or the mileage of superhighways.) There is, however, something in the German mind that prompts it to make final logical deductions from specific premises. Baron Hügel has written about this German propensity in a memorable article,[528] and Ernst Jünger has said quite rightly that Germany, due to its central location (central in a metaphysical rather than a geographical sense), is fertile ground for a symptomatic figure such as Hitler—the man, as another author said, who put the Prussian sword in the service of Austrian folly. Ernst Jünger described the situation in different fashion when he wrote in his diary (*Strahlungen II*, October 6, 1941): "After that long period of fasting the German was led by Kniébolo [Hitler] up a mountain, and the might of the world was shown to him. Not much prompting was needed that he worship his tempter."[529]

The horrors of nazism and communism have not been dealt with in detail here on the (perhaps rash) assumption that they are sufficiently well known. Yet the world, in a terrifying way, is indebted to Germany because it demonstrated vividly the ultimate reality of negative and destructive ideas. Ideas which in London or New York are repeated as seemingly harmless abstractions have been reified by the Germans in all their blood-chilling finality. In this respect national socialism has become the Gorgonian Mirror in which a decadent West might study its own features. For this absolutist characteristic is shared by the whole spine of Europe which stretches from the Straits of Gibraltar via Spain, France, Germany, and Poland into Russia, where people tend to be *pèlerins de l'absolu*, "pilgrims of the absolute," to use the phrase of Léon Bloy. While the rest of the world has only too often been engaged in small talk, the "absolutists" have transformed abstraction and theories into concrete realities. Have not American and British "liberals" repeatedly voiced ideas that lead, with ice-cold logic, directly to the gas chambers and cremation stoves of Auschwitz, the icy graves of Siberia, the gloomy forest of Katyn, the orgiastic cemeteries of Red Spain? The sad case of Germany should be a reminder to the English-speaking world that a nation admirable in so many ways, the heart of the Holy Roman Empire, the cradle of the Reformation, could become so corrupt—that the land of *Dichter und Denker* (poets and thinkers) could degenerate into the land of *Richter und Henker* (judges and hangmen).

By divorcing themselves from religion and willfully turning their backs on great traditions, the Germans fell into inferno, a fall which, historically speaking, they will never be able to forget, a fall worse than that of France, the Oldest Daughter of the Church, and equaling that of Holy Russia. All the visions of Sade and the nightmarish dreams of the French *Révolution Surréaliste*[530] came true, all the consequences of American pragmatism and universal positivism were drawn, all the eugenic blueprints of biological visionaries were carried out, all the consequences of unlimited materialism found their fulfillment. Man was conceived as a mere beast that could be crushed like an ant or a bedbug, and all the laws on the Tables of Sinai, all the words of Christ were eradicated.

Just prior to the outbreak of World War II, a leftist author under the pen name of Nicolas Calas wrote a book of essays entitled *Foyers d'incendie*,[531] which made a passionate appeal for "more sadism among leftists." He claimed that, like the early Christians, they succumbed too often to a masochistic urge for suffering. "Fascism, therefore, must be fought with Freudian as well as Marxist weapons. And, like fascism, communism will have to call on sadistic and masochistic love. Masochistic tendencies must be excited in the fascist masses, and sadistic tendencies among the Communists. . . . But we must never forget that the dominant revolutionary complex is to be sadistic. This means that hatred of the father should always be stronger than love of the brother.

"A real reeducation of the younger generation should take place for this purpose. Let the child learn to do more than admire the beauty of flowers and the intelligence of bees: let us show him the pleasure of killing animals. Let him go hunting, let him visit the butcher, let him enjoy suffering. . . .[532]

"Our holidays need no longer be those of the bourgeois calendar, for the chocolate Easter egg let us substitute chocolate guillotines.

"Excite desires! Monogamy does not yet exist. After the butcher, the prostitute! It is up to her to give the child a taste, and not a disgust for love. . . ."[533]

And a final word about the ideally educated child: "When he wants to read, put in his hands the works best calculated to excite his desire. Show him succulent dreams, the syrups of passions, the wines of blood, the burning kisses, the moist looks, all that bread of life, that whole body of love."

A poor French degenerate hiding under a pseudonym?

(And yet, who was the man who said, "I do not think that man at present is a predatory animal. It seems to me that every society rests on the death of men"? It was a justice of the United States Supreme Court—Oliver Wendell Holmes, Jr.)[534]

Nicolas Calas exhorted leftists with the words, "Comrades, be cruel!" Hitler followed the call. His *Parteigenossen* (Party Comrades) were indeed cruel. Not in vain did Charles Fourier, grandfather of socialism, write in his *Théorie de l'unité universelle*:

"The office of the butcher is held in high esteem in Harmony."

PART III

Liberalism

---

*I will not cease to hold, under
the banner of religion, in one hand the
oriflamme of monarchy and in the
other the flag of civil liberties.*

—CHATEAUBRIAND

CHAPTER 13

Real Liberalism

*. . . for the few shall save
the many, or the many are to fall
still to be wrangling in a noisy grave*

—E. A. ROBINSON, *Demos*

Another grave, this time semantic, misunderstanding between the United States and Europe lies in the concept of *liberalism*. In Europe, although the significance of the term has undergone several changes, its essential meaning has been retained. But in the United States today the word "liberalism" has a content diametrically opposed to its etymology, to its original sense as understood not only in Europe but also in Latin America, Australia, New Zealand, the Soviet Union, Southern Asia, and Japan. The deformation of the idea of liberalism has suffered nowhere more than in the United States, although the term has degenerated to some extent in Britain. The liberalism preached by the Whigs at the beginning of the last century—the liberalism of Palmerston, Asquith, Lloyd George, the younger Churchill, and, obviously, Mr. Acland-Hood—had a somewhat different meaning for each of its proponents.

In respect to the verbal meaning: the root is *liber* ("free"). The term *liberalism* (and *liberalitas*) implies generosity in intellectual and material matters. The sentence "he gave liberally" means that the person in question gave abundantly. In this sense *liberality* is an "aristocratic" virtue. An illiberal person is avaricious, petty, tight-fisted, self-centered.

Until the dawn of the nineteenth century the word "liberal" figured neither in politics nor, really, in economics. (The political content of the term has been taken up in chapter 5.) While democracy answers the question concerning *who* should rule, liberalism deals with the problem of *how* government should be exercised. The answer liberalism gives is that regardless of who rules, government must be exercised in such a way that each individual, each citizen enjoys the widest personal liberty compatible with the common good. Although the "common good" can be willfully interpreted in the narrowest way, it is nevertheless clear that liberalism rightly understood stands essentially for *freedom*.

Insofar as our research goes, the first time the term was used in a political sense was in the year 1812, and the "place of action"—not unnaturally—was Spain, a nation famous for its individualism, its inordinate sense of liberty, its strong anarchical drive. The supporters of the constitution of Cádiz were called *los liberales*, and their opponents (among them the *apostólicos*) were nicknamed *los serviles*.

It took several years for this nomenclature to make its appearance in England. Southey used it for the first time in 1816 and, significantly enough, employed the Spanish form, that is, spoke of "our liberales." Sir Walter Scott, soon afterward, copying the French, referred to the liberals as *libéraux*. In the early 1830s, when new parties emerged after the reforms of Sir Robert Peel, the Whigs became the Liberals and the Tories the Conservatives. (As noted in chapter 6, the evolution was hardly surprising.)

But the *idea* of liberalism existed well before 1812. During the eighteenth century an economic school was in the ascendancy (particularly in Britain and the Netherlands) which, without straining our semantics, can be styled *preliberal* in that it did not use the liberal label. Called the Manchester School, it had philosophical (or theological) roots deep in the soil of deism. This held that God, the Great Architect, had created the world nearly perfect; all evils were due to human intervention which upset the Divine plan. This was easily done, for the deist God had withdrawn from his creation: neither priestcraft nor white magic, neither prayers nor incantations could move Him. It was up to man to work out his own salvation, i.e., his terrestrial happiness, by interfering as little as possible (preferably, not at all) in a universe existing in a preestablished harmony that rested on divine laws. If state and society were never to intervene in commerce and industry, they would automatically flourish; but all artificial limitations, rules, or regulations—guilds, labor laws, tariffs, currency reforms, etc.—would bring prosperity to a halt.

As Alexander Rüstow has pointed out, a true theological background can be found in the thought of Adam Smith and the entire Manchester School, a "theology" that has to be understood as partly a logical continuation of Calvinism and partly its dialectical contradiction. In other words, the ideology of Manchesterism and its *laissez-faire* attitude is a synthesis of John Calvin and the Renaissance.[535] Of course, it also encompasses a good deal of practical truth and common sense. With their appeal to human egotism and ambition, the different schools of economic liberalism have produced more and better goods than the various economic orders based on a pseudomonastic collectivism and/or statism.

At the same time, Manchesterism was a truly "grand bourgeois" ideology, related to but not identical with Whiggery. The second phase of liberalism (which does bear the liberal label) can be called *early liberalism*. Though perhaps not entirely unaffected by deism, it was to a large extent led by thinkers with decided religious affiliations or who were at least strongly sympathetic to Christian tenets. This early liberalism reached its apogee in the 1850s, but its forerunners were active back in the 1820s and 1830s, and some of its exponents did not die until the end of the century. The following are but a few of them, in chronological order: Royer-Collard, Alexis de Tocqueville, Montalembert, Gladstone, Jacob Burckhardt, Lord Acton.

Half of these men, significantly enough, were aristocrats; the others belonged to what is sometimes called the patriciate (the patrician class). Count Camillo Cavour, though not a systematic thinker, was of this school, as was Achille Léonce Victor Duc de Broglie.[536] In other words, from a sociological viewpoint, these were upper-class men, none of whom had an antireligious bent. (Jacob Burckhardt, although an agnostic, developed warm feelings for the Catholic Church in his declining years.) Did early liberalism have a forerunner, a man who inspired the movement's proponents? Edmund Burke inevitably comes to mind, not as a preliberal, but certainly as an early conservative who influenced de Tocqueville as well as Metternich.

Many of these early liberals were not lovers of freedom *besides* being Christians but they did take their political inspiration either from theology or directly from Scripture. Their "religious anthropology," their picture of man, was what invited or forced them to walk the road of liberalism. Man had an immortal soul, man had a personality, man was not an accident caused by the blind forces of nature, man needed freedom because God wanted him not only to develop his personality in the right direction but to live a moral life, freely (but rightly!) choosing between good and evil. "The Christian is a bound person, but bound in freedom," as Romano Guardini put it.

Thus, obviously, the religious aspect of early liberalism was most strongly developed among Catholics, Eastern Orthodox, and those of the Reformation faiths who had broken with the strict views of the Reformers, who were "Erasmian" rather than Calvinist or Lutheran. Among the names mentioned above, there is not a single supporter of what is loosely called "Protestant orthodoxy." Calvin and Luther were certainly not liberals in the decadent American sense, but they were not "libertarians" either. "Libertarianism," that is to say, true liberalism, influenced the Reformation faiths in the eighteenth century as a result of the Enlightenment and rationalism—both late descendants of the Renaissance and therefore alien in themselves to the spirit of the Reformation. (To be sure, the man in the street more often than not associates the Enlightenment, rationalism, and individualism with the "Protestant" outlook, if not with the Reformation faiths. He knows nothing of the complete turnabout made by most of them over two hundred years ago, nor has he taken much notice of the return of a number of Reformed theologians to the orthodoxy of the sixteenth century, a relatively recent development.)

But whereas liberalism at first received support from certain Catholic *thinkers*, its supporters were probably more numerous among the Reformed *people*. In the Catholic world the early liberal parties were small and largely composed of the elite. Economic thinking and economic considerations played a rather minor role; early liberalism emphasized other sectors of human endeavor.

It was different in the Evangelical areas of Europe, where commerce and industry have always occupied a more honored position than in the *orbis catholicus*. There, the ideas and notions of a notably economic-minded preliberalism were very much alive. In the Catholic world, conversely, the businessman has enjoyed little prestige. This lack stems partly from the fact that the merchant represents the only profession which Our Lord ever physically chastised. (What a wonderful subject for our great painters in the past!) St. Thomas Aquinas's views on the trader were also frankly hostile.[537] Moreover, when the free market economy in northern Italy rose up in the fifteenth century it had many technical and psychological hurdles to overcome. (Double-entry bookkeeping was instituted by Fra Luca Pacioli di Borgo, a Franciscan, but with the rise of Calvinism, the center of business quickly shifted to the north.) No wonder the Catholic renewal in the nineteenth and twentieth centuries had certain bitterly "anticapitalist" aspects.

All that aside, it is interesting to note how the next wave of liberalism, the *old liberals* (paleoliberals, to use the phrase coined by Heddy Neumeister)[538] became as intensively interested in economic problems as had the preliberals, whereas the early liberal thinkers were rarely occupied with economics. Early liberalism was characterized by a rather limited pragmatism. It was intuitive rather than scientific. Montalembert's thinking rested squarely on Christian premises. De Tocqueville, profoundly influenced by Madame Swetchine, who was the great soul mate of Lacordaire,[539] as an older man increasingly coordinated his political and social vistas with his reviving Christian faith. Jacob Burckhardt was also deeply imbued with Christian ethics. It is indeed moving to see an agnostic solemnly choosing celibacy in his youth so as to devote himself entirely to research, knowledge, wisdom, and truth.

The early liberals seldom equated freedom with usefulness as was customary with the preliberals and the old liberals of a slightly later period. The early liberals considered freedom something to be treasured and defended because man needed it, because it was a postulate of a moral, not of a practical order, because—as many of them acknowledged—"Christ had freed us to freedom" (Galatians, V:1). An early liberal would hardly have been shaken in his belief if it had been proved that freedom was impractical, or expensive, or less apt to produce higher living standards than, say, some effective form of slavery.

Precisely because the early liberals were "idealists" in the narrow sense of the term, because their background was aristocratic or patrician, because they were intellectuals of a high order, without exception educated in the classics, because they founded their demand for freedom on religious and philosophical principles, they were not friendly toward democracy. Most of them, in truth, could be styled antidemocrats—something not often fully understood by those interested in the history of ideas. Acton's remark to Bishop Creighton in a letter addressed to him in 1887, "Power tends to corrupt, and absolute power corrupts absolutely," is frequently cited by well-meaning democrats who forget (or do not know) that Acton, quite an antidemocrat himself, would have applied this formula to parliaments or popular majorities without batting an eye.

As for de Tocqueville, the mere fact that he wrote a standard work called

Democracy in America, foretelling an extension of democracy on a worldwide scale, has made him an apologist for democracy in the eyes of many an American. But de Tocqueville was far too clever to believe that the coming upsurge of democracy spelled the end of political history and its ever-changing forms. He was fully aware that the world would outlive the democratic age, which he did not like in the least. Yet he wrote in such a detached way that, to understand him, it is necessary to read carefully between the lines. The man who, disgusted by the July Revolution of 1830, left France for the United States, then under its first Democratic adminis-tration, was not a democrat. But, admittedly, even a few of his more intelligent readers were unsure of his position. At one time, when asked peremptorily about his convictions, he replied: "I have a certain intellectual inclination for democratic institutions, but I am instinctively an aristocrat, which means that I despise and fear the masses. I passionately love liberty, legality, the respect for rights, but not democracy. . . liberty is my fore-most passion. That is the truth."[540]

This is not the de Tocqueville familiar to the average American.[541] (Nor, to be sure, is the Jacob Burckhardt featured on a Swiss stamp known to the ordinary Swiss burgher, who is unaware how much this great man loathed democracy—as did Burckhardt's liberal friend, J. J. Bachofen, similarly honored by the Swiss post office.)

Outstanding men, with a certain pride in their experience or their knowledge, are not likely to admire democracy, for it cannot distinguish between the various degrees of knowledge, is indifferent toward truth (as Berdyaev pointed out),[542] and takes its stand on the basis of quantity and biological age rather than quality. In this system of government the votes are counted rather than weighed, an observation Aristotle made well over two thousand years ago. Indeed, it would be difficult to find in Europe more than a handful of truly outstanding thinkers—and not a single giant—who believed or believes in democracy.

The aversion of the early liberals for the two democratic postulates of equality and majority rule had other important roots. These men were aware of the incompatibility between liberal and egalitarian principles, they saw all too well that the enfranchisement of the masses would inevita-bly lead to the rise of political movements that would exploit the envy of the many. They realized that the concept of the "politicized" nation was in itself *totalitarian*—a term which, if not then known or used, was certainly sensed and understood, as in de Tocqueville's vision of the new tyranny to come.[543]

It was also evident to the early liberals that the search for truth in the light of reason would be replaced in a democracy by the whim, the emotions, the naked desires of the many, expressed in numbers. Burckhardt spoke of the dangers emanating from political decisions based solely on the *Gärungen der Völker,* the "fermentations of the nations." And Royer-Collard, no less than Montalembert, emphasized that the search for lights (*les lumières*), the quest for truth, was the task of the few, not of the many. The many have neither the training, nor the time, nor the money to discover and digest the information necessary for the judgments that have to be made. (Needless to say, moral qualifications are also necessary to arrive at decisions that demand imminent sacrifices in order to ensure a better future. "Blood, sweat and tears" can usually be promised only to a people with its back to the wall.)

Not all the early liberals, of course, were immune at all times to the temptations of democracy which, as pointed out, has a paradisiacal character and all the lure of a "clear but false idea." Even Acton leaned temporarily toward democracy, and Constant de Rebecque had his own great moment of weakness when he—the brilliant essayist and politician—suddenly decided to collaborate with Napoleon during his Hundred Days. (And this although nobody had written a better or more scathing analysis of the democratic French Revolution and the Bonapartist dictatorship than Benjamin Constant de Rebeque during his exile.) These things, unfortunately, do happen. Still, the early liberals were certainly nondemocrats or antidemocrats whereas their successors, the old liberals, had as a rule a philosophical and ideological outlook which predisposed them to view democracy in more positive terms. The main reason lay with *the strong "agnostic" bent of the old liberals*.

Genuine liberals have always wanted freedom. But the quest for freedom is precisely what leads certain minds to conclude that every firm conviction, every strong affirmation will *automatically* result in intolerance. As shown in chapter 4, the *possibility* of intolerance (of "illiberality") in the thinking or actions of a truly convinced man does exist: it is a hurdle, a temptation that must be overcome. But it does not follow that those who do not believe in absolute truth or in the human ability to attain truth are thereby tolerant; no, they are merely *indifferent*. The confusion between tolerance and indifference did not seem to bother many old liberals; they preferred to "play safe" by preaching a basically agnostic attitude (to use the word in a much wider than the strictly theological sense) and by waging an intellectual and political crusade against all believers in absolutes. These were stigmatized as "dogmatists." Predictably, this attitude put the old liberals all too frequently in opposition to Christianity, especially to the Christian orthodoxy of any denomination. This "agnostic" bent was what facilitated the old liberals' armistice, even their alliance, with democracy.

Democracy—as "democratism"—is an ideology, though in its simpler form it can be seen as a mere system, a procedure for "producing," i.e., for selecting, a government. A democratic constitution offers a frame into which a picture can be fit through the voting process. The character of the picture is usually determined by the majority vote. Now, according to *standard* democratic doctrine every full citizen has the right not only to vote, but also to organize a party or to propose local candidates. The guardians of a democratic constitution have to maintain a neutral position toward all candidates, all parties, and all the ideas they represent. One man is as good as another, one opinion is as good as another, all men and all opinions are invited to participate in the race, and he who wins numerically gets the prize. Democracy as an abstract principle must insist on fair play, must express no preferences—and thus must also condone political parties that would put an end to the democratic order. If 51 percent or, better still, two-thirds of the people vote one or several antidemocratic parties into power, the end of democracy is at hand. In other words, *democracy can commit suicide democratically*.

In Europe, the old liberalism tended to enter into various alliances and combinations. On the one hand, it preached an extreme liberalism in the economic field, but on the other, it merged with nationalism which, in Europe, has an ethnic connotation. Bismarck derived his main support from the national liberals, not from the Prussian conservatives who were Prussian patriots and not nationalists with Pan-German leanings. Ethnic nationalism (except for the Irish and Polish versions) has always been anti-Catholic and antipapal. This animosity played right into the hands of the old liberals, for since they hated anything they called "dogmatism," they were naturally antagonistic to religious orthodoxy—and, above all, to Rome. Bismarck's *Kulturkampf* was almost equally pleasing to nationalists, old liberals, and national liberals. (It won *no* applause from the Prussian conservatives, although they were staunch Lutherans.)[544] Obviously then, the aristocratic character of early liberalism was not inherited by the old liberals who received their main support from the upper and middle bourgeoisie, precisely the layers of society that had anticlerical and nationalistic leanings.

Given all these alliances and connections it is not surprising that the old liberalism became illiberal. If all strong stands, all absolutes in thought, all orthodoxies are considered evil, then hostility will indeed spring up against all representatives of "absolutism" (religious, political, philosophical, whatever) and, if the chance arises, methodical and merciless persecution will follow. And since the old liberals in the second half of the nineteenth century, and frequently in the twentieth century, had great parliamentary power, thanks to the property qualifications for voting, they were also able to abuse it. Moreover, owing to their intellectual appeal, they had a near monopoly in the universities and acquired an iron grip on the press, the theater, and the entire intellectual life. Thus they could maltreat their conservative and Christian opponents. (The Holy American Illiberal Inquisition had a forerunner.)

The old liberals, moreover, had some supporters in the working class, some in the aristocracy, and, quite frequently, even some in the royal families. They were, in fact, only rarely antimonarchists. For although favorable to democracy, as a rule they considered it just one useful element in a mixed government. The Spanish aristocracy was largely liberal.[545] So was a sizable part of the Italian, Portuguese, Bavarian,[546] Hungarian, and Scottish nobility. The royal houses of Italy, Spain, and Portugal were largely liberal as well.[547] In Austria, Franz Josef's sympathies lay with the liberals and so, notoriously, did his son's, the ill-fated Crown Prince Rudolf. His brother, the tragic Maximilian of Mexico, contrary to popular belief, was an ardent liberal. "Privileges" were not decried by the old liberals provided they were held by the "right people." Whatever might be held against the old liberals—and a great deal can be—they were never really a party of the Left.

The old liberals were responsible for their own decline around the end of the century. In Austria the introduction of the one-man one-vote principle in 1907 was a great blow to them. Moreover, the rise of the Socialist parties was due partly to the anticlerical attitude that had been rather unwisely bred by the old liberals. Neither the new-type Catholic nor the socialist opposition that formed against old liberalism made any appeal to the concept of liberty. Given the ambiguous attitudes of old liberalism the word itself had been rendered suspect.[548] In France "liberty" meant expelling religious orders. In Hungary it was used to justify compulsory civil marriages. In Spain it worked as a screen for the confiscation of almost all Church property in 1857. And in Switzerland and Germany it was invoked to exile the Jesuits.

By the outbreak of World War I old liberalism was in grave crisis. It remained entrenched in certain intellectual strongholds, but it was totally beaten in the field of power politics. The liberal parties on the Continent had been decimated. What remained were certain specific positions in the universities and in the still sizable liberal press, which had become a middle-of-the-road institution promising (not always truthfully) "objectivity" to its readers. But in the practical sphere of politics, it was no longer viable. This startling turnabout could be observed all over Europe. Papers such as the *Frankfurter Zeitung*, the *Corriere della Sera*, *Le Temps*, *Die Neue Freie Presse*, and *De Algemeene Handelsblad* still held their leading positions, but they had ceased to affect elections.

When the totalitarian wave started, the old liberals were persecuted, in a sense more bitterly than the people on the Left. Those on the Left—Socialists, Communists, Jacobin democrats—were totalitarian competitors, not enemies. The social democratic worker in Essen and the socialist worker in Sesto San Giovanni or in Turin could easily switch sides. The worker in Essen, in fact, readily gave up international socialism and embraced national socialism. (The directors of his factory were now mere stewards of the state.) The worker in Turin, for his part, knew that Benito Mussolini had been a Socialist and that the fascist movement had grown out of an Italian socialism that had shed its international outlook.[549] (This is just what the Czech National Socialists had done when they seceded from the Czech Social Democratic party in 1897.) Thus the new, big totalitarian parties, which stemmed from the French Revolution, called themselves "socialist," and boasted of being "democratic." They also engaged in the perennial trick of successful leftist parties dating back to 1789—the "mobilization of envy."

The old liberals, on the other hand, had no competitors, nothing but declared enemies. They could not easily change sides. And, whatever their faults, they abstained from the tempting strategy of appealing to envy which proved so rewarding at the polls. Some of them, moreover, were aware of their aberrations. Ludwig von Mises did not hesitate to state that Burke, von Haller, de Bonald, and de Maistre were aware of the failings of the old liberalism. They were also more realistic than their adversaries in their appraisal of the masses.[550] The masses, Mises believed, were not capable of rational understanding or rational decisions.

Professor Eduard Heimann, a German religious socialist, wrote cogently during World War II: "Hitlerism proclaims itself as both a true democracy and a true socialism, and the terrible truth is that there is a grain of truth to such claims—an infinitesimal grain, to be sure, but at any rate enough to serve as a basis for such fantastic distortions. Hitlerism even goes so far as to claim the role of protector of Christianity, and the terrible truth is that even this gross misinterpretation is able to make some impression. But one fact stands out with perfect clarity in all the fog: Hitler has never claimed to represent true liberalism. Liberalism then has the distinction of being the doctrine most hated by Hitler."[551]

Heimann, who by conviction was a democrat and a Socialist, did not go far enough. Still, his thesis is correct—even in light of the curious fact that "national liberalism," peculiar to Central Europe, had and still has subtle links to nazism. Since the death of the oratorically gifted German social democrat leader Kurt Schumacher, a real nationalist, some former Nazis have come to sympathize with the Free Democratic party (FDP), aptly called by the foreign press the "Liberal party." A similar situation exists in Austria where the *Freiheitliche Partei Österreichs* (FPÖ Liberal party of Austria) is the joint party of surviving old liberals and ex-Nazis. And it is not so much their "national liberal" past as their "anticlericalism" that has joined both camps.

But the majority of ex-Nazis in Federal Germany went straight to the Social Democrats. This is clearly demonstrated by the maps in my *Narrenschiff auf Linkskurs*, which feature the statistical data of the 1932 and 1972 elections.[552] In contrast, all the German neoliberals known to this author voted not for the "liberals" but for Adenauer and Strauss.

But back to the old liberals. The Catholic Church, needless to say, energetically attacked the old liberalism, not because of its enthusiasm for liberty but because of its hostility toward organized religion in general and Christian orthodoxy in particular. Pope Pius IX in Proposition 80 of his *Syllabus errorum* (December 8, 1864) condemned the following statement: "The Roman Pontiff can and should reconcile himself and cooperate with progress, liberalism and modern civil society."[553]

This antiliberal stance remained a potent force for a long time in all (not only Catholic) orthodox Christianity. Thus, when neoliberalism developed in the 1930s and 1940s, it was often difficult to persuade freedom-loving Christian thinkers that this new phase of liberalism differed in many important and even decisive ways from its immediate predecessor, because the word "liberal" had erected a mental block in many devout Christians.

The term neoliberalism—the fourth phase of liberalism—hardly appeared before the end of World War II. In 1947 a remnant of liberal scholars met at the Park Hotel in Vevey to coordinate their forces and form an organization. It soon became evident that a certain fission had taken place, and not only in the domain of economics. Some thinkers, mostly from Central Europe, had come to view the problem of liberty in a different light from the older men, who were in many ways their teachers. (Almost all, to be sure, had been inspired by Ludwig von Mises.) But precisely in economic matters, these newer lights were less stringent in their outlook; they were willing to put curbs on mammoth power in order to preserve competition. They thought that the state had a right, and even a duty, to correct abuses of economic freedom—just as it had the right to make a person with a driving license submit to traffic laws.

Yet probably more important than this change was the reappraisal of religion, especially of Christianity. Many of the neoliberals declared that it was not sufficient to prove that liberty engendered prosperity, that freedom was more agreeable or more productive than slavery. Philosophical and even theological reasons must be invoked to show why liberty must be achieved, fostered, preserved. One of the neoliberals, perhaps the best known in the United States, the late Professor Wilhelm Röpke, maintained that even if it could be proved that a planned and collective economy was materially superior to a free one, he would still, in an "ascetic" sense, prefer the latter. Under these circumstances, sacrifices of a material order would have to be made to preserve the dignity of man. From such views it can be deduced that the neoliberals had, in a certain way, a greater affinity to the early liberals than to their immediate predecessors. Interested in economic problems, they nevertheless refused to make a fetish of them. They tried instead to integrate their economic views into a metaphysical humanism. The great early liberal thinkers, from de Tocqueville to Burckhardt, were seriously studied by these new liberals who in many cases were professing Christians.[554]

The new liberalism started in the German-speaking countries. This was no accident, because it was here that the old liberalism had helped undermine Christian civilization, from which the totalitarians derived the greatest profit; and here it had suffered its major defeats. Who were the leading neoliberals? Four of the founders of the new movement have died: Walter Eucken, professor of economics at Freiburg University in Breisgau, Alexander Rüstow, professor emeritus of Heidelberg University, and Wilhelm Röpke, professor at the École des Hautes Études in Geneva, as well as Alfred Müller-Armack of the University of Cologne, a scholar of the first order who was also state secretary under Ludwig Erhard and instrumental in "engineering" the German Economic Miracle.

Alexander Rüstow was the son of a Prussian general who, out of juvenile enthusiasm, joined the Spartacist movement in 1919.[555] Rüstow never adhered formally to a church and cultivated a somewhat anarchical outlook. At first, he was deeply interested in Greek philosophy (especially in the pre-Socratics) but later began to concentrate on economic problems within their historical, sociological, and theological context. When national socialism made research impossible and academic liberties became illusory, Rüstow emigrated to Turkey in order to remain in Europe. He taught for many years at the University of Istanbul.

Alexander Rüstow is famous not only for his essay on Manchesterism but mainly for his stupendous three-volume *Ortsbestimmung der Gegenwart*. Like all other neoliberals, Rüstow (who died in 1964) refused to deal with economics in isolation, detached from all other disciplines. His book, whose title in English, literally translated, means "Location of the Present," offers a sweeping historical view, a work in some ways more impressive than Toynbee's *A Study of History*. Forty years after it was written, his son finally published it in a radically shortened single volume.[556] But Rüstow remains little known outside Europe, just as Jacob Burckhardt (*obit* 1897) was unknown in the English-speaking world until the middle of World War II, and Max Weber only gained recognition posthumously in America. Very little indeed is known in the United States or even in Britain about rightist authors from the Continent.

The late Walter Eucken, professor of economics, and Franz Böhm, professor of law at Jena University, were both active in the German resistance. (Eucken was jailed for some time.) After the war they founded *Ordo*, a liberal (predominantly neoliberal) yearbook of essays of superior quality.

The third founder of neoliberalism, Professor Wilhelm Röpke, also fled, first to Turkey but then to Switzerland (closer to Germany), where he taught until his untimely death in Geneva in 1966. During the last years of the war he published his first stirring books. These dealt with basic economic problems as well as with political, social, and cultural questions, in all of which he espoused the cause of liberty. At war's end, he wrote a memorandum for the Allies recommending a monarchic restoration in Germany, a step advocated by Chancellor Brüning as early as 1932. But the Soviets vied with the United States in insisting on and imposing a republican form of government. Moved by self-interest, they sought a parliamentary frame, a constitutional system, within which Communist parties could work legally—to kill, in due course, the constitution.[557]

Professor Goetz Briefs, another eminent star in the galaxy of neoliberal thinkers, and a prolific writer, settled in the United States during the earliest days of national socialism and was for a long time a professor at Georgetown University. Starting as a professor at the *Technische Hochschule* in Berlin-Charlottenburg, he came originally from the school loosely identified as "Catholic Social Thought," the tradition that emanated from Ketteler and Vogelsang.

The neoliberals are not really organized and, significantly, in the Germanies they have no special love for those parties that do not actually wear the liberal label but are nevertheless usually referred to as "liberal." Many of these neoliberals are contributors to *Ordo*, published annually in Düsseldorf. They collaborate freely with the *Institut für freie Marktwirtschaft* in Heidelberg-Bonn, an organization engaged in economic research and in propagandizing for the "free market economy," i.e., free enterprise. In 1963 they held a memorable private roundtable conference in Augsburg with Catholic sociologists, but the demarcation lines were blurred inasmuch as some of the attending neoliberals were professing Catholics. Moreover, it soon became evident that the conferees' viewpoints were indeed not far apart.[558]

In a few cases it is not easy to draw the dividing line between neoliberals and certain of the later old liberals. Professor Friedrich August von Hayek, for instance, is a thinker on the borderline (but "old" rather than "new"). While Wilhelm Röpke could be called a conservative, and Alexander Rüstow was one in many ways, von Hayek declines the label.[559]

Although in Europe new liberals and modern conservatives are often practically indistinguishable, the situation in the United States is quite otherwise—not in fact but in respect to current labels. Two problems have to be solved; first, to discover how liberalism in the United States evolved (if it did "evolve") into the very opposite of what it set out to be (thereby morally forfeiting the right to call itself "liberal"), and second, to analyze what "conservatism," old and new, really stands for or, at least, ought to stand for.

(So as better to understand the four phases of genuine liberalism, it might be helpful to study a tabulation which, allowing for certain simplifications, would look roughly like the table on the following page.)

A CHART OF THE LIBERALISTS

	Period	Time	Leaders	Interest	Politics	Religion
1.	Pre-liberal	1750–1810	Adam Smith Manchester School	Economics	Libertarian	Deist
2.	Early Liberal	1812–1900	(Burke) de Tocqueville Montalembert Guizot Burckhardt Acton	Political Social	Mixed Government non- or anti-democratic	Christian pro-Christian
3.	Old Liberal (palaeo-liberal)	1840–cont.	Mazzini Gladstone Cavour Cobden Bismarck Croce Asquith v. Mises Herriot v. Hayek	Political Economical National	Parliamentary Monarchy pro-democratic	Liberal Protestant agnostic
3a.	Late British Liberalism	1900–1960	Lloyd George young Churchill	Economical Social Political	Parliamentary (symbolic) Monarchy Democratic	Indifferent
4.	New Liberal (Neo-liberal)	1945–cont.	Rüstow Röpke Eucken Rougier A. Müller-Armack L. Einaudi L. Erhard Franz Böhm Goetz Briefs Daniel Villey	Political Economical Social	Mixed Government Skeptical towards democracy	Christian or pro-Christian

NB. Obviously, a man such as Cobden might also figure as a late preliberal, Edmund Burke as an early conservative. We have omitted American names deliberately.

CHAPTER 14

False Liberalism

*A planned economy is implicit
in the spirit of democracy.*

—THE CITY OF MAN (1940)

Toward the end of World War II, the *American Mercury*, then under the editorship of Eugene Lyons, featured a series of articles in which a variety of authors defended their political-social stand. This writer's interest focused on an essay by Oswald Garrison Villard entitled "Credo of an Old-Fashioned Liberal." Villard's position was strongly analogous to the gentlemanly and Erasmian version of the old liberalism of the Continent—a liberalism not so different from the liberalism that prevailed in England and the United States during most of the nineteenth century. This is not to imply that there were no differences in the liberalism in the countries on either side of the Channel;[560] in England, the Liberals had to some extent "replaced" the Whigs and were increasingly exposed to leftist influences.

In the United States, the evolution of the term "liberal" did not take place until well into the twentieth century. And although it shows certain minor analogies with the changes in Britain it has few equivalents on the Continent. This is so because in the United States the "sectarian liberal," as Carlton J. H. Hayes defined him, might have been prejudiced, inflexible,

184

and petty, especially in his anticlericalism, but he had no leftist bent and, apart from his nationalistic proclivities, [561] no identitarian mentality. How then did the change take place? How, in the United States, did the word that means freedom-loving, generous, tolerant, open-minded, that is anti-statist and antitotalitarian, come to stand for the very contrary of these virtues and concepts?

It is, in fact, easily explained. The "old-fashioned liberal" was often the man who went along with what might be called the Wave of the Future. The conservative (and even more the "reactionary"),[562] on the other hand, as often took a stand against change. And change was largely a leftward movement. The leftist ideologies had (inevitably) assumed a "futuristic" character. They all claimed the future, utopia, they all claimed the millennium in a chiliastic spirit. They believed in the concept of near-automatic progress (which needed just a little "push"). In their eyes, this fictional road had the character of an "advance." The conservatives, meanwhile, adhered to the *status quo*, while the reactionaries looked ever backward.

The situation in this respect was not radically different on the Continent. It is surely with a sense of irony that the *Guide Bleu* (Paris: Hachette), edited by Professor Marcel N. Schveitzer of the Sorbonne, said in its 1935 edition, "Málaga is a city of very advanced ideas. On May 12 and 13, 1931, no fewer than forty-three churches and convents were burned down" (p. 562). The Spanish monarchy had fallen and the short-lived, infamous republic was moving "ahead." An unimaginative martinet such as General Franco, after some hesitation, would inevitably take steps to stop this kind of "advance."

Some old-fashioned, i.e., genuine liberals clung to their convictions; Albert Jay Nock, even H. L. Mencken, were among them. But many others dreaded being called conservative or reactionary. As long as a utopia existed at the end of the road, painted in the colors of absolute personal freedom, this sort of liberal was sure to be a "progressive." Before the 1930s the "ultraradical," the extremist (especially in America), was not the Socialist, not the Communist, but the *anarchist*. In fact, it took Americans quite some time to distinguish between a Communist and an anarchist. And, for a long time, the average American considered a *bolshevik* to be an unshaven, rowdyish creature who wanted no law, no order, but the constant overthrow of everything—in other words, an anarchist. The more spectacular acts of violence were in fact all carried out by anarchists; the Communists, who believed in mass action at the right time—in military conquest and civil war—abhorred individual action. Even in Russia the

Communists (or, to be even more exact, the radical wing of the Russian Social Democratic Workers' party) never carried out assassinations or acts of terror; the very first Communists (*bolsheviki*) who suffered death for their cause were those executed in the Civil War. *Until 1918 Russian communism had no martyrs.*

On my arrival in the United States for the first time in 1937, I had to give written assurance that I was neither a bigamist nor an anarchist. Violent, rampaging, lawless freedom still seemed to be *the* menace. It was also the direction in which the world—to the less initiated at least— gradually seemed to be moving. Respect and authority were declining, divorce laws were easing, crowned heads were toppling, censorship was disappearing, travel was becoming simpler, and liberal parties were still politically active in parts of the Western world. Thus the genuine American liberal could be fully convinced that, given his political convictions, the future belonged to him. The leniency of American and British liberals of that day toward the real leftists was precisely the reason the liberals themselves became suspect.

The Great Change, however, came in the 1930s when certain Americans, who conceived their country as not primarily their fatherland but as the "American Experiment," suddenly decided that the "Soviet Experiment" offered even more to mankind. This, in short, was the "Red Decade," to quote the title of a book by Eugene Lyons.[563] In other words, the vision of tomorrow took another form. Liberty no longer was the ideal. Security and equality—the promises of international socialism rather than individual freedom—were the new goals.

As for opposition on their part, the disease of democratic utopianism and a certain type of materialism had so deeply affected American liberals that they were unable to overcome their fear of clinging to a "lost cause." They were too afraid of "missing the boat," horrified at the thought of being considered antiquated, passé.[564] They had no consistent system of ideas, no principles, no real leadership. They were drifting, and drifts are determined by winds and currents. These now carried them toward determinism and collectivism, toward a "secular monasticism," and thus toward rank illiberality, the very opposite of their initial stand. They managed to preserve a few nonessential notions from their past and, of course, flatly refused to give up their label. It all added up to the Great American Semantic Confusion, which lives on to this very day. Genuine liberals, in resignation, dropped their label and called themselves "libertarians."

The old liberal ideas on matters such as sexual morals, capital punishment, and women's rights largely survive, but concerning their *basic* outlook on state and society, the old liberals in the United States (far more so than in Britain) have made an about-face. Liberals in all ages have looked at the state, always prone to annexations, with a great deal of suspicion. This tendency of the state is especially marked in the democratic order, not only because democracy is inherently totalitarian but also because it works (to use John Adam's term) with *largesses*, with large-scale bribes and promises rashly and shrewdly made by the *demagogoi*. Expansion, encroachment on personal rights, remains inseparable from democracy.[565] It matters little that the encroachments of the state tend in a subtle way to undermine democracy. Bureaucracy quickly assumes oligarchic and autocratic traits.

The old liberal did not necessarily like the democratic notion of the "politicized citizenry." In fact, he often suspected it of being fundamentally illiberal. But his resistance to the new winds and currents was weak for two reasons: he cherished the idea of belonging to the camp of the innovators, the progressivists, the "dawnists" (an expression of Michael de la Bedoyére), of hailing the new and damning the old; and *he had been robbed of his sense of values*. His philosophical props had been subverted long since—a generation earlier—by philosophies such as instrumentalism and behaviorism, as well as by "polite doubt," actually a refined form of positivism. This view, in the United States, had been generously represented by Oliver Wendell Holmes, Jr., grandson of a Calvinist clergyman, son of a theologically liberal physician and essayist, himself a justice of the Supreme Court of the United States—and a complete nihilist. Whereas pragmatism came on the American educational scene through that notorious institution of pedagogical training of which it has been said that false pearls were thrown to real swine, this pragmatic justice influenced legal thinking, which in the United States is equally important to education.

As a real positivist, Holmes could write, "Sovereignty is a form of power and the will of the sovereign is law because he has power to compel obedience or punish disobedience and for no other reason. The limits within which his will is law, then, are those within which he has, or is believed to have power to compel or to punish."[566]

If these were his true convictions there would be no reason at all for him to have condemned the horrors of the French Revolution, of Hitler's Dachau, or of Stalin's *kontslageri*. Or was it only a slip of the tongue? Yet Holmes could hardly have been more explicit in writing, "I think that the sacredness of human life is a purely municipal idea of no validity outside the jurisdiction; I believe that force, mitigated so far as may be by good manners, is the *ultima ratio*, and between two groups that want to make inconsistent kinds of a world I see no remedy except force. . . ." [567] What a pity, a Nazi might have mused, that Holmes (who died in 1935) was not one of the judges at Nuremberg. The Nazis could have rattled the Allies simply by quoting him.

Yet another passage to convince the truly skeptical: "I see no reason for attributing to man a significance different in kind from that which belongs to a baboon or a grain of sand. I believe that our personality is a cosmic ganglion, just as when certain rays meet and cross there is a white light at the meeting point, but the rays go on after the meeting as they did before, so, when certain other streams of energy cross at the meeting point, the cosmic ganglion can frame a syllogism or wag its tail." [568] There it is again: a grain of sand, baboon, Jew, bourgeois—let's rub them out!

Does it help to learn that the late Justice Holmes had a most humble opinion of himself? His pessimistic nihilism extended to his own person, for he wrote, "I may work a year or two but I cannot hope to add much to what I have done. I am too skeptical to think that it matters much, but too conscious of the mystery of the universe to say that it or anything else does not. I bow my head, I think serenely and say, as I told to someone the other day, O Cosmos—Now lettest thou thy ganglion dissolve in peace." [569]

The admission is no less dangerous for being melancholic in spirit. It has helped to establish a pattern that is still etched deep, witness the opinion given by Justice Vinson in 1951 in connection with a trial of Communists: "Nothing is more certain in modern society than the principle that there are no absolutes, that a name, a phrase, a standard has meaning only when associated with the considerations which give birth to nomenclature. To those who would paralyze our Government in the face of impending threat by encasing it in a semantic straitjacket, we must reply that all concepts are relative." [570]

Oliver Wendell Holmes, Jr., would have subscribed to this formulation half a century earlier. He once said that Emperor Franz Josef was a gentle-man and a "perfect illustration of my old saying that no gentleman can be a philosopher and no philosopher a gentleman: To the philosopher every-thing is fluid—even himself." [571] In his view, in other words, there is a real antithesis between philosophy and permanence—there can be no immuta-ble truths.

The consequences of such an attitude, clearly catastrophic, have shocked a number of European philosophers, [572] though others have expressed analogous ideas. An Austrian legal thinker of considerable influence on both sides of the Atlantic, Hans Kelsen, drafter of the still-valid republican constitution of Austria, has said, "Justice is an irrational ideal. However indispensable it might be for man's will and action, it cannot be reached by knowledge."[573] The real danger of this nihilism lies in the fact that its disciples find no reason to resist evil; they are intellectually defenseless in the face of such diabolical menaces as national or international socialism. Kelsen was once asked by Wilhelm Röpke what cogent argument he had against the Nazi extermination camps, whereupon Kelsen smiled cryptically and shrugged his shoulders—even though, had he stayed in Austria, he would have been a prime victim.[574]

The lack of well-grounded convictions, the absence of belief in truth create a dangerous hunger. And since nature abhors a vacuum, the absolutes of totalitarian systems find ready-made acolytes. "Isms" suddenly spring up and, as Fëdor Stepun said, they "give to the hungry demo-liberal-nihilistic world the 'truth,' but this 'truth' in reality is a lie and a travesty of religion."[575] Of course, as Keyserling has observed, there also exists a real absolutism of the relativists (who resemble Hayes's "sectarian liberals"), but they fail in emergencies.[576] They can be petty and stubborn, but they cannot take a firm stand for the true good, even if such a stand were to favor the positive values inherent in the great religions of the West.[577]

This nihilism harmonizes well with the naturalism represented by Edward Lee Thorndike, who had a great influence at Teachers College, Columbia University. Dr. S. J. Holmes has adequately summed up the philosophy of Professor Thorndike thus: "Man's traits, insofar as they are a part of his inheritance, owe their origin and biological meaning to their survival value. All natural traits and impulses of human beings must therefore be fundamentally good, if we consider the good as the biologically useful. Cruelty, selfishness, lust, cowardice, and deceit are normal ingredients of human nature which have their useful role in the struggle for existence. Intrinsically they are all virtues. It is only their excess or their exercise under the wrong conditions that justly incur our moral disapproval."[578] Was Professor Thorndike an isolated case of the lonely thinker, or was he an authentic and potent former of minds? Dean Seashore of the University of Iowa said of him: "No school is uninfluenced and no humanistic science is unaffected by (Thorndike's) labor." And Dean James E. Russell insisted that "in developing the subject of educational psychology and in making it fit study for students in all departments, Professor Thorndike has shaped the character of the college in its youth as no one else has done and as no one will ever have the opportunity of doing."[579]

There are interesting parallels between the nihilistic and materialistic undermining of the old-fashioned American liberal faith with relativist ideas, and the erosion of the faith of the French upper classes through Voltairean skepticism, which was followed by the fanatical, yet in a way consistent, philosophy of Rousseau. The nihilism inherent in the instrumentalism and pragmatism of John Dewey's philosophy also provided Marxism with an opening wedge. If all spiritual values, if Revelation, if the concept of the natural law, if the Aristotelian tradition were "illusory," if Christian existentialism from St. Augustine to Kierkegaard were "unscientific," then a naked materialism within and outside existentialism might well be the answer. As already seen, de Sade established the bridge between a subjectivist relativism and rank materialism. This inevitably leads to the thinking of a psychologist (and "philosopher") such as Professor Burrhus D. Skinner of the Behaviorist School.[580]

In other words, it was not only the "drifting" of lost old liberals, but also the corrosiveness of agnosticism that helped transform a set of ideas into their very opposite. Nor was it the first time that history had seen such a metamorphosis. Compare, for example, the ideas and ideals the Reformers stood for with the form and content of religious thought offered to students in the *average* "Protestant" theological seminary in the United States. This excepts, of course, the admirable fundamentalist and orthodox institutes of theological learning, which are unfortunately in a minority and often lack prestige. The importance of this point merits repetition. The "outstanding" theological seminaries of the Reformation faiths are by-and-large victims of rationalism; rationalism is the grandchild of Catholic scholasticism; and the Enlightenment is the grandchild of the Catholic Renaissance.

To make matters worse, there is a lamentable tendency to link modern, popular notions about "Protestantism" to the Reformers.[581] Luther would have been stunned if anybody had called him a "Protestant," a term of contempt coined during the budding Counter-Reformation,[582] and amazed at being cited as authorizing such concepts as "private interpretation"[583] (an early liberalism) and the abolition of auricular confession and of the Latin language in the ritual,[584] not to mention humanitarianism, individualism, racial equality, democracy, and all the rest. The twisting of religious concepts is cited because of its analogy to American liberalism. Although even here there are glaring exceptions. Professor Milton Friedman, for instance, who taught at the University of Chicago and acted as advisor to Senator Barry Goldwater during the latter's presidential campaign, still proudly calls himself a liberal.[585] As do others; as do I.

Since American freelance leftism, parading under the stolen liberal label, is an inversion of its former self, it cannot present a systematic and coherent picture. Like a mongrel, it suffers from inconsistencies and contradictions. Thus an American leftist,[586] in the midst of spouting his identitarian jargon, will suddenly inject ideas belonging to the liberal past. Not being a systematic thinker, but a person subconsciously torn by his various attachments—American folklore, nineteenth-century reactions to Calvinism, and radical leftism—he is not really aware of his dilemma.

And not being aware of his dilemma, he is prone to fateful miscalculations in dealing with truly systematic thought from abroad. Hence his naive belief (to cite only one instance) that should Russian Marxism be liberalized and Western "capitalism" treated with socialist hormones, the two could meet halfway. Such a meeting could, naturally, be effected, but only in such a manner that the flexible would be bent like a blade against a concrete wall. The Western world could of course be gradually socialized, communized, and sovietized: industries could be nationalized; but it is difficult to see how Russian industry or agriculture could ever be transformed into private property without (1) the collapse of the secular religion of communism, and (2) a transitional period of chaos, anarchy, or something akin to a military dictatorship. Revolution always remains a possibility (though in a totalitarian state a fairly remote one) but from an evolutionary viewpoint socialism is always a dead-end street. Yugoslavia is presently experiencing this difficulty. If you have the two long legs of free enterprise you can run; with the two short legs of socialism you can barely walk; but with one long and one short leg you might fall on your nose.

The Chinese case is entirely different. In China, at the social level, philosophy is at the top and superstition at the bottom, with hardly any religion in our sense. The Chinese are coldly pragmatic. If a system does not work, they drop it—at least in the long run. Russians, on the other hand, are a religious people. The few who are convinced Communists and have had the country in their grip are *religiously* communist. They would rather perish with their religiously held ideology than survive through fundamental compromises.

It is dangerous to believe that ideologies can be dealt with in the abstract, i.e., without any reference to national psychological situations. British and American thought looks with disfavor on "systems," airtight explanations of history, religion, psychology, economics, and so on.[587] It does not like extremes. It has a horror of reaching to the roots ("radicalism") or of embracing the Absolute.[588] Thus the confused character of American leftism is not due merely to its transitional aspect, but also to the "Anglo-Saxon" isolation that is made worse by its dislike of system, method, and logical rigidity. Witness Oliver Wendell Holmes's insistence that no gentleman can be a philosopher.[589]

In other words, American leftism derives its strength from an interplay of imported ideas, cherished American traditions, and appeals to the higher or, if need be, the lower human appetites. Communism, socialism, "welfarism"[590]—ideas sprung from the French Revolution—and "democracy" are clearly importations. The anticolonialist crusade, which has done such tremendous harm to all concerned, rests on American folklore (insofar as it does not also derive from the democratic dogma); Woodrow Wilson's program to "make the world safe for democracy" has idealistic undertones; and the "secular revolution," so dear to the non-Marxist Left everywhere, appeals to baser instincts.

The genuine liberal principle has been preserved in the domain of sex, and probably only there. (To which can be added another "biological" stand, antiracism.) American leftism is not only antipuritanical, it stands for libertinism. (To what extent the defense of homosexual practices, a cause popular with the uncommitted Left the world over, is due to the strong identitarian strain in leftism remains an element of speculation.) American non-Marxist leftism is, naturally, feminist, just as the female feminist—the ex-suffragette type—is also markedly leftist. But the American leftist is not really a lover of women; the myth of an American matriarchy is, after all, only a myth.[591] Women in America have a spacious ghetto in which they rule unhampered, but they do not have the influence of women in France, or of women in Italy, or of women in the upper layers of Central and Eastern Europe. In Spain, nay, even in misogynist England, a Queen can rule, but will there ever be a female President in America?

Feminism is an "ism," a phenomenon found almost exclusively in the lands of the Reformation. By abolishing the cult of female saints (about as numerous as males) the Reformers made Christianity an almost purely masculine religion. It was merely a matter of time for a reaction to set in.[592]

Libertinism (despite its good favor in American leftism) is frowned upon by the stricter leftist ideologies. Although homosexuality was not infrequent in certain Nazi circles and was even advocated in proto-Nazi groups,[593] it was savagely punished by the Nazi authorities. In the concentration camps homosexuals were assembled into punitive units wearing distinctive marks. In the Soviet Union, too, homosexuality is considered a crime—which makes no sense in light of the deterministic character of the official Soviet philosophy.[594] (In fact, since materialism rejects the notion of free will, why should there be any punishment for anything? De Sade asked this very question.)

The American uncommitted Left retains, apart from its sexual anti-puritanism, a few humanitarian residues from its genuinely liberal ancestors. It generally, for instance, dislikes capital punishment. Ironically, this form of retribution was first abolished in Western civilization by the Habsburgs in Tuscany[595] and Austria, and by Catherine II in Russia. It was later temporarily reintroduced in Austria and Russia, but after 1898 Emperor Franz Josef pardoned every culprit condemned to death—with one exception. (In 1898 the Empress Elizabeth, Franz Josef's wife, was murdered in Geneva by an Italian anarchist: Franz Josef's *practical* abolition of the death penalty was a Christian reply to his own loss in a great dialogue with God. Nor was Gavrilo Princip, murderer of his nephew and heir, and accidental initiator of World War I, executed.)[596] In Russia the death penalty was all but reabolished by Alexander II (it was reserved mainly for assassinations or attempted assassinations of members of the imperial family)[597] and so remained until anarchist terrorism entered the scene and the Communists became the masters of the country. It is, in fact, psychologically very difficult for a monarch to sign the death warrant of a subject with whom he is connected in a father-son relationship. (Here also lies the reason for the ready abdication of dynasties; they cannot easily fire at their "children" in times of stress and revolts.)[598] In republics the situation is radically different, because the person of the magistrate is less important; the democratic republic, moreover, works with abstractions (the constitution, the law, the general will) whereas a monarchy is a personal government.[599] According to democratic doctrine the citizen revolting against a "duly elected government" is revolting against himself. He is not a parricide; he is a suicidal maniac. He deserves no pity.

Yet, apart from these humanitarian leftovers, and although he arrogates the label "Liberal," the uncommitted American leftist (not strictly Marxist but usually Marx-tainted), is by no means a friend of liberty, of personal freedom. Even when he seemingly espouses the cause of liberation and emancipation, as in the case of the American of part African ancestry, he repeatedly invokes the strong arm of the law, the intervention of secular government in the social domain.[600] This exemplifies the radical deviation of the thinking of false liberals from the ideals of those liberals whom he brazenly claims as his ancestors; in his adulation of the ominipotent state and his genuine contempt for the independent person, he denies his own pretensions. His real or assumed "humanism" in the "biological" sphere[601] (sex, race, death penalty) is matched by a totalitarian outlook in nearly all the others. The Rousseauistic strain is even more evident than in the earlier and milder American leftist tradition as represented by Jefferson, Paine, Rush, and Jackson, which led to catastrophes everywhere, worst of all probably in the foreign policy field.

Today what is called "liberalism" in the United States, that boring mixture of modernity, mediocrity, mimicry, and naivete, still dominates the mass media—though they grow anxious about an uncertain future—and through them not only lower but predominantly higher education. The liberal "per-version" has resolved into a mixture of statism, a blind belief in total government, and populism, an equally blind trust in "the people"—seemingly a contradiction, but in reality a very feasible synthesis, if the mass media function efficiently and rightist efforts are diminished. But this issue will be expanded upon in the final chapter.

PART IV

The Left and U.S. Foreign Policy

Man is a creature who lives
not by bread alone, but
primarily by catchwords.

—R. L. Stevenson, *Virginibus puerisque*

PART IV

The Left and U.S. Foreign Policy

CHAPTER 15

The American Left and World War I

*The lights are going out all over
Europe, and we shall not see them
lit again in our lifetime.*

—Sir Edward Grey, August 13, 1914

In dealing with American, as well as with British, foreign policy in our century, this author writes as an alien, an Austrian who, during his lifetime, has been at the "receiving end" of political decisions which were largely—but by no means correctly—identified with the national interests of the United States and Britain.

Nowhere has the influence of the American and British Left been more suicidal than in matters of foreign policy. The effects of their interventions have been tragic, not only for the English-speaking countries, but for the world at large. And while the Left has vigorously participated in political and military activities that have plunged the West into decline, the more conservative forces in these countries cannot be entirely absolved from guilt—the guilt of omission rather than commission, of inaction rather than intervention.

From the viewpoint of American native mythology—which has little to do with factual history—the United States was born by those fleeing from Europe. A certain tradition likes to speak about the "American Experiment" (what is it? can it be called off if found "inconvenient"?) and tends to view America as an island where the blessed are totally removed from the rest of the world. True, the nascent American Republic needed a respite, a period in which to reconstruct, crystallize; and thanks to two oceans, its adopted policy of isolation was feasible as well as desirable.

Another myth soon took hold on *both* sides of the Atlantic: the United States was the "big democracy," the haven of the persecuted and the downtrodden, the supranational, global fatherland of equality, and so forth. And this despite the fact that the foundations of the new American Republic were Whiggish and aristocratic. Nineteenth-century America had many outstanding conservative thinkers and writers—Melville, Brownson, Sumner[602]—but a counterculture also existed. Walt Whitman, to cite only one, was a typical democrat; he was invoked *qua* homosexual as a representative of democratic *camaraderie* by Thomas Mann in his confession of faith in the Weimar Republic.[603] In *Leaves of Grass* Whitman chanted:

One's self I sing, a simple separate person
Yet after the word democratic, the word *en masse*.

Whitman's writings have the look of a solidly identitarian program, yet some passages are more pompous and less liberal, as when Whitman says in his *Democratic Vistas*: "I demand races of orbid bards, with unconditional and uncompromising sway. Come forth, sweet democratic despots of the West!"[604] The despots, of course, came from the East and they were not sweet, either. The very foundation of this democratic order was largely in the hands of "literary men" (as in today's leftism); indeed, "the priests depart, the divine literatus comes." Literature, according to Whitman, should be revolutionary, bereft of tradition, as should all other cultural manifestations. "I say that democracy can never prove itself beyond cavil, until it founds and luxuriantly grows its own forms of art, poems, schools, theology, displacing all that exists, or that has been produced anywhere in the past, under opposite influences," says another passage in the same book. This is a totalitarian, antitraditionalist program, similar to that of the spokesmen of *Proletkult* in the Soviet Union. And, again, Whitman writes that a new race should grow up in America, the "ideal race of the future—divine average!" Quite a Nazi vision. Henry Morganthau, Jr., told an Austrian friend of mine that democracy could only prevail in Europe if history were eliminated from people's minds, no longer taught in schools.

Reinhold Niebuhr has rightly pointed out in one of his best books that the United States conceived of itself as "God's American Israel" called upon to save the world.[605] Interestingly, this American national messianism has a decidedly leftist tinge which, for instance, the *earliest* Russian messianism did not have. The grandfather of American messianism was, after all, Jefferson, and its character was and still is republican (i.e., antimonarchical) and democratic (i.e., antielitist).

American nationalist feelings (which foreigners tend to feel are particularly strong), like all nationalist sentiments, have a certain "intellectual" character. Nationalism (ethnicism) is also argumentative: the nationalist will insist on the superiority of his nation by pointing to its unique characteristics, its achievements, virtues, qualities, institutions, traditions. The patriot, on the other hand, is not contentious. Just as an intelligent man would never try to argue that his parents were the "best in the world," so the patriot considers his attachment to his country a matter of loyalty. He considers being born a citizen of a specific country an accident, something over which he had no choice. Similarly, he loves his parents, although he had no part in choosing them. Or if he does not love them—if they are offensive or inferior people—he will nevertheless be loyal to them in obedience to the Fourth Commandment.

But American nationalism has been conditioned, to a large extent, by the "indoctrination" of the children of immigrants, inevitably coupled with a certain denigration of the Old World.[606] Any German, or Italian, or American gentleman will naturally defend his country against patently unjust accusations—loyalty demands this; but he will not try to convince others that his nation has the highest qualities in the world, the most gifted inventors, the most profound philosophers, the best writers, the finest painters, the fastest trains, the most beautiful women. (This uncouth boasting is reserved for the traveling salesman after a third drink, or the likes of a National Socialist or a Russian Communist.)[607]

Yet this attitude is also found in America, where moderate leftism and nativist nationalism have melded easily. Witness Whitman, witness some of Carl Sandburg's writings, witness the poem of Emma Lazarus on the Statue of Liberty. This gigantic symbol of freedom greets immigrants thus:

> "Keep, ancient lands, your storied pomp!" cried she
> With silent lips, "Give me your tired, your poor,
> Your huddled masses yearning to breathe free,
> The wretched refuse from your teeming shore,
> Send these, the homeless, tempest-tossed to me,
> I lift my lamp beside the golden door."[608]

In respect to nationalism and leftism, it is interesting to probe the ideological background of the Spanish-American War of 1898, a war in which nationalist motives were most assuredly mixed with leftist prejudices. In the United States, the highly cultivated upper crust had embraced neither the folkloric notions about European governments nor leftist ideas. But in the intellectually less ambitious a number of dangerous simplifications had taken root. In this war, the enemy was considered one of the rotten, backward, priest-ridden monarchies of the Old World. In contrast, the United States with its institutions, habits, traditions, and customs was assumed by the masses to be at the peak of evolution. The more similar a foreign country to the United States, the more "progressive"—and friendly—it was considered. The more dissimilar, the more it was deemed "backward" and worthy of contempt.

Simple or rather odd (sometimes consciously so) classifications were used; measuring rods consisted in such items as form of government, freedom of the press, formality of class distinctions, emancipation of women, literacy percentages, religious affiliation, relationship of church and state, legal status of denominational minorities, proliferation of bathtubs, cleanliness of hotels, punctuality of trains, and more. Historical elements also came into play: Britain was remembered for the year 1776 and Nathan Hale, France's role in the War of Independence somewhat improved its score, Germany's excellent record in almost all areas was offset by its monarchical form of government. And so forth.

In the case of Spain, the balance sheet in 1898 looked perfectly hopeless. The *leyenda negra*, the "Black Legend"[609] of English fabrication made it even worse. The yellow press of the United States represented the Spanish people as bigoted, fanatical, cruel, treacherous—and the Cubans as their high-minded, heroic, innocent victims.[610]

In the ensuing years, these American prejudices continued and flowered. Antimonarchism became the driving force in America's European policy during World War I and in its aftermath, and this helped crystallize American leftism to an even greater degree. Anarchists were at the so-called extreme left in the United States, but there was also a Socialist party (with a splinter) and a fair amount of "radicalism" without definite political ties. World War I actually started in Europe as a war between nations but it soon lost the character of an old-fashioned war. All participants, with the exception of Great Britain, had conscription. Moreover, in most countries, the press was instrumental in engendering broad waves of collective national hatreds.

The lights—in the words of Sir Edward Grey—were in truth going out all over Europe. In St. Petersburg a "patriotic" mob went so far as to storm the German Embassy. Collective loathing, especially in the West, reached levels that marked the decay of the Old World—dachshunds were killed in Britain, German pianos burned in America, Germans greeted each other with *Gott strafe England!*,[611] "enemy aliens" were put behind barbed wire in Germany, England, France, and Italy (but not in Austria-Hungary or Russia).[612] The Germans tried to starve out Britain, and the Western Allies tried to starve out the Central Powers. Allied propaganda represented the German armies as composed of assassins and sadists; atrocity stories were faked in droves and widely believed.[613] In short, a fanaticism, unknown in past ages, was roused.[614]

Yet by the end of 1916, when the senseless butchering had almost peaked, there was still only one European republic in the Allied camp—France; and with Russia (and Japan) fighting in the Great Coalition, the war could hardly be called ideological. Who, then, bore the main guilt for the senseless holocaust? Each nation was honestly convinced that the responsibility lay with the other side, but by any objective standard, the guilt was divided—not evenly, to be sure, but to different degrees among men, groups, and cliques in the various countries.[615]

During the latter part of 1916 and early in 1917 a compromise peace was still possible and great efforts were made to that end. In diminishing form hopes continued until early 1918, when the last Austro-Hungarian peace offensive took place. Emperor Charles I was not, of course, the only person trying desperately to end the frightful butchery. The Vatican, certain German parties (the Socialists and Conservatives), English groups, and Spain were also engaged in major efforts to put an end to the near-universal suffering. By the summer of 1917 the Russian Emperor had abdicated, the Kerenski government was tottering, the Italians awaited a major blow, Rumania had been defeated, the Western Front was locked in a stalemate, the French army had been weakened by a partial mutiny—and Lord Lansdowne's famous letter urging peace negotiations (rejected by the London *Times*) had been published by the *Daily Telegraph*.

But the non-Marxist Left in Britain and France, represented by Lloyd George, Clemenceau, and Ribot, was relentless; it also counted on American aid, for the decision over peace or war really lay with America. Never, in fact, was there a greater chance for a genuine *Pax Americana*. Had the United States been blessed at the time with an outstanding President, with a great leader endowed with real vision, it could have issued a call for a

202 THE LEFT AND U.S. FOREIGN POLICY

peace conference and treated all who refused to attend as *prima facie* partisans of the war.

Now, it could be argued that the great errors[616] committed by the German government—Franz von Papen's stupidity, the Zimmermann telegram, the sinking of the *Sussex* and the *Lusitania* (filled to the gills with arms and ammunition),[617] and those other provocative acts so severely castigated by Count Bernstorff, last Imperial ambassador to Washington[618]—had created a formidable situation. Although true, it does not mean that the United States had, inevitably, to enter the war. Quite possibly the election in 1916 of the Republican candidate, Charles Evans Hughes, so narrowly defeated by Wilson, could have changed the course of events and with it the fate of the globe.[619] (It could also be argued, of course, that Teddy Roosevelt's stubbornness in 1912, when he split the Republican vote and made Wilson's first election possible, was the beginning of the end since a reelected Taft would have made America's entry into World War I highly unlikely.)

Certainly 1917 was the most fateful year of our century. Woodrow Wilson decided to throw the American sword on the scales without realizing that he lacked the knowledge to win the peace and the power to make it last. And in fact, World War I and its seemingly permanent aftermath still haunt us. This aftermath can be laid to the monumental ignorance of the Left, its absolute nonunderstanding (rather than misunderstanding) of human nature, of the simplest facts of history, geography, psychology, economics, strategy, and politics, which led to one wrong decision after the other. Two facts stand out: Twice it was a Democratic administration (comprising the greater part of the leftist forces)[620] that engaged the United States in a global war, and twice two hierarchical organizations—industry and the military—won the wars. It was the democratically elected or appointed politicians that lost the fruits of these costly victories—costly in blood and money—at the conference tables.[621] In the long run, genuine achievements do not come from mere intuitions, but only through knowledge. The engineers and the captains of industry, the generals and the admirals, had *learned* their trade. The politicians had their jobs solely because they were popular.[622]

The collapse of the monarchical government in Russia and the advent of the Republic led by the fatuous Alexander Kerenski sharply changed the ideological picture of Europe. The revolutionary tradition continued in France, though in a moderate and "bourgeois" form. Britain, whose monarch was a mere figurehead, ranked as a "parliamentary democracy" with strong sentimental and cultural ties to America. Italy was a monarchy, but, more or less, in name only. As for the Germans, although they were considered industrious, clean, and musical, in America the myth prevailed that after 1848 all decent Germans had settled in America, leaving the mother country in the hands of arrogant, heel-clicking, monocled Junkers and the sinister autocrat, William II.[623] And although the Austro-Hungarian monarchy figured hardly at all in the popular thinking of Americans, it was uppermost in the minds of leftist intellectuals. They had not only heard of Metternich but agreed with Gladstone that "there is not an instance, there is not a spot upon the whole map, where you can lay your finger and say, 'There Austria did good.' "[624] And they remembered the tirades of Margaret Fuller, that tireless female reformer, against Vienna. No wonder, then, that the upshot of it all, the most tangible result of World War I, was the dismemberment of Austria-Hungary. It transformed the map of Europe and, incidentally, provided Germany with a masterful geopolitical position that gave Hitler an ideal start for his military and nonmilitary conquests. With the fall of the monarchy in Russia, Germany was bordered in the East by a power vacuum.

The Russian monarchical collapse made Wilson extremely happy. After the abdication of Nicholas II he praised Russia, saying, "Here is a fit partner for a League of Honor."[625] Wilson was a genuine ideologue in the narrow sense of the term; his plan, unfortunately, was not to make democracy safe for the world, but rather to make the world safe for democracy. He conducted a *jihad*, a holy war to extend the American form of government. This had already been evident in his dealings with Mexico before America's entry into World War I. About America's southern neighbor he said, "Our friendship is a disinterested friendship, so far as our aggrandizement goes. . . leaving them to work out their own destiny, but watching them narrowly and insisting that they shall take help when help is needed."[626] What sort of help can be gleaned from a conversation between Walter Hines Page, Wilson's ambassador, and Sir Edward Grey, Britain's foreign secretary. Page recorded it himself:

GREY: Suppose you have to intervene, what then?
PAGE: Make 'em vote and live by their decisions.
GREY: But suppose they will not so live?
PAGE: We'll go in again and make 'em vote again.
GREY: And keep this up for 200 years?
PAGE: Yes. The United States will be here for 200 years and it can continue to shoot men for that little space till they learn to vote and rule themselves.[627]

A variation of this policy occurred in dealings between the United States and Central Europe.

But Wilson's prejudice against monarchy was more than intellectual, it was also "folkloric," based on the conviction that monarchs, unlike democratic leaders, loved wars. (*Revanchisme*, recall, was the great *popular* passion of the Third French Republic right up until 1914, but evidence is easily ignored. Hegel, upon being told that the facts contradicted his theories, replied sternly: *Um so schlimmer für die Tatsachen*"—"all the worse for the facts.") The identification of democracy with peace was mirrored in a letter of Wilson's secretary of state, Robert Lansing, who wrote to Colonel House: "No people can desire a war, particularly an aggressive war. If the people can exercise their will, they will remain at peace. If a nation possesses democratic institutions, the popular will will be executed. Consequently, if the principle of democracy prevails in a nation, it can be counted upon to preserve peace and oppose wars. . . . If this view is correct, then the effort should be made to make democracy universal."[628]

Wilson's famous message to Benedict XV, conveyed to the Pope by Lansing before America entered the war, breathed more or less the same spirit.[629] The German people might be fine, the letter said, but its government had to go. And indeed, after the war Germany and Austria were saddled with regimes whose character was dictated by the Allies—the alternative being the hunger blockade. Any historian could have told the victors that political forms imposed by a triumphant enemy *never* last.[630] The mistake committed by the Holy Alliance in 1814-15 was repeated by the Allies in 1918-19—and by the Unholy Alliance in 1945.

Needless to say, Wilson suffered from the Great American Malady, the belief that people the world over are "more alike than unlike"; in other words, that non-Americans are nothing more than inhibited, underdeveloped could-be Americans with the misfortune of speaking a different language. At one time Wilson had been tortured by the suspicion that an alien mentality existed in other parts of the world. In an article written for the *Atlantic Monthly* in 1889 he mentioned the "restless forces of European democratic thought and anarchic turbulence" that had been brought to the United States by "alarming masses" of immigrants who were "apt to tell disastrously upon our Saxon habit of government."[631] When it came to the showdown at the conference table in Paris, Lloyd George, himself a Methodist Machiavelli, said that he was wedged in between a man who thought he was Napoleon (Clemenceau) and another who thought he was Jesus Christ (Wilson). By then, the Southern racist had developed into a savior of mankind.

The ignorance of the former president of Princeton in matters of history and geography was simply prodigious. The Italians at one point showed him a spurious map on which a mountain, fittingly named "Vetta d'Italia," appeared in the very heart of Austria; it served as proof, they claimed, that "historic Italy" (there never was such a country) extended right to that spot. As a result the Italians, for the first time ever, received the South[632] and Central Tyrol with the Brenner Pass. (The second time occurred in 1946, with the result that the shooting and dynamiting in this restless, tortured area continues to this very day.) Harold Nicolson, who was at the Peace Conference, expressed in writing the current feeling that "if Wilson would swallow the Brenner, he would swallow everything."[633] Terrified later by his own mistake, Wilson strove to prevent the annexation of Fiume (predominantly inhabited by Italians) by Italy, and somewhat undiplomatically toured the country to appeal to the Italians over the heads of their government.

As in the arrangements and treaties after 1945, following World War I almost everybody was deprived of something that was legitimately his and received something to which he really had no right. Nations were thus prevented from existing peacefully with neighbors whom they had wronged or who had wronged them.[634] The era of Pan-Democracy and Peace, in fact, started an endless series of wars—cold, lukewarm, and hot. In a way, Wilson was as "lost" at the Peace Conference as he had been before, lost in a thick fog of factual ignorance and mythological concepts. John Maynard Keynes, who as a young man had been present at the Paris Conference, gave a shattering picture of Wilson's qualities: "He not only had no proposals in detail, but he was in many respects, perhaps inevitably, ill-informed as to European conditions. And not only was he ill-informed—that was true of Mr. Lloyd George also—but his mind was slow and unadaptable. . . . There can seldom have been a statesman of the first rank more incompetent than the President in the agilities of the council chamber."[635] Thanks to the "democratization" of the Western World following the Congress of Vienna (1814–15) and the Congress of Berlin (1878), a tragic lowering of general standards had taken place. The representatives of the nations no longer spoke a common vernacular; the era of interpreters had begun. In Paris Clemenceau "alone among the Four could speak and understand both languages, Orlando knowing only French and the Prime Minister and President only English, and it is of historic importance that Orlando and the President had no direct means of communication."[636]

Woodrow Wilson's greatest guilt, nevertheless, lay in his attitude *during* the war, in his flat refusal to cooperate in any peace efforts and in his determination to carry the war to the bitter end, thus laying the foundations for the next one. (Human lives? The number of mercenaries is limited by cash and their willingness to join, but draft boards can squeeze out an almost endless number of unwilling candidates for death.) World War I, surely, is a far more crucial historic event than most Americans credit. Modern man is overoccupied with stems and leaves, he willfully disregards the roots. George F. Kennan is perfectly right when he says, "All lines of inquiry lead back to World War I." Had World War I been terminated earlier, the old Germany with certain modifications would have survived. About this Kennan wrote in 1951, "Yet, today, if one were offered the chance of having back again the Germany of 1913, a Germany run by conservative but relatively moderate people, no Nazis and no Communists, a vigorous Germany, united and unoccupied, full of energy and confidence, able to play a part again in the balancing-off of Russian power in Europe—well, there would be objections to it from many quarters, and it wouldn't make everybody happy; but in many ways it wouldn't be so bad, in comparison with our problem of today. Now, think what this means. When you tally up the total score of the two wars, in terms of their ostensible objectives, you find if there has been any gain at all, it is pretty hard to discern."[637]

The gruesome futility of this gruesome war was also perceived by Anatole France who, during the war, was menaced by Clemenceau with jail if he continued to speak out. The great novelist said: "Now we have the American war—yes, we will defeat Germany—but for this we shall need the entire world. Even if beaten, Germany will pride itself on having resisted the entire world; no other people will be so inebriated by their defeat. If peace does not bring about the United States of Europe, we will have only an armistice and everything will start anew." And again, when Austria's peace offensive failed, he said, "No one will ever persuade me that the war could not have been ended long ago. The Emperor Charles offered peace. There is the only honest man to occupy an important position during the war, but he was not listened to. In my opinion, his offer ought to have been accepted. The Emperor Charles has a sincere desire for peace, so everybody hates him. Ribot is an old scoundrel to have neglected such an opportunity. A King of France, yes, a king would have taken pity on our poor people, bled white, attenuated, at the end of their strength. But democracy is without heart, without guts. A slave to the power of money, it is pitiless and inhuman."[638]

In respect to George Kennan, his reflection was not necessarily a reaction to *two* major disappointments. For the unprejudiced mind, *one* ought surely to have sufficed. Indeed, Lord Newton could write in 1929 in connection with the failure of Lansdowne's letter in the *Daily Telegraph*: "If peace had been made at the end of 1917, it is clear that the Germans would have escaped their legitimate punishment. On the other hand, the failure of their criminal aggression would have been inconcealable, the Kaiser and the military caste would have been discredited and their disposition to embark upon another similar enterprise would have vanished. A negotiated peace, although it might have disappointed many aspirations, would certainly have effected a more permanent European settlement than exists at the present day. Millions of lives would have been saved and the load of human misery substantially reduced. We ourselves at a moderate computation would have been spared hundreds of thousands of casualties, and more than 1,500 millions of expenditure."[639]

"Objections from many quarters," "disappointed aspirations"—these would have derived exclusively from the Left, content to slaughter in order to achieve its aims: the nationalistic Left, the radically democratic Left, the socialist-communist Left looking for an oppportunity to enact a major revolution. But President Wilson's thinking, although predominantly determined by his antimonarchical bias, was also somewhat determined by his religious tradition,[640] which earned him the sympathies of the Calvinists in Europe. Nevertheless, it is questionable whether his religious position was one of affirmation or merely of negation. His Calvinism (*if* it genuinely existed in a theological sense) hardly surfaced in his speeches or writings, although his anti-Catholic attitude was quite obvious. In this respect he fully concurred with Lloyd George and Clemenceau. His hatred for Rome was such that, for its sake, he sacrificed other of his shibboleths, such as self-determination. Thus he said that "German Austria should go to Germany, as all were of one language and one race, but this would mean the establishment of a great central Roman Catholic nation which would be under the control of the Papacy."[641]

In other words, in his antimonarchism, in his endeavors to foist on Europe a form of government bound to fail (as a semihieratic, semiaristocratic Catholic monarchy would have, say, in Vermont), Wilson was perhaps not so much a scholarly professor of government as just a "plain American." He was convinced that the formula to his success in the United States—fostering American popular notions—could be repeated as successfully in the rest of the world. He once said that "the best leaders are those with ordinary opinions and extraordinary abilities, those who uphold the opinion of the generation in which they live, and hold it with such vitality, perceive it with such excessive insight, that they can walk at the front and show the paths by which the things generally purposed can be accomplished."[642] This is nothing but the despicable principle of that great demagogue, Ledru-Rollin: "I am their leader, so I have to follow them!"[643]

This is not surprising since many Americans were sensitive to the accusation that they lacked patriotism; unfortunately they had a blind belief in "democracy" (which in an altruistic nation generates the urge to disseminate it and is only too often identified, even if falsely, with patriotism). Three generations ago Hugo Münsterberg rightly said about America, "I believe sincerely that no European country knows a patriotism of such fervor and explosiveness."[644] Actually, in respect to World War I, the issue was nationalism rather than patriotism. Patriotism is never aggressive vis-à-vis other nations, but nationalism, which was reborn in the French Revolution, curiously enough "knows no borders." It incites nations to force other nations to adopt their pattern of political "happiness."

Münsterberg also discerned the deep-seated antimonarchism of Americans. Since they consider monarchy a "rotten" institution, it is extremely difficult for them to grasp monarchy's advantages and virtues in specific situations.[645] (In the youth-worshipping American mind there is a far-reaching identification between "old" and "rotten.") Another German, Ernst Bruncken, remarked that in America "every teacher of comparative government will discover what an enormous effort is required to impart a clear notion of European monarchical institutions to even quite mature students. A Napoleonic tyranny, a dictatorship—that is easily within the realm of their comprehension. But a legitimate monarchy seems to the American a simple absurdity, and he cannot understand how otherwise quite intelligent people can have faith in such a thing.[646] For too many Americans there is a mysterious-mystical connection between the monarchical and the religious concept, bolstered by the misunderstood slogan of the 'divine right of kings.' "[647] Still, there are exceptions to the rule. Reinhold Niebuhr, who did not belong to any conservative camp, has written with great acuity of the instrinsic merits of constitutional monarchy, the traditional form of European monarchical government:[648] "The institution of monarchy, shorn of its absolute power, was found to possess virtues which neither the proponents nor the opponents of the original form anticipated. It became the symbol of the continuing will and unity of a nation as distinguished from the momentary will, embodied in specific governments."[649]

During World War I American leftism in action was embodied probably not so much in Wilson himself as in George Davis Herron, his left hand (in every way) in foreign policy. (His right hand was, naturally, Colonel House, though this friendship finally foundered and failed.) Herron is barely mentioned in the *Encyclopaedia Britannica*, but he is featured in one-third of a column in the *Encyclopedia Americana*. To assess correctly Herron's *actual* importance is extremely difficult. Quite probably "he took himself more seriously than he was taken by Wilson."[650] And yet Herron's part in preventing an early peace in 1917, and much more so in February-March 1918, should not be underestimated. Herron is important in these pages both because of his historic role and because of his significance as a person, as a typical representative of the "progressive" and leftist thinking that has wreaked such harm in our century.

Herron's ideological affinitiy with Wilson was complete. Both belonged to the post-Protestant age.[651] It was easy for Herron to persuade Wilson to establish the proposed League of Nations in Geneva,[652] the city near which Herron finally made his headquarters.[653] Wilson was delighted.[654] Geneva was, after all, the city of Calvin and Rousseau, whom Herron in his confusion adored simultaneously. (Although Calvin can hardly be imagined without Luther, Herron completely rejected the German Reformer.) Herron was (quite consciously) a "national messianist," and therefore these two Genevans with their great, even if mutually contradictory, influence on America attracted him. After the war he wrote from Geneva to William Allen White, "I labored unceasingly to make America a really messianic nation in this world crisis and to help the President in his divinely appointed stature."[655]

Both Wilson and Herron were prone to dislike, if not actually hate, Austria-Hungary more than Germany. (In the 1860s, William James had also sided with Prussia against Austria and in his case too for religious motives—the typical attitude of the son of a Swedenborgian minister.)[656] Now, with America engaged in a war which Sir Denis Brogan rightly called the Second War of Austrian Succession (a third was to follow in 1939), Herron no less than Wilson was susceptible to anti-Austrian feelings and anti-Austrian propaganda. This explains the swift victory of Masaryk in his encounters with Wilson. The Czech statesman persuaded the President to break up the evil, "backward" Danubian monarchy[657] and convinced him that Austria, in declaring war against Serbia, had acted on its own and not under German pressure.[658] The enthusiasm of the Czechs for their self-appointed leaders in exile was by no means great,[659] but the American Left, quite undeterred, leaped into action. "American democracy," as Masaryk wrote, "buried the Habsburg Monarchy and the Habsburgs with it."[660] (It also helped bury hundreds of thousands of young Americans in

World War II.) Masaryk worked hand in glove with Herron, with whom he shared common quasi-religious ideological prejudices. Herron did his part in pressuring Woodrow Wilson to persuade Congress to declare war against Austria-Hungary,[661] an action not at all in the interests of the United States.[662]

To the American leftists, Austria was far more wicked than Germany. It existed in contradiction of the Mazzinian principle of the national state; it had inherited many traditions as well as symbols from the Holy Roman Empire (double-headed eagle, black-gold colors, etc.); its dynasty had once ruled over Spain (another *bête noire*); it had led the Counter-Reformation, headed the Holy Alliance, fought against the *Risorgimento*, suppressed the Magyar rebellion under Kossuth (who has a monument in New York City), and morally supported the monarchical experiment in Mexico.[663] Habsburg—the very name evoked memories of Roman Catholicism, of the Armada, the Inquisition,[664] Metternich, Lafayette jailed in Olmütz and Silvio Pellico in Brünn's Spielberg fortress. Such a state had to be shattered, such a dynasty had to disappear. Thus—finally—the House of Austria went into exile, to be replaced by a simple common man from Austria, an alleged house painter, a man who drowned the world in a flood of blood and tears.

Now, who was this George Davis Herron, who was this American who helped dig the grave of old Europe? Who was this curious, bearded, bespectacled poet, mentioned in some documents as "Reverend," in others as "Professor," and more rarely as plain "Mr. Herron"? Romain Rolland, the great pacifist, novelist, and Nobel Prize winner, referred to him at one point rather unkindly. The reason? Herron had written an article against Rolland in Geneva's *La Revue Mensuelle* (April 1917) entitled "Pacifist Immorality." At the time Herron was tortured by the fear of a compromise peace and spoke out in ringing words: "Darkness is rising rapidly over the skies of the nations. It is as if the soul of the human race were gripped by the crushing fear of a prehistoric night. Yes, it is Thor and Wotan who are now about to establish a reign of spiritual death. . . ." Romain Rolland replied by calling him a "virtuous hypocrite" and a "gigantic idiot." Herron was the latter rather than the former; he was an eternally confused youthful enthusiast, steeped in deepest ignorance and drunk with words, rather than a scoundrel. Part of the key to his behavior and his thinking was his idealistic-romantic leftism.

Herron was born on January 21, 1862, in Montezuma (halfway between Tangier and Mecca), Indiana, the son of a humble couple of Scottish descent, William Herron and Isabella Davis. In 1879-82 he went to Ripon College, a rather "progressive," coeducational, nondenominational school. In 1883, only twenty-one years old, he married Mary Everhard.[665] Herron had already decided to become a minister; it was practical humanitarianism rather than mystical or spiritual passion that determined his choice.

Herron became a minister when he was still a student of theology, subsequently received his doctorate of theology from Tabor College, was ordained minister of the First Congregational Church in Lake City, Minnesota, and was finally appointed minister in Burlington, Iowa. Apparently finding no fulfillment in his pastoral work, he turned to an academic career and embraced socialism as a secular creed. He received a professorship at Iowa (later Grinnell) College,[666] where the very wealthy Mrs. Rand[667] founded a chair for "Applied Christianity" which Herron kept until 1899. Theoretically he belonged to the ministry but he was unfrocked when his wife (who bore him five children) sued for (and was granted) a divorce on the grounds of "cruelty, culminating in desertion." But the reason for the separation seems to have been more romantic, because very soon afterward he married Carrie Rand, a girl of rather delicate health, the daughter of his kind patron. (The first Mrs. Herron received $60,000 from her former husband's new mother-in-law, a considerable sum in those days and an interesting financial transaction.) Herron was not happy about the attitude of his church and he tried to overturn the decision of the disciplinary committee with an "Open Letter," dated May 24, 1901, but his protest was to no avail.

The day after his suspension a secular celebration of his new marriage took place in New York's Gotham Hotel; America's leading Socialists (Norman Thomas among them) were invited. Poems were recited and dramatic speeches delivered. In order to get an idea of the atmosphere of this wedding a sentence from one of the addresses might suffice: "Our comrade George D. Herron arose, careworn and sorrowful as one who had passed through the Valley of the Shadows of Death, yet stronghearted and gladsome withal, and beside him stood Carrie Rand, clad in pure vestal white and bearing lillies-of-the-valley in her hand."[668] This marriage lasted until 1914 when the second Mrs. Herron died, whereupon he married Miss Frieda B. Schoeberle; he also left the more orthodox forms of socialism and pacifism.

Until World War I Herron was active in the ranks of America's Socialist party, to which many men of German descent belonged. Financially independent, he was a public orator and pamphleteer. One of his speeches, "From Revolution to Revolution: Lessons Drawn From the Paris Commune," delivered at the Boston Socialist Club on March 21, 1903, was republished in St. Petersburg.[669] During those years Herron developed the exceedingly florid style that stamped him as an ex-preacher, seer, demagogue, and hysteric. His writings abounded in hyperbolic enunciations as, for example, "Capitalism is but the survival of the animal in man."[670]

World War I surprised Herron in Italy. In the beginning Washington tried vainly to ascertain the character of this struggle, even Wilson hesitated at times to commit himself,[671] but Herron's mind was made up quickly. The Italian Socialists were just as blind as the American Socialists. This was a Holy War of all the forces of progress, enlightenment, and tolerance against the most unholy alliance of the Vatican, "Mother of Harlots," the Prussian Junkers, the wicked Habsburgs, and the Lutheran gun manufacturers of the Ruhr Valley!

The precise nature of Herron's services to the United States *and* Britain, especially before 1916, is rather ambiguous. In the voluminous *Herron Papers*, only two meager documents concern his financial dealings and official position with London and Washington. One contains an admission that he was recognized by Washington as representative of the *American Socialist Mission*, which, however, had no ties to the American Socialist party. (Its leader, Eugene V. Debs, a great idealist, was sent to the penitentiary in September 1918 for his isolationist views.)

The *Herron Papers* (1917-1924) kept in the Hoover Institution in Stanford, California, are a unique collection. They were donated to the "Hoover Library" by Herron in 1924, yet they cover nothing prior to 1917. A few letters, papers, and pamphlets are in possession of the U.S. Department of State and the Public Library in New York City. The author has read not only all the *Herron Papers* but nearly forty books and pamphlets either written by Herron or dealing with him.[672]

Wading through this mass of material is simply terrifying. A mixture of misinformation, naivete, hubris, and goodwill characterizes the activity of this fantastic person. Wilson seems not to have taken serious note of him until 1917, and their contacts remained epistolary until the Paris Peace Conference, when they finally met. There is little doubt that Wilson was deeply impressed by Herron's books—as also, perhaps, by the fulsome praise bestowed upon him by Herron.[673]

The books that pleased Wilson so much were *Germanism and the American Crusade*, *Woodrow Wilson and the World's Peace*, and *The Menace of the Peace*,[674] in which Herron cried out his desperate fear that the senseless slaughter might be shortened. Some of his words—memorable for their style and content—merit recording:

> As one who hopes passionately for the victory of the Allies, I would say that a complete Prussian triumph would be preferable to a compromise between the contending peoples and principles. For even under the baleful bondage of a German dominion mankind might still through high rebellion, through hard suffering awaken to its mission in the universe—to cosmic intimacy and infinite choice. But if the war end in universal evasion, if the race refuse its great hour of decision, then downward into long and impenetrable darkness we shall surely go. One can imagine such an issue as the very despair of the heart of God, vainly broken for a dastard and derelict humanity. [*The Menace of the Peace*, pp.9-10.]

The President wrote to Mr. Kennerley, publisher of *Woodrow Wilson and the World's Peace*, a highly congratulatory letter in which he said that he had read the book with "the deepest appreciation of Mr. Herron's singular insight into all the elements of the complicated situation and into my own motives and purposes."[675]

By late 1917 Herron sat like a spider at the center of an information network with admittedly ill-defined powers. But he undeniably met with a great number of people, emissaries from Central Europe as well as from other nations. In a way this poor, ambitious man was lost; he had the greatest trouble sizing up the character or the importance of his visitors, yet he continued to write his reports in his high-flown prose, relentlessly issuing one oracular statement, one judgment, after the other.[676]

But his great moment came when he was empowered to receive Professor Heinrich Lammasch on a confidential peace mission from Vienna. Lammasch was a personal friend of the Emperor Charles, a first-rate scholar and three-time president of the International Court of Arbitration in the Hague. It is easy to imagine what exaggerated prestige Herron enjoyed in Germany and Austria-Hungary where professors are demigods, and what importance was attached to getting the ear of a man whose opinions weighed so heavily in the White House. (Herron, according to his mood, claimed or disclaimed this importance.)

The meeting between Herron and Lammasch took place on February 3-4, 1918, on an estate near Berne that belonged to Dr. Muehlon, a self-exiled and embittered German industrialist. During one entire afternoon and evening, Lammasch explained to Herron the plans of Emperor Charles, plans which were identical with those of his uncle, the murdered Archduke Francis Ferdinand. Lammasch described the envisaged transformation of the Austro-Hungarian monarchy into a federated political body in which, entirely in keeping with one of Wilson's Fourteen Points, the individual nations (ethnic groups) would be "accorded the freest opportunity of autonomous development."[677] Actually, the picture painted by Lammasch was such that Herron at first saw no reason to reject the proposal, but he decided to reflect over it before giving an answer. During the night, he began to wrestle with this "temptation," as "Jacob wrestled with God near Yabbok."[678] By morning he knew that he had gained complete victory over himself: Lammasch had been nothing but an evil tempter. No! The Habsburg monarchy had to go because the Habsburgs as such were an obstacle to progress, democracy, and liberty. Had they remained in power, the whole war would have been fought in vain.

Lammasch returned to Austria a broken man. Herron wrote a negative report for the President, which he immediately transmitted to Hugh Wilson, American chargé d'affaires in Berne, and on February 11, the President made a speech which implicitly rejected the Austrian peace overture.[679]

Had Austria-Hungary been taken out of the war, Germany could not possibly have fought on (as in 1943, after Italy's defection) and hundreds of thousands of lives could have been saved. But Herron was a bellicose leftist: human lives meant nothing to him. His reaction to Lansdowne's one-man peace offer had been strong in the extreme. To Mr. Bland of the Foreign Office he wrote, "It had an almost shattering effect upon me. I have been sick at heart for a week—sick unto death almost. . . . I have never been as fearful of an ultimate peace and a lost world as I am now. And behind my fears are portentous forces—not merely echoes like Lansdowne, but the occultism of the international financiers in alliance with the Vatican."[680] Curiously enough, Herron liked Lammasch personally and gave him (to Lammasch's immense surprise) two of his own books against peace.[681] Herron's schizophrenia knew no limits. Later, at the Peace Conference at Saint-German-en-Laye, when Lammasch was treated almost like a criminal, Herron's indignation was overpowering.[682] After all, he was the man who had "really believed that we would come out of this war into something like an approach to the kingdom of Heaven."[683] Nothing of course came of it (as after World War II, when similar hopes were voiced), and Herron's ire now turnd against the French in wild invectives[684] paralleling Wilson's outcry: "I should like to see Germany clean up France, and I should like to see Jusserand [the French ambassador] and tell him so to his face."[685]

Herron's remark about the "occultism of the international financiers" had, as a sensitive reading might surmise, an anti-Jewish bias. The Jewish outlook is rather individualistic. Jews will join the socialist (or communist) camp wholeheartedly only in specific sociological situations and under great pressure. [686] It was therefore quite natural for Herron with his socialist background to have anti-Semitic leanings; anti-Jewish references (usually in an anticapitalist context) abound in his *Papers*.[687] Frequently these assumed the character of the vague and wild accusations heard from the National Socialists.[688] Typical of him are such baseless remarks as: "Béla Khun [sic] was the most flagrant agent of French Jew financiers and was put there by them."[689]

Herron's revulsion and disgust for the actual peace treaties were undeniably sincere. If the disappointment did not come immediately, it evolved within a year or so. Mr. Wilson's failure to rally the country in favor of the League of Nations undoubtedly had much to do with it. Herron's *Umsturz und Aufbau*, a violent diatribe against the Paris Treaties, was published in German in 1920,[690] since it could not have come out in the United States or England. His book, *The Greater War* (New York, 1919), shows his continuing worry over the danger of a "Prussian Germanization of Europe from Calais to the Gates of India."[691] But his German pamphlet, dedicated to the youth of Europe, proves that at times he was not devoid of prophetic gifts. He foretold an "age of murder and slaughter, if not a century of Tartar tortures," of the "worst wars the world has ever seen." Hitler could not have been more extreme in the denunciation of the Versailles Treaty whose "paragraphs abounding in ferocity, lust of conquest, contempt for the law, and lack of honor are as cruel, as shameless, as senseless, as vulgar. . . ." [692]

And sorrowfully he admitted that it was "Wilson's word [the Fourteen Points] which had undermined the German Reich and prepared the victory which Foch, finally, reaped with the sword."[693] In this analysis he pronounced the same judgment as a certain Captain Charles de Gaulle, who spent several years as a prisoner of war in Germany and described in his first book, *La discorde chez l'ennemi*,[694] in ringing words Germany's demoralization through enemy propaganda. There can be no doubt that the Germans and Austrians firmly believed in the sincerity and official character of the Fourteen Points. Had the Germans not accepted the Fourteen Points at face value, they probably would have fought on;[695] Max Weber had faith in Wilson but advised continuation of the war in the fall of 1918 because he thought that otherwise the wild chauvinists among the Allies would sidetrack the President.[696] And this is precisely what happened.

Herron returned to Italy after the war and visited Germany a few times. He died in Munich on October 7, 1925, on his way back to Florence. He had become disgusted with the European Socialists, not only because they had tried to make an "early peace," but because he saw men such as Ramsey MacDonald and Henderson spending up to $25 a day in exclusive hotels. About events in Russia Herron was less sure. He wrote to Norman Thomas in 1920 that the "bolsheviks" were bad, but that the "future civilization of Europe is coming out of Russia and it will be at least an approach to the Kingdom of Heaven when it comes."[697] The old leftist utopia of the Kingdom of Heaven just around the corner! To another Socialist he wrote late in 1919, "I am inclined to think that the Soviet system will ultimately prevail. But you are making a very great confusion between bolshevism and the Soviet system. . . . The Soviet system does not differ economically from the Old England town meeting, or politically from the early Christian communities"[698]—a foretaste of the bemused transformation of Mao's murderous minions into peaceful "agrarian reformers."

Slowly Herron began to see that the Italian Communists were ruining Italy economically and politically. His sights veered: force must be used against force. In a book about Italy, published back in 1922,[699] Herron had expressed the highest praise for fascism, which his friend, Roberto Michels, had already embraced.[700] Fascism, after all, had sprouted as a deviation in the socialist camp. After Mussolini took over, Herron's enthusiasm, as his correspondence with Mrs. Charles Berry shows, became almost limitless. There was nothing in the least extraordinary about his evolution. It had been duplicated in many other cases—a journey from socialism and communism to fascism and national socialism. . . and back again.

CHAPTER 16

Leftism Goes from War to War

Among the calamities of war
may be rightly remembered
the diminution of the love of truth.

—SAMUEL JOHNSON

The transformation of World War I from a conflict between nations into an ideological crusade for democracy was to bear bitter fruit. J. M. Keynes, an observer at the Paris Conference, wrote in 1919, fresh from this orgy of arrogance, incompetence, and ignorance: "If the European civil war is to end with France and Italy abusing their momentary victorious power to destroy Germany and Austria-Hungary, now prostrate, they invite their own destruction also, being so deeply and inextricably intertwined with their victims by hidden psychic and economic bonds. . . . The clock cannot be set back. You cannot restore Central Europe to 1870 without setting up such strains in the European structure and letting loose such human and spiritual forces as, pushing beyond frontiers and races, will overwhelm not only you and your 'guarantees,' but your institutions and the existing order of your society."[701]

The year 870 rather than 1870 would have been more exact an analogy, but Keynes, a controversial economist and no mean historical prophet, anticipated with great clarity the forthcoming evils. By the end of 1925,

Wilson and Herron were no longer among the living, but the seed they had sown (or helped to sow) was slowly maturing. The day was not too far distant—as Herron had foreseen—when the Germans and the Japanese would deem it possible to join hands across the Volga River. The Nazi monster had already been born, and Germany's humiliation would be instrumental in its rise.

This humiliation did not, as commonly believed, derive from military defeat. The theory, so popular in the West before 1939, that the brown evil sprang up because the Allies had held no victory parade in Berlin in 1918 is blatant nonsense. (Such a parade, if anything, might have accelerated the rise of the National Socialists.) The root of the trouble lay in the moralizing attitude of the West, especially the United States, culminating in Article 231 of the Versailles Treaty which put all the guilt squarely on Germany's shoulders.[702] The treaty was signed on June 28, 1919, exactly five years after the double murder at Sarajevo, apparently proving that crime *does* pay.[703] There is no better way to generate hatred than by forcing a person to sign a confession of guilt which he is sacredly convinced is untrue. This wanton humiliation, unprecedented up to that time in the annals of Christendom, created the thirst for revenge which the National Socialists so cleverly exploited. It was no coincidence that, on that same day, the government of the new "Czechoslovak Democracy" sent a wire to the leaders of Yugoslavia congratulating them on the anniversary of the Sarajevo murder and expressing their hopes of "similar heroic deeds in the future."

Such an article, it is argued, had to be inserted in order to provide a moral basis for Germany's reparation payments.[704] But surely it would have been not only simpler, but more honest and manly, to insist on reparations on the grounds that in a complex war, whose origins historians would dispute for decades to come, the loser, not the winner, should pay the cost. Compare the difference between the Congress of Vienna, which terminated twenty years of aggression, with the Paris Treaties. In 1815 France actually emerged slightly larger and, thanks to Talleyrand's diplomatic genius, was immediately accepted as a member of the Holy Alliance.

True, in 1918 the moral indignation game was played by Britain as well as by official America—witness the "Hang the Kaiser" campaign of Lloyd George.[705] And true, the defeat of a nation is similar to the physical defeat of a person: the victor has but two *logical* alternatives—to cut his enemy's throat or help him to his feet. But democracies at war prepare for neither; they cultivate collective hatreds, work up moral indignation against entire nations (not just against their governments, which may be perfectly warranted) and thus make it extremely difficult, if not impossible, to reach an equitable settlement.

At the outcome of World War I, the most amazing and contradictory decisions were made. Germany, not Austria-Hungary, was held up to the masses of the West as the real evildoer, although this view was not held by responsible statesmen. Clemenceau hated Austria even more than Germany,[706] and Lloyd George is said to have declared on several occasions that for denominational reasons Austria-Hungary, not Germany, had to be carved up.[707] Yet, whatever the case, it remains that after 1919 Germany bordered on only one great power, France, whereas before 1914 it had been hemmed in by three great powers—France, Russia, and Austria-Hungary—powers with a grand total of 230 million inhabitants as against Germany's 62 million. Geopolitically, Germany's situation was vastly *improved*, as bright Germans were well aware. Professor Ernst Kornemann, rector of Breslau University, declared in his inaugural address on October 15, 1926, that despite all its losses, Germany ought to be glad that it had survived the war by far the strongest and ethnically most homogeneous political unit in Central Europe: "Let us take full advantage of this situation, which our opponents have created by Balkanizing and atomizing Europe," he exhorted.[708]

Poland, which also bordered on Germany, was the only viable state with an historic background, but from the start it was handicapped by the enmity of Lloyd George (and, later, Winston Churchill). To the south and east of Germany, a political order (which made a future catastrophe inevitable) was established *conjointly* by American leftist idealism, inane British cynicism, blind French chauvinism, and Italian neoimperialism—all of them collaborating with local forces that were nationalistic and antihistoric. Elements of criminality and insanity thus achieved a perfect synthesis: *it was only a question of time before the area would fall under the sway of Berlin or Moscow or both*.

H. A. Macartney, one of the few first-rate British experts on Central Europe, said rightly: "For a very considerable proportion of the peoples of the [Danubian] Monarchy, then, the Monarchy, with all its faults, represented a degree of protection and of national security which was not lightly to be hazarded."[709] Yet, as in the case of the decolonialization of our day, the leftists of the West combined with the nationalists of other countries to break up larger units, thus giving the adjoining truly oppressive imperialist powers the chance to enslave these disjointed fragments of land, thoroughly and completely. And when Macartney said, "Of all the Danubian peoples only the Czechs have succeeded in creating anything like democracy. The rest either stuck to their old hierarchies or relapsed into despotism,"[710] he was being somewhat charitable.

The Czechs numbered 47 percent of the population of Czechoslovakia. It was only by "annexing" the Slovaks, much against their expressed will, into a hyphenated nation which had never existed historically[711] that they suddenly became a "majority." In fact, there were more Germans (24.5 percent) in Czechoslovakia than Slovaks. But by clever gerrymandering devices the Czechs maintained a parliamentary majority and exercised an oppressive rule which drove the German minority (inexactly called "Sudeten Germans") into a rebellious and disloyal nationalism that would evolve into national socialism. Czechoslovakia foundered on the fact that, although it represented a multinational state, it offered its ethnic minorities, which in sum formed a majority, no opportunity for "national fulfillment." Like Yugoslavia it was a caricature of the defunct Austro-Hungarian monarchy. And when the Czech government poured dithyrambic praise on the Czechs who had behaved treacherously against the old monarchy, they created a cult of disloyalty. The Czechs in the Czech Legion who had fought with Russia against Austria from 1914 to 1917 were praised as national heroes. With such a precedent, why should the "Sudeten Germans" not side "treasonably" with neighboring Germans?

The trick of combining several nationalities into one was repeated by the Serbs who, copying the Czechs, promulgated into existence not a "Serbocroatoslovene," but a "Yugoslav" nation, a historical, psychological, religious, and ethnic "non-sense." (Both the official "Czechoslovak" and "Southslav" atlases[712] flatly refused to distinguish between the different "ruling" nationalities—one ruled, the others obeyed.[713] The Serbs also "annexed" the Bulgars of Macedonia and ordained that the term "Macedonia" be supplanted by "Southern Serbia.") The West accepted all this without protest. The reaction would probably have been quite different had the Germans suddenly claimed that the Dutch were "Germans" on the grounds that they spoke a language based on Low German. (In fact, up until at least the sixteenth century, the Dutch considered themselves Germans inhabiting the lowlands—the *Netherlands*—of Germany; subsequently, they developed a national conscience all their own which only certain Dutch Nazis dared to question.) Yet the Slovaks had never been Czechs, the Croats and the Macedonians never Serbs, the Slovenes never ruled by the Balkan city, Belgrade.[714]

Before plunging into the maelstrom left by the breakup of the Danubian monarchy, it is well to recall Disraeli's words: "The maintenance of the Austrian Empire is necessary to the independence and, if necessary, to the civilization and even to the liberties of Europe." He feared the deep-seated antagonism of Britain's Left toward Austria, of the Liberals already influenced by radicalism, of men who measured foreign countries by their affinity to British institutions. "You looked on the English Constitution as a model form," he said to the Liberals in the House of Commons. "You forced this constitution in every country. You laid it down as the great principle that you were not to consider the interests of England or the interests of the country you were in connection with, but that you were to consider the great system of Liberalism, which has nothing to do with the interests of England, and was generally antagonistic with the interests of the country with which you were in connection."[715] How easily one could substitute "democracy" for "liberalism" and address these sentiments to American as well as British leftists who served neither the real interest of their country nor of the countries which they saddled with representative governments of democratic character.

Winston Churchill, who repeatedly crossed party lines and was by no means a "true conservative" (he was a pragmatic deist), held similar views to Disraeli. He had seen what the republican form of government in Germany and the destruction of Austria[716] had brought on the world. "For centuries," he wrote, "this surviving embodiment of the Holy Roman Empire had afforded a common life, with advantages in trade and security, to a large number of peoples, none of whom in our time had the strength or vitality to stand by themselves in the face of pressure from a revivified Germany or Russia. All these races wished to break away from the federal or imperial structure, and to encourage their desires was deemed a liberal policy. The Balkanization of Southeastern Europe proceeded apace with the consequent relative aggrandizement of Prussia and the German Reich, which, though tired and war-scarred, was intact and locally overwhelming. There is not one of the peoples or provinces that constituted the empire of the Habsburgs to whom gaining their independence had not brought the tortures which ancient poets and theologians had reserved for the damned."[717] Churchill repeated these views in a note to the Foreign Office on April 8, 1945: "This war should never have come unless, under American and modernizing pressure, we had driven the Habsburgs out of Austria and Hungary and the Hohenzollerns out of Germany. By making these vacuums we gave the opening for the Hitlerite monster to crawl out of its sewer onto the vacant thrones. No doubt these views are very unfashionable."[718]

An inventory of the state of Central Europe in 1934, half a generation after the treaties of Versailles, St. Germain-en-Laye, Neuilly, and Trianon, finds that Germany was ruled by a totalitarian dictatorship of the Nazis, that the Czechs of "Czechoslovakia" uneasily held sway over the non-Czechs who waited for a day of revenge, that Poland under Pilsudski and Austria under Dollfuss were authoritarian states, that Hungary, ruled by an oligarchy, had very limited democracy, that Rumania's Iron Guard was preparing to conquer the country, that Yugoslavia, after the murder of Radić, had been taken over by Belgrade's terror-regime which governed through assassination and execution, and that neither Bulgaria nor Albania had parliamentary governments.

In other parts of the world, Lithuania and Estonia had become dictatorships. Latvia and Greece had two more years before falling to a similar fate. Spain was girding up for its bloody civil war, and Portugal had no parliamentary government. In Russia the Duma had long since disappeared. In Japan parliamentary life had by 1935 become as farcical as in Turkey, and on and on.

In other words, the Holy Crusade to make the world safe for democracy, with its millions killed and billions spent, in the end saw the total defeat of democracy and, far worse, the destruction of the liberal principle of personal freedom.

Where did personal freedom still exist? Where was it constitutionally protected? Certainly not in Czechoslovakia, for there, on the tenth anniversary of the spurious Pittsburgh Agreement, Professor Tuka was jailed for publishing an article entitled *Vacuum Iuris* in which he posited that the terms of the agreement had come to an end. *Outside of Switzerland and France freedom existed only in the historic monarchies of Europe*, of Northern Europe to be more precise. In this connection, the text of an April 1921 decision of the Conference of (the Allied) Ambassadors, similar to a resolution on a Habsburg restoration that had been passed in February 1920, makes interesting reading: "The Principal Allied Powers consider that the restoration of a dynasty which represented in the eyes of its subjects a system of oppression and domination over other races, in alliance with Germany, would be incompatible with the achievements of the war in liberating peoples hitherto enslaved, as well as with the principle for which the war was waged."[719]

The statement is stunning in view of the fact that 22 million people in the area formerly ruled by the Habsburgs were under the control of nations of other tongues, whereas before 1918 roughly the same number were "controlled" by German-Austrians, Magyars, and Croats.[720] The Habsburgs were the villains in the eyes of the Left the world over—from Washington to Moscow (and, later, brown Berlin)—while the Karagjor-gjevićs of Serbia, who came to power through murder, governed through murder, and erected a commemorative museum in Sarajevo for the murderer, Gravrilo Princip,[721] were probably viewed as progressive and tolerant liberals. To a Central European blessed with a modicum of education and common sense this declaration by the Conference of Ambassadors of the Principal Allied Powers must have seemed the height of suicidal folly and hypocrisy.

A similar streak of stark madness characterized French strategy in Central Europe. The American folly in 1945—destroying the West's bulwark against Russian aggression—had its precedent in the French policies on the Danube.[722] Austria-Hungary had to go, leaving the successor states to act as dams against Germany *and* Russia. Austria was reduced roughly to its size in the thirteenth century; Hungary was deprived of 70 percent of its area and two-thirds of its population. Austria was allowed to keep an army of 30,000, Hungary of 35,000 men. (The Austrian army was not even permitted to use gas masks.) Austria could not feed itself; one out of three Austrians was a Viennese. And it lost all its major coal deposits.[723] As a result, the vast majority of Austrians favored reuniting with Germany; nazism flourished in Austria because the Nazis offered a speedy *Anschluss*.[724] The Hungarians, for their part, were automatically driven into the arms of the powers that promised a radical revision of the peace treaties—Italy and, later, Germany. The same was true of Bulgaria, since one-third of Bulgarians were living under a foreign flag.

Czechoslovakia, Rumania, and Yugoslavia—countries whose names before 1850 could not have been found on a map, in a dictionary or an encyclopedia[725]—formed the "Little Entente" and received an enormous amount of French military and financial aid. Billions of francs, extorted from unwilling French taxpayers, were poured into these countries in the hope of stemming Germany's *Drang nach Osten* ("impulse toward the east"). Two of them, Rumania and Yugoslavia, together with Greece and Turkey, also belonged to the Balkan League. The avowed purpose of this league was to oppose all territorial demands of Bulgaria (and Albania). The Little Entente and the Balkan League thus formed a huge "Z" stretching from the gates of Dresden to the borders of Iran. But, as any child could foresee, the French investments were squandered, the French hopes dashed. Greece and Turkey were not so much anti-German as merely anti-Bulgar, and the other three states were primarily interested in (1) preventing a Habsburg restoration, and (2) thwarting Hungarian (or Austrian) revisionism. Their common interest was their common loot, their common fear, and their common bad conscience.

When the National Socialists appeared on the scene as staunch enemies of the Habsburg restoration, Prague, Belgrade, and Bucharest immediately collaborated with them, in a way betraying their French protector. It must, moreover, have been evident (as it was to any intelligent Frenchman not belonging to the leftist establishment) that the members of the Little Entente never would nor really could fight the Germans even if so inclined. Their armies were the most heterogeneous of units, with a nucleus consisting of small groups of traitors, many from the Balkans, who had deserted from the old imperial-royal army and now served the new masters of Central Europe.[726] (How these armies stood up to the grim realities of the years 1938-42 will be discussed in due course.) Recall that Yugoslavia in 1918-19 was officially called "Kingdom of Serbs, Croats and Slovenes," *Kraljevina Srba, Hrvata i Slovenaca*—or SHS, which the German-speaking liked to translate *Sie hassen sich*, "they hate each other." To this day U.S. foreign language newspapers with a Central European background almost never refer to themselves as "Czechoslovak" or "Yugoslav," but as Slovene, Croat, Serb, Czech, Slovak, Ukrainian, Macedonian, and so on. Not even under the tremendous pressure exercised by communist dictatorship have these nationalities jelled into synthetic "nations."

However important that volatile area, however tragic American intervention in it, the fact is that the American public was never really interested in that part of the globe—not, that is, until the "Sudeten Crisis" in September 1938. This is less true of the American Left. But it was true of the Right, and therein lies the great sin of omission of the American Right—or perhaps *of conservative circles almost anywhere in the West*. When Hitler actively intervened on behalf of the Sudeten Germans in Czechoslovakia in 1938 and effectively blackmailed England, Neville Chamberlain referred to Czechoslovakia as a country "of which we know so little"—an honest and candid confession.

The study of foreign history and geography is weak in American as well as in British schools. As already mentioned, in American schools European history is often taught as "French history with frills."[727] (The usual frills are Philip II, the Reformation, Peter the Great, Bismarck, and Cavour.) And geography is the veritable stepchild of higher American education.[728]

There is yet another fateful shortcoming in conservative thought. Whereas leftists in the United States have always been internationally oriented, American conservatives have tended to be nationalistic, introspective, and isolationist. Of course, as noted, a strong and durable connection between leftism (radical democracy, socialism, communism) and nationalism exists—whether a genuine ethnic nationalism or a clever exploitation of it. But while leftism keeps one eye on national concerns, the other is busily scanning the globe.

Leftist soil also nurtured the first growth of anti-intellectualism in the United States. It all hangs together, and reaches back to the early years of the nation when attitudes were slightly different. In his remarks on foreign countries,[729] for instance, Jefferson proved he was a fanatic nationalist and, as Professor Richard Hofstadter so convincingly demonstrated, in the United States anti-intellectualism goes hand-in-hand with democracy. In America, moreover, intellectuality was originally considered an aristocratic vice.[730] Higher knowledge, training, and education were rife with anti-egalitarian characteristics, for while the American upper classes were great travelers who imbibed the rich values of foreign countries, the *early* democratic element of the United States, the frontiersmen, had neither the time nor the disposition to scan foreign horizons. The China clippers, the rise of the big banks with worldwide connections, and the international relations of the leading universities were of interest only to the upper classes of New England and the Mid-Atlantic States. Thus the United States was split between the anti-intellectual and "localist" lower classes with subtle leftist views on the one hand, and an internationally minded "brainy" upper class on the other. F. J. Grund's picture of the United States in the 1830s confirms this.[731]

A thorough study of why a change of attitudes took place would be interesting. The evolution of thought and attitudes in America has *certain* analogies and relations to shifts of emphases in Europe. In Europe, conservative thought (as opposed to mere traditionalist sentiment) developed more fully where the Reformation had triumphed than in Catholic or even Eastern-Orthodox countries. Maurras was not a conservative, de Maistre was more of a reactionary. What emanates from Southern and Eastern Europe are rather emancipated thinkers who in the sovereignty of their outlook *overcome the leftist myths*—but this is not necessarily "conservatism." The Reformers, Luther above all—and this cannot be stressed sufficiently—were anti-intellectual and antirational. And since conservatism in Northern Europe leaned heavily on religion, this antirational and antirationalist attitude crept into conservative thinking. Professor Hofstadter is emphatic about the influence of "Protestantism" on anti-intellectualism in America—especially on the purely emotional sects with ecstatic overtones.

Another factor that split American society was the international character of America's socialism as against the protectionist character of the American manufacturer. Matters worsened with the continuous flow of new ideologies imported into America by immigrants from the Continent; these new *Weltanschauungen*, strongly political and with an extremist or "radical" bias, ran counter to many facets of "Americanism" and, to a large extent, of American folklore.[732] (Similar experiences took place in England. As a child I remember a comic strip in the London *Daily Mirror* that featured a black-haired, bearded anarchist whose every word ended with "ski," thus indicating his Slavic origin.) There can be no doubt that the Mediterranean and East European elements played a very large role in the anarchist and socialist movements in America until the 1930s. To be sure, there was also a dose of the Irish influence; Anglo-Saxons do not like to throw bombs or mount the barricades. And Northern Ireland is Celtic.

By the early twentieth century the internationally minded forces in America were the Marxist Left, the anarchist Left,[733] the moderate, unorganized Left—radical democrats, suffragettes, Single Taxers, the Catholic Church (with all sorts of mental reservations)—and a great part of American Jewry. And the more these groups cast glances at Europe, Latin America, and Asia, the stiffer the average solid "conservative" American became in his retrospective parochialism.

There is, of course, a sane and even God-ordained patriotism (Our Lord cried over the fate of Jerusalem); but there is also a patriotism which, in the words of the conservative Dr. Johnson, is the refuge of scoundrels. Equally, there is a reasonable, rational, and honorable Christian internationalism as well as a perverted and irrational form. Yet, for whatever the reason, internationalism—along with the crucially important field of international relations—was "left to the Left." By default, moreover, intellectual and cultural affairs became the monopoly of long-haired professors and short-haired ladies.[734]

Thus, not surprisingly, American foreign policy increasingly followed a leftist pattern. It was indeed "left to the Left." (When F. A. von Hayek arrived in New York as a young man in 1924, a nice lady from a leftist organization was quick to ply him with information, research possibilities, and every conceivable introduction.) Originally the leftist pressures were exogenous; they emanated from well-organized groups, from the mass media—radio commentators and columnists. In 1938 the State Department was not yet the happy hunting ground of the leftists, but their critique of it was increasing by leaps and bounds. As a result a leftist administration started a series of successive purges that increasingly gave the State Department a leftist character. This, of course, was equally true of the diplomatic service which is largely under the control of the U.S. Department of State. (Since ambassadors, however, need to be confirmed by the Senate, and for one or another fortunate reason, the right man can at times actually land in the right place, as in the case of Robert Murphy.) During the crucial years from 1933 to 1953, Democratic administrations appointed many leftist professors, such as William E. Dodd,[735] as well as leftist millionaires of the Joseph E. Davies type.[736] These appointees, driven by their missionary zeal and their fatal vanity, fortunately often gave voice in print to their impressions, actions, and reactions—marvelous revelations of the monumental ignorance of the Left in the historic field of international relations.

But the monopoly in foreign affairs is not only due to conservative default, to its sour and suspicious retreat. Behind it lies something even more tragic: the suppressed fear in the noncommitted Right that the Left, so deeply rooted in American folklore, is riding the Wave of the Future. How otherwise explain those conservative college and university boards of trustees who repeatedly hire professors notorious for their leftist ideas? How else understand those archconservative American businessmen who send their sons and daughters to institutions of learning known equally for their exorbitant rates and their extreme leftism, a leftism encompassing politics, history, philosophy, economics—and morals?

How otherwise explain the fact that newspaper owners, editors-in-chief, and radio station proprietors, who have overcome their early flirtations with leftism, again and again employ wildly leftist reporters, columnists, and commentators? I especially recall a correspondent who covered the Spanish Civil War for a leading midwestern daily. The paper was well known for its strict conservativism and the correspondent for his boundless sympathies for the *mixtum compositum* known as "Republican Loyalist Spain." (The Communists were also "Republicans" and exceedingly loyal, but not exactly to Spain.) The correspondent was also blessed with an absolute ignorance of Spanish history. But then leftists are always "forward-" never "backward-looking" persons: they do not heed the maxim that those who ignore history are condemned to repeat it.[737] The paradoxical attitude of the paper can be understood only as stemming from the well-hidden inferiority complex of the American conservative who adheres to principles which he cannot intellectually defend. Moreover, because he holds to the notion of "progress," almost in the leftist sense, he feels he is fighting a rearguard action. All he can hope for is a certain *Schadenfreude*, a spiteful pleasure at the inevitable setbacks and failures of leftism. This attitude gives a petty, morose, and melancholy character to a certain type of American conservative (far more so than to his Continental cousin). He needs a somewhat lighthearted aggressiveness—humorous and magnanimous—a will to win, but coupled with the liberality of those who believe in a discreet amount of diversity.

The American Left spent the 1920s busily building up its positions. It strengthened its various camps intellectually, attained an ever-increasing control over education and the arts, and slowly gained a monopoly in fashioning public opinion on foreign issues. The Left did not seem overly anxious at the rise of Fascism in Italy; certain representatives of the Democratic party were even friendly toward Mussolini.[738] But the Soviet Union was far more successful than Italy in winning the sympathies of the writers who vaunted their "open-mindedness"—though in one direction only. And just as France had its Dreyfus case—a Jewish captain of the French army was unjustly accused and convicted of having betrayed military secrets to the German military attaché[739]—so the United States had its Sacco and Vanzetti case. It drove a great many people into the leftist camp, some of them right into the arms of communism or, at least, procommunism. (Among them was the late Eugene Lyons, a great idealist, who went as a foreign correspondent to Moscow where he was cured of his leftism. But how many Americans had the advantage of such a splendid reeducation?)

Of the many aspects of the Sacco and Vanzetti case, the *least* important to the outside world was the question of the two men's guilt or innocence. They themselves never admitted any guilt; they merely repeated their belief in political anarchism. In those days in Europe the nontotalitarian nations were very lenient toward political criminals; almost nobody cared whether the two men (and a third, a Portuguese, Celestino Madeiros) were or were not assassins.[740] By 1927 very few Continental countries retained the death penalty. What did seem intolerable to Europeans was that Sacco and Vanzetti awaited death for no fewer than seven years. While Americans argue that justice in the United States is so meticulous that every time-consuming appeal of a condemned man must be investigated, Europeans maintain that an agony lasting for several years is worse than a quick death. Thus practically all of Europe protested—rightists and leftists, monarchists and republicans, Fascists and Communists, Catholics and atheists. The Pope tried to intercede; Mussolini demanded pardon; the President of Portugal (under the "fascist dictatorship" of Salazar) also asked for grace. These details are given not only to demonstrate the importance of the Sacco and Vanzetti case to American "ideological" history, but to show how little Americans understand the Continental outlook.[741] The reaction of pious European Christians of the Right was quite simple: "Either these men are innocent, in which case their execution is a crime, or they are guilty, in which case they will hardly commit another murder. As to punishment, leave that to the afterlife." In the former German Democratic Republic, the Christian Democratic Party decided not to persecute the ex-members of the STASI (the East German KGB) for their crimes.

In Fascist Italy the execution of these two anarchists was taken as a national insult. In 1928 Luigi Rusticucci published a book in Naples, *Tragedia e supplizio di Sacco e Vanzetti*, whose preface was written by Arnaldo Mussolini, brother of the Duce. Vanzetti's earthly remains were brought back to Italy and buried, and around his grave (with the connivance of Fascist authorities) a local cult developed. That these men were Anarchists—not Communists—further aggravated European opinion. "That's what we all are," was a not infrequent reaction, "and never mind that it is an unrealistic attitude." (Americans were not so wrong when, referring to the defiant Irish immigrants in the 1860s, they spoke of "Rum, Romanism and Rebellion." *Liberty or Equality?*, by this author, mentions two banners characteristic of the Catholic world: the black Jolly Roger with skull and crossbones, and the gold-silver flag of the papacy with tiara and crossed keyes—freedom and authority.) The trial and execution of the Rosenberg couple did not create the same stir in Europe as had the Sacco-Vanzetti case, because the Rosenbergs died against the background of millions dying in red concentration camps.

The next stage in the unfolding drama of American-European relations came on the Black Friday in 1929 when the New York Stock Exchange set off powerful forces that dispersed economic distress to the far corners of the world. In the United States, this mighty blow, which struck free enterprise without warning, sparked a wave of anticapitalism, increased interest in socialist nostrums, and generated a new, benevolent attitude toward Russian communism. When I visited the Soviet Union for the first time in the summer of 1930 I was struck by the fact that 80 to 90 percent of the tourists came from the United States and that a very large sector of the *Innospyetsy*, "foreign specialists," were Americans. America's "Red Decade" was in full swing; Americans lapped up the books of Maurice Hindus. Many salient features of the USSR found fertile ground in the American mind—the fostering of community feeling, the methodical warfare against "outworn traditions," the emphasis on progress and industrialization, the demophilism in Russia (which had *always* existed), the welfare institutions from kindergartens to hospitals, the experiments in the penal system,[742] and the all-encompassing efforts to create "something new."[743] American tourists (the majority of them female) demonstrated an almost hysterical enthusiasm for the USSR.[744] For most of them communism filled the void left by their loss of faith in religion—or in Wall Street.

But of course these tourists, visitors, and "students" had no means of measuring the achievements or failures of communism. They had not known Imperial Russia, they did not know anything of Russian history, they did not speak Russian. Completely in the hands of their guides, they had no contact with the everyday Russian (contacts at that time were very difficult). They were helpless, so much so that they frequently could not distinguish between the men's room and the powder room. Had they ever been to an *obshtshezhitye*, a common apartment, seen a kitchen, or eaten in a *stolovaya*, a communal restaurant, they might have been tempted to think. But they had nothing to go on but their subconscious determination to be enthusiastic, and enthusiastic they were—one more demonstration of how a previous disposition can warp the human mind and totally destroy objectivity.

The Depression profoundly affected the patriotism of those Americans who regarded their country not as the mother to be loved even when old, fragile, and difficult, but as the provider, the "land of plenty"—the exact sentiments expressed in the poetry of Edgar Guest.[745] Mr. Hoover's presidency was drawing to a close and Mr. Franklin Delano Roosevelt, one of the most dynamic grave diggers of the Western world, succeeded on a platform not dissimilar to that of his predecessor. Though Mr. Roosevelt belonged to the Democratic party, his social background indisposed him for a time to leftist policies, both national and international. But his wife (from another branch of the Roosevelt family) was more in tune with leftist ideas, undoubtedly the aftereffect of higher feminine education in the United States.[746] Whereas Mr. Roosevelt played his politics by ear, his wife, who wielded considerable influence, was ideologically far more consistent. Mr. Roosevelt, moreover, had but the scantiest education for his task; he hardly knew Europe, and his knowledge of foreign languages[747] was as modest as his acquaintance with the mentality of other nations. Largely ignorant himself, and profoundly anti-intellectual,[748] he had no way of judging, evaluating, and coordinating expert opinion. Even worse, perhaps, his sense of objective truth was gravely impaired. His handicap was by no means predominantly of a physical nature.[749]

Hitler's takeover in Germany and Roosevelt's first inaugural speech were only a few weeks apart. In the beginning, there was a certain amount of admiration among the Nazis for President Roosevelt, his administration, and the New Deal which, as it slowly crystallized, tried to solve the economic crisis with planning and statist measures. (The end of the economic crisis in the United States, as in Germany, came of course with rearmament.) Most Nazi authors writing about American history were in fact favorable to the Jeffersonian-Jacksonian (populist-antifederalist) tradition.[750] Johst, president of the *Reichsschrifttumkammer*, the Nazi Chamber of Literature, wrote a play about Tom Paine. The German traveler, writer, and lecturer, Colin Ross, who had decidedly Nazi views, was among the admirers of the "New United States." The Roosevelt administration was after all hostile to big business, which was entirely in keeping with Nazi notions. While the Nazis tolerated manufacturers, they were especially hard on finance, which they called "grasping but not creative capital," *raffendes aber nicht schaffendes Kapital*. The Nazis, moreover, were convinced that capital in the United States was largely controlled by the Jews. They respected Henry Ford, the "history-is-bunk" man who had written an anti-Semitic book, aided Hitler with large sums, and was decorated by the German consul general in Detroit in October 1938, but they were convinced that men with names like Mellon and Morgan were Jewish. All in all, Roosevelt's high-handed dealings with the business world, Congress, and the Supreme Court, were greatly admired by the National Socialists.

Nor at the start was Roosevelt overly hostile toward Hitler or his henchmen. The *Anschluss* was immediately recognized by the United States, and the American legation in Vienna swiftly demoted to a consulate general. Nor did the *Reichsmordwoche* ("Reich Murder Week") of June-July 1934, during which the Nazis assassinated hundreds of opponents, ruffle American-German relations. The American public had not been particularly upset by Japan's invasion of Manchuria (aggression should have been stopped right there), nor by Mussolini's conquest of Ethiopia, which, incidentally, was underwritten by Herbert L. Matthews of the *New York Times*, celebrator of the Spanish Loyalists and later of Fidel Castro. (Only a black pilot in Harlem volunteered for the Abyssinian air force—a mulatto sympathetic to the Semitic Amharas under the flag of "Negro solidarity.")

It took the Spanish Civil War, which broke out in July 1936, to arouse the American people. To the American Left this was the Crusade of Crusades, a far more sacred cause than either World War I or World War II. How few, by comparison, volunteered for embattled Britain in the 1939-41 period!

Why this enthusiasm which, in a way, has not abated? As already suggested, the (British-manufactured) *leyenda negra*, the "Black Legend," about Spain was still very much alive. Spain, the pillar of the Counter-Reformation, had also been the last country at war with the United States prior to World War I. This ill feeling was exacerbated by Spain's Catholic and allegedly aristocratic character.[751] And, to top it off, Spain received aid from Germany and Italy, which proved, the reasoning went, that the Nazis and Fascists, envious of the democratic progress of Republican Spain, schemed to destroy it.

But given the fanatic and ideologically riven parties in Spain—from Anarchists to Trotskyites to Carlist Traditionalists—a parliamentary republic along classic lines was bound to fail. Such a failure was all the more certain as the parties in question preferred revolt to abiding by the rules. Modifying Clausewitz' aphorism—war is the continuation of diplomacy by other means—it may well follow that *in ideologically divided countries civil war is the continuation of parliamentary government by other means*. Miguel de Unamuno, an independent-minded and original liberal who lived in exile during Primo de Rivera's dictatorship, had advocated civil war for years[752] as necessary to purify the air and rejuvenate the country. Politically inflammable material was escalating year by year. At the last free elections, February 1936, no fewer than twenty-eight political parties competed and each received a sufficient number of votes to send representatives to the Cortes. (When I mentioned this to a Spanish friend, he pounded the table and shouted, "That's a dirty lie! We have not twenty-eight but 28 *million* different parties"—a reference to the current population in Spain.)

The birth of the republic was marred by continual strikes, endless acts of mob violence—the burning of churches and monasteries (see p. 185), repeated outbreaks of brigandage—and a rapid decline of general security. To the unbiased the Spanish Republic experiment was a grotesque parody of a democratic state. A democratic republic might work in the United States and Switzerland, but since Spaniards were radically different from Genevans or Philadelphians, the experiment was bound to fail—and fail as thoroughly as it had in Russia.

The inner division of Spain was shattering. The elections of 1934 produced a right-of-center government that prompted an uprising of the miners in the Asturias, most of them Anarcho-Syndicalists of the *Federación de Anarquistas Ibéricos* (FAI). Appalling atrocities were committed, horrors worse than those depicted by Goya in his *Desastres de la guerra*.[753] The savage outbreak could only be quelled with the aid of the Tercio, the Spanish Foreign Legion, a body of professional soldiers known for their courage and brutality. Some of them were under the command of a young general of a notoriously Republican family who had distinguished himself in the Rif War. His younger brother Ramón, the first man to cross the South Atlantic by plane, had thrown leaflets from the air in 1931 asking the King to abdicate. The Prime Minister of the Spanish Republic in 1934, Don José María Gil Robles, was of a different sort: son of a well-known professor of political science he was himself an outstanding Catholic lay leader. In light of Spain's proved inability to govern by constitutional means, he tried to persuade the young general to establish a military dictatorship. The general vehemently rejected the proposal. His name: Don Francisco Franco y Bahamonde.

Franco was certainly not the choice man in the Spanish army to emulate what has become routine in Latin America—the establishment of military rule. But General Sanjurjo, an old Republican, was. Unfortunately, Sanjurjo failed in what turned out to be a premature uprising and fled to Portugal. After the elections of 1936, matters went from bad to worse. Sanjurjo planned another attempt, while the Left plotted its own takeover, scheduled for late July.[754] Franco meanwhile had been sent to the Canary Islands by the new leftist government; he had become suspect.

Things came to a head when, in full hearing of the Cortes, Dolores Ibárruri, La Pasionaria, told the monarchist deputy José María Calvo Sotelo that he would speedily meet his end. That same night he was arrested and murdered by the Assault Guards—a new police force created by the regime, which distrusted the old Guardia Civil. Republican Spain had palpably ceased to be an *estado de derecho*, a land of constitutionality, of law and order. Sanjurjo immediately proclaimed a military dictatorship and headed for Spain in a private plane to organize the takeover. Unfortunately, the plane crashed and Sanjurjo was killed.[755] Franco's flight from the Canaries to Morocco, where he joined the Tercio, was better managed by Louis Bolín;[756] the Tercio and Moorish regiments were subsequently transferred to Spain in an action partly financed by the Jewish quarter, the Mellah of Tetuan.[757]

The army rebellions in Barcelona, Valencia, and Madrid quickly collapsed, but the commander of Seville, the quixotic Queipo de Llano, although not in the conspiracy and to everyone's surprise, rose in revolt. This unexpected help notwithstanding, the initial stage of the revolution went so badly that General Mola was prepared to surrender when the *Requetés*, the military formations of the Carlists, organized, literally over-night, and virtually forced Mola to continue to fight. The fathers and grandfathers of these men had been defeated in the war against the liberal monarchy in 1872.[758] Now, miraculously, they were once again making history, for to them belonged the lion's share of the eventual victory.[759]

General Cabanellas, another well-known Republican, was the chairman of the junta that took over, but on October 31, 1936, Franco, one of the generals in the junta, emerged as the undisputed leader.[760] Thus, Carlists aside, the "national" revolution that established a military regime was carried out, not by conservatives, but by disillusioned officers who consid-ered the republic a total failure and, as good patriots, felt they had to act honorably and vigorously.

The majority of the army and a minority of the navy joined the military rising, but the air force was almost totally Loyalist. The richest parts of Spain, almost all the industrial areas, were also Loyalist, while the poorest and most backward sections, including the historic provinces—Old Cas-tille, León, Galicia, Navarre, and part of Aragón—were pro-Franco Na-tionalists. The term "Nationalist" is not entirely spurious, for the Franco side stressed national values: "Viva España!" was a Nationalist cry, a cry totally eschewed by the Loyalists.

Indisputably, all the great lights, the great thinkers—the genius of Spain—were traditionally rightist: Spain's leftist contribution, intellec-tually and artistically, was totally insignificant. True, there was Picasso, an artist of real genius and a Communist, but he led an exceedingly bourgeois life (and, incidentally, was repudiated by the Communists *as an artist*).[761] Men such as Unamuno, José Ortega y Gasset, Federico García Lorca, Antonio Machado, Americo Castro, Salvador de Madariaga, Gregorio Marañon, and Menéndez Pidal were individualistic old liberals, but not leftists.[762] None of the great Spanish traditions was represented on the Loyalist side, except for the anarchist bent in the FAI. But in 1937 open warfare broke out between the Anarchists and the Communists; the former, defeated in street battles, were jailed and massacred en masse or murdered individually.[763] The GPU played its own brutal part by viciously persecut-ing the Trotskyite group POUM (*Partido Obrero de Unificación Marxista*).[764] Their leader, Andrés Nin, perished in one of the purges.[765]

As for population during the Civil War, the Loyalist area had about three times as many inhabitants as the Nationalist side, and, as mentioned, its wealth was far more substantial. Republican Spain had almost all the industries, by far the best agricultural lands, and to top it all, the treasury, a big gold hoard destined to go in large part to the Soviet Union with a smaller amount to Mexico. The outlook seemed dim for the Nationalists, but they had the greater faith and by far the better leaders. Besides the Carlists, the toughest of the tough, they had the *señorito* on their side and most of the officers' corps, which, among other things, prevented the fiendish massacres so prevalent in the Loyalist camp. In the confusion of the first weeks many people admittedly were shot, many innocents died. Georges Bernanos in *Les grandes cimetières sous la lune*[766] has given a terrible account of the frivolous executions in Majorca, but I know of no case of slow torture preceding death and of the sheer bestiality that abounded in the leftist sector. Here the balance is entirely in favor of the Nationalists.[767] The Loyalists, on the other hand, showed themselves faithful disciples of de Sade and the Bluecoats in the Vendée. The horrors that took place in the Congo were anticipated in this war, and the great leftist delight—the defiling of cemeteries—was practiced with exquisite artistry.

While in Spain during the war, I chanced to see the cemetery of Huesca, a city under siege between September 1936 and April 1938. Only one road connected the city to Nationalist Spain; trucks could enter only early in the morning or late at night, traveling at great speed with their lights off. Life within the city proceeded normally, but the cemetery, to the east, was in red hands. And since the forces of progress, democracy, and enlightenment could not take Huesca, they vented their spleen on the dead.[768] The vulgarities, the obscenities—the corpses torn out of their graves and assembled in obscene postures—left an unforgettable impression; they were appalling witness to the noble spirit so enthusiastically supported by the American and British Left. I saw these horrors just a few days after the liberation of the cemetery; on the way back to Huesca, riding in an army jeep, we passed a stalled ambulance that bore the insciption, "Gift of the Friends of Spanish Democracy, Tampa Florida Chapter." My Spanish companion could not forego remarking that we had just seen a splendid example of Western democracy. I tried to protest, inadequately. For in truth the "Revolution of the Eighteenth of July," as the red counterinsurgency was officially called,[769] had been an orgy of rape, sadism, and unspeakable obscenities, all perpetrated by our friend the Common Man; there are similar displays wherever leftism lifts its ugly head. A detailed account of some of the horrors would hardly befit the printed page. That they also showed the need for a spiritual reeducation of vast sectors of the Spanish people cannot be denied.[770]

As in similar ideological conflicts, the Spanish Civil War was beset by foreign intervention. The warring parties accepted help from whatever the source. In the American War of Independence, it is virtually certain that without the aid of France (also Spain, and the Netherlands) the Americans fighting against British rule would not have achieved independence, or only after a protracted struggle and at a terrible price. (There were more French than American soldiers at the siege of Yorktown.) Yet that the Founding Fathers were allies of Louis XVI and Charles III should not suggest that they were steeped in Bourbon traditions or that the United States should have felt constrained thereafter constantly to befriend the Bourbons of France and Spain.[771] One radical difference, nevertheless, does stand out between the American and the Spanish struggles. A Communist party, working hand in glove with the Soviet interventionists, *did* exist in Spain, whereas there was no big Bourbon organization in the nascent United States.[772]

With this in mind, to call the Falangists "Fascists" is far more erroneous than to call the National Socialists "Fascists" (as the Soviet do, for obvious reasons). The old Falangist doctrine, admittedly more left than right, had certain totalitarian aspects, as did the JONS (*Juntas Ofensivas Nacional-Sindicalistas*), but the political theories of José Antonio Primo de Rivera and Alfonso García Valdecasas, cofounders of the Falange, put the person first, not the state or society, a theory absolutely in keeping with the Spanish tradition.[773]

Franco used the Falange as a lure to gain German and Italian assistance. The rise of the army in July 1936 was effected by high-ranking *republican* officers who found they had been badly mistaken in their choice of government. They were neither totalitarians nor monarchists. It was a long time before Franco was persuaded that the return of the monarchy was the only solution for Spain.

Whereas the Spanish Communists, the heroes of the "Revolution of July 18th," collaborated with Moscow from the very start,[774] the military men worked independently of the Nazis and the Germans. German and Italian help, moreover, arrived only after the red air force had launched heavy aerial attacks,[775] which claimed a comparatively large number of civilian victims. Without German and Italian aid, the Nationalists would not have been assured of superiority in the air, which in any case took until the summer of 1937 to achieve. Despite outside help, red air attacks continued as late as the spring of 1938, as I can attest.

The Nationalists did not exhibit a great deal of internal unity except in their determination to assure that Spaniards settle Spain's fate and that Spanish traditions and the Spanish way of life be maintained. Unlike the Republicans, they insisted that a man be allowed to enter a church without being clubbed to death and a woman join a religious order without being publicly undressed, raped, slaughtered, and exhibited on a butcher's hook.[776] But despite these common ends, Franco had the greatest difficulty in uniting the various factions. He forced the Falange, the JONS, and the Carlists to join in a common organization (which, translated to the United States, would be like merging the Birchers with the ADA), and this led to many a local explosion.[777] The falangist leader Hedilla was *en capilla* ("in chapel," or readied for execution) three times, with intermittent pardons, prior to being executed for insubordination and revolt.[778] On the Aragón front I met with a Carlist captain who regretted in loud tones that they were fighting only the Communists, Socialists, and Anarchists, but not the Nazis, *enemigos de Nuestro Señor Jesú Cristo*. Liberal monarchists (*Alfonsinos*) and various moderate Republicans (Lerroux, etc.) also sided with Franco. In fact, the vast majority of moderate Republicans and Liberals who fled Spain because they opposed *both* warring sides either returned during the Civil War or soon thereafter.[779] The Catholics, of course, had no choice. Loyalist Spain persecuted the Church with far greater savagery than even the Russian Communists; they had to side with Franco.[780] (The situation differed only in the Basque provinces.)[781]

The Loyalist or Republic side, on the other hand, could without hesitation be called "Red" because it was dominated by the Communists and, to a lesser extent, the Socialists, the only well-coordinated international bodies within Spain. The forces of "liberal democracy" could not compete with the Second (Socialist) and Third International in respect to worldwide connections, precision of ideology, fanaticism and energy. At that time, the Communists cooperated fully with the Socialists—the Popular Front flirtation was in full swing; Largo Caballero, the socialist leader, had been called the "Spanish Lenin" by Stalin himself. The Communists gunned instead for the FAI and the Fourth International, the Trotskyites. Even Freemasonry, although officialy persecuted in Nationalist Spain, was divided in loyalty because, as a "bourgeois" movement, it knew it would face an even worse fate in a Spain gone red, as witness what had occurred in the USSR.[782]

The nonsocialist democratic element in Spain, in effect then, was impotent; it merely served as a cover for strong leftist forces. A man such as President Azaña probably disliked the savagery and executions,[783] but he was powerless to stave them off. Over six thousand priests, friars, and nuns were masssacred under his very eyes, but what could he do? He was not master in his own house. In this connection it is interesting to note that the Communist party (as also the Falange) had not shown much strength in the last elections. This is usually adduced by naive minds to demonstrate that no communist danger existed in Spain, that the threatened communist takeover was but a phantom evoked by the Right.[784] Yet, as the Russian Revolution demonstrated, a small determined minority can conquer a disorganized state and a deeply divided society. The conquest by the Spanish Communist party of the Loyalist section of the country proved it once again.

Abroad, the pro-Loyalist hysteria was loudest in Britain and the United States. Most Americans sympathized with the Loyalists; only Catholics supported the Nationalists, although even here a small segment, under the influence of Jacques Maritain,[785] either joined the majority or assumed a "neutralist" position. Only ignorance of the events, stemming from a lack of coherent reporting and the endemic failure to understand the Spanish character, could account for the faulty judgment.

If American Catholics did not know the facts, neither of course did non-Catholics. There is, in general, a dearth of reliable information in the United States. To sift the correct information from deceit, falsehood, and fabrication requires a special gift—the *ability to weigh evidence*. In Central Europe, the printed word is looked upon with the greatest suspicion in the knowledge that media editing [786] slants and distorts the news. While in Spain I met the correspondent of the *New York Times* on the Nationalist side. He regretted that only a small fraction of his reports ever got printed, whereas the cables of Herbert L. Matthews, stationed on the Loyalist side, gained wide publication. Later, the *New York Times* sent yet another correspondent, Lawrence Fernsworth, to the red side. Featured as a "liberal Catholic," he later wrote for the procommunist publication *The Protestant*.[787] From him came the glad tidings that religious tolerance was on the increase in Republican Spain. Why, only a few days previously, he personally had been permitted to attend Mass in a private home![788]

Neither the Nazis nor the Italians profited from their investments in Spain. Franco met with Hitler only once and, as an old specialist on criminals from his days in the *Tercio*, he immediately sized up the man. There never was a Madrid-Berlin Axis.

There was, on the other hand, a Rome-Berlin Axis, and it was largely the handiwork of the ineptitude of Western leftists. But Fascism and National Socialism never came close to agreeing on a common foreign policy, and Austria became the bone of contention. Austria was crucial to Hitler's expansionist plans—not because it was his (despised) land of birth, but because the geopolitical edifice of Central Europe as constructed by the Paris Treaties was such that the elimination of one brick was enough to bring it down in its entirety. With the *Anschluss*, the most important part of Czechoslovakia (Bohemia, Moravia, Silesia) was encircled and could be strangled simply by closing a few borders. With Czechoslovakia incorporated into the *Reich*, Poland would be similarly encircled, and so forth. There the domino theory worked beautifully.

But it was in Italy's interest to preserve Austrian independence, and in the crisis of the summer of 1934—after the murder of Dollfuss and the pitched battles in Central and Southern Austria between the *Heimwehr* and the illegal brown formations—Mussolini mobilized against Germany. Several divisions stood at the border of the North Tyrol and Carinthia. The Italian army, for better or for worse, had become the guarantor of Austria's survival.

In the eyes of the Left, Austria, being a "Fascist" state, was hardly worth saving. It had begun as a democratic republic in 1918, but ideological differences had soon torn the country asunder. As early as 1927 a demonstration in Vienna had degenerated into a revolt—the Palace of Justice had been burned to the ground by a mixed socialist-communist mob resulting in over a hundred casualties. The nonsocialist elements decided to form the *Heimwehr*, the "Home Defense League," to counteract the already existing Socialist private army, the *Republikanischer Schutzbund*, the "Republican Defense League," and although the forces hardly ever appeared armed in public, they were known to possess illegal weapons. The Socialist forces were strongest in the city of Vienna which, for years, had engaged in big housing programs. Enormous fortress-like buildings had been erected in a belt around the city creating the impression that, should a civil war erupt, the red-tinged city could, and would, readily defend itself against the rest of the country, which was firmly antisocialist.

In the meantime, the brown peril was flowering. The National Socialists also organized along military lines, also established paramilitary formations as they prepared for "Day X." All through 1933 and early 1934 the Nazis engaged in a terror campaign; they threw bombs, committed arson, destroyed bridges, and otherwise spread dread and fear.

The Austrian government at the time consisted only of members of the Christian Social Party and the *Heimwehr*. The parliament had ceased to function due to a technicality, i.e., the absolute equality of government and opposition mandates. The constitution stated that the largest party was to provide the Speaker, but since the government had eighty-one representatives, the opposition (Socialists, Communists, and pro-Nazi Pan-Germans) eighty, and since the Speaker was not permitted to participate in the voting, a stalemate ensued. With the aid of a war-time emergency law the Cabinet continued in power without consultation with the Parliament. But no elections were called lest a number of National Socialists win seats in Parliament and thus create a situation similar, if not quite so bad, as that of Germany in 1932. A democratic government was impossible—and the government, so far unmolested by the Socialists, desperately fought the rampaging Nazis.

The situation came to a head unexpectedly when the police received information of a large deposit of arms in Linz, in all probability belonging to the Republican Defense League. The police sent to search the premises were fired upon and counterattacked. The trade unions replied with a general strike, which was tantamount to stabbing the government in the back, a government engaged in a life-and-death struggle with the Nazis. In short, the trade unions and the Socialist (Social Democratic)[789] party had virtually become allies of the Nazis.

As foreseen, the communal apartment houses in Vienna were converted into fortresses, but the army, aided by the police and the *Heimwehr*, successfully attacked the fortified belt of buildings. And though the Socialist rebellion spread to other parts of Austria, it was suppressed in a matter of days. Significantly, the railroad and postal employees, better informed in foreign matters and domestic intrigues, helped the government by refusing to sabotage the means of communication.

At times the fighting was bitter—many Marxist leaders fled to Czechoslovakia (among them Otto Bauer), some to Russia. One local Socialist leader (Koloman Wallisch) and eight organizers were unfortunately executed; jail sentences were imposed upon others. While the moderate Socialists had opposed rising against the government, some members of the Christian Social party were dismayed by the harsh government measures; they preferred negotiation to the actions deemed necessary to quell the rebellion.[790] The result was the increased isolation of the government, which now faced a two-pronged fight—against national and international socialism. The bonds uniting the two ideologies (again, they were competitors, not enemies) was demonstrated once more when Richard Bernaschek, the red leader in Linz who started it all, was liberated from jail by the brown SA and smuggled into Germany where he gave radio speeches in Munich against Austria's clerical dictatorship. The ties between the camps were obvious: they were both anti-Austria, anti-Habsburg, anti-capitalist, anticlerical, and for the common man and the Provider State. (They were only divided by the anti-Semitism of the browns.) When the *Anschluss* was effected, red Vienna flocked to the red flags that adorned Vienna's "Heldenplatz" to acclaim Adolf Hitler.

Within leftist circles, from San Francisco to Moscow, the indignation against "Austro-Fascism" and "Clerico-Fascism" was boundless. The crackdown on the Social Democrats (often depicted as mellow democrats with social leanings) was erroneously construed as an action taken by the Dollfuss regime in obedience to Mussolini's orders. An *entente* did exist between Dollfuss and Mussolini—the only effective protector of Austrian independence—but Mussolini's sole interest was to maintain a buffer between Italy and Germany. A right-of-center government suited him well enough. Yet, in this outbreak, the Socialists, who were ideologically closer to the Nazis than to the *Heimwehr*, the Monarchists, the Catholic Church, or any genuine right-wing organization, had in fact collaborated with the Nazis; and the Nazis had orders from Berlin to stay put.[791] What the National Socialists loathed, as only they could, was the cooperation between Austria and the Latin-Catholic world; they planned to murder Dollfuss before his forthcoming meeting with Mussolini, scheduled for the last days of July 1934.

The uprising in Vienna had ominous foreign repercussions. The British and American press was in large part anti-Nazi, but it was also anti-Dollfuss. Stephen Spender wrote ringing poetry about the troubles in Vienna, and W. H. Auden, then firmly in the leftist camp, put his pen at the service of "the cause." The United Press heralded the news that some ten thousand dead littered the streets of Austria's capital, whereas fewer than three hundred had expired all told in Austria, more than one hundred of them government casualties. This piece of misinformation came from UP correspondent Robert Best, a psychologically interesting case.

Mr. Best hailed from Georgia and suffered from the scanty education prevalent among American foreign correspondents. From an early career reporting on fires and suicides in love-nests, these newsmen are suddenly jerked from their cosy surroundings to land in faraway countries, such as Austria, whose tongue is as a rule unfamiliar to them. They tend to be middle-of-the-road in their politics and to associate with the Left. Although they do not come from radical families, they are mired in the myths of their local folklore and thus inimical to the Catholic hierarchy and titled aristocrats. Nor have they sufficient ability to talk with peasant leaders— whose minds they would in any case fail to understand. The only ideological language they can *possibly* understand is that of the Left, Marxist and non-Marxist, which combines the vocabulary of the French Revolution with expressions gleaned from college courses in economics.[792]

Mr. Best could thus hardly understand talk about the *Reichsidee*, the *Ständestaat*, *organischer Staat*, *Ganzheitsphilosophie*, *Volkstumswerdung*, *Heimatverbundenheit*, or *Ordnungsbild*—concepts that cannot be translated with precision into English. But he could understand the Socialists. So he sided with the International Socialists, and when they disappeared from the political surface and went underground, he easily enough transferred his enthusiasm to the National Socialists; racial prejudices were not unfamiliar to him—he had them himself. He stayed on in Vienna after the *Anschluss*, made no move to leave after Germany declared war, became a radio announcer for the Nazis, and agitated against his land of birth. Surprising? The Nazis were progressive, built superhighways, provided the people with cheap cars and cheaper radios, and rode the wave of the future. To Best's mind they fulfilled the American dream. His kind of evolution has frequently occurred, has numerous analogies, and is perfectly natural.[793]

The murder of Dollfuss was organized in Germany, and "Millimetternich's" successor, Kurt von Schuschnigg, could not possibly stave off the final disaster. The amity between Vienna and Rome was heavily mortgaged by the South Tyrol, which the Fascists brutally tried to Italianize by all conceivable means. Nazi propaganda in Austria (which in sentiment was strongly anti-Italian) harped on the treachery of the Austrian government for inadequately countering Mussolini's policies in the South Tryol. (Not even the Austrian Nazis foresaw that in 1939 Hitler would agree with Mussolini to resettle the South Tyroleans in "Greater Germany.") Yet Italy remained the only power ready to protect Austrian independence.[794]

This anomaly was fully understood in London and Paris. It led to the Stresa Conference out of which grew the London-Paris-Rome Axis for the preservation of Austrian freedom and a public declaration of guarantee thereof. Schuschnigg, for his part, tried to counter brown propaganda in Austria and to achieve a greater understanding between the Successor States of the Old Monarchy. He knew that the *Ständestaat* ("Corporate State"), designed to overcome class antagonisms and party strife, was not enough—man does not live by bread alone. He therefore dreamed of restoring the monarchy in Austria at some future date, and in this he had many supporters—practically all the Christian Socialist Party and *Heimwehr* members, and even a few moderate Socialists. Only the National Socialists, radical Socialists, and Communists opposed the solution, and they did so with fury and violence.

But the greatest obstacles were Prague and Belgrade. These two governments collaborated closely with Hitler in the "Austrian Question." Beneš admitted in conversation that he would rather see the Nazis in Prague than the Habsburgs in Vienna.[795] Czechoslovakia and Yugoslavia seemed equally fearful that their countries would melt away the moment the Habsburgs appeared on the horizon. They melted away anyway a few years later. (In exile, Beneš acknowledged that the Central European countries had not been able to solidify, to acquire internal cohesion.)[796] Thus, as faithful minions of Hitler, these countries declared restoration a *casus belli*, which well demonstrates the brittleness of the house of cards built by the leftists at the Paris Peace Conference.[797] The hatred of the "United Left" for the Habsburgs continues to this very day;[798] it is personified in the Austrian Socialists who in many ways continue in the Nazi tradition, especially in the field of legislation.

But it was the West which, for ideological reasons, was ultimately responsible for Mussolini's withdrawal of support of Austrian independence, and the ensuing inevitable fall of Austria.[799] With the *Anschluss*, the stage was set for World War II, the Third War of Austrian Succession. At World War II's end, further opportunities arose for perpetrating even more terrible calamities. And these ideological reasons—the cause of the entire development from 1917 to our own times—bear the distinct marks of leftist beliefs.

At the Stresa Conference Mussolini informed Sir Samuel Hoare, the British foreign minister, and Monsieur Pierre Laval that he intended to attack Ethiopia, a country with whom the Italians were encountering border difficulties. He made it clear that he planned simultaneously to take revenge for the defeat of Adowa in 1896 by conquering all of Ethiopia. At first, this revelation made little impression, and since no protest was forthcoming, he proceeded to prepare for war—a war of aggression against the spirit and the letter of the League of Nations Charter. Ironically, Ethiopia had been introduced into the League by Italy, a move opposed by Britain as Ethiopia was suspected of tolerating slavery and practicing barbaric punishments (mutilations and the like).

At the buildup of Mussolini's overseas forces, the British public became restive, and leftists, who had a hold on a sector of the Conservative party, demanded that Britain adhere strictly to the League of Nations Charter and impose military-economic sanctions against Italy for breaking the agreement. Of the great powers only the Soviet Union, Germany, the United States, and Japan did not belong to the League.

From a higher moral point of view the situation was singularly complex. Italy undoubtedly infringed upon the Charter's stipulations. Equally clearly, Italy would introduce to the colonized country a life more humane and civilized;[800] the common good of Ethiopians was better served under Italian rule than under the local autocracy. People with such divergent political views as Evelyn Waugh and Herbert L. Matthews were with the Italian army in the struggle and witnessed the subsequent Italian administration.[801] They both (for different and yet similar reasons) favored the Italian side. There was, moreover, the matter of the tribes and "nationalities" that had been subjugated by the real Ethiopians, the Amharas, after their victory in 1896. The arms they had collected from the defeated Italians enabled them to confiscate vast tracts of land, especially to the east, southeast, and south of the provinces of Amhara, Tigre, and Shoa—the regions inhabited by the Dankalis, Gallas, and Somalis. Subsequently conquered by the Italians, these disparate tribes passed from one alien rule to another—but also from a harsher to a more lenient rule.

While the British public grew increasingly incensed, Sir Samuel Hoare and Pierre Laval racked their brains to discover how to maintain the "Stresa Front" (Austria!), save the League of Nations' face, and reach a compromise that would preserve order in Europe. The war was well underway with Italian troops advancing in the north when Hoare and Laval secretly drew up their famous plan to avert the worst. Their device called for the embattled Ethiopians to cede their former conquests to Italy, thus effectively consolidating the Italian colonial empire in Africa by connecting Eritrea to Somalia. Mussolini was amenable to the idea,[802] but the Hoare-Laval Plan was torpedoed, principally by the well-organized "Peace Ballot" (who, incidentally, is against peace?) and tangentially by the indiscretion of leftist journalists. The ensuing wave of moral indignation propelled Britain into adopting a rigid policy in the best League of Nations tradition; Sir Samuel Hoare was forced to resign in favor of Mr. Anthony Eden, until then minister without portfolio for League of Nations affairs.[803]

The sanctions were ineffective, Soviet oil reached Italy, and Ethiopia was defeated in 1936. Haile Selassie, the hapless Emperor, took up residence in

London, but the "Committee for the Defense of Abyssinian Democracy" refused to close shop. Whether Ethiopia (Abyssinia) was then (or has the capacity ever to be) a "democracy" is quite another question. Certainly Haile Selassie's rule was gentle compared to that of his present bolshevik successor. Mengistu Haile Mariam is a genuine Marxist monster; one of his more endearing traits was to demand thirty dollars "bullet money" from the parents of murdered high school students.

England could not possibly have assumed moral leadership in a general action to prevent Italy from acquiring colonies; being the arch-colonialist itself, it could hardly confront Italy and say something on the order of: "Colonial conquests were possible until 1919, but now that we have the League, now that we all believe in peace, democracy, equality, progress, universal brotherhood and other such niceties, you have to renounce all colonial pretensions." In Italian (and not only in Fascist) eyes England had behaved hypocritically. (Italy, of course, would not have greatly benefited from Ethiopia, but that was hardly the point. Colonies meant prestige, and only in exceptional cases eventual riches.)

The tragic results of the sanctions were soon apparent. The Nazis in Austria greeted one other with a knowing smile, substituting "Haile Selassieh!" for "Heil Hitler!" They realized that the West's recent defeat vis-à-vis Ethiopia heralded the beginning of the end of Austria's independence. And so it was.

Mr. Anthony Eden (later the Earl of Avon) thus created the Axis. He embodied the policy that drove Italy right into Germany's arms. Mussolini, a common man lacking the ways of a gentleman, who felt personally insulted by criticism of any sort, burst into obscene rantings against England. But the American public, swayed by its leftist leadership, sided with Britain and the League. Germany, of course, derived great profit—material and political—from the fracas. Isolated Italy was its fair prey.

Without effective Italian protection Austria's enslavement was only a question of time. Mussolini having displaced Hitler as chief villain in British eyes, Britain lost all interest in Austria. Above all, London wanted to avert Hitler's attention from the West and therefore gladly gave him a virtually free hand in the East. In 1940 in La Charité, the advancing Germans found a deposit of documents from the Quai d'Orsay, among them a note from Lord Halifax exhorting the French Foreign Office not to make the slightest gesture which Kurt von Schuschnigg, the Austrian Chancellor, might interpret as an encouragement to resistance.[804]

An enormous amount has been written about Schuschnigg's tactics and his "missed opportunities," but in truth the moment Italy became Germany's partner, no one, not the greatest political genius, could have saved Austria. It had been written off by the West, by the pro- as well as by the anti-Nazis, if for very different reasons. And, indeed, not too much could have been expected of the Austrian people themselves; they had lost the center around which their loyalty might have rallied—the Habsburgs. Besides, the Austrians in the majority *felt* German[805]—though not necessarily Nazi. In fact, a great deal of Austrian resistance against the *Anschluss* had the character of a struggle between the "other Germany," or "Christian Germany," as against the "Brown Greater Prussia."[806] It is too easily (and often too conveniently) forgotten that the first Austrian Constitution, promulgated under Social Democratic leadership in 1918, declared that *Deutschösterreich*, "German Austria," was part of the *Reich*.[807] The driving force against the *Anschluss* were the Monarchists, and after the calamity they paid fiercely for it. (The Austrian nobility as a whole was stigmatized as traitorous to Germandom, its members forbidden by Hitler to use their titles.)[808]

Americans and Britishers knew little about these subtleties in the overall tragic struggle. In the English-speaking world the only uneasiness was felt within Jewish circles. Ambassador Dieckhoff, who spoke to Secretary of State Cordell Hull[809] on March 12, 1938, the day after the *Anschluss*, informed the Reich's Foreign Office that Mr. Hull had evinced no disapproval of Austria's annexation, nor did he appear any the less courteous two days after the event, not too surprising given Mr. Hull's mental horizons. (Only Mr. Sumner Welles seemed bitter.)[810]

The disturbing lack of quality in the Foreign Service under Roosevelt's administration kept the American government as uninformed as the American public, whose own ignorance was nursed by leftist reporters and news commentators. The American ambassador to Germany prior to the *Anschluss* was Profesor William E. Dodd[811] whose *Diary* was published by his son William E., Jr., and daughter Martha.[812]

Reading *Ambassador Dodd's Diary* is almost as rewarding as poring over the far more voluminous *Herron Papers*; the two men vie in the sheer benightedness of their parochial leftism. There are, of course, passages of historic value, such as Ambassador Dieckhoff's admission that he would like to have seen Hitler overthrown,[813] or the Polish ambassador's belief, as early as 1934, that Hitler was secretly negotiating with Russia. William Bullitt's avowal that Lord Lothian and Lloyd George wished to give the Germans a free hand is as interesting as the Czech minister's claim that neither Czechoslovakia nor Yugoslavia would permit the Habsburgs to return to Vienna[814]—the old collaboration of Prague and Belgrade with the Nazis. More amusing aspects of the *Diary* concern Ambassador Dodd's aristophobia, his democratism. He is scandalized when his German butler packs his suitcase, shocked by Sumner Welles' fifteen servants, critical of the Harvard accents of American diplomats. And his description of a requiem for Pilsudski (which poor Dodd had to attend) is priceless. ("Candles were burning and priests were chanting in Latin which no one understood, and occasionally falling upon their knees and scattering incense, which I think Jesus never used. It was the medieval ceremony from the beginning to end. . . to me it was all half-absurd.") A hillbilly from the Shenandoah Valley lost in the neon jungle of Broadway could not have felt more bewildered. But the diary also had its terrifying aspect—the revelation of Dodd's total ignorance of history. It is one more instance of the tragic effects of specialization in learning in America. Dodd had published works on Thomas Jefferson and Woodrow Wilson—also in German—but, to him, the not inconsiderable rest of history remained a book with seven seals.

Herein but a few specimens of the ambassador's reactions to impressions and events. Interestingly, everything he considered odd or obsolete was immediately styled "medieval," a habit he shared with Franklin Delano Roosevelt. It might partially have stemmed from reading Mark Twain's *A Connecticut Yankee at King Arthur's Court*. Whatever the cause, Dodd felt that Göring, naturally, had a "medieval hunter's uniform." Savagery and barbarism, Dodd believed, were a "curious quality of the Nazi mass mind which passed away in England with the Stuart kings in 1688."[815] Himmler, in Professor Dodd's eyes, was probably another James II. And university professors who confessed to him their despair drew the comment: "They do not know the real cause of Germany's reign of terror: the failure of the 1848 movement to resolve itself into a democratic parliamentary system." As if a democratic parliamentary system had not been installed by the victorious Allies in 1918—and with what results! And again: "The Pope is in a tight place. He must help Lutherans and Lutheran universities to save Catholicism in Germany. At the same time he must support Nazi philosophy in the hope of defeating communism in Russia and checking the advance of socialism in France and Spain." Where, one wonders, were those "Lutheran universities," and how might Nazi philosophy have affected the *Front Populaire* in France or the CGT in Spain?

Professor Dodd also found time to inform Franz von Papen that "Father

Coughlin is always breaking loose," only subsequently to discover that "Von Papen is a Catholic, but he showed no sympathy with Coughlin." Should not every Catholic be enchanted by every priest? Totally perplexing sentences abound: "It is an unprecedented move to abolish such historic states as Bavaria or Saxony dating back to the time of the Caesars. Hitler, as much as he hates France, is imitating Napoleon I who abolished all French States."[816] Was Dodd raving mad? Such a man not only represented the United States in the worst trouble spot in the world, but taught history—history!—at the University of Chicago.[817] After such pronouncements it hardly surprises to read that it was Germany's "thousand-year aim to annex or at least subordinate all the Balkan countries."[818]

It is difficult to discern whether such ignorance stems from historic or geographic vacuity. Dodd of course is not alone; examples abound. Sir Robert Vansittart, GCB, GCMG, MVO, chief diplomatic advisor of the Foreign Office, published a book in 1940 replete with historic disorder,[819] but he played a significant role before and during World War II. The *New York Times*, proud of its high standards, placed not only Hungary but Czechoslovakia on the Balkan Peninsula.[820] And Raymond Moley, professor and former "braintruster" to President Roosevelt, wrote in a 1943 column in *Newsweek* a piece of pro-Soviet propaganda about the Baltic States containing a record number of historic, geographic, and political errors. After a storm of protest, Dr. Moley sent a stenciled reply to his critics that ended with the statement, "My critics are entitled to their opinions and I to mine," and so much for the sacredness of facts. If there are no absolutes, there are no facts—there are only opinions. All this is partly the practical and psychological result of our age which demands that everybody have an opinion on almost anything and be allowed to express it with limitless abandon.

The end of Austria caused little stir in the West.[821] Kurt von Schuschnigg was the *only* head of government not to flee abroad; he stayed on to make the rounds of jails and concentration camps. This failed to impress the American Left, which considered him a Fascist; and when he came to the United States in 1947 demonstrations were organized against him by native leftists and by what the French called *la résistance de la Cinquième Avenue*.

In Europe, with Austria crushed, Hitler turned on his willing collaborators—the same men and governments in Prague and Belgrade that had been "kept" by the French but, as foreseen by Jacques Bainville,[822] had failed to stand strong. Too late, Paris began to recognize the folly of having destroyed Austria-Hungary (as, in the eighteenth century, it had belatedly realized the folly of having forged Prussia).[823]

Beneš, to prevent a restoration of the Habsburgs in Vienna, secretly negotiated with the Nazis[824] and encouraged Mussolini in his anti-Habsburg stand. He opposed any type or form of Danubian Federation to stem the Nazi tide, readily admitting that his antagonism rested on reasons sentimental and psychological rather than political and economic. He went so far as to declare that the Little Entente would "always be opposed with intransigence and under all circumstances" to a union between Austria and Hungary—two sovereign states.[825] Beneš proceeded to serve notice on France that all these and similar solutions to the Central European problem were "unacceptable to Paris because, above all, they were condemned by the Little Entente." It was difficult for this little man of narrow political horizons to shed the ideological tendrils of his National Socialist Party. Nor could he appreciate the true meaning of his earlier wartime determination to prevent an early peace and thus end the senseless slaughter. "Any compromise with Vienna in the summer of 1917 would have been unmitigated disaster for us," he later shamelessly confessed.[826]

Why did this spiteful and puritanical man—a man who having helped build a synthetic country then waged a suicidal policy that led to its sovietization—gain such prestige in the West? For a variety of reasons, among them his anti-Catholicism, which, as Peter Viereck has pointed out, is the anti-Semitism of the moderate Left. Another reason was his posing as the liberator of Czechoslovakia from myriad evils—the Habsburgs, the Viennese bureaucracy, the "alien aristocracy,"[827] big landowners, Pan-Germanism—all of which were excoriated by those prejudiced in ignorance. Yet Beneš did not hesitate, in discussing the possibility that the Western Allies might not energetically support Czechoslovakia against German pressure, to tell Count Sforza, "If we should be left without support against the German menace, we will surprise the world with a limitless subservience to Berlin."[828] In the depth of his heart this petty man despised the West, longed instead for Russian cooperation. He condemned Britain more than France, for he regarded England as but a future colony of the United States, and "there is no greater impertinence than the American one."[829] A perusal of the articles he wrote for the antireligious periodical *Volná myšlenka* ("Free Thought") and *Beseda* before World War I is revealing in this respect.

But the most fatal aspect of his activity lay in his absolute determination to prevent a Habsburg restoration, even if the alternative were the

Anschluss—and with it the encirclement and the end of Czechoslovakia.[830] Better the Nazi flag over the Hradčany in the Prague than Otto in the Hofburg in Vienna! Yet, even given his limitations, how conceivably could this man have believed that Hitler would reward him for his anti-Habsburg stand?[831] A renowned American journalist who saw Beneš immediately after the *Anschluss* reported that he "pooh-poohs the idea that Hitler might succeed in any way in interfering with the affairs of the Czechoslovakian Republic."[832]

Beneš, in fact, never regretted the course he took[833]—until 1948, perhaps. He had always harbored a sneaking, at times open, admiration not only for the perennial Russia, but for the Soviet Union as well. In 1938 he must have awaited aid from Moscow, all the more so as the Third Soviet Army Air Corps was unofficially stationed in Czechoslovakia. He was convinced that "communism in its philosophy and morality has certain similarities with democracy. It is also humanitarian, universalist, intellectualist, and rationalist. It is also pacifist, internationalist, and for the League of Nations policy."[834] It also painted to perfection the picture of communism drawn by moderate leftists in the United States.

When, after his exile in London, Beneš returned to a Czechoslovakia under Russian auspices, this leader of the Czech National Socialist party proved a most docile pupil, of Hitler as well as Stalin. Personal freedom no longer seemed to interest him. While still in exile he had held Hitler up as an example in many ways. In an article in the January 1942 *Foreign Affairs* (New York), Beneš said that Hitler ought to be hailed as a "forerunner of minority settlements."[835] He repeated this thesis in March 1944 when he spoke about the "grim necessity" of transferring populations.[836] In practical terms this meant the total expropriation and deportation of fully one-third the population of the historic countries belonging to the Crown of St. Wenceslas (Bohemia, Moravia, Silesia). Dr. Beneš, being a good democrat, believed in majority rule. But as the entire German population in this area was sure to vote, it would dash all hopes of the solid majority needed for radically left experiments. The logical conclusion was quite simple: the German-speaking population had to be expelled. The Soviets agreed; in past elections the Sudeten Germans had voted Communist in tiny percentages.

Voting aside, Beneš might have been persuaded that these German-speaking Bohemians and Moravians had in some way been "disloyal." But since Messrs. Wilson, Lloyd George, and Clemenceau had handed over these areas against their wishes to the artifical state of Czechoslovakia, why *should* its inhabitants, people of German extraction, be loyal to the nationalist government of the Czech people? The Slovaks, the Hungarians, the Poles, the Ruthenians who had to join this curious state without being asked, had not been loyal.[837] In 1918-19 the Sudeten Germans had proclaimed their loyalty to Austria, but self-determination had been denied them by the Great Western Democracies,[838] and their efforts to unite with Austria had been put down by force of arms.[839] By the fall of 1938 Austria no longer existed and the Germans of the Third Reich were the only conationals of the Sudeten Germans. Had the Germans of Bohemia and Moravia appealed to the principle of self-determination it would have been highly "undemocratic" to have denied them their wish. By the same token, if after 1945 they wanted to remain under the rule of Prague, then why deport them?

But Dr. Eduard Beneš was a democrat, not a liberal. This comes through clearly in his tirade against freedom of the press in July 1945. "Unbridled freedom to publish newspapers must not be reestablished," he declared. "We all say that liberalism has been discarded. This is a fact, and we must realize that one of the factors in public life that is, above all, subject to today's socializing trends, is journalism. How to harmonize this fact with freedom of speech is another matter. But here, too, the principle that the freedom of the individual has to be subordinated to the freedom of the whole holds good."[840] Liberalism goes out, socialism comes in. Dr. Beneš headed a National Socialist, not a National Liberal party. And when Jan Masaryk was thrown out the window it was probably one of the most exquisite acts ever of subordinating the individual to the whole, in this case the Czech Communist party.

So much for Dr. Beneš, yet another grave digger of Europe, a man highly esteemed by the leftist press, a man, however, destined to die in ignominy, isolation, and despair.[841] When Hitler shrewdly whipped up the passions of the Sudeten Germans (who had genuine grievances against the Czechs) to ask more energetically for self-determination, the Western powers were thrust into a most awkward position. To cite only one instance: *Could Great Britain fight in good conscience against the realization of the principle of self-determination?* In Czechoslovakia, those who wanted to break away numbered not only the 3.5 million Sudeten Germans (as many people as the Colonies held in 1776) but also a million Hungarians and Poles—not to mention the Slovaks who, at the very least, demanded autonomy. The whole edifice of contradictions fashioned in 1918-19 was disintegrating, hard and fast. And what could a democrat say if people invoked a democratic principle in order to demand for themselves an undemocratic order?

Czechoslovakia had little to hope for from the British. But the abuse heaped upon the head of Mr. Neville Chamberlain for his surrender in Munich was unjustified. To begin with, Mr. Chamberlain inherited a totally unarmed country from his predecessor, Mr. Stanley Baldwin, one of the most insular political leaders ever produced by England. Baldwin knew little of the outside world other than that he hated it.[842] The pacifist Labour Government preceding Mr. Baldwin's premiership had worked very hard to disarm Britain; and when the Nazi danger began to loom large, the Labourites engaged in the amusing exercise of calling for disarmament while insulting the Tories for not standing up to the Nazi menace. The Liberals were worse: Lloyd George admired Hitler and declared after his visit to the Obersalzberg, "I have never seen a happier people than the Germans. Hitler is one of the greatest of the many great men I have ever met."[843] Democracy means rule by public opinion numerically arrived at. And the British public was as little prepared to fight over Czechoslovakia as over Austria. True, certain leftist cliques were highly enthusiastic over Czechoslovakia, but they were not sufficiently organized to sway the masses. Czechoslovakia was indeed a country about which the British (in the words of Mr. Neville Chamberlain) "knew so little"; neither it nor its people could be found in the 1911 edition of the *Encyclopaedia Britannica*.[844]

For Britain to declare war against Germany in September 1938 would have been suicidal. Even if untrue that at the time there were fewer than a dozen modern antiaircraft guns in Britain, there was little armament and no conscription.[845] In France, the Left was torn between pacifism and interventionism, while the Soviet Union had a military pact with Czechoslovakia dating back to 1935 but no common border. The argument that a war at that moment would have given the edge to the Allies is beyond ridicule. The Czechoslovakian army would not have resisted for forty-eight hours: Czech officers would have been killed by their own soldiers. (After defeat, moreover, the Czech population would have been scythed like the Poles.) As it happened, the Czechs were not even called to military service, full employment continued all through the war, the people received the same rations as the Germans, the birthrate rose, and in spite of isolated cases (Lidice), civilian casualties were very small and the losses through aerial warfare almost zero.

Chamberlain, in other words, although abused and ridiculed, had almost no choice—in fact, none at all other than to accept the word of the conspirators in the German General Staff.

These conspirators, the Beck-Halder group, were of themselves power-less against Hitler, who had the support of the masses.[846] He was, after all, the man who had reduced unemployment, the man who had crushed the iniquitous treaty, the man who had expanded the Reich without a single shot fired. Intellectual liberty, of course, was almost extinguished, but this was of neglible interest to the masses, who prefer bread and games to academic or artistic endeavors. The generals, on the other hand, not only despised Hitler as an upstart (Hindenburg called him the "Bohemian private first class"),[847] they grasped the ignobleness of his character, as revealed in the Fritsch case.[848] Above all, they feared that he would bring ruin on Germany in a two-front war. Generals, on the average, are far less bellicose than journalists or patriotic housewives—they know the horrors of war.

The conspirators were determined to arrest Hitler should war break out; only then would they be able to control the male population, for mobilized and under military orders, these youths could no longer obey party direc-tives.[849] The masses would also be more pliant in their disillusionment that Hitler, who had promised territorial aggrandizement without a drop of blood spilt, had inflicted on them, once again, the agonies of a war—that he had broken his pact with the German nation. The conspirators went so far as to station a division in Thuringia between Munich and Berlin to paralyze Nazi formations—specifically Hitler's bodyguard (*Leibstandarte*) stationed in Munich—in case of an emergency. (Hitler's arrest was to take place in Berlin.)

On September 5, 1938, Theodor Kordt, a German diplomat in London and brother of one of the conspirators, went to 10 Downing Street where he informed the foreign minister, Lord Halifax, of the conspiracy, urging that Britain not deal with Hitler, that the Prime Minister not negotiate but allow war to break out, thus allowing the conspirators their only chance to strike against the idol of the common man. But by then, unknown to the conspirators, Chamberlain had already consented to meet with Hitler. The German officers had put their lives at risk, but they were not considered worthy of confidence.[850]

The Beck-Halder group was desperate when Chamberlain went to Go-desberg,[851] but regained hope when matters approached a new climax. The date for Hitler's arrest was set for September 29. But when Mussolini, prompted by Chamberlain, intervened, the conspirators gave up. Hitler had gained another "moral" victory.

Britain's weakness, its lack of armament, must primarily be laid at the doorstep of democracy, of parliamentary government and elections. In their

1936 campaign the Conservatives did not dare mention the need to arm, which costs money; war talk, moreover, is unpleasant. Stanley Baldwin acknowledged as much in the House of Commons when he said that, had they told the people the truth, the Conservatives could never have won the election. "Supposing that I had gone to the country and said that Germany was rearming and that we must be armed, does anyone think that our pacific democracy would have rallied to that cry?" (*Hansard*, November 1936). And, as Lord (Charlie) Londonderry succinctly put it, Britain had a simple choice—ally with Germany or rearm. Neither was done, and war befell the nation.[852]

Why did Neville Chamberlain not collaborate with the German conspirators? Not for ideological reasons, but quite simply because of the curious inability of Britishers and Americans to project themselves into the minds and temperaments of other nations. After Theodor Kordt's departure, the men at 10 Downing Street must have glanced at each other in embarrassment, suspiciously and disdainfully, the silence perhaps broken by the exclamation, "Damn it, this is a preposterous E. Philips Oppenheim story! Can any of you chaps imagine a bloody general arresting His Majesty's Prime Minister?" Indeed, no one could. Which points to a venerable Anglo-Saxon limitation and an insoluble dilemma. The dilemma arises when the belief of the British and Americans in radical human differences, if not racial superiority, suddenly and mysteriously collapses, giving way to its very opposite—that human beings everywhere are "basically the same," that they are "more alike than unlike." Here lies the source of endless miscalculations, misinterpretations, and catastrophic errors.

Thus Chamberlain's Englishness might well have been a cause of his failure. Certainly the limitation is not a moral but a psychological disorder. No doubt the man was an English gentleman in the best sense of the word—honorable, without guile, perhaps somewhat simple-minded— and future historians will surely judge him infinitely more fairly than the strident newspapers of his day. As for the United States, was it ready to fight for Czechoslovakia or was it merely egging England on? Granted, the United States had no military alliance with the threatened country, but it was its brainchild, the joint creation of Woodrow Wilson, Thomas Masaryk, and American citizens of Czech[853] and, in some cases, of Slovak origin.[854] Yet President Roosevelt admitted that he was "not a bit upset" by the results of the Munich Agreement.[855]

The vilification of Neville Chamberlain is usually accompanied by the statement that Winston Churchill was otherwise disposed—that he had always known Hitler to be a scoundrel, and that Chamberlain's naive exclamation upon his return from Munich, "peace in our time," would never have passed the Old Bulldog's lips. Conservatives fully subscribed to this myth: Churchill, a "typical Conservative of the old school," was, in this respect at least, beyond reproach.

Yet Churchill was never a genuine conservative, but an old-fashioned eighteenth-century liberal and deist. His father, Lord Randolph Churchill, belonged to the "left-most" wing of the Tories, and young Winston, after a short flirtation with the Conservative party, became an ardent British liberal *of the leftist, the Lloyd George, dispensation.* After his switch and while stomping for the Liberal Party, he was shown by a heckler a pamphlet he had written in his conservative past. He took it and, without hesitation, tore it apart. When lured once again by the Conservative party, Sir Charles Dilcke warned: "Winston, the rat cannot leave the sinking ship twice!" But Churchill did, and twice succeeded.[856] He was considered a "radical" and supported Lloyd George after World War I, although the Welsh politician disliked the strong stand Churchill adopted toward bolshevism. Lloyd George's pro-Russian and anti-Polish attitude was due partly to his loathing for Poles (which Churchill inherited) and partly to maintaining the indirect support of the trade unions that wanted to cripple Poland's resistance in its life-and-death struggle against the Red Army.[857]

After the break with Lloyd George, Churchill worked his way back into the Conservative party where the old diehards (who valued character more than brains) never quite forgave him his vacillations.[858] But if years later, upon his return from Yalta, he believed what he told the House of Commons (February 27, 1945)—that he did not know any government that kept its obligations as faithfully as did the Soviet Union, even to its disadvantage—he was a great deal more naive than Chamberlain with his "peace in our time."[859] And his famous perspicacity about Hitler? In November 1935—well over a year after the June 1934 massacre—Churchill called the *Führer* a "highly competent, cool, well-informed functionary with an agreeable manner" and added that "the world lives on hopes that the worst is over and that we may yet live to see Hitler a gentler figure in a happier age."[860] As late as 1937 our great Epimetheus wrote about Hitler, "If our country were defeated I hope we should find a champion as indomitable to restore our courage and lead us back to our place among the nations."[861] It was yet another year before Churchill converted.

CHAPTER 17

Another Leftist War

*Thus we stumbled into what
it became fashionable to call
the "Bore War"—without arms,
without faith and without heart.*[862]

—LORD BOOTHBY

Whereas the fall of Czechoslovakia in March 1939[863] was a bitter blow to the Left, the developments later that year, though disturbing to people of good will, barely ruffled it. Churchill, as ever uninformed about the geography and history of countries at any distance from seashores, berated Hungary and Poland in his memoirs as "beasts of prey" which had devoured parts of Czechoslovakia.[864] The leftist press viewed Poland with even greater hostility: a country administered by heel-clicking army officers and Roman Catholic bishops, a country inhabited by "fascist aristocratic land-owners" and miserable serfs, a country pitted with Jew-filled ghettos.[865] But Polish realities were otherwise, and almost as complex as those of Imperial Russia. At the outbreak of World War II, this was especially true of its social conditions and structures.[866]

In 1938, pacifist feelings ran deep in France (*"Nous ne voulons pas mourir pour Dantzic!"*), and in Britain, feelings for Poland were apathetic or cool. But the British public had been outraged by Hitler's march on Prague, which it regarded quite rightly as a breach of promise, and Chamberlain was determined not to permit Hitler another "peaceful grab." Negotiations were started between the Western Allies and the Soviet Union to erect a solid front against Hitler. *Peace would almost surely have been preserved had Germany been faced with the specter of a two-front war.* Its very prospect, moreover, would have sparked a reorganization of the conspiratorial forces within the German army. But when Ribbentrop and Molotov concluded the German-Russian military pact Hitler was guaranteed a free hand in the West, and the German generals, taken off guard by the political developments, waited until November 1939 before once again closing ranks.

In September 1939 there was not the slightest reason for Hitler's attack on Poland other than his wish ultimately to attack and destroy Russia in order to wrest the great *Lebensraum* (living space) for the German people, a dream he never shed. Contrary to German propaganda, the eastern boundary of Germany, as set down in the Versailles Treaty, was not particularly unjust. In fact, certain areas scooped out of Poland by Prussia in the First and Second Partitions had not been returned. The so-called "Polish Corridor" was not an iniquity; the districts were ancient Polish lands inhabited mainly by Poles. The separation of East Prussia[867] from the rest of Germany involved a few minor hardships, but no greater than the present detachment of Alaska from the continental United States.

But Hitler had his eyes set on another triumph, another bloodless conquest. Quite probably too, he did not expect Britain to live up to its new treaty with Poland. A considerable part of the English and French press had been vituperative of Poland; a British radio commentator, Commander Stephen King-Hall, had gone so far as to announce that he would shout "Sieg-Heil!" should Hitler invade Poland. Hitler told Ciano, the Italian statesman, that he was convinced that Britain and France would never light a general conflagration in support of Poland. Ribbentrop too was confident that Britain would not move. Thus the surprise was almost boundless among the national socialist leadership when Britain declared war on September 3. Britain, of course, had been morally cornered and was literally forced to act.[868] Curiously, Hitler, suffering from the typical Continental Anglomania, continued[869] his pro-British complex even after Britain's entry into war; it accounts for his orders to the army not to destroy the remnants of the British forces cornered at Dunkirk.

All this came as a terrible surprise to the American Left, the most naive of people. A few short days before the outbreak of war, the Committee on Cultural Freedom published (August 23) a full-page advertisement in the most important national newspapers. Among the dense array of signatories ("leading intellectuals") were Jay Allen, Henry Pratt Fairchild, Waldo Frank, Leo Hubermann, George Kaufmann, Paul de Kruif, Max Lerner, Clifford Odets, Frederick L. Schumann, George Seldes, James Thurber, Richard Wright, Dashiell Hammett, Vincent Sheean, Maxwell Stuart. And here a flavor of the ad:

> The fascists. . . are intent on destroying such unity [i.e., of all "progressive forces"] at all costs [but] realizing that here in America they cannot get far with a definitely pro-Fascist appeal, they strive to pervert American anti-Fascist sentiment to their own ends. [Thus] they have encouraged the fantastic falsehood that the USSR and the totalitarian states are basically alike. . . .
>
> The Soviet Union considers political dictatorship a transitional form and has shown a steadily expanding democracy in every sphere. Its epoch-making new constitution guarantees Soviet citizens universal suffrage, civil liberties, the right to employment, to leisure, to free medical care, to material security in sickness and in old age, to equality of the sexes in all fields of activity and to equality of all races and nationalities.

The essence of this huge advertisement was that all rumors of a pact between National Socialists and International Socialists—between Hitler and Stalin—were pure fascist propaganda. Two days later the rumors were established fact. The German-Soviet alliance was in place, prepared to crush Poland, ready to trigger World War II.

As World War II began its bloody course, all those engulfed were beset by an unparalleled sadness. Germany and Austria were countries in tears, no longer capable of the spontaneous demonstrations of 1914.[870] The resistance of many German generals and rightist leaders, never fully abandoned,[871] began its slow growth, reaching its culmination in July 1944. It is untrue that they waited until Hitler's star was sinking before turning against him. A perusal of the diaries of Ulrich von Hassell[872] shows the despair created by the successive victories in the early period of the war. Rare is the country whose most distinguished citizens are driven to think, to pray, and finally to act for the defeat of their fatherland. Their actions belie the myth that Germans obey orders blindly and unconditionally. In Germany's counterintelligence, a magnificent man, Admiral Canaris—the chief, not a treacherous employee—risked his life for the downfall of the Third Reich. And it was General Oster himself who warned the Dutch and the Belgians of the coming onslaught in May 1941.[873] Indeed, a multitude of Germans were eager to put an end to their country's criminal leadership, to halt the destruction of Europe, but they fought alone, and went down in the fight, because among the Allies the forces on the Left schemed to have it happen in just that way—and the Right, feeble and confused, stood helplessly by.

At the start, the Stalin-Hitler Pact, which made the war possible, and the subsequent outbreak of fighting stunned the Left all over the world. It had apparently forgotten that the National Socialists were arch-leftists, although it fully explained the alliance with the Soviet Union, which was far from an act of political perversion. Hitler had always preferred communism to the free life, and Goebbels, especially as a younger man, genuinely admired socialist Russia, which he considered the natural ally of Germany.[874]

Though well versed in acting like sheep, many leftists in the Western World discovered that they were still human beings and decried the pact; others, clinging stubbornly to their red loyalties, decided that the National Socialists weren't so bad after all. The brown press in Germany, needless to say, made a complete *volte face*; anticommunist propaganda ceased overnight.[875] Ribbentrop[876] shocked Ciano, as well as some old National Socialists, when he recounted how well he had fared in Moscow among Stalin's henchmen, "men with strong faces."[877]

In the Soviet Union the papers gave priority to German war news and the economy worked full blast for the Nazis. After the annihilation of Poland, Vyatcheslav Molotov declared grandiloquently: "One blow from Germany, one from the Soviet Union, and this ugly duckling of a Versailles Treaty[878] was no more." He then turned on the Allies; he accused the "ruling classes" in Britain and France of "diverting attention from their colonial problems," adding that there was "absolutely no justification for a war of this kind. One may accept or reject the ideology of Hitlerism, as well as any other: That is a matter of political views. But everybody should understand that an ideology cannot be eliminated by war. It is therefore not only senseless but criminal to wage a war for the destruction of 'Hitlerism' camouflaged as a fight for 'democracy.' "

The Soviet Union had just gobbled up Eastern Poland, occupied strategic sites in the three Baltic republics (all with national socialist connivance), and was suspected of having further designs on the republics. In disavowal of the unsavory, Molotov indignantly declared: "We stand for a scrupulous and punctilious observance of pacts on the basis of complete reciprocity and we declare that all nonsense about sovietizing the Baltic countries is only in the interest of our common enemies and of all anti-Soviet provocateurs."[879]

Not much later the Soviet Union (without German protest) attacked Finland and decent people all over the world were outraged.[880] It seemed that the mere existence of Finland, sixteen short miles from Leningrad, was an "anti-Soviet provocation." Though Leningraders could not possibly visit the seaside resorts between Terijoki and Viipuri (Viborg), the news had leaked through that in Finland, a country which apart from timber had few natural resources, living standards were infinitely higher than in the Workers' Paradise. Thus the borders had to be pushed back to their temporary position in the eighteenth century, allowing the USSR (as once Imperial Russia did) to launch at will a swift attack on the heart of Finland. The Finnish Communist party, in percentage one of the largest in Europe,[881] was expected to gain by this, but nothing of the sort happened. The Finnish People's Democratic Republic under Otto Kuusinen, established in Terijoki[882] soon after the first attack, had little visible support. The Finnish Communists made it clear that they wanted their own brand of communism. After the surrender of Western Karelia in 1940 only *one* family remained in the area.

The leftist forces in the West slowly recovered from the blow. Interestingly, the shift in the German-Soviet alignment took place exactly as described by Orwell in *1984*. In the novel's permanent world war, the change of alliances occurred during a public demonstration. The orator was handed a slip of paper informing him of the startling reversal and he quickly revised his message. In real life, the Left equivocated, and in the twisting and turning, the Nazis were somehow lost from sight. (Germans stranded in America were now able to regain their *Vaterland* via Vladivostok.)[883]

Remember, only a few days before the announcement of the German-Soviet Pact, a flaming manifesto of protest against the very possibility of such a suggestion, signed by the whole shining phalanx of the leftist intelligentsia, had appeared as a full-page advertisement in leading newspapers. Now the Left had quickly to shift gears. It turned on the "forces of reaction" at home that wished to wage a "capitalist war" for bigger and better profits. National socialism? A bugbear. The American Youth Congress hooted at President Roosevelt for referring to valiant Finland. In England, "People's Congresses" sprang up overnight, drew up resolutions, demanded reforms and "peace," and protested against armaments. The Communists in the United States were entirely on the side of isolationism (so too, naturally, the members of the German-American *Bund*), and Georgi Dimitrov wrote in 1940: "The brave fight of American Communists against the United States being drawn into the war finds an ever-increasing sympathy among the labor unions and even from the ranks of the AFL run by reactionaries."[884] Symbolically, a song appeared: *The Yanks Are Not Coming.*

Yet they did come, and to repeat the old tragic performance: to win a war and to lose a peace. I do not share the opinion that a German victory in World War II would have been preferable to the ensuing state of affairs. As a Christian I could not so easily subscribe to Churchill's reported dictum: "We have slaughtered the wrong pig!" The pigs were everywhere. Hitler, among other things, would have tried to exterminate Christianity as a "Jewish religion." (To see where the brown ideology was headed, cast a glance at Rudolf Hammer's 1939 *Christentum, doch Judentum.*) A victory of the German armies, moreover, would so have enhanced Hitler's prestige as to render a revolt by the army unthinkable—and no other revolt was possible. A revolt of officers is feasible only if their soldiers will obey them. But with the progressive deification of Hitler by the success-oriented Common Man, this would no longer have been the case. The rank and file of soldiers would not have followed their officers in a rebellion against the *Führer* and "Supreme War Lord."[885] Had Britain been brought to its knees and had Russian war materiels fallen into German hands, the victorious National Socialists would have been well-nigh invincible. The argument falls flat, of course, with the completion of the A-bomb in 1945. But would it have existed without America's entry into the war? The German scientists had boycotted its manufacture in the Third Reich. In the long run, of course, it would have been most difficult to dominate the Old World with a racist ideology, a weakness of national socialism that was felt even during the war.

Still, while insisting that America's entry into war in 1917 paved the way for World War II, it does not follow that a national socialist victory in Europe would have been other than an unmitigated disaster for at least a generation or so. But nearly as disastrous was the political-psychological warfare waged by the Allies. Worse still was the order that emerged from World War II, which caused untold human suffering to generations of peoples before it began to crumble. But this hardly surprises, given the ignorance, the prejudices, and the ideologies prevalent in the West and the Soviet Union. A few intelligent American isolationists reasoned to this exact conclusion.

Mr. Churchill, as pointed out, was not a genuine conservative, but a pragmatist and deist of a certain aristocratic cast and of a terrifying cynicism. He was gifted by nature in many ways, but had a comparatively poor schooling—he had never been a *student* of anything—and was astoundingly ignorant concerning most countries. His biographer, Mr. Robert Sencourt, said that to him "Christ was a socialist" and "men who had principles were 'goody-goodies.' With one grandfather a duke and the other an American impresario, he had grandeur in his zest for adventures and huge gambles. This enabled him to seize one of the greatest occasions in history and gradually to turn it into a calamity for Europe and a triumph for America."[886] But the triumph was momentary.

His colleague, Franklin D. Roosevelt, was less gifted, less informed—in fact, totally ignorant of the big wide world. Perhaps too he was less oratorically proficient than Mr. Churchill, but he played on a far larger instrument. As Kierkegaard remarked, the preparation of a cabinet minister at present does not teach him how to be one, but how to become one.[887] In a democracy, the manifold efforts—the talks, intrigues and chats, the incessant rubbing of shoulders—necessary to attain a leading position consume so much time and energy that the factual knowledge absolutely essential for *statesmanship* (as opposed to the qualifications of a mere politician), is seldom acquired.

A rundown of various American leaders of the day is revealing. Although more cautious in his public utterances, Mr. Roosevelt knew even less than Professor Wilson. It is doubtful that he read *Mein Kampf* before 1941—if ever.[888] (To him, the National Socialists were, of course, "medieval.") His wife stood far to the left: a study of her writings is rewarding. His secretary of state, Mr. Cordell Hull, had received intellectual preparation for his exalted role in the most amazing manner.[889] He owed his wartime career largely to his specialization in trade and tariff agreements, around which American foreign policy had revolved. Yet his contribution to the profound confusion prevailing after the war was not inconsiderable. His successor, Edward R. Stettinius, an industrialist, was not much better qualified. Happily, Jan Ciechanowski, former Polish ambassador to Washington, has left history a candid glimpse of Mr. Stettinius, who was catapulted into the important position of undersecretary of state two years prior to his taking over the entire State Department. "I congratulated him on his appointment," Ciechanowski wrote, "and asked him how he felt in his new surroundings. He replied that he felt 'very bewildered.' "[890]

Barely a few days after assuming the duties of his first post in the

Department, Mr. Hull being absent, Stettinius became acting secretary of state. With boyish frankness he admitted that he felt inadequate to handling his responsibilities, and worse, that he knew nothing of most of the Department officials who had of a sudden become his subordinates and collaborators. Sheer amateurism of this sort characterized the British as well as the American war effort, whereas the Russians and the Germans suffered from a different handicap—thralldom to ideologies far removed from life. At times, a bad plan is nevertheless superior to none at all. An anti-intellectual current runs strong in "Anglo-Saxonry," as Keyserling has stated,[891] which, incidentally, is quite consistent with the democratic tradition.

American conservatives tend to compare the President unfavorably with the Prime Minister. But to the historian and moralist, this is by no means evident. Apart from the fact that Churchill was no conservative, the mythomanic tendency of the President ought be taken into account—promises broken without reason or provocation, statements made without foundation, spontaneous directions given, bare of realistic substance. In sum, they demonstrate that the man could not be held morally responsible for many of his utterances and actions. Thus he sent the Polish Premier Mikolajczyk on an irresponsible chase to Moscow, exhorting him to stand up to Stalin, to make no territorial concessions, for he, the President, and the American people stood solidly behind him. Later, Molotov told the Premier, in the presence of Eden and Harriman, that at Teheran Roosevelt had solemnly promised Eastern Poland to the Soviet Union.[892] Mikolajczyk was thunderstruck. The President's lack of responsibility was startling, his frivolity extraordinary.[893] Henry Morgenthau, Jr., relates in his *Diaries* how every morning at breakfast the President set the price of gold. One day Mr. Roosevelt proposed a rise of 21 cents because "it is a lucky number, three times seven." Finally, Montague Norman, governor of the Bank of England, protested. This outcry of indignation amused "Henry, the Morgue"; "I began to chuckle and the President roared with laughter."[894]

Roosevelt had but the haziest of ideas concerning the future order of the world, but those he had bordered on the abnormal and were characterized by a strong leftist bias. (In order to ascertain the sort of constitution the people really wanted, a plebiscite would be conducted in Norway, the Netherlands, Belgium, Italy, and Greece—but none of course in Czechoslovakia, a model democracy; according to FDR, it was Russia's great calling to dominate Europe.)[895] But these vague notions did not constitute a coherent vision. A man like Roosevelt was capable only of waging war, declaring a policy of Unconditional Surrender, and playing politics "by ear." The Russians had a plan. The Americans had none.

Nor, indeed, had Mr. Churchill and the British. It is pure myth that Churchill strongly advocated the "brilliant" strategy of invading Europe through the Balkans and thereby occupying Budapest, Vienna, and Prague ahead of the Russians. Rather, he yielded with little resistance to the "American" plan to attack Italy, calling Italy as well as the Balkans the "soft underbelly of Europe." (How many Allied soldiers, especially those Poles destined to lose their homeland, found their graves in this allegedly soft, highly mountainous, underbelly?) And it is equally untrue that Churchill opposed the Unconditional Surrender formula. His reaction to this piece of psychological strategy was the gleeful cry that "poor Goebbels is going to howl."[896]

General Albert C. Wedemeyer wrote quite tellingly about the key Allied leaders and their war aims: "Without a clearly defined political objective, war is but aimless or senseless slaughter. This fact is understood by every military man with any pretensions to professional knowledge. Winston Churchill, correctly described by his own Chief of Staff as no strategist, but as acting on intuition and impulse without regard to the implications and consequences of the courses he favored, waged war more like an Indian chieftain from the Arizona Territory intent upon obtaining the largest possible number of enemy scalps. . . In order to kill a maximum number of Germans, Winston Churchill dismissed politics or policy as a 'secondary consideration,' and on this and many other occasions said that there were 'no lengths of violence to which we would not go' in order to achieve his objective."[897]

The Russian alliance was of great psychological importance to the entire Left in Britain and the United States. The German attack on the Soviet Union was undeniably a boon to the British engaged in bitter aerial warfare with the *Reich*. Contrary to widespread opinion, air warfare was not begun by the Germans; in 1935 the Germans offered the National Labourite Government an air pact to limit the role of the air force to the support of operating ground forces. This was turned down by Air Secretary Thomson who deemed it a clever but immoral ruse to humanize warfare—a blot on humanity. Only frightfulness should terminate war! Yet Hitler at war's start acted as if it had been accepted; the first big German raids on England had the weak character of reprisals. (The attack on Rotterdam, with 945 people killed, had been erroneously unleashed after the hostilities ceased when the German troops were within nine miles of the city.)[898]

This whole issue is conclusively documented. Mr. Churchill speculated, quite rightly, that Britain eventually would win the air war because it could build an air force in safely distant lands while Germany remained vulnerable to attack. This much can in part be gathered from notes of his written July 8 and 11, 1940.[899] Documentary proof that the RAF began to bomb Germany methodically before the Germans opened their so-called *Blitz*[900] on Britain can be gleaned from such authoritative books and articles as J. M. Spaight's (assistant secretary, Air Ministry), *The Battle of Britain* and *Bombing Vindicated*,[901] and Basil Liddell-Hart's "War Limited" (*Harper's Magazine*).[902] General J. C. F. Fuller in *The Second World War, 1939–1945* states frankly that "it was Mr. Churchill who lit the fuse which detonated a war of devastation and terrorization unrivaled since the invasion of the Seljuks."[903] The air raids ravaged not only the German population (without too seriously incapacitating their industry) but also foreign laborers, concentration camp inmates, and Allied nationals.[904]

In the United States, even prior to Pearl Harbor, American public opinion had to be shaped to accept an alliance that involved the Soviet Union as well as Britain. The German attack on the USSR had an effect similar to the abdication of Nicholas II in 1917. Subsequent to it the American public could more easily be persuaded to soften its stand. In this connection Cannon Bernard Iddings Bell recorded a rather significant wartime experience: "At a dinner in New York at that time, I sat next to a high-up officer of one of the great news-collecting agencies. 'I suppose,' I ventured, 'now that the Muscovites are on our side, the American people will have to be indoctrinated so as to stop thinking of them as devils and begin to regard them as noble fellows.' 'Of course,' he replied, 'we know what our job is in respect to that. We of the press will bring about a complete and most unanimous *volte face* in the belief of the Common Man about Russians. We shall do it in three weeks.' "[905]

The trouble with deceit and untruth is not so much that misinformation is imparted as that the originators of the lies come to believe in their validity. The perpetrators, no longer able to distinguish fact from fiction, begin *to act* in accordance with their fabrications. In Britain the news of early Soviet victories came as such a relief that even people of considerable integrity lost their balance.[906] An unreal hysteria broke loose in the British Isles; visions of sturdy Cossacks, crystal-clear vodka, galloping horses, bearded muzhiks, progressive commissars, and booted girls fired the collective imagination. Britishers seemed ready to throw themselves into the arms of Unholy Mother Russia, denying the memory that, with the

Molotov-Ribbentrop Pact, Stalin had willfully started World War II (and perhaps never knowing that Stalin later shrugged off British warnings of an impending German attack as idle "capitalist" talk). A policeman, on discovering that two gangs have fallen out among themselves, does not proclaim that the weaker has been transformed into a band of cherubs and seraphs; he takes advantage of the split.

Not so the British. When the USSR demanded a much larger chunk of Poland than Hitler ever had—52 percent of Polish territory, to be precise—the British by and large failed to remember that the Polish issue was what caused them to declare war in the first place. As Lord Halifax said in December 1939: "We have tried to improve relations with Russia, but in doing so we have always maintained the position that rights of third parties must remain intact and unaffected by our negotiations. . . . I have little doubt that the people of this country would prefer to face difficulties and embarrassments rather than feel that we had compromised the honor of this country and Commonwealth."[907] The most curious part of the bill run up by the all but limitless *libido serviendi* as regards the Soviet Union was not presented until 1945. In the late spring, the majority of the British people, awaiting the millenium of the Left, sided with Labour and voted those who had brought them military victory, the Conservatives, out of power. Since Communist Russia was the epitome of all that was good, the British were drawn to its shadow, socialism—the creed of the Socialist Fatherland.[908]

In the United States, enthusiasm for the Soviet Union surfaced only after 1941. Even then, the pro-Soviet fervor seemed less strident than in Britain principally because the American citizens of East European and East Central European descent were grounded in the reality of the USSR. Since these citizens rarely mixed in high society, the Red Hysteria struck harder in Boston and Philadelphia than in Pittsburg and Wichita. I remember still a cocktail party in Manhattan in 1943 where a beminked lady, balancing a highball, declaimed that it was America's most urgent task to show itself "worthy of its gallant Soviet ally." "To think," she sobbed, after further liberal libations, "that I called them 'Bolsheviks!' " I reassured the good woman that in Russian the appellation carried no pejorative overtones.

Joseph E. Davies' *Mission to Moscow* contained deceitful propaganda and became a best-seller and a screen production.[909] It helped greatly to revise the picture of the "New Russia" for American consumption.[910] And Dorothy Thompson, perhaps America's outstanding columnist of the day, wrote in all seriousness that the Soviet Union could be counted on completely in one respect: it never broke its word or reneged on a treaty. And she was by no means the worst of the lot.

Perusing the mass of words published and uncritically accepted brings in question the probity of much of the American public. Take for instance the book of Quentin Reynolds, *Only the Stars are Neutral*,[911] published in 1942. The most telling incident in the book describes a discussion between the author, on his way home from the USSR, and Sir Miles Lampson, British ambassador to Egypt. Sir Miles plies Mr. Reynolds with questions about the USSR, to which he replies repeatedly that he does not know. " 'Sure,' I said, 'after I had been in Russia three weeks I knew everything about the place. I could have written a book about it. But I made the mistake of staying there three months. After three months I realized I didn't know a damn thing about the country.' "[912] The reader is probably moved by such modesty. But proceed.

Mr. Reynolds admits a few unsavory facts, such as the eight hundred women (political prisoners) at hard labor near Kuybishev, the sparsity of tawdry, costly goods; the great risk Soviet citizens run associating with foreigners, even the lack of freedom of speech "in spite of so much smartness." But then, he expects that youngsters will learn "soon from the older democracies."[913] Note the legerdemain—"from the older democracies" indeed! The inference—the Soviet Union as a "younger democracy"—is subtle, unobtrusive. Other lies are far less subtle and presuppose an audience immeasurably ignorant.

A few details follow to demonstrate the technique typical of the propaganda poured out during the war by the Left in the United States. Mr. Reynolds (superbly prepared for his task as a former sports reporter) wrote: "In the Czarist days the priests had a wonderful racket in Russia. They were paid by the State and collections taken up in churches went to the State. All Stalin did was to separate the church from the State. In short, he did the same thing we did in our country back in 1776. . . . Their priests are no longer government officials who have almost the power of life and death over them. . . . Had any of us ever troubled to read the Soviet Constitution (as vigorously upheld as our own) we might have got the true picture of religion in the Soviet Union. I looked it up the day after the Kremlin dinner. I talked with Father Braun. I mentally apologized as a Catholic for the things I've thought about Russia's attitude toward religion."[914]

And now for some facts. Priests in Russia were indeed paid by the state, as were *all* priests and ministers everywhere on the Continent, except in France after 1905. (And if the collections went to the state, which, incidentally, they didn't, then why call it a racket?) Stalin did not separate the Church from the state; Lenin did. Now, Mr. Reynolds is entitled to his opinion—that the Church should be separated from the state—but it happens not to be in the European tradition, least of all in Switzerland, a freedom-loving, highly democratic state. Most *free* European countries cooperate with *several* churches. And then again, in the United States, the separation clause in the First Amendment was enacted not in 1776 but in 1791; and it merely prohibited the establishment of a national church. Cooperation of state and Church is not necessarily establishment. But establishment on a *state* basis did continue well into the nineteenth century.[915] And yet again: It is totally untrue that Russian priests had "almost the power over life and death": they had neither the power nor the prestige that Catholic priests and Evangelical ministers traditionally enjoy in the West. In Russian folklore the priest (and his wife) are constantly cast in the role of the fool.

Reynolds' high praise of the Soviet Constitution is ludicrous. One can only estimate the number of concentration camp inmates at the time of Stalin, but these run beween 8 and 20 million souls.[916] In this respect, separation of Church and state is one thing, persecution quite another. When Reynolds visited the Soviet Union, the second big wave of religious persecution (1934–41) had just come to a close. (A third wave was to follow after 1958.) From 1917 until the outbreak of World War II more than 110 bishops of the Eastern Church alone were executed and more than a dozen others "disappeared."[917] This gives but a glimpse of the extent of the persecution and the savageries involved. Why in Heaven's name did Reynolds "mentally apologize as a Catholic"?

There is another choice bit: a captain in the Red Army, while talking to our author, refers to a British officer. "My friend Colonel Hill was here in Russia in Czarist days. He will tell you that only 10 percent of our citizens owned shoes then. He will tell you that only 1 percent of our people was literate. Now education—classical, scientific or industrial—is open to all. . . . Remember our world has only lasted twenty-four years. Yours in American has lasted since 1776. . . ." And then comes the climax: " 'We haven't had to chuck religion overboard,' I suggested. 'We have not chucked religion overboard,' he smiled. 'We've chucked overboard the religious abuses we suffered from. . . .' "[918]

This seemingly long digression is needed to demonstrate, among other things, the terrible naiveté of Americans. Now, Reynolds does not in fact tell us anything. He is reporting, conveying information given him by a

Red Army captain who refers him to a British colonel who is not consulted and reaffirms nothing. Fine. But according to this conversation, in czarist days, only 10 percent of the people had shoes and only 1 percent were literate. In fact, in 1917, 44 percent were literate. Hypothetically, had only 1 percent been literate at the outbreak of the Revolution, how many could have been literate in, say, 1882, the year Dostoyevski died? One in two hundred? One in five hundred? in one thousand? Just think, out of 110 million people perhaps only half a million could read and write, and yet, at the close of the nineteenth century, this illiterate country produced Europe's leading literature! Such utter nonsense, but the readers gobble it up. Just as they swallow the 10 percent shoes. Amusing to visualize Imperial Russia in the winter of 1910 with 90 percent of its people restricted to their homes between early October and late April, and then going about barefoot. Yet the greater the nonsense, the greater, apparently, the public credulity. Indeed, that same public is of the belief that American life ran along different lines before and after 1776, that a rending social and economic revolution took place. What occurred was a War of Independence, as in Greece in 1821, in Belgium in 1830, or in Finland in 1917.

In Russia, the media seers reported, nothing radical had happened in respect of religion: "abuses" had been corrected, nothing more. Yet, until very recently, a civil servant, seen regularly in church on Sundays, was fired for his reactionary tendencies; a university professor, married in church, was thereby disqualified as a scientist; an individual, teaching youngsters religion and thus alienating them from Marxism-Leninism, was judged "intolerable." In former days, the "abuse" of religion consisted in the freedom to stay home or go to church without danger of reprisal either way. Or does anyone believe that a pair of gendarmes dragged Dr. Antoni Chekhov every Sunday to attend Holy Liturgy? "In Russia, anyone who criticizes the government is an enemy of the State," Quentin Reynolds amenably states. "Harsh as Stalin's methods are, he has a complete answer, a complete justification for the ruthless quelling of opposition. Today there is not one Fifth Columnist, not one Quisling at liberty in Soviet Russia. . . Stalin knew what he was doing back in 1938. Russia's magnificent unity today and her completely unbroken spirit after the tragedy of that German advance, is proof of the fact that Russia accepted the purge and approved of Stalin's policy."[919]

Such "magnificent" unity. And almost half a million Russian *Vlassovtsy* fought under the German flag.

But then, what do we make of Mr. Reynold's message on the book's cover? This, he writes, "is a war to decide whether or not men can sit around the crackerbox in the general store and lift their voices in praise or criticism. It is a war to decide whether or not we can worship Christ or Mohammed or Buddha or a clay pigeon, or anything else which we, as individuals, want to worship." Yet, if there were Russians who worshipped navel-gazing Buddhas and others clay pigeons while sitting around a crackerbox, wherein the "magnificent unity" for which Stalin had such "complete justification"? Here lies complete schizophrenia.

There were, of course, notable exceptions in the chorus of ignoramuses, fakers, and liars who joined the government in this "moral warfare"— under the circumstances, quite a misnomer. But in a "people's war," the masses have to be whipped up to a frenzy of indignation, hatred, and fanaticism. In the event, democracies are little different from leftist dictatorships.[920] Men and women such as Thomas F. Woodlock of the *Wall Street Journal*, Henry J. Taylor, W. H. Chamberlin, Joseph Harsch, Anne O'Hare McCormick and others refused to play the evil game. Commentators such as Gabriel Heatter, Frederick L. Schumann, Raymond Gram Swing, and Lisa Sergio played quite a different role.[921] The Office of War Information (OWI), filled with refugees from all over Continental Europe, was a hotbed of leftist, procommunist and communist, propaganda. Its German department was one of the worst.[922] Since so many of these refugees had been Marxists, they plied the country with the Marxist version of global events, and the unfortunate American public swallowed the sugar-coated propaganda.

Even the dim-witted can understand political events if explained in terms of material interest, financial ambition, production, and so on. But a misreading of such events has worse consequences in the United States than elsewhere, for its civilization (and Britain's), based on commerce, lends easily to Marxist arguments. And in terms of Marxist doctrine, "fascism" was nothing but the last stand of a "dying capitalism." National socialism was the desperate defense of German industry ("monopoly capitalism") and high finance. Hitler, naturally, was but a stooge, a puppet of money-crazed monsters hired to club the trade unions into submission. Given the circumstances—the final battle for progress, liberty, and equality—what nobler ally, then, than the Soviet Union, that master at dealing with the evils of capitalism? Gustav Stolper, an exile, expanded with great insight on this danger to America.[923]

This exegesis of national socialism—this blind and irresponsible pro-Sovietism—can be linked to a piece of American folklore, the notion that "rotten backwardness" reigned supreme in a Europe[924] where misery and poverty were occasioned by the big landowners. These last were magically transformed into monocled, saber-rattling, heel-clicking officers, the natural allies of slick bankers and fat bishops. The clichés of World War I, when the United States had been at war with the Hohenzollerns, were revived, and the demoniacal shadows of aristocratic arrogance were magically projected onto the National Socialists, of all people. During my wartime years in the United States I heard not a single "morale-building" story about Central Europe that did not involve a "Nazi nobleman." Some did of course exist—as did Jews who paid conscience money to the NSDAP, and Catholic priests who held "brown" sympathies. Exceptions confirm the rule. But national socialism was a plebeian movement; significantly, at the big Nuremberg Trial, not a single nobleman was among those condemned to death.[925]

The persistence of World War I clichés was remarkable. They sparked the belief, which took hold gradually but with tenacity, that this war, like its lamentable predecessor, was fought to aid the *Common Man*—the victim of noble and arrogant Nazi-Fascists. American leftism, organized and spontaneous alike, proclaimed the emancipation of the Common Man as some sort of war aim. The century of the Common Man was in the offing! This idealism worked synchronously with anticolonialism. While the United States and Britain fought shoulder to shoulder, the President of the United States dreamed of the total destruction of the British Empire, the Commonwealth of Nations—and of the red overlordship of parts of Europe.[926] This distasteful phase of American foreign policy, never sufficiently grasped by Americans, drew deep and continuing resentment in certain European circles.

The Common Man crusade was ironic given that the real source of evil in Europe was precisely his precipitous rise to positions for which he was altogether inadequate; he was given tasks for which neither training, knowledge, nor experience had fitted him. Stalin studied a little theology, indulged in some highway robbery, and undertook an artificial, totally limited study of political science; Hitler in all likelihood hocked gifts from women admirers; Mussolini was a mason in Switzerland; Daladier was the son of a baker. Still, it is hazardous to insist on a purely sociological concept of the Common Man: the truly uncommon man, the superior man, can be born in a log cabin. In Austrian history, there were many such: Baron Joseph Sonnenfels, grandson of a little rabbinical scholar, and Baron Franz Thugut, who came from an orphanage, were both pillars of Maria

Theresa's reign; Dr. Karl Lueger, son of a school janitor, was founder of the Christian Social Party and a famous mayor of Vienna; Monsignor Ignaz Seipel, university professor and chancellor of Austria, was the son of a cabdriver; and Dr. Engelbert Dollfuss, Chancellor of Austria, was the illegitimate son of a peasant girl. But these uncommon men were men who had studied; they *were trained*.

The leftist-inspired and -directed wartime passion in the United States inundated the public with fanciful hopes about the coming of an illusory New Age. "Dawnism"—the great psychological approach of the Left— painted the best possible paradisiacal future.[927] The wartime utopia was a cornucopia of social and political blessings, and much, much more: plastic cars, every sort of new gadget, nylon hose for pretty girls, education by tape recorders, cheap transcontinental trips—limitless liberty and measured equality on an opulent globe.

Unfortunately, a few discordancies marred this promising future. Mr. Sumner Welles in a memorable book[928] advocated the total partitioning of Germany, Mr. Henry J. Morgenthau, Jr., sought to transform Germany into a goat pasture.[929] Theodore N. Kaufman showed far greater imagination: In his essay "Germany Must Perish,"[930] he proposed to sterilize all Germans and to distribute Germany and Austria among their neighbors. An accompanying map demonstrated the interesting changes: Holland and Poland would share a common boundary; France, Czechoslovakia, and Holland would touch in Thuringia.

To give due credit, the genuinely socialist camp did not participate in this unrestrained adulation of all things Soviet, this orgy mixed with outbreaks of sadistic hatred for the partly guilty, and partly innocent, German people. A socialist weekly, *The New Leader*, was absolutely honest and fair.[931] Some of its editors had been born in Eastern Europe, most were Jewish, but they knew precisely who was who and what was what. Which was not the case with the semiliterate and far more affluent rabble who gladly danced the new Carmagnole.

The euphoria was ruffled hardly at all by the Soviet Union's demand of permanent possession of the three Baltic republics as well as a large chunk of Poland. It certainly did not shock. On the contrary, Americans of nearly all political persuasions supported the shameless demands of the USSR— quickly followed by a claim to further pieces of Finland (wantonly attacked for the second time in less than two years).[932] The area "requested" by the Soviet Union was precisely thirty-four times that of Alsace-Lorraine; it comprised 482,000 square kilometers—more acreage than constituted

Germany in 1937—and over 22 million inhabitants—as many as peopled the United States in 1850. The Soviets were confident in their desires, well aware that Mr. Churchill and Mr. Roosevelt were opportunists with no real sense of honor or obligation. So long as they won the war, what matter the peace? Let us remember the famous discussions between Fitzroy MacLean and Winston Churchill recorded in *Eastern Approaches*: Brigadier MacLean, who had been with Tito's partisans, informed the Prime Minister that unlike Draža Mihajlović, the wily Croat was a true communist. In response Churchill asked him bluntly: "Do you intend to make Yugoslavia your home after the war?" "No, sir!" "Neither do I," Churchill replied, "and that being so, the less you and I worry about the form of government they set up, the better. . . . What interests us is, which of them is doing most harm to the Germans?"[933]

Luckily, cynicism is not a strong characteristic of the American people; reasons had to be found for supporting the Soviet demands. And, no matter their inanity, reasons were found. The Soviets' insistence on the Hitler-Stalin Line in Poland was suddenly bolstered by the flimsiest, most infamous argument. (The Left played its usual supporting part by stamping prewar Poland as a den of iniquity and the men who had valiantly fought the Germans as "Fascists.")[934] The Hitler-Stalin Line was identified to the gullible public with the Curzon Line, although even the congenitally anti-Polish British understood it to be merely a demarcation line of Poland's minimum demands—not a border.[935] The line extended from Central Lithuania to the Galician border, never remotely to the Carpathians. In *Time for Decision*, a manual for "peace planning," Sumner Welles, former undersecretary of state, berated Catherine the Great of Russia for having been "primarily responsible for one of the greatest international crimes in history," the first three partitions of Poland. Undeterred by his own logic, Mr. Welles proceeded to defend Stalin's present demands; and these entailed not only the Russian share of all the first three partitions, but half the Austrian share of the First Partition as well.[936] Perhaps Mr. Welles (or his ghost writer) could not read maps. For along with the mutilation of Poland, a large chunk of Czechoslovakia, larger than Connecticut, was annexed by the USSR, yet another bit of geographic intelligence that seems to have escaped general attention.

The Soviets based their claim against Poland not on ideological or historical grounds, but on a national, i.e., ethnological basis. Although the Soviet Union is basically a Great Russian State, shrewdly and methodically attempting to Russianize the lesser soviet states[937] through schooling and planned migrations, it has granted a minor ethnic autonomy to "member states" such as Byelo-Russia ("White Ruthenia") and the Ukraine. White Ruthenians and Ukrainians are thus minorities in the USSR. These same ethnic bodies are also represented in Eastern Poland, where Poles, mostly of the middle and upper classes, make up the largest ethnic group.[938] They are followed by the Ukrainians, White Ruthenians, Jews, Lithuanians, and Germans. But the point, of course, is that only a nationalist will insist on ethnic borders; one of the main charges against Hitler was that he wanted all ethnic Germans to live in the Third Reich, an objective that goes rightly under the name of Pan-Germanism. His demand for the *Anschluss*, his peremptory request for the border districts of Bohemia-Moravia-Silesia (inhabited by the so-called Sudeten Germans), his insistence on the return of various areas of Poland (which brought about World War II), his incorporation of Alsace-Lorraine in 1940—all this was based on a racist-nationalist attitude, condemned, decried, execrated, and vilified by the internationally minded Left.[939]

And now Stalin had achieved the exact same end. And in the United States (as in England) hardly a voice questioned whether the inhabitants in Eastern Poland *really wanted* to join the Soviet Union. (Imagine the indignation had Hitler declared that all of German-speaking Switzerland had to join the *Reich*.) I happened to exchange letters with a leading American journalist who defended the Soviet stand on ethnic grounds. It never entered his mind that a Ukrainian of Volhynia, despite his dislike of the Poles, might prefer to live as a member of a minority in "bourgeois" Poland than as a member of another minority in the Great Russian USSR.[940] Probably he could not imagine the chasm of difference between free Poland and Red Russia. In the United States the common perception was that the wily Poles (with French aid), having improperly defeated the Red Army, brutally wrested lands from a helpless Soviet Russia.[941]

More nonsense. In 1920 Lenin offered peace to the Poles and a boundary *a great deal further east* than that violated by Stalin in 1939.[942] The Poles did not accept because Pilsudski felt morally bound to aid Petlyura,[943] the Ukrainian nationalist leader, then engaged in a life-and-death struggle with the Russian reds. But Petlyura was nevertheless defeated, and the Red Army advanced deep into Poland, arriving at the very gates of Warsaw (which filled Lloyd George with glee[944] and made Thomas G. Masaryk very happy).[945] But at those gates, Pilsudski (*without* French aid)[946] defeated the Red Army—the "Miracle of the Vistula." The Red Army retired, and in the compromise peace of Riga the Poles regained the Russian share of the Third Partition and a few tiny fragments of the Second Partition—none from the first, and this although the partitions of Poland had been solemnly abrogated as a piece of Russian imperialism by the nascent Soviet regime (August 29, 1919). In the previous Soviet offer, cities such as Polock, Minsk, and Kamieniec-Podolski had been promised to the Poles. Since they now received less, the *Great Soviet Encyclopedia* considered the war *won by the USSR*.[947] And indeed, in the years following, a stream of refugees made the dangerous trek into Poland—Ukrainians, White Ruthenians, Jews, and naturally Poles.[948]

And now, in postwar America, it little mattered that on July 30, 1941, the Soviets had ceremoniously abrogated all treaties made with the Nazis concerning Poland's territory.[949] The pro-Soviet hysteria,[950] coupled with a mounting defamation of Poland, swept the press free of reason. Czechoslovakia and the horror of Lidice were highlighted, but the endless number of Lidices in Poland were swept aside.[951] The ungenerous treatment, at times, of Ukrainians and Jews by the Poles was rigorously condemned. Yet there is no doubt which side[952] these minorities would have chosen if permitted. A Ukrainian (or Jewish) lawyer, doctor, priest, religious, peasant, teacher, labor leader, artist, banker, shopkeeper could not possibly have preferred the Soviet regime, sure to confiscate his property and annihilate his way of life.[953]

Then news of the Katyn Massacre erupted, swiftly followed by a Soviet feint and a counterattack: Moscow alleged that the crime had been committed by the Germans after their advance into West Russia in the fall of 1941, shrugging off evidence that the horror had been perpetrated in the spring of 1940, almost a year and-a-half earlier; Moscow also ruptured relations with the Polish government-in-exile for daring to demand an impartial investigation of the Nazi charges. The American and British governments assumed a "neutral" position, but the charge nevertheless occasioned an attack of conscience by the American media.[954] Still, as late as 1946 at the Nuremberg Trial, the Soviets continued to ascribe the crime to the Germans. This so embarrassed their Western Allies that they quietly dropped the accusation.[955] The Allies probably felt that before such a mixed body of judges the Russians could not repeat the ingenious techniques used at the stage trials under Andrey Wyszynski[956] in the late 1930s. Today only a hard-bitten leftist would dare maintain that this particular iniquity belonged to the brown register of sins, and, of course, the Soviet Union has finally admitted Soviet guilt.

Katyn should have sounded the alarm—as should the establishment of the Communist Polish Committee in the Soviet Union (later transferred to Lublin); or the insidious halting of the Red Army before Warsaw leaving the heroic *Armia Krajowa*, under the leadership of Count Komorowski ("General Bor"), to bleed to death; or the murder of the two Jewish labor leaders Alter and Ehrlich;[957] or the deportation of thousands upon thousands of Poles to the Arctic and Siberia;[958] or the distrust and contempt displayed toward Allied missions. (The Soviets have but recently admitted to the slaughter of Polish prisoners of war, and not only at Katyn, but at two other sites, making a grand total of fifteen thousand murdered.) Yet all these unmistakable evils did nothing to shake the leftist adulation of the Soviets—tempering neither their admiration nor their inferiority complex. Their earlier American Messianism had transferred to the USSR.[959]

Did Mr. Roosevelt wake up to the danger? According to legend, the last months of his life were shadowed by the increasing realization that another totalitarian power was menacing the world's freedom, but no documentary evidence exists to this effect. It seems rather as if his conviction that he could "charm" the sinister Georgian never wavered.

Churchill was another case. He never really liked Bolsheviks (he disliked the Poles) and entertained no hope of ever understanding anything about Russia. Certainly his attitude towards Stalin was perplexing.[960] Before leaving for Yalta he sought to impress Stalin with the might of the Western Allies by arranging one of the ghastliest single massacres in modern history—the annihilation of Dresden. But weather conditions delayed the holocaust until the day Churchill left Yalta—where he acceded to the "Crime of the Crimea" by charting the West's suicide before its fate was sealed at Potsdam—and the dreadful slaughter at Dresden was all in vain. The number of victims in this unfortified and nonindustrial city, crammed with refugees, is estimated as between 135,000 and 204,000 people—all noncombatants, mostly women, children, and old men, including foreign slave laborers (a few thousand "only"). At least two-thirds of the victims were *burned alive*.[961] Hiroshima and Nagasaki were child's play compared with this. As for the stigmatized Inquisitors of the past, they at least sought out people who they believed were individually guilty. In Dresden, the number of those killed—in the name of progress, democracy, freedom, enlightenment, and brotherhood—in one fair afternoon, was a multiple of the Inquisitors' victims throughout the centuries. (And how it backfired; every year, until liberation in 1989, three minutes of silence were observed on the Day of Infamy in Communist-dominated Dresden for the victims of "Western Monopoly Capitalism.") When the American Mustangs appeared over the smoking ruins, they machine-gunned the fleeing fire-scarred refugees. In reference to Dresden, the term "holocaust" is exact. For the word means the ritual killing *through fire* as sacrifice to the gods, in this case (as in Hiroshima and Nagasaki) to the new pantheon of gods—democracy, progress, equality, social security, public education, sexual license, and the rest.

Back in 1943 anti-Nazi leaders in Germany had tried desperately and unsuccessfully to enlist the collaboration of the Western Allies. At the time they sought to make contact through the German Embassy in Ankara as well as through George H. Earle, former governor of Pennsylvania and U.S. naval attaché in Turkey during the war. Earle flew to Washington in May 1944 in a vain attempt to enlighten the President concerning the Russian menace.[962] Parallel efforts—constant, tireless—were made by the German opposition in Sweden, Switzerland, and Spain.[963] But the Western Allies were adamant; they refused to divulge the least detail hidden within the Unconditional Surrender formula.[964] And by their refusal they paralyzed not only the opposition groups but gave Goebbels and the Russians an undreamed-of propaganda advantage. The National Socialists were forced to fight to the bitter end in order to prolong their lives while the Soviets were assured by the West that half of defeated Germany would be theirs for the taking.[965]

Nor would the British have pursued a very different policy had they defied Washington in the matter. Churchill in the House of Commons vilified and ridiculed the conspirators.[966] Anthony Eden was hardly better; he was as adamant in rejecting the advances of the conspirators (high-level officers, labor leaders, professors, administrators, writers) as were his American counterparts—men deeply influenced by resolute traitors who valued a leftist victory far above peace or their country's welfare. Thousands of Americans were sacrificed through a mixture of vanity, treason, and stupidity, in order to pave the way for another totalitarian power to threaten another war. These young men were expendable; they were plowed under by ideological idiocies.

When on July 20, 1944, the desperate German resistance finally attempted to assassinate Hitler, the American public was fed further moral nonsense. What wisdom issued from the *New York Times*? Three weeks later, with adequate information available, an editorial appeared: "The underworld mentality and methods which the Nazis brought from their gutters and enthroned on the highest levels of German life, have begun to pervade the officers' corps as well." And the *New York Herald Tribune* wrote, August 9, "Americans as a whole will not feel sorry that the bomb spared Hitler for the liquidation of his generals. They hold no briefs for aristocrats as such, especially those given to the goosestep. . . . Let the generals kill the corporal, or vice versa, preferably both." The ensuing massacre in which not only "generals" but "goose-stepping aristocrats" were killed—Moltke! Goerdeler! Leber! Bonhoeffer! Delp! Stauffenberg!—deprived Germany of moral and intellectual luminaries from whose loss it has yet to recover.[967]

The man in the street in the United States and Britain was not aware of the possibility of an earlier peace because those he had elected to office had failed, nay, had refused to act on pertinent information out of stupidy, vanity, ideological prejudice, and subservience to the USSR.

In this connection, the question intrudes: was the West really ignorant of the extermination camps, given its elaborate system of espionage all over Nazi-occupied Europe? The Germans in their overwhelming majority, though fairly well acquainted with the horrors of the concentration camps, knew nothing of the swift mass murders. In 1947, I conducted private investigations, interviewing church leaders, and so on, and can attest to this.[968] Léon Blum, a long-time prisoner in Buchenwald, was ignorant of the camp's tortures and murders until it was bombed by the Allies, which allowed him contact with men from other sectors—and he finally realized the terrible truth.[969] For many years the Gerstein Report[970] was the only coherent eyewitness testimony of the horrors of the extermination camps in the East. Nor had the Vatican any concrete information.[971] But the Allies? By early 1943, American Jewry had conclusive reports about the extermination camps.[972] Were Washington and London unaware of this? [973] Indications point otherwise. The Western Allies, moreover, had air superiority by late 1942; they could have threatened Hitler with specific retaliatory measures; they could have enlightened the German people—but nothing of the sort was done. Stubbornly, inexorably, the war—the horror—was prolonged under the rubric of Unconditional Surrender. And the trump cards all fell into the hands of the Soviets.

The confusion in the United States was vast, and the circulating legends numerous. People clung desperately, and vainly, to the belief that in the Allied camp "at least Churchill knew better." In Yugoslavia, for instance, Churchill, not Roosevelt, was responsible for the switch from Draža Mihajlović to Tito.[974] Few people realized that Mihajlović's *Četnici* were all Serbs and that anti-Nazi Croats, historic enemies of the Serbs (who incidentally opposed the *Ustaša*) had therefore no choice but to join the *Partizani*. This they did without qualms, not least because the BBC broadcast that Tito's outfit was "really democratic." (Mihajlović had murdered Croats on a large scale, and the *Ustaši* had murdered Serbs on an equally large scale—the dragon seeds of 1918-19 producing its evil harvest[975]—and now the *Partizani* were murdering everyone in every direction.)

A government of rank amateurs could hardly cope with an immensely complex situation that required at its helm men of moral[976] and intellectual qualities such as any form of government rarely, but democracies almost never, supplies. The answer to the particular alternative— Mihajlović or Tito—was clear: Mihajlović represented the lesser evil. The cause of the entire problem was equally clear: Yugoslavia should never have been created. That it had been was due largely to the efforts of the 1914– 18 batch of emigrés, whose ranks were swollen during World War II. And, as pointed out earlier, the majority of these belonged to the leftist camp and were soon intimately tied to the American Left. More often than not, these men had previously helped undermine the fabric of traditional Christian Europe, thereby creating the frightful void that communism, socialism, and later national socialism would fill. "Deserted altars are inhabited by demons" (Ernst Jünger).

Jews and their spouses, of course, often had no choice but to emigrate; to remain meant certain death. And in 1933, the same was generally true of those who held important positions—it all but automatically put them on the list of the brown headhunters. But it can be stated with equal confidence that Marxists and those of the left-center were mobile people, a rootless element that made its way to the American fleshpots and from safety's shore wrote "courageous" anti-Nazi pamphlets and novels.[977] The valiant stayed on.[978] Hermann Borchardt, a conservative Christian writer of Jewish extraction, beaten to a pulp in a brown concentration camp, was invited to lecture by a group of moderate leftists, Marxists, and progressives in New York City. Eyeing his audience he started his speech with the remark: "Seeing you, gentlemen, sitting here, the grave diggers of Germany, I regret that Hitler permitted you to escape. . . ." He did not hear the indignant outcries; the beatings at Oranienburg had deprived him of his hearing. Indeed, truth alone offends.

America's leftists had been strongly reinforced by these newcomers, the *émigraille*, the more extreme of whom fostered the cause of the Soviet Union. Such an attitude was criminal. It was arrant treason, whatever the government's attitude. And when the treachery became apparent and the culprits were at risk, great excitement broke loose among the leftists, native and foreign born. These supporters of an alien totalitarian government of a sudden piously invoked the sacred principles of classic liberal tolerance.

Toward the end of the war, leftist follies proliferated. Secretary Cordell Hull, who went to Moscow to proclaim a resolution in favor of Austrian independence, was neatly tricked into including a declaration of Austrian war guilt. The formula was appalling: "Austria was reminded, however, that she had a responsibility which she could not evade for participation in the war on the side of Hitlerite Germany, and that in the final settlement account would inevitably be taken of her own contribution to liberation."[979] Anthony Eden apparently sponsored the declaration, and Molotov undoubtedly added the cited injunction, for it gave the Soviets "legal title" to remain in Austria and plunder at will.[980] Yet neither Molotov nor Hull seemed to realize how adversely the clever snare affected the Austrian resistance. And, too, although there were no doubt many Nazis in Austria, there were not a few in Norway, in the Netherlands, and in Belgium, as well as some eager collaborators in France.[981] But to say that these ravaged countries willingly helped the German war effort was a gross and unjust exaggeration. The Soviets knew only too well how to take advantage of the situation, and the two innocents from the West walked straight into the web.[982]

As did an American delegate in Potsdam when the Soviets demanded the "German assets" from their occupied zone in Austria.[983] This had been rejected by the Americans, partly because the Soviets demanded German real estate—oil fields, barracks, training fields. The debate over German assets in the satellite countries lasted until the small hours of the morning. By the time the agreement was finally put in writing, Mr. E. W. Pauley, head of the delegation, could hardly keep his eyes open. At this point, enumerating the countries to which the treaty would apply, the Russians surreptitiously inserted Austria. When he signed, Pauley was too exhausted to note the sleight of hand. In later years, the thirty-eighth parallel in Korea was accepted as a demarcation line in a similar state of naiveté, torpor, and confusion.

The meeting at Potsdam was a worthy culmination of its predecessors in Teheran and Yalta. Only Stalin, the Georgian highwayman, remained of the original Big Three. Roosevelt had died, replaced by Harry Truman, a man with no college education but ample political training from Tom Pendergast[984] and his associates in Kansas City, Missouri. Churchill had been voted out of power, and his successor, Clement Atlee, was a man who had greeted Spanish Loyalists with the clenched fist.

The outcome of the meeting was quite unsurprising. Most of the evils had already been agreed upon in the previous conferences. One of these, the Oder-Neisse Line, which artificially attached Poland to the Soviet Union, was surely the worst and largest wound in the fabric of Europe. The brilliant idea of moving the entire Polish nation westward (leaving Warsaw a bare 115 miles from the Soviet border) was originated by Churchilll, who even boasted of it in his memoirs.[985] Non-Britishers did not matter to Mr. Churchill, who sacrificed human beings—their lives, their welfare, their liberty—with the same elegant disdain as his colleague in the White House.

Lwów? What did Lwów mean to him? A city whose name was difficult to pronounce, inhabited by unknown East Europeans—Poles, Jews, Ukrainians, not of the Nordic race: "queer devils," to use Lloyd George's expression. Why not give it to Stalin, the "great father of his country"? Mr. Churchill, in his own words, was "not prepared to make a great squawk about Lwów."[986] And when the Polish Premier Mikolajczyk refused to sign away half his country, Churchill menaced him with its total annihilation.[987] The man who had said, "there are no lengths of violence to which we will not go,"[988] had become a terror to his allies. The Anglo-Polish Treaty of Mutual Assistance, concluded on August 25, 1939, which persuaded the Poles to fight and not "play dead" like the clever Czechs, contained eight articles: six were publicly broken by Britain.

When the three men sat down in Potsdam, the fate of Poland had already been sealed, yet further acts of folly were in the offing. One consisted in soliciting Stalin's aid in the war against Japan, enabling "Uncle Joe" to capture the entire Japanese industry in Manchuria, acquire further territories (Sakhalin, Kurile Islands), occupy North Korea and, later, help indirectly to communize China. This invitation to disaster remains a great puzzle to historians. Just prior to the meeting the first atomic bomb had been successfully exploded at White Sands, New Mexico, yet Stalin was nevertheless asked to aid the Western Allies. (Of course, men like General Henry Arnold of the AAF made no distinction between Stalin's and Roosevelt's ideologies—a delightful reflection on the New Deal. Indeed, he believed it a mistake to think of Stalin as a Communist.)[989] In asking the grizzled tyrant to join against an already doomed Japan, the Western Allies made a grave error—with tragic results for the United States.

Excuses are frequently offered for this piece of maddening stupidity, among them the uncertainty that the atomic bomb could actually be "delivered"—dropped and exploded on contact. But this flimsy reasoning was spurious, because the Japanese had already made two peace efforts, one in April 1945 through the Vatican and the other in July via Moscow. In response they received the same appalling Unconditional Surrender formula. Truman's letters reveal that he unaccountably prided himself on having persuaded Stalin in Potsdam to attack Japan. Not inconceivably, leftist circles in Washington had worked successfully to continue the murderous and costly war. After all, men such as Owen Lattimore had protested in 1941 against any *modus vivendi* with Japan.[990] Apparently, only Japan's total defeat would do. (Japan has such as Joseph C. Grew, former ambassador to Tokyo, to thank for not having been transformed into a "democratic republic" like Bulgaria and Hungary.)

The dropping of the bomb on a populated center was another totally superfluous crime. Even if callous arguments for the annihilation of Hiroshima could be made, there was no necessity for the slaughter in Nagasaki, cradle of Japanese Christianity. Within a split second the bomb wiped out one-eighth of Japan's Catholic Christians. Here the argument resurfaces—Truman wanted to impress the Soviets, just as Churchill had with Dresden.[991] Yet how could any butcher impress the arch-butcher from the Caucasus? Not even the late Adolf Hitler had succeeded.

War's end was conditioned by the preliminary arrangements and agreements—including military moves—concluded at Teheran and Yalta.[992] If Vienna could not have been occupied by the Western Allies in the last stages of the war, at least it ought not to have been savagely bombed on the anniversary of the *Anschluss*—an act of revenge that facilitated the Russian conquest.[993] And surely neither Prague nor Berlin need have been left to the Red Army. These cities were virtually given to the Soviets, who, only four years earlier, had been staunch Nazi collaborators. The Americans and British came to a halt at the Elbe[994] and later even surrendered Thuringia to the Soviets.

Berlin—as well as Prague—could easily have fallen to the Americans.[995] Under General Patton, they had advanced as far as Pilsen when ordered back.[996] In accord with leftist wishes, all important sites in Eastern and Central Europe were handed over to the Soviets leaving the West a mere toehold on the Continent. The craziest arrangements, and there were a multitude, involved Berlin and Vienna. The Western powers were to control certain sectors of those cities, but no stipulations were made regarding access to them.[997] Roosevelt is said to have been opposed to discussing details in his belief that only a complete show of confidence would soften the Soviets and create an atmosphere of "fellowship" and "goodwill." Soon, inevitably, the Americans were "undeceived," and an airlift to Berlin was organized at great cost in money and lives.

The worst stipulations of the Potsdam meeting concerned the mass transfer of Germans from east of the Oder-Neisse Line,[998] from Poland, Czechoslovakia, Rumania, Hungary, and Yugoslavia, into Germany. No fewer than 13 to 14 million people were dislocated amid heartbreak and hardship, creating demands, tensions, and hatreds from which even a de-Sovietized Europe could hardly recover. These brutal transfers, accompanied by atrocities and spoliations, continued throughout the winter of 1945-46 and into 1947. Poles from Eastern Poland were dumped into East Germany in a process whereby people from underpopulated areas were "massaged" into overpopulated centers—the height of perversity. (The Poles, moreover, have so far received no moral title over East Germany.)[999] On the trek from east to west, millions of people perished, and vast tracts of land remained fallow. [1000]

The Western Allies then pondered what to do with their part of Germany. Ironically, the Western army leaders, discussing the available measures should they meet with any resistance or sabotage, decided to take hostages and shoot them—perhaps the only "reasonable" alternative. But also precisely the "crime" for which the Germans had been pilloried when in a like predicament. [1001]

In respect of West Germany's political order and cultural institutions, a memorandum written by Professor Wilhelm Röpke, an outstanding German neoliberal, spoke of the need to restore the monarchy (an idea, incidentally, backed by practically all the heroes of the Twentieth of July). No sane person with a sense of history considered reviving parliamentary democracy, obsolete by 1919 and tragically terminated in 1933. But the American Left agitated for a constitutional arrangement that would give its forces room to flourish. Had not Engels designated a democratic republic as the form of government most conducive to the victory of Marxism?[1002] The Soviet Union had full reason to establish a democracy wherein *any* party could develop freely, gain victories—and take over the government. [1003]

The leftist establishment had its way in Germany. In many parts of the country, in Bavaria, for instance, it placed Social Democratic (i.e., Socialist) parties over a reluctant population. The civilian occupation authorities stubbornly held that clerics were reactionary, "fascist," but that Marxists were "progressive." Dorothy Thompson had announced that what Germans needed was not less, but "more socialism" (though not, presumably, "national socialism"). [1004] And now the Germans received just that, socialism, and at the expense of American capitalism, which was duly milked to spread it throughout Europe. Simultaneously, a special bias against the German nobility, many of whom had valorously opposed Hitler, was apparent. Here, once again, folklore and leftism combined against American interests. [1005] The famous *Fragebogen*—a questionnaire issued by the American authorities—had to be filled out by all Germans who wanted to do anything other than work in a factory or in the fields; and it contained questions which revealed a leftist bias, the sure little hand of Marx. [1006]

For a time the American leftists in the military occupation administration worked smoothly with their British counterparts, directed by the Labour government in London. It too was determined to create a leftist Germany—really, a "national socialist" Germany minus racism—under the rather demagogic Social Democrat Kurt Schumacher. An early victim of this combine was Dr. Konrad Adenauer. Immediately after liberation, Dr. Adenauer had become Lord Mayor (*Oberbürgermeister*) of Cologne. But one fine day he was ejected from office by the British under the (written) pretext "that he lacked the qualifications to run a city as large as Cologne." *Der Alte* kept this egregious piece of nonsense as his most cherished souvenir [1007] even as he gained national and international renown.

"Reeducation" also ran into a few snares. Luckily the leftist plans never came to fruition but what they portended can be gleaned from the "Zook Report," partly published in serial form by the *New York Times* (October 16, 1946). Dr. George F. Zook, head of a mission of nine men and women (among them a Catholic priest) sent to Germany by the Departments of War and State, declared that the goal of democracy was "democratic man." The commission found "discipline in the family" among the main German ills. "The survival of democracy would warrant an invasion of the German home," the report suggested. It spoke of the "stern German parental authority" that produced Freudian ambivalence in children—a clash of tenderness and hostility—undermining individual self-reliance and self-respect; of women confined to cooking, children, and churchgoing, and thus (somehow) converting "worthy enough functions into antidemocratic sterilities." The report went on to warn that to "shun the majority rule principle was to play into the hands of a Hitlerian 'superman.'" Since, moreover, 90 percent of Germans went to vocational schools, "this separation of children at an early age was an important factor in developing the superiority complex of the privileged class and the subservience of the trade class which had led Germany to totalitarianism and war."

An amusing light is thrown on this unamusing report by a glance at the facts: national socialism had been at core a youth movement against the older generation; the National Socialists wanted a radical revamping of the educational system to eliminate the classically educated elites; the Nazis had also tried by all available means to undermine parental authority. That is, most of the propositions of the Zook Report were clones of "Nazi" ideas. In retrospect, nazism was portrayed as a conservative and patriarchal movement: Hitler appeared to the signatories as some sort of *Patriarcha*, not the Big Brother that he actually represented. [1008]

The Zook Report and the other efforts to "democratize" German education were in some respects of a temporary nature. [1009] As soon as West Germany recovered a modicum of sovereignty, most of the various leftist experiments were dropped. But a "reinfection" took place in the mid-1960s when the New Left, the student revolt, and the hippie culture invaded Germany. The disease emanated from the Free University of West Berlin and the University of Frankfurt, amply abetted by segments of the German press and a number of intellectuals with an American background. Little wonder, for in the "Fifth Estate" the American occupation authorities found a rich field in which to sow leftist dogma. [1010] After 1945, the occupying powers favored the Left when issuing licenses for publications. To this day, the conservative forces have not caught up in the journalistic world. Ironically, the Left in Europe soon turned against its patron in wild anti-American attacks.

The calamities enacted in the years immediately following the end of the war are too numerous to detail. The most egregious, of course, were the Nuremberg Trials, which, among other failings, were badly mishandled. The notion of "legal precedent" is an Anglo-Saxon concept and fraught with danger. [1011] Even the American generals were horrified by the trials (perhaps contemplating World War III); worse perhaps, was the tragicomic picture—the assassins of Katyn sitting in judgment over the assassins of Auschwitz. Particular accusations, like the wanton attack on Norway, an accusation *per se* justified, made no sense considering that Churchill admittedly prepared an attack on Norway himself. [1012] But most importantly, the trials ought to have been held by the Germans—the Nazis ought to have been tried by German courts as *common criminals* according to the Code of Penal Law. [1013] Ignoring the principle of *Nullum crimen sine lege* was as destructive of legal purity as the lack of impartiality of the judges. The unreality of the proceedings is exquisitely captured by the memory of the Soviets condemning the German attack against Poland, an attack in which they themselves had participated.

Even worse were the minor Nuremberg Trials, thoroughly dominated by Marxist principles. A desperate effort was made to implicate German industry and high finance in Hitler's iniquities. [1014] The most astounding was the so-called Krupp trial in which Alfried Krupp von Bohlen und Halbach[1015] was placed on the bench of the accused in place of his gravely ill father. [1016] Marxism, once again financed by American taxpayers' money, was once again drinking deep in orgiastic injustice.

In the writ of accusation against Alfried Krupp von Bohlen and his ten codefendants and coworkers are the words: "The origin, the development, and the background of the crimes committed by the defendants, and the criminal plans in which they participated, can be traced back to 100 years of German militarism and 133 years—four generations—of the manufacture of arms."[1017] Apart from the fact that, on the average, arms were only one-fifth the total output of the Krupp works, the sentence, as well as other passages from the accusation, reflects the Marxian dialect. Significantly too, the director of the chief trial team was Mr. H. Russell Thayer, former assistant secretary of the North American Committee to Aid Spanish Democracy during the Spanish Civil War. At heart, the purpose of the trial was to prove in the best Leninist fashion that "big business" (especially in the form of "monopoly capitalism") abets wars. [1018] The few who were condemned were later released, and the confiscated goods returned. The trial was a farce. (On the other side of the world, the Yamashita Trial, another travesty of justice, took place. [1019] When Yamashita's lawyer, Frank A. Reel, [1020] published a book about his tragically innocent client, the director of the publishing company, the Chicago University Press, lost his position.)

Leftist forces sowed unrest almost everywhere in the world. Working through the occupation authorities (where the saner military were unable to interfere), they conducted a witch-hunt against monarchists in Austria (thus continuing brown policies). They (mainly the British Labour government) also prevented the return of the South Tyrol to Austria. Self-determination was desirable only, it seemed, if it benefited leftist causes. And it was evident that the South Tyrolians, mostly conservative agrarians, once returned to Austria, would have prevented a full socialist victory. [1021] The damage done by the *dinamitardi*, the tortures committed by the *carabinieri*, the wall of hatred between Austrians and Italians—the only "bleeding border" left in Free Europe—is primarily the work of Mr. Wilson, but also of Mr. Bevin[1022]—and of the Soviets who supported Mr. Bevin, and thus incidentally ratified the Hitler-Mussolini Agreement of

1939 pertaining to the iniquitous Brenner Border. It seems that Nazi decisions, Nazi thought, Nazi mentality, and Nazi institutions are in many ways imperishable. [1023]

True, other people, other groups, fared far worse than the Austrians, but the Austrian experience gives a fair picture of the postwar situation. The 100,000 cases of rape perpetrated by the Red Army in Eastern Austria were perhaps only a practical demonstration of "sexual democracy." [1024] (Recall Mr. Henry Wallace's charming formula: "We have political democracy, they have economic democracy.") Many Austrians were deported, some returned, but others disappeared forever. And it was on Austrian soil, in the East Tyrol, that large numbers of Russians and Cossacks who had fought against communism were clubbed half dead, packed into box cars, and sent back as "unpatriotic traitors." A British major (Davis) gave his word that England did not think to surrender the Cossacks and Russians to the Soviets. When the truth leaked out, the disarmed anticommunists resisted His Majesty's soldiers, who acted in the service of Stalin. Many Russians were killed on the spot, [1025] fifteen were killed during the trip while trying to escape, six committed suicide, and seventeen managed to disappear before reaching the Russian occupation zone. Twelve generals were in the group handed over to the USSR to placate and please the communist comrade-in-arms. But even this act of prostitution did not buy their friendship.

An Austrian eyewitness has described the scenes at Lienz, worthy of Breughel's brush. (He estimates that about three hundred Cossacks hanged themselves in the Lienz woods after being surrounded by the 8th Brigade.) Men—and many women—were subdued with bayonets and clubs. S. G. Korolkov, a Russian who escaped, later painted the *Hell of Lienz*. [1026]

The *Hell of Lienz* was followed by the surrender of the *Domobranci*, the Catholic Slovene Home Guard, which had protected Slovenes against the depredations of Tito's *partizani*. Thousands upon thousands were rounded up, shipped over the Karawanken Mountains, to be mowed down in masses, their corpses used as natural fertilizer for the fields. (Never forget: Sadism is the outstanding characteristic of the entire Left.)

And while the British perpetrated these particular deeds, the Americans were not far behind. The *New York Times* reported the ghastly scenes that took place in Dachau when the Russians, who had fought against communism, were made "ready" to be "shipped" eastward. The long somber report ended with a description of the evacuation of the second Russian barracks. "The inmates. . .barricaded themselves inside and set the building afire. Then all tore off their clothing, apparently in a vain effort to frustrate the guards and, linking arms, resisted the pushing and shoving of the Americans and Poles trying to empty the place. The soldiers then tossed in tear bombs and rushed the building. Some prisoners, they discovered, were already dead, having cut their own throats, while others had used pieces of cloth to hang themselves."[1027] The impact of these perfidious actions by the United States and Britain must have shocked the inhabitants of the USSR, but hatred and suspicion of the West were precisely the feelings that the Soviets—and their faithful collaborators in the American leftist establishment—wished to engender. The Americans at Dachau (of all places!) perpetrated these horrors three-quarters of a year *after* the end of the war—in accordance with the Yalta agreements, at least half of which the Soviets had already broken. The noble age-old American tradition in regard to political refugees was dealt a near fatal blow.

Errors proliferated.[1028] Italy in 1946 was helped back to a republican form of government, the *Repùbblica Sociale Italiana*, the same type it had enjoyed under Mussolini. A plebiscite, in which the vast majority of the noncommunist vote was cast for the monarchy, gave Italy the sort of government that could be *legally* captured by the Communists. Naturally, the communist vote was totally in favor of the Republic, which then came into being.

In Greece, a referendum—itself an impossible procedure—produced a sound majority for the monarchy.[1029] The principle of monarchy cannot be subordinated to the principle of majority decisions. In its very essence it is independent of the vagaries of the voting process.

Yugoslavia, another miscreation of World War I, was restored and even enlarged. (Yugoslavia and Bulgaria were the only countries, apart from the Soviet Union, to emerge from the war with more territory.)[1030] But since the constituent nations of Yugoslavia do not wish to live in unity, they can be held together only through coercion—either the sway of one nationality over the rest, or the rule of a harsh dictatorship, or worse.

Leftist oppression and revenge were not confined to Eastern, Central, and Southern Europe. In France, French Communists fully collaborated with Germany between 1939 and 1941, and a large number of other collaborators were recruited from the ranks of those who embraced ideologies that were "national-leftist" in character. Neither Laval nor Darnand, Déat nor Doriot, was a rightist. The Germans suspended *Le Figaro*, the conservative daily, and supported the leftist paper *L'Oeuvre*. De Gaulle, who went into opposition, had once belonged to the *Action Française*. Other French rightists and conservatives fled France (Henri de Kerillis was among them). But many in the French Right stayed and did not collaborate; some of these (rightly or mistakenly) considered it their duty to protect whatever remained of France, among them Marshal Pétain, whose patriotism was as untarnished as General Weygand's. Pétain negotiated an agreement with Churchill which, in order not to irritate de Gaulle, Downing Street tried to deny, but documentary evidence confirms its existence.[1031]

After the Germans attacked the Soviet Union, the French Communists, whose real *patrie* was the USSR, went into opposition. With more practice in clandestine activities—political and military—than the other parties, they soon assumed a sort of leadership in the resistance.[1032] After the collapse of the German occupation in 1944 the Communists began to wage terror warfare against all whom they disliked, whether politically, socially, or personally. An American observer who arrived in Southern France with the army of General Patch estimated the number of people assassinated by the *résistance* in that region as around fifty thousand.[1033] French estimates speak of about 120,000 all told. Add to this those who were "legally" condemned, often by courts staffed with communist jurors. It is quite true, of course, that many *bona fide* collaborators sacrificed French citizens in order to win a breathing spell for France. But if culpable, then what about the *résistance* men who, armed with *false* information, were given over to the Nazis by the Allies?[1034] Were they expendable? And were the Allied air massacres, butchering not only Germans,[1035] but Frenchmen, Dutch, Belgians, Serbs, and foreign laborers,[1036] morally justified?[1037] Much of de Gaulle's *ressentiment*[1038] can be explained by the gratuitous massacre of Frenchmen and women who,[1039] it seems, were at times wantonly killed by Allied ground forces.[1040]

Leftist control of foreign policy was apparent everywhere. UNRRA, an American organization designed to aid "displaced" persons, repeatedly demonstrated procommunist proclivities. The mayor of New York, Fiorello La Guardia, who directed its activities, was strongly inclined to the left. In a Yugoslav camp in Egypt he berated the inmates for not returning to their homeland.[1041] The problem of "displaced persons," those desperate refugees,[1042] was quite baffling to moderate leftists. The "Fascists" had been defeated. Whom, then, did they flee? Why, they fretted, did these people not return to their homes?[1043]

*　*　*

And now the Left—from the moderate groups to the Communists—turned their eyes toward Spain. There a fascist dictatorship still waited to be liquidated. It was a welcome "problem," a diversion of public interest from the annexationist activities of the Soviets. A little background sets the scene.

When the Allied troops landed in North Africa in November 1942, President Roosevelt wrote a letter to General Franco addressing him as "my dear friend." A "distinguished Roman Catholic layman," Professor Carlton J. H. Hayes, acted as American ambassador to Madrid and tried (successfully) to keep Spain out of the war. This was not too difficult because when Franco and Hitler first met, an immediate and mutual antipathy was born.[1044] Few recall that Spain made extraordinary efforts to protect the Jews, although predominantly those of Sephardic origin.[1045]

More than two hundred years after the Jews had been collectively expelled from Britain (1290), the Spaniards presented their Jews and Moslems with an alternative—either embrace Christianity or leave the country.[1046] Many of them left (1492), others became sincere Christians, still others only pretended to change their faith. The Jewish refugess went in part to Morocco and Algiers, in part to Turkey, while a few settled in the Netherlands, Italy, and South America. This harsh edict—a purely religious rather than racist measure—effected a great loss to Spain. In the nineteenth century a trickle of Jews returned. In 1924,[1047] under the joint rule of King Alfonso XIII, who was known for his friendly feeling toward them, and General Miguel Primo de Rivera, the dictatorial prime minister and father of José-Antonio, cofounder of the Falange, a law was issued inviting the descendants of the expelled Sephardic (i.e., Spanish) Jews[1048] to return to Spain with immediate citizenship. A few responded. When the Republic was declared, the Jews in Spain numbered over one thousand; when the civil war broke out, the Spanish Jews, most notably those living in northern Morocco, a Spanish protectorate, sided with the Right.

And when in World War II a multitude of Jews fled through Spain to the West, *not one* was surrendered to the Germans.[1049] Spain did more: its consulates and embassies throughout Europe began to issue passports to Jews of Spanish descent on the basis of the 1924 law. An estimated forty to sixty thousand passports were granted, which accords to "Franco Spain," after the Vatican, title as *the* greatest protector of Jews during the last war. The Spanish government, moreover, through economic pressure, succeeded in having the French Jews of Sephardic origin exempted from wearing the Star of David; and the Spanish consular agents sealed their apartments and houses. And even more: the Spanish government forced the Nazis to disgorge Jewish inmates from their concentration camps; whole trainloads of them were welcomed in Spain.

Mr. Maurice L. Perlzweig, in a resolution adopted at the Jewish Congress in Atlantic City (November 1944), thanked the Spanish ambassador in Washington for his government's aid and protection of Jews. "The Jews are a race of long memory; they will not easily forget the chance given to thousands of their brothers to save their lives."[1050] (Similar messages were sent to the Swiss government, the King of Sweden, and Pope Pius XII—none noted as leftist.)[1051]

But when the Allies were safely entrenched throughout Western Europe, still unaware of the threat from the East, Franco ceased being "my dear friend." Stalin, who butchered more Jews than even Franco could have saved, suggested to the Right Honourable Clement Attlee of clenched fist memory and to President Harry Truman that they blockade Spain and thus force Spaniards to rise and overthrow their "fascist" government. The result was years of misery and semistarvation for Spaniards who, whatever their private opinion of Franco, rallied to him in shared national indignation and collective pride. Luckily, the Potsdam plan miscarried, blessedly proving that, at least sometimes, God takes care of children, drunkards, fools, and U.S. foreign policy.[1052]

Meanwhile, Japan and Germany, for better or worse, played important parts in maintaining the equilibrium of Eurasia, although the United States had to fill the military void. (Happily, Japan preserved the office of emperor.)[1053] "Moderate leftist" policy was even less successful on the Asian mainland. The "agrarian reformers" of China, once in power, were found to roar like tigers; the rebellion against the colonial French in Indochina was deeply hostile to the United States and resulted in another American liability and responsibility; the untoward British-American intervention that favored Sukarno, a collaborator of the Japanese, was aimed against the Dutch, their wartime ally—these and other cases revealed the disarray of leftist policy. The leftist mind is driven by two conflicting characteristics—an impractical utopian idealism and a lack of a sense of honor. As a rule, idealism and honor are joined. Don Quixote was not practical, but he was a man of honor: Sancho Panza scoffed at honor, but he was a realist. The typical leftist is a dreamer without honor, and that is a troubling combination.

In this respect, the advice of Franklin Delano Roosevelt to Pius XII inevitably comes to mind. In various letters, the President tried to convince the Pope that he ought to face facts and realize that his picture of the Soviet Union was obsolete, no longer valid; the USSR was, under Stalin, a demonstrably liberal democracy. If nothing else, this was an interesting change from Woodrow Wilson's reply to Benedict XV's peace effort, in which he reminded the Pope that the war was a moral issue which practical considerations could never eliminate. Granted, the Vatican is not an international "power";[1054] sound Christian reasoning nevertheless has perennial value and is blessed with a profound knowledge of man in all his glory and misery, attributes which leftist emotionalism and ratiocination can never replace.

More blunders were made in the succeeding years; the failure of nerve during the Hungarian Revolution; the bungling involved in the Suez crisis; the disaster at the Bay of Pigs. . .Perhaps the worst was the horrible error perpetrated in Vietnam in the early days of that tragic war. In 1963, leftist propaganda deceitfully portrayed Ngo Dinh Diem as a "Roman Catholic dictator" oppressing benign Buddhist monks.[1055] It resulted in wild speculation concerning a possible American-supported Buddhist crusade against communism (as well imagine an American army led by Quakers, devout Mennonites, and conscientious objectors).[1056]

Needless to say, bungling American leftists have their counterparts in other parts of the world. French, Spanish, Italian, German, Austrian, and British "moderate leftists" are no less silly and superficial; but their influence, their historic importance is at present a great deal less weighty than that of their American *confrères*, who have a strong voice in a nation that drives the fate of the world. Spanish students are still filled with the most incredible nineteenth-century nonsense; sophisticated Frenchmen can relate how Texas oil millionaires murdered President Kennedy; and Mexican government officials will state publicly that the Church favors illiteracy to prevent the people from reading *Das Kapital*. The inanities uttered by Greek intellectuals, soft-headed German *literati*, and sixth-rate English university professors are just as bad, but they matter less. As for the masses; despite their inherent common sense, they only throw back what has been fed them by the information manufacturers or opinion-makers. Common sense is valuable, but without knowledge it lacks precision, just as knowledge is worthless without common sense.

Naturally, recent events have not all been black. South Korea, with American aid, resisted and is flourishing. In Taiwan an *intelligent* agrarian reform has taken place and the island is an Asian economic showcase.[1057] The Marshall Plan in Free Europe succeeded; the more scope given private initiative, the greater the success.[1058]

But the leftists, propelled by malicious impulses, have left their imprint on a troubled world. The negative, the blinding effects of leftism, even in its moderate form, derive mainly from envy and jealousy, the dynamic forces of the Left. This is the driving element that links the whole sequence of revolutions from 1789 to 1917 and 1933. Envy and jealousy can dominate not only internal politics but, even more profoundly, foreign policy. These vices support the sadistic drives that strongly sway international relations in a century that lays claim to progress and democracy. Today, the ultimate in foreign policy is total war, interrupted by methods abjured in an earlier age—the fomentation of revolutions and rebellions in foreign countries. When Sir Roger Casement in World War I asked the German Ministry of Foreign Affairs, the *Aussenamt*, to help Ireland win freedom from British rule, his plea was rejected on the grounds that it entailed meddling in internal British affairs. It was the German *army* that cooperated first with Casement and later in shipping the communist exiles back to Russia; it was a non-Junker, Erich Ludendorff, who tried to undermine the morale, discipline, and loyalty of the Russian army with revolutionary propaganda, imitating the Allies whose victory was helped by such tactics (insisted upon by the young Captain de Gaulle). [1059]

The Soviets badly needed the restoration of democracy in 1945. The following information comes from a personal source.

A prominent American general met with a Soviet leader after the war. The story follows:

> Circumstances had brought the two together on a number of occasions and the American had noticed an attitude of considerable friendliness on the part of the Russian. One day he commented on his attitude.
>
> The Soviet leader made no reply for the moment, then he drew his chair closer to the table and from a matchbox he took four matches which he placed methodically on the table, each match about an inch from the next and parallel to it. Then he said, "Now, this first match is what you call 'Capitalism'; the second is what you call 'Democracy'; the third is what you call 'Socialism'; and the fourth is what you call 'Communism.' "
>
> He paused a moment, and then, looking up at the American, said, "Now, I like your country because it is moving straight down the line from capitalism through the others to communism." [1060]

The distinguished American, according to our information, was none other than General Douglas MacArthur.

Today, world conflicts take place on several levels. The time of the old-fashioned cabinet wars is over, war has become total, partly because technology has produced staggering means of destruction, partly because of the withering away of religion, enabling totalitarian ideologies, capable of mobilizing the masses and fanaticizing pragmatists, to fill the void. Hot wars destroy bodies, cold wars destroy immortal souls. Today, more than ever, the words of Rivarol, [1061] one of the most brilliant spirits of old France, ring loud: "Politics is like the Sphinx: It devours all those who cannot solve its riddles."

CHAPTER 18

Anticolonialism

A child hates the person who
gives him everything he wants.

—AFRICAN PROVERB

Anticolonialism (or "anti-imperialism," as the Soviets prefer to call it) is one of the most harmful foreign policy snares of the century, and the United States has fallen headlong into the trap. Naturally, its foremost proponents were and are leftists, but anticolonialism has been adopted by the average American; in the United States, it takes something of an *esprit fort*, an emancipated spirit, to resist this particular mischief.

Once in Irkutsk, when asked what I thought about Eastern Siberia, I horrified my audience (by no means all convinced Communists) by replying that it was a good example of the dynamics of Russian colonialism. One of them objected to the term "colonialism": I should have called it *osvoyeniye*, which means "incorporation" (or the German *Landnahme*). I opened my notebook and with a straight face took down this invaluable piece of information—whereupon laughter broke out. Yet some among the young realized for the first time that their country was a colonial power.

I witnessed something similar in America when I began a lecture with the remark that I, native of a nation that had never had colonies, was ad-

dressing citizens of a colonial power. It was immediately pointed out to me
that the United States had never at any time possessed colonies, past or
present. By mentioning the Philippine Islands, Guam, Micronesia, and
Western Samoa, I caused a minor sensation. The fact had been known all
along, but its realization had been blocked.

There is, of course, nothing evil and nothing extraordinary about colonialism. It stems from a historic law according to which nature—as also
political geography—does not tolerate a vacuum. In the case of a geographic entity where no effective resistance is expected, other powers, other
nations, other tribes will occupy, dominate, and administer the area.
History would be unimaginable had it been bereft of constant shaping by
the forces of colonialism. Without Greek colonialism Magna Graecia would
not have existed, Stagira would not have existed (in a way, Aristotle would
not have existed); neither Paestum nor Pergamum, Ephesus nor Agrigent
would delight us with their ruins. Without Phoenician colonialism, there
would have been no Carthage—and no St. Augustine. Roman colonialism
(or "imperialism") is responsible for the French language, for Racine and
Molière, for Cervantes, Lope de Vega, and Calderón. Without Bavarian
colonialism, where would the Austrian people be? And on and on. (There
is, of course, good colonialism and bad colonialism, just as there is good
rule, a government conscious of the common good, and bad rule, a government exercised solely for the profit of the rulers.)

American anticolonialism has twin roots: (1) the insistence on self-rule
(democracy), and (2) a misinterpretation and illegitimate application of the
rationale for American independence. The mirage of self-rule (dealt with
elsewhere) admits at best to a collective, but never to a personal-existential
interpretation. The only individuals to enjoy self-rule are citizens in a direct
democracy who decide all issues unanimously (purely theoretical), and
absolute rulers—monarchs, dictators, tyrants. The dream of everybody to
become his own monarch could theoretically be fulfilled by anarchists, but
democrats can term their system a pantocracy only with the help of
mystifying abstractions, psychological arguments, and axiomatic supposi-
tions that are easily exploded.

Yet frequently it is not the democratic argument, but the memory of
history classes and an uncritical absorption of Fourth of July speeches that
compel Americans to an emotional sort of anticolonialism. The result is a
fusion of leftist and "patriotic" arguments against colonialism, fanned by
the Left. Which grants, once again, the opportunity to quote Dr. Johnson:
"Patriotism is the last refuge of the scoundrel."

Two matters tend to be forgotten in the "patriotic" (i.e., historic) appeal to anticolonialism. First, the concept involves no "ism" whatever. The term "coloni*alism*" is not found in authoritative dictionaries much before 1924. The impulse to colonize is not traceable to a systematic ideology, to a *Weltanschauung*, a philosophy, political or otherwise. And second, a great variety of situations is covered by the term "colony." One such, generally ignored, concerns the colonies that were totally without the human element before the arrival of the white man, such as a number of islands in the Indian Ocean. Is it iniquitous for such settlements to be governed by the motherland? When does their God-given right of secession and independence begin? When are they "ripe" for autonomy? With the landing of the first settler? All answers will necessarily be arbitrary.

In India, for instance, Amritsar is the sacred city that has since 1919 stood as the symbol of brutal colonial oppression. "Amritsar!" rang the battle cry. In 1919 British-led Indian troops fired at violent demonstrators and killed a few hundred; subsequently, the commander, General R. Dyer, underwent a thorough governmental investigation in London. But since 1985, Amritsar has come to mean something else: it commemorates the attack of Indira Gandhi's troops on the Sikhs, killing about one thousand and (what the British would never have dared) storming and desecrating the famous Golden Temple, a holy place for the Sikh community. The world remained virtually mute—colonialism had not been involved.

Yet another misconception concerning colonialism is the myth—accepted not only by American leftists—according to which wicked Europeans along with their missionaries brutally invaded foreign lands (which they often did) in order to destroy the idyllic life of harmless natives, a happy life of guiltless innocence, without disease, without fear. Or: these wicked settlers (with machine-guns) defeated and enslaved vastly superior civilizations (without machine-guns), civilizations of greater spirituality, intellectuality, profundity, artistry, and balance. Blatant nonsense. Anyone with a real knowledge of the world, who has not been seduced by elegiac dreams of faraway tribes and nations, realizes that the Dayaks, nay even the Japanese or the Aztecs, if they had been technically able, would have colonized Europe and established an iron rule of lasting tyranny.

Admittedly, European civilization exported hitherto unknown diseases and vices to a few islands. Yet European resourcefulness finally triumphed not only over the exported diseases but over the far more terrible local ones. The accusation that narrow-minded missionaries, in giving these "children of nature" a sense of sin, caused them mental anguish is merely silly. Most of these natural religions were based on choking fears—fear of spirits, fear of witchcraft, [1062] fear of sorcerers, fear of gods. Take one case, common in the highlands of New Guinea (Papua). There every mother must give birth to her first child in the jungle (an unwritten law that also pertains in large parts of Central Africa). She then is enjoined to take the child firmly by its feet and bash out its brains against a stone. Several sows with litters are driven to the spot, and the first sow to munch up the little corpse becomes the woman's comother. From the sow's litter the woman is made to choose a piglet to adopt and feed with her milk. Her attitude toward the piglet will determine her moral standing in the community, will demonstrate her worth as a mother. And this is by no means the most unappetizing performance in that area of the world: sucking decomposed corpses surely rivals in horror. [1063]

Now, the objection will occur that this is a "low" religion, a mere savage superstition whose like cannot be found in the more exalted religions of the East. Yet I recall a talk I had with a highly educated Hindu in Agra outside the Imperial Hotel. He was a civil engineer, with some English training. We discussed the British Raj, and he admitted that it had benefited India in many ways. But, he added, the provincialism and narrowness of the British had been harmful in many other ways, such as the prohibition of *suttee*, the burning of widows. "If a woman really loves her husband she will want to immolate herself. Besides, if she throws herself on the funeral pyre, she will become unconscious in five or ten minutes, suffocated by the fumes if not actually killed. And this gives her the chance of being reunited with her husband in another incarnation."

"You mean to say that you approve of this? Personally? For every woman?" I inquired.

"Naturally. Take the case of my married sister. Her husband had a quarrel with his father and committed suicide by taking poison, cutting his wrists and hanging himself. Two days later my sister did the same. After all, what is the alternative? There is nothing worse than to live as a widow, especially if one is of the higher castes."

"Were there any children?"

"There were three, but what are families for? They were taken care of."

In cases like these the argument has it that such errant behavior is sanctioned by religion, that the infanticide of the Papuan mother and the self-cremation of the Indian mother are merely acts that conform with their beliefs. But in reality, the Papuan mother is endowed with the same maternal instincts as Mrs. Grey or Mrs. Green of the Anti-Colonial League in Dubuque, Iowa. She *does* endure agony bashing out the brains of her firstborn baby, and, as my Indian friend admitted, his sister *did* act from a sense of duty, probably suffering anguish the while. Societies and religious systems that exact such self-inflicted cruelties have to be judged negatively. In attempting to eliminate these aberrations, colonialism does virtuous work. [1064]

But here a word of warning. These horrors are not "racially conditioned." *Ideas*, primarily specific religious ideas, are their cause. And ideas have consequences, to borrow from the title of the late Richard Weaver's book. The question arises whether we too would not still be indulging in such practices had Christianity not intervened—whether, without the British Raj, *suttee* would today be as rare as it has become.

The destruction of widows is probably an ancient Aryan rite; witness the account of Ibn Fadlan, an Arab traveler who was in a Viking town in Russia around 920, not too many hundred years ago. He watched the funeral of a Nordic chieftain whose corpse was put on a river boat. The chief's friends raped the widow in a tent on land and again on board the boat. Afterward she was held in an iron grip so that a naked old woman called the "Angel of Death" could strangle her. Finally, the boat was set on fire and the two bodies were burned in unison.

Even Christianity was strained to overcome this pagan inheritance within itself. [1065] It was a slow process and a mark of real progress (the only kind worth mentioning). Every lapse from Christian standards brought its own retribution, an immediate relapse into barbarism. Jacob Burckhardt foresaw this when he spoke of the catastrophes to come if the level of our culture were to sink only "a hand's width. Then the pale horror of death would be over us and naked power would rule supreme." [1066]

The "speed" at which the various nations progressed in different periods of history is also worth pondering. These matters, of course, can only be judged by use of subjective measuring rods. Viewing the first 4,000 years of Western history thus, how long did it take our forebears, after the collapse of the Roman Empire, to reach a level of culture and civilization roughly commensurable with that of, say, A.D. 250 or 330? Seven hundred, eight hundred, a thousand years? A similar question might be raised in connection with the termination of European colonialism in various parts of the globe. Modern times are of course telescoped but it is evident nevertheless that the old levels cannot be reached overnight. Taking this into account, a phenomenon such as apartheid must be judged more objectively than is presently the case. [1067]

It remains that we continue to move ahead along a road of Christian development—both as a faith and as a civilization—while the newly Christianized or non-Christian nations are trailing. This is true morally, it is true intellectually, and it is true economically. From the economic viewpoint, the colonizing powers have not seen their plans mature and their expectations fulfilled. The Europeans clung to their colonies for psychological and military rather than for economic reasons—even when nations nourished great hopes of economic gain. For most colonial powers, the colonies were a constant financial drain, and their independence a real blessing. Of Germany's entire colonial empire prior to 1914, only little Togo was "in the black"; even the Belgian Congo was only profitable between 1940 and 1954. Europe's present prosperity coincides with the loss of her colonies. Now, at long last, the former colonial powers can attain the material standards of the noncolonial powers—Scandinavia and Switzerland.

The colonies can be likened to adopted children of European powers. They went through adolescence, a difficult time for children and parents alike, a period when children tend to criticize those who exercise authority over them. They are convinced they are as bright, experienced, and educated as their parents. Often, they think to run away—from school, from home. Usually, they reconsider, dimly aware that their training is not finished, that it would be wiser to swallow pride and stay on.

But what would happen if just outside the home two powerful men with fat wallets were to appear and encourage the child to make the break? "The way you are being treated by your parents is a disgrace."

The two powerful men are, of course, Uncle Ivan and Uncle Sam, both of whom can reach into their taxpayers' pockets to help the elites, the *évolués* of the colonies. Uncle Ivan's subjects have no say in the matter while Uncle Sam's have been well indoctrinated by the Left. If, to makes matters worse, Uncle Sam and Uncle Ivan were to compete for the child's affections, he might easily succumb to the lure of blackmail, playing one big man off against the other.

The foster parents, for their part, although rid of an ungrateful child, of responsibilities and expenses, are naturally hurt and take umbrage at the seducers of their adopted child. Very well, let them pay through the nose! And when the two seducers—one of whom, prompted by idealism, has acted in good faith, while the other, prompted by self-interest, has been bent on pure mischief—find their financial resources unduly strained and appeal to the former parents to help support the ungrateful child, the latter are far from moved. They remember the insults, even invective, of well-meaning Americans (as, for instance, President Roosevelt and then-Senator John F. Kennedy)[1068] and are reluctant to help the Underdeveloped Countries. When even the Italians were approached by the United States for help, the Italians replied that much of their own country, the *mezzogiorno* (Italy's Deep South), was in many ways worse off than some of the new nations beyond the seas. [1069]

The reason for this aid must be probed, for it is little understood. If these hapless peoples and tribes had in truth been brutally exploited in the past and artificially stunted in their development (as were the Poles during the German occupation), then the aid can be viewed as compensation. But this was not the case. The discontent of ex-colonials tends rather to be that they have been insufficiently Westernized. Yet they do complain of exploitation, as have many Latin Americans in respect to their postliberation period. Which leads to a dual question: To what extent were the natural resources and manpower of these nations exploited before the arrival of Europeans; and what were the living standards before and at the end of the colonial period?

Europeans and Americans achieved their own high standards after struggling bitterly for 2,500 years. They went through agonies to arrive at their present levels. The Industrial Revolution, a turmoil of suffering, was but one of the many periods of large-scale sacrifice. And all this knowledge, all this thinking and planning and endless experimentation, all these fruits— of savings, of studies, of scheming, of wars (*Polemos pater chremation!*)—were put at the disposal of strange peoples in strange lands, and, in a sense, free of charge. To learn, as we all know, is not always pleasant. Remember the Greek proverb: *Ho me dereis anthropos ou paideuetai*. There is no education without tears.

But realities in politics are often less important than myths. There is a widespread feeling, from Lima to Hanoi, from Jamaica to Zanzibar, that the wealth of Europe and the United States has accrued not only from past exploitation but also from a present servitude that sails under the name of "economic imperialism" or "neocolonialism." Rare is a man such as King Hassan II of Morocco who early in 1965 dared tell his subjects that political independence did not automatically dispense wealth, which is only the fruit of hard labor. More typical is the 1961 poster of the *Unión Republicana* seen in the streets of Buenos Aires which, in respect of the natural wealth of

Argentina and the misery of the masses, said: "We are poor because a treasonable government hands over the possession of the Argentine people as a colonial tribute to Her British Majesty."[1070] This sentiment (which I have encountered in such disparate places as Egypt, Peru, Senegal, Cambodia, Ceylon, and Santo Domingo) is based on a variety of superficial impressions and propaganda rather than on concrete data.[1071]

Humanity has existed for over a million years, but living standards now considered "compatible with human dignity" have existed only, and in but a few isolated areas of the world, for the past one thousand years or so—in Europe and North American, in a more general way, for only two hundred years. The living standards of a skilled Swiss worker today are infinitely higher than those of professional people a century ago. Louis XIV might easily have exchanged his throne for the comforts and amenities enjoyed by an overseer at Peugeot—surgery, air-conditioning, modern travel, the miracle of electronics. (Versailles was very spacious and beautiful, but in summer the stench was all but unbearable; travelling was an agony, childbirth often fatal, and death in many forms ever present.)

But recent and sporadic material progress is taken for granted. Socialists violently protest the disparate conditions of people living in the same nation; they consider it "undemocratic."[1072] And in the past two decades, a tide of protest has mounted against the differences in economic levels between nations. The wealth of some nations is becoming psychologically an "act of provocation," and leftists in many a Western country speak of a *duty, a moral obligation* on the part of the richer nations toward those less well off (just as richer individuals ought to aid poorer ones).

As a call for Christian charity, this cannot be denied. But the reasons have, unfortunately, no such transcendent virtue. At times, the generosity of the West is grounded on its desire to elbow aside the influence of the Soviet Union in the poor area.[1073] But a more important reason is the drive of American leftists to foster egalitarianism. Why should economic egalitarianism be cultivated only *within* a nation? Little thought is given to the discouragement dealt (at the individual or national level) to the personal effort that alone assures progress.

Then too, the American Left is frequently energized to pour money into these new nations simply because their self-appointed leaders belong to the leftist camp. In many such countries, the masses receive little of the development grants. Great sums disappear into the pockets of the oligarchy or fund the secret police or paramilitary formations that keep the people in check. Still more money is squandered on sumptuous buildings and other objects of no economic value for no reason other than to gain prestige for the ruling group, both within the country and among the international community. (Today a newly appointed minister or ambassador in a capital such as Washington, London, Paris, Bonn, or Tokyo must make at least *one hundred* "first visits" in order to include all the various foreign representatives, [1074] demonstrating to what extent the modern world with its alleged "progress" has become balkanized, fractured.)

For decades, billions of dollars have been pumped into the Emerging Nations. Yet, with few exceptions, their votes in the United Nations show their contempt for the hand that feeds them. Americans should derive only meager consolation from the fact that the Soviets at times also "miscalculated."

The citizenry of the USSR is furious at foreign aid expenditures, an indignation for which perfectly innocent overseas students, especially Africans, suffer. Talking to Russians and Ukrainians in 1963, I was informed that the direful state of the Soviet economy was due to the selfishness of the United States which forced the Soviet Union to feed the starving two-thirds of the world. "And now 'they' have imported black students who receive scholarships that are 50 percent higher than those given our own boys." (*Oni*, "they," is the popular term for the men in the Kremlin.) These African and Asian students have available for their studies the Patrice Lumumba Friendship University, located in an old barracks. I do not remember ever having seen them in the company of their Soviet colleagues of either sex.

But back to foreign aid. Worse still are those cases when American dollars are used as a bribe, such as to nations like Yugoslavia, a self-proclaimed leader of the "nonaligned" nations (the Third World). While accepting U.S. dollars with one hand, Yugoslavia hands them out with the other; that is, the American taxpayer helps finance Yugoslavia's foreign policy. [1075] Yet even Yugoslavia has experienced what the United States and, to a lesser extent, the Soviet Union and Red China have learned: most Emerging Nations have an extremely firm character. They are for hire, but not for sale; they can be prostitutes, but not domestic animals. This is not to deny that many men of principle in the Third World nations literally beg First Worlders not to corrupt them with handouts (above all those with strings attached), but to allow them to learn to stand on their own. [1076]

(Why are the Soviets and the Chinese more successful with smaller handouts than the United States? America is more *envied* than the two communist powers. China, moreover, is "colored." And the Soviet emissaries are less "insular"; the heroes of Dostoyevski are more "universally human" than the moralizing do-gooder types who so often represent the United States abroad.) Apart from Taiwan, where the United States has tried with admirable tenacity to correct the grievous errors committed on the Chinese mainland in 1944–48, little wisdom has been employed. In its anticolonialist policy the United States, under leftist guidance, has made mistakes similar to those of Europe. And on the same old assumption— that human beings throughout the world are "more alike than unlike." Yet the typical American (or Britisher or Canadian) is radically different from the typical Khmer or Chinese or Tamil (or even Italian or Austrian). People in given situations in given countries *do* act differently.

Although I have spent a total of seventeen years all over the United States, have read more Americana than the average American, have greater knowledge of American history and geography and have perhaps a greater affection for the real United States than many an American citizen, [1077] I am still—in my thinking, acting, and reacting—quite different from the average American, and I do not fool myself that it could be otherwise. In fact, when I wrote a novel with an American background some years ago, [1078] I did not dare use as my hero a real American; I chose an immigrant. Soviet writers, who often concoct novels about the capitalist world, of necessity filled with propaganda, have provided works of fiction that are unintentionally hilarious. [1079] American writers, under no similar compulsion, have nevertheless depicted the European scene and people with equally disastrous results. A whole crop of such books, plays, and movies appeared during World War II.

As for America's Vietnam policy, "tragically typical" is the only way to describe the history of American intervention in that sad country. The French can point out with bitterness that, for as long as they were engaged in the struggle to hold North Vietnam against communist aggression, the United States did nothing to help. The French, like the Dutch in Indonesia, were convinced that Southeast Asia was not ready to resist the assault of the forces of decomposition and tyranny. They were obviously not afraid of *local* decadent ideas but of ideologies that had either failed in Europe or had imposed a variety of tyrannies, such as nationalism, socialism, communism, Jacobinism, national socialism, and others.

And after the "colonialists" had left there never was any question— whether in Southeast Asia *or any other similar nation*—of restoring forms of government or social systems that had prevailed prior to the arrival of the European powers. In fact, if such "native" forms had managed to weather colonial rule or protection, they were subsequently persecuted or crushed. Thus harsh is the hatred of the new "nationalistic" masters for their own native traditions, thus troublesome their abject admiration for the worst ideologies of all—the fecal matter of the West.

And Americans who have rejected monarchies and colonies alike as being "undemocratic" should today deplore the end of dynastic rule in Vienna, Berlin, St. Petersburg, Teheran, and Addis Ababa, and regret the end of the colonial system in Uganda, Burma, Bangladesh, Indonesia, Chad, Lebanon, Surinam, Angola, Mozambique, Eritrea, Libya, Mali, the Sudan, and Iraq. The words of Vauvenargues echo the truth: "The pretext of those who cause the misfortune of others is that they want to make them happy." (*Le prétexte ordinaire de ceux qui font le malheur des autres est qu'ils veulent leur bien.*)

The damage done by today's anticolonialism, American or other, is enormous. Few Americans realize that since 1945 an anticolonialist competition has sprung up between Washington and Moscow. India was the first victim of "liberation," with predictable results. In 1947 at the demarcation line brutally dissecting the country, Hindus and Moslems fell upon each other like beasts—knifing, mauling, castrating, strangling, kicking, killing—leaving 4 to 5 million massacred bodies to rot on the blood-soaked soil.[1080] It will take a long long time for the ill effects of this premature birth to disappear. Countries such as Haiti, Bolivia, Nicaragua, and El Salvador suffer to this day from their load of "freedom"—which took place a century-and-a-half ago. Before his death, the liberator Simón Bolívar admitted that Spanish rule had been superior to the "freedom" he had brought about. Will they or the new batch of Emerging Nations ever recover? Or will they, like a baby crippled at birth, suffer throughout their existence?

CHAPTER 19

The Outlook

"Ah!" exclaimed the baron with his
wickedest leer, "What for is my conclusion good?
You Americans believe yourselves to be
excepted from the operation of general laws.
You care not for experience."

—HENRY ADAMS, *DEMOCRACY* (1882)

I

It is characteristically American to ask after a survey: "All right, but where do we go from here?" Such a question can only be answered cogently by recalling the past, understanding the present, and allowing reason to work on a bank of solid knowledge. Disaster might otherwise easily ensue.

Imagine a typical leftist—an American "liberal" or a British Fabian— musing in the spring of 1919 about the probable future of the world.

"I am an optimist," he would remark benignly. "Progress, on the whole, is assured. Even China has become a democratic republic, and with that sort of government its wise and kind people will follow the example of Japan and adopt our enlightened way of life. Portugal, the first country since the French Revolution to become a European republic, is rid of its degenerate dynasty and will be a torchbearer of liberalism. Soon Spain will follow and Goya's dreadful pictures of the 'Disasters of War' will forever be forgotten. And Italy, once a prey to clericalism and Vatican tyranny, will follow in the footsteps of Giordano Bruno and Mazzini. Germany, the cradle and home of Kant, Fichte, Goethe, and Marx, will embrace international socialism; Austria, the 'Prison of Nations,' will surely be dismantled given the disappearance of the ramshackle Habsburg monarchy; Russia will be transformed into a pacifist democracy in accordance with the ideas of Tolstoy and the Dekabrists; and the 'Young Turks' will enlighten their countrymen and give self-government and freedom to all their ethnic groups (Greeks, Armenians, Kurds). The Islamic faith will shed its fanaticism; superstitions and colonial rule will come to an end.

"African tribes, freed from the exploitation of their brutal European masters, will enjoy unparalleled wealth in their lands so blessed by nature. The inventive and artistic spirit, the political sobriety of these dark people will stun the world. Think too what Persia could offer the world, once the Shahs are gone, what an example nonviolent India could give, what Latin America, with its century-old republican tradition, could teach of progress! And let us not forget Haiti, the first Latin country to throw off its European masters, leading the rest on the path to freedom. As for Cuba, we Americans should take pride that we helped liberate this last bastion of hateful Spanish colonialism in the Western hemisphere. We have well earned the eternal gratitude of this new nation at our door.

"True, colonialism is still expanding—Tripolitania, the old Libya—is now an Italian colony, but one nice day, after its liberation, it will carry the torch of freedom, enlightenment and progress all over Africa. The day will come when these survivals of the Middle Ages disappear not only in Europe, but in such backward countries as Persia, Afghanistan, Ethiopia, and Annam; there freedom and justice will soon reign. Technology and Science will bring unlimited happiness to mankind, and. . . "

So much for optimistic leftist daydreams.

Conservatives and reactionaries, at this juncture in history, had only the grimmest forebodings. The majority of them were religious people: For them, human existence on Earth was a period of trial, the life of a Christian a pilgrimage, his domicile elsewhere (the words of Bossuet based on Hebrews, 13, 14). They trusted in God, not in "humanity," science, or technology; they saw the twilight of the elite and the dimming of religion as the dawn of barbarism. Their views were shared by thoughtful authors. Others painted a delightful vision of a paradise on Earth, like Edward Bellamy, American socialist and founder of the "Nationalist party," in his *Looking Backward, 2000-1887* and *Equality*.[1081] But later utopian novels, like those of Aage Madelung, Aldous Huxley, and George Orwell, reflected immense fears of a collectivist slavery. [1082]

II

Actually, we are all facing a sort of huge bankruptcy. According to Maritain, the world is God's, Man's, and Satan's. But ours is an exceptionally moronic epoch of history, not only "naturally wicked," but despite our worship of science and intellectuality, a time when reason is fundamentally rejected. As a result, we are ruled by sentimentality and resentment, by clichés and slogans, by intuitions and ignoble feelings of envy, jealousy and real hatred, interspersed with frenzied, slavish adulation of this or that "leader."

In the United States, the change came with the year 1828 and the political victory of a totally un-American French import—democracy. It in turn grew into an irrational secular "ideological religion." Do most Americans believe in majority rule and equality? They do and, at the same time, they do not. They might declare insouciantly that "one man is as good as another, if not somewhat better," but if seriously ill they do not say that "one doctor is as good as another." American life is in reality very quality-conscious. The dichotomy between egalitarianism and the insistence on quality has schizoid features.

The truly great European thinkers, those who were not artists, never believed in democracy. . . nor, for all that, did most great Americans. Not a few of these *esprits forts* expressed (and express) their skepticism of democracy, which required a certain courage, surrounded, as they were, with what E. D. Adams called "the religion of democracy." [1083] Crane Brinton of Harvard and Ralph Henry Gabriel of Yale come to mind. Both proclaimed their convictions independently of each other. Gabriel remarked that the radically unscientific character of democracy forced it to become a secular (fideistic) religion. [1084] Brinton was more explicit when he wrote:

"Democracy, in short, is in part a system of judgments inconsistent with what scientists hold to be true. This inconsistency would not create difficulties—or at least would not create some of the difficulties it now creates—were not the democrat able to say that his kingdom is not of this world, able to say that his truth is not the kind that is in the least tested by the scientist. . . Democracy may become a genuinely transcendental faith, in which belief is not weakened by lack of correspondence between the propositions it lays down and the facts of life on this earth."[1085] The only trouble, Brinton added, was that a secular religion has to, but frequently cannot, deliver on its promises right here on earth.

Whereas faith in Christianity is genuinely transcendental, biblical, and ecclesiastic, belief in liberal democracy is upheld by schools, the mass media, folklore, and socio-intellectual pressures. Democracy nevertheless frequently replaces religion, too easily assuming a fanatical character. (It has its bigots as monarchy never had. Monarchy is existential: there is no monarchism as there is no parentalism. Out of "accidents" one does not build an ideology.) But all forms of leftism, including democracy, are characterized by their quasi-religious nature. They also manifest a profound irrationality. In the United States illiterates are now admitted to the polls. But this, of course, is only logical.[1086] Since knowledge, experience, wisdom and character admittedly play no role in the democratic process—the right to choose having superseded them—illiterates have a perfect right to choose a nation's leader. (Alfred Focke, S.J., remarked long ago that in democracies "defenseless illiterates are dragged to the voting urns.")[1087]

What, *objectively*, does democracy (political equality and majority rule) actually look like? The thought obtrudes that within two or three generations, historians and political scientists will shake their heads trying to discover why millions of people said "yes" to a form of government that logically made no sense, that empirically contradicted their daily experience. "Government by consent of the governed" sounds comforting and reassuring, but Hitler too ruled thus. (I, personally, have never during the past half century been ruled by a government of my choice.) Democracy, once again, is not "self-rule" of the people, but the rule of the majority over the minority. There is no least reason—neither "scientific" nor philosophical nor theological—why the majority should rule over the minority and not the other way round. In practical life, the few rule over a group, a select group over a mass, an expert over laymen, a teacher over students, a manager over employees, and so on.[1088] On the other hand, the rule of 999 people over one is more stable, less subject to change, than the rule of one over 999. The one can always be assassinated; majorities are never exterminated, only minorities, by the majorities.

Sometime in the coming century, people will rack their brains pondering how nations with tremendous scientific and intellectual achievements could have given uninstructed and untrained men and women the right to vote equally uninstructed and untrained people into responsible positions. Whereas permission to drive a car, to build a house, to teach in schools depends on examinations and countless bureaucratic documents, the right to vote or to achieve political office rests on a purely vegetative stipulation, i.e., the number of accumulated birthdays. A dogcatcher pretending to be a physician can cause limited harm—the demise of a few unfortunates. But an ignorant head of state can cause the death of countless millions, and dismal servitude for countless more.

Which leads to a further aspect of democracy. Since democratism is strongly ideological, the West has a tendency to "democratize" every conceivable domain of life—education, families, drama, stores, circuses, banks hospitals. Reflect for a moment on the matter of hospitals: patients "democratically" selecting a steering committee under a popular chairman to decide the nature of treatments, the time of a patient's release, the dosage of medicine, the number of operations, the working hours of anesthetists. This would be terribly dangerous. But further reflection reveals that it would be much less so than electing a parliament or a president. At times, elections seems to have the character of Russian roulette. [1089]

Austria's greatest poet, Franz Grillparzer, who suffered greatly from reactionary censorship in the first half of the previous century, said that "now many people believe that three asses represent a human being, but three asses *in concreto* are an ass *in abstracto*, and this is a frightful animal."

The Bible is hardly "democratic." In Ecclesiastes 38:25-38, while the intrinsic values of all trades are respectfully enumerated, the good men in the various occupations still do not qualify to sit in council. Nor did Antiquity think very differently. Plutarch relates that Phokion, a protagonist of Greek unity under Macedonian leadership, while giving a speech to avert permanent danger from the East, was interrupted by applause. Terrified, he looked around and anxiously whispered to his friends standing close: "I must have said something foolish."[1090] *Vox populi, vox Dei?* As General Sherman used to say, *Vox populi, vox humbug.*[1091]

Some people like to quote Churchill to the effect that democracy was a bad form of government, but nevertheless better than all the others. (The mature Churchill never believed in democracy, least of all, one suspects, after May 1945.) But here he is once again quoted out of context. He was merely referring to the superiority of (liberal) democracy over "all the other forms that have been tried from time to time."[1092] He knew only too well that democracy represented a relatively short interlude in world history and his reference to the other forms was aimed at the various leftist tyrannies. (He was most vocal about the value of monarchy on the Continent and deplored the end of Habsburg and Hohenzollern rule.)[1093]

III

The weakness of democracy, the Mother of Leftism, should be of deep concern. Has democracy the capacity, the qualities to deal effectively with its more wicked epigones—socialism and communism? Can one defeat a greater with a lesser evil? Democracy has several Achilles-heels, but a democratically governed country probably faces its greatest difficulties in two specific areas, in the two domains in which one nation has contact with another—that is, in *foreign affairs and defense.* Here a nation's *survival* is at stake. To be roundly defeated in this totalitarian age means to be entirely enslaved or to disappear from the map. We no longer live in the historic period of civilized cabinet wars led by internationally related monarchs. Today's wars are conducted by ideologically motivated mob-masters commanding hate-driven mobs. The Jacobins, even back then, wanted to "make the world safe for democracy"; our century has had its fill of their disciples.

Raymond Aron has said that liberal democracies do not like wars and cannot properly prepare for them, in large part because such preparations cost money.[1094] They are also unable to stop them, even when a sensible compromise is feasible. And although they are afraid of wars, they wage them in the most dreadful manner. In war, the total-totalitarian character of democracy becomes alarmingly clear. The entire citizenry, for instance, is unrelentingly "indoctrinated" to hate collectively.[1095]

The unpreparedness of liberal democracies for wars is only matched by their unpreparedness for peace. Wars, at least, are waged by hierarchic organizations, by the military, industry, and finance, but peace arrangements are carried out by politicians; and these, unlike independent statesmen, are primarily interested in themselves—their personal popularity, i.e., their reelection. To change public opinion takes months, and thus the ensuing slapdash treaties ensure future wars of revenge. (Only recall Britain's Khaki Elections in November 1918 and Lloyd George's promise to "hang the Kaiser," to make the Germans pay "until the pips squeak"!) It results in what Raymond Aron called "chain wars," a chain that is currently interrupted by the atomic balance of terror and minor deputy wars all round the globe. These conflagrations cannot even be stopped by the United Nations—these self-styled "peace-loving nations," another evasive expression in the political jargon of modernity.[1096]

Foreign policy has the task of finding allies as well as cementing peace. But these delicate tasks require secrecy, a condition that conflicts with democracy.[1097] Diplomacy is not conducive to the frank and open discussions that are conducted in the United States—and with such dire results. (It is unclear whether ignorance, innocence, or irresponsibility plays the most decisive role in these public debates.) Diplomacy in whatever guise can in *no way* be "democratized." Yet for the past seventy years the West has tended to do just that, to "democratize" foreign policy not only by increasingly "popularizing" it, subjecting it to petty party strife, legislative discussion, and opinion polls, but by demeaning the ambassadorial post, treating it at times as a political plum for men and women who have earned their reward as party hacks. In this respect, the United States has forged ahead; its enthusiasm for amateurism has had decisive and woeful effects.

Far worse, far more detrimental, is democracy's predilection for *change*. Change, a main feature of democracy, runs completely counter to *permanence*, which is essential to a constructive foreign policy. Politicians make politics, statesmen try to make history, monarchs leave political testaments in an attempt to establish consistency, to leave their successors with coherent political aims. In regard to change, two important questions: Is it possible to have a constructive foreign policy in a democratic world? and, Can mutual trust exist between democratically ruled nations? The democracies—Tokyo, Washington, Paris, Bonn, Rome, Athens, Ankara, wherever—are subject to constant changes of governments, each of which is run by distinct, and often vying, political parties. That is, international relations are in truth carried out by *parties*, whose strength and composition are subject to elections. The result is a merry-go-round of presidents, chancellors, foreign ministers, prime ministers, popping in and out of office in dizzying succession.[1098]

A monarch might break his word, but in doing so he exposes himself to formidable abuse; he can no longer claim to be a Christian gentleman. But after a change of government, neither ruler nor country can be held morally to account. This was first painfully experienced in Europe when, during the War of Spanish Succession, the Habsburgs' British ally suddenly sought peace with France. Britain did this in good faith because elections had brought the fall of the Whigs and the victory of the Tories, who were openly Francophile. The Duke of Marlborough was recalled from battle, and Spain's throne was filled by a Bourbon instead of a Habsburg (rulers of Spain for two hundred glorious years). The expression *perfidious Albion* received fresh meaning, although unjustified: it was not the British, but their system of government that earned the opprobrium.

All this means that no one democratically ruled government can trust another: the United States cannot trust its European allies, and the Free European nations cannot trust the United States—or each other.

The United States could trust Spain under Franco, or Iran under the Shah. In a sense, it could even trust the USSR; when Khrushchev told Americans, "We will bury you," they could well believe it.

All this has strong bearing on the internal situation in Western Europe. The majority of Europeans desires the federalization of Europe, but party leaders, with vested interests and ideological commitments, prevent it. (The unification of Germany in 1871 was the work of royal families, not of the plebiscite.) The Red Empire, ruled by one party, has had no such difficulties. The USSR and its satellites had, until very recently, one ideology, essentially one leadership. Above all, they have had one mission, whereas the Free World nations feel no sense of mission, have no destination; their foreign policy is purely to survive. Since 1945, the West has almost never taken a real initiative. [1099] An initiative requires conviction—grounded, uncompromising conviction—or a profound sense of honor. But loyalty, honor, and virtue belong to the vocabulary of feudalism, not to the jargon of democracy.

In the early United States, foreign affairs had little importance; they were a mere footnote of government. As in Britain, geography was (and is) hardly taught [1100] and foreign languages little encouraged. Indeed, Robert Coram, an American educator, insisted in 1791 that languages not be included in the school curriculum. (An old English proverb states that "he who speaks two languages is a rascal.") And Jefferson himself insisted that Americans who had lived more than seven years abroad ought not be employed in government service. [1101] The implication of words like "alien" and "outlandish" betray the British mentality. [1102] In respect to geography and language, Woodrow Wilson comes to mind; at the Paris Peace Conference he was a victim of forged maps [1103] and unable to communicate without the aid of interpreters. But today, for the United States, foreign policy can nevermore be a footnote; it is of crucial importance, it is a question of physical survival.

IV

To speak of governments is to speak of human beings—and of man's nature after the Fall. (Some wonder whether the institution of the state is not the result of the Fall.)[1104] Georges Bernanos confessed: "I have dreamt about the saints and the heroes, neglecting the intermediary forms of our species, and I am aware of the fact that these hardly exist in reality and that only the saints and the heroes count. The intermediary forms are a paste, a mash: he who takes a handful of it knows all the rest, and this jelly would not even deserve a name if the saints and heroes had not provided it with a name, with the name 'man.' "[1105] Even Rousseau, who together with de Sade can be regarded as a Founding Father of the French Revolution, stated in one of his brighter moments that "if a people of gods existed, they could rule themselves democratically. Such a perfect government is not for human beings."[1106]

Thanks to human weakness, democracy as "populism" is subject to corruption—legal and illegal—even greater than many other forms of government. Democracy, in fact, actively invites corruption; where else can a politician blandly promise any and every nostrum without fear of legal repercussions? The election-reelection process dominates the heart and mind of every politician. To its end he will risk all, do all. Rarely does a genuine Christian choose the political life: the temptation to lie, to break promises, to cast suspicion, to denigrate the opposition, to fan hatred and envies is too great.[1107]

William E. Simon, a former cabinet minister, has spoken with singular contempt of America's politicians, and well before him, M. Y. Ostrogorski said that "to the low types which the human race has produced, from Cain down to Tartuffe, the age of democracy has added a new one—the politician."[1108] (Isolated cases of true souls exist, of course, who from a sense of patriotism and responsibility are willing to descend to the political arena.)

These harsh judgments apply equally to heads of democratic states; unlike monarchs, moreover, they have had no preparation for their responsible tasks. Some may be fairly knowledgeable of local affairs, but at the international level, which is where death lurks, their ignorance is frightening. (I was once four hours with a presidential candidate whose grasp of the American political scene was near perfect, but as for the rest of the globe, he knew less than my preteen sister.)[1109]

A chapter in James Bryce's great classic *The American Commonwealth* is entitled "Why a Great Man Cannot be Elected President of the United States"[1110]—a shocking but true statement in respect of American history after 1828.[1111] Not a few Americans are frightened at the prospect of a truly "great" president, a man of learning and character, a man of genius. They feel easier before an ordinary, intelligent, decent sort of person, one they can trust (a bit of corruption, of the LBJ sort, is easily forgiven). Yet, if faced with serious legal problems, would these same people feel adequately safe and protected in the care of an ordinary, decent lawyer, a fellow like you and me?

Who today has the chance of becoming a great political leader (if not a statesman) in the West? In this regard, radio and (mainly) television have created a revolution. A candidate must not only be a good orator, but telegenic as well, and preferably with a certain sex appeal, or qualify for what Ernst Jünger called *der flüchtige Eros*, the "fleeting Eros." Talleyrand was clubfooted, George VI had a speech impediment, Bismarck had a piercing high voice, Cavour was too fat, and Napoleon was practically a dwarf—all would today have been gravely handicapped in the political arena.

V

Europe, probably more than the United States, suffers from a phenomenon for which the Germans have one of their long compound words: *Demokratieverdrossenheit*, meaning uneasiness, disgust, boredom, irritation with democracy. In the United States, words like "politician" and "politics" carry unfavorable connotations. Countless factors contribute to this feeling in Europe, different in many respects from those in America. Europe experienced great joy at war's end, the end of persecution, interrogations, torture, concentration camps, aerial bombings, forced migrations, and general destitution. But then something unexpected, although not at first unwanted, happened: democracy, once bankrupt, was restored. It was analogous to the restoration of the Bourbons in 1814-15, which was also effected by a victorious alliance.[1112]

Doubts later developed over the ability of democracy to endure as it became evident that democracy was essentially rule by parties. And parties, quite naturally, put their entire energies into fighting *each other* rather than serving the common good. Europeans were scandalized by the spoils-system, familiar to Americans since 1828. In the *ancien régime* prior to 1918, administrators, like personnel in the armed forces, were the Emperor's men, or the King's men. They were strictly forbidden to engage in party politics. (France, of course, being a republic, party politics was paramount and contributed directly to the shameful Dreyfus affair.)[1113]

Today, the polls in Europe draw thin crowds—the older the democracy, the fewer the voters. In Switzerland, 45 percent of the voters abstain in federal elections, as in the United States during presidential elections.[1114] The feeling grows that the people no longer understand the big issues: education cannot keep pace with global issues, whether political, economic, or technological.

And how do the people view politicians? As liars, evil compromisers who strive to enrich themselves through corruption, nepotism, and bribery.[1115] And politicians? They are not much better off. The German federal budget, printed annually, consists of two thousand pages which almost nobody reads or understands. People and politicians both seem to flounder.

The situation is dangerous because it offers tremendous advantage to the demagogues of tomorrow. The people's distrust of politicians recalls the anticlericalism of the Middle Ages. Pope Boniface VIII and the young Martin Luther, before his break with Rome, were convinced that friendship and understanding could never exist between laity and clergy.[1116] People spoke with great contempt of the clergy, characterizing them as ignorant, crafty, immoral, and egotistical—but they were nevertheless pious and faithful to the Church. For centuries this situation was taken for granted. Until one fine day the same Augustinian friar, Martin Luther, banged against the cathedral door, and like a tidal wave the Reformation swept through the greater part of Western Europe. Before the Counter-Reformation set in, the old Faith was secure only in Spain and Italy. Even countries like Austria and Poland were all but submerged by the new faith. It took the Fascists less than two-and-a-half years to conquer Italy, and the National Socialists, an insignificant group until 1929, were masters of the *Reich* by 1933. Democracy, thanks to free elections, among other things, can collapse overnight.

VI

Intelligent Americans know that their country is in grave danger. Dean Acheson,[1117] Harry Truman's last secretary of state, told Archduke Otto of Austria in December 1952: "It was my tragedy that I had to fashion and form the foreign policy of the United States, of a superpower in the atomic age, with the Constitution of an eighteenth-century small farmers' republic."[1118] But, in a way, and unrealized by most, the democratic age is over—even for the United States. "Government of the people, by the people, for the people," all talk of "checks and balances," have lost meaning in this atomic age, when at any time catastrophe can come from the hands of a madman, a Khaddafi, hurling atom bombs or chemical extinction across borders in a blind maniacal rage. Imagine a President of the United States being woken at 4:15 A.M. and presented with an emergency—to press or not to press the button. He would have time neither to convoke Congress, nor ring the editors of the *New York Times*, nor consult the latest radio or television guru. His power (and responsibility) over his country—over all mankind—would be that of one hundred Jenghiz-Khans. No, the sweet little bird of democracy fluttered from out his cage some time ago.

Americans love to quote Lord Acton's dictum that "power tends to corrupt and absolute power corrupts absolutely." This is another of the many clear but false ideas that are repeated in parrot-like fashion. A good man will not be corrupted by power, and a bad man will be corrupted with no power at all. Maria Theresa, Charles V (in whose realm the sun never set), Ferdinand and Isabel, Alexander I of Russia, Titus, Marcus Aurelius, Akbar the Great, Mutsuhito ("Meiji")—all wielded enormous power, none was thereby corrupted. The papacy was most corrupt in the tenth century when it was all but bereft of secular power.

The fear of power leads frequently to the most irrational decisions. One such is the Twenty-second Amendment limiting presidential terms. It is hard to imagine what would happen if this concept were introduced to all areas of life—religion, commerce, education, cultural affairs, and so forth.[1119] The fear of power, moreover, has set dangerous limits on presidential prerogatives, leading to such catastrophes as the conduct of the Vietnam War.

Between 1958 and 1972, I visited that embattled country five times and feel thereby qualified to write with some clarity of the gruesome war. Since the engagement was nothing but a presidential action, American armed forces were not allowed to fight properly; among other things, the generals were not permitted to engage in major actions—a big casualty list was "politically inadmissible." (Total casualties were in fact low, as cruel as that may sound.)[1120] Hanoi could theoretically have been wiped out with 5 percent of the bombs used on Dresden, but no such action was taken.

The strength of the Viet-Cong lay in their firm ideological commitment, in the bestial fear that preceded them like a black cloud paralyzing resistance. On the other side, Washington hampered any effective procedure, such as cutting off the North Vietnamese army by occupying Southern Laos.[1121] Admittedly, terrible tragedies occurred, such as My-Lai, but nothing remotely compared to the atrocities of the Viet-Cong. The obscene horrors perpetrated by them, caught in the photographs in the United States Information Center in Saigon, were too sickening for publication. When the VC took a village, they would often take the mayor and his wife, tie them to the door of their hut, behead their children before their eyes, and then slit open their abdomens. Dying in agony, the parents watched the pigs eating their own intestines. In Dak-To, the VC burned 250 "brown" aborigines alive for collaborating with the government. The fear spread by the VC has no parallel.

Only a very small segment (perhaps 5 percent) of the South Vietnamese backed the Viet-Cong. The Viet masses, many of them Catholic refugees from the north, educated and tough, flatly refused to collaborate with the invaders. The charge of the American Left that war was being waged "against the people of Vietnam" was totally without foundation. On hearing it I thought of my friend Baron Rüdt-Collenberg, the German chargé d'affaires, slaughtered like a beast during the Tet offensive, or of Père Guy de Compiègne, OSB, who was forced to dig his own grave along with two other French Benedictines of the Tien-An monastery. As his stiff hip prevented him from crouching, he was not buried alive but dug in up to his chin so the ants could eat him bit by bit.[1122]

General Westmoreland's excellent memoirs[1123] tell the story of American armed forces betrayed by the leftist network that demoralized the army of conscripts and vilified returned veterans. Television persuaded the American people that they were suitably informed concerning the war; they little realized that pictures can lie far more effectively than print.[1124]

Leftist propaganda had a fateful impact on idealistic young Americans, many of whom, overpowered by the wave of national masochism, were driven to commit treason.[1125] Riots broke out in universities, most notably at Kent, causing the embattled National Guard to fire in self-defense, killing four students. (These might or might not have had Old Glory sowed to the seats of their pants.) The cause of the demonstration was the attack of the South-Vietnamese army on the "terminus" of the Ho-Chi-Minh Trail, guarded by Pol Pot's Red Khmers.

These poor students, in reality, died for Pol Pot, for a monster who later succeeded in exterminating one-third of his country's population (he studied Marxism at the Sorbonne).[1126] He, like his red colleagues, took to its final logical conclusion the Marxist philosophy that deems man a "higher animal," a cousin, if a remote one, of rats, bedbugs, earwigs, and other pests susceptible to extermination. Pol Pot proved his convictions; he slaughtered all silversmiths and their families on discovering that their craft could not be collectivized, and slaughtered men who wore spectacles on the grounds that they were "intellectuals." All very logical; but logic applied to untruth leads straight to Hell.

Another even more revealing book (if in a different sense) on Vietnam is Leslie Gelb's *The Irony of Vietnam: The System Worked.*[1127] The thesis of Mr. Gelb—presidential advisor, former employee of the Pentagon and State Department, writer for the *New York Times*—is very simple. The irony of Vietnam is that the withdrawal of the U.S. army was simultaneously a victory for communism and for democracy. Why the latter? Because "the system worked." Because the people, mesmerized by the mass media, decided against the war and, working within the framework of the system, forced the government to retreat. In short: to wage a war in synchromesh with the oscillations of public opinion proves democracy a hugh success. The *Frankfurter Allgemeine Zeitung*, one of the world's two best papers, wrote in sarcastic comment: "we Europeans should be delighted to see, in the triumphs of communism, victories of American democracy. It seems that Franklin D. Roosevelt is not entirely dead."[1128]

It quickly became evident that the Viet-Cong were not harmless agrarian reformers,[1129] progressive liberals, and enlightened democrats, as loudly maintained by the Viet-Minh, but genuine communists, Moscow-oriented Marxists. Leftists are not bound by the Ten Commandments; they can lie as they please. As Marx said: "We Communists teach no ethics."[1130]

VII

For the average person, all problems date to World War II; for the more informed, to World War I; for the genuine historian, to the French Revolution. The mere fact that we are still living in an incredibly extended postwar period demonstrates democracy's inability to put an end to war, even in a moral and psychological sense. Forty-one years after the Napoleonic Wars (1856) nobody spoke of war criminals.[1131] Forty-one years after the fall of Robespierre (1835) nobody was interested in the main culprits of democratic savagery or even in the status of the regicides responsible for the legal murder of Louis XVI.[1132]

The order of life today is painful disorder. What sort of order might be considered ideal? (None could be perfect, of course; we are merely human beings.) Communist parties the world over, under the leadership of the USSR, had a solid program. Moscow's collaborators and sympathizers still are motivated not by hard cash but by conviction; the red ideology appeals to their hearts and minds. Ideologies are unavoidable and, in a sense, indispensable. Irving Kristol (the *Wall Street Journal*, July 17, 1980) stated that the Right needed an ideology if it hoped to win the battle against the Left. But a number of conservatives strongly protested the statement, having for generations depicted ideologies as incompatible with true conservatism, as being essentially leftist in character. Socialism, communism, liberalism, all are ideologies, intellectual constructions, whereas a genuine conservative contemplates nature, favors age-old traditions, time-honored institutions, the wisdom of his forebearers, and so on. Some conservatives speak of the terrible misfortunes ideologies have brought upon mankind, but the same could be said of religion. One ideology is not as good as any other ideology, just as, *pace* some benighted souls, one religion is not as good as another. The People's Temple supporters, the Thuggies in India, are not as good as the Quakers.

Yet missing from the conservative argument is the hard fact that man *is* an ideological animal. Hayek said quite correctly that no society could ever exist without an ideology.[1133] European conservative thinkers—Eugene Lemberg and Gerd-Klaus Kaltenbrunner come to mind—thoroughly agree with Kristol's contention that ideology cannot be fought with non-ideology. Pick any man at random, put him on a couch, and question him methodically. Soon the dim outline of an ideology will emerge, although its profile might be low, its contours barely distinguishable, its content contradictory.

The word "ideology" was originally attached to the "philosophy" of Count Destutt de Tracy, whose main work was translated by Jefferson into English. The term was soon in general use. Napoleon, who was pragmatic, erratic, and played politics by ear, once said to a group of men who had argued too logically with him: "Messieurs, you are ideologues!" They had irritated him thoroughly.

The Germans have for years used the term *Weltanschauung*.[1134] But when the National Socialists fanatically defended their *Weltanschauung*, the word took on a pejorative meaning, and it was replaced by "ideology"—even in Germany.[1135]

Ideology is a coherent, logical presentation of human existence; it is intellectual, yet it also speaks to the heart. But Anglo-Americans dislike ideology. What then is the alternative? A slogan like Bentham's, "The greatest happiness for the greatest number," might mean anything, such as the sadistic pleasure of a majority in the suffering of a minority. This is conceivable, as in Genesis 8, 12: "From his early years on the mind of man is turned towards evil."

Still, what is the alternative to an ideology that ought to be Promethean in the etymological sense of the word—that ought "to think ahead"? (Prometheus's brother, Empimetheus, married Pandora. He acted first and reflected afterward.) The alternative to an ideology is trial-and-error. It recalls lab tests on animals, where, for instance, a chimpanzee tries to reach a banana dangling from above, laying box upon box, until he succeeds almost by accident. Such a procedure should remain within the confines of the animal order.

American conservatives have carefully avoided offering to mankind an ideology—or a utopia. Yes, a utopia. There are three kinds of utopias: those that cannot be realized, those that are feasible but cost a disproportionate amount of labor, suffering, and sacrifice, and those that can reasonably be established by sober reflection and honest effort. Everything that does not yet exist, that has yet to be built, instituted, or organized is, in a certain sense, an *outopos*. Hayek deplored the fact that (genuine) liberalism never had its utopia. [1136] Every young person contemplating and planning his or her future life is a visionary, a "utopian."

As a result of their self-imposed inhibition, American conservatives, while brilliant in their critique of modern ills—pseudo-liberalism, socialism, communism, Jacobine democracy, egalitarianism, permissiveness, egotism, pacifism, progressivism, and goodness knows what other aberrations—have not provided the United States or the rest of the world with an alternative, with a blueprint for the future, with a picture of the desirable shape of things to come that could engender a real enthusiasm among the young. Most Americans, I fear, would disagree with Anatole France's statement that only extremes are bearable. In this regard I would like to cite an aphorism by Nicolás Gómez Dávila (who is proud to call himself a reactionary): conservatives are (classic) liberals who have been maltreated by democracy.

There never will be a Paradise on Earth, Edenism is nonsense, but there might conceivably be a better future. Yet only if we strive for it, not if we wait patiently for the total collapse of the present order, for we too might be buried under its debris. Professor James Buchanan, Nobel Prize laureate and a genuine liberal, has written in an article called "A Quest for a Tempered Utopia" that "it is time to again dream attainable dreams and to recover the faith that dreams can become realities. It is time to start replacing dystopia with a tempered utopia." This cannot be achieved through ordinary political channels, because "if all politicians are the servants of special interests, we must remain skeptical of political initiatives, even ours that seem aimed in the right direction."[1137]

Peter Drucker, another right-of-center thinker, said back in 1939 that "ultimately we will need a new political theory and probably a very new constitutional law. We shall need new concepts and a new social theory. Whether we shall get these and what they will look like, we cannot know today. But we can know that we are disenchanted with government, primarily because it does not perform."[1138] And Eliseo Vivas warned American conservatives: "I take it for granted that if the conservative movement is going to make more than a trivial and fugitive impact on the life of the nation, it will have to develop a philosophy that is systematic, that is comprehensive, that takes full and honest account of current positive knowledge and that is, therefore, no mean repetition of dried-up old chestnuts that appealed to men a generation or two ago, but have lost their flavor and freshness."[1139]

Over here, in the heart of Europe, I am always put into a reflective mood by the plight of former idealistic National Socialists who, when they discovered the crimes of their regime, broke with their convictions. Unless they embraced another ideology or returned to the religious faith of their earlier years, they were conscious of the void within and yearned for the glorious years when, filled with enthusiasm, they were ready to sacrifice everything for their *Weltanschauung*—money, work, time, and if necessary health and their very lives. We must realize that, beyond our hedonistic drives, we are drawn to an ascetic, some sort of sacrificial order. Joy and satisfaction have varied foundations.

A young scholar, James Jamieson, has drawn up a systematic chart showing the different types of American "conservatisms," the genuine and the fake.[1140] Some of these conservative groups cannot even cooperate among themselves. Many traditionalists are irritated by the emphasis on economic issues, while a number of libertarians are insensitive to religious values.

(It bears marking here that the Catholic Faith and the Catholic Church are not *per se* conservative. The Catholic Church is like a tree, the same trunk stands on the same spot, but the branches, twigs, and leaves change constantly—and with them the shape of the tree. The Reformers were clearly conservative, and the Eastern Church is absolutely static.)

An international conservative movement cannot exist; but a rightist one can, if prompted by the universally positive meaning of the word "right." Not a single party in Italy, Spain, Portugal, Switzerland, Germany, France, Belgium, or Austria calls itself conservative. Even some notable non-Catholics are not happy with the conservative label, men like the late Whittaker Chambers who said he did not think of himself as a conservative. "I am a man of the Right. I am a man of the Right because I mean to uphold capitalism in its American version."[1141] Looking over the record, it is evident that American conservatism—elegant, wise, clever in its critique, adroit and constructive in upholding eternal values—has not shown new ways, designed a new order; it has too often only produced what the French call *de la littérature*—although beautifully written.

VIII

In 1962 a food riot broke out in Novotsherkassk, a Russian city near the Black Sea. The riot became a rebellion, the rebellion a local revolution. The provincial Soviet regime broke down, it disappeared into thin air. The Red Army was called in and advanced to the center of the city where the inhabitants, forming a hostile human wall, refused to retreat. The commanding officer told his soldiers that he ought to give them an order to attack, but he could not do so. "Don't fire!" he yelled instead. "These are your brothers and sisters." Whereupon he pulled out his pistol and shot himself[1142]—and the soldiers retreated. In the end, the MVD arrived in jumbo planes and cleared the area, killing hundreds of people. It took seven months for the news of the massacre to reach the West.[1143]

What interests here is that these ninety thousand-odd Russians, united in their hatred for their regime, had no alternative order whatsoever around which to rally; they had no common vision of another form of government, because in a totalitarian regime it is impossible to crystallize a body of common political convictions. Each person carried his own separate answer to the Soviet system, like a secret in himself, communicated only to a handful of trusted people. Any conspiracy was out of the question. Sooner or later, when the charmed circle expanded, the secret plans would leak out. All this means that we in the West ought to have provided the Soviet people with a blueprint. A bad ideology has to be replaced with a good one. Solzhenitsyn was absolutely right when he said that for Russia, Anglo-

Saxon patterns won't do. "Russia never will be *juste-milieu*," as Alexander Herzen, the great nineteenth-century Russian revolutionary said 130 years ago.[1144] The situation has, of course, changed. Today's TV shows demonstrations in Moscow and other cities, with white-blue-red Russian flags, black-yellow-white monarchical flags, and, not infrequently, black-red *Esery*, or anarchist flags. (In all, it heralds the impossibility of installing a liberal, multiparty parliamentary system in Russia.)

Something similar is true of Latin America with its morbid cult of revolution[1145] and its short parliamentary interludes alternating with military dictatorships. Recall José San Martin's effort to persuade Simón Bolívar to imitate Brazil and adopt a monarchical government for Spanish America. All in vain. Bolívar had as a young man given his oath on Rome's Monte Sacro to establish democratic republics in South America and he was a man of honor. But he came to regret his stand, and in one of his last utterances confessed, "There is no faith nor trust in [Spanish] America, neither in individuals nor in nations. The constitutions are books, the treaties scraps of paper, the elections battles, liberty is anarchy and life a torture."[1146]

Thus in Latin America there is also need of a workable ideology to bind the people as one, perhaps even the nations. Imitations of the U.S. Constitution won't do. When attempted, they have been promptly perverted and have immediately failed. Nor would the average business suit of a man from Illinois remotely fit his colleague in Cochabamba. Latin Americans believe that the material success of the United States depends on the Constitution of 1787; *therefore* it should be adopted.[1147] This non sequitur has proved to be an enormous fallacy.

IX

Thus we should have an ideology, among other reasons because it gives us an itinerary, a destination, and a practical political ideal to live for. The American Left has an ideology, and a very fanatical one indeed. Its ideology may not encourage actual murder, but at times it leads to acts of physical violence. The students of Kent State University in their own way fought and died for Pol Pot. And, on a far less tragic level, consider the comic attack of an administrator in Dartmouth College who mauled and bit a young student for distributing the right-wing *Dartmouth Review*. (Needless to say, the college authorities censured the student, who had to be given antitetanus shots, not the indignant progressive official, although he was subsequently forced to apologize.) [1148]

But where do ideologies come from? There are various definitions of ideology, both objective and hostile. *Webster's New International Dictionary* (1967 edition) says under "3" that it is "a systematic scheme or coordinated body of ideas or concepts, especially about human life and culture." Mihajlo Mihajlov, a Yugoslav of Russian parentage, writes that "in the encyclopedic sense, ideology is a definite, all-embracing system of ideas on one's social environment [formerly and more precisely, *Weltanschauung*, or worldview]." [1149] And, after defining its inevitability, the author enumerates no fewer than eight ideologies, some of which I would contend. Religions are not ideologies, but they can serve as the basis of an ideology. The choice of a Christian, a believing Jew, or a Moslem is in each case limited. A Christian, for instance, cannot become a Marxist or a National Socialist, and an orthodox Moslem cannot evolve into a genuine liberal.

To establish a vision of a desirable future order based on an ideology is not easy in the United States. It goes against the grain of a sizeable sector of the English-speaking world because it tends to resent being guided by general ideas. But nations, like persons, must sometimes jump over their own shadows. Specific situations often make this imperative. Émile Boutmy wrote in one of his essays that a cold mind like Royer-Collard's produced the formula "I despise facts," while Burke never hid his disgust for abstractions: "I even hate the sound of the words that express them." [1150] Royer-Collard represented the Continental idea—"ideologism" in a more extreme form—while Burke stood for common sense. (It is well, however, to recall that Richard M. Weaver warned American conservatives against adopting Burke as their prophet.) The potential danger in the Royer-Collard mentality is greater, but mere common sense (although its practical value is greater) creates no dynamism whatsoever—and this is exactly what we at present need. What the West needs.

When Oliver Wendell Holmes, Jr., read Spengler's *Decline of the West*, he became so outraged by this "piece of incredible German arrogance" written by an "odious animal," that in a subsequent letter to Sir Frederick Pollock he declared that he "wished that beast were dead." [1151] A careful study of Holmes shows that he was a nihilist, an inevitable consequence if one discards divine revelation. It conforms with liberal democracy, which is equidistant from all philosophies and faiths. "Democratism," the false American ideology, is very much alive, busily fostering state subsidies for homosexual activities. [1152]

Attempts have been made in the United States to establish an ideology for the Free World on a theistic basis. One such valiant effort is the *Portland Declaration* born on the Western rim of Christendom. It could be adopted as easily by a Christian as by a Jew, or even a liberal Moslem. It was developed by the Western Humanities Institute, published in the *National Review*, and reprinted as a public service by a lay Catholic organization. [1153] Only its opening articles are philosophical in nature. The immediate purpose of the *Declaration* is (1) to offer a blueprint of state, society, and the economy based on knowledge, experience, wisdom, and ethic principles in combination with personal freedom in a "rightist" formula, adapted to a scientific and technological age that believes in God; and (2) to break the ideological monopoly that the Marxists and other materialisms exert around the globe. (It would be foolish to believe that the bankruptcy of Leninism in the East has broken the Marxist hold on mankind.)

The *Portland Declaration* consists of twenty-six articles, formulated in a longer and a shorter version. The text begins by stating a "rational" belief in God, Creator of the universe, to whom we are responsible. It then defines man as a unique *persona* with an nontransferable destiny, not as a mere "individual," created in the image of God and related to his Creator. *If God exists, everything is possible; if there is no God, everything is permitted.*

The *Declaration* emphasizes the personalistic supremacy of diversity over identity-sameness, rejects horizontalism in favor of verticality, places Right over Left; it also understands the radical difference between men and women, the importance of the family, the loving friendship between the sexes, the separateness of state and society, the moral supremacy of authority over coercion, the principle of subsidiarity, and it rejects the centralizing as well as the totalitarian Provider State.

The *Declaration* also faces the hard fact that an effective executive and a certain "technocracy" are unavoidable in an industrial society, but these have to be "humanized." Necessary too is a fruitful dialogue between governors and governed in a popular representation which, up to a point, *might* be a legislative, but never a policy-making body. The administration must be of the *highest quality and minimal size* rather than today's *lowest quality and maximum size*, its main task being to uphold law and order among the citizenry and to manage relations, friendly and hostile, with other nations—i.e., foreign affairs and defense. (A page should here be copied from the Chinese experience: the classless Mandarinate based on a combination of scholarship and practical common sense.)[1154] The *Portland* society will have freedom under the law, free discussion, free organs of expression, and many private organizations—the *corps intermédiaires*—with the most diverse and practical functions. Freedom is inseparable from the right to private property. No third way lies between free enterprise and state capitalism (or socialism). Public schools will be maintained, but parents who do not use them will not be taxed for their upkeep, or they might receive recompense transferable to private schools.

Religion must be separate from the state; no church will be established. But cooperation between religious bodies and the state in various fields is admissible since state and society have a real interest in a religiously oriented population. Religion is one of the marks distinguishing man from beast; man is a transcendent creature.

Religion should not be kept from the market place. Ethnicity must be respected. Discrimination on the basis of language, race, sex, or religion are outlawed. In some occupations, however, one or the other sex cannot legitimately be employed, such as women acting as combat soldiers, jail-wardens in men's prisons, or as coal miners.

Tolerance must be distinguished from indifference. Only those with well-grounded convictions are *able* to be tolerant, for it implies an altruistic "sacrificial discipline." He who holds no convictions, rejects value judgments and a belief in the existence of Truth, has the doubtful privilege of being indifferent.

Patriotism, not nationalism, should inspire the citizen. The ethnic nationalist who wants a linguistically and culturally uniform nation is akin to the racist who is intolerant toward those who look (and behave) differently. The patriot is a "diversitarian"; he is pleased, indeed proud of the variety within the borders of his country; he looks for loyalty from all citizens. And he looks up and down, not right and left.

Agencies and organizations of a global character are perfectly in order, and in the far future there ought, perhaps, to be a world government. But at the present time humanity is far too divided and "uneven" to contemplate such a unification. A world parliament would founder for the same reasons that today ideologically divided parliaments perform so poorly, acting merely as a forum for violent dissent. (A good marriage is a blessing for mature people, but for children marriage is inane, if not wicked.) The United Nations in its present form suffers from all these shortcomings.

Legal positivism has no place in a healthy order. Ulpian's *suum cuique* ("to everyone his due")—not equality—should be the guiding principle. Laws should not be issued arbitrarily. Justice is something to be researched, to be "discovered." Some government bodies, for instance, have declared by majority vote that a child up to twenty-four weeks after conception is not a human being and can therefore be slaughtered like a piglet. Another body has disagreed; *its* majority declared that human life begins at twenty-eight weeks. The sacredness of life (before birth as at old age)[1155] belongs to the essence of theistic ethics.

Freedom is not a goal, it is a condition in which we can live, act, and create in human dignity. The right order should be neither an umbrella nor a straitjacket, but a comfortable, well-tailored suit whose variations accord to local traditions and mentalities. "As much liberty as possible (without hurting the Common Good) and only as much restraint as necessary (to protect the Common Good)." (A certain arbitrariness in drawing the lines is unavoidable.) The demand for government by law is absolutely legitimate; in such a government the human factor will be felt, because the law can only be administered by human beings. In the Middle Ages the concept of the *rex sub lege*, "the king *under* the law," prevailed almost everywhere. The British Parliament today can theoretically decide whatever it wills.[1156] But a supreme court is generally necessary. This body should be appointed on a nonpartisan basis. On the Continent, this should be done by the legal and theological faculties of the universities, for a judge has to decide whether a law is not only legally but morally acceptable. (Abortion is fundamentally illegal as well as immoral, but we speak of what *ought* to pertain.)

Conscription, a gift of the French Revolution and totalitarian democracy, should be avoided, resorted to only in extraordinary circumstance. A professional army is preferred.

The *Portland Declaration* does not deal with the question of a republican or monarchical form of government. From a purely rational point of view a monarchy within the framework of a mixed government is preferable, as shown elsewhere in these pages.[1157] Outside of Switzerland, there has never been a republic that did not eventually become a monarchy. Only the ignorant, insular, or provincial can consider a republic or democracy— both antique forms of government—"modern," or a monarchy "obsolete." It took the Medicis (Florentine pharmacists) 225 years to become Grand Dukes of Tuscany, and the Romans four hundred years to realize that they had been living all along in a monarchy.[1158] One thing is certain, the old dictum of Plato: if philosophers do not become kings, and kings philosophers, all mankind will perish.[1159]

X

The *Portland Declaration* deserves such generous space because it is one of the few efforts made to present a right-wing utopia, ideologically colored; in doing so it departs from a habit of one-sided criticism. It takes a certain courage to offer a fairly concrete alternative to the existing order, to expose oneself to vituperation and ridicule. As Alexander Pope said in his *Epistle to Bathurst* (198-199):

> So what to shun will no great knowledge need,
> But what to follow is a task indeed.

The *Declaration* would, if accepted, provide the West with a constructive foreign policy and a coordinated concept for defense. It could become a unifying bond for all Christendom, whether the individual countries have monarchical or republican traditions. Charles Maurras, perhaps the most outspoken French defender of monarchy, said that it represented "the least evil and the possibility of something good," a sober utterance that ought be compared to the dithyrambic praise of leftists for their political dreams. Most genuine liberals, fearful of the vagaries of the multitudes, favored monarchical forms of government. [1160]

In the specifically American situation, rightism, which in a sense encompasses conservatism, is profoundly averse to breaking tradition. Whatever is inherited must be treated with tender care. The *Portland Declaration* rests in good part on the notions of the Founding Fathers and thus does not propose to "scrap" the Constitution of 1787 (which, under alien influences, has been perverted by various amendments), but to readjust and modernize it, even radically, with a number of amendments. Political institutions, unlike religions, are not supposed to be basically unchangeable or eternal. Nor were all the Founding Fathers happy about the Constitution. The most brilliant among them, Alexander Hamilton, called it "a frail and worthless fabric." [1161]

What is needed is the determination to change. An unknown Viennese coffeehouse philosopher once said that everything has an end except the sausage, which has two. We have been on the wrong track for a very long time. A Chinaman travelling in Europe in the last century even then spotted the danger in democratism: "In the past the statesmen were able to keep a stable order because they feared God and worshipped him, but today it is the people whom they fear and worship."[1162] Copernicus, centuries earlier, repeated the words of Seneca: "I never wanted to please the people. What the people want, I ignore, and what I know, the people do not realize."[1163] And Harold Nicolson, a parliamentary candidate for the British Labour Party, rather quickly woke up from his people-worshipping illusions. "It is dispiriting canvassing these idiots," he wrote in 1949. "They have no knowledge and interests at all. They are just sheep. One woman: 'I want a man who can lead me'! Hitler? *'I never liked his mustache.'* Idiot woman—it is people like her who decide elections!"[1164] All of which points to William Penn's dictum: "Let the people think they govern and they will be govern'd."[1165] The Left—always bear in mind—has a firm interest in liberal democracy, in a parliamentary government with free elections, because the Left operates with false but clear ideas, and, being clear, they can become popular. The truth, on the other hand, is immensely complex. "But our representative government has experts to rely on," we are told. Correct, but experts very often differ in their judgments, fostering among some a counsel of despair: "let us dispense with expertise altogether and trust entirely in the *vox populi.*" Others, more reasonable, want to coordinate contradictory expert views, but this again can only be done by experts. If four medical scholars of high repute discuss the possible therapy of a wealthy patient, it is the family doctor who should join them in counsel, not his loving but medically ignorant wife.

In the political arena, another leftist pitfall is its "message," whose design is to exploit materialistic envy, jealousy, hatred, resentment, and mass egotism. Yeats wrote that:

> Things fall apart; the centre cannot hold;
> Mere anarchy is loosed upon the world.
> The blood-dimned tide is loosed, and everywhere
> The ceremony of innocence is drowned;
> The best lack all convictions, while the worst
> Are full of passionate intensity. [1166]

This passionate intensity has frequently affected even otherwise intelligent men and women. Sir Karl Popper, for instance, surely one of the brightest minds of our day, considers it the indubitable advantage of democracy that it "permits reform without violence"; he believes, furthermore, that "if democracy is destroyed all rights are destroyed."[1167] Indeed? What about the reforms of Joseph II in regard to his possessions, or of Catherine II in Russia? What about the majorities that prefer "security" to freedom and vote tyrants into power? What about the democratic control of the dinner table through Prohibition? What about the rights of the unborn? (People little suspect that legalized murder in the womb constitutes a true watershed in Western history.)

Eduard von Hartmann, a German philosopher, wrote at the end of the last century that "the belief that the liberty of the people can be guaranteed by parliamentary government has ceased to exist for some time. . . The world is fed up with parliamentarian government, but nobody has a better solution, and the knowledge that this despised institution has to be carried over into the twentieth century fills the minds of the best of our contemporaries with anxiety."[1168]

This was corroborated by William Graham Sumner for the United States back in 1877 when he wrote:

"Democracy is only available as a political system in the simple society of a new country—it is not adequate for a great nation: we have reached the point at which its faults and imperfections are mischievous, and, in the growth and advance of the nation, these evils must become continually more apparent."[1169]

They have!

XI

The advance of leftism on such a broad front cannot be understood in isolation from the great moral and concomitant religious crisis shaking the globe, reaching even into the Catholic Church. Romans 12:2 bears repeating, the warning to Christians not to fall into the *aion*, the World and Spirit of the Times. The words of Alexander Pope in his *Essay on Criticism* (546-547) come to mind:

> Then unbelieving priests reformed the nation
> And taught more pleasant methods of salvation.

The crisis in the Catholic Church (as in all other Christian communities) came from the top, not from the people in the pews. As I expressed elsewhere,[1170] the calamities that befell the Catholic Church, specifically in the United States, had many parallels with those in the Netherlands, and for roughly the same reasons. Only too often those evils are attributed erroneously to the Second Vatican Council (planned, incidentally, by Pius XII) notwithstanding that the decrees of the Council are quite moderate, not very new, often rather dull, and would have caused neither harm nor confusion had it not been for the antics of the *periti* and their friends.

These theological experts had no official voice, their sole job being to advise the bishops at the council. They were frequently filled with hare-brained ideas that were, naturally enough, turned down. In great dudgeon, many of these *periti*, allied with theologians who had not even been invited, established a paramagisterium and, abetted by the mass media, caused (in the words of Eric de Saventhen) a malicious "peritonitis" in the Church. When challenged, they frequently referred to the decisions of Vatican II, invoking the "spirit" of the Council when unable to cite chapter and verse. The more humble layman was laid low by these pretentious egotists, as were many bishops, whose many attributes did not necessarily include scholarship.

The result is high season for ecclesiastic-liturgical nonsense in a Church that comprises more than half of all Christians[1171]—and this is a serious matter for every Christian. No wonder, too, that leftist ideas, representing as they do the *Zeitgeist* (spirit) of our times, have deeply penetrated clergy and laity alike. This new "spirit" thrust through religion's defense and spawned Liberation Theology, a cocktail of economic naiveté, biblical ignorance, and a longing for popularity.[1172]

Paul VI was unfortunately profoundly influenced by Jacques Maritain, who claimed in so many words to be theologically conservative but politically leftist. Pope Paul's temporary envoy to Havana, Bishop (now Cardinal) Casaroli, told the Cubans that "We too have read Marx and have learned a lot from him." The Dominican Father Joseph Lebret, who headed the team that worked on the Encyclical *Populorum Progressio*, informed seminarians in São Paulo that he thought God might be nearer to the Communists than to the capitalists. The stand of the Franciscan Father Leonard Boff, the leading "Liberation" theologian of the younger generation, is thoroughly unsound not only economically but theologically. The braying of the Trojan Asses from the theological *demi-monde* is heard today in all areas of the Catholic Church.

Politics also made nefarious inroads in the Reformation churches. Thus the World Council of Churches (WCC) for years financed Mugabe's Soviet-supported terrorists in Rhodesia. These accomplished murderers discovered a particularly effective method of terrorization. Instead of killing their victims outright, they mutilated them in a very sophisticated manner: they cut off their ears, noses, upper and lower lips, and released these "walking" advertisements of their power, thus spreading paralyzing fear. (The *Notgemeimschaft*, an association of orthodox and pious German Lutherans, collected money for cosmetic surgery for these victims of the WCC.) Is further proof needed that we live in an asylum for the criminally insane?

XII

The religious crisis affects all Christian churches, just as it affects Judaism. Although religion is infinitely more than mere ethics, today's moral crisis is intimately connected to the dwindling of theistic faiths. This is apparent in the increase of common and political crimes.

Terrorism would have been inexplicable had authority not vanished. And since the alternative to authority is coercion, it might well be that the humanitarian impulse that has spread since the end of the eighteenth century will finally be stilled. It would not surprise if not only capital punishment, but torture were to be legally reinstituted,[1173] especially if a technologically perfected terrorism leaves no alternative. (If a terrorist is caught, whose colleague is ready to explode a nuclear device on a big city, would it be legitimate to use torture to wrench the secret of his friend's whereabouts from him? I personally do not know the answer.)

The beginning of leftist *personal* terrorism in the last century can be laid to the young German National Democrat Karl Sand, murderer of the playwright August von Kotzebue, a Russian national who had exchanged letters with Alexander I of Russia. Sand had been ideologically motivated in 1817 by the Wartburg Festival, where national democratic students added the red of revolution to the Imperial black and yellow banner. They lost no time in throwing conservative books into a big bonfire; a century later, the National Socialists followed their noble example.[1174]

Terrorists might truly provoke the end of our Christian humanitarianism, which took so very long to arrive at full bloom. They are alien to our ethics, and these rest squarely and solely on God's revealed word. If there is such a thing as the natural law, whose realization can only come from human reason, it yet needs an authoritative affirmation and this, in turn, can only come from above.[1175] Modern man, in fact, tends to live an ethical life from a mere whiff of an empty bottle. Leszek Kolakowski, one of the outstanding living philosophers, has said that the ethics of nonbelievers are owed to the fact that they have grown up in a civilization that once had a sacred character.[1176] There is no such thing as a purely empirical, "natural" morality. Nature? Dog eats dog. The Auca Indians in the east of Ecuador, if their baby cries too much, dig a hole in the ground, put the baby in it, trample on it and declare, "The next baby will cry less."[1177]

The nice middle road leads to perdition. A few years ago the *New Yorker* published a grandiose cartoon by Dana Fradon showing two men in Hell. Says one to the other: "My motto was 'Go with the flow,' but I had no idea the flow would end up here." The notion that man, left to himself, is naturally good is intrinsically Rousseauistic. At the Nuremberg Trial, the Russians forbade the use of the label "National Socialist,"[1178] and it was henceforth called "The Trial of the Nazi Conspirators." It reflects the democratic ideology that embraces the notion of the good man; if good people do wrong, they can only have been cheated or seduced by a tiny group of exceptional evildoers, by a "conspiracy." In the United States, the Left, no less than the Right, has the tendency to assume that fatal turns in history are always the work of "conspirators." Yet National Socialism was most certainly not a conspiracy; it was a mass movement, operating in broad daylight and filled with people who sacrificed time, money, their very lives for a wicked and stupid cause. But democracy could not admit to any of this. The general trust in man's goodness kept people from believing not only the horrors of National Socialism, but of Communism.[1179] The truth about the inhuman crimes of the Soviet regime—the bestial *Kontslagery*, later called Gulags—was known to everyone interested in Sovietism. Yet middle-roaders only smiled when faced with the facts. Was not truth always "in between"? Things, after all, were never black and white, but grey. (Solzhenitsyn worked a real miracle when he persuaded the West of the unimagineable horrors behind the Soviet borders, and for this the Left has never forgiven him.)

Sophocles said that of all frightful creatures, man is the most terrible— the brown concentration and extermination camps (remember the lampshades of human skin?); the unspeakable scenes of China's Cultural Revolution, in which the populace participated; the annihilation of Dresden; the paperknife made of a Japanese soldier's thighbone that delighted Franklin Roosevelt;[1180] the atom bomb over Japan;[1181] the ghoulish misdeeds of African potentates; the mass murder of the unborn. To understand fully where we lie in the timetable of history, look at the list of members of the United Nations. Fewer than one-fifth of these countries have civilized governments and institutions. Mark off those where systematic torture, orgies of public executions, barbaric amputations of limbs, death by stoning, sexual mutilations of women, sadistic prison camps, human sacrifices, wholesale exterminations, and mass deportations are *not* practiced.

Ian Smith of Rhodesia was excluded from this august body, but Fernando Macias Nguema of Equatorial Guinea, who crucified his Christian opponents, was accepted with open arms. So was Idi Amin Dada, who asked his health minister if he had experienced the delicious salty flavor of human flesh,[1182] or Mengistu Haile Mariam, who demanded "bullet money" from parents for the bodies of their slaughtered high school sons.

And it all began with the French Revolution, with the dissected Princesse de Lamballe and the cook's apprentice broiled alive in butter. Oh yes, believing Christians too have committed evil deeds, but they never claimed to have acted in the spirit of God's revealed word. They acted according to the *aion* and not according to the Gospels. Nobody in the Vatican would dream of celebrating an anniversary of the Inquisition (which put priests as an inquiring body in the service of the state), nor would anybody in Geneva commemorate the burning of Servetius at the stake. Herein we betrayed the Lord, and we hang our heads in shame. But the French guillotinists will as proudly continue to celebrate the sadistic and revolting revolution of 1789 as the gulagists do the murder of countless millions on November 7th every year.

XIII

The objection might occur that to judge historic happenings with clever hindsight is cheap. Agreed. But the prophets who foresaw it all have names. My *Liberty or Equality?* contained eighty pages dedicated to the great seers of the last century who clearly envisaged our times. To foresee the basic run of history is relatively easy; to capture the timetable is difficult. Alexis de Tocqueville's vision of the coming, democratically evolving totalitarian-provider state in the Swedish pattern[1183] found no understanding in the 1830s when his *Democracy in America* appeared. By the end of the century he was nearly forgotten. But he rose from obscurity after World War II, and now that so many of his predictions have become terribly true (even the clash between the United States and the USSR), his prominence grows. Men like de Tocqueville, Jacob Burckhardt, de Maistre, Niebuhr, Donoso Cortés, Burke, Henry Adams, Leontyev or Rivarol can be infinitely better understood by our contemporaries than they were by our grandparents.

Americans, in reviewing the mistakes of their government, often blame its blunders on the youth of their country. Yet America is not a split second younger than Europe. "Young" were the ancient cultures and civilizations of the Nile, the Indus Valley, Mesopotamia, the Yang-Tse area, older the art and thought of Greece and Rome, and, later, of the Middle Ages and the Renaissance. Europe and the Americas share a common old age, even as they share some signs of senility. These are manifested in childish attitudes, such as a revolt against parents, or an overenthusiasm for games and technology, together with a touch of barbarism (the British rowdies in Brussels who slaughtered thirty-five Italian football fans). Alexis de Toqueville understood this when he said that "if the country is new, one sees at each step that it is an old people which has come to inherit it."

Youth is no excuse! Theodor Mommsen, the great historian, told a young American lady, after she explained that her country had erred frequently because it was "so young": "Madame, your nation has had open before it the whole history of Europe from the beginning; and without exception you have consistently copied every mistake Europe has ever made. I have no sympathy whatever for you, and no interest in you."[1184]

Mommsen rightly berated Americans for their insularity in time and space. But a European could not utter those same words today. We depend entirely on America. We not only desperately need its strong arm, but its leadership; and for this it is not prepared. The United States offers to the world, not a picture, but an obsolete frame. It does not reason consistently; it does not want to act globally.

There is a vacuum in the West, and no preparations have been made to fill it. Auberon Waugh, in a work of fantasy, envisioned that an Eichmann-type had been discovered in London. The Israeli secret service abducts him to Tel-Aviv where he is put on trial. Journalists standing in front of the courthouse debates in what manner he should be tortured to death. But one man, raising his voice, objects to the barbarism. "This mass murderer should be reeducated," he argues, and the crowd murmurs in agreement. Until another man asks: "Reeducated towards what?" Silence is the only answer.[1185]

IX

What of the latest Revolution? What is the significance of recent developments in Eastern Europe (and China)?

No one questions what triggered them. Marx, although a man of broad knowledge, had one blind spot: he was ignorant of the true character of economics. He did not realize that economics can only be understood in close relationship to the other humanities (and certain sciences), and therefore should not be studied *in vacuo*. Ironically, this very weakness was largely instrumental in making Marxism successful. Marxist economics—yet another instance of a false but clear idea—can be explained to the merest child in a matter of minutes. (Conversely, to explain the workings of the free market economy to an adult would take weeks of hard work.) Because it was easily grasped, Marxism flooded the world within a few decades, as had other simplistic ideologies and religions, such as Islam and the Enlightenment; this same sort of simplicity gave rise to the French Revolution and national socialism. Christianity, on the other hand, took three centuries to triumph.

The economies of the Red Empire are facing bankruptcy (foreseen by Brutzkus in 1922). This material-materialistic fact, bubbling for years among intellectuals and artists, has finally burst over the masses. (Not that they had ever completely espoused the socialist-communist pap. A sizeable communist minority existed only in the German Democratic Republic. North Germans are progressive; they believe what they imbibe at school and from the mass media.)

On coming to power, Mikhail Gorbachev was eager to make communism an economic success. To this end, he determined to rid communism of unnecessary frills as, for instance, the severe restrictions on freedom of expression. *Glasnost'* means just that. *Perestroyka*, for its part, aims at industrial and agrarian renovation by debureaucratizing the economy, but, somehow, *within* the collectivist framework of communism. Gorbachev does *not* intend to return to a free market economy. (This is not the case in Hungary and Poland, aristocratic nations to their fingertips. There, old property titles still exist, or can be reconstructed.) At this writing, the economic straits of the USSR continue, the squaring of the circle has failed. But should Gorbachev and his men unaccountably wish to return to the principles of private property and free enterprise, it is difficult to see how this could be accomplished. Under what circumstances and conditions could individuals acquire private property? How can people walk again after years and decades of being hobbled?

The Red Dinosaur is sick; of this there is no doubt. Ties with the satellites have been weakened, and nationalism—ethnicism in the Anglo-American sense—has revived. In the hearts and minds of these nationalities, which frequently fight among themselves, communism has assumed the character of a specifically Russian disease. This is making the Great Russian patriot intensely uneasy. He fears the loss of the borderlands, annexed by Russia during the past two hundred years—perhaps too the loss of the Ukraine, the cradle of Russia. He is experiencing a fierce Russianism, reacting against both communism and borderland-ethnicism. The old Imperial Russian banners have recently been carried on high by demonstrators. It is somewhat sinister to view the moral support this aspect of the nationalistic Great-Russian movement is receiving from the surviving Stalinists. Are they both headed toward something on the order of a new "national socialism"?

As difficult as it is to envisage the USSR reverting to free enterprise (despite Russia's success in the 1890–1914 period), it is impossible to conceive of its undergoing a transition to a liberal-democratic republic. When people demand "democracy" in Eastern Europe (or China), they think of liberty, not of a well-balanced multiparty system. (E. Wickert discovered that the Chinese who were demanding "democracy" were horrified at the thought of a variety of parties. "You want us to have many parties? Impossible! One party, the Communist party, has made us suffer enough!") If the Western experiment is undertaken, civil war could easily result. Recall Russia during its parliamentary period (1905–1914) and under Kerenski, recall the democratic development in Central and East Central Europe after 1918. The results were tragic. Monarchical restorations? They are desirable, and even feasible.

The dinosaur is sick, but who knows in which direction the beast will leap? In the meantime, the Red Army still stands 140 miles from the Dutch border, 35 miles from Vienna. And no one knows where the leadership of the Soviet armed forces stands. It seems that they yet have an enormous supply of nuclear weapons, that most of their officers are not communist. But what are their loyalties? Their aims?

Too many Europeans and Americans think they can, at long last, take a long holiday from history. But a sick dinosaur (which occupies one-sixth of the world) might be even more dangerous than a healthy one; and should the dinosaur die, it would present a colossal problem if it should agonize at our very doorstep. West Europeans are presently building a common house, which is immensely attractive to their brethren farther east. Gorbachev, in a clever move, has spoken of the "House of Europe" (from Lisbon to the Bering Straits?). The number of problems and emergencies growing out of the crisis in the east are legion. . .

Yet, should the menace from that direction ever come to an end, it would not solve the inner crisis of the West, above all the crisis of democracy with its deadly evolution toward the totalitarian provider state; it would not stop the mistrust between the ever-changing governments; it would not fill the deepening abyss between the *scita* and the *scienda*; it would not halt the mounting crime rates, the increasing drug consumption, the mass butchering of the unborn, the shrinking birth rates, the decline of family life, the evanescence of authority. No, this is no time for that long holiday.

X

Chesterton warned that a person who ceases to believe in God does not believe in nothing; he believes in everything. People are rarely diabolic or bent enthusiastically on evil. As a rule, they are only weak; they cannot resist temptation and thus give way to their evil drives. Evil has its own magnetism[1186] and can prove totally infectious to crowds. (The Lord's Prayer should more properly end with "And deliver us from the Evil One.")[1187] Yet some of the greatest catastrophes in history are caused not so much by weakness, by yielding to evil, as by stupidity—insane, obstinate, spiteful, fanatic, passionate stupidity. And stupidity is aided by the blinkers of false ideologies. Franco, towards the end of his rule, had two Basque assassins executed, which provoked a mass protest throughout Europe. (Today, the number of people murdered by ETA terrorists is almost legion.) In the same year, the leftist Mexican government admitted to massacring in Tlatelolco about 130 demonstrating students (the opposition claimed one thousand dead). Who protested in Europe or the United States? A leftist government can do no wrong.

Must we change? Are we obliged to break with the past? With the whole development since the French Revolution? A good American will surely object that, after all, in spite of setbacks and misunderstandings, miscalculations and irritations, the history of the United States has been a great success. Which recalls the story of the man who fell from the Empire State Building and, swishing by the sixth floor, muttered: "So far so good!"

No, the liberal-democratic combine cannot fight the children and grandchildren of the French Revolution. An ox cannot successfully fight a bull, an octogenarian a youth; the lesser evil cannot overwhelm the greater, because extremes, since they represent final, logical conclusions, have great dynamic force. Only something new, ideas of a radically different order, rejecting false premises, can set a new trend. All this is not only true ideologically, but also structurally and constitutionally.

The nations of the West have entered modernity in the swaddling clothes of nationalism and democracy, two forms of collectivist horizontalism. Let us apply to democracy what Dmitri Merezhkovski, one of the great visionaries of our century, said about nationalism—that these, our swaddling clothes, threaten to become shrouds, soon to suffocate us. We can only hope for a new life if we cast them off like the rising Lazarus.[1188]

APPENDIX

What Is Left?

1. Materialism: economic, biological, sociological
2. Messianism assigned to one group: a nation, a race, a class
3. Centralization: elimination of local administrations, traditions, characteristics, etc.
4. Totalitarianism: pervasion of all spheres of life by one doctrine
5. Brute force and terror, not authority, an *endogenous* force
6. Ideological one-party state
7. Complete state control of education
8. Socialism: the opposite of personalism
9. Provider (Welfare) State: from the cradle to the grave
10. Militarism (*not* bellicosity): conscription, people's armies, *levée en masse*
11. Rigid ideology enforced by the state: complete anti-image of "The Enemy."
12. Antimonarchical leader system: the leader (*Führer, Duce, Vozhd'*)
13. Antiliberalism: hatred of freedom
14. Antitraditionalism: against the historic past, against "reaction"
15. Territorial expansionist tendencies as form of self- realization
16. Exclusiveness: no other deities tolerated

17. Elimination of *corps intermédairs* (intermediary bodies)
18. Conformity of mass media: press, radio, television
19. Elimination or relativizing of private property: where it survives in name, it is totally under state control; the entrepreneur is merely the steward of his "property"
20. Persecution, subjection, or control of all religious bodies
21. "Right is what benefits the People" (Hitler); "Right is what benefits the Party" (*Partiynost'*, Lenin)
22. Hatred of minorities
23. Glorification of the majority and the "average man"
24. Glorification of revolution, revolt, upheaval
25. Plebeianism: fight against the former elites
26. Hunt for "traitors"; resentment against emigrants
27. Populism and "uniformism" (people's courts, people's cars, etc.)
28. Ideological roots in French Revolution
29. Constant reference to democratic principles
30. Dynamic monolithism: state, society, people become *one*
31. Coordination through slogans, poems, songs, symbols, phrases
32. Secular rites replacing religious rites
33. Conformism as vital principle
34. Incitement of mass hysteria
35. Technology in the service of power
36. Freedom—below the belt
37. Everything for, everything through the state, nothing against the state (Mussolini)
38. Totally politicized life: tourism, sports, recreation
39. Nationalism or internationalism as against patriotism
40. Struggle against extraordinary people, against "privileges"
41. Total mobilization of envy in the interest of party and state

What Is Right?

1. The opposite of all the above or its absence

Leftism characterizes all the three Great Revolutions: the French (1789), the Russian (1917), and the German (1933). But recall that political parties or systems are rarely 100 percent right or left, but an admixture of both.

Notes

1. Only a tiny "Protestant Church of the Palatinate," a Lutheran-Calvinist mixture, exists on the Continent. In the Anglican coronation ceremony, however, the monarch has to swear to "defend the Protestant faith," a term which conceivably covers the Episcopal Church of England and the Presbyterian Church of Scotland. The interpretation of *protestare* as "standing witness" is but nineteenth-century legerdemain.

2. The First Enlightenment generally refers to the intellectual movement that took place in the eighteenth century, the Second Enlightenment took place after World War II. The latter had an impact even on Catholic theologians, who ignored Romans 12: 2. What we want to do here is to contribute to a Third Enlightenment: to enlighten those who think they are enlightened.

3. Cf. Encyclical *Graves de Communi* (*A.S.S.* 33: 387). American Catholics seemed overjoyed when Pius XII allegedly "canonized" democracy in his Christmas 1944 allocution. The American translation was faulty (elite was given as "select men"), but P. Gustav Gundlach, S.J., in *Periodica*, XXXIV, Fasc. 1-2, gave an authoritative explanation of the document. In his allocution to the World Federalists (April 6, 1951) Pius XII severely criticized democratic numeralism. (*A.S.S.* II series 18:278 sq.). The delegation theory of political authority has also been condemned by Leo XIII and Pius X (in favor of the designation theory). In the *Sillon-Letter* Pius X emphasized that authority can descend, but never rise.

4. Herman Borchardt, *The Conspiracy of the Carpenters* (New York, Simon & Shuster, 1943).

5. Cf. 153.

6. Dr. Marcel Eck says in his essay "Propos de la sexualité" (in *Qu'est-ce-que l'homme*, Paris: Pierre Horay, 1955, 110) that the "hell of homosexuality" lies precisely in that it avoids genuine dialogue; homosexual love is not in quest of another but merely seeks the self.

7. José Ortega y Gasset says in *Invertebrate Spain*, trsl. Mildred Adams (New York: Norton, 1937), 170-71: "Probably the origin of this anti-individual fury lies in the fact that in their innermost hearts the masses feel themselves weak and defenceless in the face of their destiny. On a bitter and terrible page Nietzsche notes how, in primitive societies which were weak when confronted with the difficulties of existence, every individual and original act was a crime, and the man who tried to lead a solitary life was a malefactor. He must in everything comport himself according to the fashion of the tribe." On the antagonism between liberty and equality, liberalism and democracy, see also Roger G. Williams, *Free and Unequal: The Biological Basis of Individual Liberty* (Austin: University of Texas Press, 1953); A.D. Lindsay, *The Modern Democratic State* (London: Oxford University Press, 1945), 1: 46, 79; Franz Schnabel, *Deutsche Geschichte im Neunzehnten Jahrhundert* (Freiburg i. Br.: Herder, 1933), 2: 97-98; Heinz O. Ziegler, *Autoritärer oder totaler Staat* (Tübingen: J.C.B. Mohr, 1932), 10; Wilhelm Stählin, "Freiheit und Ordnung," in *Der Mensch und die Freiheit* (München: Neues Abendland, 1954), 17. Werner Jaeger in his *Paideia* (Berlin: Walter de Gruyter, 1954), 2:104, emphasizes the fact that Athens was democratic, that it laid stress on *to ison* (equality), but not on personal freedom. Professor Goetz Briefs in his *Zwischen Kapitalismus und Syndikalismus* (Bern: A. Francke, 1952), 75, reminds that all democratism (which he distinguishes from democracy) must end in despotism since it is opposed to the realities of man and society. Herbert Marcuse, referring to Hegel, came to a similar conclusion. Cf. his *Reason and Revolution* (Boston Press, 1960), 242-43.

8. Jacob Burckhardt in his letter to Friedrich von Preen dated January 1, 1879: "You are perfectly right: One wants to train people for meetings. Finally, people will start to scream if they don't form crowds of at least a hundred." (Jacob Burckhardt, *Briefe an seinen Freud Friedrich von Preen 1864-1893* (Stuttgart: Deutsche Verlaganstalt, 1922), 130.

9. Cf. Friedrich Nietzsche, *Werke* (Leipzig: Kröner, 1917), Vol. 12: 140.

10. On envy, see the magisterial works of Gonzalo Fernández de la Mora, *La envidia igualitaria* (Barcelona: Planeta, 1984), and Helmut Schoeck, *Der Neid* (Freiburg i.Br., Karl Alber, 1966), and *Recht auf Ungleichheit* (Munich: Herbig, 1979).

11. Witness President Wilson's declaration shortly before America's entry into World War I: "Conformity will be the only virtue. And every man who refuses to conform will have to pay the penalty." (Cf. Harold U. Faulkner, *From Versailles to the New Deal* (New Haven: Yale University Press, 1950), 141.
     On the dangers of standardization see Josiah Royce in *Race Questions*, 74, cited by Ralph Henry Gabriel, *The Course of American Democratic Thought: An Intellectual History since 1815* (New York: The Ronald Press, 1940), 275-76.

12. Much of modern art is simultaneously (1) a reaction against democracy and "populism," (2) a tremendous hoax at the expense of the naive, exploiting their snobbish admiration for "the Emperor's New Clothes," and (3) (at times) a bit of Satanism, a protest against God's creation. But remember that Italy's super-futurist Marinetti was a devoted Fascist, that National Socialism and Russian Communism (after a period of acceptance) turned violently against modern art. (Khrushchev thought that all modern artists were homosexuals and *therefore* belonged in jail.) There is, of course, a legitimate modern art.

13. Cf. "Monita quibus Stephanus filium Emericum instruxit, ut regnum recte pieque administraret," chap. VI, in J. P. Migne, *Patrologiae Cursus Completus, Series Latina*, 151:124ff.

14. Cf. his *Maximen und Reflexionen*, no. 953 (1907 edition).

15. See the excellent contribution of W. H. Hutt, "The Complexities of South Africa," in *The African Nettle*, Frank S. Meyer, ed. (New York: John Day, 1965), 157ff. Cf. W. H. Hutt, *The Economics of the Color Bar* (London: André Deutsch, 1964), 58ff., and Ray Marshall, *The Negro and Organized Labor* (Sydney: John Wiley, 1968). The originator of apartheid, the labor leader W. H. Andrews, later became secretary and finally chairman of the Communist party of South Africa.

16. The address of Pius XII to the World Federalists virtually condemning the one-man one-vote system and the worship of numbers received little publicity in the Catholic press—anywhere. For a full text see the *New York Times*, no. 34, 041, April 7, 1951, 3, or *Acta Apostolicae Sedis*, annus et vol. XLIII, 1951, 278ff.

17. As, for instance, John Stuart Mill, so frequently and enthusiastically quoted by leftists. Mill considered equality of vote "in principle wrong, because recognising a wrong standard and exercising a bad influence on the voter's mind. It is not useful but hurtful, that the constitution of a country should declare ignorance to be entitled to as much political power as knowlege." Cf. his "Considerations on Representative Government" included in *Utilitarianism, Liberty and Representative Government*, no. 482 of "Everyman's Library" (London: Dent, 1910), 288.

   Criticism of the one-man one-vote principle is almost universal. See also Rosalind Murray (Mrs. Arnold Toynbee), *The Good Pagan's Failure* (New York: Longmans, Green, 1939), 137-39: Sir Henry Maine in R. Sellars, *The Next Step in Democracy* (New York: Macmillan, 1916), 216: John Adams, Letter to James Madison, June 17, 1817, in *The Selected Writings of John and Quincy Adams*, A. Koch and W. Peden, eds. (New York: Knopf, 1946) 202; Jacob Burckhardt, op. cit., 200: Charles Péguy, *Pensées* (Paris: Gallimard, 1934) 21-22: Gabriel Marcel, "Considérations sur l'égalité," *Études Carmélitaines*, 24-2:164-65; *Letters from Albert Jay Nock* (Caldwell: Caxton Printers, 1949), 176: D. H. Lawrence as quoted by Witter Bynner, *Journey with Genius* (New York: John Day, 1951), 226: Antonio Rosmini-Serbati, *La società e il suo fine*, Carlo Brocca, ed. (Milan: Edizioni di Uomo, 1945), 45-46. Recently the attacks of Professor Max Horkheimer on the principle of majority rule (coming from a former supporter of the New Left) created a minor sensation in Europe. Cf. his *Zur Kritik der instrumentellen Vernunft* (Frankfurt am Main: S. Fischer, 1967), 38.

   It is true that the Rhodesian Parliament under Ian Smith was elected by a minority, but so too was the Swiss Diet. Of the entire Swiss population (residing in the country) about 29 percent (before female suffrage was introduced at the federal level) had the right to vote, and between 19 and 20 percent actually did vote. Yet nobody has thought of organizing economic warfare against Switzerland, with the possible exception of Stalin in 1945.

18. How low the Soviet birthrate actually is, is open to conjecture since reliable statistics about the USSR do not exist. Only the catastrophic decline of the birthrate in the satellite states is known at this writing. Cf. "Die Ausbeutung der Frau in Kommunistischen Osteuropa," in *Neue Zürcher Zeitung*, February 15, 1970, 19. The average Swiss family consists of 3-5 members; the average Russian family has fewer.

19. Cf. Friedrich August (von) Hayek, *Individualism and Economic Order* (Chicago: University of Chicago Press, 1947), 15.

20. Cf. Benedetto Croce, *Etica o Politica* (Bari: Laterza 1943), 288. This implies the rejection of any kind of a caste system. Castes are inherited by birth and are immovable and unchangeable: estate status is usually inherited but is changeable. A nobleman could become a priest, a burgher could be nobilitated, a peasant could receive the "freedom" of the city and thus become a burgher. Contrary to the general notion, there were no "higher" or "lower" estates; they just had different functions. (There are, of course, higher and lower classes.)

21. Marchese Vilfredo Pareto's *Trattato de sociologia universale* (Florence: G. Barbèra, 1923) also exists in an English translation by Arthur Livingston under the title *Mind and Society* (New York: Harcourt, Brace, 1935). Livingston also translated a part of Gaetano Mosca's *Elementi di Scienza Politica* (Turin, 1923) and published it as *The Ruling Class* (New York: McGraw-Hill, 1939). Robert(o) Michels' *Zur Soziologie des Parteienwesens in der modernen Democratie* (Leipzig: Duncker und Humblot, 1911) saw many editions.

The thesis that democracy is in practice oligarchical has also been defended by Enrique Gil y Robles in his *Tratado de Derecho Político según los principios de la filosofía y el derecho cristiano* (Salamanca: Imprenta Salamaticense, 1902), 2:882ff. This professor of Salamanca University was the father of Don José Maria Gil Robles, founder of the CEDA, Spain's Christian party.

22. Article 21 of the Weimar Constitution insisted that deputies are only subject to their conscience and not to the desires of the voters. This same stipulation is found in Article 91 of the Swiss Constitution. Cf. William F. Rappard, *The Government of Switzerland* (New York: Van Nostrand, 1936), 59, 64. The contrary (democratic) position had been taken by Hans Kelsen, author of the present Austrian Constitution, in his *General Theory of Law and State*, trsl. A. Wedberg (Cambridge, Mass.: Harvard University Press, 1946).

23. William Rappard reasoned that Switzerland rejected female suffrage because Switzerland is essentially middle class. Only the aristocracy and the proletarian truly accept female equality. He overlooked the Swiss equation of a citizen and an arms-bearing man.

24. The critique of proportional representation (P.R.) was the life work of Professor Ferdinand A. Hermens, formerly of Notre Dame, later of Cologne University.

25. Naturally, in old times *unanimity* was the rule and *had* to be achieved (as today among

the jurors in Britain and the United States). Unanimity was also required for the election of the King in the Polish *Rzeczpospolita*. Only the nobility (the *szlachta*) voted, and a nobleman could not possibly be subject to a man who was not his own choice but somebody else's. The Golden Bull abolished unanimity in 1356, and in 1496, in the Imperial Diet (of the Holy Roman Empire) decisions were made by majority vote. Cf. J. Stawski, *Le principe de la majorité* (Geneva: Officina Boenigiana, 1920), 29-38; see also Carl Ernst Jarcke, "Prinzipienfragen" in *Vermischte Schriften* (Paderborn: Schöningh, 1854), 175-76.

26. Cf. Herman Melville, *Mardi—And a Voyage Tither* (Boston: Small, Maynard, n.d.) p. 183. Majoritism seems to have been strongly backed by Marsiglio of Padua. Cf. Felice Battaglia, *Marsiglio da Padova e il pensiero politico medievale* (Firenze: Sansoni, 1928): Sigmund Riezler, *Die literarischen Widersacher der Päpste zur Zeit Ludwigs des Baiers* (Leipzig: Duncker und Humblot, 1874), 203. Yet Alan Gewirth insists that the majority rule character of the passage in the *Defensor Pacis* (XII, 3) is the result of mangled manuscripts. Cf. Marsilius of Padua, *The Defender of Peace*, trsl. and edit. Alan Gewirth (New York: Columbia Press, 1956), 2: 45, n 6. Orestes Brownson, the brilliant and original American Catholic thinker, rejected majorities in strong terms. Cf. the *Collected Works* (Detroit: T. Nourse, 1882-1887), 15:5, 40, quoted by Lawrence Roemer, *Brownson on Democracy and the Trend Toward Socialism* (New York: Philosophical Library, 1953), 36-37, 45: Carl Ernst Jarcke, op. cit., 172-73. Most revealing is Herman Finer, a leftist professor who, in replying to a question of F. A. von Hayek, whether the Nazi Reich should be credited with exercising rule of law if Hitler had had a clear majority in the elections, said, "The answer is 'Yes,' the majority would be right, the Rule of Law would be in operation, *if* the majority voted him into power. The majority might be unwise, and it might be wicked, but the Rule of Law would prevail. For in a democracy, right is what the majority believes it to be." Cf. *The Road to Reaction* (Boston: Little, Brown, 1945), 60. An injunction against the moral dangers of majoritarianism can be found in II. Moses, XXIII, 11; it can be summed up, "Thou shalt not follow a majority to do evil."

27. I am convinced that (contrary to the teaching of St. Thomas) the state (as we basically conceive it) is the result of original sin, i.e., of man's imperfections. Cf. also Erik von Kuehnelt-Leddihn, *Liberty or Equality* (Caldwell, Caxton Printers, 1952), 92-93, or Isdem, *Freiheit oder Gleichheit?* (Salzburg: Otto Müller, 1953), 235-37. It is commonly held that St. Augustine and Luther saw the state as a result of the Fall. Yet Otto Schilling in his magisterial work *Die Staats-und Soziallehren des hl. Augustinus* (Freiburg i Br.: Herder, 1910), 45-63 has proved the contrary, and Luther does not give an exact formulation: we can only deduce each stand. St. Bonaventure, Hugo of St. Victor and Aegydius Romanus, however, blame the state on Original Sin. (Exact sources and materials can be found in *Freiheit oder Gleichheit?*, notes 680-85 on 507-08. I am nevertheless convinced that *society* would have existed under all circumstances, and with society—leadership and arbitration.

28. The connection between love and service has been well brought out by Franz von Baader, "Vierzig Sätze aus einer religiösen Erotik," in *Gesammelte Schriften*, F. Hoffman, ed. (Leipzig: Bethman, 1853), 4:186: Gustave Thibon, "Christianisme et liberté," in *Recherches et Débats* (Paris, 1952), new series 1:16: Georges Bernanos, *La*

France contre les robots (Paris: Laffont, 1947), 87. The relationship between loyalty, law, and love was the guiding idea in the defense speech of Sir Roger Casement. Cf. Geoffrey de C. Parmiter, *Roger Casement* (London: Barker, 1936), 303ff.

29. One of the best accounts of the People's Temple was given by Boris Paramonow in the Russian dissident periodical *Kontinent*, XIX:2 (1979), 223-37. Unfortunately, all the money those fools still had was given to the USSR.

30. Is polygamy (unlike polyandry) contrary to the natural law? We doubt it.

31. Cf. The Pollock-Holmes Letters. Correspondence of Sir Frederick Pollock and Mr. Justice Holmes 1874-1932 (Cambridge: Cambridge University Press, 1942) Vol. 2, 36.

32. Cf. Elliott Roosevelt, *As Father Saw It* (New York: Duell, Sloane and Pearce, 1946) and Winston S. Churchill, *The Second World War* (London: Cassell, 1952), 5:330.

33. Cf. Peter Wust, *Ungewissheit und Wagnis* (Salzburg: Anton Pustet, 1937), *passim*.

34. See note 715.

35. Nearly all outstanding political scientists and essayists make the distinction between liberalism and democracy. Here just a few authors and works which contain references to this piece of semantics: Irving Babbitt, *Democracy and Leadership*; W. H. Chamberlin, *The World's Iron Age*; Christopher Dawson, *The Judgment of the Nations*; Luis Legaz y Lacambra, *Introducción a la teoría del Estado Nacional sindicalista*; José Ortega y Gasset, *Castilla y sus castillos*; Gustave Radbruch, *Rechtsphilosophie*; Wilhelm Röpke, *Die Gesellschaftskrise der Gegenwart*; Frank Thiess, *Das Reich der Dämonen*; Georg Freiherr von Hertling, *Recht, Staat und Gesellschaft*; Max Weber, *Grundriss der Sozialökonomik* 111, Abteilung; Franz Schnabel, op. cit.; Heinz O. Ziegler, op. cit.; Winfried Martini, *Das Ende aller Sicherheit*; Carl Schmitt, "Die geistesgeschichtliche Lage des heutigen Parlamentarismus" in *Bonner Festausgabe für E. Zittelmann*; Hermann Hefele, "Demokratie und Liberalismus," *Hochland* XXII; Georges Vedel, *Manuel élémentaire de droit constitutionnel*; Guido de Ruggiero, *Storia del liberalismo europeo*; Denis de Rougemont and Charlotte Muret, *The Heart of Europe*; Bernard Wall, *European Notebook*; Everett Dean Martin, *Liberty*; Georges Bernanos, *La liberté pour quoi faire?*; Nicholas Berdyaev, *Novoye strednovyekovye*; Petko Staynov, *Kompetentnost i narodovlastie*. Probably the best *semantic* analysis of the terms "liberalism" and "democracy" can be found in Giovanni Sartori, *Demorazia e definizioni* (Bologna: Il Mulino, 1969). The authors dealing with the incompatibility of democracy and freedom, democracy and liberty, are legion. An identification of democracy and freedom can be found, however, in the work of a strictly positivist scholar denying a hierarchy of ethical values—Hans Kelsen in his *Vom Wesen und Wert der Demokratie* (Tübingen: J. C. Mohr, 1929), 3-4.

36. Cf. J. L. Talmon, *The Origins of Totalitarianism* (London: Secker and Warburg, 1952). In this book Talmon puts the main emphasis on Gracchus Babeuf. There were plans during the Terror to put all Frenchmen into uniform, into a "national costume" (245). Similar plans were entertained by Morelly. About the educational theories of the *Babouvistes* cf. 245-47.

37. Cf. Alexis de Tocqueville, op. cit., 3:517-23.

38. J. J. Bachofen maintained that matriarchal civilizations generally consider the left superior to the right side. *Vide* his *Das Mutterrecht* (Basel, 1948), 54ff; H. Zinser, *Der Mythos des Mutterrechts* (Frankfurt a.m. Ullstein, 1981), however, denies the existence

of any matriarchy. The Gnostics identified "left" with the lower and "right" with the higher elements of creation. Cf. François M. Saguard, *La Gnose Valentinienne et le témoignage de St. Irénée* (Paris, 1947), 544-45. A very witty analysis of the leftist mind can be found in the small book of Leon Plumyène and Raymod Lasierra, *Le complexe de gauche* (Paris: Flammarion, 1967). As *leitmotif* of the leftist mentality the authors see "the murder of the father."

39. In German the sentence, "The just, saved and judged, were on the right" would sound like this: "Die *gerichteten* und *geretteten Gerechten* waren auf der *Rechten*." In Spanish and Portuguese the word for "left" is taken from another language, from the Basque *Izquierdo*.

40. The non-Latin Continental languages distinguish between citizenship, nationality, and race. The first, a legal concept, is easy to change, the second, in younger years, is difficult to transform, the third, a biological concept, is immutable *for the individual*. "Nationalism" in the Germanic and Salvic countries, therefore, implies an exaggerated emphasis on language and culture ("way of life"). In the Romance languages the same confusion prevails as in English. The Nazis, naturally, were nationalists as well as racists (and socialists), which shows their identitarian character. A Swiss, for instance, can be a patriot and might even become a racist, but he cannot become a nationalist without seriously questioning the idea of the Swiss state. *For the sake of a workable semantics (and in respect to etymology) the term nationalism in its original nonlegal connotation is employed throughout the book.*

41. Nowhere is this more evident than in the natural sciences, where one generation most visibly learns from the preceding and *adds* its own discoveries and inventions. Mortimer Adler said quite rightly, "The substitution of one thing for another would leave us going around in a circle, neither advancing nor declining. . . . Progress is conservative, because it is cumulative, not substitutional." Cf. his essay "God and Modern Man" in *The Critic* (Oct.-Nov., 1966), 402.

42. Cf. Étienne Gilson, *L'esprit de la philosophie médiévale* (Paris: Vrin, 1944), 402.

43. Cf. I. Peter, ll:9, and St. Thomas Aquinas, *De Regimine Principum*, 1,14. The origin of this concept is found in Exodus XIX:6. The uniqueness of each one of us entails our inequality in the eyes of God. Cf. also E. I. Watkin, *A Philosophy of Form* (London and New York: Sheed and Ward, 1951), 229-230.

44. Yet what about Russia, Prussia, Italy, and Portugal, the reader may ask? The Romanovs died out in the eighteenth century and were actually replaced by the German House of Holstein-Gottorp. Prussia was ruled by South German Suabians, the Hohenzollern, whose main line remained Catholic. Italy's crown belonged to the Savoys, who were French. Portugal's legitimate dynasty was in exile; the "Braganças" who ruled until 1910 were in reality Saxe-Coburg-Gothas of the Kohary branch.

45. About the death of Charles Maurras and his "reconversion," cf. Chanoine A. Cormier *Més Entretiens de Prêtre avec Charles Maurras, Mars-Novembre 1952* (Paris: Plon, 1953). The canon kissed the hands of the dying man. Cf. also Chanoine A. Cormier *La Vie Intérieure de Charles Maurras* (Paris: Plon, 1956).

46. Cf. *Konfuzius*, ed. Lin Yutang, trls. G. Coudenhove (Frankfurt: Fischer Bücher, 1957), 65-66.

47. On Socrates see the excellent article in the *Encyclopaedia Britannica* by Professor Henry

Jackson (in various editions), as well as Werner Jaeger, op. cit., 76ff., 124; A. E. Taylor, *Socrates* (Garden City, N.Y.: Doubleday-Anchor Books, 1953), 111; Heinrich Maier, *Sokrates* (Tübingen: Mohr, 1913), 133, 417ff, 419, 470: Tuttu Tarkiainen, *Die Athenische Demokratie* (Zürich: Artemis, 1966), 340.

48. Isocrates had even larger visions of unification transcending the Hellenic-Macedonian frame. Cf. Arnaldo Momigliano, "L'Europa come concetto politico presso Isocrate e gli Isocratei," in *Rivista di filologia d'istruzione classica* (Turin, 1933), 477ff. Isocrates, besides, was a confirmed monarchist. Cf. his "Nicocles" in *Isocrates*, trsl. George Norlin, The Loeb Classical Library (London: Heinemann, 1928), 1:17-18, 21, 26.

49. Cf. Polybius, *Works*, trsl. W. R. Paton, The Loeb Classical Library (London: Heinemann, 1923), 3:288 (Book VI, 2-10).

50. *Aus Metternichs nachgelassenen Papieren*, Fürst Richard Metternich-Winneburg, ed. (Vienna: Braumüuller, 1881), 3:236-37. Compare also with Henrich von Treitschke, *Politik*, Max Cornicelius, ed. (Leipzig: Hirzel, 1900) 2:196.

51. On this subject also cf. Otto Seeck, *Geschichte des Unterganges der antiken Welt* (Berlin: Siemenroth und Troschel, 1879), 1:11-14.

52. This concept is almost the tenor of the brilliant work of Fritz Kern, *Gottesgnadentum und Widerstandsrecht im früheren Mittelalter. Zur Entwicklungsgeschichte der Monarchie* (Leipzig: Koehler, 1914). There are English and Spanish translations, but they are brutally cut and do not impart the magnificent scholarship of Fritz Kern. Similar if not identical concepts also prevailed in Hispanic South America. Cf. F. Javier de Ayala, *Ideas políticas de Juan de Solórzano* (Seville: Escuela de Estudios Hispano-Americanos, 1946), 194-95, 203.

53. An "absolutistic" government will not consult its subjects. But a totalitarian government will intervene in all domains of life. A government can be absolutistic and totalitarian at the same time—but it is not necessarily so. Monarchies in their internal expansion tend to be absolutistic, democracies totalitarian. The notion of the "politicized" nation is in itself totalitarian. All forms of "populism" lead naturally to totalitarian extension.

   Thus, a free market economy and free trade might fare better in monarchies, which accounts for the political conservatism of the Physiocrats. Cf. Roberto Michels, *Introduzione alla storia delle dottrine economiche e politiche* (Bologna: Zanichelli, 1932), 15ff.

54. Cf. Josef Leo Seifert, *Die Weltrevolutionäre, Von Bogumil über Hus zu Lenin* (Vienna: Amalthea, 1930).

55. A German translation of this query was popular on the Continent. A burgher of Innsbruck nailed it to the door of the Imperial Palace where Maximilian I, famous for his genealogical mania, resided. The Emperor replied the next day in a German rhyme, "I am not better than any other man but for the honor that God did me." Maximilian knew perfectly well that, had he been born a hundred yards from the palace, he would have been in another position altogether. Yet the great mob-masters of our day believe that they owe everything to their own genius. Hence their megalomania. A German medieval proverb says: "No sword cuts more brutally than a peasant who becomes a lord."

56. Marsilius of Padua, *Defensor Pacis*, Richard Scholz, ed. (Berlin: B.G. Teubner, 1914), 16-29 (chaps. VIII-XIII).

57. Typical is the great disappearance in the arts of Christ the King, of the royal crown in favor of the Crown of Thorns. The triumph of the crowned Christ, frequent in Romanesque art, was replaced by the *Schmerzensmann*, the "Man of Pain," in the Gothic period.

58. Bishop Tunstall, in a letter to Erasmus in 1523, lamented the continuation of Lollard ideas and sentiments in Britain. Cf. also James Gairdner, *Lollardy and the Reformation of England* (London: Macmillan, 1908), 1: 314, 316, 367, and J. C. Garrick, *Wycliffe and the Lollards* (New York: Scribner's, 1908).

59. The exegetic works of Josef Schmid, *Regensburger Neues Testament* (Regensburg: Friedrich Pustet, 1954), 2: 196, has an outline of Christ's attitude toward the rich.

60. Abel Bonnard said correctly about the ancient monarchy: "The king was father of the people only because every father was king in his family." Cf. his *Le drame du présent*, vol. 1. "Les modérés" (Paris: Grasset, 1936), 35. All these concepts are ancient. The "pious king" figures in almost all political writings of the Middle Ages, such as in *De institutione regis ad Pippinum regem* of Jonas d'Orléans. See chapters II, IV, and VII in Migne, *Patres Latini*, vol. 106, col. 287, 291, 295-96. Here lies, of course, an innate connection with Christianity. Ida Görres (Coudenhove) has clearly grasped the analogies between physical and transcendental fatherhood ("in a sense more miraculous than motherhood") pointing to the God who is essentially *the* Father. Cf. Ida Friederike Görres, *Nocturnen* (Frankfurt: Knecht, 1949), 115. And the rather left French Catholic philosopher Jean Lacroix sees in democracy the revolt against God, resulting in the revolt against all fatherhood: "One could say that to a large extent the present democratic movement is the murder of the father" (his emphasis). Cf. "Paternité et démocratie," *Esprit*, vol. 15, no. 133, May 1947, 749. He would probably have the support of Jerome Frank who said that "modern civilisation demands a mind free of father-governance." (Cf. his *Law and the Modern Mind*, Boston: Peter Smith, 1930, 252.) Hence also the great American inability to understand monarchy. Mom, or even "Big Brother," can be more easily understood by the American mind. *Uncle Sam* is not a father, but essentially a New England bachelor. It is also the thesis of Friedrich Heer, another Catholic with leftist inclinations, that democracy demands brotherhood, not fatherhood. (But do brothers exist without a common parent?) The problem of fatherhood in politics, society, and family is well treated in Alexander Mitscherlich's *Auf dem Wege zur vaterlosen Gesellschaft* (Munich: R. Pieper, 1963).

61. Cf. note 53.

62. Cf. note 96.

63. Søren Kierkegaard was convinced that the "real royalists" with a homogeneous outlook all lean toward the Catholic faith. See the remark in his diary, dated October 13, 1835, in *The Journals of Søren Kierkegaard, A Selection*, Alexander Dru, trsl. and ed. (London: Oxford University Press, 1938), 21.

64. Cf. Josef Pekař, *Žižka a jého doba* (Prague: Vesmir, 1927), vols. 1-4, *passim*.

65. It is precisely in order to set the record straight that Cardinal Roncalli, when elected

pope, chose the rather odious name of this counterpope. Historians now have to cope with two John XXIIIs, a fake (who was a pirate in his younger years) and a real one.

66. Cf. note 312.

67. The term "propaganda" stems from the papal *Congregatio de Propaganda Fide*, the supreme authority for all the missions.

68. Cf. E. v Kuehnelt-Leddihn, *Liberty or Equality?*, 209-17 (*Freiheit oder Gleichheit?*, 325-33).

69. Typical of this total misrepresentation of the Reformer and of the absolute ignorance of modern scholarship is de Rochemont's American film *Martin Luther* which Germany's leading daily, the *Frankfurter Allgemeine Zeitung* (March 3, 1954) lambasted bitterly as *der amerikanische Luther.* The Catholic monthly *Herderkorrespondenz* (April 1954), under the title "Martin Luther Made in USA," called it "an intervention of alien money and an alien spirit," a film "against which Adolf von Harnack and Martin Rade would have violently protested," a "repetition of nineteenth-century platitudes," a "misdeed prompted by American naiveté" and "after all the Catholic and Evangelical efforts to come to a real understanding of Luther's personality and the spirit of the Reformation, a truly evil surprise" (col. 319). Since the Reformation is a terrible wound, dividing the German people to this day, the film, exported to Germany, rubbed salt in the wound. "The next time," a German told me grimly, "we'll make a film about the American race problem." The German Evangelicals produced a film on Luther, *The Obedient Rebel,* which was sound in scholarship and thoroughly acceptable to enlightened Catholics.

70. Walter Nigg, himself of the Reformed Church, warned, "Too often we overlook the fact that the Reformation was born in the quiet cell of a monastery." (*Rheinischer Merkur,* vol. 11, no. 21, May 25, 1956, 3.) On "Monasticism" cf. 88-89 of this book.

71. The real reason Luther broke with Zwingli was not so much over varying views of the Eucharist as on the salvation of non-Christians. Luther was furious with Zwingli's *Christianae Fidei Expositio ad Christianum Regem* in which Zwingli forcefully defended his stand. Cf. Luther's "Kurz Bekenntnis vom heiligen Sacrament" in *Werke,* Erlangen Edition (1842), 32:399-400. Bear in mind that Luther was a *Gothic man.* Cf. Alexander Rüstow, *Ortbestimmung der Gegenwart* (Erlenbach-Zurich: Eugen Rentsch, 1952), 2:235, 269-70, 299-300, and Vicente Rodriquez Casado, *De la monarquia española del barroco* (Seville: Estudios Hispano-Americanos, 1955), 52. On the traumatic importance of Luther's journey to Rome, cf. Karl August Meissinger, *Der katholische Luther* (Munich: Leo Lehnen, 1952), 55-57, 272.

   Nietzsche saw all this very clearly when he wrote about "that German monk Luther" who went to Rome and hated the Renaissance. Cf. his *Der Antichrist* no. 61.

   Friedrich Heiler saw in Luther's antipaganism one of the main roots for the reformer's stand against the Catholic faith. Cf. F. Heiler, "Luthers Bedeutung für die christliche Kirche," in *Luther in ökumenischer Sicht,* A. v. Martin, ed. (Stuttgart: Fromann, 1929) 167-68. Compare also with J. A. Möhler, *Symbolik* (Mainz: Kupferberg, 1832) 49ff. and Konrad Algermissen, *Konfessionskunde* (Celle: Giesel, 1959), 514.

72. We do not like the expression "Protestant," a term of ridicule and opprobrium invented by the Catholic Counter-Reformation. We use the term Evangelical which *is* official, although it might confuse American readers as Evangelical in the United States has a "low church" implication. In Prussia, a 1821 order of the King forbade the use of the terms "Protestant" and "Protestantism"; only the word *Evangelisch* was allowed, an adjective that has *no noun*. Cf. Franz Schnabel, op. cit. 2:263. Nor do we use the frightful term "Catholicism," which never figures in Roman documents. (Encyclicals do not even mention "Catholics" but only "*Christifideles,*" "faithful in Christ.")

73. The highest virtues in the Scholastic traditions are the "theological virtues" (faith, hope, charity), followed by the "intellectual virtues," while the "moral virtues" are of the lowest order. The lowest of all was *temperantia* which included chastity. Even *fortitude* (courage) ranked higher. Unchastity, however, is considered a "cardinal sin" because it is the *source* of so many other failings.

74. Cf. 88-89.

75. On the Anabaptists in Münster, cf. Dr. Heinrich Detmer, *Bilder aus den religiösen und sozialen Unruhen in Münster während des 16. Jahrhunderts* (Münster: Coppenrathsche Buchhandlung, 1903, 1904) 2 vols.

76. Cf. C. A. Cornelius, *Geschichte des Münsterischen Aufruhrs* (Leipzig: Weigel, 1855, 1860) 2:279ff. In all candor, tremendous preparatory studies are necessary to understand the Bible properly. Without a mastery of Greek, the New Testament is incomprehensible in parts; even the Lord's Prayer contains two major philological problems. (The complete text of the Old Testament exists only in a Greek translation, the Septuagint, completed roughly in 150 B.C. Several Hebrew originals have been lost.)

77. Ibid., 73.

78. Cf. Ludwig Keller, "Die Anfänge der Reformation und die Ketzerschulen," in *Vorträge und Aufsätze der Comenius Gesellschaft* (Berlin: R. Gaertner, n.d.), 4, 1-2:7.

79. The Pilgrim Fathers started with a short communitarian experiment, a *kibbutz* or *kolkhoz*, one is tempted to say. Yet after the starvation period in 1623, Governor Bradford ordered them to abandon the unholy experiment, "That they should set corne every man for his owne particular, and in that regarde trust to themselves."

80. Max Weber's work is *now* known in America and Britain. (The first translations came with World War II.) Still fairly unknown are the writings of Alfred Müller-Armack, professor at the University of Cologne and formerly state secretary of the German Federal Republic's Ministry of Economics. Most important is his *Religion und Wirtschaft* (Stuttgart: Kohlhammer, 1959), a work of over 600 pages in the Max Weber tradition. He implemented the German economic miracle under Ludwig Erhard.

81. Cf. the essay of Paul Kecskeméti in J. P. Mayer, *Political Thought: The European Tradition* (London: J. M. Dent, 1939).

82. Even in 1776 a correspondent of Samuel Adams informed him that, with independence gained, America could now choose a monarch from another nation. Cf. William S. Carpenter, *The Development of American Political Thought* (Princeton: Princeton University Press, 1930) 35.

83. A short look at the career and connections of Leopold of Saxe-Coburg-Gotha, first

King of the Belgians. Born as the youngest son of the ruling Duke of Saxe-Coburg-Gotha, he entered the Russian army at the age of fifteen, but managed the affairs of the Duchy during the absence of his brother. He accompanied Emperor Alexander I on many campaigns, to the Congress of Vienna, and on his visit to London. In 1816 he married the daughter of George IV of England, expecting to become Prince-Consort, and received British citizenship. But his young wife died the following year. He also became a British field marshal. Early in 1830 he was offered the crown of Greece, which he rejected. But in 1831, he accepted the crown of Belgium and married the daughter of Louis-Philippe, King of the French. He was the uncle of Queen Victoria and the father-in-law of the Emperor of Mexico, Maximilian I, brother of Franz Joseph.

84. Cf. note 44. Remember that George VI of Britain hardly had a drop of English blood, being almost all German. The same is true of Philip, Duke of Edinburgh, who was born a Greek prince without any Greek ancestry (just like King Constantine II). His real family name is not Mountbatten either, but Sonderburg-Glücksburg-Augustenburg. Theoretically, after the death or abdication of Queen Elizabeth II, the Sonderburg-Glücksburgs would rule (though under different dynastic names) in Britain, Norway, Denmark, and perhaps Greece. In 1900 the Saxe-Coburg-Gothas ruled in Saxe-Coburg, Britain, Belgium, Bulgaria, and Portugal.

85. Cf. Chester V. Easum, *Prince Henry of Prussia, Brother of Frederick the Great* (Madison: University of Wisconsin, 1942), 339.

86. Cf. F. Loraine Petre, *Simon Bolívar, "El Libertador"* (London: John Lane, The Bodley Head, 1910), 300-303, 408-09. The same is borne out by Salvador de Madariaga, *Bolívar* (Buenos Aires: Editorial Sudamericana, 1975), 2:180. The tragedy of decol-onialization took place in Africa and Asia at a time even more unfavorable to the monarchical idea than the earlier part of the nineteenth century. Hence the adoption of demo-republican forms of government. Hence the alternating chaos and dictatorhip.

    Theodor Herzl, the founder of Zionism, stated that monarchy, the best form of government, could not be applied to Israel as there were no living descendants of David; he urged study of the aristocratic rule of Venice, far preferable to democracy, which should be avoided at all costs, for it eventually leads to the tyranny of the demagogue. Cf. his "Der Judenstaat" in *Zionistische Schriften* (Berlin: Jüdischer Verlag, n.d.), 119-21.

87. Cf. John C. Miller, *Origins of the American Revolution* (Boston: Little, Brown, 1943), 499.

88. Cf. Martin Van Buren, *Inquiry into the Origin and Sources of Political Parties in the United States*, ed. by his son (New York: Hurd and Houghton, 1867), 28.

89. Cf. *The Works of Alexander Hamilton*, H. Cabot Lodge, ed. (New York-London: Putnam, 1885), 1:353ff., 372, 390, 431.

90. Cf. Francis Lieber, *On Civil Liberty and Self-Government* (Philadelphia: Lippincott, 1874), 257.

91. Cf. Russell Kirk, *The Conservative Mind* (Washington: Regnery Gateway, 1987), p. 72.

92. Cf. *The Writings of Thomas Jefferson*, Paul Lester Ford, ed. (New York: Putnam, 1896), 7:24.

93. Cf. Wyndham Lewis, *America and Cosmic Man* (London: Nicholson and Watson, 1948), 133.

94. Cf. Edmund Burke, "Observations on a Late Publication Entitled 'The Present State of the Nation' " in *Burke's Politics*, Ross J. S. Hoffman and Paul Levack, eds. (New York: Alfred Knopf, 1949), 71-72.

95. Tuffin de la Rouërie (misspelled Rouvarie or Rouverie by Jefferson), who fought in America for freedom and perished in the fight against democracy in France, a heroic and dramatic figure, a close friend of George Washington and member of the Order of the Cincinnati, is practically unknown to Americans. I devoted an appendix to him in the first edition of *Leftism*. His life is an example of the incompatibility of liberty and equality. I visited his grave near the castle of La Guyomarais in the Bretagne where he found shelter in his last days. (In consequence, the owner's entire family was guillotined.)

De Kalb was, no doubt, of humble origin. The titles of nobility in France are spurious to an incredible degree. They were never registered in the past and nothing in France exists like the *Gothaische Genealogische Taschenbücher, Debrett's,* or *Burke's.* Many French titles have been faked and arbitrarily assumed but used and accepted for centuries. A wave of "self-nobilitation" took place in the eighteenth century, often on the basis of the purchase of castles and other properties. Cf. Wilhelm Weigand, *Der Abbé Galiani* (Bonn: Röhrscheid, 1948) 199-201.

96. Cf. John C. Miller, op. cit., 190-91, 373-74.

97. Cf. Ray Allen Billington, *The Protestant Crusade 1800-1860* (New York: Macmillan, 1938), *passim*, also quoting Daniel Barber, *History of My Own Times* (Washington, 1827).

98. Many Americans have observed this. Cf. Dean Willard L. Sperry, *Religion in America* (Cambridge, England: University Press, 1945), 218-19, as also foreigners, i.e., Evelyn Waugh in his article "The American Epoch in the Catholic Church" (*Life*, International Edition, vol. 7, no. 8, October 10, 1949, 63) or the unnamed author of "Problèmes et aspects du catholicisme américain" in *La Semaine Religieuse de Paris*, vol. 97, no. 5025, September 2, 1950, 797.

99. American colleges like particularly to represent St. Robert Bellarmine as a sturdy democrat, but James Brodrick, S.J., in *The Life and Word of Blessed Robert Francis Cardinal Bellarmine S.J., 1572-1621* (London: Burns, Oates and Washbourne, 1928), 1:230, tells a different story: "Like his masters, the scholastics, he is a convinced monarchist, and goes out of his way to justify and exalt the monarchical regime." The relevant passages show St. Robert a true patriarchalist—especially *De Romano Pontifice*, lib. 1.c.2. In fact, the Cardinal was convinced that majority decisions in large communities were bad, because the wicked and the stupid are more numerous than the good and the wise (*De clericis*, VII). The basis of the Bellarmine legend in Catholic America rests on the assumption that Jefferson in writing the Declaration was profoundly influenced by Sir Robert Filmer's summing up of Bellarmine's stand in his *Patriacha*. (There was a pencil mark of uncertain origin in Jefferson's copy of the book.) But this thesis is untenable given Jefferson's letter to Madison dated August 30, 1823, his letter to Henry Lee dated May 8, 1825, and his letter to Dr. James Mease, dated

September 26, 1825. (These can be found in the Monticello Edition of his *Works*, 15:426 and 16:118-19, 123; cf. also J. C. Rager, *The Political Philosophy of Blessed Cardinal Bellarmine* Washington D.C.: Catholic University of America, 1926.)

Yet the stand taken by the other great late Scholastic, Suárez, was of a rather different character. It has been rightly said that "in the Suarezian doctrine any form of government other than direct democracy becomes substitutional—a consequence palpably opposed to the whole political doctrine of Aristotle and St. Thomas." Cf. Charles N. R. McCoy, "Note on the Origin of Political Authority," *The Thomist*, vol. 16, no. 1 (January 1953), 80-81. Compare also with Gabriel Browe, O.P., *The Origin of Political Authority* (Dublin: Clonmore and Reynolds, 1955), 94.

Efforts to "monopolize" democracy were ridiculed by Maritain in his younger years. He called them *"indiscutablement une sanglante absurdité."* Cf. his *Trois Réformateurs* (Paris: Plon, 1925), 198.

100. In connection with the efforts to establish a "political theology," read the warning sentence of Erik Peterson. Cf. his *Der Monotheismus als politisches Problem, Ein Beitrag zur Geschichte der politischen Theologie im Imperium Romanum* (Leipzig: Jakob Hegner, 1935), 98ff. *Vide* also footnote 5 in James Brodrick, S. J., op. cit., 247. A similar warning—mainly to Catholic leftists—was given by Professor Hans Maier in his essay, "Politische Theologie (Einwände eines Laien)" in *Stimmen der Zeit* (Munich), February 1969, 73-91.

101. To the classic Swiss mind a citizen is a person bearing arms. Every Swiss male must serve for a certain period biannually until the age of fifty, a commissioned officer until fifty-five. In a job application, the first question deals with a man's standing with the army. In the Swiss budget the military share is second only to Israel's.

102. Gouverneur Morris, naturally, knew about America's debt to the Bourbons, as did Alexander Hamilton. Cf. the latter's piece in the *Gazette of the United States*, signed "Pacificus," July 13, 1793, in *The Works of Alexander Hamilton*, vol.4, no.5. Still, the biggest and most important portrait in Monticello is that of Louis XVI.

103. Cf. the letter of George Washington to James McHenry, September 30, 1798: "My opinion is. . . that you would as soon scrub the blackamore white as to change the principle of a profest Democrat, and that he will leave nothing unattempted to overturn the Government of this Country." In *The Washington Papers*, Saul Padover, ed. (New York: Harper and Brothers, 1955), 389. On the difficulty of reforming a once corrupted democracy, cf. Rafael Gambra, *La Monarquía social y representativa* (Madrid: Rialp, 1954), 136-37.

104. Cf. *The Selected Writings of John and John Quincy Adams*, 129. The near-mystical fascination exercised by royal blood was founded on the attention it drew. For, as Adams said, birth creates "the indignation of the many, the envy of more and the *attention* of the world" (italics his).

105. Cf. *The Complete Jefferson*, Saul Padover, ed. (New York: Duell, Sloane and Pearce, 1943), 1276.

106. *The Works of John Adams*, Charles Adams, ed. (Boston: Little, Brown, 1851) 6:516.

107. Ibid., 520.

108. Cf. John Adams, *A Defense of the Constitution of the United States of America*, New Edition (London, 1794), 3: 493-95.

109. Letter, dated 16 July, 1814, in Jefferson's *Collected Writings*. Monticello Edition (Washington, 1904), 14: 152.

110. Cf. *The Works of John Adams*, 6:516.

111. Cf. James Madison, *Works*, Jonathan Elliot, ed., 1:501.

112. Cf. E. M. Burns, *James Madison, Philosopher of the Constitution* (New Brunswick, N.J.: Rutgers University Press, 1938), 63.

113. Cf. Madison, *Writings*, Gaillard Hunt, ed., 5:81.

114. Cf. *A Compilation of the Messages and Papers of the Presidents* (Washington, D.C.: Bureau of National Literature, 1897), 3: 493-95.

115. Cf. Ralph Adams Cram, *The End of the Democracy* (Boston: Marshall Jones, 1937), 20; Charles A. and Mary R. Beard, *America in Mid-Passage* (New York: Macmillan, 1939), 3:922-23; Andrew Cunningham MacLaughlin, *Democracy and Constitution* (Proceedings of the American Antiquarian Society, New Series, 1922), 310; Albert Jay Nock, *Our Enemy the State* (New York: Morrow, 1935) 141n.

116. Where did Hamilton, staunchest conservative among the Founding Fathers, stand "metaphysically"? Had he any religious foundations for his views? His will shows him to be a convinced Christian. Cf. *The Basic Ideas of Alexander Hamilton*, Richard B. Morris, ed. (New York: Pocket Library, 1957), 449-51.

117. Cf. Mortimer Adler in *Philosophy of the State*. Fifteenth Annual Proceedings of the American Catholic Philosophical Association, Charles Hart, ed. (Washington, 1939), 163. The same view is manifested by James N. Wood in *Democracy and the Will to Power* (New York: Knopf, 1921), 48-51. Cf. also Whittaker Chambers, *Cold Friday* (New York: Random House, 1964), 227, quoting Henry Adams to the effect that the election of Andrew Jackson was a catastrophe, not only to the initial American dream, but to the civilized West.

118. Cf. Thomas Jefferson, *Writings*, P. L. Ford, ed., 10:22 (Letter to DuPont de Nemours, written in 1816): "We in the United States are constitutionally and conscientiously Democrats." On the other hand, Dr. Benjamin Rush, a signer of the Declaration of Independence, confessed in a letter to John Adams (July 1789) that he saw in democracy "the Tivil's [devil's] government." Cf. *The Letters of Benjamin Rush*, L. H. Butterfield, ed. (Princeton: Princeton University Press, 1951), 1:523.

119. Cf. Jefferson's letter dated February 14, 1815, mentioned by Sainte-Beuve in *Premiers Lundis*, 2:147 (February 25, 1833).

120. Cf. Thomas Jefferson, *Writings*, 2: 249.

121. Cited by Russell Kirk, *The Conservative Mind* (Chicago: Regnery, 1953), 130. Compare this with the declaration of a great Swiss, J. J. Bachofen, "Because I love liberty, I loathe democracy." Cf. his "Autobiographische Aufzeichnungen," *Basler Jahrbuch* (1917), 329.

122. Cf. Thomas Jefferson, *Writings*, P.L. Ford, ed. 2:249.

123. Cf. Thomas Jefferson, Letter to Madison, December 20, 1787 in *Works*, H. A. Washington, ed. (New York: Derby and Jackson, 1859), 2:332.

124. Cf. *The Writings of Thomas Jefferson*, Lipscomb and Bergh, eds. (Washington, D.C., 1903), 5:94. (Letter to John Jay, August 23, 1785.)

125. Cf. Ibid.

126. Cf. *The Writings of Thomas Jefferson* (Washington, D.C.: 1904), 13: 401-02.

127. Ibid, 396.

128. Much of this egalitarian and revolutionary nonsense was cleared up in the controversy between Professor Mel E. Bradford and Professor Harry Jaffa, the former claiming that Abraham Lincoln, not Jefferson, fathered American egalitarianism. Cf. Mel E. Bradford *A Better Guide than Reason* (La Salle, Ill.: S. Sugden & Co., 1979). There was never an "American Revolution," only an American War of Independence. Jefferson in his letter to Henry Lee (May 8, 1823) emphasized that the Declaration contained no new or revolutionary ideas and that "all American Whigs thought alike on that subject."

129. Cf. Albert J. Nock, *Our Enemy the State* (New York: Morrow, 1935), 141n.

130. Cf. Arthur H. Vandenberg, *If Hamilton Were Here Today* (New York: Putnam, 1923) xxiv–xxvi. These confusions—in part at least—were exposed by Madison in the Federalist Paper No. 14.

131. Cf. *The Discovery of Europe*, Philip Rahv, ed. (Boston: Houghton, Mifflin, 1947).

132. Cf. *The Basic Ideas of Alexander Hamilton*, 324.

133. The juvenile "red Indian" stories of the German Karl May and Italian "Westerns" are exceptions. Knut Hamsun tried his hand at it, and I have a novel with an American background on my conscience (*Die Gottlosen*, Salzburg 1962).

134. Cf. *The Works of Alexander Hamilton*, 8:259, Letter to Colonel Edward Carrington, dated May 26, 1792.

135. Cf. *Diaries and Letters of Gouverneur Morris*, Anne Cary Morris, ed. (New York: Scribner's, 1888). 1:104.

136. Cf. Wyndham Lewis, op. cit., 135.

137. Op. cit., *Diaries*, Anne Cary Morris, 443, and Jared Sparks, *The Life of Gouverneur Morris with Selections of His Correspondence* (Boston: Gray and Bowen, 1832), 3:263.

138. Cf. Theodore Roosevelt, *Gouverneur Morris* (Boston: Houghton, Mifflin, 1898), 240-41.

139. Cf. Elizabeth Brett White, *American Opinion of France* (New York: Knopf, 1932), 24.

140. The first phase of the French Revolution, its preparatory and initial state, emphasized liberty rather than equality. Hence the nobility participated with fervor, moved by memories of the Fronde. Excessive sobriety and self-control are bourgeois-puritanical rather than aristocratic virtues, spread by English nannies in the households of the nobility on the Continent. This, at least, is the opinion of Ida Friederike Görres (née Countess Coudenhove-Kalergi) in op. cit., 33-35.

141. Maximilien de Robespierre belonged to a family of the lower nobility of relatively ancient vintage. But, as Albert Mathiez remarked in his *La Révolution Française* (Paris: Armand Colin, 1946), 1:3, the lesser nobility held an animosity toward the big, wealthy families usually centered around the court. Anglo-American readers are

reminded that the *de* in France—as in Charles de Gaulle—has almost always, as *particule*, the character of a title. This is also true of the *von* in Germany, Austria, and Switzerland, but not of the *van* in the Netherlands nor the *de* or *di* in Italy and Spain.

142. The eminent role played by the entire nobility in the French Revolution is also underlined by Alexis de Tocqueville in his "L'Ancien Régime et la Révolution" in *Oeuvres complètes*, J. P. Mayer, ed. (Paris: Gallimard, 1952), 2:68-69, 72. Count Philippe Paul Ségur also commented on this suicidal tendency of the French nobility. Cf. his *Mémoires ou souvenirs et anecdotes* (Paris: Eymery, 1824), 1:292,295. Georges Bernanos spoke in ringing terms against masochism in the political sphere, which not only characterized the French nobility prior to 1789 as also a certain element of the American upper class today. Cf. his *La liberté pour quoi faire?* (Paris: Gallimard, 1953), 129. Albert Mathiez, in op. cit., 15, says correctly that "the Revolution could not have come but from above." See also Louis Villat, *La Révolution et l'Empire* (Paris: Presses Universitaires de France, 1940), 1:ix, 3. Pierre Gaxotte in *La Révolution Française* (Paris: Fayard, 1947), puts the emphasis strongly on the ideological character of the French Revolution and discounts all economic aspects. A. de Tocqueville in his "L'Ancien Régime" insists that the mounting wealth of France prepared the way for the Revolution and that the most revolutionary regions were the richest. (Cf. *Oeuvres complètes*, 2:218ff., 222-23.)

Nor was it true that the countryside lived in misery. Serfdom survived only in a few isolated spots in the Bourbonnais and the Jura. The last remnants of serfdom had been abolished by the King in his domains in 1779. About half the area of France was in the possession of smallholders. (Cf. P. Gaxotte, op. cit., 37-38.) Foreign trade, four times greater than in 1700, reached a value of over a billion francs in 1786, a record until 1848 (ibid., 32-33). De Tocqueville comments on this in "L'Ancien Régime" (*Oeuvres complètes*, 2: 223).

143. One ought to remember the battlecry of the Polish noblemen:
Cudzych królow gromić a grozić swojemu!
Menace foreign kings, but resist your own!

144. Cf. Henry Thomas Buckle, *History of Civilisation in England* (New York: Appleton, 1880), 2:614; Augustin Gazier, *Histoire générale du Mouvement Janséniste* (Paris: Honoré Champion, 1923), 2:137, citing also Sicard, *L'Ancien clergé de France*; (Sir) Denis W. Brogan, *French Personalities and Problems* (London: Hamish Hamilton, 1946), 70.

145. Cf. Edmund Burke, "Remarks on the Policy of the Allies," in *Works* (Boston: Little, Brown, 1869), 4:452.

146. Cf. André Siegfried, "Le Protestantisme cévénol," in Marc Boegner, André Siegfried *et al. Protestantisme Français* (Paris: Plon, 1945), 43.

147. Cf. G. de Félice, *Histoire des Protestants de France* (Paris: Cherbuliez, 1856), 577, 603-04.

148. Anglomania on the Continent had and still has all sorts of versions—aristocratic, bourgeois, proletarian-socialist, Catholic, "Protestant," and Jewish. There are Anglophile sportsmen and businessmen, feminists and educationalists, technologists and male fashion designers, navy men and tourist managers. Anglophobia always

appeared as a dissenting opinion, as a "heresy," as a manifestation of bad taste, as wanton opposition against a prevailing idea.

149. Cf. Metternich, op. cit., 8: 531.

150. Ibid., 407.

151. Cf. Alfred Müller-Armack, *Das Jahrhundert ohne Gott* (Münster: Regensberg, 1948), 57-58.

152. Cf. Charles Seignobos, *Histoire sincère de la nation française* (Paris: Presses Universitaires, 1946), 291.

153. Even in the year 1896 the per capita income of the Swiss was way below that of Britain and France and only slightly above the European average. (Cf. *Handbuch der Staatswissenschaften*, 1923, 767.) Hard work and wise investments plus good organization are responsible for the Swiss economic miracle. Tourism provides only 8 percent of the Swiss national income, while in 1966 no less than 34 percent of the budget was slated for military expenditures.

  Today the Austrian *per capita* GNP is higher than Britain's. Austria, like Switzerland, has intelligent and responsible trade unions, whereas in Britain, the trade unions have done what Hitler failed to do—ruin the country.

154. Cf. *Mémoires, correspondance et manuscrits du général Lafayette*, publiés par sa famille (Brussels: Société Belge de Librairie, 1837), 1: 193, 268, 416: 2: 139-40.

155. Cf. Philippe Paul Comte de Ségur, op. cit., 1: 321.

156. Cf. la Baronne de Staël, *Considérations sur les principaux événements de la Révolution Française* (London: Baldwin, Craddock, Joy, 1818), 1:88.

157. Cf. Madame de Campan, *Mémoires sur la vie privée de Marie Antoinette* (Paris: Baudouin Frères, 1823), 1: 234. This *Déclaration* was solemnly promulgated halfway between the bestialities connected with the fall of the Bastille and the September massacres. Needless to say, God was not mentioned in it.

158. Alphonse Marie Louis de Lamartine, *Histoire des Girondins* (Paris: Furne et Cie, 1847), 1:62.

159. Cf. Chateaubriand, *Mémoires d'outre tombe*, M. Levaillant, ed. (Paris: Flammarion, 1948), 1:274.

160. Cf. Alexis de Tocqueville, "L'Ancien régime et la révolution" in *Oeuvres complètes* (Paris: Gallimard, 1952), vol. 2, t. 2, 157: "The worst imitators were those who had adopted the abstract principles of the United States Constitution without understanding the necessity of applying them in a conservative way as done in America."

161. Cf. G. E. Fasnacht, *Acton's Political Philosophy* (London: Hollis and Carter. 1952), 79.

162. Cf. H. Taine, *Les origines de la France contemporaine* (Paris: Hachette, n.d.) 2:66. Taine admits the "infection," but denies the introduction of an American political pattern in the ideology of the French Revolution. On erroneous European judgments concerning the United States, cf. Russell Kirk, op. cit., 425-26, 427-28. "The European thinks that what Americans brag, they practice," Kirk concludes wisely (428).

163. Cf. Philippe Sagnac, *La fin de l'Ancien Régime et la Révolution Americaine* (Paris: Presses Universitaires, 1941), 241, 286-300.

164. Cf. his letter "Réponse de M. Jellinek à M. Boutmy: La Déclaration des Droits de

l'homme et du Citoyen," in *Revue du Droit publique et de la Science Politique en France et à l'Etranger* (Paris), 18:385sq.

165. Cf. Felix Somary, *Krise und Zukunft der Demokratie* (Zürich-Vienna: Europa Verlag, 1952), 28-30. This brilliant book exists under the title *Democracy at Bay* (Knopf) in an American translation; it received the silent treatment.

166. Cf. *Selected Writings of John and John Quincy Adams*, 159-60.

167. Cf. *The Works of John Adams*, 485.

168. Hanns Johst even became president of the *Reichsschrifttumkammer*, the supreme Nazi organ for controlling and "guiding" writers of the Third Reich. Josef Nadler in his *Literaturgeschichte des Deutschen Volkes* (Berlin: Propyläen-Verlag, 1941), 347, calls *Thomas Paine* "the first political play of the new Germany."

169. Cf. Dr. Friedrich Schönemann, *Amerika und der Nationalsozialismus* (Berlin: Junke and Dunnhaupt, 1934), 28-29. On p.31 the author says pointedly, referring to national socialism, "For our new popular form of government, for this entire system of popular community, there is no better and more beautiful word than 'democracy.'"

170. Cf. Cornélis de Witt, *Jefferson and the American Democracy*, trsl. R. S. H. Church (London: Longmans, 1862), originally published in the *Revue des Deux Mondes*: Johann Georg Hülsemann, *Geschichte der Demokratie in den Vereinigten Staaten von Nordamerika* (Göttingen: Vandenhoeck und Ruprecht, 1832) xi. The author wrote, "The supremacy of the Democratic Party that started earlier in this century and is daily receiving momentum is for us not only of a sad interest because the hopes which Washington and Alexander Hamilton raised for the future of that country have been dashed. The evolution is far more catastrophic because the Party of Revolution has thus acquired a sure base from which to operate."

171. Cf. Le chevalier Félix de Beaujour, *Aperçu des Etats-Unis au commencement du XIXe siècle* (Paris: Michaud et Delaunay, 1814), 164.

172. Abel Bonnard, op. cit., 218, tells about Lafayette's letter to the Princesse d'Hénin in which he mentions the "delicious sensation caused by the smile of the masses." Cf. also Harold Wade Streeter, "Sainte-Beuve's Estimate of Lafayette," *The French-American Review* (Washington: 1950), vol. 3, no. 2-3, 164-86. In a letter addressed to Madison on January 30, 1787, Jefferson mentioned Lafayette's "canine appetite for popularity and fame." Cf. Th. Jefferson, *Works*, H. A. Washington, ed., vol. 2.

173. Cf. Pierre Gaxotte, op. cit., 392, depicts de Robespierre as a frustrated nobleman.

174. Maurice Heine was a prolific writer. One of his most ghoulish essays was his well-illustrated description of burnt corpses. Cf. his "L'enfer anthropoclasique," *Minuataure* (Paris), no.6.

175. Cf. Gilbert Lely, *Vie du Marquis de Sade* (Paris: Gallimard-NRF, 1952) 2 vols.

176. Cf. Gilbert Lely, op. cit., 273.

177. Cf. Paul Boudin, *Correspondance inédite du Marquis de Sade, de ses proches et de ses familiers* (Paris: Librairie de France, 1929), 269.

178. Cf. G. Lely, op. cit., 452-53, letter from Picpus to the *Sûreté Générale*, December 19, 1793.

179. Cf. G. Lely, op. cit., 2:677-85.

180. Cf. Dr. Eugen Dühren (Iwan Bloch), *Le Marquis de Sade et son temps* (Paris: Michalon, 1901), 392-93.

181. Cf. Paul Eluard, in *La Révolution Surréaliste* (Paris) vol.2, no.8, 8.

182. Cf. Bertrand d'Astorg, *Introduction au monde de la terreur* (Paris: Editions de Seuil, 1945), 32.

183. Ibid, 33. The notion of a total annihilation of the universe or, at least, of mankind is dear to leftist thought which, after all, is hostile to creation as well as to the Creator. Vide the poetry of Louise Victorine Ackermann, née Choquet (1813-1890). Cf. her *Poésies, premières poésies, poésies philosophique* (Paris, 1874). She was not an atheist but (like Louis Buñuel) an antitheist.

184. Cf. Geoffrey Gorer, *The Revolutionary Ideas of the Marquis de Sade* (London: Wisehart, 1934), 188.

185. Cf. Dr. Eugen Dühren, op. cit., 391.

186. Cf. *L'Oeuvre du Marquis de Sade*, Guillaume Apollinaire, ed. (Paris: Bibliothèque des Curieux, 1909), 227.

187. Ibid, 236ff.

188. Cf. Oswald Spengler, *Jahre der Entscheidung* (Munich: C. H. Beck, 1933 and 1953), 144.

189. These destructive left-of-centrists, without well-grounded convictions, were the special object of horror of one of the great German-American novelists, the late Hermann Borchardt. Cf. his *The Conspiracy of the Carpenters*, trsl. Barrows Mussey (New York: Simon and Schuster, 1943).

190. Cf. Louis Althusser, "Despote et monarque," in *Esprit*, vol.26, no.267, November 1958, 213-14.

191. Cf. Alexander Rüstow, *Das Versagen des Wirtschaftsliberalismus* (Düsseldorf: Küpper, 1950), 82.

192. Cf. Hugo Lang, O.S.B, *Der Historiker als Prophet* (Nuremberg: Sebaldus-Verlag, 1947), 124.

193. Cf. Voltaire, *Oeuvres Complètes*, 39:167 & 45:112.

194. Cf. *Dictionnaire de philosophie par Voltaire* (Paris: Lebigre Frères, 1834), 3: 196.

195. Cf. Franz Schnabel, op. cit., 2:186.

196. Montesquieu was of the same opinion. Cf. *Esprit des Lois*, Book 8, c. 16. Rousseau repeated these views in the *Contrat Social*, Book 3, c. 3.

197. Cf. Pierre Gaxotte, op. cit., 406.

198. Cf. George D. Herron, *Germanism and the American Crusade* (New York: Mitchell Kennerley, 1918), 21.

199. Cf. Jacques Maritain, *Principes d'une politique humaniste* (Paris: Paul Hartmann, 1945), 39.

200. Cf. Walter Lippmann, *The Public Philosophy* (Boston: Little, Brown, 1955), 73. "In America and in most of the newer liberal democracies of the Western World, the Jacobin heresy is, though not unchallenged and not universal, the popular and dominant theory in the schools." On the inherent totalitarian dangers in democracy

see also, Friedrich A. v. Hayek, "Die Anschauungen der Mehrheit und die zeitgenössische Demokratie," *Ordo*, vol. 15-16 (1965), 19-41.

201. Walter Lippmann, op. cit., 75.

202. Cf. Note 164 this edition.

203. Cf. Dr. A. J. M. Cornelissen, *Calvijn en Rousseau* (Nijmegen-Utrecht: H. V. Dekker, 1931), 229-30.

204. Cf. Calvin, *Institutiones*, I, vii, 5.

205. Cf. Corrado E. Eggers-Lecour, "Calvino y Rousseau o la ambivalencia ginebrina" in *Razón y Fé* (Madrid: vol. 165, no. 772, May 1963), 481-96.

206. The Swiss have done far more than invent the cuckoo clock—which, incidentally, is a product of the German Black Forest. Take away only one city, such as Geneva, the city of Calvin and Rousseau, and Western history, nay, *all world history is utterly changed*.

207. Cf. Georg Jellinek, *Ausgewählte Schriften* (Berlin: Häring 1911), 2:13.

208. Cf. Georg Jellinek, op. cit. 16.

209. Cf. (Baron) Ernest Seillière, *Le Peril mystique dans l'inspiration des démocraties contemporaines, Rousseau visionnaire et révélateur* (Paris: Renaissance du Livre, 1918).

210. Cf. Werner Kägi, "Rechtsstaat und Demokratie" in *Demokratie und Rechsstaat, Festgabe für Zaccaria Giacometti* (Zürich: Polygraphischer Verlag, 1953), 110. A brilliant essay by the most outstanding Swiss political scientist. On the *Rechtstaat* (constitutional state of law and order) see also Francisco Elias de Tejada, *Las doctrinas políticas en la Cataluña medieval* (Barcelona: Aymá, 1950), 196-98.

211. Cf. Irving Babbitt, *Rousseau and Romanticism* (Boston-New York: Houghton, Mifflin, 1919), 345.

212. Ibid., 436.

213. Ibid., 367.

214. Cf. Werner Kägi, loc. cit., 117.

215. Ibid., 120.

216. Ibid., 115-16.

217. Ibid., 114.

218. Cf. J. J. Rousseau, *Contrat Social*, Book 1, ch.7.

219. Ibid., Book. 4, ch.2.

220. Cf. J. J. Rousseau, "Traité de l'économie politique," in *Oeuvres complètes* (Paris: Hachette, n.d.), 2:553.

221. Cf. *The Living Thoughts of Thomas Jefferson*, John Dewey, ed. (New York: Longmans, Green, 1940), 62. "The first principle of republicanism. . . to consider the will of the society announced by the majority of the single vote, as sacred as if unanimous, is the first of all lessons in importance, yet the last, which is thoroughly learned." Jefferson thought that the alternative leads to despotism, yet adhering to such principles leads almost inevitably to totalitarianism. Cf. Angel López-Amo, *El podér político y la libertad* (Madrid: Rialp, 1952), 152, and Bertrand de Jouvenel, *Du Pouvoir: Histoire naturelle de sa croissance* (Geneva: Cheval Ailé, 1945), 25-26.

222. At the sight of a newborn babe one is not particularly struck by the thought that it is

exceedingly "free." Freedom rather seems to be the fruit of constant personal struggles. In medieval parlance, freedoms (the "freedom of a city," for instance) were privileges.

223. Cf. J. J. Rousseau, *Contrat Social*, Book 2, vii.

224. Cf. Louis Rougier, *La France à la recherche d'une constitution* (Paris: Sirey, 1952), 127.

225. Cf. Note 209. Also: T. E. Utley, "Mandatory Democracy," *Confluence* (Cambridge, Mass.) vol. 1, no. 2, (June 1952), 29-30.

226. Cf. Louis Rougier, op. cit., 132.

227. Cf. Georges Vedel, *Manuel élémentaire de droit constitutionnel* (Paris: Sirey, 1949), 196.

228. Ibid.

229. The de Broglie ducal family is one of the most gifted in France. In the last generation, brothers (one a prince, the other *the* Duke) were famous physicists (one a Nobel Prize winner), while the sister (Comtesse de Pange) was famous as a writer and historian. These are the great-grandchildren of Madame de Staël, whose daugher Hortense married a de Broglie. Originally the family came from the Piedmont side of the Matterhorn region.

230. Peter the Great, Frederick William III (through vom Stein and Hardenberg), and the Council of Trent carried out reforms with a strong hand.

231. Certainly post-Vatican II reforms in the Catholic Church were "mismanaged" insofar as they got out of hand. Hilaire Belloc might have said, "What do you expect from a bunch of clerics in Rome?" (*Vide* Diana Cooper, *Trumpets from the Steps*, 1960, 268).

232. Cf. *Athenäumsfragmente*, I, 2.

233. In *L'Île des pengouins*.

234. They can be read in Dr. A. Cabanès and L. Nass, *La névrose révolutionnaire* (Paris: Albin Michel, 1924), 88ff., and Gilbert Lely, op. cit., 2:405., n.6.

235. Cf. D. W. Brogan, *The Free State* (New York: Knopf, 1945), 2.

236. Cf. Gérard Walter, *La guerre de Vendée* (Paris: Plon, 1953), 339-41. Louis-Marie Turreau, a monstrous sadist, became a baron under Napoleon. He was French minister to the United States from 1803 to 1811. He might well have been lionized by "progressives" in the United States much as Soviet diplomats were during the honeymoon in World War II. This criminal's likeness is on the east side of the Arc de Triomphe in Paris—an unlikely decoration for the tomb of the Unknown Soldier.

237. Ibid.

238. Ibid., 311. "The big army of useless mouths." The same noble motive can be found in the Nazi extermination of the insane.

239. Cf. Otto Flake, *Marquis de Sade* (Stuttgart: Deutscher Taschenbuchverlag, 1966), 89. The frightening details of the *noyades* are still under dispute.

240. Cf. Pierre Gaxotte, op. cit., 380.

241. "The Republic needs no scientists." According to another version Coffinhal said, "The Republic needs neither scientists nor chemists."

242. This has also been deplored by John U. Nef in an essay "On the Future of American

Civilization," *The Review of Politics*, vol. 2, no. 3. Cf. also the unsigned editorial "Untragic America" in *Life*, December 2,1946.

243. Cf. Pierre Gaxotte, op. cit., 33. In the docks of Nantes, seven ships were under construction in 1738, but thirty-three in 1784.

244. Obviously, mounting wealth creates enthusiasm for a race for riches. But in a race there are losers and winners, and the bitterness of those left behind creates part of the unrest.

245. Cf. Note 142. Actually, André Maurois states in his *Histoire de France* that the provinces most attached to the *ancien régime* were precisely those where feudal traditions were strongest. It recalls Victor Hugo's cry: "Equality, political translation of the word envy!" Cf. his *Journal 1830-1848*, Henri Guillemin, ed. (Paris: Gallimard, 1954), 346. Ida F. Görres, op. cit., 53-54, speaks of the mixed fury and envy seen in the old German Youth Movement when it became evident that somebody had acquired wealth without much effort. A hundred years earlier, a great Lutheran theologian of the conservative school, A. F. C. Vilmar, made a similar observation about the younger generation. Cf. his *Schulreden über Fragen der Zeit* (Marburg: Elswerthsche Universitätsbuchhandlung, 1846), 133ff.

246. Cf. Pierre Gaxotte quoting Le Trosne, op. cit., 41-42.

247. Cf. *Burke's Politics*, 332, or *Works of the Right Honorable Edmund Burke* (Boston: Little, Brown, 1865-1867), 3:102-21. (Letter of Edmund Burke to M. Dupont.)

248. Cf. Ibid. This is corroborated by James F. Cooper in *The American Democrat* (New York: Knopf, 1931), 83 (originally published 1838 in Cooperstown, N.Y.).

249. Cf. Gérard Walter, *Histoire des Jacobins* (Paris: Aimery Somogy, 1946), 306.

250. Ibid, 268.

251. Oswald Spengler, in his *Jahre der Entscheidung* (Munich, C. H. Beck, 1933), 90, remarked: "In such times we find a certain clerical scum that drags the faith and the dignity of the Church into the dirt of party politics, which allies itself with the powers of destruction and while mouthing the phrases of altruism and protection of the poor helps the underworld to destroy the social order—the order on which the Church irrevocably and fatally rests." The revolutionary and socialistic character of a large sector of the Russian clergy and especially of the seminarians has been well described by Ernst Benz in *Geist und Leben der Ostkirche*. (Hamburg: Rowohlt, 1957), 128. The assassinating "guerrilla-priests" of Latin America were clearly foreseen by Georges Bernanos, who wrote in November 1926: "I believe that our children will see the main body of the troops of the Church on the side of the forces of death. I can see myself being executed by Bolshevik priests who carry the *Social Contract* in their pocket but have a cross dangling from their neck." Cf. his *Correspondance inédite 1904-1934* (Paris: Plon, 1971), 278. Yet Camillo Torres Restrepo was imitated (though less murderously) by Father Nicholas Riddell in St. Louis. Cf. *St.Louis Globe-Democrat*, October 19, 1971; October 20, 1971; March 9, 1972.

252. Cf. Gerard Walter, op. cit., 31.

253. Cf. *Encyclopaedia Britannica*, 11th-13th edition, 17: 487. A "definitive" work on Malesherbes is Pierre Grosclaude, *Malesherbes, témoin et interprete de son temps* (Paris: Fischbacher, 1961). The death of Malesherbes was nevertheless inspiring. Ibid., 747-48. He seems to have returned to the faith of his childhood.

Cf. Pierre Gaxotte, op. cit., 84. "The perfect type of liberal who is always afraid of being taken as a reactionary." The suicidal tendency of certain aristocrats is well illustrated by the common action of Count Michael Károlyi and Lord Bertrand Russell to get the Hungarian Communist Rákosi released from jail (February 1935). He was actually exchanged in 1940. After World War II, Rákosi established one of the grimmest communist tyrannies in Hungary. Cf. *The Autobiography of Bertrand Russell, 1914-1944* (Boston: Little, Brown, 1968), 314-15.

254. A *collège* in France is a high school that includes college (ages ten to eighteen) run by priests or a religious order. College in Britain is the equivalent of a preparatory school in America. Prep schools in Britain are schools for boys eight to twelve.

255. The town council of Strasbourg had already decided to tackle the world famous cathedral when Robespierre, luckily, was overthrown.

256. Cf. Clarence Crane Brinton, *The Jacobins* (New York: Macmillan, 1930), 149.

257. Ibid. The author quotes A. Philippe, *La Révolution dans les Vosges*, 4:133.

258. Ibid, 150. The author quotes F. Heitz, *Les sociétés politiques de Strasbourg pendant les années 1790-1795* (Strasbourg, 1863).

259. Ibid.

260. My conviction rests on investigations I made in 1947 among Austrian and German relatives and friends. Cf. 278. Actually, the slow dying in a concentration camp was an endless horror, whereas the extermination camp meant at least a sudden end in horror.

261. Did the United States Government, with excellent channels of information, know of the fate of the Jews, without doing anything about it? Arthur D. Morse, author of *Why Six Million Died* (New York: Random House, 1967), believes it did. Cf. also note 974.

262. Cf. Louis Blanc and Jacques Cretineau Joly, *Les guerres de Vendée*, Armel de Wismes, ed. (Paris: Hachette, n.d.), 284-85.

263. Ibid., 277.

264. Cf. Blanc and Crétineau-Joly, op. cit., 275., Reynald Secher, *La Chapelle-Basse, village vendéen* (Paris: Librairie Academique Perrin, 1986), 133, and *isdem, Le génocide franco-français. La Vendée-Vengé* (Paris: Presses Universitaires de France, 1986), 163. For those who do not read French, read—as an eye-opener—Simon Schama, *Citizens: A Chronicle of the French Revolution* (New York: Knopf, 1989). Especially pp. 678ff.

265. Cf. R. Secher, *Génocide* 225.

266. Cf. Dr. Hippolyte Taine, *Les Origines de la France Contemporaine* (Paris: Hachette, 1885), III:117. Taine also reports plans to burn libraries (452-453).

267. Dr. Eduard Zeller, *Das theologische System Zwinglis* (Tübingen: Fues, 1853), 163-64.

268. Cf. Martin Luther, "Tischreden," *Kritische Gesamtausgabe* (Weimar: Böhlau, 1921), 6:143, no. 6718: *Isdem*, "Predigten über etzliche Kapitel des Evangelisten Matthäi," *Gesammelte Werke* (Erlangen, 1850), 44: 156-57. Here also a disagreement between Catholic and Calvinist theological thinking. Cf. Herman Doyeweerd, *In the Twilight of Western Thought, Studies in the Pretended Autonomy of Philosophical Thought* (Philadelphia: Presbyterian and Reformed Publishing Company, 1960), 192-94.

269. Cf. Herbert Schöffler, *Die Reformation* (Frankfurt-am-Main: Klostermann, n.d.), particularly 42-60.

270. Cf. Luther's cry: "I do not concede that my teaching can be judged by anyone, not even by the angels." In *Gesammelte Werke* (Erlangen Edition), 28:144. Luther went on to say that he who does not accept his doctrine cannot be saved, because his doctrine is God's and God's is his: "Enough with all this silly humility!"

271. One of the first authors in modern times to deride the concept of Luther as an "early liberal" was Johann Friedrich Böhmer. Cf. his *Briefe und kleinere Schriften* (Freiburg i. Br.: Herder, 1868), 2:427. How the whole picture of Luther, from a stern disciplinarian to a mild liberal spirit with subjectivist-relativist leanings, has been changed and forged through the centuries is well demonstrated by Ernst Walter Zeeden in his *Martin Luther und die Reformation im Urteil des deutschen Luthertums* (Freiburg i. Br.: Herder, 1950), 2 vols. The research covers the period from Luther's death (1546) to Goethe, but unfortunately does not go beyond 1832. Cf. also Etienne Gilson, *Les idées et les lettres* (Paris: Vrin, 1932), 174, and Alexander Rüstow, *Ortsbestimmung der Gegenwart*, 2:288, where Rüstow insists that Luther's *interpretatio liberalis* is long dead among scholars, but survives in the deeper layers of public opinion. Luther's real stand explains the inherent severity of civilizations fashioned by the Reformation. Cf. Erich Fromm, *Die Furcht vor der Freiheit* (Zürich: Steinberg, 1945), *passim*.

272. Hence a country such as Lutheran Prussia is infinitely more disciplinarian than Catholic Austria or Bavaria. In the Austro-Prussian struggle over the soul and mind of Germany, the "progressive" thinkers of the West sided with Prussia—not only William James but also H. F. Amiel. Cf. his *Journal intime de l'année 1866*, Léon Bopp, ed. (Paris: Gallimard-N.R.F. 1959), 328, 376-77.

273. Here I refer the interested reader to my *Liberty or Equality?* 223-29, or to *Freiheit oder Gleichheit?* 342-48.

274. Luther's essay *De servo arbitrio*, showing quite distinctly his Augustinian heritage, can be found in vol. 18 of the Weimar *Kritische Gesamtausgabe*.

275. Was Luther a "Lutheran?" He certainly went to confession every week of his life, and once, in old age, when he spilled a few drops of the consecrated wine, he knelt down and licked up every drop from the floor. Whereupon, as the chronicler relates, the congregation wept at the sight of such piety in this holy man. And in the preface of his translation of the Mass, the *Deutsche Messe* (1525), he said he was convinced that only the Latin Mass could unite all Christians throughout the world. (Auricular confession was revived in the German Evangelical Church in 1956. Luther always considered it a possible sacrament and as such it figures in the *Confessio Augustana*.) Those who wish to learn about the real Luther should read his "Etliche Artikel von den Papisten jetz neulich verfalschet und böslich wider uns Lutherischen gerühmt," written in 1534 in *Sämtliche Werke* (Erlangen Edition, 1855), 65:57. Luther says (p. 96): "Confession is necessary in the churches, and the priest should give Absolution, because in this way Christians will be consoled, and the simple-minded as well as the ignorant will be taught and instructed in Confession." In the same essay Luther admits that good works serve as an ornament to faith (p. 97) and that "the intercession of the Saints could not be completely laid aside" (p. 98). And as to divorce,

Luther strictly forbade the remarriage of all those separated. Cf. *Werke. Briefe* (Weimar 1948), 11: 295.

276. A scholarly description of Geneva under Calvin is found in F. W. Kampschulte's *Johann Calvin, Seine Kirche und sein Staat in Genf* (Leipzig: Duncker und Himblot, 1869 and 1899), 2 vols. As for Calvin's political views, cf. Hans Baron, *Calvins Staatsanschauung und das konfessionelle Zeitalter* (Munich-Berlin: Oldenbourg, 1924).

277. The contrary was the case. The antagonism between Church and state produced a certain strife; now Church and state formed an organic whole. The sovereigns became heads of the Church—even if they were of another faith. Thus, theoretically, Emperor Franz Joseph was head of the Evangelical Church of Austria, etc. (William II as head of the Evangelical Church in Prussia even *conducted* divine services.)

278. On the disciplinary influence of the Irish monks on the Continent cf. Alfred Mirgeler, *Rückblick auf das abendländische Christentum* (Mainz: Matthias Grünewald Verlag, 1961), 7ff.

279. Cf. Alexander Rüstow, *Ortsbestimmung der Gegenwart*, 2:291.

280. Klaus J. Heinisch in his commentary to *Der utopische Staat, Morus: Utopia, Campanella: Sonnenstaat, Bacon: Neu-Atlantis* (Hamburg: Rowohlt, 1960), 226, insists that Campanella died in the "Jacobin" monastery of the rue St. Honoré, where the Jacobin Club later was located. (So does the *Encyclopedia Italiana*, 1930, 8: 568.) The book also includes a full text of the *Civitas Solis*. Cf. also J. Kvačala, *Thomas Campanella, ein Reformer der ausgehenden Renaissance* (Berlin: Trowitzsch, 1909), especially xi, 144ff. and 150. Kvačala rightly discounts Campanella's influence on the Jesuit *reducciones* in Paraguay.

On "Monasticism" cf. also my essay "El monasticismo," *Revista de Occidente* (Madrid), vol.3 (2nd series), no.32, 178-201 and "Der Monastizismus," *Civitas* (Lucerne), vol.2, no.6, 321-335. Actually, as Monsignor Otto Mauer said, today the Counsels of Perfection are imposed on the majority of the population. (Ida F. Görres, op. cit., 152.) Yet the real danger of all "monasticism" is that, especially in the realm of economics, all efforts to reach a moral level substantially higher than the existing one must provoke a wave of coercion and lies. Cf. Wilhelm Röpke, *Jenseits von Angebot und Nachfrage* (Erlenbach-Zürich: Eugen Rentsch, 1958), 165.

281. Cf. Morelly, *Code de la Nature*, introduction by V. P. Volguine (Paris: Editions Sociales, 1953). The blueprint for the ideal state and society, the "Model of legislation in conformity with the intentions of nature," is on pp. 127ff. Morelly's work has a tendency to guess a "natural order" and then to impose it by force. The analogy with Rousseau is evident. It was obviously a utilitarian materialist, Jeremy Bentham, who with the most painful accuracy outlined a totally inhuman blueprint for a totalitarian poorhouse. For details see Gertrude Himmelfarb, *Marriage and Morals Among the Victorians* (London: Faber and Faber, 1987) 111sq.

282. Comte's positivism became the "official theology" of the nascent republic of Brazil in 1888. Actually, the overthrow of the monarchy and the establishment of the republic were the result of a conspiracy of bitterly disappointed slaveholders who had not forgiven Pedro II for having abolished slavery. They were joined by Comtean Positiv-

ists (all leftists) in the army and in the administration. The slogan on the Brazilian flag: *"Ordem e Progresso"* is taken from Comte.

The pioneer of positivism in Brazil was Benjamin Constant Botelho de Magalhães. Cf. João Camillo de Oliveira Tôrres, *O Positivismo no Brasil* (Petrópolis: Editôra Vozes Limitada, 1943). Also *passim* in the magistral work of this Brazilian monarchist scholar *A Democracia Coroada, Teoria Política do Império do Brazil* (Petrópolis: Editora Vozes Limitada, 1965).

283. In fact, most manufacturers lived rather spartan lives. The lavish spenders in the large cities were the visiting big landowners, not the factory owners or managers. Even the bankers were thrifty. Thomas Mann lets one of his heroes (in *The Buddenbrooks*) remark critically that a certain burgher family in Lübeck was living from the interest on its capital rather than on the interest on interest. The drive for investments was enormous and laid the foundations for Free Europe's present wealth—and high living standards for everybody.

284. Metternich wrote to Emperor Alexander I about the general moral, intellectual, and social decay of the Paris proletariat in 1825. He also described the flood of immoral publications sold at half price to young men and women. Metternich remarked: "Here missions as among savages ought to start their work." (Cf. Metternich, op. cit., 4:164-65).

285. The Comte de Saint-Simon was a collateral descendant of the Duc de Saint-Simon, famous for his rather frivolous autobiography describing court life in the late seventeenth and early eighteenth century. The socialist Comte de Saint-Simon revolted in a very concrete sense against his class and the traditions of his family.

286. Brissot in his younger days was deeply interested in the emancipation of the Negroes (particularly in the West Indies), became an ardent Girondist, and was guillotined on October 31, 1793, along with a number of other supporters of his faction.

287. Scenes of the downfall of the high and mighty could be seen in most medieval churches over the west entrance. Popes, emperors, kings, friars, bishops, priests, nuns, and noblemen went to Hell—yet on the day of Judgment representatives of these groups could also be found among the saved.

288. This is contradicted by the enormous amount of crime in the Soviet Union. (The crime syndicates of the USSR, far larger than anything in the United States, extend from coast to coast.) The press, pre-Gorbachev, could mention individual crimes only in exceptional cases. Divorces, suicides, and accidents were also taboo. No crime statistics were available for the Soviet Union, and there is reason to believe that none exist.

289. *Vide* note 27.

290. I am partly repeating the views of Professor Paul Gaechter, S.J., professor emeritus of New Testament exegesis at Innsbruck University, author of *Maria im Erdenleben* (Innsbruck:Tyrolia, 1954) and *Das Matthäus-Evangelium* (Innsbruck: Tyrolia, 1962). Yet it frequently seems profitable to "church strategists" or Christian "democratists" to maintain that Christianity in its origins was a movement of the poor, the humble, and the ignorant. Gioberti obviously liked this thesis. Cf. Vincenzo Gioberti, *Del rinnovamento civile d'Italia*, Fausto Nicolini, ed. (Bari: Laterza, 1912), 3:7. And Montalembert with great irony described the sudden discovery of French ecclesiastics

in 1848 that republicanism took its origin at Golgotha, cf. *Montalembert, Textes choises*, Emmanuel Mounier, ed. (Paris: Egloff, 1945), 94. Friedrich Engels had the same notion (i.e., the early Church being formed by proletarian outcasts) and his view is clearly reflected by the *Bolshaya Sovyetskaya Entsiklopediya* (Moscow, 1957), 46:352 sq. For a corrective view cf. Philip Hughes, *The History of the Church* (New York: Sheed and Ward, 1949), 1:162-69. Adolf von Harnack has shown in his *Militia Christi* how Christianity successfully penetrated the Roman army (Tübingen: Mohr, 1905).

291. Cf. note 59.

292. Cf. Louis Dupré, "Marx and Religion: An Impossible Marriage," *Commonweal*, vol. 88, no. 6, April 26, 1968, pp. 171-76. This did not deter simple-minded, but slightly blood-thirsty Catholic priests from becoming Marxist guerrilla fighters, such as Camilo Torres Restrepo in Columbia (who, incidentally, was treated like a hero and a saint by Catholic editors). The same confusion existed in Uganda, where priests armed with Soviet Kalashnikovs murdered in the name of "social justice." (Cf. *Frankfurter Allgemeine Zeitung*, June 7, 1987), 3. All this was foreseen by Bernanos, see note 251.

293. The dialogue beween Christians and Marxists has largely foundered, for external reasons, among others, one of them being that up to August 1968, Czechoslovakia largely served as a bridge. The cringing attitude of some of the Christian debaters did not last too long when they became aware that they were expected to make all the concessions. On the other hand, the more enthusiastic Communists soon were anathematized by their party and expelled, as in the case of the French "Communist Humanist" Roger Garaudy.

294. There is most obviously one real contradiction between democracy and socialism; socialism stands for a planned, centralized economy; democracy rests on perpetual change. Socialism could theoretically be combined with absolute monarchy, but not with a political system that carefully registers the "fermentation of the masses" or easily yields to the cry, "let's throw the rascals out." Still, socialism, including the dictatorship of the proletariat, can be brought about by highly democratic methods, just as suicide (resulting in inaction) can be achieved by action. But the connection between political democracy and the desire for equality in all other domains was evident as far back as Aristotle. Cf. his *Politics*, V, i, 2. And when Lenin was accused by his enemies of including in his doctrines the Jacobinism of the "bourgeois" French Revolution, he replied, "What is Marxism if not Jacobinism fused with the working class movement?" Cf. Bertram D. Wolfe, *One Hundred Years in the Life of a Doctrine* (New York: Dial Press, 1965), 164. Yet in the realm of ideas filiation is no safeguard against contradiction. In fact, without a growing contradiction filiation can hardly take place.

295. Cf. Willmoore Kendall, "John Locke and the Doctrine of Majority Rule," *Illinois Studies in the Social Sciences* (1941), vol. 26, no. 2, 132.

296. Jan Czyński, a Polish socialist, in his preface to Fourier's *Théorie de l'Unité Universelle*, compared him to Christ.

297. The socialism-republic equation was not even known to Saint-Simon. Of course, the

labels attached to forms of government do not always disclose their real character. Professor Adolf Merkl says that an aristocratic republic with limited franchise can be a *Rechtsstaat*, a constitutional state of law and order, while a parliamentary monarchy with radically democratic franchise may not be. Cf. his essay, "Idee und Gestalt der politischen Freiheit," in *Demokratie und Rechtsstaat. Festgabe für Zaccaria Giacometti*, 176, quoting also Fritz Fleiner. Merkl also insists that the German Third Reich and the USSR are formally and constitutionally *republics* (177).

298. Cf. Charles Fourier, *Textes choisis*, Félix Armand, ed. (Paris: Editions Sociales, 1953), 150. ("Theorie de l'unité universelle," in *Oeuvres complètes*, 4:419.)

299. Ibid., 148 (*Oeuvres complètes*, 3:254).

300. Ibid., 149 (*Oeuvres complètes*, 3:494).

301. Ibid., 137 (*Oeuvres complètes*, 3:464).

302. Louis Napoléon himself wrote a book in 1844 entitled *L'extinction du pauperisme* in which the emperor-to-be attacked capitalism as a source of poverty. Cf. Félix Armand, *Les Fourieristes et les luttes révolutionnaires de 1848 à 1851* (Paris: Presses Universitaires, 1948).

303. Not far from San Antonio, Texas, is the town of New Braunfels, founded by a Prince Solms-Braunfels, a colorful, romantic man who wanted to establish a haven for the European nobility in America, for aristocrats who wished to escape the rising tide of democracy in their homelands.

304. Orstes A. Brownson was also loosely connected with Brook Farm. Like Isaac Hecker he became a Catholic but remained a layman; he is one of the most brilliant Catholic minds in nineteenth-century America. An outstanding conservative, he is now largely ignored by friend and foe. Cf. Doran Whalen, *Granite for God's House* (New York: Sheed and Ward, 1941); Theodore Maynard, *Orestes Brownson, Yankee, Radical, Catholic* (New York: Macmillan, 1943); H. I. Brownson, *Orestes Brownson, The Middle Life* (Detroit, 1899); Lawrence Roemer, *Brownson on Democracy and the Trend Towards Socialism* (New York: Philosophical Library, 1953). This volume gives a good synthesis of Brownson's political thought. His collected works were published toward the end of the nineteenth century in Detroit but have not since been reissued.

305. At the turn of the century, Arthur Brisbane was one of the best-known American journalists. He worked for the Hearst press and, even more than Charles A. Dana and James G. Bennett, Jr., drove his country into the sterile Cuban adventure. Hudson Strode in his *Pageant of Cuba* gave a good description of the journalistic propaganda that led to American armed intervention.

306. Cf. Th. G. Masaryk, *Zur russischen Geschichts und Religionsphilosophie* (Düsseldorf-Cologne: Eugen Diederichs, 1965; a photographic reproduction of the 1913 edition), 315.

307. Ibidem, 335n., 362.

308. The importance of this novel cannot be overestimated. Cf. N. G. Chernyshevski, *Shto dyelat'?* (Moscow-Leningrad: Dyetgiz, 1950). The preface by N. Bogoslovski keeps close to the party line. Lenin used the same title for one of his most important pamphlets, "What to do?"

309. The basic inhumanity of leftist thought, of the entire leftist mind, comés from and leads to madness. To view man merely as a gradually differing relative of termites, bedbugs, and earwigs, and to conceive of something as (virtually) dynamic as a society as if it were an arithmetic-geometric pattern inevitably leads to insanity. On the pathology of egalitarianism, cf. Sigmund Freud, *Gesammelte Werke* (London, 1940), 13:134sq. Politically Freud was a right-winger.

310. Cf. note 254.

311. The Catholic *Staatslexikon* of the "Görres-Gesellschaft" (Freiburg i. Br.: Herder, 1931), vol. 4, col. 476, says of him: "His broad intellectual interests, his untiring compassion, his life spent in purity and poverty all manifest the nobility of Proudhon's character."

312. Cf. J. P. Proudhon, *Les confessions d'un révolutionnaire* (Paris, 1849), 61. Again and again Proudhon dealt with the problem of God's existence and hotly defended the Catholic position against Feuerbach. Cf. Daniel Halévy, "Proudhon d'après ses carnets inédits (1843-1847)," *Hier et Demain* (Paris: Sequana, 1944), no. 9, 26-27.

313. Cf. Henri de Lubac, *Proudhon et le christianisme* (Paris: Editions due Seuil, 1945). (John Paul II made de Lubac a cardinal.)

314. Cf. Constantin Frantz, *Das neue Deutschland* (Leipzig: Rossberg'sche Buchhandlung, 1871), 375.

315. Cf. J. P. Proudhon, "Confessions d'un révolutionnaire," in *Oeuvres complètes* (Paris: Marcel Rivière, 1929), 353.

316. Voting by class on the basis of educational levels, taxes, or incomes, continued in Europe right into the early twentieth century. Austria, for instance, did not introduce the one-man-one-vote system until 1907, but it was still earlier than Britain. Independent Rhodesia, timocratic rather than democratic, had two "classes" ("rolls"). Cf. "State of Rhodesia," *Democracy and the Constitution* (Salisbury: Fact Papers, 1966), no. 8. (The new constitution of 1970 was not basically different.) George Bernard Shaw, a Fabian with very bright moments, said, "I do not see any way out of this difficulty as long as our democrats persist in assuming that Mr. Everyman is omniscient as well as ubiquitous, and refuse to consider the suffrage in the light of facts and common sense. How much control of the Government does Mr. Everyman need to protect himself against tyranny? How much is he capable of exercising without ruining himself and wrecking civilization? I think not. . . ." "It is a matter of simple natural history that humans vary widely in political competence. They vary not only from individual to individual but from age to age in the same individual. In the face of this flat fact it is silly to go on pretending that the voice of the people is the voice of God. When Voltaire said that Mr. Everybody was wiser than Mr. Anybody he had never seen adult suffrage at work. It takes all sorts to make a world, and to maintain civilization some of these sorts have to be killed like mad dogs while others have to be put in command of the State. Until the differences are classified we cannot have a scientific suffrage, and without a scientific suffrage every attempt at democracy will defeat itself as it has always done." (Cf. his *Everybody's Political What's What*, London, 1944, 45-46.)

317. Cf. Proudhon's letter dated April 2, 1852.

318. Cf. Proudhon, "La solution du problème social," *Oeuvres complètes* (Paris: Marpon et Flammarion, n.d.), 6:86.

319. Ibid., 75.

320. Ibid.

321. Ibid., 56.

322. Ibid., 59.

323. Ibid., 64.

324. Cf. P. J. Proudhon, "Du Principe fédératif," *Oeuvres complètes* (Paris: Marcel Rivière, 1959), 34-35. Compare with Denis de Rougemont, "Gedanken über den Föderalismus," *Mass und Wert* (Zürich, March-April 1940).

325. Cf. Proudhon, "Du principe fédératif," 375.

326. Ibid., 334.

327. Ibid., 302-03.

328. Cf. Proudhon, cited by Henri de Lubac, op. cit., 58.

329. Cf. letter to Robin, October 12, 1851, cited in Henri de Lubac, op. cit., 61n.

330. Cf. letter to A. Marc Dufraisse, cited by Emmanuel Mounier, *Liberté sous conditions* (Paris: Editions du Seuil, 1946), 213.

331. Ibid., 214.

332. Cf. Proudhon, "Du principe fédératif," 355-56.

333. Cf. P. J. Proudhon, *De la pornocratie ou Les femmes dans les temps modernes* (Paris: A. Lacroix, 1875).

334. As an ill man he went into exile to Belgium in 1858 and returned broken in 1862 to die three years later. He was befriended by Prince Joseph Bonaparte who, intellectually very active, was interested in "advanced ideas."

335. Cf. Daniel Halévy, op. cit., 52.

336. Cf. Werner Blumenberg, *Karl Marx in Selbstzeugnissen und Bilddokumenten* (Hamburg: Rowohlts Monographiem, 1962), 29. In another letter Heinrich Marx expresses his fear that his son, while having a brilliant mind, had no heart—and that the heart is more important than the brain.

337. Cf. Ernst Kux, *Karl Marx-Die revolutionäre Konfession* (Erlenbach-Zürich: Eugen Rentsch, 1967), 15. The study of this St. Gallen professor is most valuable in understanding Marx. "His practice remains theoretical," Kux adds. "He destroys only realms of ideas, of the spirit, of thought—not in order to replace them with superior constructions, but only for the sake of destruction" (25). This author also gives us a good selection of Marx's poetry which is absolutely essential to an understanding of his repulsive mentality.

338. Cf. Heinrich Heine, "Geständnisse" in *Sämtliche Werke* (Leipzig: Insel-Verlag), 10:180.

339. Cf. Karl Marx and Friedrich Engels, *Historisch-Kritische Gesamtausgabe*, D. Ryazanov, ed. (Marx-Engels Institute: Moscow, 1930), 3:120.

340. Ibid., 5:22. "Everybody in whom dwells a Raphael should have a chance to develop his art." Ibid., 372.

341. Ibid., vol. 1 part 1, 607. ("Zur Kritik der Hegelschen Rechtsphilosophie.") The term *Entfremdung* ("alienation"), on the other hand, was first used by Adam von Müller. Nietzsche might have been inspired by Marx's "Superman" notion, while he copied the "God is dead" formula from Hegel.

342. Ernst Kux, op. cit., 127, note 181.

343. This attitude is dictated by an absolute belief in an automation of the historic process, which the helpless individual cannot change. "Communism, for us, is not a situation which has to be created, an ideal, which reality will have to take into account. We call Communism a genuine motion which cancels the present state of affairs." (Marx-Engels, *Gesamtausgabe*, 5:25.)

344. Ibid., 5:227. *Vide* also the preface to *Das Kapital* (Hamburg: Otto Meissner, 1909), viii, in which the person's lack of responsibility within the pattern of society is strongly emphasized.

345. Cf. Ernst Kux, op. cit., 85.

346. Cf. Polina Vinogradskaya, "Zhenni Marks," in *Novy Mir* (Moscow), vol. 40, no. 3, March 1964, 179ff.

347. Cf. Arnold Ruge, *Briefwechsel und Tagebuchbläter*, Paul Nerrlich, ed. (Berlin: Weidmann, 1886), 381. Reading through the entire Marx correspondence (Dietz Edition, East Berlin, vol. 27-35), I have not once found a word of praise, admiration, or affection for a single human being.

348. Cf. Carl Schurz, *Lebenserinnerungen (Bis zum Jahre 1852)* (Berlin: Georg Reimer, 1906), 142-43. Very similar to this reflection of Schurz is that of an idealistic Prussian lieutenant who gave up his career in order to serve socialism. Gustav Adolf Techow (who died in Australia) said that he would sacrifice anything for Marx if that man had as much heart as he had brain, as much love as he had hatred. But Marx only laughed at the fools who parroted his "proletarian catechism" and admitted that, in reality, he respected only aristocrats. Cf. Fritz J. Raddatz, *Karl Marx, Eine Politische Biographie* (Hamburg: Hoffmann & Campe, 1975), 107, and Arnold Künzli, *Karl Marx. Eine Psychographie* (Vienna: Europa Verlag, 1966), 298. These are very important books.

Yet this mixture of spite and arrogance is due to a *ressentiment*, as Eugène Ionesco rightly guessed when he wrote in his *Journal en miettes* (Paris: Mercure de France, 1967): "Marx must have suffered from a secret wound to his pride, as did all those who wanted revolutions. It is this secret wound which he hides, consciously or not."

349. *Vide* his essay "Zur Judenfrage" in Karl Marx, *Die Frühschriften*, Siegfried Landshut, ed. (Stuttgart: Alfred Kröner, 1953), 171sq.

350. Cf. Karl Marx and Friedrich Engels, *Das kommunistische Manifest*, Rosa Luxemburg, ed. (Vienna: Verlag der Arbeiterbuchhandlung, 1921).

351. The German for it is *Gespenst* which means "ghost," "spook." *Specter* is a much milder expression. The word "bourgeois" in Continental language implies the propertied, upper part of the middle class of somewhat stuffy character. This subtle meaning developed gradually during the last two hundred years.

352. Remember that Marx believed that the proletariat made up the *majority* in most

nations. If this were the case, even the dictatorship of the proletariat could be considered democratic. Democracy *is* majority rule.

353. To Marx, especially to the younger Marx, economics serve as an intellectual explanation; but his aims and motives are always emotional. Gustave Thibon remarked rightly that "One should not forget that the totalitarian tyranny is a child of the humanitarian and democratic *mystique*. The former is not opposed to the latter as an illness to its remedy: We are dealing here rather with two successive but basically identical manifestations of the corruption of *homo politicus*." Cf. G. Thibon, "Le risque au service de la prudence," *Études Carmélitaines*, 24 year, vol. 1 (Spring 1939), 52n.

354. If we look for a more extreme but still just formulation of the difference between free enterprise and socialism-communism, we can agree with Wilhelm Röpke that the final sanction of the former is the bailiff, and of the latter the hangman. Cf. his *Die Gesellschaftskrisis der Gegenwart* (Erlenbach-Zürich: Eugen Rentsch, 1948), 147. This brilliant book of the late neoliberal thinker is still as timely as when it came out for the first time in 1942.

355. But even "right-wing" countries show a rather obsolete tendency to "carve up" large estates, although it is by now an established fact that future farming lies in large-scale farms; small ones, unless they are truck farms, are becoming increasingly uneconomic. General-President Castelo Branco enacted an agrarian reform, although no fewer than 5.5 million square kilometers are federal property, an area the size of Europe without the prewar Soviet Union.

356. Cf. Alexander Pauper (pseudonym for a high Austrian government official), "Was ist ein 'Reicher'?" *Die Industrie* (Vienna), December 23, 1960. This author mentions the statement of a budget committee of the U.S. Government in 1957 to the effect that all income tax in excess of 50 percent yields only 2 percent of the income tax revenue or 1 percent of the total revenue of the United States. The situation in Sweden is not very different. A pamphlet entitled "The Role of Taxation in the Redistribution of Income in Sweden" (edited by the Swedish Taxpayer Association, Stockholm, 1963), says that only 6 percent of the tax revenue comes from progressive taxation (p. 5). A maximum rate of 25 percent would yield 80 percent of the present revenues (p. 6) and only 1 percent of all income is redistributed by progressive taxation (p. 9). In 1962 the total income of the Swedish state from private persons in all forms was 16 billion crowns (1 crown is about 17 U.S. cents): out of this the income tax accounts for 3.45 billion crowns. Less than 10 percent of this sum (315 million crowns) comes from those who are taxed at a rate of 25 to 45 percent, and only 1.5 percent (or 45 million crowns) from those in the top bracket, i.e., 45 to 65 percent (p.7.)

The nature of most tax systems in the Western world is demagogic rather than economic: pressure is exercised by the Socialist parties and the general belief that a radical redistribution of wealth would not only remove objects of *envy* (which it would) but also raise the living standards of the lower classes (which it would not). Questions of this sort can only be answered by studying all-round statistics with paper and pencil. Were we (taking Alexander Pauper's statistics into consideration) to confiscate the total income of every Austrian earning more than 1,000 dollars a month after taxation and hand to every Austrian every day his equal share of it, he would receive 1.7 U.S. cents a day. Were we to make a similar arrangement in

Germany by confiscating everybody's income above $250.00 a month, every German would receive from the jackpot a nickel a day! Cf.Ludwig Reiners *Verdienen wir zu wenig?* (Baden-Baden: Lutzey, 1957), 4.

Reviewing the income structure of the United States shows that in 1960 the gross national income was about 100 billion dollars; of this wages and salaries account for about 65 billion, other payments 10 billion, benefits 5 billion, self-employed income almost 12 billion (farms 3.1 billion); the *total unearned income* hovered around 6 percent and Americans in all walks of life shared in it. Cf. The National Industrial Conference, *The Economic Almanack 1962* (New York), 115. Roughly the same picture emerges from Italy, noted in the full-page advertisement of the "Confederazione Generale dell'Industria italiana," Communication no. 2. in *Gente*, vol. 8, no. 48. (November 26, 1964). It shows the balance sheets of the thirteen biggest Italian companies. In 1963 these companies paid 44.5 billion lire in dividends but 526 billion lire for labor. Other sums went for taxes and reinvestments. These companies employ 258,000 people but have just over half-a-million shareholders. (Two of the companies paid no dividends. Two papers refused to publish this ad: the Communist *Unità* and the papal *Osservatore Romano*.) If, in 1960, there had been 5,000 millionaires in Mexico (in pesos of 8 cents) then the total egalitarian distribution of their wealth would have given each Mexican the sum of 18 U.S. dollars, once and for all. Yet Mexico is one of the richest nations in the Latin American community. Radical "social reforms" further south would have even less effect. Significantly, Europe's leading Catholic sociologist, Father O. von Nell-Breuning, S.J., not noted for rightist leanings, has strongly denounced the idea that the masses can be made wealthy by expropriating the wealth of the rich. (This, he insists, is equally true of the "underdeveloped nations.") Cf. his "Kritischer Rückblick auf Quadragesimo Anno," *Zur Debatte* (Munich: April 1972), vol.2, no. 4, 3.

357. People with larger incomes are thus discouraged from engaging in additional enterprises and, in these circumstances, additional jobs and additional production are thwarted. Progressive taxation, in this way, is opposed to the common good. Pauperism in the United States is well explained by Hans F. Sennholz in his *The Politics of Unemployment* (Spring Mills: Libertarian Press, 1987). In his *Deficits and Debts* (same publisher) this brilliant economist prophesied the "Black Monday" of October 1988.

358. The needless crisis of the American railroads is largely the result of the impossible labor situation with its excessive featherbedding. In Europe, the railroads, *in spite* of government ownership, are constantly improving.

359. Cf. *Karl Marx*, Franz Borkenau, ed. (Frankfurt-am-Main: Fisher Bücherei, 1956), 118. (Point 17 of the "Demands of the Communist Party in Germany," published in the *Neue Rheinische Zeitung*.) Along with the worldwide tendency toward a uniform school system is the idiotic notion that "common schools" will help eliminate class, ethnic, and racial antagonisms, cementing instead lifelong friendships across these barriers. But it is equally, if not more likely that lifelong enmities and resentments will result, especially if certain groups have higher I.Q.s than others. (*Vide* the effect of "busing" in the United States.)

360. Louis Dupré, *The Philosophical Foundations of Marxism* (New York: Harcourt, Brace

and World, 1966), ix. "Marx's early works represent one long struggle to detach Hegel's dialectic method from his idealistic system; without a solid knowledge of both, Marx cannot be understood."

361. A technological system of mass production will always go through a difficult period in its early stages, but in the world of free enterprise eventually the general levels will be raised. Interestingly, while the leftists made every excuse for the terrible sacrifices in connection with the Soviet Five-Year Plans, no such concessions were made for early capitalist enterprises in other parts of the world. "Getting ahead" always demands sacrifices, and the question is: Are the sacrifices worth it, or are they senseless? Will they or won't they help establish a way of production that assures a dignified way of life and a modicum of prosperity to all?

362. Curiously enough, all big state combines and monopolies in the Soviet Union are officially called *trusts* (*trēst*) which, of course, is part of the Soviets' morbid American fixation. When I told Soviet citizens that trusts in the United States were subject to prosecution, they could hardly believe it. Nationalized (i.e., socialized) industries offer a much greater threat to freedom than "trusts" ever did. They are as a rule condemned to party control, economic incompetence, and real corruption. The case of the permanently bankrupt Austrian state-owned industries should teach a lesson. Cf. Franz Summer, *Das Vöest-Debakel* (Vienna: Orac, 1987).

363. Cf. *Aus dem literarischen Nachlass von Karl Marx* (Stuttgart, 1902), 1:405ff.; S. M. Dubnow, *Die neueste Geschichte des jüdischen Volkes* (Berlin: Jüdischer Verlag, 1920), 2:508. Engels' letter addressed to Marx on March 7, 1856, can be found in *Karl Marx, Friedrich Engels, Kritische Gesamtausgabe*, Third Series, 2:122. Other anti-Jewish remarks of Engels in 3:192 and of Marx (all in connection with the hated Lassalle) in 2:365, 366, 371, in 3:82, 90, 91. (Lassalle was to Marx a "Jewish nigger.") See also Arnold Künzli's monumental *Karl Marx: Eine Psychographie* (Vienna-Frankfort-Zürich: Europa Verlag, 1966).

364. Cf. Erik v. Kuehnelt-Leddihn, "Do Jews tend towards Communism?" *The Catholic World*, November 1946, 107-113. A certain trait in the Jewish character perhaps directs the attention of Jews towards all ideas pointing to the future. Ida F. Görres also remarks that Jews are frequently fascinated by the "shape of things to come." Cf. her *Zwischen den Zeiten. Aus meinen Tagebüchern 1951-1959* (Olten: Walter, 1961), 202, no. 21.

365. Cf. Franz Werfel, *Between Heaven and Earth*, trsl. Maxim Newark (New York: Philosophical Library, 1944), 202, no. 21.

366. Cf. Nathaniel Weyl, *The Jew in American Politics* (New Rochelle: Arlington House, 1968), *passim*.

367. Cf. Edmund Silberner, *Sozialisten zur Judenfrage*, trsl. A. Mandel (Berlin: Colloquium, 1962). This richly documented book is largely a translation of *Western European Socialism and the Jewish Problem (1800-1918)*: A Selective Biography (Jerusalem, 1955).

368. Cf. Solomon N. Schwartz, "Anti-Semitism in the Soviet Union," in *Commentary* (New York), June 1949. See also Samuel Gringauz, "Anti-Semitism in Socialism," *Commentary* (New York), April 1950. Obviously, however, the percentage of Jews in Marxist

parties will be higher in areas where they are materially or socially depressed or oppressed. In the leadership of the French or Italian Communist parties, Jews were and are exceedingly rare. The same is true of Scandinavia. Recall that Western Europe's refugee camps after 1945 were crammed with East European Jews. Why, if Nazism had been defeated? Because these Jews (who wanted to go to Palestine) dreaded returning to Soviet- dominated areas! While America still enjoyed the red honeymoon, *they knew.* Their refusal to return where they came from—not the specter of a dead nazism—was what "made" the state of Israel.

369. Cf. Max Nomad, *Apostles of Revolution* (Boston: Little, Brown, 1939), 423, where the author mentions a dispatch of Walter Duranty, dated October 10, 1938, saying that Stalin up to then had killed more Jews than Hitler. The North American Newspaper Alliance distributed the news, but the *New York Times* on October 11, 1938, omitted the lines about the murdered Jews.

370. Two stories are current about Jewish support for the Bolshevik Revolution. One deals with the "financing" of the Soviets by Kuhn, Loeb, and Schiff of New York. But why should a "capitalist" Jewish banking house be interested in the overthrow of a democratic republic? Cf. Walter Laqueur, *Deutschland und Russland* (Berlin: Propyläen Verlag, 1965), 105-06. An earlier *canard* was a forged report, the so-called Sisson-Papers, according to which the German-Jewish banking house Warburg had financed the overthrow of the Kerenski regime. Cf. George F. Kennan, *Russia Leaves the War* (Princeton: Princeton University Press, 1956), 441sq.

371. Cf. Antonio Machado, *Obras completas* (Mexico: Edición Seneca, 1940), 702.

372. Cf. Karl Marx, *Die Frühschriften*, 201.

373. Cf. Dr. J. Goebbels, *Der Nazi-Sozi, Fragen und Antworten für den Nationalsozialisten* (Munich: Eher, 1932), 12. Alfred Rosenberg in one of his purple passages insisted that whoever wanted to be a National Socialist had to be a Socialist in order to paralyze "international capitalism" and to overcome the narrow concept of private property. Cf. his *Der Mythus des 20. Jahrhunderte* (München: Hoheneichen Verlag, 1943), 538. Hitler considered himself the "executor of Marxism" and repeatedly expressed his admiration for German socialism whose methods he was ready to copy. Cf. Hermann Rauschning, *Gespräche mit Hitler* (Zürich-New York: Europa Verlag, 1940), 174ff. See also Note 499.

374. Cf. Waldemar Gurian, *Der Bolschewismus, Einführungund Lehre* (Freiburg i. Br.: Herder, 1931), 187ff.

375. Cf. Ben Hecht, *Erik Dorn* (New York: Putnam, 1921), 381.

376. Cf. E. F. W. Tomlinson, *Criterion* (London), no. 46.

377. Nicholas I, Russian emperor, was profoundly interested in this experiment. The reader is reminded that "social" and "socialistic" are by no means the same. Socialism rests primarily on the ownership of the means of production by "society," i.e., to all practical purposes by the *state*. Sir Stafford Crips, defending the socialist viewpoint has said emphatically in his book *Towards Christian Democracy* that the injustices men create for themselves can only be removed by the state, which is "in fact, accepted as the nearest we can get to an impartial judge in any matter." Cf. John Jewkes, *Ordeal by Planning* (London: Macmillan, 1948), 210. This, naturally, is an honestly naive

statement by a naive man. The often badly misused term "social" has very aptly been analyzed by Friedrich A. v. Hayek in a brilliant and biting essay entitled, "Was ist und was heisst 'sozial'?" in *Masse und Demokratie* (Erlenbach-Zürich: Eugen Rentsch, 1957), 71-84. He quotes approvingly Charles Curran in *The Spectator* (July 6, 1956, 8) who said: "Social Justice is a semantic fraud from the same stable as People's Democracy." Yet one must read this essay in its entirely to understand an argument which, at first sight, might shock pious hypocrites.

378. Bakunin's position was severely shaken by his association with Sergey Nyechayev who had committed murder to make himself more interesting and important. Since his crime had no strictly political character, he was arrested by the Swiss and extradited to Russia where he received a life sentence. The Nyechayev case was used as a theme by Dostoyevski in *The Possessed* (*Byessy*, also called *The Demons*). On Bakunin and Nyechayev, cf. also Edward Hallett Carr, *The Romantic Exiles* (Harmondsworth: Penguin Books, 1949).

379. According to certain rumors the vaults of the Marx-Engels Institute in Moscow hold an unpublished very anti-Russian manuscript from the pen of Karl Marx. Because of the purges of the 1930s many editors of the *Gesamtausgabe* were jailed and killed and this still unfinished edition of the *Karl Marx-Friedrich Engels Gesamtausgabe* underwent considerable difficulties. In Marx's articles published by the *New York* (Daily) *Tribune* (1853-1856), his anti-Russian stand comes out clearly and prophetically.

380. *Vide* G. K. Chesterton's outcry: "Aristocrats are always anarchists." Cf. his *Man Who Was Thursday* (New York: Dodd, Mead, 1908), 190. There is, remember, a certain "anarchical" undercurrent in all genuine "rightist" thought. The French essayist Charles-Albert Cingria, flatly rejecting democracy, called himself "an anarchist of the extreme right." Cf. Marcel Bisiaux, "C. A. Cingria," in *Arts* (Paris), no. 419 (July 10-16, 1953), 5. To the Reformers, who were temperamentally disciplinarians and rigorists, the nobility was always a rather odd and unreliable estate. Cf. Luther in his "Table Talks," *Sämtliche Werke* (Erlangen Edition), 62:209-14 (no. 2751-2761). On Calvin and the aristocracy cf. Karl Holl, *Gesammelte Aufsätze zur Kirchengeschichte* (Tübingen: J. C. B. Mohr, 1928), 3: 279-80.

381. The real misery caused by financial circumstances might well have killed his only legitimate son, Edward (whom he did not particularly like), at the age of eight.

382. Cf. Werner Blumenberg, op. cit., 115-117. At that time the German workers would not have "stomached" an illegitimate child of their admired leader. Engels revealed the truth to Marx's daughters on his deathbed, causing great shock. Family life in the Marx household was unmitigated Hell for all concerned—except perhaps for the old ogre.

383. Cf. Hans Freyer, *Theorie des gegenwärtigen Zeitalters* (Stuttgart: Deutsche Verlagsanstalt, 1955), 119. Freyer points out that clever ideologists usually anticipate most criticisms and counter them with preventive arguments.

384. Cf. Otto Fürst Bismarck, *Die gesammelten Werke*, Petersdorff, ed. (Stuttgart: Deutsche Verlagsgesellschaft, 1923-1935), 15: 485, and Prinz Philipp zu Eulenburg, *Aus fünfzig Jahren* (Berlin: Paetel, 1923), 225. At one time when William II called the German Social Democrats "vaterlandslose Gesellen" ("fellows without a father-

land"), the outcry was great and the protestations vehement, but the rather un-diplomatic words of the Emperor merely echoed Marx's statement in the *Communist Manifesto*.

385. The picture of Winston S. Churchill as a leftist radical eager for nationalizations and the introduction of the Provider State in Britain is well drawn by Peter de Mendelssohn in his biography, *The Age of Churchill, 1874-1911* (London: Thames and Hudson, 1961), *passim*.

386. Professor Mark de Wolfe Howe, editing the *Holmes-Laski Letters 1916-1935* (Cambridge: Harvard University Press, 1941) was forced to admit that Mr. Laski had not always stuck to the factual truth, but engaged in interesting inventions.

387. Hobson makes rather amusing reading. Thus he tells us in his *Imperialism* (1938 edition, 57): "Does anyone seriously suppose that a great war could be undertaken by any European State, or a great State loan subscribed, if the house of Rothschild and its connections set their face against it?" Similar nonsense can be found in national socialist textbooks. The purely economic explanation of history is a facile "false but clear" idea.

388. Cf. Edward Crankshaw, "Russia in Europe: The Conflict of Values," *International Affairs* (Toronto), vol. 22, no. 4, October 1946, 509. A similar observation was made by Bruno Bauer, the ex-friend of Karl Marx, in his *Russland und das Germanenthum* (Charlottenburg: Egbert Bauer, 1835), 12, and by Joseph de Maistre in his famous *Quatre chapitres inédits sur la Russie*, published by his son.

   Analogous judgments had been made about the Spaniards. Elie Faure thought that the Inquisition for them must have been a necessary evil, an "iron belt for this undisciplined people." (Cf. his essay, "L'âme espagnole," *La Grande Revue*, vol. 33, no. 12, December 1929, 195.) It has been my thesis for a long time that the anarchical and "absolutistic" drives of the Catholic and Eastern Church nations make parliamentary democracy in the long run impossible because the latter must rest on a *basic conformity*. Ideally the various political parties (everywhere) should only be temporary. *Vide* the chapter "The Political Temper of Catholic Nations" in *Liberty or Equality?* 179ff., *Freiheit oder Gleichheit?* 285ff. The individualism and absolutism of the non-post-Reformation nations results automatically in a variety of ideologically incompatible parties and factions with no common denominator. This speedily ruins a democratic republic, although bearable in a (constitutional) monarchy where the monarch definitely has the last word and acts as a unifying force. Hence the abortive effort of America and Britain (with their great uniformity and readiness to compromise in the field of political thought) to make the countries of the "Old Church" safe for democracy.

   George Washington and Alexander Hamilton well understood this, witness the passage in Washington's Farewell Address, drafted by Hamilton, in which the great President spoke about the dangers of a strong and violent party spirit leading finally to "the absolute power of an Individual" who, as "the chief of some prevailing faction," would turn "his disposition to the purpose of his own elevation, on the ruins of Public Liberty." Washington concluded this passage with the words, "There is an opinion that parties in free countries are useful checks upon the Administration of the Government and serve to keep alive the Spirit of Liberty. . . . This within certain limits is probably true—and in Governments of a Monarchical cast, Patriotism may look with indulgence, if not with favor, upon the spirit of the party. But in those of a popular character, in Governments purely elective, it is a spirit not to be encouraged." Cf. *The Washington Papers,* Saul K. Padover, ed. (New York: Harper, 1955), 317. For Hamilton's draft cf. *The Basic Ideas of Alexander Hamilton,* R. B. Morris, ed., 387-88. All this bodes ill for hopes of a lasting restoration of parliamentary government in South, Central, or Eastern Europe.

389. Cf. N. S. Timasheff, "On the Russian Revolution," *The Review of Politics,* vol. 4, no. 3, July 1942, also citing Sir Bernard Pares, *The Fall of the Russian Monarchy,* London, 1939. Writes Timasheff, "The Russian peasants had received at the time of the liberation of the serfs more than half of the arable soil of Russia, namely 148 million hectares (versus 89 million which remained the property of the landlords and 8 million which were the property of the State). Half a century later, on the eve of World War I, the situation was quite different. Only 44 million hectares were still the property of the landlords, the rest, as well as about 6 million hectares of State land, had been bought by the peasants" (295). (One hectare equals about 2.5 acres.) The agrarian situation in Russia before the Revolution can also be gleaned from the article on "Russia, the Agrarian Question," in *Encyclopaedia Britannica,* 13th ed., 31:402-03.

Compare the agrarian situation of Russia with that of Britain. In the 1870s, 5,207 proprietors of more than 1,000 acres owned over 18 million acres, or 55 percent of the surface of Britain. Cf. *Brockhaus Lexikon,* 14th ed., 1898, 8:493. In 1902, 86.6 percent of agricultural land was rented by tenant farmers.

The history of the agrarian problem in southern Italy is characterized by *repeated* agrarian reforms—under the Bourbons, under Joseph Bonaparte and Murat, under the Bourbon restoration, and under the Fascists—and by a renewed concentration after redistribution. Absentee landlords became more numerous when a new urban class started to buy up land. Cf. Vincenzo Ricchioni, *Le leggi eversive della feudalità e la storia delle quotizzazioni demaniali nel mezzogiorno* (Istituto editoriale del mezzogiorno, n.p.n.d.), 3-4: Romualdo Trifone, *Feudi e Demani nell' Italia meridionale* (same publishing house), 12-13.

390. Cf. Manya Gordon, *Workers Before and After Lenin* (New York: Dutton, 1941), 428-30, and D. M. Odinetz and Paul Novgorodzev, *Russian Schools and Universities in the World War* (New Haven: Yale University Press, 1929). Of special interest are the statistics on the class structure of the *gymnasia* (high school-colleges), 33ff. Russia was also a real pioneer in female education. (Female students were pistol-packing revolutionaries nearly one hundred years before the advent of the female students of the Red Army Factions, who accounted for two-thirds of the wanted lists of the German police in the 1980s.)

391. This is true of the Russian classics of the nineteenth century. The relationship between servants and masters was genuinely patriarchal. Servants addressed their masters by their first names and patronymics, with peasants "thou" used mutually. When, in Chekhov's *Cherry Orchard* the lady of the house returned from Paris, she embraced the old butler and called him "sweet old man," and the snob Serpukhovski in *Anna Karenina,* after having to kiss his man servant, secretely wiped

his mouth with a silken handkerchief. Titles meant very little in Old Russia. Some princes were nothing but small farmers. The present Austrian Embassy in Moscow is located in a palace built by a sugar king for his mistress, a ballet dancer. And the sugar king had been born a serf.

A Hungarian Communist who emigrated to Russia in the 1930s was told by a long-time German resident, referring to the Imperial regime, "There was beastly brutality on the part of the ruling class, indeed, beastly brutality, but no haughtiness." Cf. Erwin Sinkó, *Roman eines Romans, Moskauer Tagebuch* (Cologne: Verlag Wissenschaft und Politik, 1969), 122. Cf. Anatole Leroy-Beaulieu, *L'Empire des Tsars et les Russes* (Paris: Hachette, 1889), vol. 1, chap. vi, 1-4, who states that class mixtures in (Imperial) Russia had no analogy whatsoever in Western society. Ivan Sergeyevitch Aksakov wrote correctly that "to the Russian national feeling the contemptuous concept of the Greek *demos* or of the Latin *plebs* is entirely alien." (Cf. the daily *Moskva*, February 10, 1867.)

392. Members of a family could never be sold into serfdom. Serfs were merely (in a very superficial way) *glebae adstricti*. And serfdom was known only in the central and western parts of Russia, not in the north, east (including Siberia), or deep south. Frank Tannenbaum's *Slave and Citizen, the Negro in the Americas* (New York: Knopf, 1947) shows that in Latin America too, the slave's position was infinitely better than in North America. He was merely a prisoner of war (or the descendant of one) who enjoyed basic human rights. He could own property and had the absolute right to freedom by paying his master the original price for which he had been bought.

393. In his doctoral dissertation *Staat, Gesellschaft und Opposition in Russland im Zeitalter Katharinas der Grossen* (Munich, 1964), Igor von Glasenapp tells of a serf who bought his freedom from the Sheremetyevs for 135,000 rubles, about 5 million dollars in present-day purchasing power. (The price of a cow was then between 1 and 2 rubles, of a horse between 3 and 5.) This man was worth about $75 million in present purchasing power. Serfs could, in turn, own serfs. Serfdom had been instituted by Russian monarchs as a means of collecting taxes.

394. Cf. Igor von Glasenapp, op. cit., 170.

395. Cf. Peter L. Lyashenko, *History of the National Economy of Russia to the 1917 Revolution* (New York: Octogon Books, 1970). The original of this revealing book appeared in the USSR.

396. Cf. Manya Gordon, op. cit., 17, mentioning Nisselovitch, *Istoriya zavodno-fabritchnego zakonodatel'stva v Rossii* (St. Petersburg, 1883). Eugene Lyons, *Workers' Paradise Lost* (New York: Paperback Library, 1967), 86, rightly points out that the annual rates of Russian industrial output between 1885 and 1889 and again between 1907 and 1914 substantially exceeded the corresponding rate of growth during the same period in the United States, Britain, and Germany. Rapid development was a characteristic feature of the whole period from 1861 to 1914. This fact was also stressed by Lenin in his book *Capitalism in Russia* written in 1899. As to the agricultural domain, peasants owned 82 percent of all cattle and 86 percent of all horses. (89)

397. Cf. Ilya E[h]renburg, "Lyudi, gody, zhizn'," *Novy Mir*, vol. 41, no. 4, April 1965, 74.

398. In the years 1945-46 sugar was still a great rarity in the USSR, and people begged prisoners-of-war for a piece. The POWs in many parts of Russia were better fed than the population: they were, after all, potential propagandists for communism in their own homelands.

399. Cf. William H. Chamberlin, in *Confessions of an Individualist* (London, 1940), 102: "I have outlived a good many early enthusiasms, but my respect and admiration for the prewar Russian intelligentsia grew steadily while I lived in Moscow." This Russian *Intelligentsiya* (to which Lenin also belonged) had a truly ascetic, nay, monastic character, which is a good breeding ground for the leftist outlook. Cf. S. I. Frank, "Etika nigilisma" in *Vyekhi*, 1909, reprinted by Possev Publishers, Frankfurt, 1967. We get a good insight of prerevolutionary Russia from V. Zhelyagin and A. Rutykh, *Rossiya w epokhu reform* (Frankfurt a. Main: Possev, 1981). Also from Richard Pipes, *Russia under the Old Regime* (London: Weidenfeld and Nicolson, 1974).

400. In a still honest trial in 1918 these two men confessed that they had secretly mobilized on the German border in August 1914 and, ordered by their Emperor to demobilize immediately, had lied to him and continued their strategic movement. William II, convinced that he was being deceived by his cousin, thereupon declared war on Russia. The two criminals defended themselves by citing "patriotic" motives, which the Emperor would neither have shared nor understood.

401. The lower nobility (*dvoryane*) had no formal titles; they could be wealthy or poor. Vladimir Nabokov, for instance, was descended from a family of rich *dvoryane*. Cf. his *Conclusive Evidence* (New York: Putnam, 1967). On the revolutionary tendencies of the nobility, old or new, poor or affluent, cf. Anatole Leroy-Beaulieu, op. cit., vols. 1, 2, and 4.

402. Cf. Comte Joseph de Maistre, *Quatre chapitres inédits sur la Russie*, Comte Rodolphe de Maistre, ed. (Paris: Vaton Frères, 1859), 27.

403. Lenin was the son of a high school-college inspector who had received the hereditary title of nobility. Moscow's Lenin Museum has his passport, issued by the police prefect of Pskov, dated February 28, 1900, in which Vladimir Ilyitch Ulyanov is described as a "hereditary nobleman." According to Louis Fischer ("Die ungleichen Brüder," *Der Monat*, Berlin, vol. 17, no. 203, August 1965, 5). Lenin's paternal grandmother was an illiterate Kalmyk. His paternal grandfather, according to Fisher, was a "Great Russian" from Astrakhan, but I think the name Ulyanov is probably of Mongol-Kalmyk (not Tartar) origin. According to C. J. Renstedt's Kalmyk Dictionary (*Kalmückisches Wörterbuch*) published by the Finnish-Ugrian Society in Helsingfors, 1935, 454, *ula, ulu* means mountain, hill. (In Mongolian *ulan* means "red"!) The Russian ending for Asian names is quite frequent. Robert Payne in his *The Life and Death of Lenin* (London: Pan Books, 1967), 39, makes the case that the name Ulyanov is frequent among the Chuvash tribe. "He was German, Swedish and Chuvash and there was not a drop of Russian blood in him" (47).

Lenin's mother was a Lutheran German-Russian, daughter of a Dr. Blank, a physician and fairly wealthy landowner. According to Stefan Possony, *Lenin, The Compulsory Revolutionary* (Chicago: Regnery, 1964), 3, Alexander Dimitriyevitch Blank also belonged to the nobility. From childhood on, Lenin spoke German fluently with his mother and aunt. Interestingly enough, the *Bolshaya Sovyetskaya Entsiklopediya* (1956), 44:216, has half a column on Lenin's mother but does not give her maiden name. This distinguished-looking lady died in 1916 and, as even the communists admit, never shared her son's political views.

Alexander, the eldest, a member of the terrorist *Narodnaya Volya*, had been executed because of his participation in an abortive attempt to assassinate Alexander III, but Vladimir Ilyitch was a prize pupil in an academy for young noblemen and earned a gold medal. His wife, incidentally, was the socialist daughter of an officer who also belonged to the nobility; he married her in an Orthodox church. Yet while many Soviet artists painted moving scenes from Lenin's life (his dramatic parting from his "unconverted" mother), nobody so far has portrayed his wedding with crowns held over the heads of bride and groom.

Vladimir Ilyitch Ulyanov, who used the pen name Lenin (but never called himself "Nikolai"), was born in Simbirsk, today's Ulyanovsk. This was also the birthplace of Gontcharov, who in his novels described the inane life of the Russian gentry, and of Kerenski, who went to the *gimnaziya* where Lenin's father was principal. Lenin, born in 1870, died in 1924, while Kerenski, born in 1881, died in 1970 in New York City, where I met him after the war.

404. Cf. Robert K. Massie, *Nicholas and Alexandra* (New York: Dell, 1969), 514ff. It describes the ghastly and ghoulish death of the Emperor and his wife. Michael, the first Romanov, was elected czar while staying with his mother at the Ipatiev Monastery near Kostroma. The house in Yekaterinburg (Sverdlovsk) where the imperial family was slaughtered belonged to a merchant by the name of Ipatiev. See also the description of this inhuman slaughter by Edward Radzinski in "Razstryel v Yekaterinburgye" (*Ogonyëk*, 21, May 1989). One maid and the family doctor were massacred along with the imperial family. The pictures in the article are heartrending.

405. R.K. Massie op. cit. 457.

406. I met the man twice in the United States. He was "nice" but, listening to his views, I could only pity him. George Katkov was absolutely right when he said that the Russian "liberals" who destroyed the old regime had no idea of the crime perpetrated, nor the least capacity to steer the ship of state on an even keel.

407. On Pyotr Arkadyevitch Stolypin cf. M. P. Bok, *Vospominaniya o moyem ottsye P. A. Stolypinye* (New York: Chekhov Publishers, 1953). For a coherent picture of Russia in the 1905-07 period, cf. *Rossiya v epokhu reform*, V. Zhelyagin and H. Rutykh, eds. (Frankfurt A.M.: Possev, 1981). In *Speak Memory* (New York: Pyramid Books, 1968), 195, Vladimir Nabokov wrote of the period before 1905: "A freedom-loving Russian had incomparably more means of expressing himself and used to run incomparably less risks in doing so than under Lenin. Since the reforms of the 1880s the country had possessed (though not always adhered to) a legislation of which any western democracy might have been proud, a vigorous public opinion that held despots at bay, widely read periodicals of all shades of political thought and, what was especially striking, fearless and independent judges." When Alexander Herzen, the great revolutionary, was exiled to eastern Russia (Perm) in 1835, he was, as an added punishment, made a civil servant in order to be "in good company." Cf. Alexander Herzen, *Byeloye i Dumy* (Kiev: Dnipro, 1976), 218. This rich man finally emigrated to London and, as editor of *Kolokol*, became leader of the Russian opposition. Yet he

regularly received revenues from his large estates. Like Pierre in *War and Peace*, he was the illegitimate son of an aristocratic father but socially accepted.

408. Cf. Fëdor Stepun, *Vergangenes und Unvergängliches aus meinem Leben 1884-1914* (Munich: Josef Kösel, 1947), 228-29.

409. In Britain (or in America) the phrase "an ambitious young man" is rather laudatory. *Un jeune ambitieux* in French (or in any Continental language) is devastating.

410. The Russian historian Michael Florenski wrote at the end of his *Russia, a History and an Interpretation* (New York: Macmillan, 1967), 2:1467, that the only way to have avoided the victory of the radical Social Democrats, the *bol'sheviki*, would have been to have made peace immediately and have given *all* land to the peasants. But Kerenski wanted to "make the world safe for democracy" and continued the war. Also, he was not the man to do anything as unreasonable as denuding the landowners totally. But the Russian peasant, unfortunately, wanted just that—and paid for it dearly.

411. Cf. Fëdor Stepun, op, cit., 73. Stepun asks the pointed question, "How could a liberal regime have any permanence if a man like Maxim Gorki, after a political banquet in 1905, could succeed in making the representatives of the business world and industry donate over a million rubles for the continuation of the Revolution and thereby for their own expropriation?" But similar stupidities are committed in the Western world by people whom Lenin liked to call "useful idiots."

412. Witness the complaint of Styepan Trophimovitch in chapters 1 and 6 of *The Possessed* about the evolution and change of his original ideas and ideals. This particular novel is (or was) unobtainable in the USSR—except as a volume of his collected works. And this is part of the reason why people will wait in line for days to buy the rather limited edition of his collected works, issued once every ten or fifteen years.

413. Dostoyevski, too, belonged to the (newer) hereditary nobility. He was deprived of his rank after receiving his death sentence (and the subsequent jail term), but was reinstated after his return from Siberia. There exists in Moscow's Dostoyevski Museum a copy of his passport where he figures in a German version as "von Dostoyevski." *The Recollections of a Death House*, Dostoyevski's great classic, depicts a terrible state of affairs, but a book such as Anatoli R. Marchenko's *My Testimony* gives with its description of torture and cannibalism an infinitely more frightening picture of post-Stalin prison camps in European Russia. It is more impressive because Alexander Solzhenitsyn's *The First Circle*, on a higher literary level, draws a comparison between Soviet and old Russian jails where (with reference to the *Recollections* of Dostoyevski) the latter are made to appear idyllic. Ilya Ehrenburg told me very interestingly about his experiences in a Russian jail when at the age of seventeen he was imprisoned for conspiratorial activities in his *gimnaziya*. "Was it very uncomfortable?" I inquired. "No, not particularly. We all only suffered from lack of sleep." "Endless interrogations?" "By no means," he replied. "But the director was interested in political and philosophical questions, so he brought the samovar to the 'politicals' and between endless cups of tea we had interminable discussions until the small hours of the morning." Leon Trotski, if his memoirs can be believed, had an equally charming recollection of his jailors. About the comforts and amenities of Lenin's exile

in Shushenskoye see also Bertram D. Wolfe's truly excellent *Three Who Made a Revolution* (New York: Penguin Books, 1966), 155-57.

414. Cf. Dmitri Myerezhkovski, *Tsarstvo Antikhrista* (Munich: Drei-Masken Verlag, 1919), 231.

415. Cf. V. Rozanov, "Apokalipsis nashego vremeni," *Vyersty* (Paris, 1927), no. 2.

416. Communism—where everybody gets goods "according to his needs"—is a state of society so unimaginable that we can safely discard this utopian vision from our speculations. Either needs are desires, or they are "fixed" by our fellowmen who thus become our superiors. This again is the "secularized monastery." Yet the Communists still have sympathy and admiration for "utopian socialism," as witness the article on Campanella and Morelly in the *Bol'shaya Sovyetskaya Entsiklopediya* (1954), 19:545-46, and 28:297.

417. Men such as Lenin, Chicherin, Lunacharski, Dzierzyński, Tukhachevski, Mayakovski, Plyekhanov, Alexei Tolstoy, Alexandra Kollontay, to name just a few. Without the collaboration of the lesser nobility in the bureaucracy the Communists would hardly have survived their first decade. Cf. Galina Berkenkopf, "Russische Elite als Wegbereiter und Opfer des Oktober" in *Ostprobleme*, 19 Year, no. 22-23 (Nov. 17, 1967), 609-13.

418. In Finland the "Red General" Antikainen reportedly boiled in a kettle all students serving in the white army who fell into his hands. He had a special dislike for them. The female red regiments in Finland, operating in the Tammerfors (Tampere) region, were also dreaded for their abysmal cruelty to male prisoners.

419. The Jewish student Kannegiesser murdered the founder of the Tshe-Ka, Moses Uritzki, because he considered him a blot on the Jewish name. The Tshe-Ka was then taken over by the Polish nobleman (*szlachcic*) Feliks Edmundowicz Dzierzyński, son of a landowner, who later became the head of the Railroad Commissariat. The Tshe-Ka was then renamed GPU ("Governmental Political Administration").

   Fanya Kaplan, who tried to assassinate Lenin, was also Jewish. So was Judas Mironovitch Stern, who tried to kill the German diplomat von Twardowski in Moscow. Stern considered German aid to the Bolsheviks as fatal to Russia. On Fanya Kaplan, cf. Stefan Possony, op. cit., 289, and Louis Fischer, *The Life of Lenin* (New York: Harper and Row, 1964), 599.

420. Stalin also complied with Hitler's request to hand over a number of leading German Communists who had fled to the Soviet Union. One of them, Heinz Neumann, had been murdered in an earlier purge by the wily Georgian. His widow, Margarete Buber-Neumann, was extradited in early 1940 to the Nazis after she had spent years in Soviet concentration camps. She then landed in Ravensbrück, a Nazi "K. Z." for women (and, to give the Devil his due, far more luxurious than its Eastern counterparts). The account of her sufferings under red and brown beasts is one of the great books of our time. Cf. Margarete Buber-Neumann, *Als Gefangene bei Stalin und Hitler* (Munich: Deutscher Taschenbuchverlag, 1962), originally Stuttgart: Deutsche Verlags-Anstalt, 1958.

421. We discount the rather widespread thesis that communism is just another form of "eternal Russian imperialism." Nor, to be sure, were the Nazis just "successors of

Frederick the Great." Of course, Russian nationalist feelings may not be entirely alien to a Russian Communist, and officers of the Imperial army (Tukhachevski, Shapotshnikov, Brussilov) have fought in the red army against "foreign interventionists."

422. Cf. Benito Mussolini, *Il Trentino veduto da un socialista* (Florence: Casa Editrice Italiana, Quaderni della Voce, 1911).

423. Mussolini, aged twenty-one, translated *Les paroles d'un révolté* of the anarchist Prince Pyotr Kropotkin. He wrote (as Duce), "Twenty years have passed, but the *Paroles* seem quite recent, so alive are they with present-day interests. . . They overflow with a great love for oppressed mankind." Cf. *Opera omnia di Benito Mussolini* (Florence: La Nuova Italia, 1951), 1:50. Mussolini was, after all, a minor intellectual who had been made an honorary doctor of the University of Lausanne in Switzerland.

424. The most radical of the whole lot—so radical that they were persecuted even by Žižka and his Taborites—were the Adamites who practiced nudism and the community of women and property. Žižka massacred them wholesale in 1421. Cf. also K. V. Adámek, "Adamité na Hlinecku v XIX věku," *Časopis Českého Musea* (Prague, 1897), part 48. Adámek ascribed the revival of the Adamites to the Toleration Law of Emperor Joseph II in the eighteenth century, documenting the tenacity of this weird sect. Cf. also Josef Dobrowsky, *Geschichte der böhmischen Adamiten* (Prague: Akademie der Wissenschaften, 1788). The main source for the entire piece is Magister Laurentius de Březina (or Březowa). *De gestis et varii accidentibus regni Boemiae 1414-1422*, which can be found, edited by Dr. Karl Höfler, in the series "Geschichtsschreiber der hussitischen Bewegung," part I in *Fontes rerum Austriacarum* (Vienna, 1856).

425. Cf. Willy Lorenz, *Monolog über Böhmen* (Vienna: Herold, 1964), 30.

426. Cf. Andreas de Broda, "Tractatus de origine Hussitarum," *Fontes rerum Austriacarum* (Vienna), 6:343-44.

427. Cf. Louis Leger, *Nouvelles Études Slaves* (Paris: Ernest Lerouex, 1886), 159.

428. Cf. Dr. Paul Tóth-Szabó, *A cseh-huszita mozgalmak és uralom története Magyarországon* (Budapest: Hornyánszky, 1917), 50.

429. While the influence of Marsiglio of Padua on Wycliffe was considerable. Cf. note 56.

430. Cf. E. v. Kuenhelt-Leddihn, *Freiheit oder Gleichheit?* 328ff.

431. Cf. Josef Pekař, *Žižka a jého doba* (Prague: Vesmir, 1927), 2 vols. Also Kamil Krofta, *Žižka a husitská revoluce* (Prague: Laicter, 1936); Th. G. Masaryk, *Jan Hus, Naše obrození a naše reformáce* (Prague: Laichter, 1925); Alois Hajn, *Jan Hus a jého vyznam v době přitomně* (Prague: Svaz Národniho Osvobozeni, 1925); František Palacký, *Dějiny národu českého w Čechach a w Morawě* (Prague: Tempský, 1877), vol. 3.

432. The *Los-von-Rom-Bewegung* ("Away from Rome Movement") was a concentrated effort by the Austrian Evangelicals to convert Catholic German-Austrians to the Lutheran faith. This allegedly religious action had a strong nationalistic flavor and enjoyed the financial support of the "Gustav Adolf Verein" centered in Germany. Georg von Schönerer, Hitler's mentor, had been intimately connected with the movement, which scored its greatest successes (roughly in the 1895-1910 period) among the Germans of Bohemia and Moravia.

433. Cf. G. Evola, *Gli uomini e le rovine* (Rome: Edizioni dell'Ascia, 1953), 106ff. The same view has been expressed by Guglielmo Ferrero in *Pouvoir, Les génies invisibles de la cité* (New York: Brentano, 1942), 297.

434. Cf. Massimo Rocca (Libero Tancredi). *Come il fascismo divenne una dittatura* (Milan: Edizioni Libraria Italiana, 1952), 329. Rocca insists that Mussolini, upon higher orders, was never sent to the front lines, whereas the King always courageously visited the trenches.

435. Cf. Jean-Jacques Chevalier, *Les grandes oeuvres politiques de Machiavel à nos jours* (Paris: Amand Colin, 1949), 331.

436. Cf. Giulio Evola, *Il fascismo* (Rome: Volpe, 1964), 53-54. Most important for a knowledge of fascism and Mussolini's mind is the Duce's personal contribution to the *Enciclopedia Italiana*, i.e., the article "Fascismo." (Cf. *Enciclopedia Italiana de scienze, lettere ed arte*, 1932, vol. 14, part II.) Mussolini invokes as "ancestors" of fascism Sorel, Péguy, and Lagardelle, but rejects de Maistre (848, 850). Péguy was the great patron saint of the *résistance* during World War II, but one of his sons publicly adhered to the Pétain regime, which shows how arbitrary the interpretation of an original thinker can be.

437. Fascist Italy's privilege (the diarchy of King and Leader) which Nazi Germany tragically lacked was strongly underlined by Pietro Silva in his *Io difendo la monarchia* (Rome: Fonseca, 1946), xii ff.

438. Cf. Hannah Arendt, *The Origins of Totalitarianism* (New York: Harcourt, Brace, 1951), 303.

439. In V. Dudintsev's novel *Nye Khlyebom yedinym* ("Not by Bread Alone"), published in *Novy Mir* (Moscow, 1956), vol. 32, no. 8, 9, 10, the bureaucratic villain, factory director Drozdov, refused to lead a private life. He has no time. "We have to overtake capitalist America," is his constant excuse. Posters all over the Soviet Union showed the comparative strength and progress of both countries, the USSR and the U.S.A.

440. The best description of the tenuous relationship between the Catholic Church and Italian fascism can be found in Daniel A. Binchy's *Church and State in Fascist Italy* (London-New York: Oxford University Press, 1941).

441. As a young man, Mussolini confessed to his wife that he had been an atheist, yet he affirmed in his last letter to her that he now believed in God. Cf. Gino de Sanctis, "La vedova dell'impero," *L'Europeo*, November 30, 1947, 9. The Duce also seemed to have a curious respect for the papacy. To the French journalist Lucien Corpechot, a *Maurassien*, Mussolini shouted in reference to the headline "Non Possumus" in *Action Française*: "Who dares to say *non possumus* to the Pope? One just does not say *non possumus* to the Pope!" Cf. Adrien Dansette, *Histoire religieuse de la France contemporaine* (Paris: Flammarion, 1951) 2:595.

442. On the Spanish Falange, cf. Bernd Nellesen, *José Antonio Primo de Rivera, der Troubadour der spanischen Falange* (Stuttgart: Deutsche Verlagsanstalt, Schriftenreihe der Vierteljahrshefte für Zeitgeschichte, 1965). The writings of Primo de Rivera (*Obras completas*, Madrid, 1942) are important, as are those of the Falange's cofounder Alfonso García Valdecasas. The Rumanian Iron Guard, on the other hand, had an essentially religious basis. Its strong anti-Judaism had no racist foundation. An authoritative work on this interesting, slightly fantastic movement has finally been

written. Cf. Alexander von Randa, *Lebende Kreuze* (Munich: Colectia "Europa," 1979).

443. Cf. Victor Serge, "Pages de Journal, 1945-1947," *Les Temps Modernes*, vol. 4, no. 45, July 1949, 78, 79. Ernst Nolte in his *Der Faschismus in seiner Epoche* (Munich: Piper, 1963), 300, shows clearly how the aging Mussolini's *Repúbblica Sociale Italiana* returned to his old ideas—Mazzini, Garibaldi, republicanism, and socialism.

444. Cf. Massimo Rocca, op. cit., 359.

445. Ibid., 360. In the English-speaking world, the newer literature on Italian fascism is little known, least of all the world's largest biography, six volumes (of about 1,000 pages each) on Mussolini written by Renzo de Felice and published by Einaudi. (The Italian Left attacked Felice violently because he correctly claimed that the majority of Italians supported the *Duce* in the thirties.) Also important is the dialogue between Renzo de Felice and the American scholar Michael Ledeen, *Intervista sul Fascismo* (Bari: Laterza, 1975). Concerning the leftist character of the "Italian Social Republic" see Silvio Bertoldi, *Vita e morte della Repùbblica Sociale Italiana* (Milano: Einaudi, 1978), especially pages 331, 380, 399, 407-418. Also Giorgio Bocca, *Mussolini Social Fascista* (Milano: Garzanti, 1983), and *isdem*, *La Repùbblica di Mussolini* (Milano: Laterza, 1977). The enthusiasm for fascism, needless to say, was greatest in Italy's reddest provinces of today (Tuscany, Emilia, etc.).

446. Cf. "Le confessioni di Vittorio Mussolini," *Il Tempo* (Rome), vol. 5, February 23, 1948, 2.

447. Cf. Guilio Evola, *Il Fascismo*, 32. The formula used by Abraham Lincoln in terminating the Gettysburg Address is supposedly taken from Wycliffe. Carefully going through Wycliffe's writings, I could not find it, though these words somewhat reflect the spirit of Wycliffe's political thinking during a certain phase of his life. They are definitely Marsiglian.

448. Cf. Jules Romains, "Le tapis magique," vol. 25 of *Les hommes de bonne volonté* (Paris: Flammarion, 1946), 151. Unfortunately, Americans were taught by the press that fascism and nazism were "aristocratic." Take, for instance, Harold Rugg in *Democracy and the Curriculum* (New York: Appleton Century, 1939), 524, "Thus the word *fascism* as currently used is really only a name for the characteristic method of government by the very 'best people'. . . . the leading citizens." As for the anti-Nazi novels manufactured in Britain and, above all, in the United States, they almost always picture a nobleman as a Nazi. The names of authors such as Sir Philip Gibbs, Ethel Vance, Louis Bromfield, Kressman Taylor, Ellin Berlin, and Nina Galen come to mind. Lillian Hellman even invented a nazi Rumanian *count*!—all a hangover from World War I. Professor Helmut Kuhn (Munich) is only too right when he speaks of four groups of victims—the Rich, Jews, Nobles, and Priests. Cf. *Der Staat* (Kösel, Munich, 1967), 443. (It was worse for those who belonged in more than one category.) National socialism, F. Reck-Malleczewen wrote, was indeed the revolt of postmen and elementary school teachers, cf. his *Tagebuch eines Verzweifelten* (Suttgart: Goverts, 1966), 180. This book was translated into English and not only published, but republished in America. Reck-Malleczewen was an East Prussian who became an enthusiastic Bavarian and a friend of Bavaria's Crown Prince.

449. Cf. *Československá Vlastivěda*, part 5, "Stát," Emil Čapek, ed. (Prague: Sfinx,

1931), 479. It contends that the National Socialist Czechoslovak party rested on the religious and social traditions of Hussitism.

450. Cf. *Masarykův Slovník Naučný* (Prague, 1925), 1:1129: See also the article of Karel Slavíček in *Ottuv slovník naučný nové doby* (Prague, 1936), 4:437, as well as the earlier edition of the same work, *Ottuv slovník naučný* (Prague, 1909), 28:984-85. Also consult *Slovník národohospodářský, sociální a politický* (Prague, 1933), part iii, 515-16.

451. *Czechoslovak Sources and Documents* (Prague: Orbis, 1936), no. 9.

452. Cf. Th. G. Masaryk, *The Making of a State*, Wickham Steed, ed. (London: Allen and Unwin, 1927), 439, and Wickham Steed, "A Programme for Peace," in *Edinburgh Review*, 1916 (separate reprint).

The anti-Jewish Czech riots in Prague are mentioned by Hermann Münch in *Böhmische Tragödie* (Braunschweig: Westermann, 1950); and H. Münch, "Panslawismus und Alldeutschtum," *Neues Abendland* (Munich, July 1950), vol. 5, no. 7, 278. German-speaking Jews in 1945 were forced by the Czechs to exchange their Star of David (enforced by the Nazis) for a swastika which then became *de rigueur* for the Sudeten-Germans. Yet while these Jews were "racially Semites" in nazi eyes, they had become "ethnically German" in Czech eyes—an "identitarian" tragicomedy!

453. Cf. A. Ciller, *Vorläufer des Nationalsozialismus* (Vienna: Ertle, 1932), 135.

454. Cf. Karel Engliš, "Le 'socialisme allemand': Programme du parti allemand des Sudètes," in *Sources et Documents Czechoslovaques* (Prague: Orbis, 1938), no. 46, 59. Further references to that period: Ingenieur Rudolf Jung, *Der nationale Sozialismus. Seine Grundlagen, sein Werdegang, sein Ziele* (Munich: Deutscher Volksverlag, 1922); Dr. Karl Siegmar Baron von Galéra, *Sudetendeutschlands Heimkehr ins Reich* (Leipzig: Nationale Verlagsanstalt, 1939); Hans Krebs, *Kampf in Böhmen* (Berlin: Volk und Reich Verlag, 1936); Hans Krebs, *Wir Sudetendeutsche* (Berlin: Runge, 1937); Hans Knirsch, *Aus der Geschichte der nationalsozialistischen Arbeiterbewegung Altösterreichs und der Tschechoslowakei* (Aussig, 1931).

Vide also Andrew Gladding Whiteside's analysis of early national socialism: "Austrian National Socialism was in essence a radical democratic movement: its official programs and propaganda emphasized social and economic equality, popular sovereignty, opposition to traditional authority, and radical changes in the existing order. Its appeal was to the poor, to the workers in ill-paid jobs, to the underdogs. National Socialism's first political program had been based on the Linz program, whose principles had by 1900 been accepted by all Austrian pan-German democratic parties." (The Linz program refers to the Social Democratic program.) Cf. A. G. Whiteside, *Austrian National Socialism* (The Hague: Martinus Nijhoff, 1962), 112.

455. Cf. A. Ciller, op. cit., 141. Of interest in this connection also are the revealing memoirs of Franz Langoth, *Kampf um Österreich, Erinnerungen eines Politikers* (Wels: Welsermühl, 1951). Langoth was an old Pan-German, republican, anticlerical fighter in the tradition of 1848 who died in his nineties in 1952. His book shows the interconnection between nascent national socialism and the "black-red-gold" heritage of the "forty-eighters" who fought the internationalism of the Habsburgs, the aristocracy, and the Catholic Church. Langoth became an ardent national socialist in a perfectly logical evolution of his ideas. As Aristotle has pointed out (*Politics*,

III,viii, 204), equality and hatred for the extraordinary man, the privileged person, is the main postulate of democracy and, therefore, of all leftist thought.

456. Count Richard Coudenhove-Kalergi, founder of the Pan-Europe Movement, frequently pointed out in the 1920s that the Jews were rapidly becoming Europe's new aristocracy, a view not without foundation at that time. Yet at the same time the Jewry of Western Europe was rapidly dwindling owing to the triple losses through conversions, mixed marriages, and low birth rates. Without further immigration from the east, the German Jews would have practially disappeared by the end of the century. The Jewish population of Germany in 1930 was only 0.9 percent. Juan Comas in his *Racial Myths* (Paris: UNESCO, 1951), 31, informs us that in Germany beween 1921 and 1925, 42 out of every 100 Jewish marriages had one gentile partner. In 1925, 851 all-Jewish and 554 mixed marriages took place in Berlin. The brown murders of Jews were mostly staged abroad.

457. This speech was published in leaflet form.

458. This proclamation is reproduced in the op. cit. of Hans Krebs (*Kampf in Böhmen*). Another facsimile shows a swastika for the first time in the history of national socialism. Yet the Nazi swastika is the reverse of the Hindu original and thus does not imply luck or success but certain doom. Baron Wilhelm Ketteler, Papen's secretary in Vienna, pointed this out at a social gathering. (He was promptly murdered after the *Anschluss*.)

459. Cf. Josef Pfitzner, *Das Sudetendeutschtum* (Cologne: Scharffstein, 1938), 23-24. Jules Monnerot in his *Sociologie du communisme* (Paris: Gallimard-N.R.F., 1949), 395-96, affirms that modern tyranny must always combine social (or socialistic) with national appeal. Analogies between socialism and nationalism were already fully realized by Nietzsche. He considered both as "dominated by envy and laziness," the laziness of the head characterizing the nationalists, the laziness of the hands characterizing the socialists. Cf. his "Menschliches, Allzumenschliches," vol. 1, no. 6, 480.

Joseph Pfitzner was executed in Prague after World War II; Rudolf Jung, who played such a fatal role in the origins of national socialism, died of starvation in Prague's Pankrac prison. Cf. *Dokumente zur Austreibung der Sudetendeutschen*, Dr. Wilhelm Turnwald, ed., published by the "Arbeitsgemeinschaft zur Wahrung sudetendeutscher Interessen," 1951, 50. (Document no 15.) Goebbels called Jung "a fine head. With him one can collaborate." Cf. *Das Tagebuch von Joseph Goebbels, 1925-1926*, Helmut Heiber, ed. (Stuttgart: Deutscher Verlagsanstalt, 1960), 64.

460. Cf. Konrad Heiden, *Geschichte des Nationalsozialismus* (Berlin: Rowohlt, 1933), 19.

461. Aussig (in Czech: Ústí-nad-Labem) was the center of early national socialism in Bohemia. Cf. *Bei unseren deutschen Brüdern in der Tschechoslowakei* (Tübingen, 1921), 38-39. (This is the collective report by a group of Tübingen students.)

The biggest spontaneous massacre of Germans in history took place in Aussig after the retreat of the German armies. At least four times as many Germans were killed there by a Czech mob as Czechs by the SS in Lidice. Cf. *Londýnské Listy* (London), vol. 2, no. 14, July 15, 1948. Decent Czechs (like the publishers and editors of the aforementioned paper) condemned such beastly horrors.

462. About Streicher's early career in the Democratic Party, cf. R. Billing. *NSDAP Geschichte eine Bewegung* (Munich: Funk, 1931), 112.

463. Cf. Professor Dr. Fanz Jetzinger, *Hitlers Jungend* (Vienna: Europa-Verlag, 1956), 25-35; Hans Frank, *Im Angesicht des Galgens* (Neuhaus bei Schliersee: Brigitte Frank, 1955), 320-21. Frank was the nazi governor of Poland, executed after the Nuremberg Trials. Hitler's father's illegitimate birth, however, was openly admitted in the Third Reich. Cf. *Die Ahnentafel des Führers. Ahnentafeln berühmter Deutscher*, III (Leipzig, 1937), 39. In the biography of Hitler by Werner Maser—cf. his *Adolf Hitler* (Munich: Bechtle, 1971)—the Führer's Jewish ancestry is denied, but without solving the riddle. The grandfather remains unknown and Hitler's *suspicion* of his own "non-Aryan" ancestry is not challenged. Joachim C. Fest in his *Hitler* (Berlin: Propyläen, 1977), 31-32, a tome of 1,190 pages, comes to the same conclusion. He also mentions, without naming the author, the blackmailing letter of his nephew Patrick Hitler, son of a half-brother and an American citizen.

464. Hitler's house of birth, a rather sinister building, now has on its ground floor the very symbol of semiliteracy—a *Volksbücherei*, a popular library. The largest single professional group in the Nazi party, elementary school teachers, traditionally veered toward the "laicist," "radical socialist," or socialist outlook; on the village level they were the sworn enemies of the priest. This development was clearly seen in the earlier part of the nineteenth century. Carl Ernst Jarcke foresaw it graphically. Cf. his op. cit., 4:229.

465. Chancellor Brüning knew quite well (he told me) about Hitler's worries concerning his father's background, but some other people "in the know" about Hitler's father were murdered on and after June 30, 1934, in Bavaria. Of course, there must have been other reasons behind Hitler's hatred for his father; *hatred* always stems from a feeling of inferiority and/or helplessness. The aged official (who was much older than Adolf and considerably older than Adolf's mother, his second wife) must have treated his dreamy, introverted, and odd son sternly and must frequently have criticized him, probably justly. Yet this is precisely what a person, tortured by an inferiority complex, cannot stand. The truth always hurts. Hitler fled his father, as he later fled Austria. When Hitler's Minister Albert Speer saw a house with a memorial tablet in the village of Spital (Lower Austria) where Hitler's father had been born, Hitler completely lost his balance and demanded its immediate removal. "Obviously, there was a reason," Speer wrote, "why he wanted to eliminate a part of his youth. Today one knows about the lack of clarity concerning his family background which gets lost in the Austrian forests." Cf. A. Speer, *Erinnerungen* (Berlin: Propyläen, 1969), 12. Even more significantly, after the *Anschluss* Hitler ordered the total destruction of Spital and the surrounding villages, the so-called Allentsteig district. The area was cleared for military maneuvers and, not so many years later (1945), claimed by the USSR as "German property."

466. Cf. August Kubizek, *Adolf Hitler, mein Jugendfreund* (Graz: Stocker, 1953). This book is invaluable for a true understanding of Hitler. Also interesting are the memoirs of Hitler's commanding officer in World War I, Captain Fritz Wiedemann's *Der Mann, der Feldherr werden wollte* (Velbert und Kettwig: Blick und Bild Verlag, 1964). Wiedemann writes that Hitler was not promoted "because we could not detect in him

qualities necessary for a leader" (26). A misjudgment? Not in the least, because military and political leadership are of an entirely different order. A general does not have need of rhetorical gifts, while demagogues often suffer from neurotic disorders. Masses are often swayed more by hysterical orators than by calm thinkers or soberly calculating managers. Hitler, moreover, a nonstop talker, was decidedly unpopular with the other soldiers. Still, there are certain legends about Hitler which, thanks to the research of Werner Maser, have been exploded. Hitler suffered material hardships only during a very short period of his life, he was a great ladies' man, he was a voracious (though unmethodical) reader, he had a modest but steady income from his pictures, and he was never a corporal but a private first class (*Gefreiter*). Not truly educated, he was nevertheless gifted in many ways. The mutual dislike between him and the General Staff grew greater after the outbreak of the war when he became increasingly sick.

467. On the Continent, four to five years of elementary school (the age group is five, six, or seven to ten) are followed either by a dead-end school lasting three or four years *or* by a high school-college lasting eight to nine years and terminating in a bachelor's degree. This school requires an entrance and a final examination. The universities have no colleges on the American pattern; they are graduate schools and impart no general instruction. The rather common belief that the junior and senior years of American colleges are the equivalent of the first two years of Continental universities is therefore quite erroneous. The Continental high school-colleges (*liceo, lycée, Gymnasium, gimnazia,* etc.) are of the classic, semiclassic, or scientific types. Hitler tried the scientific type and failed. (Hitler was always "scientific" and "antimetaphysical" in his outlook, which reminds one of Morelly's precept that only the experimental sciences should enjoy freedom in Utopia. Cf. Morelly, op. cit., 151, and chapters 4 and 5 of the *Lois des Études*.) It would be interesting to know whether the trend in favor of the Nazi ideology was more marked among those with a classic or a scientific education. The American reeducators believed that a classic education bred totalitarianism, yet all indications point in the other direction. National socialism was "biologism" and the tenor of nazism distinctly "antimediterranean," romantic rather than classic.

468. Up to the end of the monarchy there was no "German army." Bavarians gave an oath of allegiance to the King of Bavaria, Hamburgers to the Senate of the Republic of Hamburg, and so on. Some German states had their own postage stamps, and prior to the Third Reich there was no German citizenship. Diplomatic representatives were exchanged beween Bavaria, Saxony, and Prussia until 1933.

469. Foreigners accepted by the civil service of a German state automatically received citizenship. This is also true of university professors, even today. A Brazilian, for instance, receiving a chair at a German university immediately becomes a German citizen. In Europe multiple citizenship is not uncommon.

470. Hitler's other fixation concerned people whose names began with the letter "H" or one near to it in the alphabet; to wit, G, I, J, or K. Hitler also blindly believed in astrology, a fact known to the Allies. Thus, during the war, they were able to foretell some of his decisions based on the classic rules of astrology (as related by Louis de

Wohl, who worked along these lines during the war in London). Hitler and other Nazi leaders surrounded themselves with clairvoyants and soothsayers. One of these, Erik Jan Hanussen, foretold their final defeat as well as victories and paid with his life for his honesty.

471. Cf. Carl J. Burckhardt, *Meine Danziger Mission 1937-1939* (Munich: Deutscher Taschenbuch Verlag, 1962), 265 (originally Munich: Callwey, 1960). This book is of such historic importance that it has never been translated into English.

472. The role of the demotic-democratic *Führer* was stressed by Gottfried Neesse, *Die Deutsche Nationalsozialistische Arbeiterpartei. Versuch einer Rechtsdeutung* (Stuttgart: Kohlhammer, 1935), 145, and Max Irlinger, *Die Rechte des Führers und Reichskanzlers als Staatsoberhaupt des Deutschen Reichen* (Dissertation at Innsbruck University, 1939), 71. Cf. also Rodolphe Laun, *La démocratie* (Paris: Delgrave, 1933); Gerhard Leibholz, "La nature et les formes de la démocratie," *Archives de philosophie du droit et de sociologie juridique*, vol. 6 (1936), no. 3-4, 135; Alfred Weber, *Die Krise des modernen Staatsgedankens in Europa* (Stuttgart: Deutsche Verlagsanstalt, 1925), 139, 151; Gustave Le Bon, *Psychologie des foules* (Paris: Alcan-Presses Universitaires, 1939), 93ff.; Giulio Evola, *Il fascismo*, 53-54 (on the incompatibility between *ducismo*, *Führertum*, and the ideals of the rightist outlook); Karl Thieme, *Lexikon der religiösen Zeitaufgaben* (Freiburg i. Br.: Herder, 1952) citing Baldur v. Schirach's poem "Hitler" which sums up quite nicely the concept of the *Führer*:

You are many thousand people behind me,
And you are I and I am You.
I have never lived a thought
Which has not trembled in your hearts.
And if I form words, I do not know a single one
Which is not fused with your will.

There we have the *volonté générale* of Rousseau embodied in a single person— identity made flesh.

473. Careful research seems to indicate, however, that the *Lebensborne*, combining mating and parturition institutes, did not really exist in the narrow sense of the term. There were, to be sure, *Lebensborne* in the form of maternity homes in which unwed mothers, especially those producing "purely Aryan" babies, were most welcome. Yet the idea of *Mutterhöfe*, real mating and maternal institutions, proposed by Heinrich Himmler, did not come up. Cf. *Reichsführer! Briefe an und von Himmler*, Helmut Heiber, ed. (München: Deutscher Taschenbuch Verlag, 1970), 346-47. What existed were stupid, idealistic girls who "donated a child" to the *Führer*. This nice phrase was used under other circumstances also. A Viennese Nazi in a relatively high position had a neurotic daughter in a private home. She was scheduled for "liquidation" and the desperate father literally went on his knees before a top Nazi in Berlin to save his daughter. *"Nanu,"* the ogre exlaimed, "Don't you want to donate your child to the *Führer*?"

474. Cf. Dr. Henry Picker, *Hitlers Tischgespräche im Führerhauptquartier 1941-1942*, Percy Schramm, ed. (Stuttgart: Seewald, 1963).

475. Cf. Wilfried Daim, *Der Mann, der Hitler die Ideen gab* (Munich: Isar Verlag, 1958). This book by a well-known Viennese psychologist is richly documented.

476. On the *Vertretertagungen* in Salzburg, cf. Erich F. Berendt, *Soldaten der Freiheit* (Berlin, Egghofer, 1936), especially 181-210.

477. Cf. *Deutsche Arbeiter-Presse* (Vienna), August 14, 1920.

478. After the Armistice (1918) General Ludendorff fled to Sweden wearing blue spectacles with papers made out to "Herr Lindström." Following his return, he quarreled violently with Field Marshal von Hindenburg and joined Hitler's Nazi party. After the abortive *Putsch* in Munich (November 1923) he fell out with Hitler and with his new wife, a physician, founded a semireligious, semipolitical league, the *Tannenbergbund*, based on the "cognition of God through the voice of the blood." In his weekly, *Ludendorffs Volkswarte*, which saw conspiracies and secret societies everywhere, he accused nazism of being Christianity in disguise, the swastika a mere mask of the Cross. The paper was suppressed in 1934 and Ludendorff died in 1937. With a mental horizon not transcending Germany, and in light of his collaboration with Lenin, he can be included among the grave-diggers of Europe.

  August von Kahr, prime minister of Bavaria in November 1923, was murdered in the *Reichsmordwoche* (1934), an act of pure revenge against an old man for opposing Hitler as much as Cardinal von Faulhaber. Men such as Prime Minister von Kahr and General von Lossow are indirectly referred to in the lines of the party hymn, the *Horst Wessel Lied*: "Comrades who have been killed by the Red Front and Reaction are marching invisibly in our ranks."

479. In Central Europe political delinquents (just like duelists) were jailed under the older dispensation in fortresses or so-called "state prisons." There they had to be treated as gentlemen, addressed by their full titles, etc. They had the right to receive visitors at any time and their mail was not censored. In a fortress they were supervised by the army, not the police. The food came from the officers' mess. The famous cartoonist Th. Th. Heine, who lived in Bavaria and published caricatures of William II, the "King of Prussia," was arrested while making a trip through Prussia and received a six-month sentence for lampooning the Kaiser. He confessed afterward that he had never had such a wonderful opportunity for work. This form of detention naturally no longer exists in a democratic age averse to most forms of privilege. Political offenders are today treated as common criminals. "All criminals are equal."

480. Cf. E. v. Kuehnelt-Leddihn, *Liberty or Equality?* after p. 224, German edition after p. 336. The least Nazi areas were Upper Bavaria (with Munich!) and the Cologne-Aachen district. The areas most Nazi were southern East Prussia, whose population is Lutheran Polish. These maps are based on the elections of July 31, 1932. They feature the maximum votes the Nazis received in truly free elections. The elections and plebiscites after Hitler's ascent to power have little value for our purpose. The results were often "doctored." Cf. Fritz Reck-Malleczewen, op. cit., 183.

481. From this particular map, however, it also becomes evident that the demarcation line between the Soviet Zone and Western Germany was drawn carefully by the Soviets according to the local strength of the Communists in Germany's free elections. The Americans and the British, naturally, were not aware of this interesting circumstance.

482. Among non-Catholics who regarded Luther as an important spiritual ancestor of national socialism are such men as Karl Barth, Reinhold Niebuhr, Dean Inge, G. P. Gooch, Erich Fromm, Werner Hegemann, Franz Neumann, Karl Otten, et al. Cf. also *Critique* (Paris), no. 66, November 1952, which contains an interesting review of a series of books dealing with the relationship between the Evangelical Church of Germany and national socialism (981-96). The resistance of the church to national socialism, the dilemmas Christians had to face (in Germany much more than in the occupied countries), are, in a way, not open to "historical research." They can only be understood existentially and experimentally. For this very reason the books written by "fact finders" who did not live through this agony are almost worthless. Knowing the anatomy of a human being does not mean in the least knowing his person.

483. Cf. Martin Luther, *Kritische Gesamtausgabe* (Weimar Edition), 53:523ff.

484. *Philadelphia Record*, April 30, 1946. Some German Evangelicals, confused by the issues and quite ignorant of the basic tenets of their faith, tried to work out an Evangelical-Nazi synthesis. Typical of these efforts is a book that exists in English translation—Wilhelm Kraft, *Christ versus Hitler?* (New York: The Lutheran Press, 1937), particularly 32 and 75. The confusion was even greater in Austria where the Lutherans felt by-passed and ignored by Dollfuss' Christian Corporate State, distinctly Catholic in nature, and were hostile to the Habsburg traditions. They wanted the *Anschluss* because they preferred the status of a majority to that of a minority. And as they constituted in Austria a progressive (nonconservative), nationalistic, democratic, scientifically minded, "enlightened" element, they fell for nazism much more easily than their Catholic fellow citizens. They were proud of this evolution, see two books, *Die evangelische Kirche in Österreich*, Dr. Hans Eder, ed. (Berlin: Verlag des Evangelischen Bundes, 1940), and Pfarrer Endesfelder, *Evangelische Pfarrer im völkischen Freiheitskampf der Ostmark und des Sudetenlandes* (Berlin: Verlag des Evangelischen Bundes, 1939).

  Yet in all fairness, there were also German Lutherans and Calvinists who opposed nazism, not only sentimentally, but also "theologically." But, significantly, these resisters almost always had a "neo-orthodox"—a conservative or fundamentalist—background. The betrayal of Christian values and tenets was rife in the ranks of the modernists and relativists.

  Catholics have supported the fascists, the Pétain regime, Chancellor Dollfuss, or General Franco. There were and still are Catholic socialists, and Catholics who thought they could mix their religion with milder forms of national socialism, but no Catholic-Nazi "literature" exists on the subject.

485. I refer to them with a heavy heart, not only because the ecumenical spirit has always had a strong hold on me, but also because, having engaged for years in studies of Luther, I have developed a sincere affection for this true "wrestler with Christ," a compassion for this irascible and melancholy theological genius—who, moreover, created the German language. The reader is reminded that the Weimar Edition of Luther's *Collected Works* comprises 107 volumes of at least 250,000 words each. I am proud to have read more than one-fourth of this colossal work.

  The Low German dialects are spoken north of a line stretching from the Belgian border to Silesia. South of it are the High German dialects. High and Low refer to altitudes above sea level, not to classes. Thanks to Luther's choice of the idiom used in the Thuringian-Upper Saxon area for his translation of the Bible, this High German dialect became the basis of literary German. Dutch is essentially Low German; English ("Saxon") is also derived from Low German, and Low German is taught in certain North German schools twice a week. Literary works were also published in Low German.

486. At the solemn Catholic and Lutheran church services held after the first *Reichstag* session following the March 1933 elections, Hitler demonstratively refrained from attending Mass.

487. Thus my own record according to the broadcast. The official text, as so often with Hitler's speeches, shows minor deviations.

488. Cf. John Wheeler-Bennett, *Hindenburg, the Wooden Titan* (London: Macmillan, 1936), 353-68. Dr. Brüning confirmed to me the veracity of this account. (Churchill too lamented the fall of the Hohenzollerns and the Habsburgs, which resulted in the rise of the Nazis. Cf. Winston S. Churchill, *The Second World War* (London: Cassell, 1948), 1:21, 49-50.) All this was verified by Brüning in his posthumously published *Memoiren 1918-1934* (Stuttgart: Deutsche Verlagsgesellschaft, 1970), 453-55, 512-20.

489. During the war, a Hungarian refugee in America wrote a book on Papen called *The Devil in Top Hat*. The intellectual acumen of Papen was so minute that people took his lack of intelligence as a ruse, as a disguise for shrewdness. His own family considered *das Fränzchen* their least gifted member, to put it mildly. On the other hand, no doubt Papen's so-called "intrigue" was entirely in keeping with the constitution. Giselher Wirsing in "Der Herrenreiter im Morast," *Christ und Welt*, vol. 5. no. 45, November 6, 1952, 4, could write without danger of refutation, "It was the irony of history that Hitler's ascent to power was perfectly legal and that every effort to prevent it would have been illegal as, for instance, a coup of the army. Had such a move taken place, no more than 100 out of 584 deputies would have backed General von Schleicher, in any case, certainly not the Social Democrats."

Papen in his own memoirs—*Der Wahrheit eine Gasse* (Munich: Paul List, 1952)—tried to whitewash himself but his account of the events leading to the fateful January 30, 1933, is nevertheless basically correct.

Leopold Schwarzschild, a German liberal refugee, warned Americans during the last war about their misconceptions relating to nazism: "The master-race idea did not originate in the ruling class but was wedded to the democratic tendencies of the period. . . . readiness to accept such ideas showed up first in the "people". . . . It is wrong also to ascribe the growth of the Nazi movement preponderately to the money of the wealthy Hitlerites. . . . The democratic process was not falsified. It actually worked in Hitler's favor." Cf. his "Six Delusions about Germany," *New York Times Magazine*, October 1, 1944. Socialism worked in the same direction, engendering "semifascist" views. It was socialism, not "Prussianism," that Germany had in common with Russia and Italy. This was strongly emphasized by Friedrich A. von Hayek in his *The Road to Serfdom* (Chicago: University of Chicago Press, 1944), 8-9.

490. Schleicher was therefore nicknamed by the Germans "Primo de Schleicheros," cf. F. K. von Plehwe, *Reichskanzler Kurt von Schleicher, Weimars letzte Chance gegen Hitler*

(Esslingen: Bechtle, 1982). Yet the Social Democrats forbade their trade unions to support the "aristocratic general" against Hitler, a "common man"! (237-69) As for the helplessness of the German army vis-à-vis a strong Nazi working class, see note 885.

491. Cf. Hitler, *Offener Brief an Herrn von Papen*, dated Coburg, October 16, 1932, which was published in pamphlet form (Berlin, 1932). The phrase "workers of the forehead and the fist" is typical Nazi jargon. Remember the full name of the party, "National Socialist German *Workers'* party." The archetype in the Jungian sense was the worker. Only the misfortunes of the war alienated the worker from *his* party.

492. Cf. Golo Mann, *Deutsche Geschichte des 19. und 20. Jahrhunderts* (Frankfurt a.M.: S. Fischer, 1969), 799-800.

493. Cf. Harold Laski, *Parliamentary Government in England* (New York: Viking, 1938), 8, 56-57, 72-73.

494. Cf. Hermann Rauschning, op. cit., 85, 119-20. The Austrian Socialists inherited this anti-Habsburg frenzy from the Nazis. But in other domains too they have continued Nazi traditions—(German) marriage laws, prohibition of Austrian titles of nobility, etc. Even pre-*Anschluss* it was evident that they preferred Hitler to the Habsburgs, the *Anschluss* to the Restoration. Cf. Victor Reimann, *Innitzer, Kardinal zwischen Hitler und Rom* (Vienna: Molden, 1967), 80-81. The tenor of the socialist leaflets was as anticlerical and antimonarchist as the Nazis' (46-47). Both parties were suppressed by the Dollfuss regime, which had to fight a two-front war against two forms of socialism—national and international.

495. Rauschning, op. cit., 190.

496. Ibid, 174.

497. Ibid. Not only the anti-Habsburg but also the anti-Catholic bias tied Hitler to the Marxists. Victor Reimann writes about the demonstration of 200,000 people in Vienna's Heldenplatz after the *Anschluss*—"Vienna's anticlerical army consisting of National Socialists, Social Democrats, and Communists" who "celebrated the greatest triumph in their history. Into this mass of fanatical priest-haters Reichskommisar Bürckel thundered the worst demogogic speech ever uttered in this square." (V. Reimann, op. cit., 194.)

498. Cf. Wilhelm Röpke, *Civitas Humana* (Erlenbach-Zurich: Rentsch, 1946), 268. On the inner connection between socialism and nationalism in Austria prior to 1914, cf. Dr. Paul Molisch, *Die deutschen Hochschulen in Österreich und die politischnationale Entwicklung nach dem Jahre 1848* (Munich: Drei-Masken Verlag, 1922), 14-44. As you may recall, the great Austrian socialist leader, Viktor Adler, started out as a German nationalist, while Dr. Walter Riehl, cofounder of the DNSAP, was originally a social democrat. A biography extolling the merits of Dr. Riehl for the early Nazi cause was penned by Alexander Schilling-Schletter, *Dr. Walter Riehl und die Geschichte des Nationalsozialismus* (Leipzig: Forum Verlag, 1933). He writes: "Dr. Walter Riehl came to National Socialism by way of Social Democracy as did so many of our leaders. The two sources of our idea chronologically following each other can be traced in crystal clearness until they flow together and constitute today one big turbulent river destroying everything rotten and decadent" (9). Riehl's program was a socialism free

of Romish and Jewish influences. He was the great-grandson of a smith and grandson of a student who in 1848 had fought on Vienna's barricades for national democracy. His father was a lawyer like himself and a close friend of another leading German Nazi Austrian social democrat, Engelbert Pernerstorfer, whom he called "uncle." In November 1918, Riehl became director of the "Interstate National Socialist Chancellery of the German-speaking Territories." From the Munich leader, Herr Drexler, he received a letter dated March 1, 1920, informing him that "a Herr Adolf Hitler" had been appointed propaganda minister (*Werbeobmann*). Riehl and Hitler were on intimate terms, and a leading German Nazi, Hermann Esser, called him in 1933 a "Saint John of Hitlerism." But Riehl resigned in Salzburg in August 1923, was expelled from the party in 1933, and was incarcerated by the Gestapo for some time after the *Anschluss* in spring 1938—another piece of jealousy and ingratitude so frequently found in the history of leftist movements. Cf. Adam Wandruszka, "Österreichs politische Struktur" in *Geschichte der Republik Österreich*, Dr. Heinrich Benedikt, ed. (Munich: R. Oldenbourg, 1954), 406-08.

The famous Nazi slogan *Blut und Boden* (blood and soil) stems from the German Social Democrat August Winnig, cf. his *Das Reich als Republik 1918-1928* (Stuttgart and Berlin: Cotta, 1928), 3. Both Marx and Engels were highly enthusiastic over Bismarck, "convinced that he was doing their work." Cf. *Marx-Engels Kritische Gesamtausgabe*, Series III, 4:358.

499. Cf. Hermann Rauschning, op. cit., 177.

500. Ibid., 124. Jacques Ellul, op. cit., 290, writes, "Nazism, however, far from being opposed to Marxism, completes it and confirms it. It gives the solution to numerous problems of adaptation. Hitler's methods stem directly from Lenin's precepts, and conversely, Stalinism learned certain lessons about technique from the Nazis." While Erwin Sinkó (op. cit., 200), until his death an unregenerated Communist, admitted that there was a familial infection of fascism, nazism, and Stalinism, John Lukacs, though opposed to the term "Brown Communism" and "Red Fascism," insists that Hitler, Stalin, Mussolini, Nasser, Tito, Perón, Sukarno, Mao Tse-tung, etc. were all national socialists. The influence of the national factor on socialism has always been undervalued. Cf. his *Historic Consciousness and the Remembered Past* (New York: Harper and Row, 1968), 188.

501. Cf. Albert Speer, *Spandauer Tagebücher* (Frankfurt a.M.: Ullstein, 1975), 252, and Reinhard Spitzy, *So haben Wir das Reich verspielt* (Munich: Langen-Müller, 1985), 255.

502. In the series *Deutsche Forschungen* (Berlin: Juncker & Dünnhaupt, 1935).

503. Cf. Radomir Luža, *Österreich und die Grossdeutsche Idee in der NS-Zeit* (Vienna: Europa Verlag, 1965), 268.

504. Rauschning, op. cit., 265.

505. Cf. (Sir) Herbert Read, *To Hell with Culture*, no. 4 of the series "The Democratic Order" (London: Routledge and Kegan Paul, 1941), 49. Sir Herbert, born in 1893, was director of a London publishing company and had been professor of Fine Arts. Leftists have challenged the veracity of the Rauschning account, yet Theodor Schie-

der in his Rauschnings "Gespräche mit Hitler" als Geschichtsquelle (Opladen: Westdeutscher Verlag, 1972) contradicts them effectively.

506. Cf. (Sir) Herbert Read, *Politics of an Unpolitical* (London: Routledge and Kegan Paul, 1943), 4. This "Nazi-Sozi" affection was mutual. Otto Bauer, the braintruster of the Austrian Social Democrats, wrote in the Marxist monthly *Der Kampf* repeatedly about a common red-brown front against the "reactionary clerico-monarchists." Cf. Gottfried-Karl Kindermann, *Hitlers Niederlage in Österreich* (Hamburg: Hoffman & Campe, 1984), 89.

507. Speech on December 10, 1940, cf. *Völkischer Beobachter*, December 11, 1940.

508. Speech on November 8, 1938, cf. *Völkischer Beobachter*, November 10, 1938.

509. Speech on January 30, 1937, cf. *Völkischer Beobachter*, January 31, 1937.

510. Speech on May 21, 1935, cf. *Völkischer Beobachter*, May 22, 1935.

511. Cf. A. Hitler, *Mein Kampf* (Munich: Eher, n.d.), 99.

512. Dr. Paul Goebbels, speech on March 19, 1934, cf. *Völkischer Beobachter*, March 20, 1934.

513. Dr. Paul Goebbels as quoted by *Der Völkischer Beobachter*, April 25, 1933.

514. Cf. Gottfried Neesse, op. cit, 187.

515. Cf. Michael Oakeshott, *The Social and Political Doctrines of Contemporary Europe* (New York: Macmillan, 1944), xvii. The notion that democracy is a form of government favoring only the poor and ignorant is old. St. Thomas Aquinas expressed it in his commentary on Aristotle. Cf. his *Politicorum seu de rebus civilibus*, Liber 3, Lectio 6. Also: Aristotle, *Politics*, V. viii, 6-7 and V, ix, 4, where Aristotle deals with the "low class" character of tyranny and its democratic background.

516. Cf. interview in the *Petit Journal* (Paris), no. 25729, June 26, 1933.

517. Cf. Dr. Josef Goebbels, *Der Nazi-Sozi. Fragen und Antworten für den Nationalsozialisten* (Munich: Eher, 1932), 10. Goebbels wrote very candidly in his diary on October 23, 1925, "After everything is said and done, I would rather perish with Bolshevism than live in the eternal slavery of capitalism." Cf. *Das Tagebuch von Josef Goebbels*, 10. Not much later he confessed, "The destruction of Russia means that the dream of a National Socialist Germany would have to be buried once and forever." Cf. *National-sozialistische Monatshefte* (Munich: January 15, 1926.

518. Cf. *Der Hochverratsprozess gegen Dr. Guido Schmidt vor dem Volksgericht, Die gerichtlichen Protokolle* (Vienna: Österreichische Stattsdruckerei, 1947), 356.

519. Christian "anti-Judaism" resulted to a large extent from a misreading of the Gospels. *Ioudaoi* ought to be translated as "Judeans," not "Jews." St. Paul, who calls himself an "Israelite of the tribe of Benjamin," wrote a "Letter to the Hebrews." The Judeans were merely one tribe. Our Lord was a Judean by origin, a Galilean by upbringing and, as a descendant of David, a prince of the royal blood. The term "Jew" for Judean is therefore not quite legitimate. Bible translators take note!

520. For an added background study, cf. Hedwig Conrad-Martius, *Utopien der Menschenzüchtung, Der Sozialdarwinismus und seine Folgen* (Munich: Kösel, 1955). Cf. also Daniel Gasman, *The Scientific Origins of National Socialism: Social Darwinism in Ernst Haeckel and the German Monist League* (New York: American Elzevir, 1971). This

excellent book shows the nefarious effects of an obsolete explanation of evolution, such as Darwinism or Neo-Darwinism.

521. Sometimes Hitler chanced to adopt this pessimistic view, as in his reply to Speer's memorandum of March 18, 1945. General Guderian quotes Hitler to the effect that he expected that the best men, not the worst, would be killed in battle. Cf. *Der Nationalsozialismus, Dokumente 1933-1945*, Walther Hofer, ed. (Frankfurt-am-Main: Fischer-Bücherei, 1957), 260. This was certainly true of the counter-revolutionists. Those killed in connection with the German 20th-July revolt, numbering well over one thousand, all of them right-of-center, were sorely missed during Germany's reconstruction.

522. A friend of mine who got into the German Foreign Office during the war belonged to a group of officials trying to persuade the *Reichskanzlei* to give the Ukraine some autonomy. A Ukrainian national committee, situated in Berlin since 1923, considered itself the rightful group to govern the Ukraine. The Foreign Office kept asking that these men be sent to the Ukraine to establish the foundations of a local government. More than a year elapsed without any reaction from Hitler's Chancellery. At long last a reply—over the phone. My friend took the call. An unpleasant voice said, "We have to deny your plans in regard to the Ukrainians. The *Führer* on his last trip through the Ukraine was unimpressed by the race of people he met." Those whom the gods want to destroy they first deprive of their wits.

A mass slaughter of Ukrainians occurred in two phases, one by Stalin and the next by Hitler. Cf. Bohdan Wytwycky, *The Other Holocaust* (Washington, D.C.: The Novak Report, 1980).

523. Cf. Martin Bormann's strictly confidential circular letter partly reported in *Der Natinalsozialismus, Dokumente 1933-1945*, 80, 81, and in *The Tablet* (London, February 28, 1942), 179:110. Here national socialism is clearly shown as a nineteenth-century synthesis. Cf. also Alfred Müller-Armack, *Das Jahrhundert ohne Gott, Zur Kultursoziologie unserer Zeit* (Münster: Regensberg, 1948), 140.

524. Cf. Gustav Stolper, *This Age of Fable* (New York: Reynal and Hitchcock, 1942), 328. For more about the fairy tale of the "financing" of the NSDAP by German big industry and finance, cf. among others, Otto Kopp, ed. *Widerstand und Erneuerung* (Stuttgard: Seewald, 1966), Louis P. Lochner, *Tycoons and Tyrants* (Chicago: Regnery, 1954), and Konrad Heiden, *Das Zeitalter der Verantwortungslosigkeit* (Zürich, 1936), 312.

525. The latest books dealing with the financial backing of National Socialism have strongly confirmed the aforementioned authors. Cf. James and Suzanne Pool, *Who Financed Hitler?* (New York: Dial Press, 1978), and Henry Ashby Turner, *German Big Business and the Rise of Hitler* (New York: Oxford University Press, 1985). All the big enterprises gave certain sums to political parties (including the socialists, but excluding the communists). This form of corruption belongs, to this day, to the general scene of democratic corruption; yet in the Weimar Republic, the main beneficiary was the genuinely liberal German People's Party of Stresemann, not the NSDAP.

526. Cf. Felix von Papen, *Ein von Papen spricht* (Nijmwegen, 1939), 14. The same is heard

from Eugen Kogon in *Der-SS-Staat* (München: Karl Alber, 1946), 209. Yet Communist-Nazi interplay and cooperation prepared the fall of the Weimer Republic, which was keenly felt by such sharp observers as the American journalist H. R. Knickerbocker and the German novelist, essayist, and historian, Frank Thiess. Cf. his *Freiheit bis Mitternacht* (Vienna-Hamburg: Zsolnay, 1965), 509-10. But never forget that Hitler always preferred the Communists to the "decadent West" and efforts to establish a closer brown-red collaboration were made right up to June 1941. Cf. Walter Laqueur, op. cit., 68-77: Otto Ernst Schüddekopf, *Linke Leute von rechts* (Stuttgart: Kohlhammer, 1960), 199, 264, 364, 374-76. Unsurprisingly, after Hitler's takeover, many Communists tried to enroll in the Storm Trooper formations. Cf. Rudolf Diels, *Lucifer anti portas. Zwischen Severing und Heydrich.* (Zürich, n.d.) 127sq. One wonders if, after 1945, the opposite process did not take place in East Germany. Now we know it did.

527. Cf. Graf E. Reventlow, *Völkisch-kommunistische Einigung?* (Leipzig: Graphische Werke, 1924), 17-38. On Hitler's anticapitalist outlook, cf. Dr. Henry Picker, op. cit., 203. Hitler wanted to "nationalize" all stockholding companies. The richly documented volumes by Rainer Zitelmann, *Adolf Hitler* (Göttingen: Schmitt, 1989) and *Hitler. Selbstverständnis eines Revolutionärs* (Hamburg-New York: Berg-Verlag, 1987) show Hitler clearly as a typical representative of the Provider State, socialism, and the Left.

528. Cf. Baron Friedrich von Hügel, "The German Soul and the Great War," *The Quest*, vol. 6, no. 3, April 1915, 6-7.

529. Cf. Ernst Jünger, *Strahlungen* (Tübingen: Heliopolis Verlag, 1949), 562.

530. One of the most destructive leftist reviews published in Paris, totally procommunist, but not tolerated in the Soviet Union—a real product of Luciferism. Forerunners of this attitude included not only the "Divine Marquis," but also Saint-Just. Saint-Just, the alter ego of Robespierre, who wrote sexual poetry, made blueprints of totalitarian utopias reminiscent of Morelly's plans and declared that "a nation regenerated itself only on mountains of corpses." Cf. Albert Ollivier, *Saint-Just et la force des choses* (Paris: N. R. F. Gallimard, 1954), 257.

531. Cf. Nicolas Calas, *Foyers d'incendie* (Paris: Denoel, 1939).

532. Cf. translation of extracts in the *Partisan Review*, vol. 17, no. 1, January-February 1940, 45.

533. Ibid, 46-47. Calas reminds one of Franz Werfel's self-accusing cry, "I have experienced many varieties of arrogance, in myself and in others. But since I myself shared these varieties for a time in my youth, I must confess from personal experience that there is no more consuming, more insolent, more sneering, more diabolical arrogance than that of the artistic advance guard and radical intellectuals who are bursting with a vain mania to be deep and dark and subtle and to inflict pain. Amid the amused and indignant laughter of a few philistines we were the insignificant stokers who preheated the hell in which mankind is now roasting." Cf. Franz Werfel, *Between Heaven and Earth*, M. Newmark, trsl. (New York: Philosophical Library, 1944) ("Theologoumena," no. 126), 250.

534. Cf. *The Pollock-Holmes Letters, Correspondence of Sir Frederick Pollock and Mr. Justice*

Holmes, 1874-1932, Mark DeWolfe Howe, ed. (Cambridge, England: Cambridge University Press, 1942), 2:36.

535. The reference here is to an important work of this brilliant scholar, "Das Versagen des Wirtschaftsliberalismus als religionsgeschichtliches Problem," in *Istambuler Schriften (Istambul Yazilari)*, 12.

536. Napoleon III, imperial dictator, destroyed the career of Achille Charles Léonce Victor Duc de Broglie, French statesman, married to the daughter of Madame de Staël. He characterized the regime as a government which the "poorer classes desired and the rich deserved." This could be extended to the Nazis by adding, "and which leftist intellectuals unwittingly prepared." Before his death, de Broglie said, "I shall die a penitent Christian and an impenitent liberal." More pronouncedly Catholic and Christian was that other great liberal aristocrat, Montalembert, who could write in retrospect before his death, "People should know that there was at least one old soldier of the Catholic faith and of liberty who, before 1830, clearly distinguished the Catholic from the royalist cause: who under the July regime pleaded the cause of the Church's independence from civilian control: who in 1848 fought with all his energies against the alleged identity of Christianity and democracy: and who in 1852 protested the surrender of freedom to brute power under the pretext of religion." Cf. *Montalembert*, Emmanual Mounier, ed. (Paris: Egloff, 1945), 98-99.

537. Thomas Aquinas, *De Regimine Principum*, book II, ch. 3.

538. Frau Heddy Neumeister was economic editor of the *Frankfurter Allgemeine Zeitung* and the author of *Organisierte Menschlichkeit?* (Herder-Bücherei, no. 116). A description of the Augsburg Meeting can be found in my essay, "Die Augsburger Begegnung zwischen Ordo-Liberalen und katholischen Sozialethikern" in *Perspektive 2000*, Lother Bossle, ed. (Würzburg: Creator, 1987), 91-99.

539. Cf. *Correspondence du R. P. Lacordaire et de Madame Swetchine*, Comte de Falloux, ed. (Paris: Didier, 1880). As to Lacordaire's political views, he had gone through a demo-republican phase. See *Lacordaire, Sa vie par lui-même* (Marseilles: Publiroc, 1931), 225-29. His speech upon taking the *fauteuil* of de Tocqueville in the Academy, cf. ibid., 306ff. About his life in general in concise form, cf. Marc Escholier, *Lacordaire ou Dieu et la liberté* (Paris: Fleurus, 1959).

540. Cf. Antoine Redier, *Comme disait M. de Tocqueville* (Paris: Perrin, 1925), 47-48 (letter in facsimile). See also his letter to Count Leo Thun, dated February 26, 1844, quoted by Christoph Thienen-Adlerflycht, *Graf Leo Thun im Vormärz* (Graz: Böhlau, 1967), 177, in which he deplores all disestablishment of the aristocratic order.

541. As to Alexis de Tocqueville, cf. my introduction to his *Democracy in America* (New Rochelle, N.Y.: Arlington House, n.d.) v-xxii. De Tocqueville was also convinced that prerevolutionary France—where the most independent minds could develop—was much freer than mid-nineteenth-century France. Cf. his "L'Ancien régime," *Oeuvres complètes*, J. P. Mayer, ed. 2:176-77.

542. Cf. Nicholas Berdyaev, *The End of Our Time*, D. Atwater, trsl. (New York: Sheed and Ward, 1933), 174-75. Russian original: *Novoye srednovyekovye* (Paris: S.P.C.K., 1928).

543. Cf. Alexis de Tocqueville, "De la démocratie en Amérique," in *Oeuvres* (Paris, 1864), 3:516-23. In English: Arlington House edition, 2:335sq.

544. Staunch Lutherans like Ernst Ludwig von Gerlach opposed Bismarck and his National Liberals violently. So did the arch-conservative Prussian *Kreuzzeitung*. Gerlach later joined, out of sheer protest, the "Catholic" Center party. Cf. Hans Joachim Schoeps, *Das andere Preussen* (Stuttgart: Friedrich Vorwerk, 1952), *passim*.

545. This was already noted by the English volunteer officer C. F. Henningsen in his *Campaña de doce meses en Navarra y las provincias vascongadas con el general Zumalacárregui*, R. Oyarzún, trsl. (San Sebastián: Editorial Española, 1939), originally published in 1836. It was largely the gentry that was Carlist and conservative.

546. The Bavarian aristocracy turned toward the conservative (and royalist) *Bayrische Volkspartei* (Bavarian People's party, forerunner of the present C.S.U., the *Christlichsoziale Union*) only after 1918. In Bavaria, before World War I, a "gentleman" was liberal, not "clerical"! It is also significant that practically the entire Austrian School of Economics (Menger, Wieser, Böhm-Bawerk, Mises, Hayek, Haberler) with the exception of Machlup, consisted of noblemen and old liberals. When the Mont Pèlerin Society was founded—made up of both kinds of liberals—it was originally to be named the De Tocqueville-Acton Society. An American strongly protested that this would honor "Roman Catholic aristocrats," causing the members to choose the name of the mountain visible through the windows, the same name as that of the hotel wherein the meeting took place.

547. Guglielmo Ferrero rightly considered the House of Savoy the "quasilegitimate" rulers of Italy. In Spain and Portugal, the liberal branches of the royal families ruled until 1931 and 1910 respectively: in Spain the descendants of Isabel II, in Portugal those of Maria da Gloria. Today, the Carlist line (but not the Carlist tradition) has died out in Spain while true Braganças survive in Portugal, claiming the throne. (The descendants of Maria da Gloria—Maria II—were Saxe-Coburgs.)

548. It was amazing to see even *young* people disgusted by the word "liberty." And this was precisely the situation in large parts of Europe prior to World War II. The explanation is the visual impression made by the liberal camp—an agglomeration of petty, frightened mice without *positive* beliefs. European youth naively thought that it was strong enough to bear even very heavy chains.

549. When Mussolini fell into the hands of the largely communist partisans, they shouted, "Why have you betrayed socialism?" The Italian Left had never forgotten that Mussolini belonged basically to them. Cf. Paolo Monelli, *Mussolini piccolo borghese* (Milan: Garzanti, 1959), 347. Yet there were, needless to say, many Fascists who after 1944 turned Socialist or Communist as, for instance, Curzio Malaparte (whose real name was Suckert). His last book was on Red China. On his deathbed, this erstwhile Lutheran of German extraction became a Catholic.

Also among the former Socialists and Communists serving Mussolini were Nicola Bombacci, Robert Farinacci, Cesare Rossi, Massimo Rocca, Leandro Arpinati.

550. Cf. Ludwig von Mises, *Human Action* (New Haven: Yale University Press, 1949), 861. Compare also with his views in Margit von Mises, *Erinnerungen von Ludwig von Mises* (Stuttgart-New York: Gustav Fischer, 1978), 42.

551. Cf. Eduard Heimann, "The Rediscovery of Liberalism," *Social Research*, vol. 8, no. 4 (November 1941).

552. Cf. also E. von Kuehnelt-Leddihn, *Die falsch gestellten Weichen* (Vienna-Cologne: Böhlan, 1985), 495. The near-identity of the two maps is astonishing.

 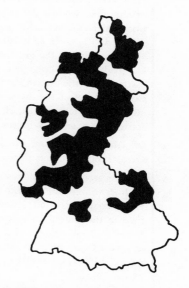

On the left: The National Socialist vote (over 40%) in the July 31, 1932, elections. (This was the greatest percentage the browns received in a truly free election.)

On the right: The areas won by the Social Democrats in direct voting in the November 19, 1972, elections.

These elections show the permanency of the "identitarian" (or socialist) tendencies in the German landscape. Originally published in my *Narrenshiff auf Linkskurs* (Graz: Styria, 1977), 114.

553. Cf. Heinrich Denzinger, *Enchiridion Symbolorum*, Karl Rahner, ed. (Freiburg i.Br.-Barcelona: Herder, 1955), 450. The *Syllabus* can be fully understood only if the individual propositions are read in their full context (Allocutions, Breves, Encyclicals, etc.) and the full context studied in relation to the historical occasion that provoked them. Without such double control the *Syllabus* (a hasty and misleading compilation in any case) makes no sense at all. When the *Syllabus* was published, the French public protested violently, but the famous liberal Bishop Dupanloup wrote a very necessary commentary that became a best-seller and earned the author a highly laudatory Breve of Pius IX. Cf. R. P. Lecanuet, *Montalembert* (Paris: Poussielgue, 1902), 386-89.

554. See the passionate plea of Wilhelm Röpke for Christianity as the last defense against totalitarianism in *Civitas Humana*, 224-25. (Cf. also 194-98.)

555. See the spirited defense of Christianity by Rüstow and his insistence that Western civilization stands and falls with it, in *Ortsbestimmung der Gegenwart* (First Edition), 2:235-36.

His grandfather's generation consisted of three brothers, all Prussian generals. They were Alexander and Cäsar, both killed in Austria in 1866, both military writers of renown, and the very colorful Wilhelm Friedrich, also an officer who wrote a pamphlet against militarism. He was arrested but fled to Switzerland before his trial in 1850. There he lectured on military affairs at the University of Zürich and became a major in the Swiss army. In 1860, he joined Garibaldi in Sicily where he was made a colonel on the general staff. He was the actual victor of the Volturno battle. After the Italian campaign he returned to Switzerland and in 1870 was elected colonel of the Swiss army—the highest rank in peacetime. He authored numerous military works. Here was a Prussian officer, intellectually and internally active, liberal and adventurous, an antimilitarist and yet a war enthusiast.

556. Cf. Alexander Rüstow, *Freedom and Domination* (Princeton: Princeton University Press, 1980). It unfortunately lacks the whole extremely rich supporting material.

557. A large group of German conspirators entrusted the American journalist Louis P. Lochner to inform President Roosevelt of their plan to restore the monarchy under Prince Louis Ferdinand, second son of the former Crown Prince who had spent some time in the United States working in Detroit. Lochner did not reach the United States until July 1942, and then was unable to see the President, who refused to hear about the German resistance. Roosevelt considered such information "highly embarrassing." Cf. Hans Rothfels, *Die deutsche Opposition gegen Hitler* (Krefeld: Scherpe, 1949), 166ff.

Austrian monarchists in 1945, some fresh out of Nazi concentration camps, were often arrested by "His Majesty's officers" and again thrown in jail. In the State Treaty of 1955, Britain, the United States, France, and the Soviet Union barred Austria from restoring the Habsburgs (and possessing submarines—in a landlocked Alpine state!). Communists of course had a vested interest in keeping the Habsburgs out of Austria. But how explain America and Britain?

558. In 1955 an enterprising young American, Patrick M. Boarman, director of the Bureau for Cultural Relations of the N.C.W.C. in Germany, organized a meeting between neoliberal and Christian thinkers in Gauting near Munich. The papers read on this occasion can be found in *Der Christ und die soziale Marktwirtschaft*, P. M. Boarman, ed. (Stuttgart: W. Kohlhammer, 1955). Nitsche too is a Catholic economic neoliberal. So is Baron Georg Bernhard Kripp who wrote an excellent thesis: *Wirtschaftsfreiheit und katholische Soziallehre* (Zürich: Polygraphischer Verlag, 1967). The work of the Dominican E. E. Nawroth (O.P.), *Die Sozial- und Wirtschaftsphilosophie des Neoliberalismus* (Heidelberg-Löwen, 1961), is practically valueless. The author, unfortunately, mistook a membership list of the Mont Pèlerin Society for a catalog of neoliberals, yet the society contained old as well as new liberals. As a result most of the authors cited made the thesis totally irrelevant. And so, therefore, his effort to identify neoliberalism with medieval nominalism.

For a further clarification of the neoliberal ethical stand in the field of economics, cf. particularly Dr. Berthold Kunze, "Wirtschaftsethik und Wirtschaftsordnung" in

Boarmann, op. cit., and Alexander Rüstow, op. cit. See also Alexander Rüstow, "Soziale Marktwirtschart als Gegenprogramm" in *Wirtschaft ohne Wunder*, A. Hunold, ed. (Erlenbach-Zürich, 1953), Alfred Müller-Armack, *Diagnose unserer Gegenwart* (Gütersloh: Bertelsmann, 1949), 293.sq., and Müller-Armack, "Die Wirtschaftsordnung sozial gesehen," in *Ordo*, vol. 1 (1948). About the compatibility of a classic and nonrelativistic liberalism with the Catholic Faith I have written in "Katholischer Glaube und Liberale Haltung" in *Ordo*, vol. 10 (1958), 337-75, and also in "Katorikku to Riberare" in *Gendaishicho to Katorishizumu* (Tokyo: Sobunshahan, 1959), 243-55.

559. Cf. F. A. v. Hayek, *The Constitution of Liberty* (London: Routledge and Kegan Paul, 1960), 397ff. Here Hayek expresses his opinion that, contrary to H. Hallam (*Constitutional History*, 1827), the origin of the political sense of the term "liberal" is not Spanish. Hayek quotes Adam Smith (*Wealth of Nations*, II, 41) on the "liberal plan of equality, liberty and justice," but I think that the term here is used in the old sense of the *liberalitas*.

560. Cf. Benjamin Disraeli, *Endymion* (London: Longmans, Green, 1920), 7. "They are trying to introduce here the continental Liberalism," said the great personage. "Now we know what Liberalism means on the Continent. It means the abolition of property and religion. Those ideas would not suit this country." These remarks were exaggerated, but not without substance since palaeoliberalism had replaced early liberalism. See the critical letter of Bishop Ketteler, "Reply to Professor Bluntschli in Heidelberg," in *Briefe von und an Wilhelm Emmanuel Freihern von Ketteler, Bishof von Mainz*, J. M. Raich, ed. (Mainz: Kirchheim, 1897), 439-44. Harsh also the judgment of Arthur Moeller van den Bruck, frequently but falsely accused of being a Nazi precursor, when he writes that "liberalism is the freedom to have no convictions and, at the same time, to maintain that this precisely is a conviction." Cf. his *Das dritte Reich* (Hamburg: Hanseatische Verlagsanstalt, 1941), 84. The book was originally published in 1924. The old liberals were obviously too optimistic about human nature. Ludwig von Mises, the great old liberal, wrote in *Human Action* (New Haven: Yale University Press, 1949), 861: "After having nullified the fable of the anointed kings, the liberals fell prey to no less illusory doctrines, to the irresistable power of reason, to the infallibility of the *volonté générale*, and to the divine inspiration of majorities."

561. The expression "sectarian liberals" for narrow-minded, anticlerical old liberals was used by Professor Carlton J. H. Hayes in *A Generation of Materialism* (New York: Harper, 1941), 49. The derivation of the term "liberal" from Spanish sources is vouchsafed by *The Oxford English Dictionary*, B. I., vol. 6, part 1, 238, and by Román Oyarzun, *Historia del carlismo* (Bilbao: Ediciones Fe, 1939), 12n.

562. The reactionary truly *reacts* in a hostile way against the existing order. He is not, in other words, a "sovereign thinker," but an emotional protester.

563. Cf. Eugene Lyons, *The Red Decade* (Indianapolis: Bobbs-Merrill, 1941). On the American pilgrims visiting the USSR, see 92-95.

564. This goes hand in hand with pedolatry, the worship of youth.

565. So is welfarism and, naturally, so is socialism. Harold Laski, who constantly

preached this, made himself rather unpopular among American democrats with no socialist inclinations—but he was right. (Only an intense tradition of freedom, as exists in Switzerland, will upset the trend.) Cf. also Harold Laski, *Reflections on the Revolution of Our Time* (London: Allen and Unwin, 1943), 128ff. Yet the realization that democracy leads naturally to socialism is fairly widespread. Cf. Ralph Henry Gabriel, op. cit., 378; Gonzague de Reynold, *La démocratie et la Suisse* (Bern: Editions de Chadelier, 1929), 298; *Joseph Conrad, Life and Letters*, G. J. Aubrey, ed. (London, 1927), 1:84.

566. Cf. Oliver Wendell Holmes, Jr., *The American Law Review*, vol. 5 (1871), 534.

567. Cf. *The Pollock-Holmes Letters*, 2:36.

568. Cf. Richard Hertz, *Chance and Symbol* (Chicago: University of Chicago Press, 1948), 107.

569. Cf. Oliver Wendell Holmes, Jr., in Harry C. Shriver, *Book Notices, Uncollected Letters and Papers* (New York: Central Book Co., 1936), 202.

570. Cf. Felix Morley, in *Barron's Magazine*, June 18, 1951.

571. Cf. *The Pollock-Holmes Letters*, 2:238-39. Letter of Holmes to Sir Frederick Pollock, February 5, 1929.

572. Cf. Eduard May, *Am Abgrund des Relativismus* (Berlin: Lüttke-Verlag, 1941), 136-38.

573. Cf. Hans Kelsen, *Reine Rechtslehre* (Leipzig and Vienna: Deuticke, 1934), 15-16.

574. Cf. Lord Percy of Newcastle, *The Heresy of Democracy* (London: Eyre and Spottiswoode, 1954), 32, 61. Also: Reinhard Steiger, "Christliche Politik und die Versuchung zur Gewalttätigkeit," *Hochland*, vol. 52, no. 4 (April 1960), 360-67. Relativism, as these two authors insist, is an essential element in Western democracy. Orestes Brownson believed that democracy was "political atheism." Cf. Lawrence Roemer, op. cit. 44.

575. Cf. Fëdor Stepun, "Die Kirche zwischen Ost und West," *Schweizer Rundschau*, vol. 52, no. 11-12 (February-March 1953), 701.

576. Cf. Graf Hermann Keyserling, *Das Reisetagebuch eines Philosophen* (Darmstadt: Otto Reichl, 1923), 1:43.

577. Cf. F. S. Campbell (E. v. Kuehnelt-Leddihn), "The Whiff from an Empty Bottle," in *The Catholic World*, October 1945, 20-27. This short story tries to dramatize my thesis. This is also Gertrude Himmelfarb's explicit message in *Marriage*, op. cit. In it, she shows the gradual decline from the passionate and evangelical James Stephen to the odious morass of Bloomsbury.

578. Cf. The *New York Times*, June 28, 1939, cited by Thomas F. Woodlock in his column "Thinking it Over," the *Wall Street Journal*, December 22, 1939.

579. Cf. *Teachers College Record*, vol. 27, no. 6. (February 1926).

580. Cf. B. F. Skinner's book, aptly called *Beyond Freedom and Dignity* (New York: Penguin-Pelican, 1973). Arthur Koestler said that it represents "a monumental triviality that has sent psychology into a modern version of the Dark Ages," while Peter Gay remarked that "the intimate naiveté, intellectual bankruptcy and half deliberate cruelty of Behaviorism manifests itself in these pages."

   In Skinner's widely read book, he says, p. 196: "What is being abolished is autonomous man. . . the man defended by the literatures of freedom and dignity. His abolition has long been overdue. . . Krutch has argued that whereas the traditional view (of man) supports Hamlet's exclamation: 'How like a god!' Pavlov, the behavioral scientist, emphasizes: 'How like a dog!' But that was a step forward."

581. Cf. p. 102. Ernst Walter Zeeden in *Martin Luther und die Reformation im Urteil des deutschen Luthertums* (Freiburg i. Br.: Herder, 1950), 1:379, speaks correctly about the "Protestant bipolarity," by which he means the evolution of the ideas of the Reformation into their opposite.

582. Cf. Chapter V, n. 25. Also, the term "Catholicism" (*Katholizismus, Catholicisme*) figures in neither the old *Catholic Encyclopedia*, nor in the *Dictionnaire apologétique de la foi catholique*, the *Dictionnaire de théologie catholique*, or the *Lexikon für Theologie und Kirche*.

The new *Der Grosse Herder*, 5:276, says clearly: "Catholicism, a term coined in imitation of the word Protestantism, describes the social phenomena of the Catholic Church. . . rather than her inner life." Pope Pius XII called the term "Catholicism" "neither customary, nor fully adequate" for the Catholic Church. (Allocution at the 10th International Congress of Historical Sciences, reported by *The Tablet* [London], vol. 206, no. 6018, September 24, 1955, 293).

583. Cf. note 270. Josef Lortz in his *Einheit der Christenheit, Unfehlbarkeit und lebendige Aussage* (Trier: Paulinus Verlag, 1959), 43, says that in Reformation theology, "not even a hint of relativistic attitude [toward truth] can be found." W. H. van de Pol in *Das reformatorische Christentum in phänomenologischer Betrachtung* (Einsiedeln-Cologne: Benziger, 1956), 66, berates severely all those who accuse the Reformation of fostering "private interpretation" or the "free exploration of Scriptures"—among whom he mentions Jaime Balmes (*El protestantismo comparado con el catolicismo*) and Henry Newman (*Lectures on the prophetical office of the Church*). Yet José Luis L. Aranguren in his *Catolicismo y Protestantismo como formas de existencia* (Madrid: Revista de Occidente, 1957), 44-48, sees more clearly that Luther's "subjectivism" is really an existentialism.

584. Cf. note 1. The introduction of the vernacular—the second such move in the Latin rite after the Vulgate, translation of the Liturgy from Greek to Latin, etc.—was, in view of the internationalization of the world, a rather "reactionary" decision. It was a late triumph of nationalism, and given the progressive "shrinking" of the globe, it will some day have to be revised.

585. Cf. Milton Friedman, *Capitalism and Freedom* (Chicago: University of Chicago Press, 1962), 6.

586. The term "left-of-center" seems to have been invented—characteristically enough—by President Franklin D. Roosevelt.

587. See p. 325.

588. W. H. Auden asked me once why I would not like to live permanently in Britain: "It's the British horror of the absolute," I said. "How right you are!" he replied. Cf. also (Sir) Compton Mackenzie's preface to Jane Lane's *King James the Last* (London: Dakers, 1942), vii-viii. The rejection of compromise and the *juste milieu* is also in the thought of the German religious philosopher Franz von Baader. Cf. his *Grundzüge der*

Societätsphilosophie (Würzburg: Stähel, 1832), 39, where Baader speaks about the "double lie of the *juste milieu.*"

589. Cf. note 571. Newman's reaction to the problem is interesting: he thought that a gentleman falls short in many respects of the Christian ideal of a complete man. (Cf. his *The Idea of a University*, Discourse VIII, chaps. 9 and 10.) Karl Löwith in his essay, "Can There Be a Christian Gentleman?" (*Theology Today*, vol. 5 no. 1, April 1948, 58-67) also gives a negative reply. Yet the reasoning of Newman and of Löwith are of an entirely different order.

590. Naturally, every state exists for the welfare, the "commonweal" of its citizens. Unfortunately, the term "welfare state" today stands largely for what Hilaire Belloc called the "servile state," in German, to be exact, *Versorgungsstaat*, "provider state." Yet the "provider state" is not inevitably socialistic even if it has totalitarian features. Sweden, for instance, is a provider state, and not a socialist state, considering that 85 percent of the means of production are privately owned.

The provider state is supplemented by another egalitarian measure, progressive taxation, which means that the state constantly has its hand in the pocket of one person in order to transfer money to another. This system conflicts with the egalitarian principle of the Left in that different sums are separated from different individuals. As Hannah Arendt has pointed out, all totalitarian systems and despotisms have always been concerned with creating equal conditions for their subjects. Cf. her *Origins of Totalitarianism* (New York: Harcourt, Brace, 1966), 322.

The excuse of the *moderate* leftist for this inequality is that progressive taxation serves to equalize living standards and wealth to a considerable extent: the *radical* leftists contend that such inequality ought to be eliminated by equal incomes. Christian sentimentalists tend to believe that such measures will do away with the proletariat. They should read the address of Pius XII given on September 14, 1952, at the Austrian Catholic Congress in Vienna. In it he stated that the proletariat in the Western World survives only in isolated areas. Real welfare lies in the cooperation of the various social layers. The main task of the Church is to "protect the individual and the family from an all-embracing socialization, a process in whose terminal stage the terrifying vision of the Leviathan State would become a gruesome reality. The Church will fight this battle without ceasing as the issue concerns final values, the dignity of man and the salvation of souls."

591. On American misogyny, cf. David L. Cohn, *Love in America* (New York: Simon and Shuster, 1943). Cf. also Francis J. Grund, *Aristocracy in America*, George E. Probst, ed. (New York: The Academy Library-Harper Torchbook, 1959), 39-40. (This book was published originally in London in 1839.) When Dr. Benjamin Rush visited France he was amazed at the mixing of the sexes and the high educational and cultural level of French women—quite at variance with the English and American tradition. Cf. *The Selected Writings by Benjamin Rush*, D. D. Runes, ed. (New York: Philosophical Library, 1947), 379-85. American misogyny is of course inherited from British patterns. Johanna Schopenhauer, mother of the German philosopher, became aware of it on her trip through the British Isles in 1805. Cf. Johanna Schopenhauer, *Reise durch England und Schottland*, L. Plakolb, ed. (Stuttgart: Steingrüben-Verlag, 1965), 186-87. The Anglo-American institution of the club is a way of escaping feminine

company. The American airline that offered flights between San Francisco and Los Angeles "for gentlemen only" was moved by the same spirit.

592. The feminist movement in the United States is largely led by lesbians, which makes for an outspoken misandry as lesbians usually hate men; male homosexuals, however, frequently like women. American feminism has also affected the Catholic minority, especially nuns who, in certain cases, have become irascible advocates of a female priesthood. But despite declaring men and women equally qualified in regard to salvation (which is *all* that should matter to a Christian), the Church Militant does not offer "careers" to both sexes. Neither does a *sane* state or society that respects the laws of nature.

593. A proto-Nazi German author, Hans Blüher, in an early book, *Die deutsche Wander-vogelbewegung als erotisches Phänomen*, preface by Dr. Magnus Hirschfeld (Berlin, 1912), proudly attributed a homosexual character to the *Wandervogel* movement which in many ways prepared the brown rebellion against the "father."

Blüher's Nazi views became clearer in a later book, *Die Erhebung Israels gegen die christlichen Güter* (Hamburg: Hanseatische Verlagsbuchhandlung, 1931), in which he accused the Jews of deriding the homosexual tendencies in non-Jews—tendencies that were essential to the founding of political units, for they rested on *Männerbünde*, male leagues. The high priest of Nazi doctrine, Alfred Rosenberg, repeated this argument in op. cit., 485.

Homosexuality was strong in the early history of National Socialism, especially among the SA. (A high Vienna police official told me in the late 1920s that youthful homosexuals frequently banded together in paramilitary Nazi formations.) The accusations against SA Chief Röhm and his friends were well founded.

594. The main reason why the Soviets persecute homosexuals is that they tend to establish small private worlds, little enchanted circles that totalitarianism automatically dislikes. For very similar reasons, it dislikes family, sex, and Eros, an attitude that finds its literary reflection in Orwell's "Anti-Sex League" in his novel *1984*. *Vide* the revolt of Soviet writers such as Olga Berggolts, Dovzhenko, and Vagarshian against the official opposition to the literary representation of all forms of love—sexual, erotic, familial, etc. Cf. E. v. Kuehnelt-Leddihn, "Contemporary Soviet Literature," *The Critic*, vol. 19, no. 1. (August-September 1960), 18, 21.

595. Dr. Benjamin Rush in a letter to Jeremy Belknap (October 13, 1789) expressed his disappointment that capital punishment had been abolished in the Duchy of Tuscany (ruled by a Habsburg who later became Emperor Leopold II). "How disgraceful for our republics," he wrote, "that the monarchs of Europe should take the lead in extending the empire of reason and humanity in this interesting part of govern-ment." Cf. *Letters of Benjamin Rush*, L. H. Butterfield, ed. (Princeton: Princeton University Press, 1951), 1:526.

596. Yet the murderer of the Archduke and the Duchess of Hohenberg, after World War I, received a monument from the Karagjorgjević dynasty to perpetuate the gloriously foul deed in Sarajevo. We are uncertain whether representatives of Britain, France, and the United States were invited to participate in the unveiling. The cult of the assassins continued until the collapse of Yugoslavia in 1941 when the statue was destroyed by the Croats, who had to suffer Serb rule for twenty-three years. After

World War II, the murderer was again honored by Tito, this time with a museum.

There are still people in the West who believe that Austria-Hungary in 1914 delivered a totally unjustified ultimatum to Serbia, which was in fact organizing and praising murder. (How would Teddy Roosevelt have reacted to the assassination of an American vice president by an organization whose head was a vice president of, say, Nicaragua? Would he not at least have demanded a personal investigation into the background of the murder?) Yet the Serbs refused to allow Austrian investigators to cooperate with their Serb colleagues on Serb territory; still when the negative Serb answer to the Austrian ultimatum arrived, not a single soldier of the imperial royal army was mobilized. Cf. Freiherr von Musulin, *Das Haus am Ballhausplatz* (Munich: Verlag für Kulturpolitik, 1924), 225-26, 241-45.

597. It recalls Raskolnikov in *Crime and Punishment*, a double murderer who received only seven years in a Siberian penitentiary. (In Britain at that time he would have been hanged, in the United States probably the same.) In connection with the revolution of 1905, the death sentence was temporarily revived. Grandduchess Elisabeth, sister of Empress Alexandra, tried to move her husband's murderer to repent, but the man only spat at her and kicked her when she visited him in prison. The Grandduchess, widow of Grandduke Sergey, later became a nun. In 1918 she was brutally beaten and thrown into the shaft of a coal mine where she died. The leftist forces of progress are pitiless.

598. In the twentieth century, the historical period when most monarchies fell and were transformed into republics, *not one monarchy* went down fighting. Not one monarch ordered the slaughter of his subjects. (And this precisely because monarchy at long last had reached its maturity.) On this subject, cf. Louis Rougier, *La France à la récherche d'une constitution* (Paris: Recueil Sirey, 1952), 124.

599. I deduce the *moral* superiority of a monarchy from the fact that it rests—far more than a republic—on the theological virtues of faith and charity. It rests on trust and affection. It is, in a wider sense, an "erotic" government. Republics rest on suspicion; democracy on envy. Cf. (Lord) Bertrand Russell, *The Conquest of Happiness* (New York: Liveright, 1930), 83-84. Montesquieu thought that monarchy's outstanding characteristic was *clemency*, the republic's *virtue*. (It is significant that the expression "the republican virtues" has been dropped from the dictionary of the French Academy.) Louis Philippe said, in exile, when he heard about General Cavaignac's brutal slaughter of the French workers: "Only democratic regimes can fire at the people because they do it in the name of the people and, in a way, by order of the people." Cf. René Gillouin, *Trois études politiques* (Paris: Ecrits de Paris, 1951), 30, and Gaetano Mosca, *Ciò che la storia potrebbe insegnare* (Milan: Giuffrè, 1958), 529, note 132.

600. Having been brought up in Europe, I haven't the slightest personal aversion to African Negroes or American mulattoes. (Brazil is made up of more than 20 percent people of mixed blood and its color problem—which I have studied—is only a shadow of that in the United States.) Yet I am convinced that a solution to this painful issue by legislation and law is as impossible as by *thoughtless* social action. The first correct step would be gradually to decrease the *mutual* inferiority complexes and to arrange a subsequent meeting of the "races" at the top—not at the bottom. Trying to solve the "Negro problem" through "busing" is childish. All real meetings of

nations have been meetings of elites, not of the masses who tend to be strongly "identitarian" in sentiment and to hate all manifestations of otherness.

601. Yet during the Spanish Civil War leftists tried to rouse popular passions against the *Franquistas* by reminding Americans that the wicked Generalissimo fought with the help of evil blackamoors against lily-white democrats.

602. Melville's political ideas are found in a number of his novels and epics (especially in *Clarel*): on Orestes Brownson cf. Lawrence Roemer, op cit.; on William Graham Sumner cf. W. G. Sumner, *Challenge of Facts and Other Essays*, A. G. Keller, ed. (New Haven: Yale University Press, 1914), 264, 271, 286.

603. Cf. Thomas Mann, *Von Deutscher Republik* (Berlin: S. Fischer, 1923), 399. On the intrinsic connection between homosexuality and democratic (as well as leftist) trends *vide* also Donald Webster Cory, *The Homosexual in America* (New York: Greenberg, 1953), 152, 163, 164. On homosexuality and nazism cf. note 594.

604. Walt Whitman, *Democratic Vistas* (London: Walter Scott, 1888), 58.

605. Cf. Reinhold Niebuhr, *The Irony of American History* (New York: Scribner's, 1952), 24-25. In conjunction with this read also the brilliant book of Thomas Molnar, *The Two Faces of American Foreign Policy* (Indianapolis-New York: Bobbs-Merrill, 1962), 51ff.

606. Cf. in this connection Vianna Moog, *Bandeirantes and Pioneers*, L. I. Barnett, trsl. (New York: G. Braziller, 1964), 263. At the International Conference of Christians and Jews in August 1948 in Fribourg, Switzerland, the American delegation showed short films to demonstrate how they combated racism in the United States. The tenor of these films shocked the Europeans as they debunked racist prejudices, preferring flamboyant nationalism under the "We're All Americans!" slogan. Nationalism more than anything else—even more than racism—ruined Europe.

607. This is sweetly and directly expressed in Edgar A. Guest's poem: "The Best Land," which begins with the ringing lines:

If I knew a better land on this glorious world of ours,
Where a man gets bigger money and is working shorter hours;
If the Briton or the Frenchman had an easier life than mine,
I'd pack my goods this minute and I'd sail across the brine

608. This attitude created in the mid-nineteenth century an anti-American literature in Europe. Anti-American utterances were not rare in the works of Heinrich Heine, Gustave de Beaumont, Ferdinand Kürnberger, Nikolaus Lenau, etc.

609. The *leyenda negra*, the "Black Legend" about Spain always had numerous American devotees, cf. Julián Juderías, *La leyenda negra* (Barcelona: Casa Editorial Araluce, n.d.) 315ff. Salvador de Madariaga informs that the Hispano-American Inquisition, having dealt with over three thousand cases during centuries of activity passed not more than thirty death sentences. Thus less than 1 percent were punished by death. English courts dealing with sorcery generally condemned 19 percent of those accused; in the first four years of the rule of James I, 41 percent faced the supreme penalty. During the Hopkins campaign in 1645, 19 of 29 indicted women were executed. The Scotch courts were far more severe; the last witch in Scotland paid

with her life in 1780! Cf. de Madariaga's *El auge del imperio español en América* (Buenos Aires: Editorial Sudamericana, 1959), 220-21.

610. A good account of the American press propaganda against Spain at the time of the Cuban crisis is found in Hudson Strode's *Pageant of Cuba*. It mattered little that the Spaniards were far more tolerant toward Cuba's colored population than the American "liberators" toward their own. In 1965-1966 the American leftist press once again found reason to rant, this time against Rhodesia, a newly independent country which, despite its proximity to the Republic of South Africa, was markedly more "color blind" than many Western countries. Yet Britain's Labour government could do no wrong, nor the "progressive" new African nations from Zambia to Ghana, from Nigeria to the black slaughterers from Khartoum. Ideological blindness is the worst of all.

611. It would be worth investigating why in Germany during World War I the hatred for Britain was far more intensive than any other. Was it perhaps the hatred of disillusioned Anglophiles, which the Germans decidedly were—and in a sense still are?

612. During these years I was a boy living in Baden bei Wien, headquarters of the Austrian-Hungarian army (AOK). My "Sunday best" was a British sailor suit with a cap bearing the inscription "H. M. S. Renown." I had, needless to say, a French governess. National hatred was for the mob. The feelings for the Italians were harsher: they had been members of the Triple Alliance and, having tried unsuccessfully to blackmail their Austrian ally in a desperate situation, they had gone over to the enemy. This was, in a sense, unforgivable. The Russians, too, behaved in an old-fashioned—that is, civilized—way. Having conquered the fortress of Przemyśl in March 1915, they invited the defeated Austrian officers to their banquet. Enlisted men with some skills, if made prisoners, were often released to practice their trade and made small fortunes until, that is, the Communists took over. A Prince Radziwiłł, ethnically a Pole but a member of the Prussian Senate, was permitted to return to Berlin to take up his duties. Countess Nora Kinsky (future mother-in-law of the late ruling Prince of Liechtenstein), an Austrian Red Cross nurse, was allowed in 1916-18 to inspect conditions in Russian prison camps containing Austrians. She was received by the Empress Alexandra who, in the course of the conversation, asked her if she did not hate the Germans. The young nurse, aged twenty-six, stiffened and replied: "Your Majesty is speaking of *our* allies." The Empress apologized. Cf. Nora Kinsky, *Russisches Tagebuch* (Stuttgart: Seewald, 1976), 87.

613. The most widely believed story was about German soldiers cutting off the hands of Belgian babies; it was sufficiently stupid to be believed.

614. The Napoleanic Wars were still highly civilized. When Baron Wintzingerode, a Hanoverian in the Russian service, was arrested near Mozhaisk as a spy, the French officers restrained Napoleon who lost his temper at the insolence of the German. The latter finally ate in the officers' mess and Napoleon sulked alone in his tent. Cf. *Mémoires du Général de Caulaincourt*, Jean Hanoteau, ed. (Paris: Plon, 1933), 2:100-08. Baron Haugwitz, political advisor to the King of Prussia, told the Abbé Siéyès, French Ambassador to Berlin, confidentially, "Our real interests are those of the monarchy against the republican system. . . between monarchies one will always

wage a few wars but without destroying one another." Cf. René Gillouin, *Aristarchie ou Recherche d'un gouvernement* (Geneva: Cheval Aile, 1946), 305. Yet how brutal and stupid the war propaganda waged in France during World War I, is described in Georges Bernanos, *La Grande Peur des Bien-Pensants* (Paris: Grasset, 1949), 414-18.

615. Soon after World War I, the historians in the United States became divided in their opinion as to the guilt for the horrendous blunder. The spectrum reached all the way from Bernadotte Schmitt (condemning the Germans almost unilaterally) to Harry Elmer Barnes. Charles Callan Tansill leaned toward Barnes' position, as did Sidney B. Fay, who in his *Origins of the World War* (New York: Macmillan, 1928), opined that a further investigation of Serb documents would tend to strengthen the case for Serbia's initial guilt. (In this field of research, the real weakness of most Western historians lies in their lack of knowledge of Slav languages.)

Fay also warned (*Current Events*, vol. 6, no. 34, October 1939, 241) not to confuse the origins of World War I with those of World War II. As expected, a leftist school, not long since, tried to exonerate Hitler. Its most prominent British representative was Professor A. J. P. Taylor, known for his strong leftist inclinations and his dislike of the Habsburg monarchy. Cf. his *The Origins of the Second World War* (Greenwich, Conn.: Fawcett Publications, 1963). Yet even in World War II, guilt cannot be laid entirely on the Axis. The outbreak of the war is unimaginable without Soviet connivance—just as fascism and nazism are unthinkable without communist inspiration and challenge. The thesis that Stalin expected to come out on top in the war has many sound arguments; Stalin's armaments (if not his strategy) were far superior to Germany's, and some of his arms were of even higher quality. Cf. Ernest Topitsch, *Stalins Sieg* (Herford: Busse-Seewald, 1990).

616. Franz von Papen's intelligence is highlighted by the account of Franz von Rintelen, his collaborator in the United States, who describes Papen's role in diplomacy as more comic than tragic. Cf. his *The Dark Invader* (Harmondsworth: Penguin Books, 1936).

617. Cf. Colin Simpson, *The Lusitania* (Boston: Little Brown, 1972), especially 104sq. In paid advertisements in American newspapers, the Germans warned the public against travelling on the boat. Allan Welsh Dulles, brother of John Foster Dulles, knew well that the *Lusitania* tragedy had been engineered to "ease" America's entry into the war—a joint British-American operation at the expense of nearly 1,200 human lives. Cf. Leonard Mosley, *Dulles* (London: Hodder & Stoughton, 1978), 37-38. Emperor Charles I of Austria strongly opposed unlimited U-boat warfare. Cf. Peter Broucek, *Ein General im Zwielicht, Die Erinnerungen Edmund Glaises von Horstenau* (Vienna: Böhlau, 1980), 1:395.

618. Count Bernstorff's nephew, Count Albrecht Bernstorff, who during World War II served in the German Foreign Office, was a staunch anti-Nazi; he was executed in 1944.

619. George D. Herron insisted that Wilson's reelection "was not only opposed by all Germans between Potsdam and San Francisco, but also by the Roman Catholic hierarchy." (*La Semaine Littéraire*, Geneva, December 19, 1916.) Woodrow Wilson was quite anti-Catholic as well as something of a racist, fearing the "dirty white" immigration.

620. Cf. Harry Elmer Barnes, *Perpetual War for Perpetual Peace* (Caldwell, Idaho: Caxton Printers, 1953), 35: "The columnist Jay Franklin gave us a good picture of the fruits of interventionism. Since 1900 under five Republican Presidents *no* casualties, under three Democratic Presidents (Theodore Roosevelt, Taft, Harding, Coolidge, Hoover, versus Wilson, Roosevelt, and Truman) 'O' versus 1,628, 480 casualties." (Here the casualties under J. F. Kennedy and L. B. Johnson obviously are not included.) Americans are by nature isolationists—as are the Russians, if not driven by specific ideologies. Felix Somary in his op. cit. discusses this in a brilliant passage, adding: "Americans like to be judges of the world, not its rulers, but do not realize that the former position cannot be achieved without the latter" (101). Viewed from this angle the Republican party is "naturally" the more American party.

621. Ben Hecht in his *Erik Dorn* likened Wilson in Paris to a "long-faced virgin trapped in a bawdy house and calling in valiant tones for a glass of lemonade." Cf. Oscar Cargill, *Intellectual America: Ideas on the March* (New York: Macmillan, 1941), 504. John Maynard Keynes described the three main figures at the Paris Peace Conference as: "Clemenceau, aesthetically the noblest; the President, morally the most admirable; Lloyd George, intellectually the subtlest. Out of their disparities and weaknesses the Treaty was born, child of the least worthy attributes of its parents, without nobility, without morality, without intellect." Cf. J. M. Keynes, "David Lloyd George" in *Essays and Sketches in Biography* (New York: Meridian Books, 1956), 180.

622. Woodrow Wilson, to be sure, had not only been a professor, but a professor of government and president of a leading American university. A defender of democratic amateurism and a critic of expertise could point this out triumphantly and use it as an argument. Wilson knew nothing of geography, history, sociology, or theology. The humanities (and perhaps not only they) can never be properly understood outside their wider context. In these domains specialization has always been fatal. On the American professor *vide* also C. Wright Mills, *White Collar: The American Middle Classes* (New York: Oxford University Press, 1951), 129ff.

623. Whatever the faults and shortcomings of William II (and there were many), he never actively prepared World War I. We have this on the authority of several historians, among them G. P. Gooch and Arthur Rosenberg, who in 1923 were charged by the German Social Democratic party to investigate the German Emperor's responsibility for the holocaust. Their negative conclusions can be found in their *Die Entstehung der deutschen Republic, 1871-1918* (Berlin: Rowohlt, 1930), 66-67. Yet, according to American folklore, "Kaiser Bill" was the villain, the good boys were the forty-eighters. Hence Mr. Walt W. Rostow, a professional planner in the State Department, declared on September 9, 1963, that the Federal Republic was the fulfillment of the dream of the men who in 1848 produced the liberal Frankfurt Parliament, although the revolution was crushed by Prussians and German nationalists. Statements like these are screamingly funny given that the liberal Frankfurt Parliament offered a (hitherto nonexistent) German crown to the King of Prussia, whereas the forty-eighters *were* the nationalists who worked for a German *national* state which would exclude nationally pluralistic Austria.

624. Cf. Gladstone's election speech at Edinburgh, March 17, 1880, quoted by Carlton J. H. Hayes, op. cit., 38.

625. Wilson's misunderstanding of Russia was only part and parcel of his misreading of the European mind. For a Continental Russia is more comprehensible than the United States (even if he prefers the latter to the former). Cf. the admission of Ida F. Görres in *Zwischen den Zeiten* (Olten and Freiburg i. Br.:Walter, 1961), 429-30.

626. Quoted by Carlos Pereyra, *El crimen de Woodrow Wilson*, Madrid, 1917.

627. Cf. Burton J. Hendrick, *The Life and Letters of Walter H. Page* (Garden City, N.Y.: Doubleday, Page and Co., 1925), 1:188. Page's most interesting views on Europe ("In all the humanities, we are a thousand years ahead of any people here...") can be found in a long letter to Frank N. Doubleday, dated Bournemouth, May 29, 1916.

628. Cf. *The Intimate Papers of Colonel House*, Charles Seymour, ed. (Boston: Houghton, Mifflin, 1928), 4:13-14.

629. Cf. Walter H. Peters, *The Life of Benedict XV* (Milwaukee: Bruce, 1959), 149-51.

630. Fénélon said that "peace treaties are meaningless if you are the stronger one and if you force your neighbor to sign a treaty to avoid greater evil; then he signs in the same way as a person who surrenders his purse to a brigand who points a pistol at his throat." Cf. Fénélon, "Direction pour la conscience d'un roi," in *Oeuvres* (Paris, 1787), vol. 25, t. 3, 489.

631. Cf. Charles A. Beard and Mary R. Beard, *The Rise of American Civilization* (New York: Macmillan, 1948), vol. 4 ("The American Spirit"), 357. See also Woodrow Wilson, *A History of the American People* (New York: William Wise, 1931), 5:212. Such utterances were made repeatedly by Wilson. His outlook was strictly "Anglo-Saxon" but his pride was his own Scotch-Irish Presbyterian descent.

632. The "far south Tyrol," the *Trentino*, is Italian by language, but the vast majority of the Trentinese did not want to join Italy. When in 1915 the Italians demanded territories from their embattled Austrian (former) ally, Vienna reluctantly promised them the *Trentino* after the war.

633. Cf. Thomas A. Bailey, *Woodrow Wilson and the Lost Peace* (New York: Macmillan, 1944), 252.

634. Cf. S. Miles Bouton, Robert Dell and Charles H. Herford, *English and American Voices about the German Tyrol* (New York: C. J. Bernard, 1925).

635. Cf. J. M. Keynes, *The Economic Consequences of the Peace (1919)* (New York: Harcourt, Brace, 1920), 43.

636. Ibid., 31n. But few people realized that Wilson had, prior to his first election in 1912, already suffered two, possibly three, strokes: a minor one in 1891 and major ones in 1896 and 1906; the latter left him blind in his right eye and able to write only with his left hand. The stroke in October 1919 incapacitated him almost completely. It was a gravely ill man who dragged America to a "historically losing" war. Cf. Edwin A. W. Weinstein, *Woodrow Wilson, A Medical and Psychologic Biography* (Princeton: Princeton University Press, 1981).

637. Cf. George F. Kennan, *American Diplomacy 1900-1950* (Chicago: University of Chicago Press, 1951), 55-56. World War II had been initiated in 1939 to save Poland and in 1941 to save China. In both cases, the countries involved were in the end delivered over to totalitarian slavery.

638. Cf. René Schickelé's *Die Grenze* (Berlin: Rowohlt, 1932), 146, and Sir Charles Petrie, *Twenty Years' Armistice and After* (London: Eyre & Spottiswood, 1940), 12. Ribot was the foreign minister of France. Emperor Charles's ("Servant of God") canonization has been initiated in Rome.

639. Lord Lansdowne's letter was published in the (London) *Daily Telegraph* on November 29, 1917. It had been turned down by the *Times*. A year earlier, it had been sent to the Prime Minister. For the passage cited in the text, cf. Lord Newton, *Lord Lansdowne* (London: Macmillan, 1929), 482-83. Walter Lippmann described the situation in 1917, prior to American intervention: "The existing governments had exhausted their imperium—their authority to bind and their power to command. With their traditional means they were no longer able to carry on their hyperbolic war, yet they were unable to negotiate peace. They had, therefore, to turn to the people. They had to ask still greater exertions and sacrifices. They obtained them by 'democratizing' the conduct and the aims of the war, by pursuing total victory and by promising total peace." Cf. op. cit., 12. Hence the "Holy War." André Malraux clearly saw that the French Revolution with its republicanism for export had to end in a bellicose "Islamic" expansion. (*La Nouvelle Revue Française*, vol. 3 no. 25, 18.)

640. Wilson was born, to be sure, on the Day of the Innocents, on Childermass. As expected, he was hailed by Calvinists all over Europe as their Savior. Cf. Émile Doumergue, "Calvin et l'entente de Wilson à Calvin," *Revue de Métaphysique et de Morale*, vol. 25 (September-December, 1918), especially 825.

641. Cf. *Letters of Franklin Lane*, A. W. Lane and L. H. Hall, eds. (Boston: Houghton, Mifflin, 1922), 297. Profesor F. A. Hermens in his book *Democracy or Anarchy* (Notre Dame: University Press, 1941) claims that the *Anschluss* after the war would have prevented (numerically) the Nazi electoral victories. If, in all-German elections, the Austrians had voted like their Bavarian neighbors with whom they were linked by ethnic, racial, religious, and cultural ties, Professor Hermens' thesis would seem to have been correct.

642. Cf. Stanley A. Hunter, *The Religious Ideals of the President* (Allahabad: Mission Press, 1914), 8.

643. Cf. E. I. Woodward, *Three Studies in European Conservatism* (London: Constable, 1929), 228: "Je suis leur chef: il faut hien que je les suive." We naturally like to see in the statesman that *rara avis*, the scholarly trained practitioner—or a practically trained scholar. Neither the pure scholar nor the uneducated pragmatist will do. . . which is equally true of great medical men. Cf. the views of the Arab sage, Ibn Khaldun, quoted in chapter 3 of his "Prolegomena," in *Arab Philosophy*, Charles Issawi, ed. (London, 1950), 64-66.

644. Hugo Münsterberg, *American Patriotism and Other Social Studies* (New York: Moffat, Yard and Co., 1913), 3.

645. Ibid, 15-16. Also cf. Denis W. Brogan, *The American Character* (New York: Knopf, 1944), 146.

646. Cf. Ernst Bruncken, *Die amerikanische Volksseele*, quoted by Elias Hurwicz, *Die Seelen der Völker, ihre Eigenarten und Bedeutung im Völkerleben* (Gotha: Andreas Perthes, 1920), 91-92. Joseph de Maistre said that "the prejudices of the nations are like

boils, one has to touch them gently so as not to break the tissue." Cf. Sainte-Beuve, *Causeries de lundi* (Paris: Garnier Frères, 1927) 15:80.

647. Cf. Richard M. Weaver, *Ideas Have Consequences* (Chicago: University of Chicago Press, 1948), 76. On the medieval concept of the "Divine Right of Kings," see particularly Fritz Kern, op. cit., 10-11, 283, 84.

648. Absolutism, including monarchical absolutism, is a political aberration rejected by European "conservatives." C. L. von Haller, to name only one typical representative of romantic conservatism (no less than Ludwig von Gerlach), equated royal absolutism with Jacobinism. Cf. Franz Schnabel, op. cit., 4:175.

649. Cf. Reinhold Niebuhr, op. cit., 77-78. For a rational defense of monarchy, cf. also C. Northcote Parkinson, *The Evolution of Political Thought* (London: University of London Press, 1958), with pertinent quotes from Simón Bolívar (253), Alberdi (259), and others. The arguments of this famous inventor of "Parkinson's Law" are on 315-16.

650. According to a letter from Walter Lippmann (who knew Herron) addressed to this writer, dated Washington, D. C., May 17, 1956.

651. The term "post-Protestant era" figures (as a possibility, not as a certainty) in Paul Tillich's theological thinking. Cf. his *The Protestant Era*, trsl. and edit J. L. Adams (Chicago: University of Chicago Press, 1948). "Post-Protestant" defines a mentality and outlook containing essential characteristics from the Reformation and the post-Reformation period in a secularized form. All great religions have such a "version" wherever they have (or had) great cultural force or cohesion. Yet this is rarely the case with religious bodies in the dispersion where they often try to combine their own "factual" theology with mind patterns of the majority. A Spanish Presbyterian—however fervent—is in a certain way a "Catholic," and a Danish Catholic a "Lutheran."

652. Compton McKenzie called the League of Nations quite aptly a "typist's dream of the Holy Roman Empire, for politicians a new hypocrisy, for diplomats a sitting on addled eggs." Cf. *My Religion* (New York: Appleton, 1926), 52.

653. Cf. Document VII a, of vol. 12 of the *Herron Papers*. (In manuscript, Hoover Institution, Stanford, California.) Letter of Herron to Wilson, dated Geneva, March 20, 1919. Calvin, Herron insisted, not Luther, was the father of the Scottish Covenanters and the English Puritans.

654. Reply of Wilson to Herron, Document XIII, ibid. Letter dated Paris, April 17, 1919. Wilson was delighted with this proposition.

655. Ibid., Document XXVII, vol. 12. Letter dated Geneva, April 17, 1920. There are thirteen large cardboard boxes filled with the *Herron Papers*, most of them retyped. To read them over the years took a major effort on my part.

656. Cf. *The Letters of William James*, Henry James, ed. (Boston: Atlantic Monthly Press, 1920), 1:139. Sir Charles Petrie, very much to the contrary, called the major tragedy of Central Europe the fact that German unity was accomplished under the leadership of Prussia rather than Austria. Cf. his *Twenty Years Armistice and After*, op. cit., 126.

657. Cf. Th. G. Masaryk, *The Making of a State*, Henry Wickham Steed, ed. (New York: Stokes and Co., 1927), 308-09.

658. Ibid, 375.

659. Cf. Raymond Aron, *Les guerres en chaîne* (Paris: Gallimard, 1951), 34. Th. G. Masaryk's son, Jan Masaryk (the later, ill-fated foreign minister murdered by "defenestration") was captain in an Imperial Royal regiment until the collapse of the Danubian monarchy. He had nothing but praise for the old regime. Cf. Indro Montanelli, "La sua insomnia si chiama Gottwald," *Il Nuovo Corriere della Sera*, March 11, 1948, 1. An excellent summing up of anti-Habsburg sentiments, disastrous for everybody in their final consequences, has been given by Carl J. Burckhardt in a letter to Hugo von Hofmansthal. Cf. H. v. Hofmansthal, Carl J. Burckhardt, *Briefwechsel* (Frankfurt: S. Fischer, 1956), 75 (letter dated November 1921).

660. Cf. Th. G. Masaryk, op. cit., 309.

661. Mitchell Pirie Briggs, *George Herron and the European Settlement* (Palo Alto: Stanford University Press, 1932), 29.

662. The United States first declared war on Germany, then on Austria-Hungary, and finally on Turkey. *Bulgaria was left out.* The Bulgar minister in Washington during World War I tried to make himself as inconspicuous as possible. (In World War II the United States refused to declare war on Finland, etc.)

   Still, George D. Herron, in a letter to Hugh R. Wilson, American *chargé d'affaires* in Berne, urged a declaration of war against Bulgaria, "the worst enemy, after Prussia, of Americanism in Europe." (Dateline, Geneva, May 25, 1918.) Cf. *Herron Papers*, vol. 9, document I. No explanation of why "Americanism" was so uniquely incompatible with "Bulgarianism". . . and how Herron could discern this by long distance.

663. Actually, Maximilian of Mexico, who sympathized with every "progressive" cause in Europe, was an extreme liberal. Thus he had "ideological differences" with his brother Franz Joseph who was a moderate liberal. (Maximilian was quite possibly a Freemason.) Benito Juárez, on the other hand, played up by recent Mexican regimes as a fierce nationalist, was in fact an agent of the hated *gringos* and enjoyed full American support. Popular historiography is at least as confused as politics.

664. The Inquisition, naturally, never operated in Austria. In fact, a Lutheran in the eighteenth century was much freer in Austria than a Catholic at that time in England.

665. Cf. *Dictionary of American Biography* (New York: Scribner's, 1932), 8:594-95.

666. Iowa College was founded by Congregationalists in 1847. The town of Grinnell where the college was located had been named after Josiah Grinnell (1821-1891), a Congregationalist minister and close friend of John Brown of Harper's Ferry fame.

667. The *Rand School of Social Science* in New York, which always had a strong socialist flavor, was founded by this wealthy family.

668. Cf. *A Socialist Wedding, Being an Account of a Marriage of George D. Herron and Carrie Rand* (New York: Knickerbocker Press, n.d.).

669. Cf. George D. Herron, *Ot revolyutsii k revolyutsii, Uroki parizhskoy kommuny 1871 g.* (St. Petersburg, O. N. Rutenberg, 1906). After 1905 Russia was nearly as liberal as most nations in Western Europe. *Pravda* was founded in 1912 and the Bolsheviks were members of the Duma.

670. Cf. George D. Herron, *The Day of Judgment* (Chicago: Kerr and Co., 1906), 29. Walter Lippmann told me that Herron was a monument to himself, and Robert F. Grunder in his *Ministers of Reform* (New York: Basic Books, 1982) 44, 49, wrote that Herron saw himself as a "suffering Christ." Chapter VIII of this book is aptly named "A Presbyterian Foreign Policy."

671. Cf. Thomas A. Bailey, op. cit., 330. Two days after the German declaration of limitless submarine warfare, February 2, 1917, Wilson declared, "in response to a question as to which side he 'wished to win,' that 'he didn't wish either side to win.' " But was he sincere? Mr. Irwin Laughlin, attaché to the American Embassy in London in 1914, told this writer in 1937 about Wilson's offers to aid Britain in every way possible, short of declaring war on Germany, which he could not do without congressional approval, offers which Ambassador Page refused to pass on, informing the President that his messages were incompatible with diplomatic usage.

672. Pressure of time prevented me from using my research material fully. In the meantime, the Austrian historian, Professor Heinrich Benedikt (Vienna), published salient parts of Herron's dealings in *Die Friedensaktion der Meinl-Gruppe 1917- 1918* (Graz-Cologne: Hermann Böhlau, 1962). His book also contains a portrait of Herron, who looked exactly as one would expect.

673. Cf. Herron's cable to the President after news of his illness reached Europe: "Multitudes beyond number rejoice with me in the supreme news of your recovery. You are still the hope of the world. You are the living barrier against universal reaction and dark ages. For the sake of all mankind you must and will get well and fight on." (*Herron Papers*, vol. 5, document XXII.)

What were the reactions of intelligent Europeans to Wilson after his intervention in Europe? Max Eastman cites the words of Freud, who was anything but a Catholic legitimist arch-reactionary: " 'You should not have gone to war at all. Your Woodrow Wilson was the silliest fool of the century, if not of all centuries.' He paused for an answer which got stuck accidentally in my throat. 'And he was probably the greatest criminal—unconsciously, I am sure.' " Cf. Max Eastman, *Einstein, Trotzky, Hemingway, Freud* (New York: Collier Books, 1942), 127.

674. Cf. George D. Herron, *Germanism and the American Crusade* (New York: Kennerley, 1918); *Woodrow Wilson and the World's Peace* (New York: Kennerley, 1917); *The Menace of Peace* (London: Allen and Unwin, 1917).

675. Cf. Wilson's letter, dated October 1, 1917, in *Herron Papers*, vol. 12, document I.

676. Letter from Herron to Hugh Wilson, dated July 11, 1918. (*Herron Papers*, vol. 2, document XXVIII.) It deals with Admiral von Hintze, whom he had met before the war:

I regard Admiral von Hintze as one of the most sinister figures in the political world of today. Indeed, I am convinced there is no other such dangerous character in any place of great power. He is unqualifiedly a cynic, and his mind is clearly medieval in its constitution and methods; his conception of world politics differs not from the conception that prevailed in the courts of Borgia and Sforza . . . He is clever to the last degree; and not only Machiavellian, but positively diabolical in both his thinking and acting: and his mental and tactical diabolism are clothed with medieval refinement.

All of which clearly sheds a new light on the Middle Ages and the Devil. Hintze, just an ordinary civil servant with a naval and diplomatic background, must have frightened Herron out of his wits.

677. According to Walter Lippmann, the main drafter of the Fourteen Points, the original plan of the President merely foresaw a federalization of Austria-Hungary—precisely the plan of Emperor Charles—not its destruction. (Personal information.) Influences and events changed his original plan, thus laying the foundations of World War II. In German, "autonomy" implies local prerogatives, whereas in English it can also mean total separation.

678. Cf. Stefan Osuský, *George D. Herron, Dôvernik Wilsonov počas vojny* (Pressburg: Naklad "Prudov": 1925), 25. He was then minister in Paris. Osuský, once a Slovak student at the University of Chicago, knew Herron intimately. Much of the book is dedicated to Herron's political philosophy.

679. Even stronger were the reactions of Clemenceau and Ribot, the French foreign minister, to the Austrian peace action aided by Prince Sixtus of Parma, the brother of Empress Zita. Lansing decried Clemenceau's action as "a piece of the most outstanding stupidity . . . an unpardonable blunder." Cf. *The War Memoirs of Robert Lansing* (Indianapolis-New York: Bobbs Merrill, 1935), 265.

680. Cf. *Herron Papers*, vol. 1, document XXVI, letter to Hugh R. Wilson.

681. Cf. Heinrich Lammasch, *Seine Aufzeichnungen, sein Wirken und seine Politik*, Marga Lammasch and Hans Sperl, ed. (Vienna: Deuticke, 1922), 99-102.

682. Cf. George D. Herron, *Defeat in Victory* (Boston: Christopher Publishing House, 1924), 53.

683. Cf. *Herron Papers*, vol. 12, document XXVII, letter to William A. White, dated April 17, 1920.

684. Cf. letter of G. D. Herron to Stewart E. Bruce, dated November 1, 1923, published in *Fight for Light Leaflet*, R. I. Orchelle, ed. (Hamburg: Antikriegsschuldlügenliga).

685. Cf. James Kerney, *The Political Education of Woodrow Wilson* (New York: The Century Press, 1925), 476.

686. That so many Jews accept democracy and believe in it with almost religious fervor can only be explained by the fact that they become fascinated with its egalitarian aspect while ignoring democracy's majoritarian nature, for, other than in Israel, they will always be a minority. An eminent German sociologist, Winfried Martini, has commented on the paradox in his crucially important work *Das Ende aller Sicherheit, Eine Kritik des Westens* (Stuttgart: Deutsche Verlagsanstalt, 1954), 16-19. In a sermon I gave in New York City's Temple Emanu-El, the world's largest synagogue, December 12, 1981, I touched upon this subject, emphasizing that the *true* interest of Hebrews lies in a vertical rather than a horizontal social and political order. Later, at the reception, the congregation evinced a positive reaction.

687. Cf. *Herron Papers*, vol. 13, document IX. Letter to Leo Ragaz, dated April 1, 1919. Naturally, it was Herron's argument (at that time) that "International Finance," with its center in Paris, was dominated by German Jews acting on Germany's behalf. Hitler's argument was that international Jewry was intrinsically and congenitally anti-German. The theory that the Jews are nearly always the scapegoats is certainly not without substance.

688. Cf. *Herron Papers*, vol. 13, document IX and VII, and vol. 11, document II. In typical Nazi fashion, Herron thought that international Jewish finance was collaborating with the Vatican and that the emissaries of these dark forces met in Fribourg.

689. Ibid., vol. 11, document XVII. Letter dated Geneva, October 15, 1919, addressed to the socialist leader George Strobell, on the early socialist contacts of Herron and his second marriage. Cf. also Philip M. Crane, *The Democrat's Dilemma* (Chicago: Regnery, 1964), 75-78.

690. Cf. George D. Herron, *Umsturz und Aufbau. Der Pariser Friede und die Jugend Europas* (Berlin: Rowohlt, 1920). No translator mentioned.

691. Cf. George D. Herron, *The Greater War*, 27.

692. Cf. George D. Herron, *Umsturz und Aufbau*, 7.

693. Ibid, 16-17.

694. Cf. Le Capitaine de Gaulle, *La discorde chez l'ennemi* (Paris: Berger-Levrault, 1924), particularly p. vi. The (London) *Times* in October 1918 also admitted in an editorial that the impending end of the war was in part caused by the effectiveness of Allied propaganda.

695. Cf. Thomas A. Bailey, op. cit., 49.

696. Cf. Max Weber in the *Frankfurter Zeitung,* October 27, 1918.

697. Cf. *Herron Papers*, vol. 10, document XXV. Letter to Norman Thomas, dated Geneva, April 27, 1920.

698. Cf. *Herron Papers*, vol. 11, document XVII. Letter to George Strobell, dated Geneva, October 15, 1920.

699. Cf. George D. Herron, *The Revival of Italy* (London: Allen and Unwin, 1922), 76-87.

700. Robert (Roberto) Michels, born in Cologne in 1876, was a German Social Democrat who finally migrated to Italy where he received a professorship. Together with Gaetano Mosca and Marchese Vilfredo Pareto, he fathered the thesis that every democracy is, in fact, a party oligarchy. Later, like so many other Socialists, he supported fascism. Curiously enough, the original (Fascist) *Enciclopedia Italiana* omits his name, but he is mentioned in the "Third Supplement" (1961). He died in Rome in 1936. His main work was *Zur Soziologie des Parteienwesens in der modernen Demokratie* (Leipzig: Kröner, 1925). Cf. also his "Studii sulla democrazia e sull'autorità" in *Collana di Studi Fascisti* (Florence: La Nuova Italia, 1923), no. 24-25; and *Sozialismus und Faschismus in Italien* (Munich-Karlsruhe: G. Braun, 1925), 2 vols. (The information on Robert Michels in *Chi è? Dizionario degli Italiani d'oggi*, Rome: Formiggini, 1931, 495-96, is not too revealing.)

701. Cf. John Maynard Keynes, *The Economic Consequences of the Peace 1919* (London, 1919, and New York: Harcourt, Brace & Howe, 1920), 4-5, 36-37.

702. The crux of the accusation was the "Potsdam Crown Council" on July 5, 1914, in which the decision was allegedly taken to start a world war. Except that this meeting never took place. It figures in Article 231, but to his merit, G. P. Gooch destroyed this evil legend. Lloyd George at least was honest when he declared on March 3, 1921, that the entire Versailles Treaty rested squarely on Germany's war guilt. "We want to make it clear," he said, "that the German responsibility for the war has to be treated by the Allies as a *cause jugée*."

703. On the same day, the day of the anniversary, Štranský, prime minister of highly democratic Czechoslovakia, sent a telegram of congratulations to the government of the Kingdom of the Serbs, Croats, and Slovenes in which he expressed the hope that similar heroic deeds by the South Slavs might eventuate in the future. Cf. *Neue Freie Presse* (Vienna, June 30, 1919), 3.

704. Cf. Algernon Cecil, *Facing Hard Facts in Foreign Policy* (London: Eyre and Spottiswoode, 1941), 59: "For the scene of their labour the peace-makers fixed upon Paris, which was of all places the least likely to countenance a dispassionate peace, and as a result secured for their chairman an old tiger of a man whose lack of religious opinions assured the absence of any spiritual quality in the settlement. They dictated instead of negotiating peace, which was a blunder if the goodwill of the parties was desired, and they failed to occupy the Rhine frontier, which was a crime if in the alternative they hoped to keep the enemy in permanent subjection. They assumed that a hard peace would produce hard cash, which it never did, and that a confession of guilt extorted by pressure would provoke repentance, which it never has." Stephen Bonsal in his *Unfinished Business* (New York: Doubleday, 1944), 48, writes that at the Versailles Peace Conference the Portuguese delegate, Professor Batalha Reis of Coimbra University, protested the omission of the traditional invocation of the Holy Trinity. But, to soothe the feelings of the Japanese, who had not succeeded in getting a clause against racial discrimination (California laws) accepted, the protest was rejected. Lord Hugh Cecil thereupon remarked flippantly, "one will take a chance." One should, indeed, not have taken it!

705. Mr. J. O. B. Bland, Herron's contact man in the British Foreign Office, wrote to Herron on September 10, 1918: "If they want any suggestion what to do with the Germans after the war, they are welcome to my idea, which is that for five years they should only be admitted in civilized countries on taking out a dog license. And that is rough on the dogs." (*Herron Papers*, vol. 11, document XVIII.) Germans, deemed unworthy to join in civilized sports, were not admitted to the Geneva golf links, controlled by the League of Nations, until 1927.

706. Cf. *The Memoirs of Raymond Poincaré*, Sir George Arthur, trsl. (London: Heinemann, 1929), 3:11-12.

707. When I lived in England in 1935-36, I wrote the Rt. Hon. David Lloyd George a letter to the effect that he was widely quoted as saying that Germany could not be carved up since it was a "Protestant country," while there could be no such qualms about Catholic Austria-Hungary. I asked him to confirm or to deny this rumor. He replied through his secretary Frances Stevenson (whom he subsequently married) that he was unfortunately too busy to answer my query. This letter, to my regret, was destroyed during an Allied air raid that prepared Vienna for the Russian occupation in March 1945. On the general ignorance of Lloyd George see also *World Within World: The Autobiography of Stephen Spender* (London: Hamish Hamilton, 1951), 79-80.

708. Cf. Ernst Kornemann, "Vom antiken Staat," *Breslauer Universitätsreden* (Breslau: Ferdinand Hirt, 1927), no. 1, 35.

709. Cf. H. A. Macartney, *Problems of the Danube Basin* (Cambridge, England: Cambridge University Press, 1942), 98.

710. Ibid., 71.

711. In 1918, Czech exile politicians concluded a treaty in Pittsburgh with Slovak representatives (some of them American citizens) stipulating that the two ethnic units should form a common state for ten years. When the Slovak professor Vojtěch Tuka in 1928 declared in a newspaper article that there now existed a *vacuum iuris*, he was promptly tried for high treason and condemned by the Czech authorities. (This was not the end of Tuka's political career; nearly blind, he left jail when Slovakia became almost independent, was hailed as a national martyr, became prime minister of the Slovak Republic, and was executed in 1947 as a "traitor" by the then half-communist Prague government. His tragedy mirrors the calamitous situation in which an ill-conceived and ill-constructed Central Europe has been ever since 1918.) The country has recently been renamed the Czecho-Slovak Federal Republic.

712. The Czech Atlas, *Atlas Republiky Ceskoslovenské*, Jaroslav Pantoflíček, ed. (Prague: Nakladatelstvo Orbis, 1935), refused to distinguish between Czechs and Slovaks. The official language of Czechoslovakia was "Czechoslovak"—a nonexisting language.

713. The official Yugoslav atlases showed no difference beween Slovenes, Croats, Serbs, and Macedo-Bulgars either. Only Germans, Magyars, Albanians, Rumanians, and Italians figured separately on the ethnic maps. Even Roosevelt knew better. Robert E. Sherwood tells that "the President expressed his often repeated opinion that the Croats and Serbs had nothing in common and that it is ridiculous to try to force such antagonistic peoples to live together under one government." Cf. his *Roosevelt and Hopkins* (New York: Harper Brothers, 1948), 711.

714. Here is the tragic realization of Mazzini's dream: "the indisputable tendency of our epoch is to reconstitute Europe into a certain number of homogeneous states as nearly as possible equal in population and in area." Cf. Graham Wallas, *Human Nature in Politics* (New York: Crofts, 1921), 290. This led, unfortunately, to the artificial coalescing of related but hostile nations in order that they might stand up to their bigger neighbors. These artificial combinations were bound to fail.

715. Cf. William Flavelle Monypenny and George Earle Buckle, *The Life of Benjamin Disraeli, Earl of Beaconsfield* (London: John Murray, 1929), 1:998-99. In his *The Fall of the House of Habsburg* (Harmondsworth: Penquin Books, 1983), 303, Edward Crankshaw says that by 1904, the Austrian half of the empire already "enjoyed a very high level of freedom for the individual and a much higher level of social welfare than, for example, England. Politics and administration were open to all talents. Government was very largely a middle-class affair." As for Austrian society, it was much more democratic than England's (81-83); and, I add, in many ways much more so than that of America.

716. Cf. Winston S. Churchill, *The Second World War* (London: Cassell, 1948), 1:9, 21-50.

717. Ibid, 8.

718. Cf. Winston S. Churchill, op. cit. (1954), 6:640.

719. Cf. H. A. Macartney, *Hungary and Her Successors* (London: Oxford University Press, 1937).

720. The Croats then had a very substantial amount of autonomy: they ruled over a Serb and a (very small) Italian minority.

721. This is not the only public glorification of a murderer. The Italians used to name streets and places after Wilhelm Oberdank (Guglielmo Oberdan), who tried to assassinate the Emperor Francis Joseph.

722. Nothing in history is entirely new. As a precedent there was the French folly, all through the sixteenth and seventeenth centuries, and even during the first half of the eighteenth century, of strengthening the power of Brandenburg-Prussia. After 1766, Prussia became politically and morally a British protectorate and a friend of the United States. (Cf. note 656.) When the news of the Franco-Prussian War reached the House of Representatives in Washington, spontaneous applause broke out. Cf. Othon Guerlac, "Le suicide de Prévost-Paradol à Washington et l'opinion américaine," *Revue de littérature comparée*, 8:1 (January-March 1928), 116.

723. Today the Austrian payment balance is nearly in the black because for the past forty years, industrialization and agrarian improvements have made great strides; the rather substantial tourist trade has also acted as an equalizing factor, thus making up for imports which are still larger than exports. In 1985, Austria even exported wheat to the USSR!

724. The *Anschluss*, the union of Austria with Germany, had more than mere identitarian-ethnic motives. Vienna had been the capital of the Holy Roman Empire, the "First Reich," whose insignia remained in Vienna's imperial treasury. The Habsburgs, not the Hohenzollerns, were the old German dynasty. When Madame de Staël came to Vienna, she commented that, at last, she had arrived at the *capitale de l'Allemagne*. Even Franz Joseph called himself in 1908 "a German prince." Most Austrians today have an independent feeling of statehood but not necessarily of what we over here call "nationality."

725. No country called Czechoslovakia, Yugoslavia, or Rumania existed before 1850. "Rumania" was founded in 1857 (without historic precedence) through the union of Wallachia and Moldavia. Czechoslovakia was established in 1918. "Yugoslavia" was the new official name (1929) for the "Kingdom of Serbs, Croats, and Slovenes" founded in 1918. (Hungary, Poland, Lithuania, and Bulgaria, on the other hand, were ancient historic realms.)

726. There was a "Czech Legion," consisting of ex-prisoners-of-war, in Russia. They fought at the start against Austro-Hungarian armies, but later against the Communists. Placed finally in a tight spot in Siberia, they "bought" their free passage to Vladivostok by surrendering the "white" Admiral Koltshak to the Red Army, which promptly shot him. Cf. Generalleutnant Konstantin W. Sakharov, *Die verratene Armee* (Berlin: Reichel, 1939), 358-61. Another "Czech Legion" was established in Italy and commanded by Colonel Graziani, who played a big (and fatal) role in the fascist movement, in the Ethiopian War, and in Mussolini's "Italian Social Republic." The officers taken from the Austro-Hungarian army were not overly trusted and played secondary role in the Czechoslovak army. (The Austro-Hungarian army, on the other hand, had little ethnic or religious prejudice. The last generalissimo of the Imperial-Royal army was a Transylvanian Lutheran, the last chief admiral a Hungarian Calvinist, and the commander on the Italian front a Greek-Orthodox Serb.)

727. Cf. Professor Caroline Robbins (Bryn Mawr), "The Teaching of European History in the United States," *Bulletin of the Polish Institute of Arts and Sciences in America*, vol. 2, no. 4 (July 1944), 1110-11.

728. I remember that, of America's leading universities in 1937, only Harvard had a minor geography department. (The only university with a reputation in geography was Clark University in Worcester, Mass.) Geography at best eked out a humble existence as a poorly endowed chair in the Department of Geology. On the Continent, two hours a week are dedicated to geography (an obligatory subject) in every high school-college. The same is true of history. From the age of ten or eleven on, boys and girls have both geographic and historic atlases.

In the United States atlases of quality were printed only after World War II. In the fall of 1987, the U.S. Secretary for Education, William Bennett, loudly deplored the almost total lack of geographic education in American schools. Something similar is true concerning world history.

729. In this Jefferson insists that Americans are better than anybody else. "If all the sovereigns of Europe were to set themselves to work to emancipate the minds of their subjects from their present ignorance and prejudice and that as zealously as now they attempt the contrary, a thousand years could not place them on the high ground on which our people are now setting out." This recalls sharply the thousand-year backwardness accredited to Europeans by Walter H. Page. Did Jefferson conceive of Americans as *racially* superior? It seems that our great democrat advocated harems so that the elite could spread their superior qualities. Cf. Lester J. Cappon, *The Adams-Jefferson Letters* (Chapel Hill: University of North Carolina Press, 1959), 2:387ff. American nationalism was stronger in the past than today. Clara von Gerstner heard an orator in Charleston over 120 years ago affirm that Americans "possess an intelligence not exceeded by any portion of the world." Cf. her *Beschreibung einer Reise durch die Vereinigten Staaten in den Jahren 1838 bis 1840* (Leipzig: J. C. Hinrich, 1842), 295. And Lincoln, in an address to the New Jersey State Senate in 1861, referred to Americans as the "almost chosen people of God." Cf. *Collected Works of Abraham Lincoln* (New Brunswick, N. J.: Rutgers University Press, 1953), 4:236. Today the Left (and near Left) preach an American-style masochism, criticizing and denigrating all American values and traditions.

730. Cf. Richard Hofstadter, *Anti-Intellectualism in American Life* (London: Jonathan Cape, 1964), 50-51.

731. An American aristocracy? The expression might not be popular, but Grund wrote in 1839, "I have heard more talk about aristocracy and family in the United States than during my whole previous life in Europe" (op. cit. 145).

732. "Post-Protestant" civilizations instinctively reject extremes, but the "radical," as the word implies, wants to go to the "roots." As I have pointed out in *Liberty or Equality?* "radicalism" disappeared in Europe's *Orbis Reformatus* by the eighteenth century— except in denominationally mixed Germany. Yet, significantly, certain Germans spoke in jest about *Radikalinskis*, as though they were Slavs. The Catholic and Eastern Church world never had the cult of the *juste milieu* (as Herzen and Leontyev remarked). Cf. note 588.

733. An anarchical tendency is not *per se* a leftist one. Henry Adams called himself quite aptly a "Christian Conservative Anarchist," and I would not be too reluctant to use this term for myself. Cf. the letter of Henry Adams to Elizabeth Cameron, in *Letters of Henry Adams (1892-1918)*, W. C. Ford, ed. (Boston: Houghton Mifflin, 1938), 364. Anarchism pure and simple, after all, is nothing but extreme liberalism and individualism. Political anarchism in the nineteenth and twentieth centuries, however, had strong leftist implications.

734. The male mind, of course, is the measuring rod used in this statement. Thanks to biological-anatomical research of the past fifteen to twenty years, it is now known that nature, much more than nurture, makes up sex differences. Brains, not only glands, work in different ways. These differences do not necessarily imply superiorities or inferiorities. *Sex Differences in the Brain*, Ed. G. J. de Vries (Amsterdam—New York: Elzevier, 1984).

735. The views and ideas of William E. Dodd will be discussed in due course.

736. Ambassador Joseph E. Davies thought that the purge trials in the 1930s were absolutely genuine. Cf. his *Mission to Moscow* (New York: Simon and Schuster, 1941), 155sq. The book was filmed. As for Stalin, Mr. Davies opined that "a child would like to sit on his lap and a dog would sidle up to him."

737. A curiously antihistoric feeling pervades the leftist creeds. Gerrard Winstanley in *The Laws of Freedom* (1952) not only insisted that science (and not metaphysics) alone should be taught, but also that history should be kept out of the curricula of schools because history looked "backward" and not "forward." Cf. Friedrich Heer, op. cit., 46-47. Henry Morgenthau, Jr., told Archduke Otto of Austria that historic ignorance is necessary for a healthy democracy. On the other hand, Yves Simon correctly pointed out that there is no proper and fruitful understanding of history without theology. ("Philosophie chrétienne, Notes complémentaires," *Études Carmélitaines*, XIX, 1:114-15.) And Duff Cooper is right when he says, "Perhaps one of the reasons why so little is learned from experience is that the men who conduct the affairs of nations are always changing and that too few of them read history. This is particularly true of democracy." Cf. *Old Men Forget* (London: Hart, Davis, 1953), 193-94.

   History irks leftists because, if they do not ignore it altogether, they have to "rewrite" it, which means that they have to forge it. This is necessary because they have a concrete concept of the future and the (artificially adapted) past must appear to be an organic and logical preparation for the "shape of things to come." Leftists (and this includes radical democrats), are suspicious of history because their program calls for the "end of history"—at least of history as we understand the term. Even the perfect global democracy of the convinced "democratist" is utopian, a paradise on earth. Insofar as history is generally taught in "programmatic democracies," it assumes the character of an evolution (interspread with revolutions) toward a specific goal: beatitude for the millions. This view is also deeply imbedded in American popular feelings. Writes Professor Eugene N. Anderson, "European history in the hundred years after Napoleon has been regarded in the United States as the story of the slow but certain victory of liberalism over the *ancien régime*. In writing this history the episodes emphasized have been those in which liberalism clashed with the old order and either overcame it or, unfortunately, was temporarily defeated by it.

American historians have assumed that the goal of the century was to establish the ascendancy of the American social and political ideals: they have interpreted European history according to their own wishes, and they have been abetted in this work by the memoirs and biographies of liberal exiles from the Continent and the tendency to translate these works about Continental history which fitted their own theories." (*Social Education*, May 1938.) All this optimism, needless to say, is equally applicable to the Asian scene. Today democratism and socialism have replaced the old liberal outlook.

738. Representative Sol Bloom of the Democratic party, to quote one instance, was a warm admirer of Mussolini.

739. William II knew about Dreyfus's innocence but could not publicly intervene. Had he done so, he would only have aggravated Dreyfus's position. But he informed Queen Victoria of the truth. H. B. von Bülow, the German chargé d'affaires in Paris, wrote to Chancellor Prince Hohenlohe that the verdict against Dreyfus was a "mixture of vulgarity and cowardice, the surest sign of barbarism," and that France "has therewith excluded herself from the family of civilized nations." Cf. Wilhelm Herzog, *Der Kampf einer Republik* (Zürich, 1933), cited by Hannah Arendt, *The Origins of Totalitarianism* (New York: Harcourt, Brace, 1951), 91, n.6

740. The Russian philosopher Vladimir Solovyov, after the assassination of Emperor Alexander II, demanded that the murderer be handed over to the Holy Synod for religious instruction and spiritual regeneration. This sensible proposal was rejected and the law carried out: for a successful or unsuccessful attempt to murder a member of the Imperial family, Russia had a statutory death sentence (and at certain times for this crime alone). Cf. Fëdor Stepun, "Poet—providyets, K stolyetiyu so dnya rozhdyeniya Vladimira Solovyova," *Za Svobodu*, 1953, no. 7, 7. The high-strung Irish lady who wounded Mussolini was returned for medical attention to the British Isles. Drtil, who failed to kill Dollfuss, got a slight jail sentence, as did Jawurek who gravely wounded the Austrian chancellor, Monsignor Ignaz Seipel (and thus eventually caused his death). The assassin of Empress Elizabeth was imprisoned for life. Friedrich Adler, who murdered Prime Minister Count Stürgkh during World War I, was formally condemned to death but released from jail a year later. Austria's Socialist party celebrated with great pomp the hundredth birthday of this assassin who, for years, was general secretary of the Socialist International. (Leftists seem to have a weakness for political murder.)

The French, to be sure, were more spiteful: Gorgulov, the mentally deranged Russian assassin of President Doumer, was actually executed. Anatole Leroy-Beaulieu in op. cit., vol. 2, iv. 7, tells that during the rule of Alexander II, from 1855 to the first months of 1879, only one execution took place in Russia, that of Karakosov, would-be assassin of the Emperor (1866). Nor had the number of murders increased since the days of Nicholas I. Percentagewise, they were fewer than either in France or Prussia.

Were Sacco and Vanzetti guilty? The best book on this issue is Francis Russell's *Tragedy at Dedham* (New York: McGraw Hill, 1962). The author is convinced that Sacco either fired the fatal shot or knew who the assassin was, but deems Vanzetti as probably innocent (466). The book, by an American conservative writer, is based on serious research.

741. I experienced this in connection with the Chessman case when I wrote a column for a Catholic American monthly in which I merely *explained* the psychological reasons for the European reaction. I even carefully avoided taking sides. As a result, the editorial staff (mostly female) threated to walk out should the editor publish the column. (Chessman had been indicted for rape, not for murder, and received the death sentence on a technicality: he had *dragged* his victim a few yards from the car. Cases like these highlight, above all, the fact that "East is East and West is West, and never the twain shall meet.")

742. One wonders whether much-heralded experiments like those of the humane reformatory camp (in Bolshevo, for instance) did not serve as a smokescreen for less humanitarian "experiments"—further east and further north—in the form of the Gulag.

743. One ought to say: something the Communists considered to be "new," nay, to be "American." The fascination that the long distance (and thoroughly distorted) picture of America exercised on Russian communism has so far never been a subject of serious research. The writings of Lenin and Stalin are replete with expressions of boundless admiration for America and the subconscious thought that all the United States needed to make things right was to eliminate Wall Street. To Stalin, the "style" of communism consisted in "Russian Revolutionary Dynamism" and "American Pragmatism" (*Delovitost'* is best translated thus, but it can also mean sobriety, work-readiness, industriousness). Cf. I. Stalin, *Ob osnovakh Lyeninizma, K voprosam lyeninizma* (Moscow: Partizdat, WKP-b, 1935), 75-75. Immediately after the Russian Revolution, a new artistic and architectural style sprang up, called *Chicagizm*, based on the notion of a new city in a new world without a past. Needless to say, *Chicagizm* had nothing to do with the reality of Chicago.

     The Soviets knew how to impress their American visitors with the label "new," and this although, as I hinted, an American is not truly a friend of the radically new, but rather of familiar things in a "bigger and better" edition. Nor was or is the USSR anything genuinely modern. It breathes the spirit of nineteenth-century bourgeois culture, *vide* the Moscow subway stations, replicas of great-grandmother's drawing room. Or the railroad station of Sotchi which resembles an oversexed Munich beer brewer's dream of an Oriental harem. Still, there is a certain type of American or British leftist whose heart beats faster when he sees travel folders inviting him to come to the "New Czechoslovakia," the "New Libya," or the "New Algeria" where he can admire uniformed women and girls marching with broad smiles and shouldering submachine guns.

744. I was told in Moscow in 1930 by an American woman that never ever would I see in the United States such fine, modern, clean, streamlined streetcars as in the USSR. I could not prove the contrary as I had not yet been in America, but I could show her a metal plate in one of the trolley cars indicating that it had been built prior to 1917. Was the good lady a Socialist or a Communist? Probably not. But she suffered from the modern malady of accepting unthinkingly the "axiom" of socialist inevitability. This has been impugned by Gaetano Mosca in his *Elementi di scienza politica* (Turin: Fratelli Bocca, 1923), 319. It is surely better to rejoice in the shape of things to come than to deplore them.

745. See note 607.

746. In the United States higher female education, public or private, is more markedly leftist than its male counterpart. "Conservative Clubs" are more frowned upon by the administrations. This is not only due to the leftist *ressentiment* as delineated by Werner Sombart, but to the close links between leftism and militant feminism, which is particularly strong in the English-speaking world. There feminism is not unrelated to the misogyny so strongly entrenched in America and Britain. It is naturally impossible to evaluate the position of women in a country by studying its laws. Were this the "key," women in English-speaking countries would have a higher position than in the old Russia or in France, which is not the case. Cf. Randolph Bourne's letter in *Twice a Year* (New York), no. 2 (Spring-Summer 1939), and no. 5-6 (Spring-Summer 1941). Cf. also note 591.

747. I heard the President's French only once. It was a unique experience. Still he was certain that he could "charm Stalin." Without a means of direct communication?

748. According to Frances Perkins, secretary of Labor, Roosevelt relied on mere hunches and he rarely read serious books. Cf. her *The Roosevelt I Knew* (New York: Viking, 1946), 34, 352. To William C. Bullitt, the President also confessed that he relied primarily on hunches, intuitions. Cf. W. C. Bullit, "How We Won the War and Lost the Peace," *Life*, International Edition, vol. 5, no. 7 (September 27, 1948), 48. The author tells how Roosevelt insisted that Woodrow Wilson's decisions were also prompted by mere feelings. "Intuitionism" is a worldwide disease, prevalent in democracies and personal dictatorships, where people with no training, study, or experience achieve ruling positions. Not only FDR and Wilson, but also Beneš and Hitler (with his *traumwandlerische Sicherheit*, the "inner security of a sleepwalker") boasted of it—and all failed fatally. There is no substitute for knowledge *and* experience. In the male, the predominance of sheer intuition is always coupled with mediocrity. This also pertains to Napoleon, whose intellectual mediocrity startled Léon Bloy. Cf. his *Le mendiant ingrat (Journal de l'auteur 1892-1895)* (Paris: Mercure de France, 1946), 127.

749. He was actually what psychiatrists call a mythomaniac. With no aim to personal profit, he invented stories and made statements and promises with no basis in fact.

750. This Nazi enthusiasm for the populist American tradition (the Jeffersonian-Jacksonian trend) had deep psychological and theological roots, which become apparent on reading Søren Kierkegaard's violent strictures on democracy and his praise for monarchy, found in his diaries. Cf. *Die Tagebücher*, Hayo Gerdes, trsl. and ed. (Düsseldorf-Köln: Eugen Diederichs, 1963), 2: 218, 220, 245-47, and *Christentum und Christenheit*, Eva Schlechta, ed. (Munich: Kösel, 1957), 87, 286. Cf. also chapter VII, note 30.

751. The Spanish character is aristocratic only in the sense that the people are proud and have a deep sense of spirituality. A beggar might address the passer-by as *hermanito*, "little brother," and upper-class arrogance is rare in Spain. Cf. also Salvador de Madariaga, *Hernán Cortés* (New York: Macmillan, 1941), 40-41, Orestes Brownson, *Equality and Democracy* (Detroit: H. F. Brownson, 1897), 22, or Havelock Ellis, *The Soul of Spain* (New York: Houghton, Mifflin, 1909), 12-13.

752. Cf. Miguel de Unamuno y Jugo, *Vida de Don Quijote y Sancho* (Madrid: Renacimiento, 1914), 213-14.

753. Salvador de Madariaga in his *Spain* (New York: Creative Age Press, 1943), 332, after describing the 1934 uprising, added: "I shall not dwell on atrocities. Both sides flooded Spain and even foreign countries with harrowing tales, both unfortunately true though both possibly exaggerated." (I knew reliable eye witnesses who had seen carved-up priests in the windows of butcheries.) And then Madariaga adds: "The revolt of 1934 is unpardonable. . . . As for the Asturian miners, their revolt was entirely due to doctrinaire and theoretical prepossessions. Had the hungry Andalusian peasants risen in revolt, what could one do but sympathize with their despair? But the Asturian miners were well paid and, in fact, the whole industry, by a collusion between employers and workers, was kept working at an artificial level by state subsidies." (Here again I warn the reader not to expect too much sense or reason from history but to remember man's fallen and irrational nature; he is a sinner and a half-wit. I am amazed at historians, above all Christian historians, who overlook this fact. Who are the staunchest Communists in Sweden? The best-paid workers in all of Europe, the steel workers in Lapland.) Cf. Winfried Martini, *Freiheit auf Abruf, Die Lebenserwartung der Bundesrepublik* (Cologne-Berlin: Kiepenheuer und Witsch, 1960), 114. *Vide* also Fredrick B. Pike, "The Modernized Church in Peru: Two Aspects," *The Review of Politics*, vol. 26, no. 3 (July 1964), 316, where he speaks of the strong communist domination of the Peruvian stevedores' trade union, of men who earn between $400 and $600 a month, a royal wage for Latin America. "Throughout Latin America," he adds, "it is those members of the middle class who have grown indifferent or hostile to spiritual forces that furnish the most recruits to communism. The Communist promise to bring about the fall of the upper class feeds the envy of the spiritually adrift but often economically securely anchored middle class." There is nothing more ridiculous than the naive cause-effect school in history, which, above all, refuses to consider Grace and Evil.

754. When General Sanjurjo declared for the Republic in 1931, King Alfonso considered the monarchy definitely lost.

755. The pilot, Juan Antonio Ansaldo, wrote a book of recollections, *Mémoires d'un monarchiste espagnol, 1931-1952*, J. Viet, trsl. (Monaco: Editions due Rocher, 1953). The memoirs are as violently anti-Republican as they are anti-Franco.

756. After World War II, Louis Bolín, who was half-British, organized modern Spanish tourism attracting millions, which made Spanish economic reconstruction in the late fifties possible. Without his groundwork, the Neo-Liberals (mostly *Opus Dei*) could never have effected it.

757. The vast majority of Spanish "Protestants" sided with the Republic, the Jews (who knew something about communism elsewhere) supported Franco, whom Hitler considered "a Freemason." Cf. Dr. Henry Picker, op. cit., 49. During the Civil War I had occasion to talk in Seville with Pastor Santos y Molina (the Evangelical bishop in Madrid) who spoke to me frankly in the presence of a Press and Propaganda official about the grievances he had against the Nationalist government. About Franco and the Jews, cf. 290-91.

758. According to the Carlists (and to the serious historian), the monarchy has belonged to the liberal order ever since the days of Isabel II. In the opinion of the conservative Iberian, the Spanish monarchy that fell in 1931 and the Portuguese monarchy that collapsed in 1910 were usurped by illegitimate, leftist-liberal monarchs. While in Portugal the liberal branch died out with Dom Manuel, the Carlist branch in Spain came to an end with the accidental death of Don Alfonso de Borbón in Vienna late in 1936.

759. In Hemingway's (historically valuable) novel, *For Whom the Bell Tolls*, there is symbolic value in the killing by the confused American hero of a Carlist wearing a Sacred Heart of Jesus badge.

760. Franco had a brilliant record in the Rif War. He was known for his courage. *Vide* the thumbnail sketch of Franco in Arturo Barea's *The Forging of a Rebel*, Ilse Barea, trsl. (New York: Reynal and Hitchcock, 1946). Barea fought in that war with the *Tercio* and was able to see Franco in action. "I've seen murderers go white in the face because Franco had looked at them out of the corner of his eye" (365). Franco's relationship with the National Socialists is partly handled in Dr. Picker's *Tischgespräche*, partly in the *Akten zur deutschen auswärtigen Politik 1918-1945* (Baden-Baden: Imprimerie Nationale, 1951), series D, vol. 3. From these documents it appears that there was no Nazi support of Franco prior to the rebellion (3), that Franco was furious about Italian aerial attacks on Barcelona (552), and that the German ambassador in Paris (January 8, 1937) was certain that the Spanish government would show no gratitude for the aid accorded it during the civil war (181-82). The *Tischgespräche* tell about Hitler's contempt, if not hatred, for Franco and for Catholic Spain.

761. There was (and still is) a beautiful Picasso Museum in Barcelona, right in "Francospain." Military dictatorship is rarely ideology-ridden.

762. The old influential liberal monthly, *Revista de Occidente*, founded by José Ortega y Gasset, was revived in Franco's days. Its editor-in-chief was Ortega's son, José Ortega Spottorno.

763. The persecution and massacre of nonorthodox Communists and other leftists is well described by George Orwell in his *Homage to Catalonia* (London: Secker and Warburg, 1938; Penguin, 1962).

764. Most of the organizers of these "inner-leftist" massacres, men like Vladimir Antonov-Ovseyenko, were later killed in the Stalinist purges. Executions, like those of Nin, were part of the *Yezhovshtshina*, the bloody rule of Nikolay Ivanovitch Yezhov, who later also perished. (His substitute was Beriya.) At least half the men Ilya Ehrenburg knew in Spain became Stalin's victims—as he later admitted. Others who survived subsequently played infamous roles, like Ernö Gerö, the bloodhound of Budapest. But the man who was Stalin's chief prosecutor (and who knew the truth throughout) was the renegade Pole Andrzej Wyszyński, who for years represented the USSR at the United Nations in New York City. The UN provided no disinfectant for those who, in the line of duty, had to shake hands with him.

765. Cf. Madariaga, op. cit., 397. Nin was a relative of Anais Nin, noted American writer.

766. Despite his violent condemnation of the warfare of the "Nationalists," Bernanos

remained until his death a confirmed right-winger. One of his sons was, to the very end, a volunteer in the Spanish National army. Simone Weil, who knew only too well the horrors of the other side, replied to Bernanos in a long letter that can be found in Georges Bernanos, *Correspondance* (Paris: Plon, 1971), 2:200-04.

767. Hugh Thomas, a British Labourite, in his *The Spanish Civil War* (London: Eyre and Spottiswoode, 1961), part II, chap. 19, reflects on the many assassinations and executions carried out by the Franco forces, but he obviously cannot speak about the elaborate cruelties committed by the "Nationalists." The delirious atrocities perpetrated by the forces of enlightenment, progress, and democracy are honestly dealt with in the following chapters and make gruesome reading. Ilya Ehrenburg in his memoirs, "Lyudi, gody, zhizn'," published in Summer 1962 in *Novy Mir* (Moscow), gives a less detailed picture of the atrocities and attributes them almost exclusively to the Anarchists. But Hugh Thomas is emphatic on the horrors committed by the "Chekas."

768. This recalls the desecrations during the French Revolution in St. Denis, where the tombs of the French Kings are found. In 1793, a revolutionary mob performed ghoulish acts on the remains of the "sons of St. Louis". . . a real throwback to the practice of past ages. Hatred always comes from helplessness mixed with envy. Of course, to "punish the dead" is a time-honored pastime, but in the last two hundred years it has become a privilege of the Left—including the Nazis, who desecrated Jewish cemeteries.

769. I have a red Spanish poster celebrating the "Revolution of the 18th of July."

770. Unfortunately, these horrors are not purely Spanish—or German, or Russian. The inhumanities in Spain were perpetrated more often than not by large crowds, a fact our Rousseauists do not like to face. According to Reinhold Niebuhr, it is far more difficult for a group than for an individual to be ethical. Cf. his *Moral Man and Immoral Society* (New York: Scribner's, 1941), xi. Half a century before the discovery of America, revolutionary German peasants, congregating in Worms in 1428, voted for a program they entitled "Postulates of the Common Man." The most salient points were the abolition of all private property and the exiling or killing of all Jews. These demands have been echoed in our progressive century. Cf. Felix Somary, op. cit., 80.

771. The United States at least showed gratitude in the beginning. Ségur writes that after his arrival in the United States during the War of Independence, "at all solemn occasions, during all festivities, in all toasts one never forgets to mention the names of Louis XVI and of France." He adds, "America indeed has always avoided ingratitude, of which history has charged almost all republican governments." Cf. Monsieur le Comte de Ségur, op. cit, 1:446-47.

772. The Spanish Socialists, unlike their northern brethren, were very orthodox in their Marxism: they were really Bolsheviks rather than Mensheviks. Margarita Nelken, a leading Socialist, said, "We want the Revolution, but the Russian Revolution to us is insufficient. There must be enormous flames which can be seen throughout the entire world and rivers of blood have to color the sea." Largo Caballero, another Socialist leader, announced: "If the Popular Front collapses, which we expect, the victory of

the proletariat is certain. Then we will establish the dictatorship of the proletariat."
Cf. Hugh Thomas, op. cit., book 1, chap. 11.

773. Cf. Alfonso García Valdecasas, "Los Estados totalitarios y el Estado Español," in *La Revista de Estudios Políticos* (January 1942), 5sq. In this article the cofounder of the Falange (and rector of the University of Barcelona) declared (9) that Spain refused to follow the general political trend in Europe (in 1942!), that the new movements were totalitarian in nature (20-21), but that Spain always believed in immutable moral principles and that the state was merely in the service of those values: "These are, for us, as an example, the liberty, the dignity, and the integrity of man, and it is the strict duty of the state to respect them and to make them respected" (27). A more outspoken rejection of Nazi and Fascist ideas can hardly be imagined—and yet these words were written at the height of Nazi victories. Such views, of course, are typically Spanish; hence the leftist dislike for traditional Spain. No wonder Alfred Rosenberg, the Nazi "ideologist" chief, said that "nowhere else in Europe could one find such psychological and intellectual backwardness as in Spain before April 1931." (Cf. op. cit., 186.) Such views were shared by most "progressive" people in the West.

774. Cf. Salvador de Madariaga, op. cit., 368: "During the Eighth Congress of the Communist International which took place in Moscow in 1935, the 'Trojan Horse' policy to be adopted by the Comintern from then on was formulated and expounded by Comrade Dimitrov. This was the policy which led Russia to Geneva, to the International Peace Campaign, and to the Popular Front. The chief agent for the policy in Spain was to be Señor Álvarez del Vayo, stronger and more efficient for remaining officially a Socialist. His trips to Moscow had begun in 1930, a year before the fall of the Spanish monarchy. In April 1936 a party of over a hundred Spaniards and pseudo-Spaniards who had been living in Moscow passed through Paris and were sent to Spain with every possible care and attention by the Spanish Embassy." Significantly, Señor Álvarez del Vayo for years handled a foreign policy column for *The Nation*, a respected "liberal" paper. Cf. also Hugh Thomas, op. cit., book I, chap. 11, note 18.

775. Cf. Salvador de Madariaga, op. cit., 402, note 1, "I believe the first time a Spanish airplane bombed a Spanish town was on July 20th at Toledo, where Don Francisco Caballéro had the city bombed at regular intervals for three days in the hope of regaining it from the Rebels." Guernica still poses a problem for the historian. Was it bombed by the Germans, or not? Hugh Thomas is convinced it was, but recent research points in the opposite direction. Cf. Helene Schreiber, "Guernica—Mythos von Malerhand," *Rheinischer Merkur*, January 17, 1969, no. 3, 32. Harold G. Cardozo, correspondent for the London *Times* denied the bombardment in the May 5, 1937, issue. In my opinion, a certain number of bombs fell, but the *dinamiteros* played a full part in the destruction, as in Irún.

776. Again, was the Church so bad that such a dreadful reaction could be expected? And *again* be warned—even at the risk of sounding repetitious—against the theory that where there is smoke there is fire. Big fires can produce little smoke and vice versa. Among priests, the best (since they were a major "provocation") usually suffered more than the bad, lazy, or stupid ones who, from the red viewpoint, were harmless and lowered the prestige of the Church. Some in the West insist that all these

problems could have been avoided had there been separation of Church and state. Yet, considering the intrinsic character of the Church and the modern state, strict separation is not really feasible; this was well understood by Reinhold Niebuhr. Cf. Jerome G. Kerwin, "The Church and the State," *Commonweal*, vol. 62, no. 14, 342-44.

777. Franco tried vainly to embody the synthesis by sporting the blue shirt of the Falangists with the *boina roja*, the red beret, of the Carlists. The synthesis did not work. Later Franco appeared either in civilian clothes or in a plain military uniform. It is little known that Franco *most* hesitantly responded to the call of Sanjurjo. Cf. Luis Suárez Fernández, "Der Weg in den Bürgerkrieg von 1936," *Criticón*, no. 98, November-December 1986, 250-51.

778. This much he told to his friend, the famous Italian journalist Indro Montanelli, who published it in January 1948 in the *Corriere della Sera*. Yet some of the Falangists later drifted into violent opposition of the Franco government, among them Dionisio Ridruejo, author of the Falangist hymn *Cara al sol*. Others, such as García Valdecasas, broke with the Falange.

779. Among them are Don Gregorio Marañón, medical expert, historian, politician, and writer who took a hand in the abdication of Alfonso XIII, and José Ortega y Gasset. Salvador de Madariaga held out for a long time. Pablo Casals refused to return but is said to have had a Spanish passport.

780. Cf. Salvador de Madariaga, *Spain*, 376-77, "The fact that the Church was being ruthlessly persecuted by the Revolutionists can only be disputed or contested by ignorant or prejudiced critics. Whether the priests murdered were 16,000 or 1,600 time will tell. But that for months, years perhaps, the mere fact of being a priest was tantamount to a capital sentence, and the fact that no Catholic worship was allowed at all till the end of the war or very nearly, and that churches and cathedrals were used as markets and thoroughfares for animal-driven vehicles cannot be disputed." (Madariaga considered the Basque nationalist attitude a case of schizophrenia.) A group of non-Catholic clergymen visiting Spain in the winter of 1937 reported laconically about Spanish priests: "Many certainly have been killed. [Unless] the parish priest was actively unpopular, he was not killed by his own people." (Cf. *Report of a Group of Anglican and Free Churchmen who Visited Spain, January 29 to February 9, 1937*, cited by E. Allison Peers, *Spain, the Church and the Orders* (London: Burns, Oates and Washbourne, 1945), 254.

781. In large parts of the Basque Provinces the population wanted autonomy, and since the Cortes of the Republic voted for the Basque Statute, the Basques, led by their priests and ignorant of the persecution of the Church in the rest of Republican Spain, sided with the Republic. Territorially they were cut from the main area and thus took the stories of the persecution of their Church farther south as mere propaganda of the Burgos government. Basque exiles, later on, fanatially spread the anti-Franco gospel in Catholic circles abroad—and successfully. It cannot be doubted, however, that the Basques had a just grievance.

The state, as such (and the modern state even more so), is essentially "annexationist" and decentralizes only with the greatest reluctance (and with a minimum of sincerity). Cf. Rafael Gambra, *La monarquía social y representativa* (Madrid: Rialp,

1954), 204. Our democratic age is basically opposed to minorities. Says Winfried Martini, "From the concentration camps and later from the gas chambers which—though unaware—the will of the people had brought on, the frightening yelling screams of our century could be heard: 'Woe to the minorities!' " Cf. *Das Ende aller Sicherheit*, 118.

782. Leon Trotsky was a Freemason, but neither Lenin nor Stalin nor Khruschchev belonged to the Brothers. *Any* organization not "of the State" was forbidden in the USSR, and thus the religious communities were an anomaly scheduled for liquidation. (Hence also the pressure on Zionism.)

783. Harold Laski wrote to Oliver Wendell Holmes on August 6, 1933, that he had spoken to Azaña and that this politician's "resonant anticlericalism" went to his heart. Cf. *Holmes-Laski Letters, 1916-1035*, 1446. The joint letter of Stalin, Molotov, and Voroshilov to Largo Caballero, dated December 21, 1936, advising him to use democracy, republicanism, and Azaña as a convenient camouflage against the accusation of a communist takeover, can be found in S. de Madariaga, *Spain*, 472.74.

784. Numerically the Communists in Spain were then relatively not more numerous than the Communists in Russia in 1917, but in Spain, unlike Russia, the Socialists were hardly distinguishable from the Communists. The Russian *Bolsheviki* totally disregarded democratic procedures, whereas the *Mensheviki* still clung to the time-honored notion of legality. On January 23, 1936, Largo Caballero said in Madrid: "When things change, the Right need not ask for our benevolence. We will not respect the lives of our enemies as we did on April 4, 1931, when the Republic came in. If the Right is not defeated at the polls, we will find other means to beat them: means to obtain the total triumph of the red flag, because, and I emphasize this, if the Right wins, we shall be forced to turn to civil war." Cf. Richard Pattee, *This is Spain* (Milwaukee: Bruce, 1951), 177. The chapters of this book dealing with the events leading to the civil war are well documented.

785. As previously stated, this was largely due to Basque influence, particularly to the friendship that bound Señor José Antonio Aguirre y Lecube, the former President of the Basque Republic, to Jacques Maritain. And yet an English observer could state unequivocally, "The attack on religion has been more radical in loyalist Spain than anywhere else in the world, even Mexico and Russia. All Roman Catholic churches have been closed down as places of worship and nearly all have been completely destroyed. . . .In loyalist Spain there is nothing left to persecute." Cf. Arthur Loveday, *Spain 1923-1948* (London: Boswell, 1949), 119, quoting the liberal *Manchester Guardian*. Of course, some readers might think that the Church in Spain created boundless envy, displaying such wealth amidst poverty. Yet prior to the outbreak of the civil war, priests received about eight dollars a month, bishops about $1,500 a year. The vast majority of the clergy was living on a proletarian level. In this respect, the situation today is not much different.

786. Curiously enough there is no equivalent term with this particular meaning in Continental idioms.

787. *The Protestant*, edited by Kenneth Leslie and published during World War II in New York, was an amazing publication. A number of Communists and fellow travellers were on its editorial board, among them Pierre van Paassen. It fought a valiant battle

against the Nazis and the Catholic Church (considering them nearly identical) and declared (vol. 5, no. 6, June-July 1942, 3) that the two most hated men of our time were not Hitler and Mussolini, but Franco and Pétain. On the last page of that number an appeal was printed for additional subscribers because "the Fascists, whichever side wins, plan to win the peace. If the Fascists or the Falangists win the peace, the war will have been fought in vain. Their victory would mean the renewed and intensified persecution of the Jews and of all those who have become in any way identified with the age-old struggle for democracy." One of the editors of this delightful periodical, Heinz Pol, in a letter published in the *New York Times*, demanded the mass slaughter of "German militarists and junkers," a demand reiterated by Stalin during the Teheran Conference. Yet the main target of the attack of *The Protestant* was never national socialism, but "Franco Spain" and Pétain's regime, which was also considered "clerico-Fascist."

788. A Spanish Catholic was also used by the Republic as an alibi: Angel Ossorio y Gallardo, who served as a representative of Republican Spain in Paris. One of the archbishops who opposed Franco increasingly down the years was Cardinal Segura of Seville. He attacked Franco, Americans, "Protestants," Falangists, modern dance (beginning with the waltz and polka) and, finally, Pope Pius XII. His case was *really* unique. Luckily, he died before he had a chance to hear about the bikinis on the Costa del Sol. But he was no danger to the Church—and today, as Bernanos foresaw clearly, the trap is no longer the throne-and-altar-complex but leftism. Cf. his *Le Chemin de la Croix des Âmes* (Paris: Gallimard-NRF, 1948), 452.

789. In the Germanic and Slavic countries the Socialist parties called themselves "Social Democratic," but they were originally pledged to the Marxist program. The Russian Social Democrats were split into Mensheviks and Bolsheviks. Until 1917, Lenin figures, naturally, as a Social Democrat, a term that sounds harmless to Anglo-American ears. In Latin countries these parties are plainly called "Socialists." (The French *Radicaux Socialistes* were never Socialists, but radical liberals claiming a social outlook: they were very bourgeois, anticlerical middle-of-the-roaders and, in a way, the ideological backbone of the Third Republic.) In Austria, after World War II, the Social Democrats reconstituted themselves as "Socialists," probably in order to emphasize their Marxist heritage vis-à-vis the heavily Soviet-supported Communists. This Marxist heritage can be found deep in the heart of the Labour party. A photo exists of the late Lord Attlee giving the Communist clenched fist salute while in Loyalist Spain.

790. A good and impartial description of these events can be found in Hellmut Andics's *Der Staat, den keiner wollte* (Vienna: Herder, 1962), 431ff.

791. The hero in the defense of the Linz arms cache, Richard Bernaschek, was arrested, but liberated by the National Socialist illegal underground and smuggled into Germany, where he gave speeches on Munich Radio against the Dollfuss regime. Later he broke with the National Socialists, fled to Czechoslovakia, and returned later to Austria only to be arrested by the SS and executed. He probably knew too much about the red-brown collaboration. Cf. Hans von Hammerstein, *Im Anfang war der Mord* (Vienna: Verlag für Geschichte und Politik, 1981.) 148-51.

792. British journalists on the Continent, needless to say, have similar mental-intellectual

handicaps. *The abyss, as always, is the Channel, not the Atlantic.* Of course, journalism *per se* has many pitfalls. Michael Clark, a one-time *New York Times* correspondent, wrote that according to the advice given by a "most experienced" American reporter, young journalists should always write what the folks "back home" want to hear and always play up to their bias. In Clark's particular area (Northwest Africa) these items were scandals involving American air bases and the bad treatment of natives by the French colonialists. Cf. Thomas Molnar, *The Decline of the Intellectual* (Cleveland and New York: Meridian Books, 1961), 226n.

793. After the war he was tried in Boston and received a stiff jail sentence.

794. Cf. Heinrich Benedikt, ed. *Geschichte der Republik Österreich* (Munich: R. Oldenbourg, 1954), 10-11: "The First Austrian Republic had been a sovereign state, yet it was so in name only. Subjected to the control of the League of Nations—the typical example of power politics in disguise—Austria's self-government was only another name for the administration of the country by the Allies. In the Tripartite Conference from March 14 to 17, 1934, and in the Protocols of Rome, Italy took over the role of a tacit agent of the League of Nations and deputy of the Great Powers." And Benedikt adds, "The Abyssinian venture resulted in the surrendering of Austria to Hitler" (11). Compare also with Kurt von Schuschnigg, "Neuösterreichische Geschichtsschreibung," *Wissenschaft und Weltbild*, vol. 4 (1951).

795. He repeatedly made these and similar statements. I also have oral information from Professor von Schuschnigg. Yet in his doctoral thesis published in Paris in 1908 (for the University of Dijon) entitled *Le problème autrichien et la question tchèque, Étude sur les luttes politiques des nationalités slaves en Autriche*, Beneš demanded the "federalization," not the destruction of Austria-Hungary. His growing anti-Catholic and anti-Habsburg bias drove him finally simultaneously into the arms of Hitler and Stalin and thus into political suicide. His fanatical anti-Habsburg stand, preferring the *Anschluss* to restoration, is also testified to by his admirers. Cf. Jaroslav Papoušek, *Eduard Beneš, Třicet let práce v boje pro národ a stát* (Prague: Orbis, 1934), and Louis Eisenmann, *Un grand Européen: Edouard Beneš* (Paris: Hartmann, 1934), 111-14. Cf. also Sisley Huddleston, *The Tragic Years, 1939-1947* (New York: Devin Adair, 1955), 12; Jean de Pange, *Les meules de Dieu* (Paris: Alsatia, 1951), 182; Comte de Sainte-Aulaire, *François-Joseph* (Paris: Fayard, 1945), 583. Beneš, unlike Masaryk, was a Freemason, belonging to the lodge *Pravda Vitězi* in Prague; its ideology might have colored his political thinking. Cf. Eugen Lennhoff and Oskar Posner, *Internationales Freimaurerlexikon* (Vienna: Amalthea, 1932), col. 164-165. (These authors were Masons.) I suspect that *Pravda Vitězi* might have been connected to the *Grand Orient* rather than to the *Grande Loge Nationale Indépendante et Regulière pour la France.*

In dealing with the political effects of Freemasonry on the Continent, beware of three pitfalls: to underrate them, to overrate them, to fail to distinguish between the various trends, lodges, organizations. The book by Roger Peyrefitte, *Les fils de la lumière* (Paris: Flammarion, 1961), though not of a scholarly nature, gives at least an inkling of the large variety of Masonic dogmatic positions. On Freemasonry in French politics, cf. also D. W. Brogan, *French Personalities and Problems* (London: Hamish Hamilton, 1946), 37-40.

Take care not to see history as nothing but a chain of conspiracies. Count Prokesch-

Osten remarked that in "Metternich's heart there lived the ineradicable mania (Gentz called it the *Urlüge*, the original lie), that all revolutions are the work of secret societies and that Lafayette could have organized the revolt in Poland no less than in Paris." Cf. *Aus den Tagebüchern des Grafen Prokesch von Osten* (Vienna: Christoph Reisser, 1909), 68 (entry of December 7, 1830).

796. Cf. Eduard Beneš, "The Organization of Post-War Europe," *Foreign Affairs*, vol. 20, no. 2 (January 1942), 231.

797. Cf. *Der Hochverratsprozess gegen Dr. Guido Schmidt,* 367, 393, 397, 399. Franz von Papen, as seen, fought valiantly on the side of the Little Entente. Professor von Schuschnigg (former chancellor) told me of his encounter with the Yugoslav foreign minister Boško Jevtić in Geneva, where Jevtić informed him in all candor that Belgrade would never consent to a Habsburg restoration in Austria because such a challenge would render the difficult Croats totally recalcitrant. Restoration would be a *casus belli* since it would be a questioon of life-and-death for Yugoslavia.

798. In the mid-1930s, Paris considered a Habsburg restoration a minor evil, but Britain seemed totally opposed. Cf. *Der Hochverratsprozess gegen Dr. Guido Schmidt*, 397-99. Edward VIII might have been personally in favor of a restoration, but his reign was short-lived.

799. Cf. Elizabeth Wiskemann, *The Rome-Berlin Axis* (London: Oxford University Press, 1949), 52: "The remarkable and admirable reaction of the British against the Hoare-Laval plan was all the greater, the Stresa front was dissolved and Hitler unshackled, let loose to advance step by step, from the militarization of the Rhineland to the invasion of Poland. History has perhaps never played a stranger trick upon Man than to allow British indignation against international lawlessness and imperialist and racialist bullying to have smoothed the plan for Adolf Hitler. Out of this misconception was born that deformity, the Italo-German alliance, of which Hitler had so long dreamed."

It was not at all a "strange trick," but the inability of the well-meaning masses to grasp an immensely complex political situation that stretched from the Somali Desert to the Bavarian border. Starry-eyed idealism has often played a more disastrous role in history than diabolical malice. For the same good reason that St. Thomas considers the intellectual virtues to be higher than the moral ones, Fouché (though hardly a reader of the *Summa*) exclaimed when Napoleon ordered the execution of the Duc d'Enghien, "This is worse than a crime, it's a blunder!" I visited Miss Wiskemann and asked her point-blank why she did not name Eden as the forger of the Rome-Berlin Axis. She replied coyly: "Sir Athony is such a nice man, I would never say anything of the sort about him."

It is worth noting that in David Carlton's *Anthony Eden, A Biography* (London: Allan Lane, 1982), which is very critical of "Lord Avon," nothing is mentioned about Eden's responsibility concerning Austria. Eden in fact hated Mussolini more than Hitler or Stalin. (Op cit., 96, 124.) Hence the lack of a common front against Hitler's invasion of Austria. Mussolini confided to Prince Starhemberg, leader of Austria's *Heimwehr* ("Home Guard"), that France and Britain had left him in the lurch: "I cannot alone resist Hitler!" Cf. Gottfried-Karl Kindermann, op. cit., 175.

800. Admittedly, however, Haile Selassie's rule was ultra-humanitarian in comparison to

the savageries of his massacring, "republican," Bolshevik successor, whose subjects have to be fed by "capitalist" nations.

801. Cf. Herbert L. Matthews, *Eyewitness in Abyssinia* (London: Secker and Warburg, 1937), 319. "Yesterday I wrote an article about the resources of the country, and what the Italians hope to get out of it. I wish them luck. They have earned the place." Later Mr. Matthews became an apologist for Republican Spain and, quite naturally, Castro's Cuba.

802. According to a reliable estimate the Hoare-Laval Agreement would have left to Ethiopia 200,000 out of 350,000 square miles—the higher, wetter, and better lands.

803. Elizabeth Wiskemann thought that it was Pertinax and Madame Tabouis "who learnt of the Hoare-Laval Plan from Herriot, but Laval afterwards told Cerutti (the Italian Ambassador in Berlin) that Herriot did not know, and that he (Laval) suspected a Quai d'Orsay official: naturally he himself disclaimed all responsibility for betraying Hoare to the press" (op. cit., 52n). The author continues, "It has often been supposed—and to this the present writer pleads guilty—that Abyssinia, the Rhineland and Spain formed a chain of Nazi-Fascist connivance. This is not true—how untrue in the case of Ethiopia has already been seen. But from the moment the Hoare-Laval Plan existed Ethiopia became a trump card for Hitler, because it had split the Stresa front and freed him from 'encirclements' " (53).

Duff Cooper, strongly anti-German, was convinced that "the half-hearted sanctions that we imposed served only to infuriate Mussolini and drive him into the arms of Hitler. Doing a minimum of harm we incurred a maximum of ill-will." (Duff Cooper, op. cit., 193.) And later he remarks, "I was unhappy about Anthony Eden's departure. I wrote him to tell him so and to say that I had always found myself in agreement with him, except on this one question of Italy." There was a real personal enmity between Eden and Mussolini that grew as time went on. Eden himself in his memoirs—The Rt. Hon. Earl of Avon, *The Eden Memoirs* (London: Cassell, 1965), vol. 3, "The Reckoning"—is singularly reticent about his blunder but regrets the *Anschluss* in several passages. Neville Chamberlain, on the other hand, thought that Halifax (in Eden's place) could have saved Austria by cooperating with Mussolini more closely. Cf. Keith Feiling, *The Life of Neville Chamberlain* (London: Macmillan, 1946).

804. Cf. Erich Kordt, *Wahn und Wirklichkeit* (Stuttgart: Union Deutsche Verlagsgesellschaft, 1948), 102, n. 2. Halifax was a natural fumbler. He told the German refugee banker Max Warburg, who warned him against Hitler, that the *Führer* was a very honest man and that Warburg's feelings as an emigrant were prejudiced. Cf. Jacques Attali, *Banker in wirrer Zeit. Vom Emigranten zum europäischen Banker* (Düsseldorf: Econ, 1986).

805. Cf. Gordon Brook-Shephard, *Der Anschluss*, G. Coudenhove, trsl. (Graz: Styria, 1963). This author strongly criticizes the pro-German bent of the anti-Nazi leaders of independent Austria. Yet anyone familiar with the history of Austria could hardly expect otherwise. After 1945 the Allied occupation authorities made an effort to eradicate all pro-German sentiments. In the school report cards the word "German" could not be mentioned, and thus the subject was called *Unterrichtssprache*, "language of instruction." Antimilitarism was also written with capital letters, and Austrian

public libraries were not even permitted to handle books pertaining to the history of World War I.

806. The role of Austria as the "other German State" was precisely what created in German Nazi circles the feeling of an "intolerable provocation." It ran counter to the formula, "One people, one realm, one leader": Peter F. Drucker in *The End of Economic Man* (New York: John Day, 1939) understood well that pre-*Anschluss* Austria was valuable as a "psychological alternative" for many a German.

807. Dr. Karl Renner, a Socialist and first President of the Austrian Republic after World War II, stated on April 3, 1938, three weeks after the *Anschluss*, in an interview (*Tagblatt*, Vienna) that he would vote "yes" for Austria's inclusion into Germany. Having been Austria's State Chancellor in 1919, he admitted to feeling a real satisfaction for the humiliations of 1918 and 1919 as well as for the treaties of Versailles and St. Germain-en-Laye. Cardinal Innitzer (despite his courageous protest in November 1938) was "morally dead" after his unfortunate declaration at the plebiscite, while Renner (who wrote a letter to Stalin in 1945 addressing him as "dear comrade") became President of Austria with the blessing of the Allies. Cf. Hellmut Andics, in *Die Presse* (Vienna), July 4, 1962, no. 4231, 8.

808. Cf. G. E. R. Gedye, *Fallen Bastions* (London: Gollancz, 1939), 235. "Except for the Jews, the aristocracy which remained loyal to the old ruling House met perhaps with the worst treatment of any class from Hitler, Bürckel, and Globočnik: there was not even the brief attempt to flatter and cajole them which the Reds 'enjoyed.' "

This policy was supported by Hitler's ingrained antimonarchism. He was always grateful to the Social Democrats for having destroyed the German monarchy. He said verbally about the Republic: "It was a big step forward. It, above all, prepared our way." Cf. Hans Frank, op. cit., 288, and Albert Speer, op. cit., 67. But he really feared the survival of monarchist feelings in Austria, which had been very strong up to November, 1918. Cf. Ludwig A. Windisch-Graetz, *Der Kaiser kämpft für die Freiheit* (Vienna: Herold, 1957), 86-105.

809. Cordell Hull was born in a hamlet in Tennessee. His higher education consisted of one year in the National Normal University, Lebanon, Ohio—all traces have been lost of this educational institution—and one year in the Cumberland University Law School in Lebanon, Tennessee. That same year he was admitted to the bar of Tennessee. This man who, to say the least, passively contributed to laying the foundations of a potential World War III, received the Nobel Peace Prize in 1945.

810. Cf. *Documents on German Foreign Relations, 1918-1945*, series D. I, 604-05. He had good reason to react as he did. Laval, too, knew only too well that the great fatality was not the Munich pact but the surrender of Austria (due to Italy's alienation), for Austria was the bastion of Central Europe. Cf. *Boothby: Recollections of a Rebel* (London: Hutchinson, 1978), 137-38.

811. Cf. *Ambassador Dodd's Diary*, William E. Dodd, Jr., and Martha Dodd, eds. (New York: Harcourt, Brace, 1941), introd. Charles A. Beard.

812. Martha Dodd, years later, fled to Prague to escape arrest by the FBI. She had become an active Communist.

813. Cf. *Ambassador Dodd's Diary*, 101.

814. Ibid., 309 and 396. Lord Lothian became wartime British Ambassador to Washington. According to Dodd, Lothian was thoroughly pro-Hitler (406).

815. Ibid., 119.

816. Ibid., 360.

817. Talking to a professor of a big American university, a specialist in modern German history, I remarked that Hitler was a demagogue like Cleon. "Cleon?" "Yes, Cleon of Athens." "Ah, that's antiquity. It's none of my business." This phenomenon of specialization is by no means restricted to the United States; it is beginning to be worldwide, invading *all* studies and knowledge as a new form of *docta ignorantia*.

818. Cf. *Ambassador Dodd's Diary*, 413.

819. Cf. his *The Black Record* (London, 1940).

820. The geographical-historical confusions created by journalists are worth a separate study. The Near East, for instance, in World War II mysteriously became the Middle East. (The Far East, some time earlier, had became the Orient.) Hitler's West Wall was suddenly named the Siegfried Line by a reporter who remembered the *Siegfried-Linie* ("Victorious Peace Line") of trenches across northern France in World War I. Thus a new mixup took place. The *Blitz* ("Blitzkrieg") refers to the rapid advance of the (German) motorized units. The term had nothing to do with air attacks on more or less defenseless cities. (The German word *Blitz*, lightning, metaphorically refers to speed, not to a blow from the skies.) To call the mass murder of Hebrews, perpetrated by the National Socialists, a "holocaust" only betrays Hollywood's bottomless ignorance and the mass media's parrotlike character. In Greek mythology, a holocaust is a burning sacrifice that seeks both to please the gods and to ask for their intercession.

821. William E. Dodd tells (op. cit., 422) about a conversation between the British Ambassador in Berlin, Henderson, and a high Austrian official. "The British Ambassador said Austria, being Nazi, must be annexed to Germany. This was at once reported to Schuschnigg, the Chancellor of Austria, and that led to immediate telegraphic inquiries in London. Schuschnigg was satisfied by denials from Eden." There is little doubt that Henderson sympathized profoundly with the Third Reich's incorporation plans. Cf. *The Eden Memoirs*, 3:8.

About the desperate efforts of the Austrian foreign minister Guido Schmidt to get British (and French) aid to save Austrian independence, or even to move Sir Robert Vansittart, cf. Hellmut Andics, op. cit., 537-38. The mood in London's Foreign Office is well documented in a passage of Cadogan's diary, dated February 15, 1938: "Was summoned early to the FO as there was a flap about Austria. Personally, I almost wish Germany would swallow Austria and get it over. She is probably going to do so anyway—anyhow we can't stop her. What's all the fuss about?. . . Should not mind if Austria were *gleichgeschaltet*." Cf. *The Diaries of Sir Alexander Cadogen 1938-1945* (London: Cassell, 1971). The same man later on ridiculed the information about Auschwitz and referred to Poles and Jews as notoriously hysterical.

822. Jacques Bainville had ridiculed in 1918 (*Action Française*, February 14) the idea that the disappearance of the Austro-Hungarian monarchy would mean "any progress." It rather would result in endless German ethnic revindications. And in his *Conséquences politiques de la paix* (Paris: Nouvelle Librairie Nationale, 1920), 119-120, he said

about the successor states: "They are not at all disposed to make themselves instruments of the too simple and really naive system imagined by the designers of the peace. These people will wake up and reexamine the situation. They feel, they know that their States are fragile, that they are, in a way, amorphous, that they will immediately be shattered if they clash with a power stronger than themselves. They will assume a prudent neutrality and will take great pains to avoid a conflict with Germany." Only Yugoslavia was imprudent and paid dearly for it (though it saved Moscow by delaying the German attack against Russia). And, as Bainville clearly foresaw, none of the successor states lifted a finger for France in its hour of distress. The poor French taxpayer had again been milked in vain.

823. Cf. Roger Peyrefitte, *Les Ambassades* (Paris: Flammarion), 237-38.

About Beneš's secret negotiations with the Nazis, cf. the letter of Dr. Štefan Osuský in the *New York Times*, October 20, 1958. Beneš was ready to cede the Friedland, Rumburg, and Eger districts to Germany.

824. An Austrian Socialist deputy, Dr. Robert Danneberg, who tried to flee after the *Anschluss*, was extradited to the German authorities who first brought him to Dachau and then to the gas chambers in Poland. Cf. *Neue Volkszeitung*, New York, April 10, 1943. Naturally, many such cases resulted from Dr. Beneš's efforts to ingratiate himself with the Nazis.

825. Cf. Beneš's speech before the Foreign Affairs Committee of the Czechoslovak Parliament. Cf. *Sources et documents tchécoslovaques*, no. 24, 49, 51. See also Lois Eisenmann, op. cit., 111. In early 1932, while working for an influential Hungarian newspaper, I tried through the aid of the Czech Minister in Vienna, Hugo Vavrečka, to get an interview with Dr. Beneš for my paper, hoping to achieve a *détente* between the two countries. The brown danger in Germany, at that time, was mounting. The answer from Prague was negative, and Vavrečka told me frankly that it was his country's policy to bring Hungary economically to its knees: the "democratic" Hungarian peasant would then march on Budapest and destroy the "feudal government" which aimed to revise the iniquitous peace treaty. Vavrečka also acknowledged the German menace, but fully defended the stubbornness and ideological blindness of his country. Even at the ripe old age of twenty-three, I was aghast at the stupidity and hatred.

826. Cf. Dr. Eduard Beneš, *My War Memoirs*, P. Selver, trsl. (London: Allen and Unwin, 1928), 258.

827. One instance of Czech propaganda in the West insisted that the Czechs (who had, relatively, the largest Communist party in free Europe prior to 1930) were "born democrats" because they had no aristocracy. Their old nobility allegedly had all been exterminated after the Battle of the White Mountain. *This is totally untrue.* A large segment of the Bohemia-Moravian nobility was either Czech in origin or sentiment. Families of German extraction had greatly assisted in the revival of the Czech language. A Czech "Almanack de Gotha" was published by Z. R. Kinský, *U nás*, Leopold Novák, ed. (Chlumec: Knihtiskarna V. Klemens, 1933). In fact, the Bohemian-Moravian nobility had always been richer and more influential than the more indigent aristocracy of Alpine Austria. (The old Slovak upper crust, on the other hand, had been Magyarized.) The concept of the "nonaristocratic Czechs" is an integral part of twentieth-century mythology.

828. Cf. László V. Taubinger, "Beneschs Vermächtnis," *Neues Abendland* (Munich), vols. 9, 11 (February 1954), 91, quoting Count Carlo Sforza's *The Totalitarian War and After* (London: Allen and Unwin, 1942).

829. Cf. Fritz Weil, *Das Werden eines Volkes und der Weg eines Mannes: Eduard Beneš* (Dresden: Reissner, 1930), 132.

830. Cf. Kurt von Schuschnigg, *Austrian Requiem*, Franz v. Hildebrand, trsl. (New York: Putnam, 1946), 153, 195.

831. He was also the clever man who apparently passed on the Gestapo-fabricated documents "proving" the treason of Tukhachevski to Stalin. (Cf. Winston S. Churchill, *The Second World War*, 1:225n.) Yet to get a real grasp of the man's ignorance, read his *Democracy Today and Tomorrow* (New York: Macmillan, 1939). Page 8 relates that Alexander Hamilton and John Adams were "pioneers of democracy"—and so forth.

832. Cf. Louis P. Lochner, *What about Germany?* (New York, 1942), 48-49. (This occurred in March 1938.) Compare with the account of Beneš's stubbornness and unpopularity in John de Courcy's *Behind the Battle* (London: Eyre and Spottiswoode, 1942), 241. Sir John Addison, British Minister to Prague, warned Beneš even before the *Anschluss* that only a close association with Austria and Hungary would save his country. But Beneš (then Foreign Minister) declared this would be "the end of Czechoslovakia," which in any case had nothing to fear from Germany. (*Documents of British Foreign Policy*, vol. 6, no. 328, 514-17.) He was sufficiently ignorant and petty to figure in the West as a "great statesman." His foreign minister, Kamil Krofta, viewed the incorporation of Austria in August 1938 as a real improvement of Czechoslovakia's geopolitical situation as it destroyed the alliance between Rome, Vienna, and Budapest. Whom the gods want to destroy. . .

833. Cf. Eduard Beneš, "The Organization of Post-War Europe," op. cit., 242.

834. Cf. Eduard Beneš, *Democracy Today and Tomorrow*, 182.

835. Cf. Eduard Beneš, "The Organization of Post-War Europe," op. cit., 237-38.

836. Cf. Eduard Beneš, "Toward Peace in Central and Eastern Europe," in *The Annals of the American Academy of Political and Social Science* (Philadelphia), March 1944, 165-66. Here one can see how one National Socialism learns from another.

837. Jan Masaryk told Halifax on May 2, 1938, that his father had not wanted to include the Sudeten Germans in the new republic, but Lloyd George insisted on it. Cf. *Documents on British Foreign Policy*, III, 1, 237. This is difficult to believe, but not out of the question.

838. Cf. Francis Deák, *Hungary at the Paris Peace Conference* (New York: Columbia University Press, 1942), 531. The murder of German-speaking Bohemians and Moravians in armed attacks during the transition period (1918-1919) shook world opinion as little as the large-scale massacres in 1945.

839. The late Wenzel Jaksch, former leader of the Social Democratic party of the German minority in Czechoslovakia, wrote that during the mobilization in 1921, only 30 percent of the *Czech* population answered the call to arms when an invasion of Hungary was planned to foil the attempted restoration of Emperor-King Charles. Jaksch later was witness to the failure of this brand new "loyalty." Cf. his *Europas Weg nach Potsdam* (Cologne: Verlag für Wissenschaft und Politik, n.d.), 528.

840. Cf. Daniel Seligman, "The Collapse of Czech Democracy," *The American Mercury*, March 1948, 313.

841. Yet Beneš's popularity was great only in Western leftist circles; at home he was unpopular and he knew it: "Don't you realize that I am the most unpopular man in Czechoslovakia?" he asked a Swiss journalist. Cf. Robert de Traz, "M. Masaryk et M. Beneš," *La Revue de Paris*, vol. 37, no. 5 (March 1, 1930), 58.

842. Douglas Woodruff tells in his column in *The Tablet* (London, December 20, 1947, 394) about Stanley Baldwin: "He was, it must be admitted, intensely insular: I recall this, for instance: 'That was the first thing, I said on packing up my traps and leaving Downing Street, now I never need speak to another foreigner again!'," And about the nomination of Eden, Baldwin had remarked, "Nobody else knew all the foreigners about whom it was necessary to be informed, and there was no time for anyone else to get to know them." Churchill also spoke about the "marked ignorance of Europe and aversions from its problems in Mr. Baldwin." (*The Second World War*, 1:69.)

843. Cf. AP report, dated London, September 21,1936, in the *New York Herald Tribune*, September 22, 1936. When Lloyd George returned to his hotel in Berchtesgaden, his daughter greeted him facetiously with "Heil Hitler"! The old gentleman became very serious and replied earnestly and with gravity, "Yes, indeed, Heil Hitler, this is what I say to myself, because he is, in fact, a great man." Cf. Dr. Paul Schmidt, *Statist auf diplomatischer Bühne, 1923-1945* (Vienna: Ullstein Verlag, 1953), 346.

844. Cf. note 725.

845. Viscount Templewood (Sir Samuel Hoare) informed that in October 1938 the British air force had one hundred fighter planes as against one thousand German bombers, cf. his *Nine Troubled Years* (London: Collins, 1954), 333. Ian McLeod says that in October 1938, Britain only had two, in September 1939, five fully armed divisions, cf. his *Neville Chamberlain* (London: Atheneum, 1962), 264. In October 1938, Britain had only one-tenth of the necessary antiaircraft guns and only 1,430 searchlights; in London there were only sixty fire engines. (Ibid., 266.) Thus the bitter fruits of the pacifism of the preceding Labourite government, eager to antagonize Hitler, but not to rearm.

846. On the "democratic," mass character of the dictatorships born in the first half of the century, cf. Emil Lederer, *State of the Masses: The Threat of the Classless Society* (New York: W. W. Norton, 1940), 98, 110, and Gyula Szekfü, *Három nemzedék es ami utana következik* (Budapest: Egyetemi nyomda, 1934), 497. Also Frank Thiess, *Freiheit bis Mitternacht* (Zsolnay: Vienna-Hamburg, 1965), 474sq.

847. Cf. end of note 820. *"Der böhmische Gefreite"* is the German version.

848. The National Socialists tried unsuccessfully to frame General von Fritsch with a homosexual agent provocateur. Baron Fritsch was killed during the siege of Warsaw in September 1939. Fritsch's removal was necessary in order to eliminate a generalissimo (*Oberbefehlshaber der Wehrmacht*) who opposed armed German intervention in Austria. At this juncture, the German General Staff should have acted—despite the much larger SA and SS formations—but it did not.

849. After the abortive attempt to assassinate Hitler in July 1944, three German army regulations were changed: instead of saluting the military way, soldiers and officers had to use the *deutscher Gruss.*, i.e., had to say *Heil Hitler*; non-Christians (*Gott-*

gläubige, mere theists), were permitted to become commissioned officers; soldiers in the *Wehrmacht* no longer had to deposit their party membership cards with the NSDAP before entering military service. That is, prior to this, no active party member could be a soldier in the German army. This Army-Party dualism must be understood in the light of the anti-Nazi sentiment of the bulk of the officers' corps, of the so-called "Junkers and Militarists."

850. Cf. Eberhard Zeller, *Geist der Freiheit. Der Zwanzigste Juli* (Munich: Hermann Rinn, 1954), 37; Gerhard Ritter, *Carl Goerdeler und die deutsche Widerstandsbewegung* (Munich: Deutscher Taschenbuchverlag, 1964), 195-96; Franklin L. Ford, "The Twentieth of July in the History of the German Resistance," *The American Historical Review*, vol. 51, July 1946, 616-17; Allen Welsh Dulles, "Le complot qui eu fait échouer Munich," *France-Illustration*, no. 110 (November 8, 1947), 415-19. Ewald von Kleist (later executed) had also gone to London, and at a time when Churchill was still fairly cooperative. Kleist informed Churchill that the aim of the conspiracy was peace and the restoration of the monarchy. (G. Ritter, op. cit., 188.) By now the literature on this tragic chapter in the history of the German resistance is enormous. What has been cited is a small fraction of the whole.

851. (Sir) Ivone Kirkpatrick told me in July 1939 about the Godesberg meeting at which he had been present in his capacity as a British diplomat accredited in Berlin. Hitler ranted and shouted, spoke about the German spirit embodied in Marienburg Castle in Prussia, invoked philosophers, theologians, kings, and generals. Dr. Paul Schmidt, official German interpreter, questioned Kirkpatrick with his eyes, asking whether he should translate the rot. Throughout, Neville Chamberlain looked like a little boy waiting to receive some nasty medicine. There was not the slightest meeting of minds. (Sir Ivone Kirkpatrick became British High Commissioner in Germany after the war.)

It was also true that the Sudeten Germans had a real case. H. N. Brailsford, famous British leftist journalist, had pointed out back in 1920 that more than 3 million Sudeten Germans, placed under Czech rule against their wills, were a serious handicap to world peace. Arnold J. Toynbee in a long article published on July 10, 1937, in *The Economist* had to admit that "in Czechoslovakia today the methods by which the Czechs are keeping the upper hand over the Sudetendeutsche are not democratic." The Dean of St. Paul's Cathedral (W. R. Matthews), in a letter to the *Times* on June 2, 1938, advocated "self-determination" for the Sudenten Germans and protested against the possibility of Britain fighting a war to prevent self-determination. The same ideas were expressed by Lord Noel Buxton, a true liberal, in a letter to the *Times* on March 22, 1938. These facts have to be viewed in relation to Göring's boast to Sir Nevile Henderson that "London had only fourteen anti-aircraft guns and nothing to prevent Germany from dropping 1,000 to 2,000 bombs a day on London." (The *London Times*, November 25, 1940.)

852. Cf. *Chips: the Diaries of Sir Henry Channon*, R. R. James, ed. (Harmondsworth: Penquin, 1970), 529.

853. To understand some of the more sinister or ironical aspects of the peace treaties of 1919, the reader should turn to Harold Nicolson, *Peacemaking 1919* (Boston: Houghton Mifflin, 1933); H. W. V. Temperley, *A History of the Peace Conference of Paris* (London: H. Frowde, 1920-1924, 6 vols.); André P. Tardieu, *La Paix* (Paris: Payot,

1933); Francesco Nitti, *La Pace* (Turin: P. Gobetti, 1925); and Henri Pozzi, *Les coupables* (Paris: Editions Européennes, 1935) (not always reliable but with valuable details), and *La guerre revient* (Paris: P. Berger, 1933). Hatred, prejudice, and ignorance found a new synthesis. Often the Peace Treaty of Brest-Litovsk (1918) is referred to as proof that, had the Central Powers won, they would have been neither more prudent nor more lenient. John Wheeler-Bennett (*The Foreign Peace*, New York, 1948), made this point. But the Central Powers in 1918 were not prepared to hand over a maximum of territory to red tyranny; in fact, in 1920, Lenin offered *additional* territory to Poland. The Treaty of Brest-Litovsk left to Soviet Russia and the Ukraine (unjustly, to be sure) *more* than the Russian share of all the three partitions of Poland.

854. Almost all these Americans of Slovak origin belonged to the (pro-Czech) Lutheran minority. Of course, Czechoslovaks exist no more than do "Bulgaroserbs." Henri Pozzi tells that Wilson, unsurprisingly, confused the Slovaks with the Slovenes (and Silesia with Cilicia). Not only do Slovaks and Slovenes exist, but also Slovyaks, Slavs, Slavonians, and Slovintsians. There is also Old Slavonic, a dead, liturgical language (which has nothing to do with Slavonia).

855. Cf. *Franklin D. Roosevelt: His Personal Letters, 1928-1945*, Elliott Roosevelt, ed. (New York: Duell, Sloane, Pearce, 1950), 2:818. Letter of the President to Ambassador William Phillips in Rome, dated October 17, 1938. The President expressed his satisfaction in letters to the Canadian Prime Minister. Cf. ibid., 816. Sumner Welles was also in favor of the Munich Agreement. Cf. the *New York Times*, October 4, 1938. (The *New York Times* itself in an editorial on September 30, 1938, had a few reservations, but, by and large, it accepted the pact.)

856. Cf. Peter de Mendelssohn, *The Age of Churchill* (London: Thames & Hudson, 1961), 274-75.

857. Cf. Harold Nicolson, *Curzon: The Last Phase* (London: Constable, 1934), 204. Mr. Bevin, later Foreign Minister (1945), then a TUC leader, went so far as to threaten a general strike were the British Government to assist Poland "directly or indirectly."

858. Of Churchill's political meanderings in his earlier years, cf. Peter de Mendelssohn, *The Age of Churchill 1874-1911* (London: Thames and Hudson, 1961), *passim*. Churchill's religious practice was unnoticeable. Cf. Randolph S. Churchill, *Winston Spencer Churchill* (London: Heinemann, 1966), 1:157-58.

859. Recalling that Churchill demonstrated to Stalin, with the help of three matches, how Poland could easily be "moved" westward at the expense of Germany (vol. 5 of his *Second World War*) one wonders at his words in the famous Fulton speech (March 5, 1946): "I have a strong admiration and regard for the valiant Russian people and for my wartime comrade Marshal Stalin. . . . The Russian-dominated Polish Government has been encouraged to make enormous and wrongful inroads upon Germany, and mass expulsions of Germans on a scale grievous and undreamed of are taking place." (The mass deportations had of course been agreed upon in Potsdam!)

860. Cf. Winston S. Churchill, "The Truth about Hitler," *Strand Magazine* (London), November 1935, 19-20.

861. Cf. Winston S. Churchill, *Step by Step* (New York, 1939), 143-44. This was written in 1937.

862. Cf. *Boothby*, op. cit., 135.

863. Throughout the fourteenth and fifteenth centuries Prague had been the capital of the first German *Reich*; it was where the Holy Roman Emperors (of the Luxemburg and Habsburg dynasties) resided. Prague had a Germanic character; before Luther's translation of the Bible, the only standardized German was the language used by the Imperial Chancellery in Prague (*Prager Kanzleisprache*). Czech history is an integral part of German history; Polish, Hungarian, Croat history is not.

864. Cf. Winston S. Churchill, *The Second World War*, 1:252. Czechoslovakia, created in 1918 (without historic precedent), was considered a temporary arrangement by Hungary and Poland. The Teschen region occupied by Poland in October 1938 had a clear Polish majority (Polish deputies were in the parliaments in Vienna and later in Prague). It was given over to Czechoslovakia by the conference of the ambassadors in July 28, 1920, as the Red Army marched on Warsaw. Poland protested in vain. The Hungarians reoccupied Magyar-inhabited areas, which had belonged to Hungary for over one thousand years until 1920 (Treaty of Trianon). Not to occupy these areas would have meant leaving them to the Germans. If the French had annexed Kent and Sussex at the time of the Congress of Vienna, would it have been immoral in 1871 for Britain to have wrenched these areas from a "prostrate France"?

We now know from Lord Moran how gravely ill Churchill was during and after World War II and should in consequence view his words and actions with some leniency. Cf. his *Churchill* (London: Constable, 1966). That in the Great Emergency there was no one else endowed with manliness, authority, and courage is merely one more proof that the qualities of the pre-World War I generation were (and are) missing in our times. Around 1960 Europe was ruled by septuagenarians and octagenarians. They have been succeeded by "small fry."

As to the Teschen (Cieszyn) area, cf. the letter of Ignacy Jan Paderewski, addressed on July 28, 1920, to the President of the Council of Ambassadors, A. Miller, and quoted by W. Kulski and M. Potulicki in *Recueil de textes de droit international* (Warsaw, 1939), 278ff.

865. Polish Jews did not live in ghettos prior to World War II: there were, quite naturally, Jewish quarters, or neighborhoods, predominantly populated by Jews, a phenomenon prevalent in Western Europe and North America, just as in Dutch cities there are Catholic, or in New York German quarters. Nor was the medieval Jewish quarter in its origin an institution imposed by the Christian authorities. Jews, according to their religion, were not permitted to live in *trefen*, gentile houses. Cf. Guido Kisch, *The Jews in Medieval Germany* (Chicago: The University of Chicago Press, 1949), 292: "There can no longer be any doubt that the separation of the Jewish from the general settlements in medieval cities had its origin in the free will of the early Jewish settlers and by no means in compulsory measures imposed on them. Such measures would be absolutely contradictory to the alluring conditions of settlement offered at times to Jewish immigrants, such as those included in the old Rhenish Jewry privileges. . . . Inclosure within walls or behind a gate was at first considered a particular favor by the Jews." When in the 1860s the walls of the Jewish *borghetto* in Rome were torn down at the behest of Pius IX, the rabbis protested vigorously. The walls had made them feel protected and privileged. (The term "ghetto" was derived from that wall.)

866. The Polish "Fascist aristocratic landowner" (with monarchist, clerical, and plutocratic innuendos) is a bugbear in the Western world. Yet large land ownership in Poland

prior to 1939 was by no means substantial. Before the agrarian reform, enacted by the old "reactionary" government, 73 percent of the arable land belonged to the peasants, rich or poor, i.e., to persons holding fewer than one hundred hectares or 247 acres. After the land reform which divided just over 8 million or 47 percent of the bigger holdings, more than 87 percent of the arable territory belonged to small and middle-size holders of not more than the aforementioned 247 acres. These data do not include forests. Cf. R. Krygier, "Poland's Agrarian Policy," *The Polish Review* (New York), vol. 3, no. 38 (October 18, 1943), 11.

867. This is the real Prussia. (West Prussia was a nonhistoric name given to the lands that had been Polish between 1446 and 1776.) East Prussia is a much maligned area of Germany. Cf. the nice sentence, "In view of East Prussia's long history of leadership in German militarism its complete euthanasia is, on the whole, justified." Where did this bright remark come from? John Kenneth Galbraith's *Reconstruction in Europe* (Washington, D. C.: The National Planning Association, 1947), 21. What about Kant, Herder, Simson, Hamann, and Wiechert? Were they militarists? The humanitarian wisdom of Mr. Galbraith, an economist of note, has its counterpart in the representation of East Prussia in the *New Yorker's* "Our Own Baedeker" (vol. 20, no. 23, July 22, 1944, 12). These facetious irresponsibilities often have disastrous effects in the long run.

868. Cf. Dr. Paul Schmidt, op. cit., 473-74. Ribbentrop despised England and was deeply impressed by Russia. He was desperate when Hitler declared war on the USSR. Cf. Henry Picker, op. cit., 238-39, and Valentin Byerezhkov, "Na rubyezhe mira i voyny (S diplomaticheskoy missiyey v Berlinye 1940-1941)," *Novy Mir*, vol. 41 no. 7 (July 1965), 143-84.

869. Hitler's Anglomania knew no bounds. This much emerges clearly from his "Table Talks." Cf. Dr. Henry Picker, op. cit., *passim*. On p. 145 (September 8-10, 1941), for instance, Hitler spoke about the glorious day he probably would not live to see, when the British and the Germans, shoulder to shoulder, would fight against the United States. Needless to say, he knew neither England nor the United States.

870. Cf. Joseph C. Harsch, *Germany at War* (New York: Foreign Policy Association, 1942), 7-8, and Albert Speer, op. cit., 180-81. Having spent the first three days of World War II in Germany and seen the general despair (compared to the enthusiasm and clear conscience in 1914), I told everyone upon returning to the United States that such a melancholy nation could not possibly win a war. I was *basically* right. Yet, while relatively easy to foretell events, it is most difficult to forecast their timing. I could not guess that defeat would not come until 1945 (nor could I guess the chief cause for the delay: unconditional surrender).

   Lack of enthusiasm was especially strong in the army. Harsch (op. cit., 46-47) said correctly, "Thinking back over a year and a half in wartime Germany, I am impressed by the fact that the most intelligent, the most interesting, the most fair-minded—in fact, in all respects the most honorable—men I met were in the army, serving people they despised to an end in which they did not believe, but welcoming the opportunity to forget their feelings about these men and those ends in what seemed to them a last means of serving their country." This frightening dichotomy under which the army suffered is highlighted by a conversation in Russia between Ernst Jünger and Colonel Ravenstein, an acquaintance from World War I. "I asked him about the 'torture huts' (*Schinderhütten*) and how he could square their evidence with the honor of arms and the wearing of military decorations. Without entering into the matter he gave me a reply which to me came unexpectedly: 'For this, perhaps, my youngest daughter will have to pay some day in a Negro brothel.'" Cf. his *Strahlungen*, 330. See also the memoirs of R. C. Baron Gersdorff, *Soldat im Untergang* (Berlin: Ullstein, 1977), 62. After the outbreak of the war, young officers took up the sport of using a portrait of Hitler for pistol practice. (The riddled picture was then burned in the garden off the officers' mess.)

871. Another American observer was convinced that the generals felt more bitter enmity toward Hitler than toward the Communists. Cf. Howard K. Smith, *Last Train from Berlin* (New York: Knopf, 1942), 280. Hitler suspected quite rightly that nobody among the bourgeoisie or the Marxists would dare assassinate him. (Dr. Henry Picker, op.cit., 307, May 3,1942.) Actually, the man who came nearest to killing him was a Catholic officer, Count Klaus Schenk von Stauffenberg, neither a bourgeois nor a Marxist.

   Another good account of Germany during the war was given by the Swedish journalist Arvid Fredborg in his book *Bakom Stälvallen*, American edition: *Behind the Steel Wall (A Swedish Jounalist in Berlin 1941-1943)* (New York: The Viking Press, 1944), especially 74-75, 239, 241, 248, 275.

872. The diaries of Ulrich von Hassell, a German diplomat executed by the National Socialists, make the most melancholy reading. Every victory of Hitler, every success of his country ("My country wrong, not right!") plunged him into a new fit of depression. Cf. his *Vom anderen Deutschland. Aus den nachgelassenen Tagebüchern 1938-1944* (Zürich: Atlantis, 1946).

873. By far the best biography of Canaris is K.H. Abshagen, *Canaris, Patriot und Weltbürger* (Stuttgart: Union Deutsche Verlagsgesellschaft, 1949). This splendid book not only brings out the facts, but also presents the man's character. It sounds incredible, but I heard about Canaris's role in New York in 1943, while the Admiral was still active. His widow was invited by Franco to come to Spain where she was given a pension. As for General Oster, who paid with his life in 1944, cf. Roger Keyes, *Outrageous Fortune: The Tragedy of Leopold III of the Belgians* (London: Secker & Warburg, 1984), 133. This well-documented volume repeatedly gives credit to the forces of resistance in the German army.

874. See his book, *Die Zweite Revolution* (München-Zwickau: Franz Eher, 1927), 47, where he writes, "We are looking to Russia because she is most likely to march with us in the direction of socialism—because Russia is for us the natural ally against the diabolic infection and corruption coming from the West."

875. Hitler repeatedly boasted about the speed with which the opinion of his press on political matters could "make a 180 degree turn." He cited the case of his attack on Russia, cf. Henry Picker, op. cit., 344. The press, of course, is enabled to change its viewpoint with such speed only because the masses are fickle, their loyalties ephemeral, their convictions ungrounded, their factual knowledge imperceptible. In January 1945 the people of Milan cheered Mussolini wildly; a few months later they were

spitting on his corpse. Cf. Luigi Barzini, *The Italians* (London: Hamish Hamilton, 1964), 155.

876. Joachim Ribbentrop was adopted by a titled aunt and used the name "von Ribbentrop." He figures in the *Genealogisches Handbuch der adeligen Häuser* (Limburg: Starke, 1961), 5:306, as "nonnoble user of the name." This means that in the defunct monarchy he would have been prosecuted for using a title without the monarch's patent or permission.

877. Cf. Paul Schmidt, op. cit., 481.

878. While the western border of Poland was fixed at Versailles, the eastern one resulted from the Treaty of Riga (1921) between Poland and Soviet Russia. The Versailles Treaty, as Americans and British (and news editors) should bear in mind, dealt only with *Germany*—and with no other country. Many other treaties were made in the 1919-1923 period: St. Germain-en-Laye (Austria), Neuilly (Bulgaria), Sèvres (first treaty with Turkey), Trianon (Hungary), Lausanne (second treaty with Turkey).

879. Molotov's speech was made before the Ts.I.K. (Central Executive Committee of the USSR) on October 31, 1939. It was reprinted in *Soviet Russia Today* (New York), November 1939.

880. Not only Portuguese and Spanish volunteers went to fight with the Finns, but even Britishers. (An English friend of mine lost his leg in Karelia.) Actually, London and Paris were preparing an expeditionary corps to come to the aid of Finland when the armistice was declared.

881. The *relatively* largest organized Communist parties west of the Iron Curtain are in Iceland and Finland. Iceland is a very prosperous country with high living standards, as is Finland, which even "enjoys" being the immediate neighbor of Russia. Yet ideology is blind to experience. It is autonomous. And Nordic communism (as in Swedish Lapland) is based on convictions, not, as in Italy, on mere grudges or a sort of collective blackmail (bigger red votes mean bigger wages).

882. Terijoki is a resort about halfway between Viborg (Viipuri) and Leningrad on the Karelian Isthmus, now part of the USSR. Here the first "People's Democratic Republic," a delightful pleonasm coined by an illiterate, was established. The next step could only be a "Popular People's Democratic Republic"—with no rights whatsoever for the people.

883. Sir Owen O'Malley, British Minister to Hungary, was also evacuated through Vladivostok, making the trip from Hungary through the Soviet Union eastward. He and his party were treated like criminals in early 1941, whereas the Germans trying to reach their fatherland were practically guests of honor.

884. Cf. Georgi Dimitrov, *Der Kampf gegen den imperialistischen Krieg* (Stockholm: Weltbibliothek, 1940), 14. On Georgi M. Dimitrov, cf. *The Fate of East Central Europe* (Notre Dame: The University of Notre Dame Press, 1956), 275-76. The late Georgi Dimitrov, like all the Communists of the older generation, had been a Social Democrat in his earlier years.

885. An anonymous German author wrote in 1949, cf., "La responsabilité des officiers," in *Temps Modernes*, 5 year, no. 46-47, August-September 1949, 495-96.

National Socialism could have been overcome from inside by a revolution, but only if an important opposition had existed among the lower classes, prepared to sacrifice everything to the revolution, to follow the officers, flag-bearers of the revolt. Any other attempt at rebellion would have been considered reactionary by the masses and passionately resisted. . . There is no revolution of leaders without the people. Yet, aside from the fact that an ideology in favor of an uprising was lacking among the people, those men who today lay the entire blame on the German officer should instead feel themselves responsible. One must also assume that they believed that a new revolutionary uprising would mature years after the events of 1933.

886. Cf. letter in *The Commonweal*, March 12, 1965, 751. The conclusion is inescapable after a reading of the post-victory plans of Himmler, which include periodic shooting parties with human victims in the Eastern Marches of the great German Reich. I admittedly reason as a Christian: the liquidation of Christianity was a definite Nazi plan. On February 2, 1942, Hitler declared he would exterminate Christianity— just as effectively as another superstition, witchcraft, had been wiped out. He called Christianity *eine Kulturschande*, a "cultural scandal." Cf. Henry Picker, op. cit., 176.

887. Cf. *The Journals of Søren Kierkegaard*, a selection of Alexander Dru, ed. (London-New York: Oxford University Press, 1938), no. 1210 (April 1951).

888. A complete English translation of *Mein Kampf* did not exist before 1941. Of course, the *modern* statesman cannot (or can hardly) be a scholar or at least a real *student* of world affairs: vote-getting consumes half his time. Nor, for that matter, were all leading National Socialists avid readers of *Mein Kampf*. Fritz Wiedemann says that many people in Hitler's entourage had never perused this fateful book (op. cit., 56). Göring also admitted this in 1946 during the Nuremberg Trial. We obviously are going through an interesting period of semiliteracy, where everybody can write, but few people will or can read.

889. Cf. note 810. And, as Robert Murphy pointed out, "Hull was often depicted as the most anti-Soviet member of the Roosevelt Cabinet, whereas he was virtually cocreator with the President of the 'Grand Design' for the postwar world, a plan which assumed that the United States and Soviet Russia could become partners in peace because circumstances had made them partners in war." Murphy quotes Hull's address to Congress after his return from the Foreign Ministers' Conference in Algiers during which the Secretary of State said, "There will no longer be need for spheres of influence, for alliances, for balance of power, or any other of the special arrangements through which, in the unhappy past, the nations strove to safeguard their security or to promote their interests." Cf. Robert Murphy, *Diplomat Among Warriors* (London: Collins, 1964), 259. The Nobel Peace Prize was indeed a shabby reward for such a brilliant mind.

890. Cf. Jan Ciechanowski, *Defeat in Victory* (Gardon City, N.Y.: Doubleday, 1947), 223.

891. Cf. Graf Hermann Keyerling, *Das Spektrum Europas* (Heidelberg: Niels Kampmann, 1928), 23-33.

892. Cf. Jan Ciechanowski, op. cit., 330-31.

893. *Vide*, for instance, *The Stilwell Papers* (New York: William Sloane, 1948), 251-54.

894. Cf. *The Economist* (London), vol. 152, no. 5393 (January 4, 1947), 20-21.

895. Cf. Robert I. Gannon, S.J., *The Cardinal Spellman Story* (New York; Doubleday, 1962), 222-25. See also note 926.

896. Cf. Elliot Roosevelt, *As Father Saw It* (New York: Duell, Sloane and Pearce, 1946), 117. On Churchill and unconditional surrender cf. also Emrys Hughes, *Winston Churchill in War and Peace* (Glasgow: Unity Publishing, 1950), 206ff. The formula, which Roosevelt thought had terminated the Civil War, was actually used by U.S. Grant in February 1862 during the siege of Fort Donelson in Tennessee. Impossible as it seems, the unconditional surrender formula was defended as recently as 1955 by an American scholar: "On all counts and contemporary criticisms notwithstanding, it was one of the most effective achievements of American statesmanship of the entire war period." Cf. John L. Chase, "Unconditional Surrender," *The Political Science Quarterly*, Summer 1955, 279.

897. Cf. General Albert C. Wedemeyer, *Wedemeyer Reports!* (New York: Henry Holt, 1958), 90-91. Churchill's quoted remark was made on February 27, 1945, in the House of Commons. (Cf. also his speech on September 31, 1943.)

898. Cf. David Irving, *The Destruction of Dresden* (London: William Kimber, 1963), 20-25. Irving points out that under the terms of Article 25 of the 1907 Hague Convention, Rotterdam could be attacked because it was not an undefended city. (The same could be said of Warsaw.) Only forty of the hundred attacking planes heard the signal canceling the attack. The number of people killed, according to the American press, was forty thousand. The rectified data were supplied to David Irving by Rotterdam authorities in 1962.

899. Cf. Winston S. Churchill, *The Second World War*, 2:567.

900. Cf. note 820.

901. Cf. J. M. Spaight, *The Battle of Britain* (London: Geoffrey Bles, 1941), 22-24, 30, 34, 217, 220, and *isdem, Bombing Vindicated* (London: Geoffrey Bles, 1944), 74.

902. Cf. Basil Liddell-Hart, "War Limited," *Harper's*, March 1946, 198-99.

903. Cf. J. C. F. Fuller, *The Second World War, 1935-1945* (New York: Duell, Sloane and Pearce, 1949), 222-23.

904. In Buchenwald concentration camp Princess Mafalda, daughter of King Victor Emmanuel III and wife of Prince Philip of Hesse, was severely wounded and died a few days later. In an Allied attack on the Hague eight hundred Dutchmen were killed (almost as many as by the Germans in Rotterdam) and twenty thousand left homeless. Cf. *New York Times*, March 25, 1945. The air massacre of Belgrade on April 17, 1944, turned many Serbs against the Western Allies. Only one-half the Allied bombs were dropped on Germany; one-eighth landed on Italy and *one-fifth on France*. More Frenchmen were killed by Allied than by German bombs. According to a semiofficial statistic, no fewer than 67,078 Frenchmen were killed and 75,660 wounded by the Allied air warfare between 1941 and 1944. Cf. Robert Aron, *Histoire de Vichy 1940-1944* (Paris: Fayard, 1954), 604.

905. Cf. Bernard Iddings Bell, *Crowd Culture* (New York: Harper, 1952), 25-26.

906. Even Sir Compton MacKenzie did. This great Conservative, Scottish Nationalist, and Catholic convert suddenly developed pro-Soviet sympathies, as seen in the last volume of his *Winds of Love*. The fascination undoubtedly transcended the leftist camp.

907. As quoted by Oswald Garrison Villard in the *Christian Century*, March 14, 1945, 334. (Speech of December 5, 1939.)

908. This is why the Socialist (Social Democratic) parties are always susceptible to the "Call of the Wild." (The term Social Democrat was coined by the near-anarchist Bakunin.) It is true that the East German, Hungarian, Czech, Polish, and Rumanian Socialists have often fled the dominion of Moscow, but the Communists have forced Socialists (Social Democrats) into the camp of "Socialist Unity"—not other parties. There are two kinds of run-of-the-mill Socialists: those who have really watered the Marxist wine, and those who are Marxists but want to achieve the Great Goal democratically by parliamentary majorities. In an emergency, i.e., in case of a Communist takeover, the former usually emigrate and the latter collaborate. Yet Socialists who want to establish a collectivist state and society by persuasion (i.e., by "cerebral conquest") are just as much enemies of the right order as the revolutionaries who want to achieve an evil social system by the "dictatorship of the proletariat." The ends are always reprehensible, only the means differ morally. And, in a deeper sense, popular feelings notwithstanding, the seducer is more diabolic and destructive than the rapist.

909. Eugene Lyons called this film the intellectual abdication of America. It probably was the grossest piece of propaganda ever projected on the American screen.

910. Miss Lillian Hellman also helped to direct a film with idyllic scenes of Russian collective farms.

911. Cf. Quentin Reynolds, *Only the Stars Are Neutral* (New York: Random House, 1942).

912. Ibid., 284.

913. Ibid., 207.

914. Ibid., 98. Considering the highly critical public utterances of Father Braun after his return, one wonders what he told or did not tell Mr. Reynolds. As to religion in the USSR, the authoritative books of Walter Kolarz (*Religion in the Soviet Union*, London: Macmillan, 1962) and Nikita Struve (*Les chrétiens en USSR*, Paris: Seuil, 1964), paint a depressing and frightful picture.

915. Only Rhode Island among the original states had no establishment or religious tests for office. Disestablishment in Massachusetts came only in 1833. In New Hampshire only "Protestants" could be elected to Congress until 1877, and in New Jersey only a Protestant could hold public office until 1844. Congress also continued to vote public funds for Protestant missions among Indians. Here again is a potent myth. Cf. also Joseph McSorley, CSP, *Father Hecker and His Friends* (St. Louis: B. Herder Book Co., 1952), 69. See also the letter by H. J. Freeman in *The Commonweal*, vol. 76, no. 20, September 7, 1962, 495-96, full of specific data and referring to a recent decision of the Supreme Court proving its irrational stand on the First Amendment. "If the Black-Rutledge interpretation of the amendment was correct," he wrote, "then Congress had been acting unconstitutionally for 160 years during which it passed law after law concerning religion or religious institutions, and Madison did not know the meaning of the amendment he himself had drafted."

916. Those who read Alexander Solzhenitsyn's splendid novel *The First Circle* about a "swank" concentration camp (for technological specialists) in 1949 should also delve

into the even more terrifying account of Anatoli Marchenko, *My Testimony*, which deals with concentration camps in the 1970s. Only the very naive think that they have disappeared. (Marchenko died in jail in 1986.)

917. Cf. the terrible statistics of Nikita Struve's op. cit., Annex IV, dealing with the martyred bishops of the USSR.

918. Cf. Quentin Reynolds, op. cit., 173.

919. Ibid., 110.

920. In 1914 people in England stoned dachshunds, German shepherds were renamed alsatians, and German pianos were burned; in Paris German-owned shops were destroyed; in Germany patriots greeted each other with "*Gott strafe England*"; and in the United States *sauerkraut* was renamed "liberty cabbage"—previously unthinkable phenomena.

921. Lisa Sergio was a fanatical "anti-Fascist," leftist radio commentator, yet in a book of hers published a few years earlier in Italy—*From Intervention to Empire* (Rome: Novissima, 1937)—she wrote, "Notwithstanding the many deficiencies in this first book of Fascist Dates, I dedicate it to the memory of all the Black Shirts who, within Italy and abroad, have written in their blood the glorious dates of the Fascist Era." This historic calendar is not uninteresting. Thus on page 177, under the heading July 25, 1934: "Herr Dollfuss, Austrian Chancellor, is assassinated by the Reds in Vienna." That the reds were National Socialists is a piece of newspeak.

922. When I asked a Hungarian refugee and noted Iranian scholar who I heard was working in the OWI (Office of War Information), whether he was in the German department, he answered somberly, "*Je ne suis pas encore tombé si bas*"—"I have not as yet fallen so low."

923. Cf. Erik v. Kuehnelt-Leddihn, *Black Banners* (Caldwell: Caxton Printers, 1954), 279-80. Brazen lies, needless to say, are usually the most successful ones, especially if they are savagely stupid and contradict truth. Take, for instance, the review of Abel Plenn's *Wind in Olive Trees* by W. E. Garrison in the *Christian Century*, June 1946, 781. It includes the statement that "most Spanish liberal leaders, including 30,000 Protestants, had been exterminated" (i.e., by the Franco regime). I immediately wrote Garrison, who was literary editor of the *Christian Century*, inquiring why nobody had previously reported the biggest "sectarian massacre" in all history. I never received a reply and, naturally, my letter never appeared in the worthy (leftist) magazine.

　　Cf. also Gustav Stolper, *This Age of Fable* (New York: Reynal and Hitchcock, 1942), 328. "The position of Hitlerism in public discussions has been largely fixed by the fact that the bulk of anti-Hitler literature . . . was written by Marxist authors of various denominations. As their political thinking was tied down to the Procrustean bed of primitive social philosophy, all they had to do was to fit the phenomenon of Hitlerism into their ready-made scheme. Since Hitler was anti-Marxist—whatever that meant—he must be the puppet of Capitalists. Once that was taken for granted, the details of the story were freely invented." Again bear in mind that the connection between class and ideology or financial interest is very flimsy. The three "Angels" of the New York *Daily Worker* were wealthy women: Susan Homans Woodruff, a DAR member; Anne Whitacker Pennypacker, daughter of Samuel

Pennypacker, governor of Pennsylvania; and Mrs. Fernando W. Reed, daughter of a Cambridge physician.

924. In the earlier 1940s, General Electric published in leading American periodicals a full-page ad featuring a miserable crowd of women and children dragging a plow. The text called this a common sight in Central Europe. Yet a poster showing American schoolchildren, two of them barefoot, drew violent protests. And I know of American teachers who tried to bolster the patriotism of their pupils by telling them that their ancestors in Europe ate *black* bread. As indeed they did; and today it is sold as a delicacy.

925. Ribbentrop was neither a nobleman nor a noble man. Cf. note 876. Three of the accused were acquitted—Franz von Papen, Hjalmar Greeley Schacht (born in Brooklyn), and H. Fritzsche. Papen had, after all, nearly been killed by the Nazis, and Schacht had been liberated from a concentration camp in 1945.

926. There are other tidbits about Roosevelt's mental problems in the *Eden Memoirs*, 3:464 (the Mikolajczyk wild goose chase), and p. 373. It includes the president's plan to carve out a new state to be called "Wallonia," consisting of southern Belgium, Luxembourg, Alsace-Lorraine, and parts of northern France. Eden "politely poured water on it."

927. Cf. Walter Lippmann, op. cit., 21: "The masses have first to be frightened. . . the enemy has to be portrayed as evil incarnate, as absolute and congenital wickedness. The people wanted to be told that when this particular enemy had been forced to unconditional surrender, they would reenter the golden age. This unique war would end all wars. This last war would make the world safe for democracy. This crusade would make the whole world a democracy." Remember Lord Bryce, who warned against the idea that democracy is "here to stay." Cf. Viscount Bryce, *Modern Democracy* (London: Macmillian, 1921), 1:47.

928. Cf. his *Time for Decision* (New York: Harper, 1944). The following year another volume came out, a sort of guide to the postwar world, written more or less by two confirmed leftists and merely "edited" by the old gentleman. It was Muscovite propaganda pure and simple. (*An Intelligent Man's Guide to the Peace*, Sumner Welles, ed., New York: Dryden, 1945).

929. Cf. Henry Morgenthau, *Germany Is Our Problem* (New York: Harper, 1945). His book has a plan showing a partitioned Germany. Morgenthau's propositions, from a purely territorial viewpoint, were far less harsh than the reality: Morgenthau gave only Upper Silesia and East Prussia to Poland. Typical is the remark (p. 57) that the Junkers were "backward in their social outlook."

930. Cf. Theodore N. Kaufman, *Germany Must Perish!* (Newark: Argyle Press, 1941), particularly 97-98. This book was a "godsend" to Goebbels. In a preface written for *Men at War*, an anthology, Ernest Hemingway also proposed the sterilization of all Germans.

931. By 1939 the *New Leader* was, to be sure, a socially minded rather than a Socialist paper. It had shed its original Marxism.

932. Cf. William H. Chamberlin, "The Tragic Case of Finland," *The American Mercury*, vol. 59, no. 247, July 1941, 7-15.

Here is the record in the *New York Times*: Monday, June 23, 1941, p. 2: Finnish communiqué; Soviet flyers start bombing, AP; clashes not yet recorded, UP; Russians violate Finnish territory, p.3; Finland declared not to be at war; UP relates interview of Soviet Minister Orlov in Helsinki: "We are convinced that neither side wants to fight." Tuesday, June 24, 1941: Gripenberg, Finnish minister to London, enlightens Eden on Russian attacks, p. 5; Finland professes neutrality in war. Wednesday, June 25, 1941, p. 2: continuous aerial bombardments in entire south of Finland (information of *New York Times* correspondent). Thursday, June 26, 1941, pp. 1-2: AP describes the big damage caused by Soviet bombardments. Friday, June 27, 1941: five days after German attack, Finland declares war (June 26); the declaration decided after a plenary session of the *Eduskunta* (parliament); Soviets protest against Finnish "Fascist militarism."

933. Cf. Fitzroy How MacLean, *Escape to Adventure: Eastern Approaches* (Boston: Little, Brown and Co., 1951), 309-12. Another observer, the American Leigh White, wrote, "Surely the Serbs were as precious as the lives of Britons and Americans—or were they? Let us face it: they were not. We fought the war according to a double standard of human values. In Western Europe we allowed the *guerrilleros* to husband their resources, human lives included, until the eve of victory. In Eastern Europe we demanded increasingly suicidal adventures in the unexpressed conviction that Slavic and Balkan blood was less valuable than the blood of Saxons, Latins, and Scandinavians." Cf. *Balkan Caesar* (New York: Scribner's, 1951).

934. On Mussolini's authoritative views on the collectivist and leftist nature of fascism, cf. Hans Sennholz, "Who Is the Fascist?" *Human Events*, December 25, 1965. This essay is carefully documented.

935. Cf. Harold Nicolson, *Curzon: The Last Phase*, 205-207: H. W. V. Temperley, op. cit., 6:267, 275; Ferdinand Lot, *Les invasions barbares et le peuplement de l'Europe* (Paris: Payot, 1937), 191n; Leszek Kirkien, *Russia, Poland and the Curzon Line* (London: Caldra House, n.d.); Stanislaw Grabski, *The Polish-Soviet Frontier* (London: 1943, no publisher mentioned); Hans Roos, *Geschichte der polnischen Nation 1916-1960* (Stuttgart: W. Kohlhammer, 1961), 78-79.

But there seems to exist an old British-Polish incompatibility of character and outlook that also affects the political scene. This is partly due to the confrontation between the Catholic thirst for the Absolute and the post-Protestant delight in the *juste milieu* and compromise. Even Disraeli disliked the Polish refugees and resented their activities. Cf. W. F. Monypenny and G. E. Buckle, op. cit., 2:71. But the great "professional" hater of the Poles was Lloyd George, the friend of Hitler, great Franco-baiter, and erstwhile protector of Winston Churchill. In all Polish border disputes, Lloyd George opposed the Poles violently, and in the Polish-Soviet war of 1919-1920, the Premier stood solidly on the side of Bolshevism. Cf. *Lord Riddell's Intimate Diary of the Paris Peace Conference 1918-1923* (New York: Reynal and Hitchcock, 1934), 221-24. When the Poles defeated the Red Army, Lloyd George (who had danced with joy when he heard in Chequers that the reds were in the suburbs of Warsaw), was deeply disappointed (ibid., 233). To him the Poles were mad and arrogant, they were hopeless, they were a menace to the peace of Europe (ibid., 191, 227, 198). His hatred for the Poles never abated. Count Kessler heard him (March 24, 1925) rant against the Poles in the House of Commons and was disgusted by the "grotesque sight of an old ham actor demagogically attacking his own work." Cf. Graf Harry Kessler, *Tagebücher 1918-1937* (Frankfurt: Insel-Verlag, 1961), 427. The (London) *Sunday Express* published on September 24, 1939, an article by Lloyd George entitled, "What is Stalin up to?" in which the former premier reviled the "class-ridden" Polish government and "Polish Imperialism" and praised the Soviets for "liberating their kinsmen from the Polish yoke." Cf. Count Edward Raczyński, *In Allied London* (London: Weidenfeld and Nicolson, 1962), 37. Worse still, on September 27, Lloyd George attacked prostrate Poland in the House of Commons as the "worst feudal system in Europe," a line which his friend Adolf Hitler took up on October 7 in the *Reichstag* calling Poland a country "ruled by aristocrats since 1919." Cf. the *New York Times*, September 28, 1939, 5:6, and October 7, 1939, 8:3. The root of this attitude is to be found elsewhere. When Virginia Cowles asked him why he was so anti-Franco while approving of Hitler, he replied with a twinkle, "I always line up on the side against the priests." Cf. Virginia Cowles, *Looking for Trouble*, (London: Hamish Hamilton, 1941), 107.

936. Cf. Sumner Welles, op. cit., 310. Malcolm Muggeridge, one of the wittiest of contemporary British writers, wrote a brilliant parody on Winston Churchill's attitude toward Poland in *Punch* (1953), cf. Burling and Lowrey, eds. *Twentieth Century Parody: American and British Anthology* (New York: Harcourt, Brace, 1960), 133-35.

937. Once a member republic of the USSR has its artificially boosted Russian majority, it is regularly disestablished. Thus the Karelo-Finnish Soviet Socialist Republic was first deprived of Western Karelia and the rest was then placed under the RSFSR, the Russian Soviet Federal Socialist Republic. What will happen once Kazakhstan achieves a Russian majority? A foretaste came in December 1986 in the murderous riots in Alma Ata, quelled only after a number of Kasakh students had been killed, jailed, or deported. Subsequent demonstrations of various ethnic groups with the USSR have since taken place.

938. Cf. *Concise Statistical Year Book of Poland* (London, 1941), 9, F. A. Doubek, "Die Ostgrenze der polnischen Volkstumsmehrheit," *Jomburg* (Leipzig), 2:1. Among eminent Poles born east of the Hitler-Stalin Line, herein a few: King Jan III Sobieski, who saved Vienna and Europe in 1683; Henryk Siemiradzki, the painter; Kościuszko and Pulaski, national heroes; Ignacy Jan Paderewski, pianist and statesman; Mickiewicz and Slowacki, Poland's two greatest poets; Joseph Conrad, the writer; Cieszkowski, the philosopher; General Pilsudski; and the Nobel Prize Laureate Czeslaw Milosz. In fact, very few Poles known to educated Americans or Britishers were born *west* of the Hitler-Stalin line. (Sienkiewicz and Leszek Kolakowski are the exceptions proving the rule.)

939. Indeed, the great liberal, Franz Grillparzer, was right when he wrote in 1849 under the impact of the revolution:

The way of civilization goes
From humanitarianism
Over nationalism
To beastliness.

940. Peoples speaking an identical (or very similar) language have often fought bitterly among themselves: the Irish and the English, the Americans and the British, the Union forces and the Confederates, the Austrians and the Prussians, the Chileans and the Peruvians, and so on.

941. On the natural borders of Poland with Russia, cf. Albrecht Penck, "Die natürliche Grenze Russlands," *Meereskunde* (Berlin, 1917), vol. 12, no. 1.

942. Cf. Viscount d'Abernon, *The Eighteenth Decisive Battle of the World, Warsaw, 1920* (London: Hodder and Stoughton, 1931), 81; Harold Nicolson, *Curzon: The Last Phase*, 205; H. W. V. Temperley, op. cit., 6:320; Stanislaw Grabski, op. cit., 21-25; Hans Roos, op. cit.,79-80.

943. Hetman Simon Petlyura was assassinated years later in Paris by a Jewish emigrant as revenge for the pogroms carried out by Ukrainian troops during the war. The Ukrainian troops were certainly not innocent in sacking Jewish quarters, but if the Polish army was guilty in thirty or so cases, the Red Army committed no fewer than 106 *pogromy*. (Cf. *The Jewish Encyclopedia*, New York, 1943, 8:562.) Did the borderland Jews prefer "Red Freedom" to Polish "Military Fascism?" Between November 11, 1918, and June 30, 1924, no fewer than 33,000 "ethnic" Jews fled from the East to the West. This number excludes Jews who thought of themselves as Poles, Ukrainians, Russians, etc. Cf. *Maly Rocznik Statystyczny*, Warsaw, 1939, 52. (There were also 122,000 Ukrainians, 492,000 White Ruthenians, and 121,000 Russians fleeing in the same direction.)

944. Cf. note 934. Also Frank H. Simonds, in the (London) *Times*, April 25, 1919.

945. Cf. Viscount d'Abernon, op. cit., 20-21.

946. General Weygand always disclaimed a share in the victory. Cf. Winston S. Churchill, *The World Crisis* (London: Thornton Butterworth, 1929), 5:271-72; Ferdinand Lot, op. cit., 194. Général Camoin, *La Maneuvre libératrice du maréchal Pilsudski contre les bolchéviks en août 1920* (Paris, 1929); Hans Roos, op. cit., 88-89. Roos says that the idea of Weygand's exclusive merits came from the Polish National Democrats who hated Pilsudski. De Gaulle, who accompanied Weygand on his mission, was deeply impressed by the strategic genius of Pilsudski, and General Hans von Seeckt, the reorganizer of the German army, saw in him a "Polish Frederick the Great." But the Polish historian Jedrzej Giertych insists that the real military genius in this decisive battle was General Tadeusz (von) Rozwadowski who, like the father of John Paul II, had served in the Austro-Hungarian army. Cf. his *In Defense of My Country* (London: Roman Dmowski Society, 1981), 713sq.

947. Cf. *Bolshaya Sovyetskaya Entsiklopediya* (Moscow: Gossudarstvenny Institut, 1940), 46:247.

948. Cf. note 944.

949. Cf. *Vnyeshnaya politika sovyetskogo soyuza v periodye otyechestvennoy voiny* (Moscow: Ogiz, 1944), 1:121.

950. Typical was an editorial in the *New Republic* on February 20, 1943, dealing with the Soviet claims on the Baltic States: "Yet, however forceful or dubious the Russian legal claims, the crux of the problem must be sought not in legal genealogies, but in the need of an enduring friendship between Russia and America."

951. The Ukrainians in Poland had just grievances. They wanted, for instance, a university of their own in Lwów (Lviv, Lemberg), but the Polish government offered them one elsewhere. Still, the Ukrainian language was taught in certain ethnically Polish schools. The literary life of the Ukrainians in Southeast Poland was flourishing. Take only the number of Ukrainian periodicals: 64 in 1932, 72 in 1934, 116 in 1936. Cf. Bocheński, Loś, and Baczkowski, *Problem polsko-ukraiński w Zemiej Czerwieńskiej* (Warsaw, 1938). On the schools cf. Stanislaw Sobiński, *L'enseignement public en Petite Pologne orientale au point de vue national* (Lwów, 1923), especially p. 12 and Tables 1, 2, 3. These two books represent a Polish viewpoint. Still, Professor Chubatyj was right when he said in 1944 that no more than 5 percent of the population of East Poland would freely vote for the USSR. Cf. "The Ukraine and the Polish-Russian Boundary Dispute," *The Ukraine Quarterly*, vol. 1 (October, 1944), 70.

952. Recall that the Ukrainians (Ruthenians) from Polish-dominated Eastern Galicia were in many ways different from the Ukrainians who had for a long time been under Russian rule. (Those from Eastern Galicia were predominantly Catholics of the Eastern Rite, those from the "Russian" Ukraine were "Orthodox.") The Russian *Entsiklopedicheski Slovar* (St. Petersburg, 1892), 7-A:907, insisted that these differences were marked. It added that many Jews in that area considered themselves Poles (p. 908). The Ukrainian Encyclopedia *Ukrainska Zagalna Entsiklopediya* (Lviv), 2:567, dealing with Lwów, provides the following statistics: 50 percent Poles, 35 percent Jews, and 15 percent Ukrainians.

953. From being a minority in Poland these people would have become nothing more than minorities in the USSR. Today, due to Soviet demographic policies, the Ukrainians are a minority even in Kiev, their own capital.

954. In fact, none of the more respectable American papers expressed positive belief in Soviet innocence. At the Nuremberg Trial, the accusation that the Germans had perpetrated the crime was quietly dropped. In view of the Katyn crime, Ernst Jünger could write about the Nuremberg Trial: "The worst thing of all is to put yourself into the wrong vis-à-vis a scoundrel. He will talk to you of morals and there is no more pitiless judge than one who is in the right, and a scoundrel to boot. Shylock gives us a pale notion of such a person.

"In this respect the non-plus-ultra is a court consisting of murderers and Puritans. Then the slaughter knife is given a moral handle." Cf. his *Strahlungen III* (Munich: Deutscher Taschenbuchverlag, 1966), 254.

955. The Katyn crime was discovered at a rather early date by the Germans. The janitor of the GPU-NKVD building in Smolensk, where the German staff was quartered, babbled about it when he was drunk. But a regular investigation was not instigated until Berlin ordered it. (Nobody had believed the janitor's story until be began to furnish details.) First, the German authorities tried to determine the date of the mass murder by analyzing the decomposed brains of the victims, but they soon discovered that the age of the trees planted over the huge mass graves gave a more exact clue. (Information was given to the author by the late Prince Erich Waldburg zu Zeil.) When the Poles demanded an impartial inquiry through the Red Cross, the Soviets broke relations with the Polish Government-in-Exile. The discussion between Sikorski, Anders, Stalin, and Molotov the previous year about the fate of the missing

officers (as reported by Anders) must have been amazing. Stalin maintained that these officers must have fled somewhere, perhaps to Manchuria. The older lie—that the boats carrying them to Solovki had been torpedoed in the White Sea—had already been jettisoned. Cf. Général W. Anders, *Mémoires* (Paris: La Jeune Parque, 1948), I. Rzewuska, trsl, 119-20. Anders' book can only be read with an intense feeling of moral nausea. The Soviets have recently admitted to mass slaughter, sociological rather than ethnic, in three camps, with over 15,000 victims.

In order to get a vivid, if horrible picture of the exhumations in Katyn, cf. the novel by Wlodzimierz Odojewski, *Zasypie wszystke, zawieje*, published in German as *Katharina oder alles verwehen wird der Schnee* (Vienna: Zsolnay, 1977), 96-108, and in French (Paris: Seuil, 1969).

956. There is no reason to assume that Andrzej Wyszyński, the Soviet prosecutor and delegate at the United Nations, one of the vilest creatures in modern history, is in any way related to the late Cardinal Wyszyński. Andrzej Wyszyński, also of Polish extraction, was a Menshevik who did not join the Bolsheviks until 1920. Thus he had to make extraordinary efforts to prove his loyalty—to the Soviet Union and to communism.

957. Cf. *The Case of Henryk Erlich and Victor Alter*, foreword by Camille Huysmans (New York: General Jewish Workers' Union of Poland, 1943).

958. One of the most moving documents on the efforts to escape from the huge Soviet dungeon is Slawomir Rawicz's book, *The Long Walk* (New York: Harper and Row, 1956), describing the flight of three Poles, two men and one girl, from Siberia over Mongolia and Tibet to India.

959. A big mass rally of the Congress of American-Soviet Friendship was held in New York's Madison Square Garden on November 7, 1942, to celebrate the twenty-fifth birthday of the Soviet Union. Congratulations came from President Roosevelt and General Eisenhower. Twenty thousand delegates attended. It became a love feast.

960. In a letter to Eden (December 3, 1944), Churchill called Stalin a "great and good man"—although totally aware of the Soviets' crimes. Cf. Winston S. Churchill, *The Second World War*, 6:616. Yet even Churchill had his moments of truth. Archduke Otto of Austria in his *Naissance d'un Continent* (Paris: Grassett, 1975), 175, describes a heated debate beween Winston Churchill and his son Randolph who accused his father of having totally misrepresented the role of Leopold III in World War II, calling the pertinent passages "a pack of lies." "Of course, they were lies," the old man retorted, "but you must not forget that the history of a period is what its best authors write about it. I am and will remain that author and consequently what I have written will be accepted as the truth." About Churchill's weakness see the voluminous tome by Martin Gilbert, *Road to Victory, Winston Churchill 1941-1945* (London: Heinemann, 1986).

961. David Irving in op. cit., 112, talking about the high degree of saturation bombing: "Every time it had been employed before, it had caused a fire-storm of some degree. Previously the fire-storm had been merely an unfortunate result of the attack: In the double-blow on Dresden the fire-storm was to be an integral part of the strategy." And let nobody believe that Mr. Churchill was innocent concerning the A-bomb on Hiroshima. He agreed to its use. Cf. the Earl of Avon, *The Eden Memoirs*, 3:547. But he knew nothing about Harry S. Truman's additional designs on the cradle of Christianity in Japan, the impending devastation of Nagasaki.

962. Cf. Albert C. Wedemeyer, op. cit., 416-18.

963. On these efforts, cf. Allen Welsh Dulles, Gerhart Ritter, Eberhard Zeller, op. cit.

964. Cf. B. H. Liddell-Hart, *The German Generals Talk* (New York: Morrow, 1948), 292-93, referring to Germans and the German troops during the war: " 'black-listening' to the Allied radio service was widespread. But the Allied propaganda never said anything positive about the peace conditions in the way of encouraging them to give up the struggle. Its silence on the subject was so marked that it tended to confirm what Nazi propaganda told them as to the dire fate in store for them if they surrendered. So it greatly helped the Nazis to keep the German troops and people to continue fighting—long after they were ready to give up." Thus Roosevelt's "originality" cost the lives of countless Americans. Government-by-brainwaves is sometimes murder.

   The U.S. army was anything but enthusiastic about the Unconditional Surrender formula as it had to pay the price in blood. Cf. Captain Harry C. Butcher, *My Three Years with Eisenhower* (New York: Simon and Schuster, 1946), entry of August 12, 1943. The real beneficiaries were the brown Socialists and the USSR.

965. The efforts of Louis P. Lochner, an American journalist (AP), to inform President Roosevelt in 1942 about the German conspiracy against Hitler proved totally abortive. The President refused to receive him because such a meeting would have been "highly embarrassing." Cf. H. Rothfels, *Die deutsche Oposition gegen Hitler* (Krefeld: Scherpe, 1949), 166sq. One could add, cynically, the well-known adage, "Don't confuse me with facts; I have already made up my mind." But this was an *indoctrinated* leftist mind.

966. Cf. Allen Welsh Dulles, op. cit., 42; George A. Bell, Bishop of Chichester, in the *Contemporary Review* (London), October 1945. Eden's reply to the bishop can be found in *20. Juli 1944* (Freiburg i. Br.: Herder, 1961), "Herder-Bücherei," 96:52. Regrettably, it cannot be found in the *Eden Memoirs*.

967. Yet Churchill was ceaselessly informed about the German opposition by Dr. Bell, Anglican Bishop of Chichester. Dr. Bell in turn was in permanent contact with the now-famous German theologian, Pastor Dietrich Bonhoeffer, via the latter's brother-in-law, Dr. Leibholz, a refugee in Britain. (Bonhoeffer, now erroneously claimed by God-is-dead theologians abroad, was an intimate friend of the conspirators; he was executed in Flossenbürg.) The Bishop of Chichester wrote to Leibholz on August 8, 1944: "I heard Churchill. . . but he is living in a world of battles only, and seeing time with the mind of a child with regard to deep policy—for Home affairs as well as the far graver matters. And disaster gets nearer and nearer. One feels so powerless. . . ." Cf. Eberhard Bethge, *Dietrich Bonhoeffer, Theologe, Christ, Zeitgenosse* (Munich: Chr. Kaiser-Verlag, 1967), 1004.

968. I spoke with Cardinal Count Preysing in Berlin a few weeks before his death. He assured me that neither he nor Cardinal von Galen had had any concrete facts about the extermination camps in the East. They had had information about the extermination of the insane, and thus had protested against this leftist-humanitarian atrocity, the sort that sails under the label of "euthanasia" in the West. Had they known of the genocide in Polish camps, they most certainly would have protested with equal vigor. Karl Jaspers, the German philosopher, and Herr Rudolf Augstein, editor-in-chief of

the leftist *Der Spiegel*, were similarly ignorant. They only had vague notions of the horrors and were not aware of the truth until 1945. Cf. Karl Jaspers, *Wohin treibt die Bundesrepublik?* (Munich: R. Piper and Co., 1966), 36. Albert Speer admitted to having heard rumors, but failed to have them confirmed or denied—for which he felt guilt. Cf. op. cit., 385-86.

　　Cf. also George N. Shuster (former president of Hunter College and U.S. Commissioner of Bavaria), "Catholic Resistance in Nazi Germany," in *Thought*, vol. 22, no. 84 (March 1947), 13, talking about Msgr. Johann Neuhäusler's book *Kreuz und Hakenkreuz*: "He goes on to conclude that if the bishops were not afraid to attack euthanasia as a means for disposing of the mentally sick, they most assuredly would have spoken out against the gas ovens of Auschwitz had they known of their existence. With this I am in agreement. The Cardinal of Cologne as well as the late Cardinal of Münster, whose courage none will doubt, assured me that they were without an inkling of the nefarious acts committed during the final years of the Third Reich." Again the question arises: how many Americans knew about the manufacturing of the A-bomb, although a multitude of people were engaged in the work?

969. Cf. Léon Blum, in the *New Leader* (New York), July 21, 1946. Constantin Silens in *Irrweg und Umkehr. Betrachtung über das Schicksal Deutschlands* (Basel: Birkhäuser, 1946), 216, thinks that Niemoeller's assumption, that one in 100,000 Germans knew of the extermination camps, is an overstatement. There were fewer. The *bulk* of the personnel in the extermination camps were undoubtedly East Europeans.

970. The "Gerstein Report" (a German translation from the French, the German original having been lost) was published for the first time by the *Vierteljahrshefte für Zeitgeschichte*, vol. 1 (Stuttgart, 1953). Gerstein was a former SS man who left the organization before the war, became a devout Lutheran, and was redrafted after the outbreak of the war. Arrested by the French, he gave a full description of the horrors of the extermination camps. Brought to Paris, he perhaps committed suicide by hanging, but there is a distinct possibility that he was murdered by other National Socialists in jail.

971. Cf. the letter by William N. Harrigan in *Commonweal*, April 3, 1964, 48. In this letter the official publication *Foreign Relations 1942* (Washington, D.C.: United States Government Printing Office, 1961), 3:772-78, is cited. Cardinal Maglione insisted that the Vatican had no detailed or certain knowledge of large-scale Nazi atrocities. Cardinal Tisserant insisted that the Vatican knew nothing about the mass slaughter and cremation of Jews until the advancing Allied armies began to reach Rome. Cf. N.C. "Cardinal Says He Criticized Curia, Not Pius, on Hitler," in *The Catholic Universe Bulletin*, April 3, 1964 (vol. 90, no. 51), 1-2. It is necessary to bring up this matter because a German playwright, Rolf Hochhuth, has fabricated a drama that rather conveniently makes Pius XII morally the most responsible man for that terrible slaughter. Significantly, concerning the deep ignorance of the period in which we live, a play such as Hochhuth's *Der Stellvertreter* ("The Deputy") can be staged throughout the world without the public being in the least aware of the ignorance and inanity of the text. Cf. my review of the play in *The Timeless Christian* (Chicago: Franciscan Herald Press, 1969), 184-94. (German original: *Hirn, Herz and Rückgrat*, Osnabrück, Fromm, 1968, 221-33.) The audience of a modern theater in

our age of affluence and illiteracy is made up of people unable to judge history, past or contemporary.

972. I was present when one of my Jewish friends debated this issue in New York with a Red Cross delegate who had come out of Germany in late 1943. The Red Cross official, a man of unquestionable antitotalitarian conviction, poo-poohed the idea that extermination camps existed. He considered euthanasia, such as death in a gas chamber, more humane than slow death by beatings in a concentration camp, but he warned my friend not to spread false information, which would merely aid the Nazis. Did I believe the Red Cross man's tale? Being a "logician," I considered it factually possible. For someone with no firm religious ground to stand on, there is no reason whatsoever to refrain from even the worst atrocities—exterminating certain groups of people, or, without waiting for them to be born, massacring them in their mothers' wombs (a current legal procedure in most "progressive" countries). In my novel *Moscow 1979* (New York: Sheed & Ward, 1940), I foretold the use of human bodies for commercial purposes, especially skins. The National Socialists used human skin for lampshades, although the evidence in the trial of Ilse Koch was only circumstantial. But in the French Revolution, the democrats established a whole factory in Meudon (using the corpses of the guillotined), which was later moved to the Pont-de-Cé in the Vendée, where the "material" was more plentiful.

973. One wonders what was known—and duly noted—about the Soviets' concentration camps by their Western Allies. *Vide* the rather comprehensive picture in Robert Conquest's account *The Great Terror: Stalin's Purge of the Thirties* (New York: Macmillan, 1968). And that horror continued, though at a more modest level. Much was known by 1932-1943, but not "digested," nor was the scanty information accepted as truth. The same was true within the Third Reich. Cf. Martin Gilbert, *Auschwitz and the Allies* (London: Michael Joseph, 1981), esp. 110, 170, 179, 339.

974. Andreas Graf Razumovsky, in his magisterial *Ein Kampf um Belgrad* (Berlin: Ullstein, 1980), makes Churchill primarily responsible for bolshevizing Yugoslavia, which so significantly shared with Cuba the leadership of the "uncommitted" nations. (Cuba was as uncommitted as pre-1989 Czechoslovakia.)

975. Even today these wounds have far from healed. The old hatreds, as I found during a trip through Yugoslavia, have lost none of their hideous strength. In fact, the resistance against the Communist regime is paralyzed by the subconscious (and sometimes conscious) fear that with the collapse of the red dictatorship, the various artificially united nationalities and nations of Yugoslavia would again be at each other's throats. Thus the foundation of Yugoslavia in 1918 actively fostered the survival of communism.

But the worst mutual massacres did not take place between Serbs and Croats, but between Albanians and Serbs in the Kosovo region, which had been annexed by Serbia in 1912-1913, but got a "breathing spell" under German occupation. The Albanian minority then found the opportunity for revenge. In 1944, the Serb Communists took their revenge, slaughtering between 40,000 and 50,500 Albanians; another massacre took place (this one methodical and organized) in the winter of 1955-1956 under the "Stalinist" Minister of the Interior, Ranković. The details of these crimes were revealed at a session of the *Savez Komunista* (League of Communists) in 1966 in Priština. The violent unrest in the Kosovo region during the past eight years is due to these mass murders as well as to the rapid numerical growth of the Albanian element demanding political rights.

976. This does not mean that situations do not arise in which a man of integrity and knowledge is incapable of finding a way out. Count Paul Teleki, a great scholar and statesman, my former teacher and personal friend, was forced by the Germans, while he was Hungarian Prime Minister in 1941, to choose between dishonor and the ruin of his country. In a fit of depression, this devout Catholic committed suicide.

977. Though I was not a political refugee in the United States (having left Austria for Hungary in 1929) I still regret that I did not stay in Europe—whatever the cost—to resist the evil on the spot.

978. I think of authors such as Frank Thiess (*Das Reich der Dämonen*), Ernst Wiechert, Werner Bergengruen (*Im Himmel und auf Erden*), Reinhold Schneider, Ernst Jünger (*Auf den Marmorklippen*), Friedrich Georg Jünger (*Der Mohn*), and, above all, Fritz Reck-Malleczewen, who wrote a bit too obviously. His *Bockelsohn: Geschichte eines Massenwahns* is a description of Hitler under the mask of Jan van Leiden. He perished heroically in a concentration camp.

979. The valiant not only stayed on, but some worked as protectors of "U-boats," the wartime name for Jews that hid in Aryan "households" during those years. About five thousand "U-boats" survived. If their hosts were caught, they faced certain death. (The hosts also had to share their food tickets with the Jews.) This particular story has yet to be fully aired.

980. Cf. *The Memoirs of Cordell Hull* (New York: Macmillan, 1948), 2:1297. In his memoirs, Hull stated (p. 1293) that Eden was the driving force in the "Austrian Declaration." And James F. Byrnes in his *Speaking Frankly* (New York: Harper, 1947), 161, could not refrain from remarking, "It is not unfair to describe this policy now as one that seems to punish the Austrians for their association with the Germans during the Nazi occupation, and one that tries to make Austria an economic if not political dependence of the Soviet Union." The Austrian resistance, coming mainly from Monarchists and Catholics, was very substantial; in the meantime, a number of books have been published on the subject. The first coherent account was given by Wilhelm Schmidt SVD in *Gegenwart und Zukunft des Abendlandes* (Luzern:Stocker, 1949), 214-322. More detailed: Otto Molden, *Der Ruf des Gewissens* (Vienna: Herold, 1959). The weakest resistance came from the Social Democrats (p. 226). Cordell Hull excused the recognition of Germany's grab saying that the United States wanted to collect the Austrian debts from Germany, the "incorporator." (*The Memoirs*, 575-76). Naturally, the main culprit in the *Anschluss* (after the National Socialists themselves) were the Western Powers, mainly England. Cf. also L v. Tončić-Sorinj (chairman of the Council of Europe in Strasbourg), "Die Kollaboration Europa. Die unteilbare Schuld der Mächte am Aufstieg Hitlers," *Berichte und Informationen*, vol. 2 (1947), no. 59.

When I protested after the "Declaration" in a letter to the *New York Times* (signed by my pen name, F. S. Campbell), the editor of the pro-Communist *Austro-American Tribune* took issue. He contended that Austrian munition plants worked for the Germans. (And what about the Škoda Works in Czechoslovakia, Schneider-Creuzot in France, and so on?) These and other criticisms so infuriated Cordell Hull that he became violently anti-Austrian, as demonstrated by George Creel, who had an acrimonious discussion with him on the subject. (Verbal communication with the late G. Creel.) Eden was right when he wrote about Hull: "Yet it was impossible to forget the beak and the claws. I could never watch him without recalling the song of his native Tennessee about the Martins and the Coys. I felt that he too could pursue a vendetta to the end." (*The Eden Memoirs*, 3:380.) His vindictiveness was fully focused on Austria.

981. The involuntary French contribution to the German war effort was considerable. Not only did a French Legion fight in Russia, but the French war industry worked full blast for Germany. A comprehensive picture of Paris under German domination can be found in David Pryce-Jones, *Paris in the Third Reich* (London: Collins, 1981).

982. One of Hull's last public acts was to demand of the Austrians that they rebel openly against the Germans, as an active contribution to their liberation, because the final judgment of the Allies would depend on whether Austria in some way had atoned for "having participated in the war on Hitler's side." He ended by remarking, "I want to say that the time for Austria to make that contribution is almost up." (Cf. the *New York Times*, September 12, 1944, 6:1.) General Eisenhower was furious at the political interference, which impinged on his plans. He sent a blistering note to Washington, while a spokesman for the General exhorted the Austrians over the radio to dissociate themselves from their brown masters, to form clandestine committees, to gather food in order in time to help the Allied administration—but not to revolt. (Cf. the *New York Times*, October 2, 1944, 3.) A few days later, Cordell Hull resigned and was replaced by Edward R. Stettinius, Jr.

983. A good psychological thumbnail sketch of the Potsdam Conference can be found in Robert Murphy's *Diplomat Among Warriors* (London: Collins, 1964), 326-43.

984. Soon after he became President, H. Truman pardoned his former associates in the Pendergast administration in Kansas City (Mo.), thus releasing them from jail. A reading of Jack Lait's and Lee Mortimer's *U.S.A. Confidential* (New York: Crown, 1952) suggests that Truman had the right kind of training to deal with a man like Stalin. Even more horrifying is Jules Abels *The Truman Scandals* (Chicago: Regnery, 1956). The manuscript was sent to the former President prior to publication; Truman greeted it with furious expletives but no arguments.

985. Cf. Winston S. Churchill, *The Second World War*, 5:320.

986. Ibid., 351.

987. Cf. Jan Ciechanowski, op. cit., 332-35.

988. Cf. note 897. When General Anders, the admirable Polish leader who with his valiant men fought on the Italian front for the greater glory of the Western democracies, pointed out to Churchill that the mass migrations would be inhuman to the Germans as well, Churchill remarked cynically that 6 million Germans had already perished and some more would soon join them. Cf. Wladyslaw Anders, op. cit., 308.

989. Cf. Jan Ciechanowski, op. cit., 249.

990. Cf. William L. Neumann, "How American Policy Toward Japan Contributed to War in the Pacific," in *Perpetual War for Perpetual Peace*, H. E. Barnes, ed., 306: "Hull was

hell-bent for War. The constant needling by Chiang Kai-shek had gotten under his skin and President Roosevelt felt pressured by his administrative assistant, Lauchlin Currie, also a warm admirer of Soviet Russia. At this point Owen Lattimore, American adviser to Chiang Kai-shek, sent a strongly worded cablegram against any modus vivendi or truce with Japan." (This cable was received on November 26, 1941.) The next day Cordell Hull handed the Japanese diplomats, Kurusu and Nomura, the ultimatum that—in the words of Albert Jay Nock—would have been a deadly insult even to a state such as Luxembourg.

Also cf. Harold L. Ickes, "The Lowering Cloud, 1939-1941," vol. II of *The Secret Diaries of Harold J. Ickes* (New York: Simon and Schuster, 1954), 630: "For a long time I have believed that our best entrance into the war would be by way of Japan. . . And, of course, if we go to war against Japan, it will inevitably lead to a war against Germany." Secretary of War Henry L. Stimson noted about the meeting of the War Cabinet in the White House on November 25, 1941: "The question was how we should maneuver them into the position of firing the first shot without allowing too much danger to ourselves." Cf. Henry Regnery, *Memoirs of a Dissident Publisher* (New York: Harcourt, Brace, 1979), 80. To Robert Sherwood's despair, as Roosevelt's ghost writer he had to repeat again and again the patent lie that the President would never send young Americans overseas. Cf. his *Roosevelt and Hopkins* (New York: Harper, 1948), 874.

But the *sequitur* was added by Hitler who arbitrarily, for no cogent reason, declared war against the United States. There might otherwise have been two separate wars. In fact, the Germans hoped that Japan would attack the USSR. George N. Shuster, America's civilian governor in Bavaria (he had a German background), visited Göring in his death cell and asked him why Hitler had declared war on the United States. "Obviously only as a gesture to anticipate America's move," was the answer. Shuster then explained that, unlike 1917, a majority in Congress would never have agreed to this. (With a Pacific war underway, the majority of Americans would have opposed an Atlantic venture.) Whereupon Göring threw up his hands in despair and exlaimed: "*Mein Gott!*"

991. This is the thesis in the well-reasoned article of Gar Alperovitz, "Why We Dropped the Bomb," *The Progressive*, August 1965, 11-14. On p. 12, Alperovitz cites Admirals William D. Leahy and Ernest J. King, and Generals Henry A. Arnold, Dwight D. Eisenhower, and Curtis E. LeMay as convinced that the actual dropping of the bomb on an inhabited center was superfluous. Einstein himself was opposed to the Atomic Board in 1945 and declared: "We can only hope that we have not put dynamite into the hands of children." He was a religious man, believed in God, and was profoundly afraid of the technological development. Cf. Antonina Vallentin, *Das Drama Albert Einsteins* (Stuttgart: Günther Verlag, 1955), 259, 261, 149-50, 163, and Graf Harry Kessler, op.cit., 242. Yet Truman, while knowing that the A-bomb worked, wrote triumphantly to his wife from Berlin on July 16, 1945, that he had succeeded in persuading "Uncle Joe" to break his nonaggression pact with the Japanese and attack them on August 15. One's mind boggles at such great statesmanship. Cf. *Dear Bess: The Letters of Harry to Bess Truman*, R. M. Ferrel, ed. (New York: Norton, 1983), 519.

992. Cf. Walter Lippmann, op. cit., 24.

993. There were tens of thousands of rapes in Vienna and surroundings. Females between the ages of three and ninety were victimized. The spread of venereal diseases became uncontrollable. Yet, according to the protesting Milovan Djilas, Stalin thought that raping in liberated Yugoslavia by the Red Army was "natural."

994. If only the Elbe had been the demarcation line reaching to the Czech border. But it was only a boundary for thirty-three miles, after which the Soviet-controlled area extended west, coming within 180 miles of the Netherlands. John Gunther said of Roosevelt at Yalta, "his exhaustion was so complete that, on occasion, he could not answer simple questions and talked what was close to nonsense." Cf. Noah Fabricant, M.D., *Thirteen Famous Patients* (Philadelphia: Chiltern, 1966), 36. As we know, Roosevelt never read books, he was quite illiterate, but Alger Hiss, who "assisted" him at Yalta, in all likelihood was an "intellectual" and a reader.

995. General Eisenhower, by refusing to advance on Berlin and, later, by evacuating Thuringia and parts of Saxony, not only did great disservice to his country, but also struck a mighty blow against the Free West. One argument holds that he only obeyed his Commander-in-Chief. (An analogous order was given to General MacArthur a few years later during the Korean War.) Did General Eisenhower have to obey the President? Then what about the German generals who were tried in Nuremberg for obeying Hitler? According to General Hobart R. Gay, Patton begged Eisenhower to take Berlin. The latter refused, asking, "Of what use is Berlin, anyhow?" Patton replied, "Eisenhower, history will answer this question for you." Cf. Henry Regnery, op. cit., 247.

996. Robert Murphy told how the Czechs implored the Americans, when in sight of Prague, to advance even further. But Eisenhower, knowing that the commander of the Russian troops had demanded that the American army be halted, declared at a staff meeting, "Why should we endanger the life of a single American or Briton to capture areas we shall soon be handing over to the Russians?" (R. Murphy, op. cit., 312-13.) The matter, unfortunately, had been settled by the politicians at Yalta, with Alger Hiss advising the ailing President. According to one source, prior to Yalta, Roosevelt had assured an agent of Stalin that the USSR would control Central Europe. The so-called Zabrousky letter can only be found in José R. Doussinague's *España tenía razón* (Madrid: Espasa-Calpe, 1950).

997. Robert Murphy relates how he brought up the subject of a formal definition of the Western Allies' rights to their communication routes to Berlin. Whereupon Ambassador John Winant exlaimed vehemently that the Russians were "inclined to suspect our motives, and if we insisted on this technicality, we should intensify their distrust." Thus this crucial matter could not be settled. Not much later, Ambassador Winant committed suicide. (Cf. R. Murphy, op. cit., 285-86.)

998. Cf. Winston S. Churchill (*The Second World War*, 5:359), insisted that the Allies envision the Eastern Neisse, not the Western Neisse, as a boundary line, saying "this is still our position." The evil might have been lessened (the left bank of the city of Breslau might have been retained by Germany), but rivers—as geographers know only too well—are not ideal boundaries. Rivers not only sometimes change their

course, they are means of communication and thus they *unite*: they do not divide. With the exception of a longer stretch of the Lower Danube between Bulgaria and Rumania, no river has ever separated language groups. (Thus the boundary between the German and the French idioms is the Vosges mountains, not the Rhine.)

999. It is a mistake to think this was some sort of punishment for the Germans who "had turned Nazi en bloc." Consider East Prussia, whose center was German, Catholic, and (as the last free election proved) "anti-Nazi." The highest Nazi percentages in the Weimer Republic were in Southern East Prussia, where the people are Lutheran by religion but Polish by language. Yet while the anti-Nazi Catholic Germans were expelled, the pro-Nazi Masurian Poles were allowed to stay in their ancestral homes. Historic justice is not just.

1000. It is difficult to verify whether cannibalism was actually practiced during these terrible months. Cf. also the authentic report: "Germania Deserta" in *The Catholic World* (New York), April 1947, 17-25. About this tragedy Bishop (later Cardinal) Muench of Fargo, N.D., papal coordinator of Catholic Affairs and later nuncio to Germany, wrote: "The one thing which is perhaps even a greater atrocity than the Allied looting and expulsion of 12 million people is the conspiracy of silence about it." (Cf. *The Catholic Action News*, Fargo, N.D., November 1946.)

1001. The word "reasonable" is in quotation marks because politics is the belief in the possible, Christianity is the belief in the impossible.

1002. Cf. Friedrich Engels, *Der Ursprung der Familie, des Privateigentums des Staates* (Stuttgart: Dietz, 1894), 181. The idea that democracy is in an evolutionary and/or revolutionary way the matrix, the preparatory school, of tyranny was stated by Plato, Aristotle, and Polybius. In our time the fear of a natural metamorphosis has been expressed by a host of writers and concretely enumerated in my *Freiheit oder Gleichheit?* To their number I would like to add Gustav Gundlach, "Vom Wesen der Demokratie," *Gregorianum*, vol. 28 (1947), 572-73; Werner Kägi, op. cit., 119-20; Winfried Martini, *Das Ende aller Sicherheit*, 79-82; Thomas Gilby, O.P., *Between Community and Society: A Philosophy and Theology of the State* (London: Longmans, Green, 1953), 171ff.; Angel López-Amo, op. cit., 89, 152; Jürgen Rausch, *In einer Stunde wie dieser* (Stuttgart: Deutsche Verlagsanstalt, 1955), 424; and in the last century two rather divergent thinkers and acute observers: Bismarck, *Gedanken und Erinnerungen* (Stuttgart: Cotta, 1898), 2:60; and Rosmini-Serbati, *La società e il suo fine* (Milan: Edizioni di Uomo, 1945), 102.

1003. David J. Dallin wrote in *Russia and Post-War Europe* (New Haven: Yale University Press, 1943) that the USSR wanted democratic orders outside its borders because "democracy provides special ways and opportunities for an unhampered building up of a Communist party—for its propaganda activity, its press, and its congresses. Not until there is formed a firm party framework will it be possible to proceed with the major task of the Communist program." This is why Communists everywhere hope for a full and unhampered democracy and prefer a republican to an authoritarian or even a constitutional monarchy. In this respect, their desires only too often meet with popular trends and desires in America—if not in Britain. In 1946, not only the Communists but even influential Americans fostered the cause of republicanism in the Italian referendum; and in the Austrian State Treaty of 1955, the insistence that Austria should have a republican form of government came not only from the Soviet delegation. Cf. also Walter Lippmann, op. cit., 56-57. Maritain is quite right in stating that the normal form of expression for democracy is the republic. Cf. J. Maritain, *Christianisme et démocratie* (Paris: Paul Hartmann, 1947), 65.

1004. Cf. Dorothy Thompson, *Listen Hans* (New York: 1942), 117.

1005. See note 448. The policy to foster leftist administrations was evident all over American-occupied Germany. Thus Baron Franckenstein with a fine anti-Nazi record, who had been elected mayor of a Bavarian village, was immediately deposed by the horrified American *Gauleiter* who nominated (by nondemocratic *fiat*) a Social Democrat. But, yielding to the *vox populi*, the poor man quickly abdicated, and the baron with the truly monstrous name emerged victorious.

1006. The interminable questionnaire can be found in Ernst von Salomon's *Der Fragebogen*, published in a Ro-Ro-Ro pocket edition. The most important question, of course, could not be asked: "How did you vote?" This would have been considered "undemocratic." But the funniest question—there were 131—was number 18, which asked whether the person or his wife had a titled grandparent. The author had obviously seen all the anti-Nazi films produced in America.

1007. It is little known that the British also came close to arresting Cardinal Count Galen, Bishop of Münster, probably the most outstanding anti-Nazi in the defeated country. The manly protest of a British officer, Major Rolf Elwes, prevented this enormous *gaffe*. Despite such setbacks, Labourite leftism had a field day in the British zone of occupied Germany.

1008. Former Judge Leibowitz, interested in the reasons for the low rate of juvenile delinquency in Italy, made a personal investigation in the Appenine Peninsula. He found that paternal authority was largely responsible for good juvenile behavior. Yet the charge that German paternal authority was largely responsible for Nazism was made by Bertram Schaffner in his Columbia University Press: *Fatherland, a Study of Authoritarianism in the German Family* (New York: 1948). Face it: certain American influences and habits are harmful to Europe. (The reverse is also possible.) A Russian proverb says, "What is healthy for the Russian is deadly for the German." (*Shto russkomu zdorovo, to nyemtsomu smert'*.) Values, concepts, institutions cannot always be harmlessly exchanged between nations. Wilhelm von Schütze was an early German critic of American influences on Europe. Cf. his *Russland und Deutschland oder über den Sinn des Memoirs von Aachen* (Leipzig: Gerhard Fleischer, 1819), 161-63.

1009. Mr. Robert Hutchins, after World War II, was asked in Frankfurt by American "reeducationists" to address German teachers and professors. He shocked the organizers by imploring the Germans to hold fast to their old, traditional ideals and not yield to their reeducators. (The classic high school-colleges, the *Humanistische Gymnasien*, were specifically picked out for strong criticism by the occupiers for strengthening "class-consciousness.")

By far the best book on the American effort to cast the German mind into a leftist pattern is C. von Schrenck-Notzing's *Die Charakterwäsche* (Stuttgart: Seewald,

1965). It describes brilliantly the work of American leftism, partly paralyzed at home by the late Truman and Eisenhower administrations, but highly active in the malleable German postwar world. The most amusing parts of the book deal with the psychological-ideological tests used by the reeducators. In 1945 and 1946, the American "reeducators" continued to insist that Communist journalists be included in the editorial boards of the newly licensed newspapers. It was some time before this regulation was aborted.

1010. Still, the best newspapers today in Germany and Austria, as well as in Switzerland and Italy, are in "right" hands—*Frankfurter Allgemeine Zeitung, Die Presse, Neue Zürcher Zeitung* and *Il Giornale*. The *Frankfurter* and the *Zürcher* are the best newspapers in the world.

1011. I personally know the man who conceived the idea of the Nuremberg Trials. I am certain that the notion of mere revenge never entered his mind. He thought that a "precedent" should be set, a common law notion that would, of course, have no meaning in the non-English-speaking world, since most of Europe is wedded to the Roman principle of codified law and the *nullum crimen sine lege* concept. He stated to a mutual friend that he realized the gamble involved, but that the risk ought to be taken: he admitted that the thing could misfire. It did. C. von Schrenck-Notzing remarked that since the amnesty of 1951 by McCloy, the "Nuremberg Law, just like the Potsdam Agreement, is a 'Sleeping Beauty' waiting for the day when a Red Prince will kiss it awake." (Op. cit., 195).

1012. Cf. Winston S. Churchill, *The Second World War*, 1:456-58.

1013. President Wilson was rather eager to have William II tried. On July 1, 1919, Pope Benedict XV wrote a letter to the President and added a clipping from the *Osservatore Romano* of June 2, 1919. The extract from the Vatican daily reproduced the views of a professor of Bologna University who spoke about the legality of bringing the German Emperor to trial. Point One of his observation: "that the accusers themselves should constitute the Tribunal of Justice is unprecedented in the history of criminal law."

1014. The widow of one of the leading German chemical industrialists informed me that the judge told her at Nuremberg after her husband's acquittal: "I can assure you, Madam, your husband is a most perfect gentleman." The aged gentleman had spent four years in a very strict jail waiting for the verdict while his wife worked as a laundress. "We always knew it," she replied to the judge. In the "little Nuremberg Trials," one could see the popular (folkloric and unsystematic) Marxist mind at work. The big Nuremberg Trials were officially leveled against the "Nazi conspirators." The Soviets forbade use of the term "National Socialists" and the Allies were opposed to "Fascists." They compromised on the term "Nazis." Goebbels called his followers "Nazi-Sozis."

1015. The male line of the Krupps died out. Bertha Krupp married a Herr von Bohlen und Halbach: the oldest son uses the name "Krupp von Bohlen und Halbach" while all other males are Herren von Bohlen und Halbach.

1016. Cf. Thilo Freiherr von Wilmowsky, *Warum wurde Krupp verurteilt?* (Stuttgart: Vorwerk, 1950). This book is very informative on the ideological background of the process. The comparison between the attorney's "anticapitalistic" writ in the Flick trial and Andzej Wyszyński's tirades on pp. 37-38 is amusing. Wars—who dared doubt it?—were made by capitalists.

1017. Cf. Thilo von Wilmowsky, op. cit., 9.

1018. The supporters of this theory forget that in modern wars the sons and brothers of the "war-mongering" manufacturers are drafted into armies just like everybody else. Old Krupp von Bohlen (related to the American diplomat Charles E. Bohlen) had five sons. One, who had to stay behind to manage the firm, faced death from the skies and later a jail sentence in his father's stead at Nuremberg; four were at the front, two of these were killed, one spent eleven years in Soviet prisons (three of them in solitary confinement). I knew both survivors. What is the use of further millions if you lose your sons and other relatives? The egregious nonsense of seeking purely (or predominantly) economic reasons for wars, particularly during this age of continuous wars, has been dealt with by Felix Somary, op. cit., 33-34; Morris Ginsberg, *Reason and Unreason in Society* (London: Longmans, Green, 1947), 184-85; Wilhelm Röpke, *Internationale Ordnung* (Erlenbach-Zürich: Rentsch, 1945), 73ff.; 2nd ed., 1954, 101ff. Here Röpke says: "The statement that imperialism is an unavoidable consequence of capitalism would only be convincing if empirical proof of two sorts were offered: (1) that imperialism without capitalism and (2) that capitalism without imperialism never existed. One only has to ask for these proofs to know that they can never be produced" (116). Sidney Fay in his op. cit. states that during his endless research into the origins of the "Great War," he discovered practically no economic motives for the conflagration.

1019. Since I knew Yamashita personally I wrote an article about him for a "liberal" Catholic publication which purported to be eager to come to the aid of the innocently persecuted. The article was turned down.

1020. Cf. A. Frank Reel, *The Case of General Yamashita* (Chicago: University of Chicago Press, 1949). The author ends his book with these words: "We have been unjust, hypocritical and vindictive. We have defeated our enemies on the battlefield, but we have let their spirit triumph in our hearts" (247).

1021. Mr. Bevin, who in this instance was one of the most important decision-makers, had a fine ultraleftist record (cf. note 857). He was not overly encumbered by knowledge and preliminary studies, as can be gleaned from Joseph Frayman's sketch: "Careers of Bevin and Morrison Reveal Background Similarities," *New York Times*, March 10, 1951, 5. The decline in the quality of parliamentarians seems to be unavoidable. Cf. René Gillouin, op. cit., 142-43.

1022. Even Winston Churchill protested against the renewed enslavement of the South Tyrol in a speech before the House of Commons. Cf. *New York Times*, June 6, 1946.

1023. Other Nazi hangovers were the anti-Habsburg stipulations in the Austrian State Treaty of 1955—interesting in the light of the democratic principle of self-determination. Yet, as stated previously, the Western Powers gladly acceded to this brown-red demand. American antimonarchism has always been lively and popular. This attitude is highlighted by Dr. Benjamin Rush, op. cit., 264, 65. Yet Rush, who wanted to frighten naughty children with the specter of a king, saw the future in a rather different light. In a letter to John Adams (July 21, 1789), he admitted that "a hundred years hence, absolute monarchy will probably be rendered necessary in our country by the corruption of our people. But why should we precipitate an event for which we are not yet prepared?" (522).

1024. Needless to say, the victims were predominantly women, adolescents, and small children of the lower classes, most of whom were Social Democrats who had boasted of their "proletarian status"; this did not protect them in the least. "You want to be proletarians, but you live like bourgeois!" they were told in surprise and indignation.

In the Napoleonic Wars, the Russian armies fought all over Europe. At that time, the majority of the soldiers were Christians and illiterate. In 1944, they were largely literate, but lacked a Christian upbringing. Fritz Reck-Malleczewen speaks about the Christian spirit of Russian soldiers in World War I in his *Tagebuch eines Verzweifelten* (Stuttgart: Henry Goverts, 1966), 80-81.

1025. They were buried by Austrian peasants.

1026. A description of the events near Lienz can be found in Nikolay Nikolayevitch Krasnov, *The Hidden Russia* (New York: Henry Holt, 1960).

1027. Nikolai Tolstoy, "The Klagenfurt Conspiracy: War Crimes and Diplomatic Secrets," in *Encounter* (May 1983), 24-37. The Yugoslav purgatory established after World War I was transformed into a Hell, moving from "democracy" via royal dictatorship to socialist and communist tyranny, again thanks to the progressive West. (Tito's rise was aided by Churchill, but also, psychologically, by the merciless bombardment of Belgrade in April 1944—apparently to "chastize" General Nedić's Quisling government.)

1028. When the British entered (Austrian) Carinthia from the South, Sir Harold Alexander issued a declaration to the local population which began, "We have come as conquerors, not as liberators." But "conqueror" (*Eroberer*) in German implies lasting territorial conquest. To make matters worse, the soldiers and officers were forbidden to extend "common courtesy" to the inhabitants, i.e., to greet them, to say "thank you," etc. A few weeks later it dawned upon the British that this was nonsense, that such treatment of Austrians was not at all in their best interest, that they should distinguish between Austrians, Nazis, and Germans. Everything was reversed. Austrians were told that *all* the Allies were their good friends and that they should not believe the lies told them by the Nazis about communism in Russia and Yugoslavia. Communism was just in the last stage of developing into a liberal democracy!

Thus the Austrians, who as neighbors of the Communist world knew a great deal about communism, finally woke up from the National Socialist hell to find themselves in an insane asylum—admittedly an improvement.

1029. Unlike Italy in 1922-1943, the diarchy in Greece did not work at all; in 1973, military dictators destroyed the Greek monarchy.

1030. France *eventually* lost most of its colonial possessions but gained a few square kilometers along the Italian frontier in the Alps.

1031. Cf. Louis Rougier, *Les Accords Pétain-Churchill, Histoire d'une mission* (Montreal: Beauchemin, 1945). As expected, nobody from Britain's Foreign Office dared testify at the Pétain trial that, behind de Gaulle's back, Britain had made secret agreements with the Marshal. The facsimile documents published by Louis Rougier, the go-between, were declared forgeries by the British; the General, a nonagenarian, was given a life sentence in 1946. But in the 1980s, the London Foreign Office admitted—"now it can be told"—the existence of the agreement, which had been largely adhered to by Pétain.

1032. There were, of course, noncommunist and even rightist groups in the *résistance*. One of these, on the Right, was led by the ex-Maurassian Guillain de Bénouville. Cf. his *Le sacrifice du matin* (Paris: Laffont, 1946), especially 65-69. Bénouville became a close associate of de Gaulle in the late 1940s.

Nor were the members of the House of Bourbon spared by the Nazis in their leftist furor. Prince Xavier de Bourbon-Parma, brother of the Empress Zita, was nearly beaten to a pulp in the Struthof (Alsace) concentration camp. The notion that the Right collaborated while the Left resisted is simply not true. Laval, a Radical Socialist, for instance, was clearly a leftist. A terrifying picture of the bestialities committed by the left *résistance* comes from one of its "heroes," all in the best tradition of the French Revolution. Cf. Dominique Ponchardier, *Les Pavés de l'Enfer* (Paris: Gallimard, 1950). This charming lady describes how she cut the throat of a Monsieur Durand (22-23). "We really practiced slaughtering rather than assassinating," she recalls. A zealous *maquisard* called Simon slaughtered an SS officer in front of his soldiers and then forced them to eat little cakes dipped in the victim's blood. A very original Dominican, Père Bruckberger, who fought in the *résistance*, described the misdeeds of his companions in a book, whereupon his Order sent him into exile in America. (The scandal was too great.) Bruckberger, incidentally, has recently published an excellent book *Le capitalisme, mais c'est la vie* in which he boldly declares that the New Testament is a manifesto of human inequality.

1033. Cf. Louis Rougier, *La France Jacobine* (Paris and Brussels: Diffusion du Libre, 1947), 169-71, and Donald B. Robinson, "Blood Bath in France," *The American Mercury*, April 1946.

1034. Cf. Gilles Perrault, "Fallait-il sacrifier ces résistants?" *Historia*, June 1965, 765ff.

1035. Cf. Gallicus, "Terror in the Air," *Politics*, New York, November 1945, vol. 2, no. 11.

1036. Cf. Thilo. v. Wilmowsky, op. cit., 182-83.

1037. Cf. Winston S. Churchill, *The Second World War*, 1:482. Churchill gave the following instructions to Major General Macksey, selected on April 5, 1940, to command an expedition to Narvik: "It is clearly illegal to bombard a populated area in the hope of hitting a legitimate target which is known to be in the area but which cannot be precisely located and identified." This injunction was later blithely overlooked.

1038. After prisoners of war were repeatedly killed in Germany by Allied raids, Brigadier General B. M. Bryan declared that these incidents were regrettable, but "the pilots' instructions are to disrupt transportation and strafe every German vehicle they can see on the road." Cf. *New York Times*, April 8, 1945, AP dispatch.

1039. The destruction of Le Havre *after* the Germans had evacuated the city cost the lives of 3,500 Frenchmen; it was described by Anne O'Hare MacCormick in the *New York Times*, October 9, 1944. De Gaulle was present at the mass burial. When he protested, he was informed that it had been *thought* that Germans were still in the area. De Gaulle almost hit the ceiling; it explains in part his *ressentiment* against the English-speaking world. (Some of Couve de Murville's actions are understandable given the treatment he received in North Africa by Messrs. Roosevelt and Morgenthau, accompanied and advised by the Soviet spy Harry Dexter White. Cf. Robert Murphy, op. cit., 188-89.)

1040. The wanton destruction of a French village (in Alsace) was mentioned *passim* in an article in the *New York Times*.

The village had not seemed particularly enthusiastic about the American liberators. They were on the whole "unconcerned," but some boys were seen "spitting in the tracks of the Army trucks" and "there were those three, husky women strolling down arm in arm, singing and laughing and mocking everyone else." When the Nazi counterpush came, the inhabitants kissed the German soldiers and removed the American and French flags. "Somehow a few soldiers got back and told the story to the colonel. The colonel suddenly remembered that there were a lot of enemy tanks in the village and told the artillery to pound it to rubble. And so they did." Killing how many French citizens? Or only the three husky blondes? Cf. Ralph G. Martin, "What Kind of Peace? The Soldiers' Viewpoint," *New York Times Magazine*, March 11, 1945, 43-44.

1041. This frightening confusion was not restricted to the United States. I heard a famous French Catholic philosopher with leftist leanings speak about the "Fascist" Polish army in Italy.

1042. There were millions of "displaced persons"—an expression that marks a record in the realm of understatements, much like "relocation center" for concentration camp.

1043. Significantly, Jewish refugees were the least eager to return to the red paradise, and for a variety of reasons. When the Soviet regime broke down in Odessa and Kiev, history's most terrible spontaneous slaughter of Jews took place. Many of the Jews in the Ukraine had, however, fled, not believing the Soviet tales of brown anti-Semitism. Tragically enough, quite a number of Jewish soldiers in the Red Army were even *eager* to surrender to the Germans. The pro-German sympathies of Russian Jews had always been quite marked.

1044. Cf. note 760. Also Henry Picker, op. cit., 390, 394-95, 447-49.

1045. An official Spanish publication on its Jews can be found in the series *Temas Españoles*, no. 252, "Los Sefardíes," by Jesús Cantera Ortiz de Urbina (Madrid, 1958).

1046. Jews were not admitted into Sweden until the end of the eighteenth century (in Norway not until the end of the nineteenth century). Jews could become Swedish citizens in isolated cases only at the end of the nineteenth century. Jesuits were admitted to Norway twenty or so years ago. A great liberalization of the civic laws pertaining to non-Lutherans in Sweden took place in 1952. Cf. Peter Hornung, "Das schwedische Gesetz über Religionsfreiheit," *Stimmen der Zeit*, vol. 150, no. 8 (May 1952), 122-33. Until 1952, even the Catholic Bishop of Sweden had to submit a certificate of good conduct from *his* Lutheran pastor in order to get a passport. Finland, on the other hand, has had diplomatic relations with the Vatican since 1939, although it has only three thousand Catholic citizens.

1047. The year 1924 symbolizes the expiation—with rearranged numbers—of the year of expulsion, 1492.

1048. Sephardic descent could easily be proved by the family name. Proof of an (unbroken) genealogical tree was never required by the Spanish authorities.

1049. Admittedly, the camp of Miranda de Ebro, where many of the Jewish (and non-Jewish) refugees were temporarily located, was anything but a swank resort. The food was miserable. But at that time many in Spain were actually starving. In 1920, there were roughly eight hundred Jews in Spain; today there are over twelve thousand.

1050. I wrote a long paper on the efforts of the "Fascist" Spanish Government to save Jewish lives during World War II. For about a half year I negotiated with a leading American-Jewish "liberal" (now very conservative) monthly to have it accepted. But exception was taken to this or the other statement. Wanting to get the facts across, I compromised on stylistic matters. The answer was nevertheless a "No." Spain was "fascist," and that was that. Thus I had the essay published in France, "L'Espagne et les Juifs," *Études* (Paris, April 1956), vol. 289, no. 4, and in the *Catholic World* (Oct. 1956). Needless to say, I was thoroughly disgusted by the petty and, in a deeper sense, dishonest American "liberal" publication. This bit of truth was in the end communicated to the American public at large when in 1970 Rabbi Chaim Lipschitz divulged it to *Newsweek* magazine.

1051. The French Sephardic community, about three thousand families, thanked Franco in a letter (October 1941) for his effective aid. The Spanish government saw to it that these Sephardic Jews with their property were placed under the protection of the Spanish consulate. They were also exempt from wearing the Star of David.

1052. Which resembles a statement about another republic: *"Hominum confusione et divina providentia regnatur Helvetia."* Yet Switzerland no less than the United States exercised in the eighteenth century an immense political-social fascination on romantic minds—a fascination mobilized by Jean-Jacques Rousseau who became a spokesman for *la libre Helvétie*. Cf. Gonzague de Reynold, *La démocratie et la Suisse* (Bern: Editions du Chandelier, 1929), 191-92.

1053. The trouble with Japan in the remote past was the weakness of its monarch, which resulted in an oligarchic military dictatorship (*bakufu*, literally, "rule of the tent") headed by the Shôgun. The Restoration of 1868 meant the return of the Emperor to full power, after its abeyance for many centuries. In 1935 a new *bakufu* arose casting the Emperor in the role of a sacred cow, remote and ineffective, emasculating the parliament. Prince Mikasa, the late Emperor's youngest brother and a noted historian, gave me a vivid account of how the militarists deified the *Tennô* and even warned people not to look at him directly for fear of being blinded. At the present time, the role of the Emperor is greatly weakened, the army is reduced to a minimum, and the country is in some danger if, in a grave economic crisis (certainly not evident today), extremist parties should arise. (Japanese who have lost their common sense and self-control can be terrifying.) Due to the nature of

American intervention, not only the balance of power in East Asia, but also the internal balance of Japan, which needs a sound imperial authority, have been lost. The warnings of Gaetano Mosca in his *Ciò che la storia potrebbe insegnare* (Milan, 1958) 289-90, 308, have not been heeded. Still, the evolution (through constitutional reform) of a stronger imperial center is still possible.

1054. The words of St. Augustine—that the Church is *paupera et inops*, poor and helpless—are true at all times. Canossa? The end of that long story was that Gregory VII died in Salerno fleeing from the Emperor. The notion that the Church was powerful only when the sun of the state shone upon it totally misinterprets the "power" of Pius XII who, according to Pinchas E. Lapide's excellent book, *Rom und die Juden* (Freiburg i. Br: Herder, 1967), 188, saved between 700,000 and 900,000 Jews. But the Pope (wisely) did not protest publicly against the horrors of the extermination camps, about which, in any case, he had no exact knowledge. Such a protest would have exacted terrible payment from other members of his flock. The National Socialists had learned from Bismarck to spare the hierarchy while making the laymen and women pay for the courage of their leaders. When the Dutch Catholic bishops protested the deportation of the Jews, the brown monsters murdered Dutch Jews of the Catholic faith. Blessed Edith Stein, a Carmelite nun and philosopher who died in Auschwitz, was among them. A "bad record" in the public eye is preferable to the agony of innocents. (The public eye? Listen to Rivarol: "The public, the public? How many idiots does it take to form a public?") In this connection, I am frequently reminded of a conversation in F. Scott Fitzgerald's *The Beautiful and the Damned* (Garden City, N.Y.: Perma-Books, 1951), 239:

Maury: I imagined you were broad-minded.
Paramore: I am.
Muriel: Me, too. I believe one religion's as good as another and everything.
Paramore: There's some good in all religions.
Muriel: I'm a Catholic but, as I always say, I'm not working at it.
Paramore (with a tremendous burst of tolerance): The Catholic religion is a very—a very powerful religion.

Luckily (or unluckily) this is a widespread illusion—an illusion related to the belief that the Church is a purely dogmatic monolith. Writes a Lutheran theologian: "There is probably no other Church which has the capacity for harboring so many widely divergent theological points of view as the Roman Church. . . There is a fixed dogmatic limit, but within this limit there is room for divergent and often contradictory opinions." Cf. F. E. Mayer, *The Religious Bodies of America* (St. Louis: Concordia Publishing House, n.d., 2nd ed.) 32, 38.

1055. The writer of this volume had been to Vietnam five times (twice during the Ngo Dinh Diem regime) and the last time in 1972. He emphatically rejects the story of the "suppression of the Buddhists." The United Nations sent a commission to Vietnam after the violent death of the Ngo brothers: It reported that there was not a shred of evidence of persecution of the Buddhists, past or present. To much of the American public, it made little sense to place the main burden of the war effort on the shoulders of the "Buddhist" majority (instead of the Catholic minority). The

Buddhists—the anti-Christian Mahayana-Buddhists plus the far more spiritual Hinayana (Teravada) Buddhists—do not form a majority. The estimates are: 35 to 40 percent Mahayana and Hinayana-Buddhists, 12 to 18 percent Catholics, the rest Caodaists, Hao-Hoa supporters and, above all, Animists. Cf. also Piero Gheddo, *Cattolici e Buddisti nel Vietnam* (Florence: Vallecchi, 1968).

Mr. David Halberstam, an American journalist who "substantiated" the myth, was given the Pulitzer Prize for his achievement. He claimed that he had toppled Ngo Dinh Diem and, no doubt, he actually did. Thus the best leader South Vietnam ever had was doomed by the *New York Times*, which was religiously read in the White House. Henry Kissinger rightly called the fall and murder of Diem "a real folly, although the war correspondents were for it." Cf. his *The White House Years* (Boston: Little, Brown, 1979), 231. General Samuel T. Williams called Ngo Dinh Diem "the most dedicated man I have ever known in Asia for two generations. It will set back religious freedom and Christianity in Vietnam." Cf. *U.S. News & World Report*, November 9, 1964, 62-72.

1056. The weakness of the countries bordering on Vietnam, Cambodia, and Laos, is due precisely to their intense Buddhist character, which involves peacefulness, absent-mindedness, indifference, and lack of aggression. (Merchants and entrepreneurs in these delightful countries were almost exclusively Chinese, Viets, Indians, and Europeans.) A fierce minority led by a Marxist monster like Pol Pot can commit dreadful atrocities against such a soft population, just as the Aztecs did in Central Mexico among their subject tribes.

1057. Taiwan presently has a population of well over 21 million in an area 15 percent smaller than Switzerland, and with a somewhat similar distribution of high mountains and lowlands. (The highest mountains in Switzerland are over 15,000 feet, in Taiwan over 12,000 feet.) The Taiwanese have the third highest living standards in all of Asia, lower than those of Israel and Japan and about equal to those of Korea.

1058. Again, a warning note not to confuse the Provider State (the correct name for the Welfare State) with the Socialist State, although all Socialist States (including a National Socialist State like Hitler's Third Reich) have the added character of being Provider States—the Santa Claus parties having transformed it.

1059. Cf. Le Capitaine Charles De Gaulle, *La discorde chez l'ennemi* (Paris: Berger-Levrault, 1924).

1060. Cf. *Economic Council Letter* (New York), no. 271, September 15, 1951, 1. The author of the article had it directly from General MacArthur.

1061. Antoine de Rivarol, who died in 1801 in his Berlin exile, was a French Royalist, the son of an innkeeper, and bearer of one of the many fake French titles. He was unexcelled in his witty and profound remarks, many of a political or social nature. Ernst Jünger has written a profound book about him.

1062. Witchcraft is by no means based purely on superstition. In the nineteenth century, at the time of our "enlightened" grandparents, black magic was relegated to the realm of fairy tales. Yet modern ethnologists and anthropologists of the first order accept it. Cf. for instance Hans Findeisen, *Schamanentum* (Stuttgart: Kohlhammer, 1957), 13- 14. The cases of Navajo witchcraft which I have related or alluded to in

Die Gottlosen (Salzburg: Berglandbuch, 1962) are also authentic. Compare also with André Dupeyrat, *Savage Papua*, E. and D. Demauny, trsl. (New York: Dutton, 1954), 145ff. At the same time, genuine superstition might live side-by-side with the truly supernatural. The partly ludicrous, partly tragic "Cargo-Cult" in New Guinea is a point in question. Cf. Joseph Höltker, SVD, "Der Cargo-Kult in Neuguineas lebt noch," *Neue Zeitshrift für Missionswissenschaft*, vol. 18, no. 3, 223-26. The same: "Die Mambu-Bewegung in Neuguineas. Zum Prophetentum in Melanesia," *Annali Lateranensi*, vol. 5 (1941), 181-219.

1063. Cf. André Dupeyrat, op. cit., 217ff. and 246ff.

1064. For this very reason an honest man such as President Tubman of Liberia admitted that many of Liberia's ills stem from the fact that his country never had "the benefits of colonialism" (*Time*, January 17, 1969, 28). Emperor Haile Selassie expressed a similar sentiment. Cf. Michel Croce-Spinelli, *Les Enfants de Poto-Poto* (Paris: Grasset, 1967), 338.

1065. Cf. Sigrid Undset, *Selvportretter og Landskapsbilleder* (Oslo: H. Aschehoug, 1938), 195-96.

1066. Cf. Jacob Burckhardt, *Briefe an seinen Freund Friedrich von Preen 1864-1893* (Stuttgart: Deutsche Verlagsanstalt, 1922), 248 (letter dated Baden, July 24, 1889).

1067. Big *Apartheid* stood for the territorial separation of whites and non-whites in South Africa. Its practicality could be questioned, but it is not so easy to attack on moral grounds. Little *Apartheid*, which regulated the "coexistence" between the various tribes, involving separate school buses, elevators, post office windows, etc., was different. It involved real discrimination and should be rejected. *This, however, is a piece of historical reminiscence.* In South Africa today, there are hardly more vestiges of apartheid than in the United States. To discover in which direction South Africa is moving, it ought to be visited regularly, at least every other year.

1068. As Senator, John F. Kennedy delivered a blistering speech in early 1957 against the continued French presence in Algeria. (One wonders what specific knowledge he had of the Algerian situation.) The result? An increase of anti-American feeling in France and no gratitude whatsoever from the "New Algeria," which retained a strong anti-American foreign policy. To assure the survival of a French cultural influence (above all the French language), France continued to pay enormous subsidies to its ex-colonies, i.e., between 1 and 2 percent of its GNP. Algeria, for instance, is wholly dependent upon France. If, in the case of serious economic crisis, France were to send home its Algerian workers, Algeria would quietly collapse.

1069. The Swiss diplomat and scholar Jacques Albert Cuttat, a man with great knowledge and affection for Asia, in his lecture, "Die geistige Bedeutung Asiens und des Abendlandes für einander," in *Münchner Universitätsreden* (Munich: Max Hueber, 1961), 26-27, pointed out the danger of a misplaced guilt complex by the West. Having studied conditions in Southern Italy with the aid of the *Cassa per il mezzogiorno* and knowing Nigeria, I can sympathize with Naomi Mitchison who said that living standards in Eastern Nigeria (the ill-fated Biafra) were higher than in Southern Italy. Cf. her *Other Peoples' Worlds: Impressions of Ghana and Nigeria* (London: Secker and Warburg, 1958), 94.

1070. Original text: "Estamos pobres porque un estado *traidor* entrega los bienes del pueblo argentino como un tributo colonial a su majestad británica!" Hardly had Perón nationalized British-owned railroads than they went into a decline from which they have not recovered to this day.

1071. This remark might be extended to the United States. Although Americans of part-African ancestry are emphatically not Negroes, Peter F. Drucker is right when he says that "Black Harlem is one of the world's wealthiest communities—fifth or so in per capita income of all communities outside of North America and Europe, and easily the richest of all Negro communities in the world." Cf. his *The Age of Discontinuity* (New York: Harper & Row, 1968), 123.

1072. But what happens if one person is very industrious and the other "takes it easy"? The ambitious man automatically creates an "undemocratic" situation. In Austria at present the law foresees the 38-40-hour week for the working class and a 5-week annual vacation. I work 75 hours a week. A statistic compiled in 1969 revealed that the self-employed in Austria work an average of 62-and-a-half hours a week. To level the inequality, the ambitious worker must be punished through progressive taxation, thus rendering intensive or extensive work materially unattractive.

1073. The Soviets, quite obviously, do not suffer the widespread modern evil of Western masochism. Cf. Helmut Schoeck, "Der Masochismus des Abendlands" in *Europa—Besinnung und Hoffnung,* A. Hunold, ed. (Erlenbach-Zürich: Rentsch, 1957), 221-56. These brilliant pages require a supplementary reading of H. Fortmann's book on "cultures of shame" and "cultures of guilt." (Cf. H. Fortmann, *Schuldcultuuren en Schaamtecultuuren*, Hertogenbosch, 1962). Ours obviously is a culture of guilt, and our "friends" and enemies know very well indeed how to exploit it.

1074. Embassies (representing the heads of states) and legations (representing merely the heads of governments); before World War I only world powers (including the Vatican and Turkey) had *mutual* representations with embassy rank. (Thus the United States had an embassy in Paris, but only a legation in Brussels or Monrovia.) During and after World War II the megalomania of newly created nations changed the order. There are very few legations left. It is delightful to see an embassy of Trinidad and Tobago in Addis Ababa, but then, too, enormous sums are squandered by the new small nations on their diplomatic service.

1075. Almost immediately after the Six-Day War in the Near East, Mrs. Indira Gandhi handed a check of 50 million U.S. Dollars to the Government of the United Arab Republic. It is surely surprising to see an emerging nation, plagued by bitter poverty and clamoring for aid, being so generous with its funds.

1076. This was also the opinion of two Central American speakers at a Conference on Constructive Alternatives (CCA) in Hillsdale College, Michigan.

1077. After a television debate on the Vietnam War, I remarked to the three other participants, college and university professors: "I am surprised to see that, although an alien, I was the only one here loyal to *your* country." They were furious and one of them even refused to shake hands with me. "You are offended?" I asked him. "Indeed, I am." This gave me great satisfaction because, as Napoleon said, truth alone offends—and I had told him just that.

1078. I refer to the novel, *Die Gottlosen*. (A Dutch translation was published in 1965.) Hemingway was careful, of course. In novels with European backgrounds, his heroes were always American.

1079. One of the most priceless books of this sort is Dmitri Sergeyevitch's *Na golubom Dunaye* (Odessa: Oblastnoye Izdatelstvo, 1955), a novel about postwar Vienna, concocted with the help of encyclopedias. It is even funnier than Hochhuth's *The Deputy*, and ought to be published in English, perhaps funded by a foundation. Even those unacquainted with Austria would be exhilarated.

Americans might be more amused by the play *Shakaly*, written by an Estonian Communist, Jakobson, trsl. into Russian by L. Toom (Moscow: Iskusstvo, 1953), as it speaks of the South in the United States. The villain is an American general, McKennedy by name, who is assisted by an evil college professor, whose wealth and power allow him to dominate a whole city. Phrases like "Now they go to the lynchings in their smart sports cars while their ancestors went with covered wagons" add flavor to the play. (As do the "Imperialist War Hymns" in praise of the A-bomb sung by the Salvation Army.) A Western reader could also derive the most devastating fun from Ivan Kurchavov's *Moskovskoye Vremya* (Tallin: Estonskoye Gosudarstvennoye Izdatelstvo, 1956), which describes an Estonian ne'er-do-well being trained in the Vatican to disrupt labor organizations. He becomes a friend of the Pope, learns to use poison, pistols, and false signatures, studies the history of the Inquisition, and makes himself popular by shouting: "We have to burn them all on the stake—from the Communists to the Metropolit of Moscow" (293). Yet it is quite unsurprising, given the sources. The article "Jesuits" in the *Bolshaya Sovyetskaya Entsiklopediya* (Moscow, 1952), 27:341-42, is also a priceless piece; it could have appeared in any Nazi magazine.

1080. Cf. Larry Collins and Dominique Lapierre, *Freedom at Midnight* (London: Pan Books, 1975), 329sq. This bestial massacre was not ordered by a bloodthirsty tyrant, a totalitarian regime, or a fanatical government; it came about *spontaneously*—no propaganda, no conspiracy, no influence from above was involved. It was an extremely popular "happening."

1081. It is significant that in nineteenth-century America a *socialist* author established a *nationalist* party. This neatly prefigures "horizontal" national socialism.

1082. One of the first authors to voice fears of a coming leftist tyranny was the Hungarian poet Imre Madách (1828-1864), who wrote the drama *Az ember tragédiája* ("The Tragedy of Man"), which pictured the existence of man from the Fall in Paradise to the establishment in the future of a terrifying socialist state. His classic play was translated into many languages and is frequently called "the Hungarian Faust."

1083. Cf. Ephraim D. Adams, *Power Ideals in American Society* (New Haven: Yale University Press, 1913).

1084. Cf. Ralph Henry Gabriel, *The Course of American Democratic Thought* (New York: Ronald Press, 1940), 382.

1085. Cf. Crane Brinton, *Ideas and Men: The Story of Western Thought* (New York: Prentice Hall, 1950), 549. Yet Brinton was also convinced that the triad of democracy, "fascism," and socialism works effectively as a surrogate for religion (538).

1086. In India and large parts of Africa, the vast majority of voters is illiterate and thus the voting ballots are marked with symbols, especially animal symbols. Since knowledge is not a prerequisite for voting, why not lower the voting age to eight, when most children can read?

1087. In certain countries (Belgium, the Tyrol) the nonvoter has to pay a fine. The outcomes of elections seem "most impressive" and are hailed as signs of "political maturity."

1088. Belief in the sacredness of the principle of majority rule (one of the two dogmas of democracy) is so strong that the expression "minority government" is one of the most pejorative in the language of the mass media. "A white minority government" has taken to sounding more devastating than "a totalitarian party dictatorship."

1089. In the Athenian democracy, too, the inanity of elections was felt to the extent that the lot was also used.

1090. Cf. *Plutarchus Vitae*, Lindskog & Ziegler, ed. (Leipzig: Teubner, 1932), viii, 1-2 (10).

1091. The origin of this saying must be a distortion of Hesiod's *Works and Days* (763), according to which "rumor always survives because he is a god." Alcuin contradicted the *vox populi, vox Dei* formula, writing in his *Capitulare admonitionis ad Carolum* that it is best to ignore it because the mob's mania for noise approaches insanity. Alexander Hamilton thought similarly when he said on June 18, 1787, at the Federal Convention: "The voice of the people has been said to be the voice of God, and however generally this maxim has been quoted or believed, it is not true to fact. The people. . . seldom judge or determine right."

1092. Cf. *Hansard*, November 10, 1947.

1093. Cf. notes 717 and 718.

1094. Cf. Raymond Aron, *Le grand schisme* (Paris: Gallimard-NRF, 1948), 28. By the 1860s, Austria already had a well-functioning parliament, the *Reichsrath*, which was averse to raising taxes. It held the purse strings and vetoed the money necessary to exchange the muzzle loaders of the Imperial army for breach loaders. The result was fatal: in the German-Prussian War of 1866, the firing capacity of the Prussian army was four times that of the Austrians and their German allies. Thus the Battle of Königgrätz was lost and Germany was eventually unified by Berlin instead of Vienna. Had the German League, headed by Austria, won, world history would have been totally different.

1095. For a variety of reasons a government can, of course, fail to propagandize the masses, and the enemy, with the aid of the mass media, can persuade the people and those in power to change course and terminate a war which might otherwise have been won. This was the case in the Vietnam War. In the late sixties I spoke at various universities on the war (duly warned by the "authorities" of possible violence to myself) and was greeted once with a standing ovation. Various students, veterans of the conflict, later shook my hand and told me that they at long last knew what it was they had been fighting for.

  The worst crimes in Vietnam were perpetrated by the retreating Viet-Cong after their failure (little noted by the American and European Left) in the Têt offensive.

The sadistic cruelties are described vividly by Dan Oberdorfer in his *Têt* (New York: Da Capo, 1984).

1096. Is the United States a "peace-loving nation"? Yes, in a way; nevertheless, in the nineteenth century the U.S. fought no fewer than four foreign wars (Tripolitania, Britain, Mexico, Spain) and its own "War Between the States"—only one less than Prussia. (In the war against Britain, the United States was *de facto* allied with Napoleon, certainly no liberal, democratic, peace-loving sovereign.)

1097. Toward the end of World War I, a wave of protest in the democracies broke out against "secret diplomacy." President Wilson took the lead. One could as well propose to play poker by laying all the cards on the table.

1098. The statesmen or, rather, the strong leaders of the postwar period were all born before World War I—men as different as de Gaulle, Adenauer, Franco, Salazar, Schuman, Tito, Stalin, Churchill, Mao (some undoubtedly monstrous). But in the apparent calm of a liberal democracy, outstanding people with a strong nature no longer seem to enter politics; and the totalitarian red bureaucracies became visibly sclerotic. The time for great men seems to belong to the past.

1099. The only exception is probably the successful Marshall Plan, which was opposed by various neoliberals. They argued that devastated Europe ought to get back on its feet without aid.

1100. In the leading old universities on the East coast, geography was at times an inconspicuous shadow of the geology department. In Continental high school-colleges (ages ten to eighteen or nineteen), students take geography twice a week and must own a geography atlas (the same pertains to history). Geography is much more than memorizing maps; it demands "geographic thinking."

1101. This, to Jefferson's mind, included Americans who were in diplomatic service in Europe. Cf. Francis J. Grund, *Aristocracy in America* (New York: Harper Torch Books, 1959), 128. The book was originally published in London in 1839.

1102. The German words *Ausländer* and *ausländisch*, on the other hand, almost denote distinction.

1103. Wilson was won over to Italy's incorporation of the German-speaking South Tyrol, a real wound in the body politic of Europe, by means of a fake map showing a mountain called "Vetta d'Italia" on the very border of the Tyrol and Salzburg.

1104. See note 27.

1105. Cf. Georges Bernanos, *Les enfants humiliés* (Paris: Gallimard, 1949), 199-200. Is this only the view of a Catholic monarchist? Sigmund Freud thought in a similar way when he wrote that the masses, hellbent on gratification and destruction, have to be kept down forcefully by soberly thinking superior people. Cf. his *Gesammelte Werke* (Vienna: Psychoanalytischer Verlag, 1934), 12: Freud has been totally misunderstood in America. The translation of his works into English, according to Bruno Bettelheim, is a scandal. (Needless to say, Freud never preached promiscuity and praised ascetic Christianity for having saved true Eros.) Freud spoke about the "soul" (*Seele*), not the "psyche," and he had one besetting fear: that his cultural and educational theories should fall into the hands of psychiatric therapists. Cf. Bruno Bettelheim, "Freud and the Soul," *The New Yorker,* March 1, 1982, 52-93.

1106. Cf. J. J. Rousseau, *Du contrat social*, book III, chap. 4.

1107. Cf. my *Liberty or Equality?* 110-116.

1108. Cf. Moses Yakovlevitch Ostrogorski, *Democracy and the Organization of Political Parties* (Macmillan: London, 1902), 632. The moral losers are the voters, too. Karl Mannheim observed that the voting masses now shoulder the moral responsibility that was formerly the concern of the "sophisticated (aristocratic) elites" and crowned rulers. The effects are definitely evil. See his "Rational and Irrational Elements in Contemporary Society," *L. T. Hobhouse Lectures* (London: Oxford University Press, 1934), Lecture IV, 33.

1109. It was *not* Senator Goldwater whom I met in Spain. I told the defeated Senator that I could not understand his candidacy, for if I were suddenly to wake up and find myself President of the United States, it would take four strong male nurses to keep me from jumping out of the nearest window. He just smiled.

1110. Cf. (Lord) James Bryce, *The American Commonwealth* (New York: Macmillan, 1911), 1:77sq.

1111. Abraham Lincoln? He did not prevent the worst war in history prior to 1914, i.e., the American Civil War of 1861-1865, which cost the lives of over half a million men.

1112. This view was also held by Raymond Aron, cf. *Les guerres en chaîne*, 313.

1113. The French army, as a result of the "Original Sin of French Conservatism," remained split for decades. The French Government in World War I refused to accept Foch as commander-in-chief of the Allied armies because his brother was a Jesuit and he had had a Catholic education. Thanks to Britain's virtual ultimatum, the rabidly anticlerical Clemenceau finally yielded in 1918.

1114. The higher voting participation in the Swiss canton elections is not surprising. Local affairs are far better understood than more universal matters.

1115. It is significant that the Spanish language has no word for "compromise"; *compromiso* has the opposite meaning: it means "fixed engagement." Equally significant, the English expression "fifty-fifty" is now being used colloquially on the Continent, untranslated.

1116. Pope Boniface VIII in his *Bull to the French Clergy* (1296) and Luther's *Vorlesungen über den Römerbrief 1515-1516* (Scholion for Romans 13, 1).

1117. Dean Acheson was not too popular among conservatives, not only because he started out being left-of-center and a member of a Democratic Cabinet, but also because he sported a Homburg hat, grey mustache (at that time considered "aristocratic" and snobbish), dark jacket, striped trousers, and a Harvard accent. To make matters worse, his parents were born in Canada. He was not, of course, infallible.

1118. Cf. Otto v. Habsburg, "Gute USA-Aussenpolitik," *Zeitbühne* (July 1976), 13.

1119. The reason for the Twenty-Second Amendment was President Roosevelt's fourth term, overturning the time-honored two-term limit. Fear arose that the citizenry would become accustomed to the near-permanent rule of one man, a psychological move in the direction of a monarchy.

1120. But if one's own father, brother, husband, or son had been killed during some sort of "experimental" warfare which had been broken off because it "displeased" the leftist media, the reaction might well have been a mixture of fury, despair, and rancor. Defeats do happen in history, and they are tragic and sometimes unavoidable, but a vain sacrifice due to a lack of aim, purpose, and determination, is quite another matter.

1121. I went to Vientiane flying criss-cross over the Ho-Chi-Minh Trail in order to investigate the situation. The discussions with the Laotian officials were hopeless, because Far Eastern logic works along lines quite different from ours.

1122. The Europeans, by and large, were fed by information from American news agencies (which in turn received it from newsmen who could not even speak French, the only means of contact with part of the local population). American officialdom showed real inertia in regard to telling Europeans the truth and informing them of their country's aims. (Was this passivity accidental, or had treason become fashionable?) The anti-American and pro-Viet-Cong attitude even affected ecclesiastic circles. The German Catholic News Agency (KNA) openly sympathized with the red sadists, and the Vatican donated $1.5 million to the North Vietnamese for "humanitarain purposes." An account of how this money was spent has never, to my knowledge, reached Rome.

1123. Cf. General William C. Westmoreland, *A Soldier Reports* (Garden City: Doubleday, 1976). Needless to say, the author never recommended use of the A-bomb; he was not another Harry S Truman. The war there could have been won in a much more conventional manner. Even before the betrayal of South Vietnam, intelligent American generals had protested Washington's policies in the area. *Vide* Lieutenant General Samuel T. Williams: "Why U.S. is losing in Vietnam. An Inside Story," *U.S. News & World Report*, November 9, 1964. General Williams was not alone in deploring the fall and assassination of the valiant Ngo Dinh Diem. Henry Kissinger, cf. his *The White House* (Boston: Little, Brown, 1979), 231, was well aware of the guilt in this matter incurred by American war reporters.

1124. Lies can of course also be told in print. There is a South-German–Austrian expression: "He lies like print" (or a printed text) (*Er lügt wie gedruckt*). Northern Europeans and Americans are far more gullible than most when presented with printed information. This conceivably has something to do with bibliolatry. The tragic effects of the pro-Communist propaganda in the United States were watched with a sinking heart by the last South Vietnamese ambassador to Washington. Cf. Bui-Diem and David Charnoff, *In the Jaws of History* (New York: Harper & Row, 1987), 286-87.

1125. The singer Joan Baez found out relatively early that she had been tricked by the mass media into taking her antiwar stand, Jane Fonda did not concede her error until 1989. The "boat people" were great eye-openers. Unlike Americans, South or East Europeans, on opening the daily newspaper, say to themselves: "These, then, are the lies the newspapermen (government) want us to believe today."

1126. Significantly, many Asian communities received their intellectual formation in that birthplace of modern democracy: not only Pol Pot, but also Ho-Chi-Minh and Dzhu-Enlai studied in Paris. Cf. F. Sitte, *Die roten Khmer* (Graz: Styria, 1982), 47.

1127. Cf. Leslie Gelb, *The Irony of Vietnam. The System Worked* (Washington, D.C.: Brookings Institution, 1978).

1128. Cf. Adelbert Weinstein, "Der heimliche Krieg der Sowjets," *Frankfurter Allgemeine Zeitung*, August 9, 1980, 4. Also remember that Richard Nixon as President of the United States gave South Vietnam a solemn guarantee of renewed American intervention should the Communists break the Paris Treaty. Cf. Nguyen Tien Hung and Jerrol L. Schecter, *The Palace File* (New York: Harper & Row, 1986), 812. *Democratica fides!* Yet no democratic body or politician can make promises for the future. Eternal change is democracy's iron principle. Hence a constructive, historically oriented foreign policy is completely out of the question.

1129. Actually, large landholdings were never characteristic of the agrarian scene in Vietnam. When the American advisors came, they thought that communism in Vietnam was the result of "feudal conditions" and were thus surprised when they found no large estates. (The same pertained in China. In old China, farms of one hundred acres or more were extremely rare; in Taiwan today, the maximum acreage permitted is 7.5.)

1130. Cf. Marx-Engels, *Historisch-kritiche Gesamtausgabe* (MEGA), (Berlin, 1932), 5:227.

1131. A well-documented book on the attack against Dr. Kurt Waldheim, the successful Austrian presidential candidate in 1986, would be well worth writing. It could serve as a first-class exhibit of the monumental ignorance of the mass media and of the organizations backing them, as well as of the helpless millions who blindly believe all they are offered. The campaign originated in Austrian Socialist circles, cf. Günther Ofner, "Die Rolle der SPÖ in der Waldheim-Kampagne" in Khol, Faulhaber and Ofner, *Die Kampagne Kurt Waldheim. Opfer oder Täter?* (Munich: Herbig, 1987), 110-75. Americans, in this case, were the "fall guys." Their propaganda, mixed with threats, greatly helped Waldheim to win the election. Unlike his opponent, he was, and is, no "father figure."

1132. The Abbé Siéyès finally returned to Paris, where he died in peace; another regicide, Fouché, became a diplomat under Louis XVIII.

1133. Cf. Friedrich A. von Hayek, *Law, Legislation and Liberty* (London: Routledge & Kegan Paul, 1976), 2:54.

1134. In the East European languages, *Weltanschauung* was almost always literally translated. (In Russia it even has two versions.)

1135. Even in combinations like *Ideologiekritik, ideiologielos* or *ideologieverdächtig* ("suspected of having an ideological foundation").

1136. Cf. F. A. von Hayek, "The Intellectuals and Socialism" in *The Intellectuals*, G. R. de Huszár, ed. (Glencoe: Free Press, 1960), 386, and *Law, Legislation and Liberty*, 1:65.

1137. Cf. his article "Quest for a Tempered Utopia," *Wall Street Journal*, November 14, 1986.

1138. Cf. Peter F. Drucker, *The End of Economic Man* (New York: John Day, 1939), 241-42.

1139. Cf. Eliseo Vivas, "On the Conservative Demonology," *Modern Age* (Spring 1964), 121.

488   *Notes*

1140. His useful chart has not yet been published. It is considered preposterous by Europeans to call Adam Smith a "conservative thinker." As to my own evaluation of genuine and fake conservatism in the United States, cf. E. v. Kuehnelt-Leddihn, "An Alien Looks at American Conservatism," the *St. Croix Review*, June 1990.

1141. Cf. *Odyssey of a Friend: Whittaker Chambers' Letters to William F. Buckley* (Washington: Regnery Gateway, 1987), 230. Chambers was also convinced that capitalism and conservatism do not mix. This is a rather primitive mistake of European conservatives, with the shadow of a Third Way in the background.

1142. Cf. Cornelia I. Gerstenmaier, *Der Stimme der Stummen* (Stuttgart: Seewald, 1971), 65. These events are not surprising. In 1953, seventeen Russian Red Army officers refused to fire at rebellious workers in Berlin. They were executed and received a memorial for their courage in West Berlin.

1143. In the heart of the Ukraine is an area of "scheduled cities," i.e., cities not accessible to visitors. In 1963, pitched battles between Ukrainians and Soviet units took place around Krivoy Rog; they were never reported. Armed resistance in the Western Ukraine continued right up to the late 1950s.

1144. Cf. Herzen's letter to Jules Michelet, written in 1851, found in *Sochineniya A. I. Gertsena* (Geneva: Georg, 1878), 5:209. He said textually that Russia would never be "Protestant," never *juste-milieu*. From ignorance, "Protestantism" has for the past two hundred years generally been viewed as a middle-of-the-road religion. Nobody in France admires *un modéré*. (Hence, too, in Spain the popularity of the *exaltados*.)

1145. Even the right-wing military government of Brazil, after the overthrow of the Goulart regime in 1964, talked about *A Revolução*. One out of three parties in Latin America calls itself "revolutionary."

1146. Cf. Salvador de Madariaga, *Bolívar* (Madrid: Espasa-Calpe, 1958), 2:215. An equally desperate letter is found on p. 490.

1147. This brings to mind the story of a diplomat in Kinshasa who was attacked by three robbers. The athletic man knocked them out, and the next day the chief of police wanted to buy his shirt, convinced that it had empowered the diplomat with extraordinary strength. (Cf. Michel Croce-Spinelli, op. cit., 40.)

    A free and healthy economy can flourish in a tolerant dictatorship and perish in a narrow-minded, restrictive democracy.

1148. Cf. Benjamin Hart, *Poisoned Ivy* (New York: Stein & Day, 1987), 15-18.

1149. Cf. Mihajlo Mihajlov, *Underground Notes* (New Rochelle: Caratzas Brothers, 1982), 79. This chapter is called "The Absurdity of Nonideology." Whittaker Chambers, op. cit., 84, wrote about the need for an alternative. Freedom, he insisted, was not enough.

1150. Cf. Émile Boutmy, *Essai d'une psychologie politique du peuple anglais du XIXe siècle* (Paris: Armand Colin, 1901), 27. This recalls Hegel's reaction to a student's observation that the facts contradicted his theory. Hegel looked at the man severely over his spectacles and said: "All the worse for the facts." Trotski's outlook was quite similar. He confessed: "The feeling of the pre-eminence of the general over the particular, the law over the facts, the theory over the personal experience, originated in me at an early age and was strengthened with the years." Cf. his *Moya zhizn'* (Berlin: Granit, 1930), 1:27. This is a far cry from the trial-and-error method.

1151. Cf. Holmes-Pollock, op. cit., 2:307, 309. Holmes added significantly that he preferred to read P. G. Wodehouse.

1152. There are "Gay Clubs" in state universities, subsidized by the authorities. Taxpayers' money is thus being used to finance the spread of homosexuality, which can, up to a point, become fashionable. Cf. my essay, "Homosexuality: A Christian Point of View," *The Human Life Review* (Spring 1978). Benjamin Hart tells (op. cit., 166-67) how right-wingers tried in Dartmouth (as a provocation) to establish a college-subsidized "Dartmouth Bestiality Association," but the authorities quite irrationally refused to legitimize the club as an "alternative lifestyle." On Thomas Mann, democracy and homosexuality, cf. p. 198.

1153. It was published in *National Review* on October 16, 1980, and by the National Committee of Catholic Laymen (NYC) the following year as a public service. There are Spanish and German versions.

1154. The Mandarin System lasted in China for countless generations. It is still being practiced in the (Taiwanese) Republic of China. I had the opportunity to talk to Dr. Sun Fô, son of Sun Yatsen and director of the examination board; here, the sons of the Prime Minister and the small farmer have exactly the same chances. (College or university degrees are ignored.) On the Continent, civil servants are "finalized" only after a number of probationary years.

1155. Dr. Francis B. Crick, the British protagonist of abortion and Nobel Prize winner, proposed the mandatory extermination of those over eighty. The Lutheran Bishop of Austria, Dr. O. Sakrausky, called Austria's abortion law, issued by a Socialist government, the "Royal Road Back to Auschwitz." In both cases—Jews or the unborn—the victims were considered "unwanted life."

1156. The British monarch could *theoretically* refuse to sign a law, but such a feat has become unthinkable.

1157. In my *Liberty or Equality?* 150-64, I gave no fewer than thirty favorable reasons for a hereditary monarchical government within the framework of a *regimen mixtum*. In that chapter, I cited Rivarol, who said that a monarch can be a Nero or a Marcus Aurelius, the people can collectively be a Nero, but they can never, ever, be a Marcus Aurelius.

1158. A Roman in the year 260 A.D. might have hotly denied that his country was a monarchy. The official inscriptions read: SENATUS POPULUSQUE ROMANUS. "Imperator" only meant "general." But when in 280 Diocletian donned a gold crown, demanded that the people kneel before him, and abolished the Senate, it finally became evident that the republic had gone the way of all flesh. Recently? No, three hundred years previously.

1159. The monarchy is at one and the same time a patriarchy and a matriarchy. In the popular mind, the royal couple figure as additional parents. Ruling queens and empresses have, moreover, always existed.

1160. Ludwig von Mises, former financial adviser to the Dollfuss regime and a pillar of the Austrian School of Economics, was decidedly a monarchist. Most of the Italian

Liberals I have known were monarchists, as were the German National Liberals (including Stresemann). And so too was the neoliberal Wilhelm Röpke, who, in a memorandum to the Allies, proposed Crown Prince Rupprecht of Bavaria for the German monarchy. Cf. also W. Röpke, *Die deutsche Frage* (Erlenbach-Zürich: Rentsch, 1945), 227.

1161. In a letter to Gouverneur Morris, dated New York, February 29, 1802, cf. *The Papers of Alexander Hamilton* (New York: Columbia University Press, 1977), 25:544. Hamilton was clearly a monarchist, as noted in his speech before the Federal Convention of June 18, 1787 (as reported by James Madison). A strict republicanism was rare among Americans of wide horizons even in those days. Cf. James Fenimore Cooper, "On the Advantages of a Monarchy" in his *The American Democrat* (New York: Knopf, Vintage Books, 1956), 56.

1162. Cf. André Shih, *L'Occident 'chrétien' vue par les Chinois vers la fin du 19e siècle 1870-1900* (Paris: Presses Universitaires, 1962), 226.

1163. Seneca: *Epistola ad Lucilium*, XXIX.

1164. Cf. *Harold Nicolson's Diaries 1930-1964* (London: Collins, 1980), 331 (March 4, 1949).

1165. Cf. his *Some Fruits of Solitude*, no. 337. William E. Simon has described cogently how politicians act in public to deceive voters. Cf. his *A Time for Truth* (New York: Reader's Digest Press, 1978), 166.

1166. John Harrison in his *The Reactionaries* (New York: Schocken, 1967) laments the "fact" that the greatest literary figures of the century—Yeats, Wyndham Lewis, Pound, Eliot, and Lawrence—were "attracted by Italian and German Fascism" before World War II (and in Pound's case during and after the war). There are two reasons for this overly stressed situation: revulsion against democracy, and the English difficulty in understanding Continental issues.

1167. Cf. Karl R. Popper, *The Open Society and its Enemies* (London: Routledge and Kegan Paul, 1962), 1:160.

1168. Cf. Eduard von Hartmann, *Zur Zeitgeschichte. Neue Tagesfragen. Gedanken über Staat, Politik und Sozialismus* (Leipzig: Kröner, n.d.), 14, 15. The burden of an obsolete form of government is felt in Latin America more than elsewhere. Thus the words of a former Uruguayan President, Juan Bordaberry, to the effect that "liberal democracy is irrevocably doomed," merit special attention. Cf. *La Busqueda* (Montevideo), August 27, 1987. The problems of that country, "redemocratized" prior to the establishment of a military dictatorship in 1973, have returned, intact in their old tragic insolubility.

1169. Cf. William Graham Sumner, *Challenge of Facts and Other Essays*, A. G. Keller, ed. (New Haven: Yale University Press, 1914), 286.

1170. Cf. my "Trojan Asses" in *Chronicles*, July 1986. The major theological reason for this confusion in the Catholic Church (and others) is that our "Christian Left," instead of striving to refashion the world in the spirit of Christ, wants to "assimilate" it to the prevailing currents in a conformist and purely masochistic spirit. The Church is to be "democratized," hitched to the wagon of doomed ideologies. Bear in mind that the Church is *in*, not *of*, the world. Scripture leaves no doubt as to who the Prince of the World is, and Luther was not far off when he called the world "the Devil's Inn."

1171. Uninformed people believe that Vatican II abolished the Mass in Latin, but Article 54 of the Decree on the Holy Liturgy says merely that the bishops have the right to permit the use of the vernacular; they must also, however, insure the use of the Latin, something rarely done in the United States. The "People's Altar?" It is nowhere mentioned in the decrees.

1172. The *Declaración de los Andes*, denying the theological, political, and economic validity of the so-called Liberation Theology, can be found in *El Mercurio* (Santiago de Chile), July 23, 1985. The Swiss theologian Cardinal Hans Urs von Balthasar was even more explicit and called the theologies of both Hans Küng and Leonardo Boff "strictly non-Christian"—not just "non-Catholic." Cf. *Die Welt*, October 16, 1985. Indeed, many voices in the Catholic Church run counter to these leftist inroads. A book like *Le capitalisme, mais c'est la vie* (Paris: Plon, 1983), written by the independent Dominican thinker R. L. Bruckberger, will probably never appear in the United States, as so often happens with truly important Continental works. Therein lies a whole world, hidden from Americans!

1173. Torture, unfortunately, is a recurrent phenomenon in all Latin American countries. In Chile, General Pinochet tried to suppress it, but the police were "uncontrollable." Torture was used so extensively by the police under Allende that the weekly, *La Portada* (Santiago, November 1970), published an ironic article proposing to systematize torture and advocating the presence of a priest for the 4th and 5th degrees.

1174. August von Kotzebue was the father of the Russo-German Pacific explorer Otto von Kotzebue, after whom a town in Alaska was named. The Wartburg Festival was initially organized to celebrate the third centenary of the Reformation, but Luther would have condemned it as a perversion of nearly everything he stood for. The misrepresentation of the Reformation was already in full swing.

1175. This is also the view of the well-known defender of the natural law, Johannes Messner. Cf. *Das Naturrecht* (Innsbruck: Tyrolia, 1950), 99. Cf. also my essay "Where do Ethics Come From?" in *The Human Life Review*, Summer 1986, 79-93. Professor Allan Bloom said correctly in his *The Closing of the American Mind* (New York: Simon and Schuster, 1987), 194, that "reason cannot establish values, and the belief that it can is the stupidest and most pernicious illusion."

1176. Cf. Leszek Kolakowski, *Religion* (London: Fontana-Collins, 1982), 188. Ethically inclined nonbelievers are truly living off the whiff of an empty bottle.

1177. Cf. Rosemary Kingsland, *A Saint Among Savages* (London: Collins, 1980), 44. This book makes frightening reading and reveals the inanity of the proposition that these "children of Nature" are blissfully happy and should be left alone.

1178. Leftists always loyally obey this Muscovite veto and merely refer to "German Fascism"—the word can be pronounced with an eery, hissing sound. One looks in vain in the newest "dual" *Encyclopaedia Britannica* for "National Socialism" or "National Socialists." All that appears is "Nazi Party." I proposed that they write about the "Bolshies" rather than the "Communists." Incidentally, this particular encyclopedia delegated all the articles involving the Soviet Empire to "collaborators" from inside the Iron Curtain. *Caveat emptor!*

1179. Lies about the Germans during World War I—Belgian babies with their hands cut off, or a naked girl crucified near Suippes with unshaved German soldiers spitting on her martyred body (a famous etching by Louis Raemaekers)—were nevertheless believed.

1180. Japan protested via the Vatican against the President's utterances, worthy of a cannibal chieftain on the Upper Ubangi, whereupon the President returned the object to the patriotic gentlemen for burial.

1181. General Eisenhower, too, opposed this ghastly deed. The opposition among scientists was considerable. Cf. Daniel F. Boorstin, *The American Democratic Experience* (New York: Random House, 1973), 588-89. The argument that the bomb was really humane because it shorted the war is worthless: Japan had twice—via the Vatican and Moscow—desperately tried to get humanly acceptable armistice conditions. All they received was the nefarious Unconditional Surrender formula.

1182. Cf. Henry Kyemba, *State of Blood* (London: Corgi Books, 1977), 108.

1183. Cf. Roland Huntford, *The New Totalitarians* (London: Allan Lane, 1971). Life in Sweden has become so dull that crime seems a welcome change. Between 1950 and 1966, crime in Sweden increased 25 percent (p. 343).

1184. Cf. Albert Jay Nock, *Memoirs of a Superfluous Man* (Washington: Regnery Gateway, 1991), 256-57. "History is bunk" was not only Henry Ford's opinion; it is subconsciously believed by many Americans. They think that their history and situation is so unique as to preclude their learning from other nations and other historic periods. Hence also the neglect of foreign languages.

1185. Cf. Auberon Waugh, *Who Are the Violets Now?* (London: Chapman & Hall, 1965), 244.

1186. In a *Samizdat* article of 1980, Joseph Dyad'kin mentions the figures 43-53 million victims attributable to Stalin's regime alone, 20 million of them killed on the battlefield. (Stalin admitted to only 10 million dead during the Patriotic War, a war he had started with Hitler.) An article by William T. Corson and Robert T. Crowley, the *Wall Street Journal* (July 23, 1980), listed 10 million victims prior to Stalin's rule; Robert Conquest speaks of 41,400,000 killed in the 1917-1953 period. Even larger numbers are mentioned by Ivan Kurganov, a professor of statistics, who claims about 110,700,000 murdered between 1917 and 1958. (Other estimates seem modest by comparison.) All these data do not include the hideous loss of human life in the satellite states, in Afghanistan, China, Southest Asia, and even in Latin America. If the horrors of National Socialism are added, the tally reaches the 200 million mark!

1187. The new Oxford Bible speaks about the "Evil One" and this is the correct translation from the Greek.

1188. Cf. Dmitri Merezhkovski, *Tsarstvo Antikhrista* (Munich: Dreimasken-Verlag, 1919), 251.

Index

JC 571 .K793 1990 c.1
Kuehnelt-Leddihn, Erik von,
1909-
Leftism revisited

DATE DUE

GAYLORD

PRINTED IN U.S.A.